# Official Guide to Financial Accounting using Tally.ERP 9

Fourth Revised & Updated Edition

*By*

**Tally Education Private Limited**

**Bengaluru**

**BPB PUBLICATIONS**

First Edition 2017
Second Revised & Updated Edition 2017
Third Revised & Updated Edition 2018
**Fourth Revised & Updated Edition 2018**



**ISBN : 978-93-87284-03-6**



LIMITS OF LIABILITY AND DISCLAIMER OF WARRANTY

This information contained in tis book is true and correct and the best of Author's and publisher's knowledge. We are committed to serve students with best of out knowledge and resources. We have taken utmost care and attention while editing and printing of this book but Author and publisher should not be held responsible for errors, omission and any other unintentional mistake that might have crept in However, errors brought to out notice shall be gratefully acknowledged and attended to.

All trademarks referred to in the book are acknowledged as properties of their respective owners. This book is written solely for the benefit and guidance of the students.

**Distributors:**

BPB PUBLICATIONS
20, Ansari Road, Darya Ganj
New Delhi-110002
Ph: 23254990/23254991

BPB BOOK CENTRE
376 Old Lajpat Rai Market,
Delhi-110006
Ph: 23861747

MICRO MEDIA
Shop No. 5, Mahendra Chambers, 150
DN Rd. Next to Capital Cinema, V.T.
(C.S.T.) Station, MUMBAI-400 001 Ph:
22078296/22078297

DECCAN AGENCIES
4-3-329, Bank Street,
Hyderabad-500195
Ph: 24756967/24756400

Published by Manish Jain for BPB Publications, 20, Ansari Road, Darya Ganj, New Delhi- 110002 and Printed him at Repro India Ltd, Mumbai

# Preface

Tally Education, subsidiary of Tally Solutions (creators and developers of Tally software), has been traversing the journey of an assiduous mission to enhance the employability of learners. We continuously envisage to blend conceptual learning with business applications to develop true professional competence.

Tally Solutions Pvt. Ltd. is a pioneer in the business software products arena. Since its inception in 1986, Tally's simple yet powerful products have been revolutionising the way businesses run. Having delivered path breaking technology consistently for more than 30 years, Tally symbolises unmatched innovation and leadership. Today, it caters to millions of users across industries and continues unchallenged as the industry leader in the enterprise resource planning software domain.

In this age of intense economic competition and rapid technological developments, it has become customary for employers to place a premium on computer skills and abilities to enhance business productivity. This makes it imperative for job seekers and employees to stay abreast of developments in their areas of expertise and constantly update and upgrade their skills to stay relevant in the workplace. Tally Education is committed to bridging the gap between education and employment in the country.

Over the years, the success of Tally software has fueled the demand for Tally trained professionals across the globe. Catering to this demand has always been a priority for us and this courseware is one more step towards the same.

Written as an official guide of the UGC curriculum of Financial Accounting, this book can be adapted to the needs of learners with diverse interests and backgrounds. It shall lead the learner towards varied career goals ranging from entrepreneurship to finance professionals.

Fundamentals of Financial Accounting using Tally.ERP 9 have been explained with the help of diverse business scenarios which provide the learners a clearer insight on the real-life business situations. Thereby preparing the candidates to experience and understand the real life implementation of the theoretical knowledge.

Sections of this book have been kept independent from each other, thus providing additional flexibility to the advanced readers to choose their own way around the book.

Enriched with numerous figures, illustrations and practice scenarios, it enables candidates to understand the intricacies of business operations and nuances of financial accounting with ease and prepares them to handle business transactions in the daily work environment more confidently.

# Table of Contents

## Chapter 1

# Basics of Accountancy

### LEARNING OBJECTIVES

After studying this chapter, you will understand:

- Meaning and Purpose of Financial Accounting
- Advantages and Disadvantages of Financial Accounting
- Meaning of Key Accounting Terms
- Convention of Double-Entry System of Bookkeeping
- Different Types of Accounts

## 1.1 INTRODUCTION

**Accounting is the process of classifying, recording and reporting a**n enterprise's business transactions over a period of time. Financial Accounting is a branch of accounting that is primarily concerned with the preparation of financial statements, based on the business transactions, and communication of the same to person interested in the information.

Financial accounting helps in determining the results (i.e., profit or loss) of business operations during the particular period and the financial position of the enterprise as on a date at the end of the period.

## 1.2 OBJECTIVES OF FINANCIAL ACCOUNTING

The objective of financial accounting is to keep a record of all business transactions so that:

- The profit earned or loss sustained by the business during an accounting period can be determined;
- The financial position of the business at the end of the accounting period can be ascertained; and
- The financial information required by the owners of business, Government and other interested parties such as employees or investors can be provided.

## 1.3 ADVANTAGES OF FINANCIAL ACCOUNTING

Financial Accounting has many advantages, the main advantages being:

1. **Record of Business Transactions:** The record of business transactions maintained by an enterprise serves as a permanent record of transactions, and a future reference.
2. **Determination of Profit or Loss:** The availability of the complete record of business transactions, specifically income and expense, helps in the determination of profit or loss of an enterprise.
3. **Determination of Financial Position:** The availability of the complete record of business transactions, specifically information regarding what the enterprise owns, invests and owes, helps in the determination of the financial position of the enterprise. Further, it also helps the enterprise to maintain a clear record of debtors (amounts to be collected) and creditors (amounts to be paid).
4. **Track Progress of Business:** Maintenance of business records on a yearly basis facilitates the comparison of performance over the years. This helps to keep track of the progress made by the organisation year-on-year and over the years.
5. **Compliance with Legal Requirements:** Business concerns are required to comply with certain statutory requirements such as paying and filing of tax returns. Maintenance of financial accounting as per accounting standards, facilitates compliance with such legal requirements.
6. **Documentary Evidence:** Accounting records of a concern can be used as documentary evidence in case of litigation, like seeking claims against debtors.

## 1.4 LIMITATIONS OF FINANCIAL ACCOUNTING

Financial Accounting has numerous advantages; at the same time, it also suffers from certain limitations. Some of the limitations are:

1. **Record Monetary Transactions:** A major limitation of financial accounting is that, it record monetary transactions only. Non-monetary transactions (i.e., transactions that cannot be expressed in terms of money) are ignored in financial accounting. Thus, important information like technological innovations of the business concern, or competition faced, which have an impact on business are not reflected in financial accounting.
2. **Does Not Provide Exact Information:** Financial accounting reports do not necessarily give exact information. This is because, at times, estimates are used in accounting; thus, the information in such cases is at best, approximate.
3. **Does Not Reflect Present Value of Business:** Balance Sheet, the financial report that reflects the financial position of a business, is prepared by taking into account the historical cost (book value) of assets and not the market value. Hence, financial accounting fails to accurately reflect the present value of a business.
4. **Does Not Provide Timely Information:** The focus of Financial Accounting is provision of information in the form of financial statements for a defined period, normally,

one year. This means that the information is, of a historical nature, that may not be of much use for handling the current situation.

## 1.5 ACCOUNTING TERMS

Some of the most commonly used accounting terms are:

- **Account:** An account is a statement of transactions affecting any particular asset, liability, expense, or income. Example: cash account, bank account, etc.
- **Accounting Period:** A regular period of time such as a quarter or year, for which a financial statement is generated, is called an accounting period. Example: 01 April 2016 to 31 March, 2016.
- **Chart of Accounts:** A chart of accounts is a list of all account titles used by an organisation. The chart of accounts of the business shows the categorisation and grouping of its accounts.
- **Entity:** An entity is a person, partnership, organization, or business that has a legal and separate existence. Example: Rajesh Jewellers, Vriddhi Traders Pvt Ltd., etc. An accounting system is always devised for a specific business entity (also called accounting entity).
- **Transaction:** A transaction is an event involving some value between two or more entities. Purchase of goods, receipt of money, payments to creditors, expenses, are all examples of transactions. Transactions can be cash transactions or credit transactions.
- **Assets:** Assets are economic resources of an organisation that can be expressed in terms of money. Assets are items of value used by the business in its operations. Example: Deepak Travels owns a fleet of buses. These buses provide economic benefit to the enterprise and so are shown on the asset side of the balance sheet of Deepak Travels. Assets can be broadly classified as:
  - **Fixed assets:** Assets held on a long term basis such as land, buildings, machinery, plant, furniture, and fixtures. Fixed assets are used in regular business operations of a company.
  - **Current assets:** Assets held on a short term basis. Such as, debtors, bills receivables, stock, cash and bank balances.
- **Liabilities:** Financial obligations (amounts which a business owes to others) of a business organisation are called liabilities. Examples include loans from banks or other persons, creditors for goods supplied, bank overdraft etc.
- **Capital:** Capital is the amount invested by the owner/s (proprietor/s) in a business. Capital increases when a company earns profits; and decreases if a company incurs losses or if any amount is withdrawn.
- **Income:** The difference between business revenues and expenses is called income.
- **Expenditure:** Expenditure refers to all the expenses or amounts spent to produce and sell the goods and services. Examples include, purchase of raw materials, payment of salaries, office expenses, etc.
- **Profit:** Profit refers to the excess of revenues over expenses during an accounting period. Profit increases the investment of the owners.
- **Gain:** Gain refers to the profit earned from events or transactions which are incidental to business such as sale of fixed assets, winning a court case, appreciation in the value of an asset, etc.
- **Loss:** Loss refers to the excess of expenses over related revenues during an accounting period. It also refers to money or money's worth lost, without any benefit in return. Examples include, cash or goods lost due to theft, fire, and so on.
- **Discount:** Discount is the deduction in the price of goods on sale. If the deduction is given at an agreed percentage on the list price at the time of the sale it is called a 'trade discount'. Trade discounts are generally offered by manufactures to wholesalers and by wholesalers to retailers.

  Another type of discount is cash discount, which is an incentive that encourages debtors to make prompt payments. In this case, after selling the goods on credit basis, debtors may be given a certain deduction in the amount due if they pay the amount within a stipulated period. Such deduction is given at the time of payment on the amount payable.
- **Voucher:** The documentary evidence in support of a transaction is called a Voucher. Examples include cash memos (when goods are bought for cash), invoices (when goods are bought on credit), receipts (for payments), and so on.
- **Goods:** Goods refer to the products in which a business unit deals or manufactures. For example, for a furniture dealer-chairs and tables are goods, while for others it is furniture and is treated as an asset.
- **Drawings:** Withdrawals of money and/or goods by the owner from the business for personal use is called drawings. Drawings reduce the investment of the owners.
- **Purchases:** Purchase refers the goods procured by a business for use or sale. Purchases may either be cash or credit.
- **Sales:** Sales refers to goods sold after being purchased or manufactured by the business. If goods are sold for cash, they are called cash sales and if goods are sold and payment is not received after sale, it is called credit sales.
- **Stock:** Stock or inventory refers to the goods or merchandise kept in the premises of a shop or warehouse and offered for sale or distribution. In a trading concern, the amount of goods that lie unsold at the end of an accounting period is called closing stock. Similarly, opening stock is the amount of stock at the beginning of the accounting period.
- **Debtors:** Persons and/or other entities who owe an enterprise money, on having bought goods and services on credit are called debtors of the enterprise.

- **Creditors:** Persons and/or other entities who have to be paid by an enterprise for providing goods and services on credit are called creditors.
- **Receivables:** Receivables refer to a business concern's claims to future collection of cash or other assets. In other words, receivables are assets of a concern in the form of debts or monetary obligations owed to it from debtors or customers.
- **Payables:** Payables refer to the debts owed by a business concern to its creditors or suppliers. Payables are liabilities.
- **Journal:** A journal is a book of original entry in which business transactions are entered in chronological order. A record of a single business transaction is called a journal entry.
- **Ledger:** A ledger is the book in which all journal entries, are classified into accounts, are posted.

## 1.6 SYSTEMS OF ACCOUNTING

An Accounting System refers to the way or method of recording business transactions in the books of accounts of a business concern. Based on the system of recording transactions, accounting systems are classified in two types:

1. Single Entry System, and
2. Double Entry System

A brief explanation of both systems follows:

### 1.6.1 Single Entry System

Though the Double Entry system of accounting is more popular system of accounting, some small business proprietors still use the single entry system for accounting. It is a system of accounting under which only one aspect (debit or credit) of the transaction is recorded. It is usually used by small concerns which have very few transactions.

The Single Entry system is considered an incomplete and unscientific system of entry, as all business transactions are not recorded under it. Usually, only cash, bank, and a few debtors and creditors accounts are maintained under this system.

### 1.6.2 Double Entry System

The Double Entry system of accounting is more scientific and systematic method of accounting and hence is popularly used by big and small business organisations all over the world.

This system is based on the premise that every business transaction has two aspects, i.e., the receiving aspect or debit aspect, and the giving aspect or the credit aspect. Each of these aspects of every transaction affects two accounts in opposite ways (increase or decrease in monetary terms). Therefore, under this system, a complete record of both the aspects of every transaction (i.e., debit and credit) is maintained.

#### *Accounting Equation*

The double entry system of accounting is based on accounting equations where the relationship between assets, liabilities, and capital can be expressed in form of an equation. The accounting equation signifies that the assets of a business are always equal to the total of its liabilities and capital (owner's equity).

The accounting equation is:

**Assets = Liabilities + Capital**

As the accounting equation depicts the fundamental relationship among the components of the balance sheet, it is also called the balance sheet equation.

*(A detailed explanation of the Double Entry System of Accounting is available in Chapter 3 of this book.)*

## 1.7 CLASSIFICATION OF ACCOUNTS

The essential function of accounting is to record transactions to ascertain the financial status of a company as on a particular date. The usual transactions of a business are:

- Purchase of goods, either as raw material for further processing or as finished goods for resale
- Payment of expenses incurred towards business
- Sale of goods or services
- Receipts, in cash or by cheque
- Other payments, in cash or by cheque

In order to record transactions, ledger accounts are created.

The accounts can be classified into three types, namely, Real accounts, Personal accounts and Nominal accounts.

### 1.7.1 Real Accounts

Real accounts are accounts maintained as assets owned or possessed by the business. Real accounts include both tangible (things that can be touched) and intangible (things that cannot be touched) accounts. Examples: Buildings, Furniture, Cash, Purchases, Sales, Goodwill, etc.

### 1.7.2 Personal Accounts

Personal accounts are the accounts of persons with whom the business is required to deal with. Personal accounts are further classified as:

- **Natural Personal Accounts**: Accounts of individuals or natural persons. Examples: Ram's account, Vikram's account, etc.
- **Artificial Personal Accounts:** Accounts of companies, banks or other institutions (not persons). Examples: State Bank of India, Mahendra Club, etc.
- **Representative Personal Accounts**: Represnsentative Personal Accounts refer to accounts that satisfy the following two conditions:
  (i) it relates to the particular head of expenditure or income (nominal account), and
  (ii) it represents persons to whom it is payable or from whom it is receivable. Examples: Outstanding Salaries, Pre-paid Insurance, etc.

### 1.7.3 Nominal Accounts

Nominal accounts are accounts where income and expenses are recorded. Examples: Sales, Rent expenses, Salary expenses, etc.

**Note:** All those accounts which are not personal accounts (ie., real and nominal accounts) are called impersonal accounts.

**All accounts** can be broadly classified under the following **five** groups:

- Assets – Examples: buildings, stock, debtors
- Liabilities – Examples: loan, creditors
- Capital – Example: share capital of Rs. 100,000/-
- Revenue – Examples: commission received, dividend received
- Expenses – Examples: rent, salaries, electricity

Assets, liabilities, and capital are taken to the balance sheet. Revenue and expenditure accounts are shown in the profit and loss statement.

## KEY TAKEAWAYS

- Accounting is the process of classifying, recording and reporting an enterprise's business transactions over a period of time.
- Financial Accounting is a branch of accounting that is primarily concerned with the preparation of financial statements, based on the business transactions, and communication of the same to person interested in the information.
- Accounting systems are classified into two types, namely, Single Entry System, and Double Entry System.
- The double entry system of accounting is based on the accounting equation, viz., Assets = Liabilities + Capital
- Accounts can be classified into three types, namely, Real accounts, Personal accounts and Nominal accounts.

## PRACTICE EXERCISES

### Section A: Review Questions

1. What do you understand by the term 'Financial Accounting'?
2. Discuss the advantages and limitation of accounting information.
3. Explain the three types of accounts with two examples each.
4. Differentiate between the terms 'profit and gain'.
5. Classify the following on the type of Account (Personal, Real or Nominal):

| S. No. | Name of Account | Type of Account |
|---|---|---|
| 1 | Building Account | |
| 2 | Capital Account | |
| 3 | Outstanding Wages Account | |
| 4 | Cash Account | |
| 5 | Stationery Account | |
| 6 | Prepaid Insurance Account | |
| 7 | Dr. Ambedkar College Account | |
| 8 | Interest Account | |
| 9 | Vijay's Account | |
| 10 | Sales Account | |

### Section B: Multiple Choice Questions

Select the most appropriate answer from the choices given below:

1. _____________ refers to the difference between business revenues and expense.
   a. Expense b. Liability
   c. Asset d. **Income**
2. Canara Bank account is an example of a _______________.
   a. Real Personal Account
   b. **Artificial Personal Account**
   c. Representative Personal Account
   d. Natural Personal Account
3. A _____________ is a book in which business transactions are first entered in a chronological order.
   a. Asset b. Account
   c. **Journal** d. Ledger
4. If Debtors : Creditors, then Profit :______.
   a. Gain b. Expense
   c. **Loss** d. Income
5. Drawings __________ the investment of owners in a business concern.
   a. Increase b. **Decrease**
   c. Double d. Do not affect

Chapter 2

# Principles, Concepts and Conventions of Accounting

## LEARNING OBJECTIVES

After studying this chapter, you will understand:

- Need for Accounting Principles, Conventions And Concepts
- Fundamental Principles of Accounting
- Concepts of Accounting
- Conventions of Accounting

## 2.1 INTRODUCTION

Accounting is considered as the language of business. In other words, accounting is the language used by business enterprises to communicate its financial position with the world. So, this language must be understood by all and there are certain uniform guidelines and standards that are followed as a part of accounting practice. Such rules of action are adopted universally, while recording accounting transactions and preparing accounting statements such rules are called 'Generally Accept Accounting Principles' (GAAP).

It may be noted that GAAP differs from country to country based on legislative requirements and accounting practices therefore.

The accounting principles are designed to ensure that financial statements are:

- **Accurate:** i.e., free from errors related to content and principle
- **Reliable:** i.e., represent the information that users consider it to represent
- **Timely:** i.e., available when required to support decision-making, and
- **Relevant:** i.e., applicable to the purpose required.

Accounting principles can be classified into two broad categories:

1. Accounting Concepts, and
2. Accounting Conventions

| ACCOUNTING PRINCIPLES | |
|---|---|
| **Accounting Concepts** | **Accounting Conventions** |
| 1. Money Measurement Concept | 1. Convention of Consistency |
| 2. Separate Entity Concept | 2. Convention of Full Disclosure |
| 3. Going Concern Concept | 3. Convention of Conservatism |
| 4. Cost Concept | 4. Convention of Materiality |
| 5. Dual Aspect Concept | |
| 6. Periodicity Concept | |
| 7. Objective Evidence Concept | |
| 8. Matching Concept | |
| 9. Realisation Concept | |
| 10. Legal Aspect Concept | |
| 11. Accrual Concept | |

## 2.2 ACCOUNTING CONCEPTS

Accounting assumptions are premises or notions on which the accounting process is based. Also called 'Accounting Concepts', these assumptions form the basis of systematic accounting practices. The following are some important accounting concepts:

1. **Money Measurement Concept:** In accounting, all transactions are measured by using a common unit of measurement, which is money. Under the money measurement concept, only those transactions or events which can be measured or expressed in terms of money are recorded. Hence, factors such as the skill of the human resources, employer-employee relationship cannot be recorded in books of accounts in spite of their importance to the success of a business.
2. **Separate Entity Concept:** The business entity concept views the business as an entity, separate from its owners, i.e. business is assumed to have a distinct entity (existence) other than the existence of its proprietors. Thus, if an owner of a business is interested in playing badminton and so pays a subscription as a member of a local badminton club, this activity will be considered as completely outside the activities of the business. Such personal transactions will be kept separate from the accounts of the business. Based on this concept, a firm can sue and also be sued in its own name.
3. **Going-Concern Concept:** The going-concern concept, also known as the Continue of Activity Concept, assumes that a business concern will continue to exist for a long period. Thus, transactions are recorded on the assumption that a business will remain in operation long enough for all its current plans to be carried out.
4. **Cost Concept:** As per the cost concept or historical cost concept, cost of assets should be recorded at their original acquisition cost (cost price). This is an accounting concept which is used only for fixed assets. For example, if a piece of furniture is purchased for Rs. 50,000, it must be recorded in the books of the company at the invoiced and paid price of Rs. 50,000 even after two years.
5. **Dual-Aspect Concept:** Every business transaction involves a dual or double aspect of equal value. Under the dual-aspect concept, both these debit and credit aspects of a transaction are recorded. For instance, when a business

purchases goods for cash, it receives goods of some value and gives cash of equal value.

6. **Periodicity Concept:** The periodicity concept, also called the time interval concept, requires business enterprises to produce financial statements at set time intervals. As per this concept, financial statements are generated at relatively short periods such as a year or quarter, so that performance can be measured and compared.
7. **Objective Evidence Concept:** According to the objective evidence concept, all accounting entries should be evidenced and supported by business documents such as invoices, vouchers, and so on. Such documents serve as evidence in a court of law.
8. **Matching Concept:** According to the matching concept, the revenue that is reported must be set off against the expenses incurred to generate revenues during the accounting period. This gives a true picture of the profit earned during that period.
9. **Realisation Concept:** The realisation concept deals with how revenue is recognised by a business. Revenue is recognised when goods and services are delivered in quantities/amounts that are reasonably certain to be realised.
10. **Legal Aspect Concept:** According to the legal aspect concept, all accounting records and statements must conform to legal requirements, i.e. accounting records should be maintained and statements should be prepared as prescribed by law.
11. **Accrual Concept:** Under the accrual concept of accounting, revenue is recognised only when earned rather than when due or collected, and expenses when incurred rather than when paid. Thus, transactions are recorded on the basis of income earned or expense incurred, irrespective of actual receipt or payment. For example, the salary of an employee becomes due from the first of the month, while it is paid at the end of the month.

## 2.3 ACCOUNTING CONVENTIONS

Accounting Conventions refer to customs and traditions followed by accountants in preparing accounting statements. In other words, these are guidelines for preparing accounting statements.

1. **Consistency:** According to convention of consistency, accounting practices and policies of a business entity must be consistent from one period to another.
2. **Full Disclosure:** According to the full disclosure convention, accounts should be prepared in such a way that all material information, including facts and figures, is clearly disclosed. The disclosure of financial information is useful to different parties interested in the progress and developments of an enterprise.
3. **Conservatism:** The convention of conservatism is related to the policy of playing safe. It states that uncertainties and risks inherent in business transactions should be given proper consideration.
4. **Materiality:** Under the convention of materiality any item should be regarded important (i.e., material) if there is reason to believe that its knowledge would influence the decision of the user of the information. Thus, all unimportant items are either left out or merged with other items.

## KEY TAKEAWAYS

- Rules of action adopted universally while recording accounting transactions and preparing accounting statements are called Accounting Principles.
- Accounting principles can be classified into two broad categories called Accounting Concepts and Accounting Conventions.
- Accounting Concepts are assumptions that form the basis of systematic accounting practices.
- Accounting conventions are customs and traditions that guide accountants in preparing accounting statements.

## PRACTICE EXERCISES

### Section A: Review Questions

1. What is the purpose of Accounting Principles?
2. Differentiate between Accounting Concepts and Accounting Conventions.
3. Briefly explain the Objective Evidence Concept.

### Section B: Multiple Choice Questions

Select the most appropriate answer from the choices given below:

1. 'The owners of a business enterprise can rely on the regularity with which the reporting of financial information takes place.' – Which accounting concept does this statement refer to?
   a. Separate Entity Concept
   b. Going Concern Concept
   c. Cost Concept Dual Aspect Concept
   d. **Periodicity Concept**
2. Under which accounting concept can a company sue a debtor?
   a. Going Concern Concept
   b. Legal Aspect Concept
   c. **Separate Entity Concept**
   d. Accrual Concept
3. Anand, an accountant at a company, recorded the cost of land purchased in the year 2013 for Rs. 50 lakh as Rs. 80,000 in 2016, as he felt that it is the current market price. Which accounting concept did Anand violate?
   a. Going Concern Concept
   b. **Cost Concept**
   c. Dual Aspect Concept
   d. Periodicity Concept

4. The _______________ is the recording and measurement rule that provides the basis for double entry system of book-keeping.
   a. **Dual aspect concept**
   b. Going Concern Concept
   c. Cost Concept
   d. Accrual Concept

5. The practice of considering bad and doubtful debts in the books of accounts before ascertaining the profit is based on the Convention of _____________.
   a. Consistency
   b. Full Disclosure
   c. **Conservatism**
   d. Materiality

Chapter 3

# Recording Procedure in Accounting

## LEARNING OBJECTIVES

After studying this chapter, you will understand:

- Meaning of Transaction
- Phases of Accounting Cycle
- Meaning and Uses of Voucher
- Different Methods of Recording Business Transactions
- How to Journalise Day to Day Business Transactions
- How to Record Compound Journal Entry
- Meaning of Ledger & Posting
- Rules of Ledger Posting
- How to Post Journal Entries into ledger/Book of Final Entry
- How to Prepare Trial Balance
- Meaning of Subsidiary Books
- Different Types of Subsidiary Books
- How to Record Transactions in Subsidiary Books
- Meaning of Journal Proper
- Type of transactions recorded in Journal Proper

## 3.1 INTRODUCTION

This chapter deals with the phases of the Accounting Cycle like recording, classifying and summarising of financial transactions. The first step is to identify the transactions that should be recorded and prepare the source documents which are, in turn, recorded in the book of original entry called journal. The transactions are then posted to individual accounts in the principal book called ledger. Finally, the balance amounts from the different ledger accounts are transferred to the Trial Balance.

## 3.2 DIFFERENT PHASES OF ACCOUNTING CYCLE

Accounting is the art of recording, classifying and summarising the financial transactions and presenting the useful information like financial performance, financial position to internal person like management and external person like owners/stockholders and vendors.

Different phases of the Accounting cycle are:

1. **Recording of Financial Transactions:** Transactions are recorded in the book of original entry called Journal Book.
2. **Classifying the Financial Transactions**: The recorded transactions are next posted to the Ledger.
3. **Summarising the Financial Transactions:** Once the Posting is complete, reports like Trial Balance, Profit & Loss Account and Balance Sheet are prepared.
4. **Analysis of the results:** After preparation of reports financial performance and position of the company is analysed.

## 3.3 BUSINESS TRANSACTIONS AND SOURCE DOCUMENT

### 3.3.1 Business Transaction

A Business Transaction is an event or happening which takes place between the business and clients, suppliers and others with whom they do the business and this event will change the financial statements of the business. For example, when you purchase the goods for cash, your cash balance reduces and the stock balance increases. This transaction will involve the aspect of 'give and take'. Thus, business transactions are exchanges of economic consideration between parties and have two-fold effects that are recorded in at least two accounts.

### 3.3.2 Source Document or Voucher

Business transactions should be evidenced by appropriate documents such as cash memo, invoice, sales bill, pay-in slip, cheque, salary slip, and so on. A document which provides evidence of the transactions is called the source document or voucher.

## 3.4 RECORDING BUSINESS TRANSACTIONS

Recording of financial transaction is the first step in the accounting cycle. Business concerns everyday are involved in making Purchases, Sales, Payments to Vendors, Receiving Payments from customers on a day to day basis. If any one of the transactions is not recorded then the final financial statements and business financial position of the company will be wrongly interpreted. *For example:* A company sells goods for ₹ 50,000 and receives cash immediately; if this transaction is not recorded, then the income statement will give a wrong picture. Hence, it is very important to record the day to day transactions.

### 3.4.1 Methods of Recording Business Transactions

Under the double-entry system of accounting, one can record the day to day business transactions in the books of accounts in two ways or methods, based on their size of the business and the number of business transactions recorded by the business concern.

The two methods of recording business transactions are:

- Conventional Method or Theoretical Method
- Modern Method, Practical Method or English Method

#### *3.4.1.1 Conventional Method or Theoretical Method*

This method is followed by the small scale business concerns, who have less number of transactions to record in the books of accounts.

Under Conventional Method the following steps are considered while recording the business transactions in books of accounts

**Step 1:** Firstly, business transactions are recorded in the Journal, which is also called as *Book of Original Entry.*

**Step 2:** Secondly, the business transactions recorded in the Journal are posted or transferred to the Ledger, which is also called as *Book of Final Entry*. All the ledger accounts are closed periodically

**Step 3:** Thirdly, by calculating the totals of debit and credit sides of a ledger, the balanced figure or the difference between the sum of credits and debits is listed in the statement called Trial Balance.

**Note:** The left out amount (Negative or positive) in the ledger account or the difference between the debits and credits in the ledger at the end of the accounting period is known as Closing Balance

**Step 4:** Fourthly, final accounts like Profit & Loss Account and Balance Sheet are prepared from the Trial Balance.

**Step 5:** After the preparation of Trial Balance, Profit & Loss Account and Balance Sheet, the interpreted Accounting Information is communicated to the end users like Vendors, Customers, Investors and Management etc.

### *3.4.1.2 Modern Method, Practical Method or English Method*

This method is followed by large scale business concerns, who have more number of transactions to record in the books of accounts.

Under Modern Method the following steps are considered while recording the business transactions in books of accounts

**Step 1:** Firstly, business transactions are recorded in the number of books of original entry called Subsidiary Books or Special Journals.

**Step 2:** Secondly, the business transactions recorded in the Subsidiary Books are posted or transferred to the Ledger, which is also called as *Book of Final Entry.*

**Step 3:** Thirdly, by calculating the totals of debit and credit sides of a ledger, the balanced figure or the difference between the sum of credits and debits is listed in the statement called Trial Balance.

**Step 4:** Fourthly, final accounts like Profit & Loss Account and Balance Sheet are prepared from the Trial Balance.

**Step 5:** After the preparation of Trial Balance, Profit & Loss Account and Balance Sheet, the interpreted Accounting Information is communicated to the end users like Vendors, Customers, Investors and Management etc.

## 3.4.2 Recording of Business Transactions in Journal/ Book of Original Entry

In accounting systems, transactions recorded in source documents are analysed and recorded for the first time in a journal, also called the book of original entry. Journal is a day book or a daily record wherein the transactions are recorded in chronological order, i.e. as and when they take place.

A **Specimen journal** is shown below in Table 1.1.

| Journal | | | | |
|---|---|---|---|---|
| Date | Particulars | L.F | Dr. | Cr. |
| | | | | |
| | | | | |

*Table 1.1 Specimen of Journal*

Details of specimen of journal are:

- **Date:** The date column is used to record the date on which a particular transaction takes place.
- **Particulars:** In the particulars column the account title to be debited is written in the first line, beginning from the left corner and the word **Dr.** is written at the end of the column. The account title to be credited is written in the second line, leaving a margin on the left with a prefix **To.** Below the account titles, a brief explanation of the transaction is given which is called **narration**. After the narration, a line is drawn in the particulars column which indicates the end of recording of the specific journal entry.
- **Ledger Folio (L.F):** In the Ledger Folio (L.F.) column, the page number of the ledger book on which relevant account appears is recorded.
- **Debit (Dr.):** The debit column is meant to record the amount against the account to be debited.
- **Credit (Cr.):** The credit column is meant to record the amount against the account to be credited.

The process of recording transactions in the journal is called journalising. The process of transferring a journal entry to individual accounts is called posting. This sequence causes the journal to be called the **Book of original entry** and the ledger account as the **Book of Final Entry**.

### *3.4.2.1 Use of Debit and Credit*

Every transaction involves two aspects – give and take. In the double entry system of accounting, every transaction is recorded in at least two accounts. While recording transactions, the total amount debited and credited must be equal. In accounting, the terms debit (abbreviated as Dr.) and credit (abbreviated as Cr.) indicate whether the transactions are to be recorded on the left or right of the account.

### *3.4.2.2 Rules of Debit and Credit*

Two fundamental rules are followed to record the changes in these accounts.

For recording changes in assets or expenses (losses)

- **Debit:** Increase in assets, increase in expenses (losses)
- **Credit:** Decrease in assets, decrease in expenses (losses)

For recording changes in liabilities, capital, or revenues (gains)

- **Debit:** Decrease in liabilities, decrease in capital, decrease in revenue (gain)
- **Credit:** Increase in liabilities, increase in capital, increase in revenues (gains). The following table 1.2, summarises the rules applicable to different kinds of accounts.

| | Increase | Decrease |
|---|---|---|
| Asset | Debit | Credit |
| Liability | Credit | Debit |
| Income/Revenue | Credit | Debit |
| Expense/Losses | Debit | Credit |
| Capital/Stock Holders' Equity | Credit | Debit |
| Dividends | Debit | Credit |

*Table 1.2 Rules of Credit and Debit*

The following illustration will help you to understand the Rules of Debit and Credit.

### *Illustration 1: Application of Rules of Debit and Credit*

1. As on 1st April, 2016, Deepak commenced the business with ₹ 50,000
2. As on 1st April 2016, Ashok bought furniture for his business by paying cash ₹ 20,000.
3. As on 2nd April 2016, purchased goods from Pradeep on credit for ₹ 10,000
4. As on 3rd April 2016, sold good to Murthy Traders on credit ₹ 5,000

### *Solution:*

1. Deepak commenced the business with ₹ 50,000

   This transaction increases the capital as well as the cash. Increase in assets is debited and increase in capital is credited. Therefore, record the transaction with debit to cash account and credit to Deepak's capital account.

| Journal | | | | | |
|---|---|---|---|---|---|
| Date 2016 | Particulars | | L.F | Dr. | Cr. |
| Apr. 1 | Cash Account | Dr. | | 50,000 | |
| | To Capital Account | | | | 50,000 |
| | (Being cash invested by the proprietor) | | | | |
| | | | | | |

2. Ashok bought furniture for his business by paying cash ₹ 20,000.

   This transaction increases furniture (assets) and decreases cash by ₹ 20,000. The increase in assets is debited and the decrease in cash is credited. Therefore, record the transaction with debit to furniture account and credit to cash account.

| Journal | | | | | |
|---|---|---|---|---|---|
| Date 2016 | Particulars | | L.F | Dr. | Cr. |
| Apr. 1 | Furniture Account | Dr. | | 20,000 | |
| | To Cash Account | | | | 20,000 |
| | (Being furniture bought for business use) | | | | |
| | | | | | |

3. Purchased goods from Pradeep Traders on credit for ₹ 10,000

   This transaction increases purchases (increases assets) and liabilities (Pradeep Traders as creditors). Increase in assets is debited and increase in liabilities is credited. Therefore, record the transaction with debit to purchases account and credit to Samrat Traders account.

| Journal | | | | | |
|---|---|---|---|---|---|
| Date 2016 | Particulars | | L.F | Dr. | Cr. |
| Apr. 2 | Purchase Account | Dr. | | 10,000 | |
| | To Pradeep Traders Account | | | | 10,000 |
| | (Being goods purchased from Pradeep Traders on credit) | | | | |
| | | | | | |

4. Sold good to Murthy Traders on credit ₹ 5,000

   This transaction increases sales (decreases assets) and assets (Murthy Traders as debtors). Decrease in assets is credited and increase in assets is debited. Therefore, record the transaction with credit to sales account and debit to Murthy Traders account.

| Journal | | | | | |
|---|---|---|---|---|---|
| Date 2016 | Particulars | | L.F | Dr. | Cr. |
| Apr. 3 | Murthy Traders Account | Dr. | | 50,000 | |
| | To Sales Account | | | | 50,000 |
| | (Being goods sold to Murthy Traders on credit) | | | | |
| | | | | | |

### 3.4.2.3 *Steps to be followed while recording the Business Transactions in Journal*

While recording Business Transactions in a journal, one must follow the below given steps.

1. **Identify Two Accounts Involved in Transaction:** Every Business Transactions involves two accounts. One of the account is the receiver of the benefit and the other account is giver of the benefit **(While identifying the accounts involved in the transactions, ignore the account of the firm because business transactions are recorded in the books of firms)**
2. **Identify Nature of Account Involved in Transaction:** After identifying the two accounts involved in the transaction, next identify the nature or find out to which classes of accounts these two accounts belong.
3. **Apply Rules of Debit and Credit:** Next step is to find out which account should be debited and credited
4. **Recording the Transaction in Journal:** Finally, after identifying the account to be debited and account to be credited, the entry should be recorded in the Journal or Book of Original Entry, by debiting the account which has to be debited and crediting the account which has to be credited.

The journal entry is the basic record of a business transaction. It may be simple or compound. When two accounts are involved to record a transaction, it is called a simple journal entry.

### *Illustration 2: Application of the Steps to be followed while recording Business Transactions in Journal*

1. As on 21st May, 2016, Ashok commenced the business with ₹ 40,000

2. As on 21st May 2016, bought furniture for business by paying cash ₹ 10,000.
3. As on 22nd May 2016, purchased goods from Shuhas on credit for ₹ 5,000
4. As on 23rd May 2016, sold good to TT Traders on credit ₹ 2,000

***Solution:***

The below given table shows the Steps to be followed before recording the transaction in Journal or book of original entry.

| | Step 1 | Step 2 | Step 3 | | |
|---|---|---|---|---|---|
| Serial No. | Two Accounts Involved in the Transaction | Nature of Account Involved in Transaction | Rules of Debit and Credit | Accounts to be Debited | Accounts to be Credited |
| 1 | a. Cash A/c<br>b. Capital A/c | a. Asset A/c<br>b. Capital A/c | Debit Increase in an Asset<br>Credit Increase in a Capital | Cash A/c | Capital A/c |
| 2 | a. Furniture A/c<br>b. Cash A/c | a. Asset A/c<br>b. Asset A/c | Debit Increase in an Asset<br>Credit Decrease in an Asset | Furniture A/c | Cash A/c |
| 3 | a. Purchase A/c<br>b. Shuhas A/c | a. Expense A/c<br>b. Liability A/c | Debit Increase in an Expense<br>Credit Increase in a Liability | Purchase A/c | Shuhas A/c |
| 4 | a. TT Traders A/c<br>b. Sales A/c | a. Asset A/c<br>b. Income A/c | Debit Increase in an Asset<br>Credit Increase in an Income | TT Traders A/c | Sales A/c |

After following the above steps, the entries can be recorded in Journal as shown below:

| Journal | | | | | |
|---|---|---|---|---|---|
| Date 2016 | Particulars | | L.F | Dr. | Cr. |
| May. 21 | Cash Account | Dr. | | 40,000 | |
| | To Capital Account | | | | 40,000 |
| | (Being cash invested by the proprietor) | | | | |
| May. 21 | Furniture Account | Dr. | | 10,000 | |
| | To Cash Account | | | | 10,000 |
| | (Being furniture bought for business use) | | | | |
| May. 22 | Purchase Account | Dr. | | 5,000 | |
| | To Shuhas Account | | | | 5,000 |
| | (Being goods purchased from Shuhas Traders on credit) | | | | |
| May. 23 | TT Traders Account | Dr. | | 2,000 | |
| | To Sales Account | | | | 2,000 |
| | (Being goods sold to TT Traders on credit) | | | | |

***Illustration 3:*** *TARA Enterprises furnishes the following information regarding transactions for the month of April, 2016.*

| Date (2016) | Transactions |
|---|---|
| Apr. 1 | Business started with cash of ₹ 5,00,000 |
| Apr. 5 | Goods purchased from Mohan on credit for ₹ 50,000 |
| Apr. 6 | Stationery purchased for cash ₹ 4,000 |
| Apr. 10 | Opened a bank account with Kotak Bank by depositing cash of ₹ 1,00,000 |
| Apr. 11 | Goods sold to Siya Manufacturers on credit for ₹ 50,000 |
| Apr. 12 | Received a cheque of ₹ 50,000 from Siya Manufacturers |
| Apr. 13 | Insurance paid by cheque ₹ 10,000 |
| Apr. 14 | Sold goods to Nidhi Manufacturers ₹ 20,000 |
| Apr. 15 | Nidhi pays ₹ 20,000 cash |
| Apr. 16 | Goods purchased for ₹ 30,000 on credit from Gita Traders |
| Apr. 17 | Purchased office furniture for ₹ 10,000 in cash |
| Apr. 18 | Goods costing ₹ 5,000 given as charity |
| Apr. 19 | Paid ₹ 10,000 towards rent by cash |
| Apr 30 | Cash withdrawn for household purposes ₹ 5,000 |

Record the above given business transactions in Journal

***Solution:***

| Books of TARA Traders Journal | | | | | |
|---|---|---|---|---|---|
| Date 2016 | Particulars | | L.F | Dr. | Cr. |
| Apr. 1 | Cash A/c | Dr. | | 5,00,000 | |
| | To Capital A/c | | | | 5,00,000 |
| | (Being cash used by Proprietor) | | | | |
| | | | | | |
| Apr. 5 | Purchase A/c | Dr. | | 50,000 | |
| | To Mohan A/c | | | | 50,000 |
| | (Being goods purchased on credit) | | | | |
| | | | | | |
| Apr. 6 | Stationery A/c | Dr. | | 4,000 | |
| | To Cash A/c | | | | 4,000 |
| | (Being purchase of stationer for cash) | | | | |
| | | | | | |
| Apr. 10 | Kotak A/c | Dr. | | 1,00,000 | |
| | To Cash A/c | | | | 1,00,000 |
| | (Being opened a bank A/c with Kotak) | | | | |
| | | | | | |
| Apr. 11 | Siya Manufacturers A/c | Dr. | | 50,000 | |
| | To Sales A/c | | | | 50,000 |
| | (Being goods sold to Siya on credit) | | | | |
| | | | | | |
| Apr. 12 | Kotak Bank A/c | Dr. | | 50,000 | |
| | To Siya Manufactures A/c | | | | 50,000 |
| | (Being Cheque received from Siya) | | | | |
| | | | | | |
| Apr. 13 | Insurance Premium A/c | Dr. | | 10,000 | |

| | | | | |
|---|---|---|---|---|
| | To Kotak Bank A/c | | | 10,000 |
| | (Being Insurance premium paid by cheque) | | | |
| | | | | |
| Apr. 14 | Nidhi Manufacturers A/c Dr. | | 20,000 | |
| | To Sales A/c | | | 20,000 |
| | (Being goods sold to Nidhi on credit) | | | |
| Apr. 15 | Cash A/c Dr. | | 20,000 | |
| | To Nidhi Manufacturers A/c | | | 20,000 |
| | (Being Cash Received from Nidhi) | | | |
| | | | | |
| Apr. 16 | Purchase A/c Dr. | | 30,000 | |
| | To Gita Traders A/c | | | 30,000 |
| | (Being goods purchased on credit) | | | |
| | | | | |
| Apr. 17 | Furniture A/c Dr. | | 10,000 | |
| | To Cash A/c | | | 10,000 |
| | (Being furniture purchased) | | | |
| | | | | |
| Apr. 18 | Charity A/c Dr. | | 5,000 | |
| | To Purchase A/c | | | 5,000 |
| | (Being goods given as charity) | | | |
| | | | | |
| Apr. 19 | Rent A/c Dr. | | 10,000 | |
| | To Cash A/c | | | 10,000 |
| | (Being rent paid) | | | |
| | | | | |
| Apr. 30 | Drawings A/c Dr. | | 5,000 | |
| | To Cash A/c | | | 5,000 |
| | | | | |
| | | | 8,64,000 | 8,64,000 |

**Note:** When there are many transactions recorded in a number of pages in the journal book, then at the end of each page of the journal book, the amount columns are totalled and carried forward (c/f) to the next page where such amounts are recorded as brought forward (b/f) balances.

### 3.4.3 Compound Journal Entry

A journal entry in which more than one debit account, more than one credit account or more than one of both debit and credit accounts are involved in the transactions on the same date related to one particular account or one particular Nature of account is termed as Compound Entry.

Instead of recording several Journal entries we can record the transaction which involves more than one debit or credit in a single journal entry called Compound Journal Entry.

Compound Journal Entry can be recorded in any one of the following manner.

1. One account will be debited and multiple accounts will be credited.
2. Multiple accounts will be debited and one accounts will be credited.
3. Multiple accounts will be debited and multiple accounts will be credited.

***Illustration 4:** Recording business transactions in Compound Journal.*

1. As on 1st June 2016, payment made to Raghav for ₹ 10,000 and discount received for ₹ 1,000
2. As on 2nd June 2016, cash of ₹ 20,000 was received from Mohan and discount allowed for ₹ 2,000
3. As on 4th June 2016, running business was purchased by Rakesh and the following assets and liabilities details are shown below.

   Cash ₹ 10,000; Furniture; ₹ 5,000; Land ₹ 20,000; Creditors ₹ 7,000; Bank Overdraft ₹ 2,000; Capital ₹ 26,000

***Solution:***

| Compound Journal Entry | | | | |
|---|---|---|---|---|
| Date 2016 | Particulars | L.F | Dr. | Cr. |
| Jun. 1 | Raghav A/c Dr. | | 11,000 | |
| | To Cash A/c | | | 10,000 |
| | To Discount Received A/c | | | 1,000 |
| | (Being payment made to Raghav after discount) | | | |
| | | | | |
| Jun. 2 | Cash A/c Dr. | | 20,000 | |
| | Discount Allowed A/c Dr. | | 2,000 | |
| | To Mohan's A/c | | | 22,000 |
| | (Being cash received from Mohan and discount allowed) | | | |
| | | | | |
| Jun. 4 | Cash A/c Dr. | | 10,000 | |
| | Furniture A/c Dr. | | 5,000 | |
| | Land A/c Dr. | | 20,000 | |
| | To Bank Overdraft A/c | | | 2,000 |
| | To Creditors A/c | | | 7,000 |
| | To Capital A/c | | | 26,000 |
| | (Being commencement of business by taking over) | | | |
| | | | 68,000 | 68,000 |

***Illustration 5:** TARA Enterprises furnishes the following information regarding transactions for the month of July, 2016.*

| Date (2016) | Transactions |
|---|---|
| Jul. 5 | Purchased goods from Mohan for ₹ 1, 00,000 for cash 80,000 and on credit ₹20,000. |
| Jul. 6 | Sold Goods for ₹ 50,000 to RK Traders for cash ₹ 30,000 and on credit ₹ 20,000. |
| Jul. 15 | Cash payment made to Mohan for ₹20,000. |
| Jul. 17 | Cash of ₹ 20,000 was received from RK Traders. |
| Jul. 18 | Purchased goods from Mohan for ₹ 1, 00,000 for cash and discount of ₹ 5,000 was received. |
| Jul. 20 | Sold goods to TT Traders for ₹ 2, 00,000 for cash and discount of ₹ 10,000 was allowed. |

## *Solution:*

| Date 2016 | Particulars | | L.F | Dr. | Cr. |
|---|---|---|---|---|---|
| Jul. 5 | Purchase A/c | Dr. | | 1,00,000 | |
| | To Cash A/c | | | | 80,000 |
| | To Mohan's A/c | | | | 20,000 |
| | (Being goods purchased on cash and credit from Mohan) | | | | |
| | | | | | |
| Jul. 6 | Cash Account | Dr. | | 30,000 | |
| | RK Traders A/c | Dr. | | 20,000 | |
| | To Sales A/c | | | | 50,000 |
| | (Being goods sold on credit and cash to RK Traders) | | | | |
| | | | | | |
| Jul. 15 | Mohan's A/c | | | 20,000 | |
| | To Cash A/c | | | | 20,000 |
| | (Being Cash paid to Mohan for the purchases made) | | | | |
| | | | | | |
| Jul. 17 | Cash A/c | | | 20,000 | |
| | To RK Traders A/c | | | | 20,000 |
| | (Being cash received from RK Traders) | | | | |
| Jul. 18 | Purchase A/c | | | 1,00,000 | |
| | To Mohan's A/c | | | | 95,000 |
| | To Discount Received A/c | | | | 5,000 |
| | (Being goods purchased from Mohan and received discount) | | | | |
| | | | | | |
| Jul-20 | TT Traders A/c | | | 2,00,000 | |
| | To Sales A/c | | | | 1,90,000 |
| | To Discount Received A/c | | | | 10,000 |
| | | | | **4,90,000** | **4,90,000** |

### 3.4.4 Opening Entry

Opening entry is the first entry recorded in the Journal, in case of continuous business the assets and Liabilities appearing in the previous year's balance sheet will have to be bought forward to the current year, these details are recorded in the Journal and this is called as Opening Entry.

Even in case of new business when the capital is introduced by the proprietor into the business, this will be the first entry to be recorded in the Journal.

Rule of recording Opening Entry is *all assets accounts are debited* and *all liabilities accounts are credited* and *the excess of Assets or Debits over Liabilities or Credits represents Capital* and it is *credited to the Capital Account*. Thus in an Illustration or question, if the capital Balance is not given then the same can be found out by the following Accounting Equation:

Assets – Liabilities = Capital

The opening entry illustration is given below for clear understanding.

***Illustration 6:*** *Record the opening entry as on 1st April, 2016 on the basis of the following information taken from the business of KAR Traders.*

| Closing Balance as on 31st March, 2016 | Amounts (₹) |
|---|---|
| Cash in Hand | 5,000 Dr. |
| Stock of Goods | 10,000 Dr. |
| Plant | 20,000 Dr. |
| Sundry Debtors | 15,000 Dr. |
| Land and Machinery | 20,000 Dr. |
| Sundry Creditors | 25,000 Cr. |

## *Solution:*

| Journal | | | | | |
|---|---|---|---|---|---|
| **Date 2016** | **Particulars** | | **L.F** | **Dr.** | **Cr.** |
| Apr. 1 | Cash A/c | Dr. | | 5,000 | |
| | Stock of Goods | Dr. | | 10,000 | |
| | Plant | Dr. | | 20,000 | |
| | Sundry Debtors | Dr. | | 15,000 | |
| | Land and Machinery | Dr. | | 20,000 | |
| | To Sundry Creditors | | | | 25,000 |
| | To Capital A/c (Balancing Figure) | | | | 45,000 |
| | (Being Balances bought forwards from the last year) | | | | |
| | | | | **70,000** | **70,000** |

**Note:** Capital A/c Balancing figure shows as ₹ 45,000, because Total Asset is ₹ 70,000 and Total Liability is ₹ 25,000. After applying Accounting Equation (Assets – Liability = Capital), we will get the Capital A/c values as ₹ 45,000.

***Illustration 7:*** *Record the following transaction in Books of TS Traders as on 1st April 2016*

1. The following table shows the closing balance of TS Traders.

| Opening Entry | |
|---|---|
| **Closing Balance as on 31st March, 2016** | **Amounts (₹)** |
| Cash in Hand | 10,000 Dr. |
| Stock of Goods | 11,000 Dr. |
| Plant | 10,000 Dr. |
| Cash in Bank | 20,000 Dr. |
| Sundry Debtors | 10,000 Dr. |
| Land and Machinery | 10,000 Dr. |
| Sundry Creditors | 25,000 Cr. |
| Loan from JK | 20,000 Cr. |

2. As on 2nd April 2016, purchased goods for cash ₹ 50,000 and discount of ₹ 5,000 was received from the Supplier on the total purchase value.
3. As on 3rd of April 2016, sold goods to TMB traders on credit for ₹ 20,000
4. As on 4th of April 2016, sold goods to TR Traders for cash ₹ 20,000 and discount of ₹ 2,000 was allowed on total sales value.
5. As on 10th of April 2016, received Cash ₹ 20,000 from TMB Traders
6. As on 23rd of April 2016, interest received from Madhukar ₹ 1,000

| Journal | | | | | |
|---|---|---|---|---|---|
| Date 2016 | Particulars | | L.F | Dr. | Cr. |
| Apr. 1 | Cash in Hand A/c | Dr. | | 10,000 | |
| | Stock of goods A/c | Dr. | | 11,000 | |
| | Plant A/c | Dr. | | 10,000 | |
| | Cash in Bank A/c | Dr. | | 20,000 | |
| | Sundry Debtors A/c | Dr. | | 10,000 | |
| | Land and Machinery A/c | Dr. | | 10,000 | |
| | To Sundry Creditors A/c | | | | 25,000 |
| | To Loan from JK A/c | | | | 20,000 |
| | To Capital A/c (Balancing figure) | | | | 26,000 |
| | (Being balances bought forward from last year.) | | | | |
| | | | | | |
| Apr. 2 | Purchase A/c | Dr. | | 50,000 | |
| | To Cash A/c | | | | 45,000 |
| | To Discount Received A/c | | | | 5,000 |
| | (Being Purchased goods for cash and received discount.) | | | | |
| | | | | | |
| Apr. 3 | TMB Traders A/c | Dr. | | 20,000 | |
| | To Sales A/c | | | | 20,000 |
| | (Being goods sold to TMB Traders on credit.) | | | | |
| | | | | | |
| Apr. 4 | Cash A/c | Dr. | | 18,000 | |
| | Discount Allowed A/c | Dr. | | 2,000 | |
| | To Sales A/c | | | | 20,000 |
| | (Being goods sold for cash and discount was allowed.) | | | | |
| | | | | | |
| Apr. 10 | Cash A/c | Dr. | | 20,000 | |
| | To TMB Traders | | | | 20,000 |
| | (Being cash received from TMB Traders.) | | | | |
| | | | | | |
| Apr. 23 | Cash A/c | Dr. | | 1,000 | |
| | To Interest Received A/c | | | | 1,000 |
| | (Being interest received from Madhukar) | | | | |
| | | | | 1,82,000 | 1,82,000 |

## 3.5 LEDGER

Ledger is the principal book of the accounting system and is also called the Book of Final Entry. This Book contains all the accounts of a business or all the accounts of a particular type. In a ledger, the transactions of the same nature are classified and grouped together at one place in the form of accounts. Ledgers may be in the form of a bound register, cards, or separate sheets maintained in a loose leaf binder.

### 3.5.1 Need of Ledger

A well-maintained accounting system plays a significant role in the growth of an organisation. The ledger, is a record of the transactions, assumes great importance in the process. The net result of all transactions in respect of a particular account on a given date can be ascertained only from the ledger.

For example, the organisation can ascertain the amount due from a customer only from the ledger. Ledgers, thus act as a reference for the transactions of an organisation on any given date. Accounts are opened in the ledger in a specific order, facilitating easy posting and location. For example, accounts may be opened in the same order as they appear in the profit and loss account or balance sheet.

The format of the Ledger is shown below:

| Dr. | | Title of the Account | | | | | Cr. |
|---|---|---|---|---|---|---|---|
| Date 2016 | Particulars | J.F | Amount (₹) | Date 2016 | Particulars | J.F | Amount (₹) |
| | | | | | | | |
| | | | | | | | |

The columns contain the following information:

- **Title of the account:** The name of the item is written at the top as the title of the account. The title of the account ends with the suffix, 'Account'.
- **Dr./Cr.:** Dr.is the debit side of the account, i.e. the left side and Cr. is the credit side of the account, i.e. the right side.
- **Date:** Year, month, and date of transactions are posted in chronological order in this column.
- **Particulars:** Name of the item with reference to the original book of entry is written on debit/credit side of the account.
- **Journal Folio (J.F.):** It records the page number of the original book of entry on which the relevant transaction is recorded. This column is filled in at the time of posting.
- **Amount:** It records the amount in numerical figures, corresponding to what has been entered in the amount column of the original book of entry.

### 3.5.2 Difference between Journal and Ledger

Journal and ledger are the most important books of the double entry system of accounting. The following table highlights the differences between a journal and a ledger.

| Journal | Ledger |
|---|---|
| It is a Book of Original Entry or Primary Entry, as all transactions are first recorded in the Journal. | It is a Book of Final Entry or Secondary Entry, as all transactions are finally recorded in the Ledger. |
| It is the book for chronological record. | It is the book for analytical record. |
| Journal, as a book of source entry, gets greater importance as legal evidence. | Ledger gets lesser importance as legal evidence. |
| Transaction is the basis of classification of data. | Account is the basis of classification of data. |
| The process of recording in the journal is known as journalising. | The process of recording in the ledger is known as posting. |
| In the journal, information related to one particular account is not found in one place. | In the Ledger, the information related to one particular account is found in one place. |
| In journal, transactions are recorded every day, hence it is a daily record. | Ledger posting is done periodically like weekly, fortnightly, monthly or quarterly based on the requirement of the business concerns. |
| In Journal the values are totalled not balanced. | In the Ledger the values are balanced. |

### 3.5.3 Classification of Ledger Accounts

Ledger accounts are classified into five categories. They are:

- Assets
- Liabilities
- Capital
- Revenues/gains
- Expense/losses

All these accounts may further be classified into two groups, namely:

- Permanent accounts (assets, liabilities, and capital accounts)
- Temporary accounts (revenue and expense accounts)

Permanent accounts are balanced and carried forward to the next accounting period. The temporary accounts are closed at the end of the accounting period by transferring them to the trading account and profit and loss account. All permanent accounts appear in the balance sheet.

### 3.5.4 Posting from Journal

The process of transferring entries from the books of original entry (journal) to the ledger is called posting. In other words, posting is the process of grouping all the transactions in respect to a particular account at one place for a meaningful conclusion and to further the accounting process. Depending on the requirement and convenience of the business, posting from the journal may be done periodically, i.e. weekly, fortnightly, or monthly.

The process of posting from journal to the ledger involves the following steps.

**Step 1:** Locate in the ledger, the account to be debited as entered in the journal.

**Step 2:** Enter the date of transaction in the date column on the debit side.

**Step 3:** In the particulars column, write the name of the account through which it has been debited in the journal. For example, sold books for cash ₹ 25,000. Now, in the cash account on the debit side in the particulars column, 'Books' is entered, signifying that cash is received from the sale of books. In the books account, in the ledger on the credit side in the particulars column, the word, cash is recorded. The same procedure is followed for all the entries recorded in the journal.

**Step 4:** Enter the page number of the journal in the folio column and in the journal, write the page number of the ledger on which a particular account appears.

**Step 5:** Enter the relevant amount in the amount column on the debit side. It may be noted that the same procedure is followed for making the entry on the credit side of that account to be credited. An account is opened only once the ledger and all entries relating to a particular account are posted on the debit side or credit side, as the case may be.

### 3.5.5 Rules of Posting

1. **Separate accounts should be opened:** In journal different accounts are recorded in the chronological manner, while posting these accounts into the Ledger a separate accounts should be maintained or opened. For Example a separate accounts may be opened for Sales, Purchase, Cash, Capital, Sales Returns and Purchases Returns etc.
2. **Particular Account which is debited in the Journal:** The particular account which is debited in Journal, should also be debited in the Ledger and a reference should be made for other account which is credited in the journal. For example, for Cash Purchases, the Purchase account should be debited in the Ledger and a reference should be given of the Cash account, which is credited in Ledger.
3. **Particular Account which is credited in the Journal:** The particular account which is credited in Journal, should also be credited in the Ledger and a reference should be made for other account which is debited in the journal. For example, for Cash Purchases, the Cash account should be credited in the Ledger and a reference should be given of the Purchase account in the Ledger.

From the above details we will come to know that the accounts which are debited and credited in Journal should also be debited and credited in the Ledger while posting and also proper reference should be given for the other account which is credited or debited in the Journal

The following illustration will demonstrate how the transactions are posted to Ledger from Journal i.e., how the transactions are moved from Book of original entry to Book of final entry.

***Illustration 8:*** *Record the following transactions in the journal and post them into the Ledger.*

1. As on 2nd April 2016, purchased goods for cash ₹ 20,000.
2. As on 3rd April 2016, sold goods for cash ₹ 30,000.

***Solution:***

The above entries will be recorded in the books of original entry i.e. Journal as shown below;

Journal

| Date 2016 | Particulars | | L.F | Dr. | Cr. |
|---|---|---|---|---|---|
| Apr. 2 | Purchase A/c | Dr. | | 20,000 | |
| | To Cash Account | | | | 20,000 |
| | (Being purchased goods for cash) | | | | |
| | | | | | |
| Apr. 3 | Cash A/c | Dr. | | 30,000 | |
| | To Sales A/c | | | | 30,000 |
| | (Being goods sold for cash) | | | | |
| | | | | | |

In the Ledger three accounts will be opened that is Purchase A/c, Cash A/c and Sales A/c. In the Journal Purchase A/c is debited, hence while preparing the ledger the same account will be debited and the Cash account is credited in the Journal and the same account will be credited in the Ledger as shown below:

Dr. Purchase Account Cr.

| Date 2016 | Particulars | J.F | ₹ | Date 2016 | Particulars | J.F | ₹ |
|---|---|---|---|---|---|---|---|
| Apr. 2 | Cash A/c | | 20,000 | | | | |
| | | | | | | | |

Dr. Cash Account Cr.

| Date 2016 | Particulars | | ₹ | Date 2016 | Particulars | | ₹ |
|---|---|---|---|---|---|---|---|
| Apr. 3 | Sales A/c | | 30,000 | Apr. 2 | Purchase | | 20,000 |
| | | | | | | | |

| Dr. | | | Sales Account | | | | Cr. |
|---|---|---|---|---|---|---|---|
| Date 2016 | Particulars | | ₹ | Date 2016 | Particulars | | ₹ |
| | | | | Apr. 3 | Cash A/c | | 30,000 |
| | | | | | | | |

**Note:** Purchase A/c is debited in Journal and the same is debited in the Ledger, Cash A/c is credited in the Journal (Purchase transaction) and the same is credited in Ledger.

Sales A/c is credited in the Journal and the same is credited in the Ledger, Cash A/c debited in the Journal (Sales transaction) and the same is debited in Ledger

### 3.5.6 'To' and 'By' Usage

While posting in the Ledger the words "To" and "By" are used regularly. "To" is used for the accounts which are to be debited in the Ledger and "By" is used for the accounts which are to be credited in the Ledger.

**For Example:** In the above illustration the first Ledger account shows the Cash A/ c on the debit side of the ledger, here we can use "To Cash A/c" instead of Cash A/c, similarly in case of second ledger account purchase is credited in the ledger, here we can use "By Purchase A/c" instead of Purchase A/c.

The following illustration will explain how the word "To" and "By" are used while posting the Transaction into Ledger.

***Illustration 9:*** *Recording the following transactions in Journal and Post them into the Ledger, while posting use the words "To" and "By"*

1. As on 22nd April 2016, purchased goods for cash ₹ 10,000.
2. As on 23rd April 2016, sold goods for cash ₹ 20,000.

***Solution:***

| Journal | | | | | |
|---|---|---|---|---|---|
| Date 2016 | Particulars | | L.F | Dr. | Cr. |
| Apr. 22 | Purchase A/c | Dr. | | 10,000 | |
| | To Cash Account | | | | 10,000 |
| | (Being purchased goods for cash) | | | | |
| | | | | | |
| Apr. 23 | Cash A/c | Dr. | | 20,000 | |
| | To Sales A/c | | | | 20,000 |
| | (Being goods sold for cash) | | | | |
| | | | | | |

| Dr. | | | Purchase Account | | | | Cr. |
|---|---|---|---|---|---|---|---|
| Date 2016 | Particulars | J.F | ₹ | Date 2016 | Particulars | J.F | ₹ |
| Apr. 22 | To Cash A/c | | 10,000 | | | | |
| | | | | | | | |

| Dr. | | | Cash Account | | | | Cr. |
|---|---|---|---|---|---|---|---|
| Date 2016 | Particulars | | ₹ | Date 2016 | Particulars | | ₹ |
| Apr. 23 | To Sales A/c | | 20,000 | Apr. 22 | By Purchase | | 10,000 |
| | | | | | | | |

| Dr. | | | Sales Account | | | | Cr. |
|---|---|---|---|---|---|---|---|
| Date 2016 | Particulars | | ₹ | Date 2016 | Particulars | | ₹ |
| | | | | Apr. 23 | By Cash A/c | | 20,000 |
| | | | | | | | |

### 3.5.7 Balancing of Ledger Account

Transactions in the ledger Account are arranged in the classified manner. At a certain period like Monthly, Quarterly or Yearly, the business concern will be interested in knowing the position of the particular account, so to know the position of the Particular account we should total up the debits and credits separately and find out the net balance amount, this process of finding the net balance of a particular account after considering debits and credits of an account is termed as Balancing of Ledger Account.

So, there is the need to find out whether the particular Ledger account has received benefit more than it has given or it has given more benefit than it has received as on any particular date. In other words to find out the position of an account, it is very important to balance the account on the given date.

#### *3.5.7.1 Steps to be followed while balancing the Ledger Account*

1. **Find out the difference between the debits and credits:** Total up both the sides of the account and find out the difference.
2. **Enter the difference amount on the side of the account which is smaller with the reference:** Once the difference is found out enter the difference amount on the side of the account which is smaller with a reference stating that To Balance carried forward or carries down (c/f or c/d) to the next period. On the other side in the beginning of the next balancing period a reference is used to state that the opening balance has been brought forward or brought down (b/f or b/d), from the previous period.

**Note:** A ledger account will have a debit balance or a credit balance. If the credit side of the ledger account is more than its debit side total, then the difference is called as Credit balance. On the other side if the debit side of the account is more than its credit side total, then the difference is called as Debit Balance

The following illustration will demonstrate how the ledger accounts are balanced.

***Illustration 10:*** *Record the following transactions in the books of SP Traders and post them into Ledger and balance the accounts on 30th April 2016.*

1. As on 1st April 2016, Ashok started a business with a capital of ₹ 20,000.
2. As on 2nd April 2016, purchased goods from SK Traders on credit for ₹ 10,000.
3. As on 10th April 2016, paid cash of ₹ 10,000 to SK Traders.
4. As on 12th April 2016, sold goods to Shobha Enterprises for ₹ 30,000

5. As on 15th April 2016, received cash of ₹ 30,000 from Shobha Enterprises.
6. As on 16th April 2016, purchase goods from SK Traders for ₹ 20,000
7. As on 17th April 2016, paid cash of ₹ 20,000 to SK Traders.
8. As on 18th April 2016, sold goods to Shobha Enterprises for ₹ 20,000
9. As on 30th April 2016, received a cash of ₹ 20,000 from Shobha Enterprises.

***Solution:***

Recording the transactions in the books of SP Traders for the month of April 2016.

**Journal**

| Date 2016 | Particulars | | L.F | Dr. | Cr. |
|---|---|---|---|---|---|
| Apr. 1 | Cash A/c | Dr. | | 20,000 | |
| | To Capital A/c | | | | 20,000 |
| | (Being Commencement of business) | | | | |
| | | | | | |
| Apr. 2 | Purchase A/c | Dr. | | 10,000 | |
| | To SK Traders A/c | | | | 10,000 |
| | (Being goods sold on credit to SK Traders) | | | | |
| | | | | | |
| Apr. 10 | SK Traders A/c | Dr. | | 10,000 | |
| | To Cash A/c | | | | 10,000 |
| | (Being Cash paid to SK Traders for the purchases made) | | | | |
| | | | | | |
| Apr. 12 | Shobha Enterprises A/c | Dr. | | 30,000 | |
| | To Sales A/c | | | | 30,000 |
| | (Being goods sold on credit) | | | | |
| | | | | | |
| Apr. 15 | Cash A/c | Dr. | | 30,000 | |
| | To Shobha Enterprises A/c | | | | 30,000 |
| | (Being cash received from Shobha Enterprises) | | | | |
| | **Total c/f** | | | **1,00,000** | **1,00,000** |
| | **Total b/f** | | | **1,00,000** | **1,00,000** |
| Apr. 16 | Purchase A/c | Dr. | | 20,000 | |
| | To SK Traders A/c | | | | 20,000 |
| | (Being goods sold on credit to SK Traders) | | | | |
| | | | | | |
| Apr. 17 | SK Traders A/c | Dr. | | 20,000 | |
| | To Cash A/c | | | | 20,000 |
| | (Being Cash paid to SK Traders for the purchases made) | | | | |
| | | | | | |
| Apr. 18 | Shobha Enterprises A/c | Dr. | | 20,000 | |
| | To Sales A/c | | | | 20,000 |
| | (Being goods sold on credit) | | | | |
| | | | | | |
| Apr. 30 | Cash A/c | Dr. | | 20,000 | |
| | To Shobha Enterprises A/c | | | | 20,000 |
| | (Being cash received from Shobha Enterprises) | | | | |
| | **Total** | | | **1,80,000** | **1,80,000** |

## *Posting in ledger*

**Cash Account**

| Dr. Date 2016 | Particulars | J.F | ₹ | Date 2016 | Particulars | J.F | ₹ Cr. |
|---|---|---|---|---|---|---|---|
| Apr. 1 | To Capital A/c | | 20,000 | Apr. 10 | By SK Traders A/c | | 10,000 |
| Apr. 15 | To Shobha Enterprises A/c | | 30,000 | Apr. 17 | By SK Traders A/c | | 20,000 |
| Apr. 30 | To Shobha Enterprises A/c | | 20,000 | Apr. 30 | By Balance c/d | | 40,000 |
| | | | 70,000 | | | | 70,000 |
| May. 1 | To Balance b/d | | 40,000 | | | | |

**Note:** In the above Ledger Cash Account, we can find out that the cash account is having Debit Balance of ₹ 40,000 because the balance of the account is always known by the side which is greater, in the above account debit side is greater than the credit side.

**Capital Account**

| Date 2016 | Particulars | J.F | ₹ | Date 2016 | Particulars | J.F | ₹ |
|---|---|---|---|---|---|---|---|
| Apr. 30 | To Balance c/d | | 20,000 | Apr. 1 | By Cash A/c | | 20,000 |
| | | | 20,000 | | | | 20,000 |
| | | | | May. 1 | By Balance b/d | | 20,000 |

**Note:** In the above Ledger Capital Account, we can find out that the capital account is having credit Balance of ₹ 20,000, because credit side of capital account is more than the debit side.

**Purchases Account**

| Date 2016 | Particulars | J.F | ₹ | Date 2016 | Particulars | J.F | ₹ |
|---|---|---|---|---|---|---|---|
| Apr. 2 | To SK Traders A/c | | 10,000 | Apr. 30 | By Balance c/d | | 30,000 |
| Apr. 16 | To SK Traders A/c | | 20,000 | | | | |
| | | | 30,000 | | | | 30,000 |
| May. 1 | To Balance b/d | | 30,000 | | | | |

**SK Trader's Account**

| Date 2016 | Particulars | J.F | ₹ | Date 2016 | Particulars | J.F | ₹ |
|---|---|---|---|---|---|---|---|
| Apr. 10 | To Cash A/c | | 10,000 | Apr. 2 | By Purchase A/c | | 10,000 |
| Apr. 17 | To Cash A/c | | 20,000 | Apr. 16 | By Purchase A/c | | 20,000 |
| | | | 30,000 | | | | 30,000 |

**Shobha Enterprises Account**

| Date 2016 | Particulars | J.F | ₹ | Date 2016 | Particulars | J.F | ₹ |
|---|---|---|---|---|---|---|---|
| Apr. 12 | To Sales A/c | | 30,000 | Apr. 15 | By Cash A/c | | 30,000 |
| Apr. 18 | To Sales A/c | | 20,000 | Apr. 30 | By Cash A/c | | 20,000 |
| | | | 50,000 | | | | 50,000 |

**Sales Account**

| Date 2016 | Particulars | J.F | ₹ | Date 2016 | Particulars | J.F | ₹ |
|---|---|---|---|---|---|---|---|
| Apr. 30 | By Balance c/d | | 50,000 | Apr. 12 | By Shobha Enterprises | | 30,000 |
| | | | | Apr. 18 | By Shobha Enterprises | | 20,000 |
| | | | 50,000 | | | | 50,000 |
| | | | | May. 1 | By Balance b/d | | 50,000 |

## 3.6 TRIAL BALANCE

In Trial Balance, the balances of various accounts (debit balances and credit balances) are listed in a sheet or a statement at the end of the accounting period. In the previous sections you have learnt how to record the transactions in Journal or Book of Original Entry and then posted these transactions in Ledger or Book of Final Entry and balanced the accounts, now to complete the accounting cycle, accounts have to be compiled by preparing a trial balance.

A trial balance is the conclusion of the accounting process. It is the link between primary and final accounting work. The finalisation of accounts cannot be made directly from a journal or ledger as it requires a summary of all ledger account balances of a particular period. The task of preparing the statements is simplified as the accountant can take the account balances from the trial balance instead of looking them up in the ledger.

The trial balance is a statement showing the balances or total of debits and credits of all the accounts in the ledger, with a view to verify the arithmetical accuracy of posting to the ledger accounts.

### 3.6.1 Objectives of Trial Balance:

1. **Ascertains the Arithmetical Accuracy of the accounting entries:** As per dual aspect concept for every debit, there must be an equivalent credit. Trial balance contains the details of all debit balance and credit balance of all the accounts involved in the transactions, in short it is a summary of all the ledger balances, therefore if two sides of the ledger are equal, then it is an indication that the books of accounts are arithmetically accurate
2. **Helps in preparation of financial statements:** The trial balance is a link between accounting records and financial statements. When preparing a financial statement, the ledger need not be referred. In fact, the availability of a trial balance is the first step in the preparation of financial statements. All revenue and expense accounts appearing in the trial balance are transferred to the trading and profit and loss accounts and all liabilities, capital, and asset accounts are transferred to the balance sheet.
3. **Summarised Ledger:** Trial Balances contains the ledger balances on a particular date, the position of the particular account can be found out by looking at the Trial Balance.
4. **Helps in identifying the errors:** In Trial Balance, when the totals of the debit and credit columns are not equal then this indicates that there is an error.

   The error may have occurred at any of the following stages of the accounting process:

   - While posting the Journal entries in Ledger.
   - While balancing ledger accounts
   - While carrying the ledger account balance to the Trial Balance.
   - While totalling the Trial Balance debit and credit columns
   - While totalling of Subsidiary Books

### 3.6.2 Steps to be followed while preparing Trial Balance

1. Determine the balances of each ledger account
2. Place each ledger account balance in the debit or credit column, as the case may be. (If an account has zero balance, it can be included in the trial balance with zero in the column for its normal balance.)
3. Calculate the total of the debit balances column.
4. Calculate the total of the credit balances column.
5. Verify that the sum of debit balances equals the sum of credit balances. All assets, expenses, and receivables accounts shall have debit balances, while all liabilities, revenues, and payables accounts shall have credit balances.

### 3.6.3 Methods of Preparing Trial Balance

Trial Balance can be prepared by any one of the below given methods.

1. **Total Method:** In this method, the total of each side in the ledger (debit and credit) is ascertained separately and shown in the trial balance, in the respective columns. The total of the debit column should agree with the total of the credit column as the accounts are based on the double entry system.
2. **Balance Method:** Balances method is the most widely used method in practice. In this method, the trial balance is prepared by showing the balances of all ledger accounts and then totalling the debit and credit columns to ensure that they are correct. The account balances are used because the balance summarises the net effect of all transactions related to an account and helps in preparing financial statements.
3. **Total and Balance Method:** This method is a combination of the totals method and balance method. In this method, four columns are prepared for amount. Two columns are meant for the debit and credit totals of various accounts and the other two are for the debit and credit balances of these accounts.

   Sample format of Trial Balance is as shown below:

| Trial Balance as on 31st March, 2016 | | | |
|---|---|---|---|
| Particulars | L.F | Debit (₹) | Credit (₹) |
| | | | |
| | | | |

**Particulars Column:** In this column names of various ledger accounts are recorded like Capital Account, Sales Account, Purchase Account, Cash Account etc.

**Ledger Folio (L.F):** In this column the page number of ledger accounts will be recorded, these are number where a particular ledger is found.

**Debit Column:** In this column Debit Balance of various ledger accounts are recorded.

**Credit Column:** In this column Credit Balance of various ledger accounts are recorded.

The following illustration will demonstrate how to prepare different types of Trial balance.

***Illustration 11:** Record the following transactions in the books of account of MSK Traders, then post them into the ledger and Prepare Trial Balance based on Balance Method as on 31st May 2016.*

| Date (2016) | Transactions |
|---|---|
| May. 1 | Ashok started a business with a capital of ₹ 30,000. |
| May. 2 | Purchased goods from SK Traders on credit for ₹ 20,000. |
| May. 10 | Paid cash of ₹ 20,000 to SK Traders. |
| May. 12 | Sold goods to Shobha Enterprises on credit for ₹ 40,000 |
| May. 15 | Received cash of ₹ 40,000 from Shobha Enterprises. |
| May. 16 | Purchase goods from SK Traders for ₹ 30,000 |
| May. 17 | Paid cash of ₹ 30,000 to SK Traders. |
| May. 18 | Sold goods to Shobha Enterprises on credit for ₹ 30,000. |
| May. 20 | Received a cash of ₹ 30,000 from Shobha Enterprises. |
| May. 21 | Sold goods to Ramesh Industries for cash ₹50,000. |
| May. 23 | Ramesh Industries returned goods of ₹10,000. |
| May. 24 | Paid Salaries through cheque for ₹ 20,000. |
| May. 25 | Received interest of ₹ 2,000. |
| May. 26 | Purchases Stationery for Cash ₹ 3,000. |
| May. 31 | Prepaid insurance for cash ₹ 5,000. |

## *Solution:*

1. Journalising the transactions in the books of MSK Traders for the Month of May 2016

| Date 2016 | Particulars | L.F | Dr. | Cr. |
|---|---|---|---|---|
| May. 1 | Cash A/c Dr. | | 30,000 | |
| | To Capital A/c | | | 30,000 |
| | (Being Commencement of business) | | | |
| | | | | |
| May. 2 | Purchase A/c Dr. | | 20,000 | |
| | To SK Traders A/c | | | 20,000 |
| | (Being goods sold on credit to SK Traders) | | | |
| | | | | |
| May. 10 | SK Traders A/c Dr. | | 20,000 | |
| | To Cash A/c | | | 20,000 |
| | (Being Cash paid to SK Traders for the purchases made) | | | |
| | | | | |
| May. 12 | Shobha Enterprises A/c Dr. | | 40,000 | |
| | To Sales A/c | | | 40,000 |
| | (Being goods sold on credit) | | | |
| | | | | |
| May. 15 | Cash A/c Dr. | | 40,000 | |
| | To Shobha Enterprises A/c | | | 40,000 |
| | (Being cash received from Shobha Enterprises) | | | |
| | | | | |
| May. 16 | Purchase A/c Dr. | | 30,000 | |
| | To SK Traders A/c | | | 30,000 |
| | (Being goods sold on credit to SK Traders) | | | |
| | | | | |
| May. 17 | SK Traders A/c Dr. | | 30,000 | |
| | To Cash A/c | | | 30,000 |
| | (Being Cash paid to SK Traders for the purchases made) | | | |
| | | | | |
| May. 18 | Shobha Enterprises A/c Dr. | | 30,000 | |
| | To Sales A/c | | | 30,000 |
| | (Being goods sold on credit) | | | |
| | | | | |
| May. 20 | Cash A/c Dr. | | 30,000 | |
| | To Shobha Enterprises A/c | | | 30,000 |
| | (Being cash received from Shobha Enterprises) | | | |
| | **Total c/f** | | **2,70,000** | **2,70,000** |
| | **Total b/d** | | **2,70,000** | **2,70,000** |
| May. 21 | Cash A/c Dr. | | 50,000 | |
| | To Sales A/c | | | 50,000 |
| | (Being goods sold on cash to Ramesh Industries) | | | |
| | | | | |
| May. 23 | Sales Return A/c Dr. | | 10,000 | |
| | To Cash A/c | | | 10,000 |
| | (Being goods return by the customer) | | | |
| | | | | |
| May 24. | Salaries A/c Dr. | | 20,000 | |
| | To Bank A/c | | | 20,000 |
| | (Being salaries paid through Bank) | | | |
| | | | | |
| May. 25 | Cash A/c Dr. | | 2,000 | |
| | To Interest Received A/c | | | 2,000 |
| | (Being Interest Received) | | | |
| | | | | |
| May. 26 | Stationery A/c Dr. | | 3,000 | |
| | To Cash A/c | | | 3,000 |
| | (Being Stationery purchased) | | | |
| | | | | |
| May. 31 | Insurance A/c Dr. | | 5,000 | |
| | To Cash A/c | | | 5,000 |
| | **Total** | | **3,60,000** | **3,60,000** |

2. After journalising the transaction it should be posted to Ledger.

**Cash Account**

| Date 2016 | Particulars | J.F | ₹ | Date 2016 | Particulars | J.F | ₹ |
|---|---|---|---|---|---|---|---|
| May. 1 | To Capital A/c | | 30,000 | May. 10 | By SK Traders A/c | | 20,000 |
| May. 15 | To Shobha Enterprises A/c | | 40,000 | May. 17 | By SK Traders A/c | | 30,000 |
| May. 20 | To Shobha Enterprises A/c | | 30,000 | May. 23 | By Sales Return A/c | | 10,000 |
| May. 21 | To Sales A/c | | 50,000 | May. 26 | By Stationery A/c | | 3,000 |
| May. 25 | To Interest Received A/c | | 2,000 | May. 31 | By Insurance A/c | | 5,000 |
| | | | | | By Balance c/d | | 84,000 |
| | | | 1,52,000 | | | | 1,52,000 |
| Jun. 1 | To Balance b/d | | 84,000 | | | | |

**Capital Account**

| Date 2016 | Particulars | J.F | ₹ | Date 2016 | Particulars | J.F | ₹ |
|---|---|---|---|---|---|---|---|
| May. 31 | To Balance c/d | | 30,000 | May. 1 | By Cash A/c | | 30,000 |
| | | | 30,000 | | | | 30,000 |
| | | | | Jun. 1 | By Balance b/d | | 30,000 |

**Purchases Account**

| Date 2016 | Particulars | J.F | ₹ | Date 2016 | Particulars | J.F | ₹ |
|---|---|---|---|---|---|---|---|
| May. 2 | To SK Traders A/c | | 20,000 | May.31 | By Balance c/d | | 50,000 |
| May.16 | To SK Traders A/c | | 30,000 | | | | |
| | | | 50,000 | | | | 50,000 |
| Jun. 1 | To Balance b/d | | 50,000 | | | | |

**SK Trader's Account**

| Date 2016 | Particulars | J.F | ₹ | Date 2016 | Particulars | J.F | ₹ |
|---|---|---|---|---|---|---|---|
| May.10 | To Cash A/c | | 20,000 | May.2 | By Purchase A/c | | 20,000 |
| May.17 | To Cash A/c | | 30,000 | May.16 | By Purchase A/c | | 30,000 |
| | | | 50,000 | | | | 50,000 |

**Shobha Enterprises Account**

| Date 2016 | Particulars | J.F | ₹ | Date 2016 | Particulars | J.F | ₹ |
|---|---|---|---|---|---|---|---|
| May.12 | To Sales A/c | | 40,000 | May.15 | By Cash A/c | | 40,000 |
| May.18 | To Sales A/c | | 30,000 | May.20 | By Cash A/c | | 30,000 |
| | | | 70,000 | | | | 70,000 |

**Sales Account**

| Date 2016 | Particulars | J.F | ₹ | Date 2016 | Particulars | J.F | ₹ |
|---|---|---|---|---|---|---|---|
| May.31 | By Balance c/d | | 1,20,000 | May.12 | By Shobha Enterprises A/c | | 40,000 |
| | | | | May.18 | By Shobha Enterprises A/c | | 30,000 |
| | | | | May.21 | By Cash A/c | | 50,000 |
| | | | | | | | 1,20,000 |
| | | | | Jun. 1 | By Balance b/d | | 1,20,000 |

**Sales Return Account**

| Date 2016 | Particulars | J.F | ₹ | Date 2016 | Particulars | J.F | ₹ |
|---|---|---|---|---|---|---|---|
| May.23 | To Cash A/c | | 10,000 | May.31 | By Balance c/d | | 10,000 |
| | | | 10,000 | | | | 10,000 |
| Jun. 1 | To Balance b/d | | 10,000 | | | | |

**Salaries Account**

| Date 2016 | Particulars | J.F | ₹ | Date 2016 | Particulars | J.F | ₹ |
|---|---|---|---|---|---|---|---|
| May.24 | To Bank A/c | | 20,000 | May.31 | By Balance c/d | | 20,000 |
| | | | 20,000 | | | | 20,000 |
| Jun. 1 | To Balance b/d | | 20,000 | | | | |

**Bank Account**

| Date 2016 | Particulars | J.F | ₹ | Date 2016 | Particulars | J.F | ₹ |
|---|---|---|---|---|---|---|---|
| May.31 | To Balance c/d | | 20,000 | May.24 | By Salaries A/c | | 20,000 |
| | | | 20,000 | | | | 20,000 |
| | | | | Jun.1 | By Balance b/d | | 20,000 |

**Interest Received Account**

| Date 2016 | Particulars | J.F | ₹ | Date 2016 | Particulars | J.F | ₹ |
|---|---|---|---|---|---|---|---|
| May.31 | To Balance c/d | | 2,000 | May.25 | By Cash A/c | | 2,000 |
| | | | 2,000 | | | | 2,000 |
| | | | | Jun. 1 | By Balance b/d | | 2,000 |

**Stationery Account**

| Date 2016 | Particulars | J.F | ₹ | Date 2016 | Particulars | J.F | ₹ |
|---|---|---|---|---|---|---|---|
| May.26 | To Cash A/c | | 3,000 | May.31 | By Balance c/d | | 3,000 |
| | | | 3,000 | | | | 3,000 |
| Jun. 1 | By Balance b/d | | 3,000 | | | | |

**Insurance Account**

| Date 2016 | Particulars | J.F | ₹ | Date 2016 | Particulars | J.F | ₹ |
|---|---|---|---|---|---|---|---|
| May.31 | To Cash A/c | | 5,000 | May.31 | By Balance c/d | | 5,000 |
| | | | 5,000 | | | | 5,000 |
| Jun. 1 | By Balance b/d | | 5,000 | | | | |

3. Preparation of Trial Balance.

**MSK Traders**
**Trial Balance as on 31st May, 2016**

| Particulars | L.F | Debit (₹) | Credit (₹) |
|---|---|---|---|
| Cash Account | | 84,000 | |
| Capital Account | | | 30,000 |
| Purchase Account | | 50,000 | |
| SK Traders Account | | 0 | 0 |
| Shobha Enterprises Account | | 0 | 0 |
| Sales Account | | | 1,20,000 |
| Sales Return Account | | 10,000 | |
| Salaries Account | | 20,000 | |
| Bank Account | | | 20,000 |
| Interest Received Account | | | 2,000 |
| Stationery Account | | 3,000 | |
| Insurance Account | | 5,000 | |
| **Total** | | **1,72,000** | **1,72,000** |

**Note:** The above Trial Balance is in the Balance Method format i.e., in the above trial balance the Ledger account balances (Difference amount) are taken and it is widely used format.

In this chapter we have studied about the Accounting cycle like recording the transactions in Journal and posting of the recorded transaction into the Ledger and preparation of Trial balance, which will further help in preparation of Final Statements like Balance Sheet and Profit and Loss Account.

## 3.7 SUBSIDIARY BOOKS

The business having small number of transactions is easy to record in journal. But, when the business transactions of large numbers are recorded in one journal then it becomes bulk and results in complexities. Therefore, in the modern book-keeping the journal is divided into separate journals, to record the transactions of similar nature together.

These separate journals are known as subsidiary books.

### 3.7.1 Concept/ Fundamental

These are separate books of original entry, which is based on the earlier practices of **Journal,** where a single book is used to record all the transactions of the business.

In large business enterprises, it would be difficult to record all the business transaction into a single book called journal, hence to avoid the complexity, the concept of subsidiary books were introduced which is the modern approach of book-keeping.

### 3.7.2 Advantages of Subsidiary Books

- The complexity during recording of transactions is eliminated.
- It saves the time of the accountant.
- It avoids the duplication of transactions.
- Easy to find particular transaction and post it into ledger accounts.
- It helps to rectify the manual errors and mistakes.

## 3.8 TYPES OF SUBSIDIARY BOOKS & RELATED ASPECTS

- Purchase Book/ Register
  - o Purchase Bill Specimen (**Specimen** to be **Prepare** or **Show**)
  - o Purchase Ledger Account
- Sales Book/ Register
  - o Sales Invoice Specimen (**Specimen** to be **Prepare** or **Show**)
  - o Sales Ledger Account
- Purchase Return Book/ Register
  - o Debit Notes Specimen (**Specimen** to be **Prepare** or **Show**)
  - o Purchase Return Ledger Account
- Sales Return Book/ Register
  - o Credit Notes Specimen (**Specimen** to be **Prepare** or **Show**)
  - o Sales Return Ledger Account
- Cash Book/ Register
  - o Single/ Simple/ Only Cash Column
  - o With Discount Column
  - o With Bank Column
- Petty Cash Book/ Register
  - o Imprest System
- Journal Proper

### 3.8.1 Purchase Books

This book is maintained to record all the credit purchases only, of the company. It is prepared on the basis of purchase bills received from the supplier which contains the details of the purchase transaction which are as follows:

- Date of the transaction
- Inward Invoice Number/ Bill Number
- Description of goods
  - o Quantity
  - o Rate
  - o Amt
- Terms of sales
- Any other references

The purchase book total of a particular period, is transferred to purchase account as **"To Sundries as per purchase book"** and every supplier ledger account is maintained to track the value of goods purchased from purchase account.

***Illustration 12:*** *In the books of Garuda Traders Pvt Ltd., record the following transactions in the purchase book and further prepare the respective ledger account and post entries from purchase book.*

Below is the transactions details of, 2016-April month

1. On 1-04-16, purchased goods from **Ritin Traders.**
   **Quantity:** 100 Nos
   **Rate:** 50 Nos
2. Goods received from **Ammu Wholesaler** dated on 4-04-16.
   **Quantity:** 200 Nos
   **Rate:** 40 Nos
3. Goods worth Rs. 800/- were purchased on cash from **Vertical International Traders** dated 13-04-16.
4. Bought goods from Wind Fast Pvt Ltd on 22-04-16
   **Quantity:** 140
   **Rate:** 50
5. Computer of Rs. 40000/- were purchased on 30-04-16, for office purpose from Solo Info Systems.

**Note:** 1. Kindly check the transaction no 3, will not be recorded in the purchase book.
2. Transaction no 5, will not be recorded in purchase book.

Let us see how to prepare the necessary books and applicable ledger accounts

| In the books of Garuda Traders | | | |
|---|---|---|---|
| **Purchase Book** | | | |
| **Date** | **Particulars** | **Description** | **Amt** |
| 01-04-16 | Ritin Trader | Goods<br>**Quantity:** 100 Nos<br>**Rate:** 50 Nos | 5000 |
| 04-04-16 | Ammu Wholesaler | Goods<br>**Quantity:** 200 Nos<br>**Rate:** 40 Nos | 8000 |
| 22-04-16 | Wind Fast Pvt Ltd | Goods<br>**Quantity:** 140 Nos<br>**Rate:** 50 Nos | 7000 |

| In the books of Garuda Traders | | | | | | |
|---|---|---|---|---|---|---|
| Purchase A/c | | | | | | |
| Dr | | | | | | Cr |
| Date | | Particulars | Amt | Date | Particulars | Amt |
| | | Sundries as per purchase book | | | By | |
| 01-04-16 | To | Ritin Traders | 5000 | | By | |
| 04-04-16 | To | Ammu Wholesaler | 8000 | | By | |
| 22-04-16 | To | Wind Fast Pvt Ltd | 7000 | | By | |

| In the books of Garuda Traders | | | | | | | |
|---|---|---|---|---|---|---|---|
| Ritin Trader A/c | | | | | | | |
| Dr | | | | | | | Cr |
| Date | | Particulars | Amt | Date | | Particulars | Amt |
| | To | | | 01-04-16 | By | Purchase A/c | 5000 |
| | To | | | | By | | |

| In the books of Garuda Traders | | | | | | | |
|---|---|---|---|---|---|---|---|
| Ammu Wholesaler A/c | | | | | | | |
| Dr | | | | | | | Cr |
| Date | | Particulars | Amt | Date | | Particulars | Amt |
| | To | | | 04-04-16 | By | Purchase A/c | 8000 |
| | To | | | | By | | |

### 3.8.2 Sales Book

This book is maintained to record all the credit sales only, of the company. It is prepared on the basis of sales invoices issued to the customers which contains the details of the sales transaction which is as follows:

- Date of the transaction
- Outward Invoice Number/ Invoice Number
- Description of goods
  - o Quantity
  - o Rate
  - o Amt
- Terms of sales
- Any other references

The sales book total of a particular period, is transferred to sales account as **"By Sundries as per sales book"** and every customer ledger account is maintained to track the value of goods sold from sales account.

***Illustration 13:*** *In the books of Harsha Enterprises Pvt Ltd., record the following transactions in the sales book and further prepare the respective ledger account and post entries from sales book.*

Below is the transactions details of, 2016-April month

1. On 3-04-16, sold goods to **Swami Electronics,** find the details below.

   **Quantity:** 70 Nos

   **Rate:** 80 Nos

2. Sold goods to **Neeta Garments** on 14-04-16 details as follows.

   **Quantity:** 95 Nos

   **Rate:** 80 Nos

3. Goods worth Rs. 1,000/- were sold on cash on 14-04-16 to **Nav Jeevan Society**.

4. Sold old office printer @ Rs. 1000/- to **Shantanu Enterprises** on 20-04-2016.

**Note:** 1. Kindly check the transaction no 3, will not be recorded in the purchase book.

2. Transaction no 5, will not be recorded in purchase book.

Let us see how to prepare the necessary books and applicable ledger accounts

| In the books of Harsh Enterprises | | | |
|---|---|---|---|
| Sales Book | | | |
| Date | Particulars | Description | Amt |
| 03-04-16 | Swami Electronics | Goods<br>**Quantity:** 70 Nos<br>**Rate:** 80 Nos | 5600 |
| 07-04-16 | Neeta Garments | Goods<br>**Quantity:** 95 Nos<br>**Rate:** 80 Nos | 7600 |

| In the books of Harsh Enterprises | | | | | | | |
|---|---|---|---|---|---|---|---|
| Sales A/c | | | | | | | |
| Dr | | | | | | | Cr |
| Date | | Particulars | Amt | Date | | Particulars | Amt |
| | To | | | | | Sundries as per sales book | |
| | To | | | 03-04-16 | By | Swami Electronics | 5600 |
| | To | | | 07-04-16 | By | Neeta Garments | 7600 |
| | To | | | | By | | |

| In the books of Harsh Enterprises | | | | | | | |
|---|---|---|---|---|---|---|---|
| Swami Electronics A/c | | | | | | | |
| Dr | | | | | | | Cr |
| Date | | Particulars | Amt | Date | | Particulars | Amt |
| 03-04-16 | To | Sales A/c | 5600 | | By | | |
| | To | | | | By | | |

| In the books of Harsh Enterprises | | | | | | | |
|---|---|---|---|---|---|---|---|
| Neeta Garments A/c | | | | | | | |
| Dr | | | | | | | Cr |
| Date | | Particulars | Amt | Date | | Particulars | Amt |
| 03-04-16 | To | Sales A/c | 7600 | | By | | |
| | To | | | | By | | |

### 3.8.3 Purchase Return Book

This book is maintained to record all the transactions concerned to return outwards of goods purchased on credit to its original supplier

Some of the common reason for sending back the whole of the goods or partial goods are as follows:

- Damage
- Defective
- Delay
- Not up to the mark or unsatisfied
- Incompatible

The debit note is issued mentioning remarks (**reason for goods returned**) and sent along with goods to its original supplier, stating that supplier accounts is debited respectively. Hence on the basis of this debit note, the transaction is thus recorded in the purchase return book.

***Illustration 14:*** *In the books of Vivek Enterprises Pvt Ltd., record the following transactions in the purchase return book and further prepare the respective ledger account and post entries from purchase return book.*

Below is the transactions details of, 2016-April month

1. On 2-04-16, some goods were returned to **Ritin Traders** along with **debit note no: 001**, mentioning **remarks** stating the reason – goods were found damaged on reception.

   **Quantity:** 20 Nos

   **Rate:** 50 Nos

2. On 6-04-16, partial goods were returned to **Ammu Wholesaler** along with **debit note no: 002**, mentioning **remarks** stating the reason – goods were not up to the mark.

   **Quantity:** 110 Nos

   **Rate:** 40 Nos

3. On the same day of 22-04-16, whole of goods were returned to **Wind Fast Pvt Ltd** along with **debit note no: 003**, mentioning **remarks** stating the reason – all goods were defective

   **Quantity:** 140

   **Rate:** 50

Let us see how to prepare the necessary books and applicable ledger accounts

| In the books of Vivek Enterprises Pvt Ltd. | | | | |
|---|---|---|---|---|
| Purchase Returns Book | | | | |
| Date | Particulars | D/N No | Description | Amt |
| 02-04-16 | Ritin Trader | 001 | Goods<br>Quantity: 20 Nos<br>Rate: 50 Nos | 1000 |
| 06-04-16 | Ammu Wholesaler | 002 | Goods<br>Quantity: 110 Nos<br>Rate: 40 Nos | 4400 |
| 22-04-16 | Wind Fast Pvt Ltd | 003 | Goods<br>Quantity: 140 Nos<br>Rate: 50 Nos | 7000 |

| In the books of Vivek Enterprises Pvt Ltd. | | | | | | | |
|---|---|---|---|---|---|---|---|
| Purchase Returns A/c | | | | | | | |
| Dr | | | | | | | Cr |
| Date | | Particulars | Amt | Date | | Particulars | Amt |
| | To | | | | | Sundries as per purchase returns book | |
| | To | | | 02-04-16 | By | Ritin Traders | 1000 |
| | To | | | 06-04-16 | By | Ammu Wholesaler | 4400 |
| | To | | | 22-04-16 | By | Wind Fast Pvt Ltd | 7000 |
| | To | | | | By | | |

| In the books of Vivek Enterprises Pvt Ltd. | | | | | | | |
|---|---|---|---|---|---|---|---|
| Ritin Trader A/c | | | | | | | |
| Dr | | | | | | | Cr |
| Date | | Particulars | Amt | Date | | Particulars | Amt |
| 02-04-16 | To | Purchase Returns A/c | 1000 | 01-04-16 | By | Purchase A/c | 5000 |
| | To | | | | By | | |

| In the books of Vivek Enterprises Pvt Ltd. | | | | | | | |
|---|---|---|---|---|---|---|---|
| Ammu Wholesaler A/c | | | | | | | |
| Dr | | | | | | | Cr |
| Date | | Particulars | Amt | Date | | Particulars | Amt |
| 06-04-16 | To | Purchase Returns A/c | 4400 | 04-04-16 | By | Purchase A/c | 8000 |
| | To | | | | By | | |

### 3.8.4 Sales Return Book

This book is maintained to record all the transactions concerned to return inwards of sold goods on credit from the original customer

Some of the common reason for getting back the whole of the goods or partial goods are as follows:

- Damage
- Defective
- Delay
- Not up to the mark or unsatisfied
- Incompatible

The credit note is provided to the customer as a confirmation, that the return inward goods given by the customer is accepted, mentioning remarks (**reason for goods returned**) and stating that, the customer accounts is credited respectively. Hence on the basis of this credit note, the transaction is thus recorded in the sales return book.

***Illustration 15:*** *In the books of Keerthi Trader Pvt Ltd., record the following transactions in the sales return book and further prepare the respective ledger account and post entries from sales return book.*

Below is the transactions details of, 2016-April month

1. On 5-04-16, partial goods were returned by **Swami Electronics** hence a **credit note no: 101**, were issued to the customer, mentioning **remarks** stating the reason – customer found goods damaged on reception.

   **Quantity:** 4 Nos

   **Rate:** 80 Nos

2. On 8-04-16, goods were returned by **Neeta Garments** thus a **credit note no: 102**, were issued to the customer, mentioning **remarks** stating the reason – goods were found damaged due to poor packaging.

   **Quantity:** 5 Nos

   **Rate:** 80 Nos

Let us see how to prepare the necessary books and applicable ledger accounts

| In the books of Keerthi Trader Pvt Ltd | | | | |
|---|---|---|---|---|
| Sales Returns Book | | | | |
| Date | Particulars | C/N No | Description | Amt |
| 05-04-16 | Swami Electronics | 101 | Goods<br>Quantity: 4 Nos<br>Rate: 80 Nos | 320 |
| 08-04-16 | Neeta Garments | 102 | Goods<br>Quantity: 5 Nos<br>Rate: 80 Nos | 400 |

| In the books of Keerthi Trader Pvt Ltd | | | | | | | |
|---|---|---|---|---|---|---|---|
| Sales Returns A/c | | | | | | | |
| Dr | | | | | | | Cr |
| Date | | Particulars | Amt | Date | | Particulars | Amt |
| | | Sundries as per sales return book | | | | | |
| 05-04-16 | To | Swami Electronics | 320 | | By | | |
| 08-04-16 | To | Neeta Garments | 400 | | By | | |
| | To | | | | By | | |

| In the books of Keerthi Trader Pvt Ltd | | | | | | | |
|---|---|---|---|---|---|---|---|
| Swami Electronics A/c | | | | | | | |
| Dr | | | | | | | Cr |
| Date | | Particulars | Amt | Date | | Particulars | Amt |
| 03-04-16 | To | Sales A/c | 5600 | 01-04-16 | By | Sales Return A/c | 320 |
| | To | | | | By | | |

| In the books of Keerthi Trader Pvt Ltd | | | | | | | |
|---|---|---|---|---|---|---|---|
| Neeta Garments A/c | | | | | | | |
| Dr | | | | | | | Cr |
| Date | | Particulars | Amt | Date | | Particulars | Amt |
| 03-04-16 | To | Sales A/c | 7600 | 08-04-16 | By | Sales Return A/c | 400 |
| | To | | | | By | | |

### 3.8.5 Cash Book

In any business when a transaction involve flow of cash due to payments or receipts, by means of liquid cash or through bank cheque or any other negotiable instrument, hence to record cash transactions cash book is used. It is opened with a cash or bank balance at the beginning of the period. The entries are balanced on a monthly basis. Cash book, also known as book of original entry, is maintained by all organisations, big or small, profit or not-for-profit. It serves the purpose of both journal as well as the ledger (cash) account. When a cash book is maintained, transactions of cash are not recorded in the journal and no separate account for cash or bank is required in the ledger.

Cash book is maintained in three kinds

- Single Column
- With Discount Column
- Bank Column

#### *Single Column Cash book*

It is very simple in form where receipts amount column is maintained in the debit side of the cash book and payments amount column is maintained in credit side of the cash book

#### *With Discount Column*

This is a separate column included in the cash book to records all the discounts, the discount allowed column is in the debit side and the discount received column is in the credit side.

#### *With Bank Column*

This is an additional column included in the cash book, to record all the cash receipts deposited in the bank are recorded in the debit column and all the cash payment withdrawals from bank are recorded on credit side

#### *Illustration 16:*

#### *Single Column Cash book*

In the books of SP Enterprises Pvt Ltd., record the following transactions in the cash book. Below is the transactions details of, 2016-June month.

1. Cash in hand as at 1-6-2016 is Rs. 10000/-
2. On 2-6-2016, Payment made for Printing & Stationery Rs 800/-
3. Loan taken from Maxis Fin Corp of Rs 25000/- dated 14-06-2016.
4. Paid for Tea & Snacks of Rs 5000/- dated 22-06-2016.
5. Bank Interest Received on Bank Deposits of Rs 1900/- 30-06-2016.
6. Office Maintenance Charges per month is Rs 4000/- on 30-06-2016.

| In the Cash Book of SP Enterprises Pvt Ltd | | | | | |
|---|---|---|---|---|---|
| Dr | | | | | Cr |
| Date | Particulars | Cash Column | Date | Particulars | Cash Column |
| 1-6-16 | To Balance c/f | 10000 | 2-6-16 | By Printing & Stationery | 800 |
| 14-6-16 | To Loan from Maxis Fin Corp | 25000 | 22-6-16 | By Tea & Snacks Expenses A/c | 5000 |
| 30-6-16 | To Bank Interest Received A/c | 1900 | 30-6-16 | By Office Maintenance Expenses A/c | 4000 |
| | | | 30-6-16 | By Balance c/d | 27100 |
| | Total | 36900 | | Total | 36900 |

#### *With Discount Column*

In the books of Neeraj Traders Pvt Ltd., record the following transactions in the cash book. Below is the transactions details of, 2016-July month.

1. Cash in hand as at 1-7-2016 is Rs. 27100/-
2. On 10-7-2016, Cash purchases of goods worth Rs. 8000/- were made with Virat Traders with a Trade Discount of 5% on purchases.
3. Goods were purchased on cash of Rs 15000/- from Deepak Traders on 12-07-2016, were made with a cash discount received @ 10% on purchases.
4. On 12-07-2016, cash paid to supplier Ancient Tech for the outstanding amount of Rs 5000/- and got 5% cash discount.
5. On 13-07-2016, Sales of goods Rs 12000/- were done and 5% cash discount were provided on total sales
6. Purchased goods worth Rs 10000/- on 14-07-2016, from Virat Traders and received trade discount of 5% and cash discount of 5%.
7. Sold goods worth Rs 25000/- on 18-07-2016, to Yash Mesh Retailers with 2% trade discount allowed and 5% cash discount on total sales.
8. On 31-07-2016, received cash of Rs. 5900 from customer Kenben Traders for outstanding account Rs 6000/-

| In the Cash Book of Neeraj Traders Pvt Ltd | | | | | | | |
|---|---|---|---|---|---|---|---|
| Dr | | | | | | | Cr |
| Date | Particulars | Discount Allowed | Cash Column | Date | Particulars | Discount Received | Cash Column |
| 1-7-16 | To Balance c/f | | 27100 | 10-7-16 | By Purchase of Goods A/c | | 7600 |
| 13-7-16 | To Sales of Goods A/c | 600 | 11400 | 12-7-16 | By Purchase of Goods A/c | 1500 | 13500 |
| 18-7-16 | To Sales of Goods A/c | 1225 | 23275 | 12-7-16 | By Ancient Tech A/c | 250 | 4750 |
| 31-7-16 | To Kenben Traders A/c | 100 | 5900 | 14-7-16 | By Purchase of Goods A/c | 475 | 9025 |
| | | | | 14-7-16 | By Balance c/d | | 32800 |
| | Total | 1925 | 67675 | | Total | 2225 | 67675 |

#### *With Bank Column*

In the books of Vinod Traders Pvt Ltd., record the following transactions in the cash book. Below is the transactions details of, 2016-August month.

1. Cash in hand as at 1-8-2016 is Rs. 32800/- and Bank Balance of Rs 10,000/-
2. Sold goods worth Rs 20000/- on 2-08-2016, to Yash Mesh Retailers with 5% trade discount allowed and 1% cash

discount on total sales. Payment is received by cheque and deposited to bank

3. Purchased goods worth Rs 12000/- on 5-08-2016, from Virat Traders and received trade discount of 10% and cash discount of 5%, payment were done by issuing bank cheque.
4. On 10-08-2016, cash withdrawn from bank for office maintenance of Rs 4000/-
5. For tea and snacks amount of Rs 7000/- were paid through cash on 12-08-2016.
6. On 31-08-2016, bank charges of Rs 500/- were recognised
7. Cheque deposited by one of the customer named Wilson Traker were recognised on 31 - 08-2016 of Rs 15000/-

In the Cash Book of Vinod Traders Pvt Ltd

| Dr | | | | | | | | | Cr |
|---|---|---|---|---|---|---|---|---|---|
| **Date** | **Particulars** | **Dis Allw** | **Cash** | **Bank** | **Date** | **Particulars** | **Dis Rec** | **Cash** | **Bank** |
| 1-8-16 | To Balance C/f | | 32800 | 10000 | 5-8-16 | To Purchase of Goods A/c | 540 | | 10800 |
| 2-8-16 | To Sales of Goods A/c | 190 | | 18810 | 10-8-16 | To Office Maintenance A/c | | | 4000 |
| 31-8-16 | To Wilson Traker A/c | | | 15000 | 12-8-16 | To Tea and Snacks A/c | | 7000 | 15000 |
| | | | | | 31-8-16 | To Bank Charges | | | 500 |
| | | | | | 31-8-16 | To Balance c/d | | 25800 | 13510 |
| **Total** | | **190** | **32800** | **43810** | **Total** | | **540** | **32800** | **43810** |

### 3.8.6 Petty Cash Book

In any business, there are various small cash payments which are very often or recurring in nature, hence it is very difficult to record these petty transactions in main cash book which results in complexities for the cashier. To overcome this a special book is maintained which is called as petty cash book, thus this book is maintained by petty cash

#### *Imprest System*

In this a fixed amount is allocated to the petty cashier in advance at the beginning of the specific period, usually a month, to meet various small expenses of the business.

At the end of a particular period when the petty cashier is running out of cash balance, petty cashier is reimbursed with the remaining balance of fixed amount for the next month.

Examples of common often and recurring expenses

- Postage and Telegram
- Printing and Stationery
- Carriage Charges
- Local Travelling Conveyance
- Sundry Expenses
- Personal Account

***Illustration 17:*** *In the books of Suraj Enterprises record the following transactions in the cash book. Below is the transactions details of, 2016-May month.*

Petty Cash is fixed to Rs 1000/- per month

1. Cash in hand as on 1-5-2016 is Rs. 100/-
2. Petty cashier received Rs 900/- on 1-5-2016
3. Paid on 2-5-16, for Postage/ Courier and Telegram of Rs 80
4. Paid on 5-5-16, Local Travelling Conveyance of Rs 50/-
5. Paid on 8-5-16, for Postage/ Courier of Rs 150/-
6. Paid on 11-5-16, for Carriage Charges of Rs 100/-
7. Paid on 15-5-16, Local Travelling Conveyance of Rs 70/-
8. Paid on 19-5-16, Miscellaneous office expenses of Rs 100/-
9. Paid on 26-5-16, for Postage/ Courier and Telegram of Rs 150
10. Paid on 28-5-16, Local Travelling Conveyance of Rs 40/-
11. Paid on 31-5-16, Mohan for Conveyance of Rs 50/-

In the Petty Cash Book of Suraj Enterprises

| Dr | | | Cr | | | | | |
|---|---|---|---|---|---|---|---|---|
| Receipts | Date | Particulars | Payments | Postage and Telegram | Carriage Charges | Local Travelling Conveyance | Sundry Expenses | Personal Account |
| 100 | 1-5-16 | To Balance b/d | | | | | | |
| 900 | 1-5-16 | To Cash | | | | | | |
| | 2-5-16 | By Postage | 80 | 80 | | | | |
| | 5-5-16 | By Local Travelling | 50 | | | 50 | | |
| | 8-5-16 | By Postage | 150 | 150 | | | | |
| | 11-5-16 | By Carriage | 100 | | 100 | | | |
| | 15-5-16 | By Local Travelling | 70 | | | 70 | | |
| | 19-5-16 | By Misc office expenses | 100 | | | | 100 | |
| | 26-5-16 | By Postage | 150 | 150 | | | | |
| | 28-5-16 | By Local Travelling | 40 | | | 40 | | |
| | 31-5-16 | By Mohan A/c | 50 | | | | | 50 |
| 1000 | Total | | 790 | 380 | 100 | 160 | 100 | 50 |
| 210 | 31-5-16 | By Balance b/d | | | | | | |
| | 1-6-16 | To Balance c/d | 210 | | | | | |
| 790 | 1-6-16 | To Cash | | | | | | |

## 3.9 JOURNAL PROPER

The transactions which are different in nature and cannot be recorded in any regular subsidiary books, such transactions are recorded in the book called as Journal Proper. It is also known as Modern Journal or Miscellaneous Journal.

The following is a list of transactions which can be recorded in a Journal Proper:

- Opening Entries & Closing Entries

- Transfer Entries
- Rectifying Entries
- Adjusting Entries
- Credit Sales (other than goods)
- Credit Purchase (other than goods)
- Withdrawal of Goods or Assets by the owner or proprietor
- Loss of Goods or Assets (by fire, flood, accident, theft etc.)
- Joint Venture Transactions
- Consignment Transactions
- Dishonour of Promissory Notes
- Dishonour of Bills of Exchange

### 3.9.1 Difference between Journal and Journal Proper

The main difference between Journal and Journal Proper is given bellow:

| Journal | Journal Proper |
|---|---|
| This is maintained under conventional or traditional methods of accounting. | This is maintained under practical or modern method of accounting. |
| All the transactions are recorded in Journal. | Only those transactions are recorded which cannot be recorded in the subsidiary books. |

***Illustration 18:*** *Record the following transactions in the Journal Proper.*

| Date (2016) | Transactions |
|---|---|
| Jul. 1 | Furniture of ₹ 10,000 was lost by fire. |
| Jul. 3 | Goods withdrawn by owner for his personal use ₹ 5,000 |
| Jul. 4 | Bought office furniture from SKC Mart for ₹ 10,000 |
| Jul. 5 | Bought Machinery from NC Trading Company for ₹ 10,000 |
| Jul.6 | Sold Furniture to Shubhashine for ₹ 5,000 |
| Jul.7 | Net Profit of ₹ 1,000 is transferred to Reserve |
| Jul. 8 | A Debit Balance of ₹ 3,000 from CK account to be transferred to M&M account. |
| Jul.18 | Goods given away as charity for ₹ 2,000 |
| Jul. 19 | Goods given away as sample for ₹ 3,000 |
| Jul.20 | Interest on capital ₹ 4,000 |

*Solution:*

Journal

| Date 2016 | Particulars | | L.F | Dr. | Cr. |
|---|---|---|---|---|---|
| Jul. 1 | Loss of furniture A/c | Dr. | | 10,000 | |
| | To Furniture A/c | | | | 10,000 |
| | (Being the furniture lost by fire) | | | | |
| | | | | | |
| Jul. 3 | Drawings A/c | Dr. | | 5,000 | |
| | To Purchase A/c | | | | 5,000 |
| | (Being the goods withdrawn by the owner) | | | | |
| | | | | | |
| Jul. 4 | Furniture A/c | Dr. | | 10,000 | |
| | To SKC Mart A/c | | | | 10,000 |
| | (Being furniture bought from SKC Mart) | | | | |
| | | | | | |
| Jul. 5 | Machinery A/c | Dr. | | 10,000 | |
| | To NC Trading Company A/c | | | | 10,000 |
| | (Being machinery bought from NC Company) | | | | |
| | | | | | |
| Jul. 6 | Shubhashine A/c | Dr. | | 5,000 | |
| | To furniture A/c | | | | 5,000 |
| | (Being furniture sold to Shubhashine) | | | | |
| | | | | | |
| Jul. 7 | Profit & Loss A/c or Profit & Loss Appropriation A/c | Dr. | | 1,000 | |
| | To Reserve A/c | | | | 1,000 |
| | (Being goods sold on credit to SK Traders) | | | | |
| | | | | | |
| Jul. 8 | M&M A/c | Dr. | | 3,000 | |
| | To CK account A/c | | | | 3,000 |
| | (Being debit balance transferred from CK A/c to M&M A/c) | | | | |
| | | | | | |
| Jul. 18 | Charity A/c | Dr. | | 2,000 | |
| | To Purchase A/c | | | | 2,000 |
| | (Being goods given away as charity) | | | | |
| | | | | | |
| Jul. 19 | Free Sample A/c | Dr. | | 3,000 | |
| | To Purchase A/c | | | | 3,000 |
| | (Being goods given away as sample) | | | | |
| | | | | | |
| Jul. 20 | Interest on Capital A/c | Dr. | | 4,000 | |
| | To Capital A/c | | | | 4,000 |
| | (Being interest allowed on capital) | | | | |
| | | | | | |
| | Total | | | 53,000 | 53,000 |

## KEY TAKEAWAYS

- Business Transactions are first recorded in the Journal.
- Recording of transactions in Journal is known as Journalising.
- Journal Transactions are posted in Ledger.
- Ledger is also known as Book of Final Entry.
- Trial Balance is the listing of Balances Ledger Accounts.
- In modern book-keeping, a journal is divided into separate journals, to record the transactions of similar nature together. These separate journals are known as subsidiary books.

## Trial Balance Format

| Balance as on ___________ | | | |
|---|---|---|---|
| **Particulars** | **L.F** | **Debit (₹)** | **Credit (₹)** |
| Cash Account | | xxxx | -- |
| Capital Account | | -- | xxxx |
| Purchase Account | | xxxx | -- |
| Sales Account | | -- | xxxx |
| Sales Return Account | | xxxx | -- |
| Wages Account | | xxxx | -- |
| Land and Building | | -- | -- |
| Plant and Machinery | | -- | -- |
| Bills Receivable | | xxxx | -- |
| Bills Payable | | -- | xxxx |
| Opening Stock of Raw Materials | | xxxx | -- |
| Work in Progress | | xxxx | |
| Salaries Account | | xxxx | -- |
| Bank Account | | xxxx | -- |
| Interest Received Account | | -- | xxxx |
| Advance from customers | | -- | xxxx |
| Stationery Account | | xxxx | -- |
| Insurance Account | | xxxx | -- |
| Total | | xxxx | xxxx |

# PRACTICE EXERCISES

## Section A: Review Questions

1. What is a Business Transaction?
2. What is a Journal?
3. What is a Ledger posting and why it is needed?
4. What is the Difference between the Journal and Ledger?
5. What is a Trial Balance and list down the objectives of Trial Balance?
6. Write down the different methods of preparing trial Balance.
7. What is the difference between Journal and Ledger?
8. Why journal is known as Book of Original Entry?
9. What is a Compound Journal Entry?
10. What is a Journal Proper?
11. Record the following transactions in the books of Mani Enterprises for the Month of April.

| Date (2016) | Transactions |
|---|---|
| Apr. 1 | Business started with cash of ₹ 10,00,000 |
| Apr. 5 | Goods purchased from Karthik for cash ₹ 2,00,000 |
| Apr. 6 | Stationery purchased for cash ₹ 10,000 |
| Apr. 10 | Opened a bank account with SBI Bank by depositing cash of ₹ 5,00,000 |
| Apr. 11 | Goods sold to Ram& Sons Manufacturers on credit for ₹ 80,000 |

12. Record the following transactions in a Journal:

| Date | Transactions |
|---|---|
| Apr. 12 | Received a cheque of ₹ 50,000 from Ram & Sons Manufacturers |
| Apr. 13 | Insurance paid by cheque ₹ 20,000 |
| Apr. 14 | Sold goods to Nandini Manufacturers ₹ 2,00,000 |
| Apr. 15 | Nandini pays ₹ 2, 00,000 through cheque. |
| Apr. 16 | Goods purchased for ₹ 3, 00,000 from GG Traders and paid through cheque. |
| Apr. 17 | Purchased office furniture for ₹ 50,000 in cash |
| Apr. 18 | Goods costing ₹ 30,000 given as charity |
| Apr. 19 | Paid ₹ 50,000 towards rent through cheque |
| Apr. 20 | Cash withdrawn for household purposes ₹ 20,000 |
| Apr. 21 | Damaged goods returned to GG Traders ₹ 50,000 |
| Apr. 30 | Salaries paid ₹ 30,000 through Cash |

| Date (2016) | Transactions |
|---|---|
| Jun. 6 | Payment made to Sugriv for ₹1,00,000 and discount received for ₹10,000 |
| Jun 7 | Cash of ₹ 2,00,000 was received from Star Traders and discount allowed for ₹ 20,000 |
| Jun. 9 | Running business was purchased by Rakesh and the following assets and liabilities details are shown below. Cash ₹ 50,000; Furniture; 25,000; Land ₹ 2,00,000; Creditors ₹70,000; Bank Overdraft ₹ 20,000; Capital ₹ 66,000 |

13. Record the Following Transaction in Journal and then post them into the Ledgers for the month of May 2016.

| Date (2016) | Transactions |
|---|---|
| May. 1 | Triveni started a business with a capital of ₹ 2, 00,000. |
| May. 2 | Purchased goods from KS Traders on credit for ₹ 1, 00,000. |
| May. 3 | Paid cash of ₹ 50,000 to KS Traders. |
| May. 10 | Sold goods to S&S Enterprises for ₹ 3, 00,000. |
| May. 15 | Purchase goods from KS Traders for ₹ 2, 00,000. |
| May. 16 | Returned damaged goods to KS Traders for ₹ 5,000. |
| May. 18 | Salaries paid for ₹ 20,000 through cheque. |

14. Record the Following Transaction in Journal and then post them into the Ledgers and prepare the Trial Balance.

| Date (2016) | Transactions |
|---|---|
| May. 1 | Bhuvan started a business with a capital of ₹ 5, 00,000. |
| May. 2 | Purchased goods from TT Traders on credit for ₹ 2, 00,000. |
| May. 3 | Paid cash of ₹ 30,000 to TT Traders. |
| May. 10 | Sold goods to SWOS Enterprises for ₹ 6, 00,000. |
| May. 15 | Purchase goods from TT Traders for ₹ 2, 00,000. |
| May. 16 | Returned damaged goods to TT Traders for ₹ 50,000. |
| May. 18 | Salaries paid for ₹ 30,000 through cheque. |
| May. 31 | Purchased furniture for ₹ 1,00,000 and the payment I made through cash |

## Section B: Multiple Choice Questions

Select the most appropriate answer from the choices given below:

1. ____________ is the Book of original Entry.
   - a. Ledger
   - b. **Journal**
   - c. Trial Balance
   - d. Balance Sheet
2. ____________ is the Book of Final Entry.
   - a. **Ledger**
   - b. Journal
   - c. Trial Balance
   - d. Balance Sheet
3. ____________ is the base of Financial Statements.
   - a. Balance Sheet
   - b. Profit & Loss Account
   - c. **Trial Balance**
   - d. Cash Balance
4. ____________ entry is recorded in the beginning in Journal.
   - a. Closing Entry
   - b. Purchase Entry
   - c. Sales Entry
   - d. **Opening Entry**
5. "To" word will be used by the account which will be?
   - a. **Debited**
   - b. Credited
   - c. Balanced
   - d. Removed

Chapter 4

# Bank Reconciliation

## LEARNING OBJECTIVES

After studying this chapter, you will be able to:

- Understand to examine bank balance as per statements and company cash book
- Correcting the difference between bank account funds and company cash book
- To prepare bank reconciliation statement

## 4.1 INTRODUCTION

Every business organisation maintains a cash book in which it records both cash and bank transactions. The cash book shows the balance of both cash and bank transactions at the end of a given period. Once the cash book is balanced, the business must check the details with the records of its bank transactions. For this purpose, the cashier needs to update the cash book and obtain a recent statement from the bank. The balance shown in the passbook must tally with the balance shown in the cash book. Invariably, there is a difference between these balances and it is necessary to ascertain the reasons for such a difference. Once the difference is known, a bank reconciliation statement is prepared to reconcile the balances

## 4.2 MEANING

A bank reconciliation statement is prepared by a customer (i.e. account holder) to ascertain the items or reasons responsible for the difference between the bank balance shown in the cash book and the bank balance shown in the passbook as on a particular date

## 4.3 CAUSES OF DIFFERENCE IN COMPANY CASH BOOK AND BANK PASS BOOK

The differences which occur between company cash book balances and bank pass book are as follows

1. **Cheques issued but not presented for payment**

   Cheques issued by a company to its suppliers or some party are immediately entered on the credit side of the cash book. However, the cheques may not be immediately presented to the bank for payment by the receiving party. The bank will debit the company's account only when it actually honors these cheques. Hence, the time gap between the issue of a cheque and it to be honored by the bank causes the difference between the balance as per the cash book and the balance as per the passbook.

2. **Cheques deposited into the bank but not cleared and credited.**

   When a company receives cheques from some party or from its customers (debtors), these cheques are immediately recorded on the debit side of the cash book. This increases the bank balance as per the cash book. However, the amounts on the cheques will only realised, when bank credit the funds to customer's account. Clearing of cheques usually takes a few days, especially in case of outstation cheques or when the cheques are paid-in at a branch other than the one wherein the business has an account. This causes a difference between the balances.

3. **Interest gained and dividend collected and credited by bank but not recognized thus remains unrecorded in company cash book**

   The company is unaware when the dividend are collected by bank, or when bank provide interest by crediting sum of money into company's account, until it confirm the bank statement, Hence this transaction is not recorded in company's cash book. As a result, the balance shown in the bank passbook will be more than the balance shown in the company's cash book.

4. **Bank Charges or Interest charged and debited by bank but not recognized thus remains unrecorded in company cash book**

   The bank interest and any other charges of the company are debited to the company's bank account, the company will acknowledge these transactions and record those in its cash book, only when it receives a bank statement, until then the balances will differ.

5. **Direct payment by the bank on behalf of company's standing instructions.**

   Sometimes, the company may give directions to the bank to make specific payments regularly on particular days to third parties. For example, telephone bills, insurance premiums, rent, and taxes, and so on are directly paid by the bank on behalf of the company and debited to the company's bank account. As a result, the balance as per the passbook would be less than the one shown in the cash book.

6. **Direct deposit by the customer**

   At times, debtors (customers) of the business may directly deposit money into the company's bank account. But, the company is unaware and does not receive the intimation until it confirms the bank statement. In this case, the bank credits the amount in the company's account, but the same is not recorded in the company's cash book. As a result, the balance shown in the bank passbook will be more than the balance shown in the company's cash book.

7. **Dishonor of Cheque or Bills discounted with the bank**

   If a cheque deposited by the company is dishonored or a bill of exchange drawn by the business organisation, discounted with the bank, is dishonored on the date of maturity, the same is debited to the company's account by the bank. As this information is not immediately available to the company, hence there will be no entry in the company's cash book reflecting the same. This will be known to the organisation only when it receives a statement from the bank. As a result, the balance as per the passbook would be less than the balance as per the cash book.

8. **Errors caused in recording transaction by the company**

   Any omission or incorrect recording of transactions relating to cheques issued/cheques deposited and wrong totaling by an organisation while recording entries in the cash book can cause a difference between cash book and passbook balances

9. **Errors caused in recording transaction by the company**

   Any omission or incorrect recording of transactions relating to cheques deposited and wrong totaling by the bank while posting entries in the passbook can also cause differences between passbook and cash book balances.

## 4.4 HOW TO PREPARE A BANK RECONCILIATION STATEMENT

To prepare a bank reconciliation statement, the bank balance as per the cash book and cash balance as per bank passbook or statement as on a particular day are required along with transaction details of both the books.

1. Compare the values in the bank column on the **debit** (**receipts**) side in the **cash book** with the values of the bank **pass book** or **statement** on **credit** (**deposit**) side.
2. Compare the values in the bank column on the **credit** (**payments**) side in the **cash book** with the values of the bank **pass book** or **statement** on **credit** (**withdrawals**) side.

### *Bank Over-Draft:*

This is a facility provided by banking institution only for those who holds current account in the bank. With this facility the current account holder can withdraw money in excess of their balance in the account in simple these type of account holder can overdraw the money from their account

Proforma of Bank Reconciliation Statement

| Date | Effect | Ref | Particulars | Amount |
|---|---|---|---|---|
| | | | Balance as per | XX |
| | Add: | | | |
| | | (a) | Total | XXXXX |
| | Less: | | | |
| | | (b) | Total | XXXXX |
| | | (c) = (a-b) | Balance as per | XXXX |

### 4.4.1 Using Bank Balance as per Company Cash Book Method

When bank balance of the cash book is available as base then

#### *Add these below items*

a. Anything which is **not debited** (**withdrawals**) in the bank
b. Anything which **have credited** (**deposits**) in the bank and not observed/ unknown

#### *Deduct these below items*

c. Anything which is **not credited** (**deposits**) in the bank
d. Anything which **have debited** (**withdrawals**) in the bank and not observed/ unknown

#### 4.4.1.1 *Illustration*

In the books of Premsung Pvt Ltd, prepare **bank reconciliation statement** as on 30th September 2016, with the following details of **September** month.

- **Bank balance** as per company's **cash book** is Rs. 9000/- as on 30th September 2016.
  1. 05-09-2016 – Cheque of Rs. 4000/- was issued to the vendor, Mr. Ram, which he has not presented in the bank.
  2. 06-09-2016 – Cheque of Rs. 1200/- deposited in the bank account was dishonored.
  3. 09-09-2016 – Mangal Motors is customer of the, company has deposited sum of Rs. 5000/- in company bank account which was not yet accounted in cash book.
  4. 21-09-2016 – Rs. 50/- was debited by the bank in the company's account, for bank charges which was unknown and not recorded in cash book.
  5. 25-09-2016 – Sum of Rs. 900/- was late fee towards credit card was debited in the bank account.
  6. 30-09-2016 – Bank credited sum of Rs. 450/- as quarterly interest, this was not identified.

**Bank reconciliation statement of Premsung Pvt Ltd as on 30th September 2016**

| Date | Effect | Ref | Particulars | Amount |
|---|---|---|---|---|
| | | | Balance as per cash book | **9000** |
| | Add: | | **Anything which is not debited in the bank** | |
| 05-09-16 | | (i) | Cheque issued to Mr. Ram not presented | 4000 |
| | Add: | | **Anything which have credited in the bank and not observed** | |
| 09-09-16 | | (ii) | Mangal motors deposited cheque not identified | 5000 |
| 30-09-16 | | (iii) | Quarterly interest credited in the account | 450 |
| | | **(a)** | **Total** | **18450** |
| | Less: | | **Anything which is not credited in the bank** | |
| 06-09-16 | | (i) | Cheque deposited but dishonored | 1200 |
| | Less: | | **Anything which have debited in the bank and not observed** | |
| 21-09-16 | | (ii) | Bank charges debited | 50 |
| 25-09-16 | | (iii) | Credit card late fee debited | 900 |
| | | **(b)** | **Total** | **2150** |
| | | **(c) = (a-b)** | Balance as per pass book | **16300** |

### 4.4.2 Using Cash Balance as per Bank Pass Book Method

When cash balance of the bank pass book is available as base then

*Add these below items*

a. Anything which is **not credited** (**deposits**) in the bank

b. Anything which **have debited** (**withdrawals**) in the bank and not observed/ unknown

*Deduct these below items*

c. Anything which is **not debited** (**withdrawals**) in the bank

d. Anything which **have credited** (**deposits**) in the bank and not observed/ unknown

### 4.4.2.1 *Illustration*

In the books of **Tim-Tom Traders**, prepare **bank reconciliation statement** as on 30th June 2016, with the following details of **June** month.

- **Cash balance** as per bank **pass book** is Rs. 16300/- as on 30th June 2016.

1. 01-06-2016 – Insurance premium of Rs. 699/- and bank charges of Rs. 251/- was debited by the bank directly.
2. 08-06-2016 – Dividend of Rs. 3500/- was directly credited by bank account which was not identified.
3. 15-06-2016 – Cheque payment of Rs. 1300/- were made to C.A. Kotwal Associates towards auditing services were not yet cleared.
4. 20-06-2016 – Cheque Rs. 1200/- received by the customer was deposited in bank was got dishonored.
5. 22-06-2016 – Company had issued cheque of Rs. 2700/- to the supplier M/s Karmel Electronics, was not presented in the bank.
6. 30-06-2016 – Bank credited sum of Rs. 1950/- as quarterly interest, this was not identified.

**Bank reconciliation statement of Tim-Tom Traders as on 30th June 2016**

| Date | Effect | Ref | Particulars | Amount |
|---|---|---|---|---|
| | | | Balance as per **Pass Book** | **16300** |
| | Add: | | **Anything which is not credited in the bank** | |
| 20-06-16 | | (i) | Deposited cheque of customer got dishonored | 1200 |
| | | | **Anything which have debited in the bank and not observed** | |
| 01-06-16 | | (ii) | Insurance premium debited by bank directly | 699 |
| 01-06-16 | | (iii) | Bank charges debited for the month | 251 |
| | | **(a)** | **Total** | **18450** |
| | Less: | | **Anything which is not debited in the bank** | |
| 15-06-16 | | (i) | Cheque issued to C.A. Kotwal Associates not cleared | 1300 |
| 22-06-16 | | (ii) | Cheque issued but not presented by the supplier | 2700 |
| | | | **Anything which have credited in the bank and not observed** | |
| 08-06-16 | | (i) | Dividend collected by bank directly | 3500 |
| 30-06-16 | | (ii) | Bank interest credited unidentified | 1950 |
| | | **(b)** | **Total** | **9450** |
| | | (c) = (a-b) | Balance as per **Cash Book** | **9000** |

### 4.4.3 Using Overdraft Balance as per Company Cash Book Method

When overdraft balance of the cash book is available as base then

*Add these below items*

a. Anything which is **not credited** (**deposits**) in the bank

b. Anything which **have debited** (**withdrawals**) in the bank and not observed/ unknown

*Deduct these below items*

c. Anything which is **not debited** (**withdrawals**) in the bank

d. Anything which **have credited** (**deposits**) in the bank and not observed/ unknown

### 4.4.3.1 *Illustration*

In the books of **Ekta Enterprises**, prepare **bank reconciliation statement** as on 31st August 2016, with the following details of **August** month.

- **Bank Overdraft/ credit balance** as per **cash book** is Rs. 6700/- as on 31st August 2016.

1. 01-08-2016 – Bank credited sum of Rs. 3200/- towards refund from IRCTC, which was not recorded in the cash book.
2. 03-08-2016 – Subscribed Govt investment scheme of Rs. 1000/- were auto debited by bank.
3. 11-08-2016 – Bonus of Rs. 500/- on share trading was directly credited by bank which was not identified.
4. 16-08-2016 – Company issued cheque of Rs. 5000/- to a supplier, which was not presented in the bank.
5. 21-08-2016 – Amount of Rs. 1500/- was wrongly debited by the bank.
6. 27-08-2016 – Cheque of Rs. 4000/- was deposited by the company was dishonored due to insufficient funds in the customer's bank account.
7. 31-08-2016 – Commission of Rs. 350/- was credited by bank into company's bank account.
8. 01-09-2016 – Bank has rectified the wrong debited entry and reversed the value of Rs. 1400/- by crediting it.

**Bank reconciliation statement of Ekta Enterprises as on 31st August 2016**

| Date | Effect | Ref | Particulars | Amount |
|---|---|---|---|---|
| | | | Overdraft balance as per **Cash Book** | **6700** |
| | Add: | | **Anything which is not credited in the bank** | |
| 27-08-16 | | (i) | Cheque deposited got dishonored due to insufficient funds in customer bank account. | 4000 |
| | | | **Anything which have debited in the bank and not observed** | |
| 03-08-16 | | (ii) | Investment in Govt Scheme debited | 1000 |
| 21-08-16 | | (iii) | Bank wrongly debited, reason not yet validated | 1500 |
| | | **(a)** | **Total** | **13200** |
| | Less: | | **Anything which is not debited in the bank** | |
| 16-08-16 | | (i) | Cheque issued but not presented by the supplier | 5000 |
| | | | **Anything which have credited in the bank and not observed** | |
| 01-08-16 | | (i) | Refund from IRCTC credited in bank | 3200 |
| 11-08-16 | | (ii) | Share Trading bonus credited in bank | 500 |
| 11-08-16 | | (iii) | Commission credited by bank | 350 |
| | | **(b)** | **Total** | **9050** |
| | | (c) = (a-b) | **Overdraft** balance as per **Pass Book** | **4150** |

### 4.4.4 Using Overdraft Balance as per Bank Pass Book Method

When overdraft balance of the bank pass book is available as base then

*Add these below items*

a. Anything which is **not debited (withdrawals)** in the bank
b. Anything which **have credited (deposits)** in the bank and not observed/ unknown

*Deduct these below items*

c. Anything which is **not credited (deposits)** in the bank
d. Anything which **have debited (withdrawals)** in the bank and not observed/ unknown

#### 4.4.4.1 *Illustration*

In the books of **Roshni Com**, prepare **bank reconciliation statement** as on 31st November 2016, with the following details of **August** month.

- **Bank Overdraft/ credit balance** as per **pass book** is Rs. 4150/- as on 31st November 2016.
  1. 02-11-2016 – Company received cheque from its customer of Rs. 1900/- which was deposited in the bank but not yet cleared.
  2. 06-11-2016 – Cheque of Rs. 2000/- issued to a vendor was not yet cleared.
  3. 11-11-2016 – Bank charges of Rs. 500/- was debited by bank was not recorded.
  4. 15-11-2016 – Bank collected dividend on behalf of the company, sum of Rs. 4000/- and credited it into company bank account, which was not identified.
  5. 22-11-2016 – Cheque of Rs. 2100/- was deposited by the company was dishonored due to insufficient funds in the customer's bank account.
  6. 25-11-2016 – Company issued cheque of Rs. 3000/- to a supplier, which was not presented in the bank.
  7. 28-11-2016 – Bank had wrongly credited sum of Rs. 50/- in the company's bank account
  8. 30-11-2016 – Insurance premium of Rs. 2000/- was auto debited by bank.
  9. 04-12-2016 – Bank has rectified the wrong credited entry and reversed the value of Rs. 50/- by debiting company's bank account.

**Bank reconciliation statement** of **Roshni Com** as on **31st November 2016**

| Date | Effect | Ref | Particulars | Amount |
|---|---|---|---|---|
| | | | **Overdraft** balance as per **Pass Book** | **4150** |
| | Add: | | **Anything which is not debited in the bank** | |
| 06-11-16 | | (i) | Cheque issued to vendor not yet cleared | 2000 |
| 25-11-16 | | (ii) | Cheque issued to supplier not yet presented | 3000 |
| | | | **Anything which have credited in the bank and not observed** | |
| 15-11-16 | | (iii) | Dividend collected and credited by bank | 4000 |
| 28-11-16 | | (iv) | Bank wrongly credited | 50 |
| | | **(a)** | **Total** | |
| | Less: | | **Anything which is not credited in the bank** | |
| 02-11-16 | | (i) | Cheque deposited of the customer not yet cleared | 1900 |
| 22-11-16 | | (ii) | Deposited cheque got dishonored | 2100 |
| | | | **Anything which have debited in the bank and not observed** | |
| 11-11-16 | | (iii) | Bank charges debited was not recorded in cash book | 500 |
| 30-11-16 | | (iv) | Insurance Premium debited by bank not recorded | 2000 |
| | | **(b)** | **Total** | |
| | | **(c) = (a-b)** | **Overdraft** balance as per **Cash Book** | **6700** |

## PRACTICE EXERCISE

In the books of **Magnatus Int**, prepare **bank reconciliation statement** as on 31st December 2016, with the following details of **December** month.

- **Cash balance** as per **pass book** is Rs. 6250/- as on 31st December 2016.
  1. 03-12-2016 – Cheque of Rs. 2000/- issued to a vendor was not yet cleared.
  2. 05-12-2016 – Bank charges of Rs. 500/- was debited by bank was not recorded.
  3. 09-12-2016 – Customer of the, company has deposited sum of Rs. 5000/- in company bank account which was not yet accounted in cash book.
  4. 21-12-2016 – Rs. 50/- was debited by the bank in the company's account, for bank charges which was unknown and not recorded in cash book.
  5. 25-12-2016 – Sum of Rs. 710/- was late fee towards credit card was debited in the bank account.
  6. 15-12-2016 – Bank collected dividend on behalf of the company, sum of Rs. 4000/- and credited it into company bank account, which was not identified.

7. 27-12-2016 – Cheque of Rs. 5000/- was deposited by the company was dishonored due to insufficient funds in the customer's bank account.
8. 31-12-2016 – Commission of Rs. 250/- was credited by bank into company's bank account.
9. 20-12-2016 – Cheque Rs. 3100/- received by the customer was deposited in bank was got dishonored.
10. 28-11-2016 – Bank had wrongly credited sum of Rs. 900/- in the company's bank account, which was got reversed in next month.
11. 22-12-2016 – Company had issued cheque of Rs. 2700/- to the supplier, which was not presented in the bank.
12. 31-12-2016 – Bank credited sum of Rs. 550/- as quarterly interest, this was not identified.

Chapter 5

# Preparation of Final Accounts

## LEARNING OBJECTIVES

After studying this chapter, you will understand:

- Meaning of Final Accounts
- Trading Account and Profit and Loss Account
- To Prepare Trading Account and Profit and Loss Account
- Balance Sheet
- To Prepare Balance Sheet

## 5.1 INTRODUCTION

Final accounts are the statements prepared at the end of a year, which present the final results of the operations of a business, in financial terms. The two important aspects of the final results of a business include ascertaining the profit or loss made by the business and determining the financial position of business as on the last date of the accounting period. Final accounts include the following two reports:

- Income Statement or Trading and Profit and Loss account: It is prepared to ascertain the results of a business operation, i.e. the net profit or net loss of the business for an accounting year.
- Position Statement or Balance Sheet: It indicates the financial position, i.e. the assets, liabilities, and owner's capital of a business at the end of an accounting year.

The final accounts prepared at the end of a year are useful for most of the stakeholders in an organisation. Stakeholders can be classified into two broad categories namely i) Internal Stakeholders such as management, shareholders or owners and ii) External Stakeholders such as creditors, employees, consumers, government etc.

While management gets to assess performance and progress of the organisation and decide the future course of action, shareholders or owners use the information to ascertain profits and credit worthiness of the concern.

## 5.2 OBJECTIVES OF PREPARING FINAL ACCOUNTS

The primary objectives of preparing Final Accounts are as follows:

a. To provide a fair and clear view of the Financial Performance of the business for the accounting period, which includes information about the profit or loss made by the business.

b. To provide a fair and clear view of the Financial Position of the business as on the last date of the accounting period, which includes information about the assets, liabilities and the capital.

## 5.3 TRADING AND PROFIT AND LOSS ACCOUNT

Profit and loss account is an accounting statement that shows an organisation's trading position over a given period of time, usually the financial year. A profit and loss account has two sections namely trading account and profit and loss account.

At the organisation's discretion (trading or manufacturing), these two accounts may be put together in one account or shown separately. However, the usual practice is that a single account is prepared with two sections, viz. trading account and profit and loss account.

### 5.3.1 Trading Account

A trading account merely indicates the result of buying and selling of goods, i.e. the gross profit or gross loss on trading, without considering administration, selling and financial expenses incurred in running the business.

The format of trading account is given below:

***Trading Account***

| Trading Account for the year ending __________ (e.g. 31st March, 2016) | | | | | |
|---|---|---|---|---|---|
| Particulars | | Amount (₹) | Particulars | | Amount (₹) |
| To opening Stock | | xxxxx | By Sales | xxxxx | |
| To Purchase | xxxxx | | *Less:* Returns | xxxxx | xxxxx |
| *Less:* Returns | xxxxx | xxxxx | By Closing Stock | | xxxxx |
| To Direct Expense (Eg: Wages, Carriage Charges, Octroi, Import Duty etc.) | | xxxxx | By Gross Loss* | | xxxxx |
| To Gross Profit* | | xxxxx | | | |
| | | | | | |
| | | xxxxx | | | xxxxx |

### *Explanation of the items in the above format*

**Opening stock:** It is the first item on the debit side of the trading account. In case of manufacturing business, opening stock includes the stock of raw materials, partly finished goods, and finished goods at the beginning of the trading period. In case of trading business, it includes only the stock of finished goods at the beginning of the trading period.

**Purchases and purchase returns:** Purchases refer to finished goods purchased for resale or raw materials purchased for manufacture. It includes both cash and credit purchases. Net purchases are entered in the outer column by deducting the purchase returns from the total purchases.

**Cartage, carriage inwards, and freight:** The details of transportation charges incurred for the movement of goods are entered in these fields. They may be inwards or outwards. Carriage, carriage inwards, and freight incurred on the goods purchased are entered on the debit side of the trading account. When these expenses are incurred on goods sold, they are entered in the profit and loss account. When it is not stated whether cartage, carriage, and freight are inward or outward, the common practice is to treat them as inwards.

**Import duty, Excise duty, Octroi:** The import duty, export duty, and octroi paid on the goods purchased are shown on the debit side of the trading account. Such duties paid on goods sold are entered in the profit and loss account. If there is no specification as to whether these duties are paid on purchases or on sales, it is considered to have been paid on purchases.

**Wages:** Wages incurred while manufacturing goods or making purchased goods ready for sale are considered direct expenses and entered on the debit side of the trading account. Indirect and non-manufacturing wages are entered in the profit and loss account. The wages, of which the nature (direct or indirect) is not mentioned, are treated as direct wages. Certain organisations combine wages and salaries. They treat them as direct expenses and enter the details on the debit side of the trading account.

**Other factory expenses:** Other factory expenses such as factory rent, factory insurance are direct expenses. They appear on the debit side of the trading account.

**Sales and sales returns:** Sales is the first item on the credit side of the trading account. Sales include both cash and credit sales. Net sales are entered in the outer column by deducting the sales returns from the total sales.

**Sales tax:** Sales tax refers to the tax paid by a businessman to the government on the sales made by him. It can be deducted from sales on the credit side of the trading account. Alternatively, it can also be treated as a selling expense and entered on the debit side of the profit and loss account.

**Closing stock:** Closing stock represents the stock of finished goods in case of a trading business. Whereas in case of a manufacturing business, it represents the stock of raw materials, partly finished goods, and finished goods at the end of the trading period. Closing stock generally does not appear in the trial balance but it has to be calculated and brought into the books of accounts

## 5.3.2 Objective of Trading Account

The Main objectives of trading account are:

i. To ascertain the gross profit or gross loss as a result of trading (sale and purchase) goods during the current period.

ii. To furnish information about the direct expenses like wages, cartage, freight etc.

## 5.3.3 Preparation of Trading Account

The trading account shows only the gross profit or gross loss. The gross profit or gross loss is the difference between net sales (sales – sales returns) and the cost of goods sold.

The cost of goods sold refers to the cost of the portion of goods actually sold during the year rather than the cost of goods purchased during the year.

**Cost of Goods =**

**Opening Stock + Net Purchase (Purchase – Purchase Returns) + Direct Expenses – Closing Stock**

Here, Direct Expenses refer to the expenses incurred in obtaining the goods and in converting and maintaining the goods into saleable condition such as freight, wages, electricity, rent etc. Net sale is arrived at by subtracting the sales returns from gross sales. Gross profit or gross loss is determined by the excess of net sale over cost of goods and vice-versa.

Opening stock, net purchase, and direct expenses are taken in debit side of the trading account whereas net sale and closing stock appear on the credit side.

Credit side exceeding debit side results in "gross profit" while the debit side exceeding credit side results in "gross loss". The gross profit or loss as shown by the trading account is transferred to the profit and loss account.

## 5.3.4 Illustrations

### *Illustration 1*

Let's prepare the trading account for the year ended 31.03.2016 from the following particulars.

| Particulars | Amount |
|---|---|
| Opening stock | 15,000 |
| Purchases | 80,000 |
| Sales | 1,25,000 |
| Sales returns | 8,000 |
| Fuel | 500 |
| Freight | 1,000 |
| Octroi | 800 |
| Wages | 7,000 |
| Electricity | 1200 |
| Premises rent | 8,500 |
| Packing materials | 2,000 |
| Closing stock on 31.03.2016 | 12,000 |
| Purchase Returns | 5000 |

| Trading Account for the year ending 31st March, 2016 | | | | | |
|---|---|---|---|---|---|
| Particulars | | Amount (₹) | Particulars | | Amount (₹) |
| To opening Stock | | 15,000 | By Sales | 1,25,000 | |
| To Purchase | 80,000 | | *Less:* Returns | 8,000 | 1,17,000 |
| *Less:* Returns | 5,000 | 75,000 | By Closing Stock | | 12,000 |
| To Direct Expense (E.g: Wages, Carriage Charges, Octroi, Import Duty etc.) | | 21,000 | By Gross Loss* | | |
| To Gross Profit* | | 18000 | | | |
| | | | | | |
| | | 1,29,000 | | | 1,29,000 |

### *Illustration 2*

Let's prepare the trading account for the year ended 31.03.2016 from the following particulars.

| Particulars | Amount |
|---|---|
| Opening stock | 20,000 |
| Purchases | 1,20,000 |
| Sales | 75,000 |
| Sales returns | 5,000 |
| Fuel | 800 |
| Freight | 1,200 |
| Octroi | 900 |
| Wages | 9,000 |
| Electricity | 1600 |
| Premises rent | 7,000 |
| Packing materials | 1,500 |
| Closing stock on 31.03.2016 | 20,000 |
| Purchase Returns | 2000 |

| Trading Account for the year ending 31st March, 2016 | | | | | |
|---|---|---|---|---|---|
| Particulars | | Amount (₹) | Particulars | | Amount (₹) |
| To opening Stock | | 20,000 | By Sales | 75,000 | |
| To Purchase | 1,20,000 | | *Less:* Returns | 5,000 | 70,000 |
| *Less:* Returns | 2,000 | 1,18,000 | By Closing Stock | | 20,000 |
| To Direct Expense (E.g: Wages, Carriage Charges, Octroi, Import Duty etc.) | | 22,000 | By Gross Loss* | | 70,000 |
| To Gross Profit* | | | | | |
| | | | | | |
| | | 1,60,000 | | | 1,60,000 |

### 5.3.5 Manufacturing Account

A business which manufactures goods would require to know the cost of goods manufactured by them before ascertaining the gross profit or loss acquired by selling the goods. Such businesses have to prepare an additional account called manufacturing account in addition to the trading account.

The format of manufacturing account is as follows:

| Manufacturing Account for the year ending ________ (e.g. 31st March, 2016) | | | | |
|---|---|---|---|---|
| **Particulars** | | **Amount (₹)** | **Particulars** | **Amount (₹)** |
| **To Raw Materials Consumed** | | | By Work-in-Progress (Closing) | xxxx |
| *Opening Stock of Raw Materials* | xxxx | | | |
| *Purchase of raw materials* | xxxx | | | |
| *Carriage and freight on purchase of raw materials* | xxxx | | By Cost of Goods Manufactured transferred to Trading Account | xxxx |
| *Less: Closing Stock of Raw Materials* | xxxx | | | |
| | | xxxx | | |
| To Manufacturing Wages | | xxxx | | |
| **To Factory Expenses:** | | | | |
| *Electricity bill* | xxxx | | | |
| *Factory Rent* | xxxx | | | |
| | | xxxx | | |
| | | | | |
| Opening work in progress | | xxxx | | |
| | | xxxx | | xxxx |

### 5.3.5.1 *Illustrations*

### *Illustration 3*

Let's prepare the manufacturing account for the year ended 31.03.2016 from the following particulars

| Particulars | Amount |
|---|---|
| Opening stock of raw materials | 15,000 |
| Purchase of raw materials | 90,000 |
| Closing stock of raw materials | 7,500 |
| Carriage and freight on purchase of raw materials | 15,000 |
| Manufacturing wages | 37,500 |
| Factory Rent | 7,500 |
| Electricity bill | 22,500 |
| Opening work in progress | 12,000 |
| Closing work in progress | 8,500 |

| Manufacturing Account for the year ending 31st March, 2016 | | | | |
|---|---|---|---|---|
| **Particulars** | | **Amount (₹)** | **Particulars** | **Amount (₹)** |
| **To Raw Materials Consumed** | | | By Work-in-Progress (Closing) | 8,500 |
| *Opening Stock of Raw Materials* | *15,000* | | | |
| *Purchase of raw materials* | *80,000* | | | |
| *Carriage and freight on purchase of raw materials* | *12,000* | | By Cost of Goods Manufactured transferred to Trading Account | 1,70,000 |
| *Less: Closing Stock of Raw Materials* | *8,000* | | | |
| | | 99,000 | | |
| To Manufacturing Wages | | 37,500 | | |
| **To Factory Expenses:** | | | | |
| *Electricity bill* | *22,500* | | | |
| *Factory Rent* | *7,500* | | | |
| | | 30,000 | | |
| | | | | |
| Opening work in progress | | 12,000 | | |
| | | 1,78,500 | | 1,78,500 |

## 5.4 PROFIT AND LOSS ACCOUNT

Profit and loss account is an accounting statement that shows the organisation's trading position. It helps in ascertaining the net profit or net loss of a business for a given trading period, usually a financial year. It is the profit earned or loss incurred after charging all business expenses including all depreciation and provisions.

The format of Profit and Loss account is as follows:

| **Profit & Loss Account for the year ending ____________ (e.g. 31st March, 2016)** | | | |
|---|---|---|---|
| **Particulars** | **Amount (₹)** | **Particulars** | **Amount (₹)** |
| To Gross Loss b/d | xxxxx | By Gross Profit b/d | xxxxx |
| *To Selling and Distribution Expenses* | | By Discount Received | xxxxx |
| Advertisement | xxxxx | By Commission Received | xxxxx |
| Travellers' Salaries, Expenses and commission | xxxxx | By Income from Investments | xxxxx |
| Bad Debts | xxxxx | By Rent From Tenants | xxxxx |
| Godown Rent | xxxxx | By Income from Investments | xxxxx |
| Export Expenses | xxxxx | By Miscellaneous Revenue Receipts | xxxxx |
| Carriage Outward | | By Interest Received | xxxxx |
| Bank Charges | xxxxx | By Apprenticeship Premium | xxxxx |
| Agent's Commission | xxxxx | By Interest on Debentures | xxxxx |
| Upkeep of Motor Lorries | xxxxx | By Income from any other source | xxxxx |
| *To Management Expenses* | | By Net loss Transferred to Capital Account | xxxxx |
| Rent, Rates and Taxes | xxxxx | | |
| Heating and Lighting | xxxxx | | |
| Office Salaries | xxxxx | | |
| Printing Stationery | xxxxx | | |
| Postage and Telegrams | xxxxx | | |
| Telephone Charges | xxxxx | | |
| Legal Charges | xxxxx | | |
| Audit Fee | xxxxx | | |
| Insurance | xxxxx | | |
| General Expenses | xxxxx | | |
| *To Depreciation and Maintenance* | | | |
| Depreciation | xxxxx | | |
| Repairs and Maintenance | xxxxx | | |
| *To Financial Expenses* | | | |
| Discount Allowed | xxxxx | | |
| Interest on Capital | xxxxx | | |
| Interest on Loans | xxxxx | | |
| Discount on Bills | xxxxx | | |
| *To Extraordinary Expenses* | | | |
| Loss by Fire (Not covered by insurance) | xxxxx | | |
| Cash Defalcations | xxxxx | | |
| To Net Profit to Capital A/c | xxxxx | | |
| | xxxxx | | xxxxx |

### 5.4.1 Classification of Incomes and Expenses

Income is defined as the amount a business receives in exchange of providing a service or good. Expenses are defined as the economic costs a business incurs to earn revenue.

#### *Explanation of a few important items in the above format*

**Office and Maintenance Expenses**

**Salaries**: This refers to the salaries paid to office staff.

**Rent and taxes**: Rent and taxes refers to municipal taxes and the rent paid for the office building.

**Insurance**: This refers to the premium paid for insuring buildings, machinery, stock, and so on against risks.

**Office lighting and heating**: This refers to lighting and heating expenses incurred in providing lighting and heating for the office.

**Printing and stationery**: This indicates the printing and stationery expenses incurred in the office.

**Repairs and renewals**: This refers to repair charges incurred for repairing the properties of the business.

**Depreciation:** Depreciation refers to the wear and tear, i.e. the reduction in the value of an asset, resulting out of its use.

**Selling and Distribution Expenses**

**Carriage outwards or Freight outwards:** It refers to the transportation expenses incurred in carrying the goods to the market for sale.

**Bad debts:** Bad debts refers to the debts that are considered to be irrecoverable.

**Commission paid:** This is the commission paid to the salesmen and distributors for their services.

**Financial Expenses**

**Discount on sales or Discount allowed:** This indicates the cash discount allowed to the debtors for the prompt payment made by them.

**Interest paid:** This refers to the interest paid on loans.

**Interest on capital:** Interest allowed to the proprietor on his capital is entered under interest on capital.

**Incomes**

**Non-trading incomes**: It refers to all incomes other than trading incomes, such as rent received, commission received, interest received, and so on.

**Interest on drawings:** It refers to the interest charged on the amount withdrawn by the proprietor from the business for his personal use. It is an income of the business and appears on the credit side of profit and loss account.

**Note**: Personal expenses such as life insurance premium, income tax, and so on, incurred by the business owner should not be included in the profit and loss account. Such expenses are treated as drawings, which has to be deducted from the capital

### 5.4.2 Objective of Profit and Loss Account

The main objectives of Profit and Loss Account are as follows:

i. To get the final profit or loss (net profit or net loss) of the business for the current period

ii. To provide information on different classes of indirect expenses of the business such as financial expenses, maintenance expenses, office expenses etc.

### 5.4.3 Preparation of Profit and Loss Account

Preparation of profit and loss account can be performed in the following steps:

i. The gross profit or gross loss as shown in the trading account is entered in the profit and loss account. Gross profit is entered on the credit side whereas the gross loss is entered on the debit side.

ii All indirect expenses of the business such as rent, repairs, depreciation, electricity bills, taxes etc. are entered on the debit side of the profit and loss account

iii. All indirect or non-trading incomes such as interest or commission received, bad debts recovered etc. are entered on the credit side of the profit and loss account

After all the indirect incomes and expenses are entered in the profit and loss account, the account is balanced. If the total of the credit side of the profit and loss account is more than the debit side, the balance is called 'net profit'. Conversely, if the debit side is higher than the credit side, the balance is called 'net loss'.

### 5.4.4 Illustrations

#### *Illustration 4*

Let's prepare the profit and loss account for the year ended 31.12.2016 from the given particulars

| Particulars | Amount |
|---|---|
| Gross profit | 2,25,000 |
| Salaries | 37,500 |
| Commission received | 2,700 |
| Rent paid | 15,000 |
| Office lighting | 3,750 |
| Advertisement | 8,400 |
| Printing and stationery | 4,500 |
| Repairs and Maintenance | 6,300 |
| Interest Received | 2,700 |
| Interest on loans | 1,350 |
| Discount allowed | 3,000 |
| Interest on Debentures | 375 |
| Bad debts | 3,300 |
| Carriage outwards | 1,800 |
| Travelling outwards | 2,775 |
| Telephone Charges | 825 |
| Discount received | 900 |
| Insurance | 1,000 |
| Depreciation | 2,000 |
| | |

| Profit & Loss Account for the year ending 31st March, 2016 | | | |
|---|---|---|---|
| Particulars | Amount (₹) | Particulars | Amount (₹) |
| | | By Gross Profit b/d | 2,25,000 |
| ***To Selling and Distribution Expenses*** | | By Discount Received | 900 |
| Advertisement | 8,400 | By Commission Received | 2,700 |
| Travellers' Salaries, Expenses and commission | 2,775 | By Interest Received | 2,700 |
| Bad Debts | 3,300 | By Interest on Debentures | 375 |
| Godown Rent | 15,000 | | |
| Carriage Outward | 1,800 | | |
| | | | |
| ***To Management Expenses*** | | | |
| | | | |
| Heating and Lighting | 3,750 | | |
| Office Salaries | 37,500 | | |
| Printing Stationery | 4,500 | | |
| Telephone Charges | 825 | | |
| Insurance | 1,000 | | |
| ***To Depreciation and Maintenance*** | | | |
| Depreciation | 2,000 | | |
| Repairs and Maintenance | 6,300 | | |
| ***To Financial Expenses*** | | | |
| Discount Allowed | 2,000 | | |
| Interest on Loans | 1,350 | | |
| | | | |
| To Net Profit to Capital A/c | 1,41,175 | | |
| | 2,31,675 | | 2,31,675 |

*Illustration 5*

Let's prepare the profit and loss account for the year ended 31.12.2016 from the given particulars:

| Particulars | Amounts |
|---|---|
| Gross profit | 3,15,000 |
| Office Salaries | 52,500 |
| Commission received | 3,780 |
| Office lighting | 5,250 |
| Advertisement | 11,760 |
| Printing and stationery | 6,300 |
| Repairs and Maintenance | 8,820 |
| Interest Received | 5,000 |
| Interest on loans | 1,890 |
| Interest on Debentures | 525 |
| Bad debts | 4,620 |
| Carriage outwards | 2,520 |
| Travelling outwards | 3,885 |
| Telephone Charges | 1,155 |
| Discount received | 1,260 |
| Insurance | 1,400 |
| Depreciation | 2,800 |

## 5.5 BALANCE SHEET

Balance sheet is a quantitative summary of a business organisation's financial condition at a specific point of time presenting a complete picture of a company's assets, liabilities, and net worth. In other words, it is a statement of the total assets and liabilities (including capital) of an organisation as on a particular date - usually the last date of an accounting period.

The first part of a balance sheet shows all the productive assets a company owns, and the second part shows all the financing methods (such as liabilities and shareholders' equity). It is also called the statement of condition.

Following is a format of Balance Sheet:

| Balance sheet as on ______________ (e.g. 31st March, 2016) | | | |
|---|---|---|---|
| **Liabilities** | **Amount ₹** | **Assets** | **Amount ₹** |
| *Capital* | xxxxx | *Fixed Assets:* | |
| *Fixed Liabilities:* | xxxxx | Plant and Machinery | xxxxx |
| Long-Term Loans | xxxxx | Land and Building | xxxxx |
| Long-Term deposits | xxxxx | Furniture & Fixtures | xxxxx |
| *Long Term Liabilities:* | | | |
| Loan From Bank | xxxxx | Vehicles | xxxxx |
| Debentures | xxxxx | | |
| *Current Liabilities:* | | Goodwill | xxxxx |
| Bills Payable | xxxxx | Patent | xxxxx |
| Sundry Creditors | | Copyright | xxxxx |
| Bank Overdraft | | *Current Assets:* | |
| Income received in advance | | Cash in Hand | xxxxx |
| Short Term Loans | | Cash at Bank | xxxxx |
| | | *Floating Assets:* | |
| | | Sundry Debtors | xxxxx |
| | | Investments | xxxxx |
| | | Bills Receivables | xxxxx |
| | | Stock in Trade | xxxxx |
| | | Prepaid Expenses | xxxxx |
| | | | |
| | | | |
| | | | |
| | | Profit & Loss A/c | xxxxx |
| | | | |
| | xxxxx | | xxxxx |

### 5.5.1 Objective of Balance Sheet

A balance sheet is prepared with a view to ascertain the financial position or soundness of a business as on a given date. The assets and liabilities of the organisation reflect its financial position or soundness. A business can be called sound when its assets are more than its liabilities. On the other hand, if the liabilities are more than its asset, it is considered unsound.

### 5.5.2 Classification of Assets & Liabilities

**Assets** are defined as any item of economic value owned by an individual or corporation, provided it can be measured in terms of money. In other words, assets are the properties owned by an organisation and the debts (i.e. amounts) due to an organisation from other parties. Examples are cash, securities, accounts receivable, inventory, office equipment, and other properties.

From an accounting perspective, assets are divided into the following categories namely current assets (cash and other liquid items), long-term assets (real estate, plant, equipment), prepaid and deferred assets (expenditures for future costs such as insurance, rent, interest), and intangible assets (trademarks, patents, copyrights, goodwill).

**Current assets, circulating, floating or fluctuating assets:** These refer to cash or other temporary assets which can be converted into cash in a short period. Examples are cash in hand, cash at bank, bills receivable, and other liquid items.

**Liquid assets:** Liquid assets are the current assets which are either in the form of cash or can be converted into cash immediately without incurring high losses. Examples are cash in hand, cash at bank, and sundry debtors.

**Investments:** This refers to the amount invested by the business on government bonds, on shares and debentures of companies for the purpose of earning interest and dividends.

Investments may be for a short-term or long-term. Short-term investments are grouped with current assets and long-term investments are shown as a separate item.

**Fixed assets:** These are the assets held by a business organisation for its use, and not for sale. These are relatively permanent in nature. Examples are buildings, furniture, and machinery.

**Wasting assets:** Wasting assets are the fixed assets lost through use or exhausted. Examples are mines and quarries.

**Intangible assets:** Intangible assets are the fixed assets which do not have a physical existence, i.e. it cannot be seen or touched, but the possession of which yields benefit to the business or the possessor. Examples are copyright, patent, and goodwill.

**Fictitious assets:** Fictitious assets are the debit balances, i.e. expenses and losses, carried forward from one accounting period to another. These are fictitious and not represented by any tangible or concrete property. Examples are heavy advertisement expenses not written off and preliminary expenses.

**Liabilities** are amounts owed by a business to other parties. This amount can be owed for various reasons such as purchase of assets on credit, services received on credit or purchase of goods on credit. Examples of liabilities are sundry creditors, loans borrowed, bills payable etc. Liabilities of a concern may be classified into the following categories:

**Current Liabilities** are those liabilities that require to be repaid in a short period. Examples of current liabilities include bills payable, short term loans borrowed, sundry creditors etc.

**Fixed Liabilities** are those liabilities which are more permanent in nature and require to be repaid after a long period which may extend the current accounting period.

### 5.5.3 Preparation of Balance Sheet

Balance sheet is prepared only after the trading and profit and loss account has been prepared since the net profit or loss requires to be added to or subtracted from the capital. The liabilities are put on the left hand side of balance sheet while the assets are put on the right. The sides of balance sheet are not called debit or credit side since it is a statement and not an account. There are multiple ways in which the assets and liabilities are arranged on a balance sheet. Assets can be arranged either in the order of liquidity or order of permanence. The first method puts current assets on the top and fixed assets at the end whereas the second method puts fixed assets on the top and current assets at the end. Liabilities can be arranged either in the order of urgency of payment or in the order of permanence. The first method puts current liabilities on the top whereas the second one puts the fixed liabilities at the beginning.

### 5.5.4 Illustrations

#### *Illustration 6*

Let's prepare a balance sheet as on 31.03.2016 using the particulars given below.

| Particulars | Amount |
|---|---|
| Capital | 1,05,000 |
| Long term loan | 70,000 |
| Sundry creditors | 28,000 |
| Sundry debtors | 52,500 |
| Investments | 35,000 |
| Bills receivable | 8,750 |
| Plant and machinery | 39375 |
| Land and building | 43,750 |
| Goodwill | 17,500 |
| Patents | 8,750 |
| Bills payable | 22,750 |
| Cash in hand | 9,800 |
| Cash at bank | 18,200 |
| Net profit | 26,250 |
| Closing stock | 27,125 |
| Bank overdraft | 8,750 |

| Balance sheet as on 31st March, 2016 | | | |
|---|---|---|---|
| Liabilities | Amount ₹ | Assets | Amount ₹ |
| *Capital* | 1,05,000 | *Fixed Assets:* | |
| *Fixed Liabilities:* | | Plant and Machinery | 39,375 |
| Long-Term Loans | 70,000 | Land and Building | 43,750 |
| | | Goodwill | 17,500 |
| *Current Liabilities:* | | Patent | 8,750 |
| Bills Payable | 22,750 | | |
| Sundry Creditors | 28,000 | *Current Assets:* | |
| Bank Overdraft | 8,750 | Cash in Hand | 9,800 |
| Income received in advance | | Cash at Bank | 18,200 |
| Short Term Loans | | | |
| Profit & Loss A/c | 26,250 | *Floating Assets:* | |
| | | Sundry Debtors | 52,500 |
| | | Investments | 35,000 |
| | | Bills Receivables | 8,750 |
| | | Closing Stock | 27,125 |
| | | | |
| | 2,60,750 | | 2,60,750 |

| Particulars | Amount |
|---|---|
| Capital | 1,84,000 |
| Long term loan | 56,000 |
| Sundry creditors | 22,400 |
| Drawings | 10,000 |
| Sundry debtors | 42,000 |
| Investments | 28,000 |
| Bills receivable | 7,000 |
| Plant and machinery | 31500 |
| Goodwill | 14,000 |
| Patents | 7,000 |
| Bills payable | 18,200 |
| Cash in hand | 7,840 |
| Cash at bank | 14,560 |
| Net profit | 21,000 |
| Closing stock | 21,700 |
| Bank overdraft | 7,000 |

### *Illustration 7*

Let's prepare a balance sheet as on 31.03.2016 using the particulars given below.

## KEY TAKEAWAYS

- Final accounts are the statements prepared which indicates the final results of the operations of a business organisation, in financial terms.
- Final accounts include trading and profit and loss account and balance sheet.
- Profit and loss account is an accounting statement that shows an organisation's trading position over a given period of time.
- Trading account indicates the result of buying and selling of goods.
- Balance sheet is a quantitative summary of an organisation's financial condition at a specific point of time, including assets, liabilities, and net worth.
- Assets can be defined as any item of economic value owned by an individual or corporation, especially that which could be converted into cash.
- Liability can be defined as any item of economic value owed by an individual or an organization.

**Balance sheet as on 31st March, 2016**

| Liabilities | Amount ₹ | Assets | Amount ₹ |
|---|---|---|---|
| *Capital* | | *Fixed Assets:* | |
| *Opening Capital* | 1,84,000 | Plant and Machinery | 31,500 |
| *Less: Drawings* | 10,000 | Land and Building | 43,750 |
| | 1,74,000 | Goodwill | 14,000 |
| | | Patent | 7,000 |
| *Fixed Liabilities:* | | | |
| Long-Term Loans | 56,000 | *Current Assets:* | |
| | | Cash in Hand | 7,840 |
| *Current Liabilities:* | | Cash at Bank | 14,560 |
| Bills Payable | 18,200 | | |
| Sundry Creditors | 22,400 | *Floating Assets:* | |
| Bank Overdraft | 7,000 | Sundry Debtors | 42,000 |
| | | Investments | 28,000 |
| | | Bills Receivables | 7,000 |
| | | Closing Stock | 21,700 |
| | | | |
| | | Profit & Loss A/c | 60,250 |
| | | | |
| | 2,77,600 | | 2,77,600 |

## PRACTICE EXERCISES

1. From the following trial balance of Smart Electricals, prepare trading and profit and loss account for the year ending 31.03.2016, and a balance sheet as on that date:

| Particulars | Debit | Credit |
|---|---|---|
| Owner's drawings | 24,500 | |
| Furniture | 9,100 | |
| Land and buildings | 70,000 | |
| Opening stock | 77,000 | |
| Debtors | 65,100 | |
| Purchases | 3,85,000 | |
| Sales returns | 7,000 | |
| Discount | 5,600 | |
| Taxes and insurance | 7,000 | |
| General expenses | 14,000 | |
| Salaries | 31,500 | |
| Commission | 7,700 | |
| Carriage | 6,300 | |
| Bad debts | 2,800 | |
| Owner's capital account | | 1,05,000 |
| Bank overdraft | | 14,700 |
| Rent received from tenants | | 58,800 |
| Sales | | 5,25,000 |
| Discount received | | 7,000 |
| Provision for doubtful debts | | 2,100 |
| Total | 7,12,600 | 7,12,600 |

2. Use the trial balance of Surekha Enterprises below and prepare the trading and profit and loss account for the year that ended on 31.03.2016.

| Particulars | Debit | Credit |
|---|---|---|
| Opening stock | 1,20,000 | |
| Purchases | 3,30,000 | |
| Purchase returns | | 12,000 |
| Sales | | 5,85,000 |
| Sales returns | 19,500 | |
| Carriage inwards | 5,250 | |
| Wages | 24,000 | |
| Freight | 3,600 | |
| Factory rent | 15,000 | |
| Water and electricity | 2,400 | |
| Salaries | 40,500 | |
| Rent | 18,000 | |
| Advertisement | 3,600 | |
| Carriage outwards | 2,400 | |
| Discount allowed | 2,250 | |
| Discount received | | 3,600 |
| Bad debts | 3,000 | |
| Rent received | | 7,200 |
| Bad debts recovered | | 3,300 |
| Lighting and heating | 2100 | |
| Telephone expenses | 4,350 | |
| Building | 1,35,000 | |
| Furniture | 36,000 | |
| Goodwill | 45,000 | |
| Patents and trademarks | 24,000 | |
| Secured loan | | 60,000 |
| Debentures | | 1,50,000 |
| Capital | | 6,00,000 |
| Sundry creditors | | 72,000 |
| Sundry debtors | 1,20,000 | |
| Bills receivable | 1,49,400 | |
| Bills payable | | 27,000 |
| Cash in hand | 36,000 | |
| Cash at bank | 84,000 | |
| Bank overdraft | | 15000 |
| Investments | 3,09,750 | |
| Total | 15,35,100 | 15,35,100 |

3. From the following trial balance of Hinduja and co., prepare trading and profit and loss account for the year ending 31.03.2016, and a balance sheet as on that date:

| Particulars | Debit | Credit |
|---|---|---|
| Opening stock | 85,000 | |
| Purchases | 2,51,000 | |
| Purchase returns | | 25,000 |
| Sales | | 6,50,000 |
| Sales returns | 12,000 | |
| Carriage inwards | 4,000 | |
| Wages | 23,000 | |
| Freight | 3,500 | |
| Water and electricity | 3,000 | |
| Salaries | 56,000 | |
| Rent | 24,000 | |
| Carriage outwards | 3,500 | |
| Discount allowed | 2,600 | |
| Discount received | | 4,000 |
| Bad debts | 4,000 | |
| Rent received | | 8,500 |
| Telephone expenses | 4,200 | |
| Building | 2,50,000 | |
| Furniture | 40,000 | |
| Goodwill | 1,00,000 | |
| Capital | | 7,00,000 |
| Sundry creditors | | 93,300 |
| Sundry debtors | 1,10,000 | |
| Bills receivable | 75,000 | |
| Bills payable | | 34,000 |
| Cash in hand | 15,000 | |
| Cash at bank | 94,000 | |
| Bank overdraft | | 45000 |
| Investments | 4,00,000 | |
| Total | 15,59,800 | 15,59,800 |

Chapter 6

# Concepts of Goods and Services Tax (GST)

## 6.1 INTRODUCTION

India is a federal country where both the centre and the states have the powers to levy and collect taxes through appropriate legislations. They have distinct responsibilities to perform according to the powers prescribed by the constitution. Accordingly,

- The centre can levy tax on the manufacture of goods and rendering of services.
- The state can levy tax on the sale of goods.

## 6.2 INDIRECT TAX SYSTEM IN INDIA BEFORE GST

**Central Levied Taxes**

| Type of Tax | Levied on | Goods/ Services |
|---|---|---|
| Central Excise Duty | Manufacture of goods in India | Goods |
| Additional Excise Duty (AED) | Manufacture of specific goods in the schedule specified by the Central Excise Tariff Act (CETA) in addition to Excise Duty | Goods |
| Counter-vailing Duty (CVD) | Import of Goods | Goods |
| Special Additional Duty (SAD) | Import of goods in addition to Customs Duty | Goods |
| Service Tax | Taxable services rendered | Services |
| Surcharge and Cess | Addition to Tax | Both |

**State Levied Taxes**

| Type of Tax | Levied on | Goods/ Services |
|---|---|---|
| VAT | Sale of goods within the state | Goods |
| Central Sales Tax | Sale of goods outside the state | Goods |
| Purchase Tax | Purchase of goods from unregistered dealer | Goods |
| Luxury Tax | Charged on Luxury Products | Goods |
| Entry Tax | Levied on goods entered from outside state | Goods |
| Octroi | Tax Levied by Municipalities on entry of goods | Goods |
| Surcharge and Cess | Addition to Tax | Both |

## 6.3 WHY GST?

The indirect taxation system had inefficiencies and limitations due to:

- Multiple taxes (Central levies like Excise Duty, Service Tax, and other Cesses, state levies like VAT, Entry Taxes, Octroi, Luxury Tax, Entertainment Tax, Purchase tax)
- Multiple tax rates
- Multiple points of taxation (during manufacture, trader, rendering services, and so on)

In 2005, VAT was introduced to overcome the cascading effect (tax-on-tax) of sales tax. By setting-off the tax paid on purchases with the tax collected, the cascading effect was to be eliminated. CENVAT, similarly, was an enhanced system of Central Excise with provisions to set-off duties.

However, both CENVAT and VAT had their own limitations and couldn't eliminate the cascading effect of tax completely. When Excise Duty is charged by a manufacturer to a dealer, the dealer can't claim input tax credit. Similarly, input tax credit can't be availed on the Central Sales Tax (CST) charged on interstate purchases. Often, this led to taxes being a part of the product cost.

GST allows seamless flow of tax credit, and eliminates the cascading effect of all the indirect taxes in the supply chain - from manufacturers to retailers, and across state borders.

Here are some reasons to explain why:

a. **Simple Tax Structure:** GST replaces a number of indirect taxes. Further, uniformity in tax rates, and structure of taxation makes GST simpler to understand and easy to administer.

b. **Eliminates cascading effect of taxes:** The input credit set-off process is seamless, and the benefit is duly passed on to consumers.

c. **Technology Driven System:** A robust and comprehensive IT system would be the foundation of the GST regime in India. Therefore, all tax payer services such as registrations, returns, payments, selfassessment, and so on would be available to the taxpayer's online, making compliance easy and transparent.

d. **Increased Revenue:** A simpler tax structure can bring about greater compliance, thus increasing the number of tax payers and in turn tax revenues for the Government. The elimination of the cascading effect will directly result in price reduction of products which will benefit the end consumer.

Now that we know the advantages of GST, let us understand more about GST

## 6.4 WHAT IS GST

GST is tax on supply of goods and services with input credit set off available at the next stage of value addition from manufacturer to distributor to retailer until the end consumer. This means, suppliers at each stage are permitted to set-off the GST paid on the purchase of goods or services against the GST to be paid on the supply of goods or services respectively. The end consumer will thus pay only the GST charged by the last dealer in the supply chain. Since taxes at each stage are set-off, cascading effect gets eliminated.

### 6.4.1 Dual GST Model

In the dual GST model, both federal (the center) and provincial (the states) governments will levy GST separately rather than the center levying the taxes and sharing the revenue with the states.

Dual GST is preferred in federal systems, where the power is divided between the centre and the states. This means, the center and the states can levy and collect taxes. The states don't have to depend on the centre to share the revenues.

Since India is a federal country, the dual GST model will be implemented. Under this system, tax is administered, collected and shared by both the Centre and States based on the nature of transaction (Within a state or interstate).

### 6.4.2 Structure of GST

On every supply of goods and services, a tax component of the Centre and State will be applicable.

| Tax Component | Tax Applicability | Revenue Sharing |
|---|---|---|
| Central GST (CGST) | On intra-state supply of goods or services or both | Centre |
| State GST (SGST) | On intra-state supply of goods or services or both | State |
| Union Territory GST (UTGST) | On intra-union territory supply of goods or services or both | Union Territory |
| Integrated GST (IGST) | On interstate and import transactions | Centre |

**Note:** As per Final GST act, the terminologies have changed from CGST to Central Tax, SGST to State Tax, UTGST to Union Territory Tax and IGST to Integrated Tax.

### WHY UTGST?

Under GST, the SGST Act applies to all the states of India. The definition of 'States' as per the constitution of India includes union territories with their own legislature. Hence, the SGST act can't be applicable on union territories without its own legislature. The GST council has therefore introduced the UTGST Act to levy tax from the union territories that don't have a legislature. UTGST will be levied in Chandigarh, Lakshadweep, Daman and Diu, Dadra and Nagar Haveli and Andaman and Nicobar Islands instead of SGST.

**Note:** Delhi and Puducherry have their own legislatures and the SGST Act will be applicable for these territories.

### 6.4.3 TAXES SUBSUMED UNDER GST

All central taxes are subsumed under Central GST (CGST), state taxes under State GST (SGST)/Union Territory GST, and the Central Sales Tax, and CVD and SAD applicable on imports are subsumed under the Integrated GST (IGST)

| Central Tax | State Tax/ Union Territory Tax | Integrated Tax |
|---|---|---|
| Excise Duty | VAT | CVD & SAD |
| Additional Excise Duty (AED) | Purchase Tax | CST |
| Service Tax | Entry Tax | |
| Surcharge and Cess | Luxury Tax | |
| | Surcharge and Cess | |

### 6.4.4 DETERMINATION OF TAX

The structure of indirect taxes was origin based, and with GST we moved to a destination based tax system. Let us understand the difference:

| Origin Based | Destination Based |
|---|---|
| The revenue collected as tax will reach to the State where the supplier is located. | The revenue collected as tax will reach the State where the supply/consumption happens |
| For example, Ram Trading Ltd, located inKarnataka, supplies goods to M/s GaneshTrading Ltd based in TamilNadu. | For example, Ram Trading Ltd, located inKarnataka, supplies goods to M/s GaneshTrading Ltd based in TamilNadu. |
| Tax revenue will reach Karnataka sinceRam Trading Ltd. is located in Karnataka. | Tax revenue will reach TamilNadu since the place of supply is TamilNadu. |

## 6.5 REGISTRATION

In the pre-GST tax structure, businesses registered under VAT were assigned TIN, and service providers had service tax registration numbers. Now, all businesses will be unified under the 'One Tax' - GST. This leads to unified tax registration of all businesses.

Being registered under the GST law means a business is acknowledged by the government of India, as a supplier of Goods and Services. Only registered businesses are allowed to claim Input Tax Credit.

On registration, each business will be allocated a unique 15 digit PAN based registration number. This is called the GST Identification Number (GSTIN).

Let us now understand the structure of GSTIN.

| State Code | | PAN | | | | | | | | | | Entity Code | Blank | Checksum Digit |
|---|---|---|---|---|---|---|---|---|---|---|---|---|---|---|
| 1 | 2 | X | X | X | X | X | 1 | 2 | 3 | 4 | X | 1 | 2 | 3 |

### 6.5.1 Liability to Register

Are all businesses liable to register under GST? The next section will explain on what terms a business becomes liable to register under GST.

#### *Threshold Limit*

Businesses crossing the defined annual aggregate turnover threshold are liable to register under GST. Aggregate turnover includes the value of all taxable, exempt, and export supplies made across India by a business with the same PAN.

The annual aggregate turnover threshold beyond which a business becomes liable to be charged GST is as follows:

| Region | Turnover Threshold (₹ ) |
|---|---|
| **Special Category State**Arunachal Pradesh, Assam, Manipur, Meghalaya, Mizoram,Nagaland, Sikkim, Tripura and Himachal Pradesh | 10 Lakh |
| The Rest of India | 20 Lakh |

### 6.5.2 Mandatory Registration

The following category of persons have to mandatorily register, irrespective of their turnover:

- Persons doing taxable, interstate supply.
- Casual and non-resident taxable persons
- Businesses liable to pay tax under reverse charge
- Agents supplying on behalf of taxable persons
- Input service distributors
- Sellers on ecommerce platforms
- E-commerce operators
- Person supplying online information and database access or retrieval services from outside India to an unregistered person in India
- Persons responsible to deduct TDS (Government Departments)

This means that the persons will have to register even if they made a turnover of 1.

### 6.5.3 Composition Tax Payer

To ease the process of compliance for small dealers in the states, the composition scheme is provided. Under this scheme, a dealer:

- Is required to pay tax at certain percentage of turnover.
- Need not maintain detailed records and documents nor follow the rules and procedures of issuing a tax invoice, maintaining stock, filing of invoice-wise sales and purchase, and so on.
- Only needs to file periodic returns, usually on a quarterly basis.
- Will not be allowed to avail ITC
- Is not allowed to collect tax on sales.

Thus for small businesses, it is simpler to calculate tax liability and save lot of time in maintaining detailed records.

Let us understand how composition scheme is different from regular with an example:

| S/N | Composition Dealer | | Regular Dealer | |
|---|---|---|---|---|
| 1 | **Purchase** | 25,000 | **Purchase** | 25,000 |
| 2 | GST @ 5% | 1,250 | GST @ 5% | 1,250 |
| 3 | **Composite Dealer Cost** | 26,250 | Regular Dealer | 26,250 |
| 4 | Margin (10%) | 2625 | Margin (10%) | 2500 |
| 5 | **Sales Price** (Dealer Cost + Margin) | 28,875 | **Sales Price** (Purchase + Margin) | 27,500 |
| 6 | GST Tax (composite dealer can't charge tax | 0 | GST @ 5% | 1,375 |
| 7 | **Customer Price** | 28,875 | **Customer Price** | 28,875 |
| 8 | Tax Payable @ 1% on turnover of 28,875 | 289 | Tax Payable (Output GST – Input GST; 1375 – 1250) | 125 |

You can see that both the composite dealer and the regular dealer pay 5% GST on their purchase. However, since the regular dealer can claim ITC, GST doesn't get added to the cost of the product. The composite dealer can't claim ITC and this amount gets added to the cost of the product.

The composite dealer can't collect GST, but the regular dealer can charge GST from his customers and issue a tax invoice.

The composite dealer will pay tax on a fixed percentage of his turnover but has no input tax credit to set off but the regular dealer can set off the input GST and the input GST.

#### *Composition levy in GST*

In GST also, a similar benefit will be extended to small dealers, who can opt for compliance under the composition scheme. In GST, this is referred to as 'Composition Levy' and the registered taxable person who is allowed pay tax at a certain percentage of the turnover during the year is called the Composition tax payer.

| Region | Turnover Threshold (₹t) |
|---|---|
| **Special Category State**Arunachal Pradesh, Assam, Manipur, Meghalaya, Mizoram,Nagaland, Sikkim, Tripura and Himachal Pradesh | 50 Lakh |
| The Rest of India | 75 Lakh |

### *Rate of Levy*

The composite rate of levy is as below:

| Nature of Business | Percentile of Turnover |
|---|---|
| Traders | 1% |
| Manufacturers | 2% |
| Supplier of food and drinks for human consumption | 5% |

**Note:** As per the recommendation by the council, the government may increase the threshold limit, but not exceeding 1 crore.

Apart from the threshold limit, the following conditions are critical in determining the eligibility for composition levy:

A composite dealer cannot:

- be engaged in supply of services
- be engaged in the manufacture of specific notified goods (Yet to be notified)
- supply goods not taxable under GST
- be a casual taxable person and a non-resident taxable person
- be engaged in interstate supply of goods or services and imports

This implies that if a dealer wants to choose to be a 'composition dealer', then all supply of goods and/or services dealt by him should be restricted within the state.

- Opt the composite scheme for goods and regular for services or the vice versa, if he is a supplier of both goods and services.
- Opt for composite scheme in one vertical and regular in another when he deals with multiple verticals, for businesses under the same PAN.

This means an individual can own multiple businesses under different verticals like,

- Sale of mobile and accessories
- Sale of stationeries
- Franchisee of KFC

In the above scenario, the composition scheme will be applicable for all the 3 business verticals. The dealer cannot opt for the composition scheme for one business, and regular for another.

- Collect tax on all his outward supply of goods and/or services.
- Claim input tax credit, and is not eligible for input tax credit on all his inward supply of goods and/or services. This implies that when the composition dealer receives goods (purchases) from a regular taxable person, though tax is charged in the tax invoice, the dealer cannot claim input tax credit. This will form a part of the cost to composition dealer.
- On the top of bill (Bill of supply), he need to mention 'composition taxable person, not eligible to collect tax on supplies'
- The words 'composition taxable person' should be mentioned on every notice or signboard displayed at a prominent place at his principal place of business and at every additional place or places of business.

## 6.6 SUPPLY OF GOODS AND SERVICES

We know that all the different indirect taxes are subsumed under GST. This means, the concept of manufacture of goods, sale of goods, and provision of services will no longer be relevant. This makes the determination of point of taxation for GST simple. The taxable event under GST is the supply of goods and/or services.

Thus, for every business, it is important to understand the relevance of supply. Supply sets the scope of transactions as liable for the levy of GST.

### 6.6.1 Scope of Supply

The term Supply includes all forms of supply of goods or services, supplied or to be supplied, for a consideration, in the course of or for furtherance of business.

However, there are specific types of supplies mentioned in the law which need to be considered as supply even without a consideration.

Let us understand by categorising the different types of supply as:

- Supplies made for a consideration in the course of or for furtherance of business
- Supplies without consideration
- Supplies made for a consideration whether or not in the course of or for furtherance of business

Supplies made for a consideration in the course of or for furtherance of business

The following are considered as supply with consideration:

| | |
|---|---|
| **Sale** | Any sale of goods or services which broadly result in the transfer of title in case of goods, and transfer of right to use in case of services. |
| **Transfer** | Any transfers between braches form a part of supply and are taxable. However, GST paid on branch transfers are fully available as Input Tax Credit. |
| **Barter/ Exchange** | When the consideration is paid through goods instead of money. For example:A seller has supplied goods and the buyer, supplies goods to the extent of payment.Or when one product is exchanged with another product. |
| **License** | Any grant of license to use forms part of supply. For example: online subscriptions. |
| **Rental** | Renting of property fully or partially is a supply under GST. |
| **Lease** | Letting out the building or property on lease is a supply under GST. |
| **Disposal** | Disposal of business assets forms part of supply. |

### *Supplies without consideration*

1. Permanent transfer/disposal of business assets on which input tax credit has been availed
    a. In the event of sale or transfer of business assets i.e. capital goods on which Input Tax Credit was availed – the transaction shall be treated as supply even when these are cleared or transferred without consideration, and the business is liable to pay GST.
2. Supply of goods or services between related persons and distinct persons.

### *Related person*

When is supply of goods or services between related persons?

- In a supply, if the supplier and the recipient are actually officers or directors of each other's business.
- The supplier and the recipient are legally recognized partners in the same business or associated business.
- Any supply of goods and services between employer and employee. However, gifts not exceeding 50,000 in value in a financial year by an employer to an employee shall not be treated as supply of goods or services or both and GST will not be levied.
- The supplier or recipient directly or indirectly owns, controls or holds twenty-five per cent or more of the outstanding voting stock or shares. For example, the recipient holds 25% of equity in the supplier's business.
- If in any supply, the supplier or the recipient directly or indirectly controls the other, then it is considered as supply between related persons.
    - o Direct Control
    - o Indirect Control
- If in any supply, the supplier and the recipient are directly or indirectly controlled by a third person
- If in any supply, the supplier and the recipient, together, directly or indirectly control a third person
- A supply made between the members of the same family is considered as supply between related persons.

### *Distinct Person*

A distinct person can be defined as a taxable person who has obtained or is required to obtain more than one registration in the same state or a different state or an establishment of a person who has obtained or is required to obtain a registration, and also has the establishment in another state.

Each of his/her registration and establishment will be treated as a distinct Person, and any supply between them will be taxable.

Therefore, any stock transfer or branch transfers are taxable in the following two cases:

- Intrastate stock transfer: Only when an entity has more than one registration in one state.
- Inter State Stock transfer: Transfer between two entities located in different states is taxable.

**Supply of goods between principal and his agent**

Supply of goods under the following scenario is considered as taxable supply even without consideration:

Supply by the Agent to the Principal: When the agent undertakes to receive such goods on behalf of the principal.

**Import of services in the course or for furtherance of business, by a taxable person from a related person or from any of his other establishments outside India.**

This implies that services imported without consideration from related persons situated outside India will be subject to levy of GST only if it is in the course of or for furtherance of business.

**Supplies made for a consideration whether or not in the course or for furtherance of business**

The import of service for a consideration whether or not in the course or for furtherance of business is considered as taxable supply. This implies that if the services are imported for a consideration, either for business purpose or for personal use, you are liable to pay GST.

## 6.7 MIXED SUPPLY AND COMPOSITE SUPPLY

If you look at the market today, you will notice how, very often, two or more goods, or a combination of goods and services, are supplied together. This could be due to either of the following reasons:

- A sales strategy – to attract more customers
- The nature or type of goods or services, requires them to be bundled or supplied together

Under Service Tax, this mechanism is called Bundled Service – which is the rendering of a service or services with another element of service or services.

Under GST, supplies which are bundled with two or more supplies of goods or services or combination of goods and services are classified, with distinct characteristics, as:

### 6.7.1 Mixed Supply

The supply of two or more individual supplies of goods or services, or any combination of goods and services, by a taxable person, for a single price, is called mixed supply.

In a mixed supply, the combination of goods and/or services are not bundled due to natural necessities, and they can be supplied individually in the ordinary course of business.

### *Determining Mixed Supply*

Let us understand this with an example.

Consider a kit which contains a tie, a watch, a wallet, and a pen as a combo for ₹ 4,500/-

Tie @12%, Watch @ 18%, Wallet @ 12%, Pen @ 5%

**Note:** Bundled as a kit

The supply of a tie does not naturally necessitate the supply of other elements (watch, wallet, and pen) and vice versa the kit is supplied for a single price

### *Tax liability on mixed supply*

To calculate the tax liability on Mixed Supply, the tax rate applicable on the goods or services attracting the highest rate of tax, in the combination of goods and services, will be considered

In the example of the kit, the wallet attracts the highest rate of tax in the mixed supply i.e., 18%. Hence, the mixed supply will be taxed at 18%.

### 6.7.2 Composite Supply

Composite Supply of goods and services is made by a taxable person to a recipient, and:

- It comprises two or more supplies of goods or services, or
- A combination of goods and services, which are naturally bundled and supplied, in the ordinary course of business.

This means that the goods and services are bundled owing to natural necessities. The elements in a composite supply of goods and services are dependent elements on the 'principal supply' of goods or services.

#### *What is a Principal Supply?*

The pre-dominant element in the supply of goods or services, forming part of composite supply, is principal supply, and any other dependent supply, forming part of composite supplies, are secondary to principal supply.

#### *Determination of Composite Supply*

Let us understand this with an example,

1. A 5-star hotel in Mumbai provides a 4 days/3 night's package, with breakfast.

   This is a composite supply as the package of accommodation facilities and breakfast is natural combination in the ordinary course of business for a hotel. In this case, the hotel accommodation is the principal supply, and breakfast is ancillary to the hotel accommodation.
2. A 5-star hotel in Mumbai provides a 4 day/3 night's package with the breakfast and one day Mumbai Darshan.

   The inclusion of Mumbai Darshan in this package is not a natural requisite to accommodation in the hotel. Hence, this does not amount to composite supply. This is a mixed supply.
3. Sale of Laptop with Bag.

   This is a composite supply because laptop bag is natural requisite to carry the laptop. But if the customer opts for a multipurpose bag like backpack bag, it is not a composite supply since it is not naturally bundled

#### *Tax liability of composite supply*

For the purpose of calculating tax liability, the rate of tax applicable on the principal supply of such goods and services will be effected on the composite supply. Let us consider the same example,

1. A 5-star hotel in Mumbai provides a 4 days/3 night's package with the breakfast. Let us assume, the hotel accommodation attracts 12% tax and the restaurant service attracts 18% tax.

As per the example, hotel accommodation is the principal supply, and the entire supply will be taxed at 12%.

## 6.8 PLACE OF SUPPLY

Two key aspects to be considered while levying taxes based on place of supply:

- Location of supplier
- Place of supply

Determining the place of supply is critical to:

- Know taxable jurisdiction where tax should reach
- Determine if the nature of transaction is intrastate (subject CGST + SGST/UTGST) or interstate (subject to IGST)

| Criteria | Nature of Transaction | Tax Components |
|---|---|---|
| Location of supplier and place of supply are the same.For example, location of supplier and theplace of supply is Karnataka | Intra-State | Centre Tax + State Tax/ Union Territory Tax |
| Location of supplier and place of supplyare two different statesFor example, location of supplier isKarnataka and the place of supply is Tamil Nadu | Inter-State | Integrated Tax |

Apart from the place of supply, the following are also treated as interstate supplies:

- Import of goods or services
- Export of goods or services
- Supply of goods manufactured by a unit in the Special Economic Zone (SEZ), even if the location of the SEZ and the place of supply are the same.

We will discuss determining place of supply of goods and services in two separate heads

### 6.8.1 Determining the place of Supply of Goods

Goods being tangible, determining the place of supply is far more direct. Services are intangible, and with the uncertainty involved in knowing the mode of delivery of the service, place of supply or the location of the supplier or recipient, the provisions are different for determining the place of supply of services.

#### *What happens when goods are installed or assembled at site?*

The place of supply is where the location where the installation or assembling happens.

#### *What happens when goods are sold on board during conveyance?*

Place of supply is the location from where the good were taken on board.

#### *What happens in a Bill to - Ship To Scenarios?*

A Bill to - Ship to scenario is where the goods are delivered by a supplier to a recipient on the direction of a third person. This third person can be an agent or a seller. The third person is the principal, and is deemed to have received the goods, while the actual transfer may happen between the supplier and the recipient only.

### 6.8.2 Determining the place of Supply of Services

Place of supply of services is the location where the services have been rendered, when the address of the recipient is available. This is most often relevant in a business-to-business scenario. When taxable services are rendered to a registered person or entity within the same state, then the supply is intrastate and will attract CGST and SGST

***When taxable services are rendered to a registered person or entity outside the state***

Then the supply is interstate and will attract IGST

***Supply of Services to a registered person or entity within the state***

When services are supplied to registered person, the Place of supply of services will be the place of registered person. This is most often relevant in a business-to-business scenario. When taxable services are rendered to a registered person or entity within the same state, then the supply is intrastate and will attract CGST and SGST.

## 6.9 TIME OF SUPPLY

Under GST, the taxable event is 'Supply' of goods and services. The point in time when goods or services are supplied will be determined in terms of 'Time of Supply' provisions.

Let us understand time of supply under two heads:

- Time of Supply of Goods
- Time of Supply of Services

### 6.9.1 Time of Supply of Goods

***Forward Charge on Supply of Goods***

Forward Charge is a mechanism by which the supplier has to levy tax and remit the same to the credit of the Central or State Government.

Let us understand 'Time of Supply of Goods' under GST on Forward Charge

The liability of GST (CGST and SGST or IGST, as applicable) will arise as shown below:

| Earliest of the following | |
|---|---|
| **Date of invoice** | The date on which the supplier issues the invoice |
| **Due date to issue invoice** | The last date on which the supplier is required to issue the invoice with respect to the supply of goods. In case of supply of goods involving the movement goods, the invoice needs to be issued at the time of removal. In other cases, at the time of delivery of goods to the recipient. |
| **Receipt of payment** | The date on which payment is received. The point of taxation in this case will be the earliest of the date on which payment is accounted in the books of accounts of the recipient or the date on which payment is credited to his bank account. |

***Reverse Charge on supply of Goods***

In order to ensure that the tax is collected on the sale of goods or services from various unorganised sectors, the government introduced the Reverse Charge Mechanism. Under this, the recipient or buyer of goods or services has to pay the tax to the credit of the Government, unlike in the forward charge, where the supplier is liable to pay the tax. The key change is the shift in the responsibility of paying tax, which has moved from the supplier to the buyer.

Under GST, a similar concept of reverse charge mechanism is being introduced. This is applicable on specified supply of goods and services, which will be notified.

Let us understand time of supply for goods under Reverse Charge Mechanism.

The liability of GST (CGST and SGST or IGST as applicable) will arise as shown below

| Earliest of the following | |
|---|---|
| **Date of Receipt of Goods** | The date on which the goods are received by the recipient |
| **Due date to issue invoice** | The date on which payment is made. The earliest of the date on which the payment is accounted for in the books of accounts of the recipient or the date on which the payment is credited to his bank account. |
| **Receipt of payment** | The date immediately following 30 days from the date of issue of invoice by the supplier. |

## 6.10 VALUE OF SUPPLY

Under GST, the value of taxable supply of goods and services will be the transaction value. Transaction value refers to the price actually paid or payable for the supply of goods and services.

***The effect of additional charges on transaction value***

| Charges/expenses related to supply | Effect on transaction value |
|---|---|
| Incidental expenses such as commission and packing | Included in transaction value |
| Interest/late fee/penalty charged by supplier for delayed payment | Included in transaction value |
| Subsidies excluding those provided by the Central and State governments | Included in transaction value |
| Any tax other than GST | Included in transaction value |
| Any amount payable by supplier, but incurredby receiver | Included in transaction value |

The effect of discount on transaction value

| Type of Discount | Effect on transaction value |
|---|---|
| If the discount is given before or at the time of supply, and is recorded in the invoice | Can be claimed as deduction fromtransaction value |
| If the discount is given after supply, but agreed upon before or at the time of supply, and can be specifically linked to relevant invoices | Can be claimed as deduction fromtransaction value |
| If the discount is given after supply, and not known at the time of supply | Cannot be claimed as deduction fromtransaction value |

## 6.11 INVOICING

Invoicing is an important aspect of tax compliance for every business. It is necessary to be aware of the rules of invoicing under GST. Let us understand these in detail.

In the GST regime too, two types of invoices will be issued:

1. Tax invoice
2. Bill of Supply

When a registered taxable person supplies taxable goods or services, a tax invoice is issued. Based on the rules of the details required in a tax invoice, a sample tax invoice is shown below:

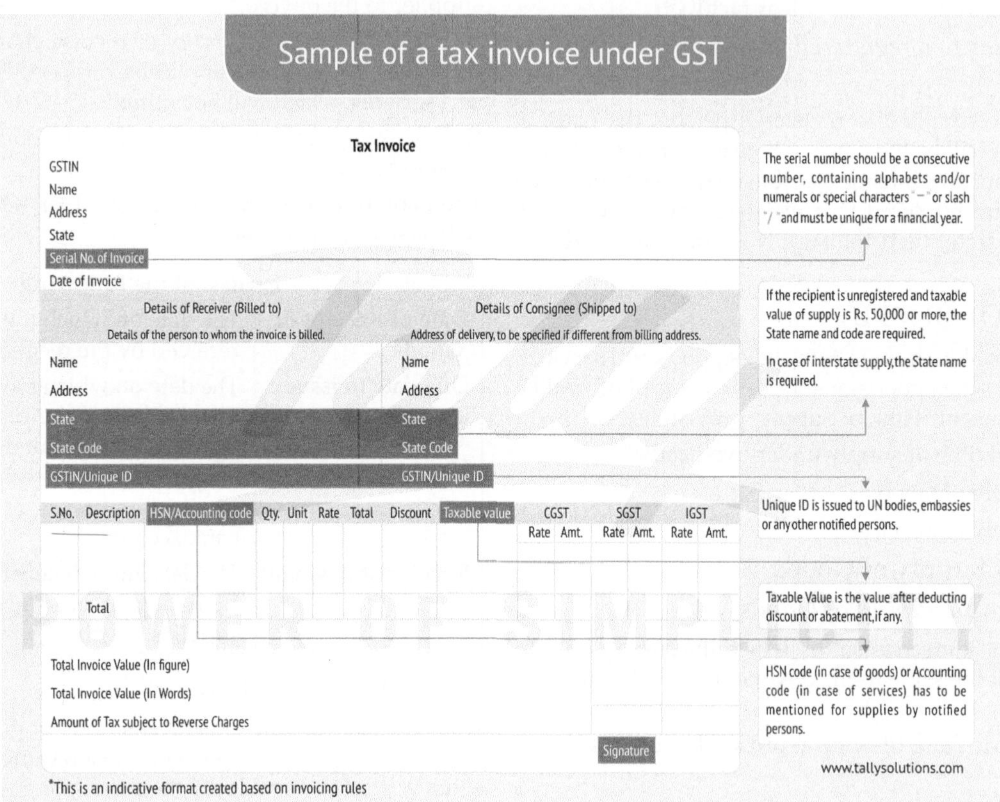


### 6.11.1 Timelines to issue Tax Invoice

*Supply of goods*

The tax invoice must be issued before or at the time of:

**Removal of goods, where supply involves movement of goods.**

For example, when Super Cars Ltd, a car manufacturer, supplies cars to its dealer Ravindra Automobiles, the invoice must be issued at the time of removal of the cars from the premises of Super Cars Ltd. This is because the supply involves movement of the cars to the premises of Ravindra Automobiles.

**Delivery of goods to the recipient, where supply does not require movement of goods.**

For example, Super Cars Ltd purchases a generator set, which will be assembled and installed at the factory premises by the supplier. Here, since the supply does not require movement of the generator set, the invoice must be issued at the time when the generator set is made available to Super Cars Ltd.

*Supply of services*

The tax invoice must be issued within 30 days from the date of supply of the service. Where the supplier is a bank or any financial institution, the invoice must be issued within 45 days of the supply of service.

### 6.11.2 Copies of Invoices

*Supply of goods*

For supply of goods, three copies of the invoice are required – Original, Duplicate, and

*Triplicate.*

- **Original Invoice:** The original invoice is issued to the receiver, and is marked as 'Original for recipient'.

- **Duplicate Copy:** The duplicate copy is issued to the transporter, and is marked as 'Duplicate for transporter'. This is not required if the supplier has obtained an invoice reference number. The invoice reference number is given to a supplier when he uploads a tax invoice issued by him in the GST portal. It is valid for 30 days from the date of upload of invoice.
- **Triplicate Copy:** This copy is retained by the supplier, and is marked as 'Triplicate for supplier'.

### *Supply of Services*

For supply of services, two copies of the invoice are required:

- **Original Invoice:** The original copy of the invoice is to be given to the receiver, and is marked as 'Original for recipient'.
- **Duplicate Copy:** The duplicate copy is for the supplier, and is marked as 'Duplicate for supplier'

### *Bills of Supply*

Bill of Supply is to be issued by a registered supplier in the following cases:

- Supply of exempted goods or services
- Supplier is paying tax under the composition scheme

Based on the rules of details required in a Bill of supply, a sample Bill of Supply is shown below:

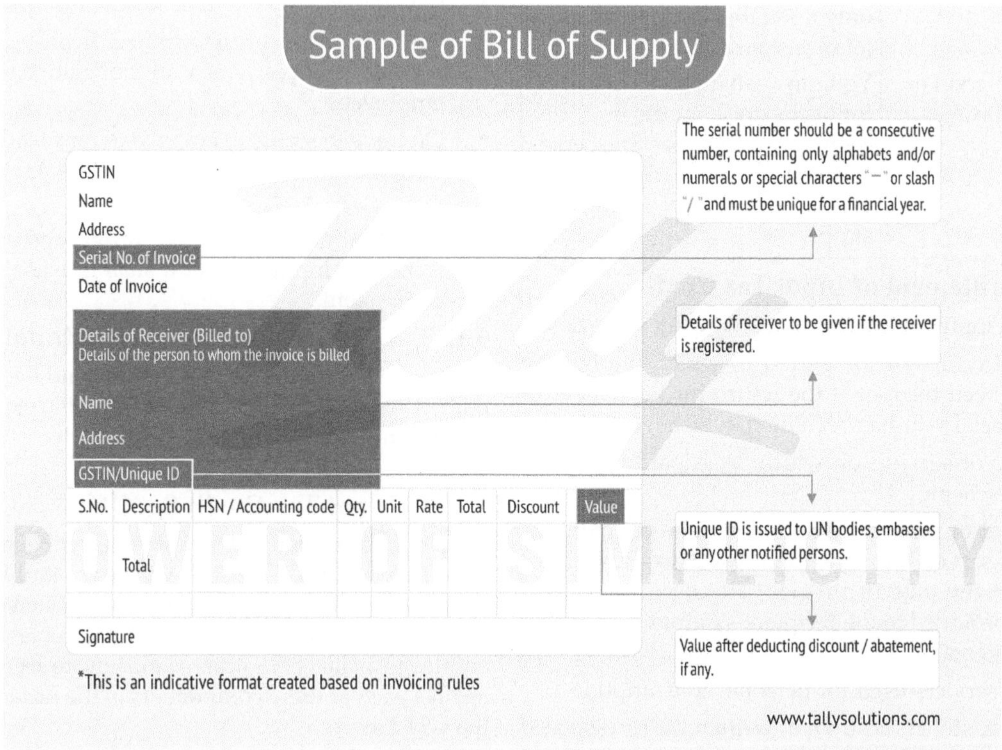


Bill of supply need not be issued when the value of goods or services supplied is less than 100, unless the receiver insists for the bill. However, a consolidated bill of supply should be prepared at the end of the business day for all such supplies for which the bill of supply was not issued.

## 6.12 INPUT CREDIT MECHANISM

One of the fundamental features of GST is the seamless flow of input credit across the chain (from the manufacturer to the consumer) and across the country.

Under the GST regime, input tax credit can be availed by every registered taxable person on all the inputs used or intended to be used for the furtherance of business.

### 6.12.1 Entitlement of Input Tax Credit

| Scenario | Input Tax Eligibility |
|---|---|
| Applying for new registration under GST - On becoming liable to register. Conditions:<br>1. Applied for registration within30 days from the date of beingdeemed as liable to register<br>2. Registration Granted | Entitled to avail input tax credit on the inputs in stock, inputs in semi-finished state or finished goods from the date on which youbecome liable to pay tax |
| Voluntarily apply for registration: | You can avail input tax credit on inputs in stock, inputs in semifinished state, or finished goods in stock on the day before the date of grant of registration |

| | |
|---|---|
| A registered dealer ceased to pay tax under the composition levy | You can avail input tax credit on inputs in stock, inputs in semifinished state, finished goods and capital goods in stock on the day before the date from when you become liable to pay tax |
| Sale/merger/demerger/ amalgamation/lease/ transfer of the business | The unutilized input tax credit can be transferred to the sold, merged, demerged, amalgamated, leased, or transferred business |
| Goods are received in lots or instalments | Input tax credit can be claimed only upon the receipt of the last lot or instalment |
| When an exempt good or servicebecomes taxable | You can avail input tax credit on inputs in stock, inputs in semifinishedstate, or finished goods in stock, and capital goods exclusively used for exempt supply |

### 6.12.2 Non Entitlement of Input Tax Credit

You cannot claim input tax credit in the following scenarios:

- If the annual return of the period to which the invoice pertains has been filed, or if the return for September of the next financial year has been filed, whichever is earlier
- On the goods or services on which tax is paid under the composition scheme
- If the recipient of the service does not make payment for the supply of services along with the tax payable, within 3 months from the date of invoice. The input tax credit availed will be added to the recipient's output tax liability along with interest
- On goods or services used for personal consumption
- On goods lost, stolen, destroyed, written off or disposed as gift or free samples
- On input tax credit wrongly availed
- On motor vehicles and other conveyance. Input tax credit is not allowed on motor vehicles and other conveyance unless they are:
  - o Further supplied or
  - o Used for transport of passengers or goods or
  - o Used for imparting training on driving, flying, or navigating such vehicles or conveyances
- **For example:** Super Cars Pvt Ltd purchased a Tempo Traveller for the purpose of transporting its employees within the factory premises. Super Cars Pvt Ltd cannot avail input credit on the Tempo Traveller as it does not satisfy the above conditions. In contrast, Mukesh Travels, a tour operator, purchased a Tempo Traveller for the purpose of transporting tourists. Mukesh Travels can avail input credit on the Tempo Traveller, as it is used for transporting passengers – a business activity for Mukesh Travels.
- On food and beverages, outdoor catering, beauty treatment, health services, cosmetic and plastic surgery except where they have been used for making outward supply of the same category of goods or services. For example: Super Cars Pvt Ltd took the services of Rakesh Caterers, a caterer in Bangalore, for their Diwali celebration. Here, Super Cars Pvt Ltd cannot avail input tax credit on the catering service received, as they are not supplying the service any further. In contrast, Rakesh Caterers purchase cold drinks from Coca Cola India and supply them to Super Cars Ltd for the Diwali celebration. In this case, Rakesh Caterers can avail input tax credit on the cold drinks purchased, as they have been further supplied to Super Cars Pvt Ltd.
- On membership of clubs, health and fitness centres
- On rent-a-cab, life insurance, health insurance, except notified services which are obligatory to be provided to employees
- On travel benefits to employees on vacation, such as leave or home travel concession
- If depreciation is claimed on the tax component of the cost of capital goods under the provisions of the Income Tax Act, 1961, input tax credit shall not be allowed on the tax component

### 6.12.3 Determining the Eligible Input Tax Credit

In the above sections, we have understand the various scenarios related to entailment of input tax credit, partial allowance of ITC and negative list of goods and service for which ITC is not allowed.

### 6.12.4 Input Tax Credit Set Off

On every transaction within a state, a component of Central GST (CGST) and State GST (SGST) will be applicable. Integrated GST (IGST) is for interstate transactions. A registered dealer's liability to pay can be set off against the input tax credit that he/she is entitled to avail. Let us understand how to set off the input credit against each of these components in the order as prescribed by the GST Law.

| Input Tax Credit | Set-Off Against Liability |
|---|---|
| Central Tax | CGST and IGST (in that order) |
| State Tax | SGST and IGST (in that order) |
| Union Territory Tax | UTGST and IGST (in that order) |
| Integrated Tax | IGST, CGST, SGST (in that order) |

### 6.12.5 Input Tax Credit Claim

Let us now discuss about various conditions laid down by the GST law to avail input credit on the supply of goods or services. All of the following conditions need to be satisfied to avail input credit:

- The dealer should be in possession of the Tax Invoice/Debit or Credit Note/Supplementary Invoice issued by a supplier registered under the GST Act.
- The said goods/services have been received.
- Returns (Form GSTR-3) have been filed.

- The tax charged has been paid to the government by the supplier.

## 6.13 RETURNS

With GST in place, it does not matter whether you are a trader, manufacturer, reseller or a service provider. You only need to file GST returns.

Let us understand different types of return forms in GST.

All the forms are required to be e-filed. The details of each form are listed below along with details of applicability and periodicity.

### 6.13.1 Regular Dealer

Let us now discuss about various conditions laid down by the GST law to avail input credit on the supply of goods or services.

| Form Type | Frequency | Due Date | Details to be Furnished |
|---|---|---|---|
| Form GSTR-1 | Monthly | **10th** of the succeeding month | Furnish details of outward supplies of taxable goods and/or services effected |
| Form GSTR-2A | Monthly | **11th** of the succeeding month | Auto-populated details of inward supplies made available to the recipient, on the basis of Form GSTR-1 furnished by the supplier |
| Form GSTR-2 | Monthly | **15th** of the succeeding month | Details of inward supplies of taxable goods and/or services claiming input tax credit. Addition or modification in Form GSTR-1 should be submitted in Form GSTR-2 |
| Form GSTR-1A | Monthly | **17th** of the succeeding month | Details of outward supplies as added, corrected or deleted by the recipient in Form GSTR-2 will be made available to the supplier |
| Form GSTR-3 | Monthly | **20th** of the succeeding month | Monthly return on the basis of finalization of details of outward supplies and inward supplies along with the payment of amount of tax |
| Form GSTR MIS-1 | Monthly | — | Communication of acceptance, discrepancy or duplication of the input tax credit claim |
| Form GSTR-3A | Monthly | **15 Days** from default | Notice to a registered taxable person who fails to furnish return |
| Form GSTR-9 | Monthly | **31st** Dec of Next Fiscal | Annual Return - Furnish the details of the ITC availed and GST paid which includes the local and interstate transactions and import/exports |

### 6.13.2 Composite Dealer

| Form Type | Frequency | Due Date | Details to be Furnished |
|---|---|---|---|
| Form GSTR-4A | Quarterly | — | Auto-populated details of the inward supplies made available to the recipient registered under the composition scheme, on the basis of the FORM GSTR-1 furnished by the supplier |
| Form GSTR-4 | Quarterly | **18th** of the succeeding month | All outward supplies of goods and services, including auto-populated details from Form GSTR-4A and tax payable details. Details of any additions, modifications, or deletions in Form GSTR-4A should also be submitted in Form GSTR-4 |
| Form GSTR-9A | Annually | **31st** of the succeeding month | Consolidated details of the quarterly returns filed along with tax payment details. |

## 6.14 PAYMENT OF TAX

The liability of tax, input tax credit and deposits of every registered taxable person is maintained and administered on a common portal under the following accounts:

- Electronic Tax Liability Register
- Electronic Credit Ledger
- Electronic Cash Ledger

### *Electronic Tax Liability Register*

All the amount payable by a taxable person will be debited (added) to an electronic tax liability register. The register will be added with:

- The amount payable towards tax, as per the return filed by the registered taxable person
- Interest, late fee or any other amount payable by the registered taxable per

- The amount of tax and interest payable as a result of mismatch of ITC and tax liability

The electronic tax liability registered will be credited to the extent of the payment made by utilizing the input tax credit or by depositing the amount to the said registerbe e-filed. The details of each form are listed below along with details of applicability and periodicity.

### *Electronic Credit Ledger*

The electronic credit ledger will be maintained for each registered taxable person on the common portal and every claim of input tax credit under it shall be credited to the said ledger.

The ledger will be debited to the extent of utilization of input tax credit to discharge the tax liability, and incase refund claim.

### *Electronic Cash Ledger*

The electronic cash ledger will be maintained for each registered taxable person on the common portal for crediting the amount deposited. This account will be debited to the extent of payment made towards tax, interest, penalty, fee or any other amount.

### 6.14.1 Timeline for Payment of Tax

| Type of Dealer | Due Date |
|---|---|
| Regular | 20th of the subsequent month |
| Composite Dealer | 18th of the subsequent month |

### 6.14.2 Modes of Payment

The payment of tax and other dues can either be paid online or offline.

### *Online Mode*

- Internet banking through authorized banks
- Credit card or Debit card after registering the same in the common portal through the authorized bank
- National Electronic Fund Transfer (NEFT) from any bank
- Real Time Gross Settlement (RTGS) from any bank

For payments made by NEFT or RTGS mode from any bank, a mandate form shall be generated along with the challan and the same needs to be submitted to the bank (from where the payment has to be made).

### *Offline Mode*

Offline payment can be done by cash, cheque or demand draft by depositing through Over the Counter Payment (OTC) from authorized banks. Offline payment can be done only if the payment is up to 10,000 /- per challan per tax period.

## 6.15 CONSEQUENCES OF NON-COMPLIANCE

Various measures have been laid down to check non-compliance under GST. These vary based on the severity of the offence. Penalties have been made stricter for tax evaders under GST.

Let us understand the various penalties laid down for non-compliance under GST

### 6.15.1 Late Fee

Late fee will be applicable if the returns are not furnished within the due date

| Type of Return | Late |
|---|---|
| Monthly/ Quarterly Return | ₹ 100/- per day for every day during whichsuch failure continues, subject to a maximumof ₹ 5000/- |
| Annual Return | ₹ 100/- per day for every day during which suchfailure continues subject to a maximum of ₹ 0.25% of aggregate turnover |

### 6.15.2 Interest

The following are the circumstances for levy of interest

| Offence | Interest | Rate of Interest |
|---|---|---|
| A person liable to pay tax fails to pay the tax | Interest on the tax due will becalculated from the first day on which the tax was due to be paid | Maximum 18% |
| A person makes an undueor excess claim of inputtax credit or undue or excess reduction in outputtax liability | Interest on the undue excessclaim or undue or excess reduction | Maximum 24% |

### 6.15.3 Cancellation of Registration

The registration can be cancelled when:

- A regular dealer has not furnished returns for a continuous period of 6 months.
- A composition dealer has not furnished returns for 3 quarters.
- A person who has taken voluntary registration has not commenced business within 6 months from the date of registration.
- Registration has been obtained by fraud, wilful misstatement or suppression of facts.

### 6.15.4 Fines

Offences on which penalty will be levied have been specifically laid down under GST

| Offence | Penalty |
|---|---|
| Supplies goods and/or services without issuing an invoice or issues an incorrect or false invoice<br>• Issues an invoice without supply of goods and/or services<br>• Collects tax but fails to pay the same to the government beyond a period of 3 months from the date on which the payment becomes due<br>• Is an e-commerce operator, and fails to collect tax or collects lesser than the amount required to be collected or fails to pay the tax to the government | ₹ 10,000/- or an amount equivalent to the tax evaded |

| | |
|---|---|
| • Takes input tax credit without actual receipt of goods and/or services either fully or partially<br>• Obtains refund of tax by fraud<br>• Falsifies or substitutes financial records or produces fake accounts and/or documents or furnishes a false return<br>• Liable to be registered, but fails to obtain<br>• Furnishes false information with regard to registration<br>• Transports taxable goods without documents<br>• Suppresses turnover leading to evasion of tax<br>• Fails to maintain books of accounts and documents<br>• Issues an invoice or document by using the identification number of another person | |
| A person who aids or abets any of the offences listed above | May extend to ₹ 25,000/- |
| Any offence for which a penalty is not separately provided under the law | May extend to ₹ 25,000/- |

### 6.15.5 Imprisonment and Fines

| Offence | Imprisonment |
|---|---|
| Commits or abets the following:<br>• Obstructing or preventing any officer in the discharge of his duties<br>• Tampering with or destroying any evidence or documents<br>Failing to supply any information required of him under the law or supplying false information | 6 months imprisonment with fine |
| • Tax evaded or input tax credit wrongly availed or refund wrongly taken of an amount exceeding ₹ 100 Lakhs, but not exceeding ₹ 2 Crore<br>• Tax evaded or input tax credit wrongly availed or refund wrongly taken of an amount exceeding ₹ 2 crore , but not exceeding ₹ 5 Crore<br>• Tax evaded or input tax credit wrongly availed or refund wrongly taken of an amount exceeding ₹ 5 Crore | Imprisonment which may extend to 1 year with fine |

## 6.16 ACCOUNTS AND OTHER RECORDS

Accounts and records are the primary source of data for any organization's financial reporting. Every law of Direct and Indirect Tax in our country also mandates that information in a prescribed manner has to be captured and preserved for a certain period of time Under GST, every registered taxable person is required to maintain correct accounts of the following details at the principal place of business specified in the registration certificate:

- Production or manufacture of goods
- Inward or outward supply of goods and/or services
- Stock of goods
- Input tax credit availed
- Output tax payable and paid
- Any other particulars as may be prescribed in this behalf

When there is more than one place of business, as specified in the certificate of registration, the accounts relating to each place of business should be kept at such places of business concerned.

Accounts and records should be maintained separately for each activity, such as manufacturing, trading, and provision of service. Any entry in registers, accounts and documents should not be erased or overwritten and incorrect entries should be scored out under attestation and then, the correct entry should be recorded. Where the registers and other documents are maintained electronically, a log of every entry edited or deleted should be maintained.

Every registered dealer whose turnover during a financial year exceeds of 2 crore should get his accounts audited by a practising Chartered Accountant, Cost Accountant or Company Secretary

### 6.16.1 Documents as Evidence

Printed records of any sort and electronic records are admissible as documents. Broadly the following electronic records are admissible as documents:

- Micro film or reproduction of the image of a document
- A facsimile (duplicate) copy of the document
- Printed material produced by a computer (computer printout)

The computer printout should be from the computer being used regularly to store or process information for any activity regularly carried on over the period

### 6.16.2 Period of Accounts

Every registered taxable person should retain the accounts and records until the end of 72 months from the last of date of filing of annual return for the said year. For example,For the financial year 2017-18, if the annual return has to be submitted by December 2018, the books will be kept till the end of December 2024.

## 6.17 TAX RATE STRUCTURE

A four tier tax structure of 5%, 12%, 18% and 28% was finalized by the GST council on 3rd November, 2016. Additionally, a cess would be applicable on luxury cars, tobacco, and aerated drinks.

On the 18th of May, 2017, the GST council convened to fix and finalise the much awaited GST rates the following table contains details few important products.

| Type | Rate | Products & Services |
|---|---|---|
| Zero Rated | 0% | Fresh Meat, Fish, Chicken, Eggs, Curd, Butter Milk, Jaggery (Gur), Lassi, unpacked Panner, Handloom Products, Contra-ceptives, Hotel Services priced at less than INR 1000, Education, Healthcare etc. |
| Merit Rate | 5% | Skimmed Milk Powder, Milk food for babies, Condensed milk,Packaged Panner, Cream, Frozen Vegetables, Coffee, Tea, Juices,Kerosene, LPG, Coal, Lifeboats, Railway Travel, Economy Class Air -Travel, Cab Aggregators (e.g. Uber & Ola) etc. |
| Standard Rate | 12% | Butter, Cheese, Ghee, Packaged Dry Fruits, Snacks (Namkeen &Bhujia), Packaged Chicken, Sausages, Fruit Juices, Packed CoconutWater, Tooth Powder, Sewing Machine, Umbrella, Ayurvedic -Medicine, Mobile Phones, Non-AC Hotels & Restaurants etc. |
| Standard Rate | 18% | Preserved Vegetables, Flavoured refined sugar, Pasta, Corn Flakes,Pastries, Cakes, Jams, Sauces, Soups, Instant Food Mixes,Processed Foods, Edible Oil, issues, Toilet Paper, Hair Oil, Soap Bars,Toothpaste, Mineral Water Printed Circuits, Speakers, Monitors,Iron & Steel Products, AC Hotels & Restaurants that serveliquor, Telecom Services, IT Services, Financial Services etc |
| Demerit Rate | 28% | Chocolates, Chewing Gum, Custard Powder, Aerated Water,Deodorants, Shaving Cream, After Shave, Hair Shampoo, Dye,Sunscreen, Perfume, Face Creams, Detergents, Vaccum Cleaner, Shavers, Hair Clippers, Washing Machines, Dish Washers, Water -Heaters & other Home Appliances, Automobiles & Motor Vehicles,Pan Masala, Tobacco, Aerated Drinks & Motor Vehicles, Rooms and Restaurants in 5-star hotels, Race course betting, etc |
| Additional Cess over and above 28% Rate | | Pan Masala, Tobacco, Aerated Drinks & Motor Vehicles, Automobiles & Motor Vehicles etc |

## 6.18 REFUND OF TAX

A tax refund refers to any amount that is due or returnable to the tax payer from the tax department. There are specific scenarios in which refund is allowed and dealers can claim tax refund only in these scenarios, such as excess payment of taxes, unutilized input tax credit on account of output supplies being exports, rate of tax on inputs being higher than the rate of tax on outputs (Inverted duty structure)

Following are the most common scenarios where refund is allowed under GST:

1. Unutilized input tax credit due to inverted duty structure: This is when the rate of tax on inputs is higher than the rate of tax on output supplies. Before GST this was not allowed for refund. However, in the GST regime, this scenario is eligible for claim of tax refund. Note that in this case, refund is not applicable when supplies are nil rated or fully exempt.
2. Unutilized input tax credit due to outward supplies are exported at zero rate. If goods are exported out of India, and are subject to export duty, no refund can be claimed.
3. Tax paid on inward supply of goods and/or services which have been exported or on inputs or input services used in goods and/or services exported. Note that if the goods are subjected to export duty, refund will not be allowed.
4. Tax has been paid on a supply which has not been provided, either wholly or partially, and for which an invoice has not been issued. For example, a supplier has received an advance from the recipient on 28th November '17 for a supply to be made on 20th December '17, however, the supply wasn't fulfilled owin to a disagreement. While filing the return for November '17, the supplier has to pay tax on the advance received. This tax is eligible for refund.
5. Tax wrongly collected and deposited with the Central or State Government- If a person has paid CGST and SGST on an interstate supply or IGST on an intrastate supply, the person is eligible for refund of the amount once the tax has been remitted correctly.
6. IGST paid on supply of goods to tourists traveling out of India, if the goods are taken out of India.

The application for refund of tax should be made within 2 years from the relevant date (broadly when the goods leave/passes outside India). 90% of the claim will be refunded on a provisional basis on receipt of application, and the remaining 10% after due verification of documents furnished by the applicant.

If the amount of refund claimed is less than 2 lakhs, the person needs to file a declaration, based on the documents or other evidence available with him, certifying that the incidence of tax or interest being claimed as refund has not been passed on to another person. In case, the refund is more than 2 lakhs, the application for refund must be accompanied by documentary evidence to establish that the refund is due to the person and Documentary or other evidence to establish that the amount was paid by him/her, and that the incidence of the tax or interest has not been passed on to another person

## 6.19 TRANSITION TO GST

The first and foremost task for you, as a business is transitioning to GST. While it is important to know the fundamentals of GST, it is also very critical for you to understand the transition provisions available, and take the necessary actions to ensure a smooth transition to GST, and leverage on transition benefits. You will need to review your accounting and reporting procedures, procurement, logistics decisions, and so on, in advance, to avail the appropriate input tax credit. Today, the manufacturing, sales and service activity are governed by a separate indirect tax system. The manufacturing activity is covered by Central Excise, sales is covered under State VAT/ CST, and the services activity is covered under the Service Tax Act.

Let us understand the carry forward of input tax credit for business and availing input tax credit on closing stock held on the last day prior to implementation of GST.

### 6.19.1 Registered Business

For ease of understanding, we have categorized the transition provisions for each of the below tax types:

- Central Excise
- VAT
- Service Tax

*Central Excise*

*Manufacturer*

A manufacturer can carry forward the balance CENVAT credit available on the last day, prior to date on which GST is implemented, as input credit. This will be allowed as credit only if the following conditions are met by the manufacturer:

- The closing balance of CENVAT credit should reflect in the last return filed by you
- It should be allowed as input tax credit under GST
- All the returns as required to be furnished, filed for last 6 months from the date of implementation of GST

Today, any manufacturer other than Small Scale Industries (SSI- whose turnover does not exceed 4 crores) should file their monthly returns in Form ER-1, and SSI quarterly returns in Form ER-3. The amount of CENVAT carried forward in Form ER-1 or Form ER-3 as on the last day i.e., the day before GST is implemented, will be allowed to be carried forward as CGST input tax credit

*Excise Dealer*

You are liable for registration under Central Excise if you trade in excisable goods. Today, the excise duty you pay will not be available as credit. A first stage or second stage dealer adds the excise duty paid to the price of the product. When the product is sold to a manufacturer, the excise duty passed on will be claimed as CENVAT credit by the buying manufacturer.

On the date of transitioning to GST, the excise duty paid in respect of closing stock held, will be allowed to be carried forward as CGST input tax credit. The eligibility conditions are discussed in the next section availing the input credit held in closing stock

*VAT*

A business registered under VAT needs to file monthly or quarterly VAT return forms, as prescribed by their respective states. The input VAT credit in VAT return forms will be carried forward as SGST input tax credit.

*Service Tax*

A service provider was liable for registration, if his aggregate value of taxable services exceeded ' 10 lakhs. The following are the types of service tax levied on taxable services

| Tax | Rate of Tax | Input Credit Available? | Set-Off Against? |
|---|---|---|---|
| Service Tax | 14% | Yes | Service Tax and Excise Liability |
| Swachh Bharat Cess | 0.5% | No | — |
| Krishi Kalyan Cess | 0.5% | Yes | Only against Krishi Kalyan Cess Liability |

A service provider needs to file half yearly returns in Form ST-3. The closing balance of service tax input credit will be carried forward as CGST input tax credit.

### 6.19.2 Unavailed CENVAT credit and Input VAT on capital goods

Before GST, under Central Excise, CENVAT credit was availed to the extent of 50% in the current year, and the remaining was availed in the subsequent year. Similarly, VAT paid on purchase of capital goods will not be fully available as input VAT immediately.

Depending upon the state VAT laws, and the type of capital goods purchased, the input VAT can be availed:

- In instalments spread over different financial years or
- As credit after commencement of commercial production and so on.

Due to this prevailing restriction for availing CENVAT credit on capital goods, there could be some Unavailed CENVAT and input VAT on the date of transitioning to GST

### 6.19.3 Availing the Input Credit held In Closing Stock

On the date of transitioning to GST, broadly, there will be businesses which are:

**Not liable to be registered under the current law, but are liable for registration under GST**

As per the Central Excise Act and Rules, a manufacturing unit is required to register if its aggregate clearance value crosses 1.5 crores, and needs to discharge the duty. Similarly, under VAT, you are liable for registration if your turnover during the financial year crosses the threshold limit. The threshold limit differs from state to state.

Today, you may not be liable for registration as your threshold limit does not exceed the prescribed limit. However, you become liable to register under GST if your threshold limit exceeds ' 10 lakhs for Special Category States (Arunachal Pradesh, Assam, Jammu and Kashmir, Manipur, Meghalaya, Mizoram, Nagaland, Sikkim, Tripura, Himachal Pradesh and Uttarakhand) and 20 lakhs for the rest of India.

**Engaged in the manufacture or sale of exempted goods or services**

You may currently be engaged in the manufacture, sale of exempted goods or provision of exempted service, but on transition to GST, these are taxable.

**First stage dealer or a second stage dealer or a registered importer**

As a dealer, you are liable for registration under Central Excise if you trade in excisable goods. The excise duty paid was not available as credit, as a first stage or second stage dealer adds the excise duty paid to the price of the product. If it was sold to a manufacturer, the excise duty passed on will be claimed as CENVAT credit by the buying manufacturer.

Similarly, you need to register under Central Excise as an importer if you are importing the goods, and if you discharge the applicable import duty.

In all the above mentioned scenarios, input tax credit (CENVAT, input VAT, entry tax and Service Tax) held in the closing stock of inputs (raw- materials), semi- finished goods, and finished goods can be availed. However, there are conditions that you need to meet to be eligible to avail input tax credit held in your closing stock

**Eligibility Conditions to Avail Input Tax Credit for Your Closing Stock**

You can avail input tax credit for your closing stock only if:

- The closing stock is held either in the form of raw materials, semi-finished goods, or finished goods, and must be used or intended to be used for taxable supplies.
- The benefit of such credit is passed on, by way of reduced prices, to the recipient.

  Before GST, duty/tax is added to product cost as input tax credit is not allowed. On transitioning to GST, ITC will be allowed, and this should naturally result in the reduction of base cost, and subsequently reduce the final price to customers.
- You are eligible for input tax credit under GST

  In GST, you are eligible for input tax credit if you are a regular tax payer only. A taxable person opting for composition levy under GST is not allowed to claim input tax credit.
- You have invoices or any other prescribed duty/tax paying documents in respect of the closing stock of inputs (including semi-finished goods and finished goods). 100 % input tax credit will be allowed if you have invoice or any other document evidencing tax payment. In the absence of such document, 60 % of CGST or SGT will be allowed, if the rate of tax is 18% or higher. If rate of tax is less than 18%, 40% of CGST or SGST will be allowed. In case of IGST, it will be 30% and 20 % respectively
- The date of invoices or any other prescribed duty/tax paying documents is within 12 months from the date of transitioning to GST.
- The supplier of services is not eligible for any abatement under the act

## 6.20 COMPLIANCE RATING

GST compliance rating is a new concept being introduced under GST. Under this system, every taxable person will be assigned a GST compliance rating score based on his historical record of compliance. The score will be determined on the basis of set parameters which is yet to be prescribed. This compliance rating score will be available to taxpayers and also would be placed in the public domain. The scores will be updated at periodically. Under GST, the input tax credit will be available based on the supplier's compliance and matching of invoice, the system of rating of concept will help the recipient view the complete compliance profile of supplier and choose the suppliers who are better compliant.

## 6.21 GST PRACTITIONERS (GSTP)

In the pre-GST regime, there were accounting and tax professionals who are authorized to file returns on behalf of taxable persons. This role was performed by Chartered Accountants (CAs), Sales Tax Practitioners (STPs) and advocates. The GST Act seeks to formalize this association between a tax payer and the return preparer and make the three-way association between a tax payer, a GST Practitioner and GSTN transparent.

Let us understand who a GST Practitioner is, under GST.

A GST Practitioner is a person approved by the Central or State Government to perform any or all of the following activities, on behalf of a taxable person:

- File an application for fresh registration
- File an application for amendment or cancellation of registration
- Furnish details of outward and inward supplies
- Furnish monthly, quarterly, annual or final return

  Make payments for credit into the electronic cash ledger, i.e. payments for tax, interest, penalty, fees or any other amount
- File a claim for refund
- Represent the taxable person in any proceeding under the Act, other than inspection, search, seizure and arrest
- File an appeal to the First Appellate Authority
- File an appeal to the Appellate Tribunal

### 6.21.1 Who can become a GST Practitioner?

A person can become a GST Practitioner under GST if he/she satisfies the conditions listed below:

- Should be a citizen of India
- Should be a person of sound mind
- Has not been declared as insolvent
- Has not been convicted for an offence with imprisonment for more than two years
- Meets the required education or work experience criteria, given below:
- Should be a retired officer of the Commercial Tax Department of any State Government or of the Central

Board of Excise and Customs, having worked in a post not lower in rank than of a Group-B gazetted officer, for a period not less than two years

OR

Has Passed –

a. A graduate or postgraduate degree or its equivalent examination, having a degree in Commerce, Law, Banking including Higher Auditing, or Business Administration or Business Management from any Indian University established by any law for the time being in force

OR

b. a degree examination of any Foreign University recognized by any Indian University as equivalent to the degree examination mentioned above

OR

c. any other examination notified by the Government for this purpose

OR

d. any degree examination of an Indian University or of any Foreign University recognized by any Indian University as equivalent of the degree examination, and has also passed any of the following examinations
   - final examination of the Institute of Chartered Accountants of India OR
   - final examination of the Institute of Cost Accountants of India OR
   - final examination of the Institute of Company Secretaries of India

## 6.22 GSTN AND GSP

GST Network (GSTN), a Non-profit- Non-Government company appointed by State and Central government to provide shared IT infrastructure and services to the Centre and State Governments and tax payers'.

While GSTN, is going to have a portal for taxpayers to interact, it also provides flexibility for taxpayers to file the return via their choice of third party application through desktop, mobile and Software. This will be extended by GST Suvidha Providers (GSP). Thus, there will be two set of interactions, one between the Tax payers 'application and the GSP and the other between the GSP and the GSTN

**The GSTN is expected provide the following service:**

- Registration related services including enrolment and transition of existing tax payers
- Challan Generation
- Run the matching engine for matching, reversal and reclaiming input tax credit.
- Provide various MIS reports to the Central and the State Governments based on the taxpayer return information
- Maintain the e-ledger (Electronic liability register, Electronic cash ledger and Electronic credit ledger) of all the tax payers
- Matching of tax payment details with banking network

**GSP is expected to provide the following services:**

- Uploading Form GSTR-1 containing invoice wise details
- Download data on inward supplies (receipts or purchase) in Form GSTR-2A from GST Portal, generated based on Form GSTR-1 filed by corresponding suppliers.
- Communication of Input tax credit, acceptance and discrepancies post matching of invoices

## PRACTICE EXERCISES

1. In India the GST is ____________ based principal.
   a. Destination b. Origin
   c. Manufacturing d. Assembling
2. Since in India the GST is destination based principal, the revenue should belong to the ____________ in which the goods are finally consumed.
   a. Consulate b. Customs
   c. State d. Union
3. The supply of two or more individual supplies of goods or services, or any combination of goods or services, by taxable person is termed as ____________.
   a. Composite Supply b. Continuous Supply
   c. Mixed Supply d. Bill of Supply
4. ____________ is a combination of goods and services, which are naturally bundled and supplied, in the ordinary course of business.
   a. Composite Supply b. Continuous Supply
   c. Mixed Supply d. Bill of Supply

### Answers

1. (a) 2. (c) 3. (c) 4. (a)

Chapter 7

# Computerised Accounting Systems using Tally.ERP 9

## PART A

### LEARNING OBJECTIVES

After studying this chapter, you will learn about:

- Creating a Company
- Configurations and Features
- Creating Accounting Ledgers and Groups
- Creating Stock Items and Groups
- Voucher Entry
- Generating Reports – Cash Book, Ledger Accounts, Trial Balance, Profit and Loss Account, Balance Sheet, Funds Flow Statement, Cash Flow Statement
- Banking
- Cost Centres and Cost Categories
- Order Processing & Pre-closure of Orders

### 7.1 INTRODUCTION

Tally.ERP 9 is one of the most widely used financial software. Tally.ERP 9 reports can help a business owner make informed decisions to increase efficiency, reduce costs, and organise business operations.

With Tally.ERP 9, accurate, up-to-date business information is available at your fingertips anytime. It provides a comprehensive solution for the accounting and inventory needs of a business. It provides the capability to extract, interpret and present financial data.

#### 7.1.1 Getting started with Tally.ERP 9

Tally.ERP 9 can be started by double clicking the Tally.ERP 9 icon on desktop.

***Components of Gateway of Tally***

The Gateway of Tally is Tally.ERP 9's main screen. It appears as shown below

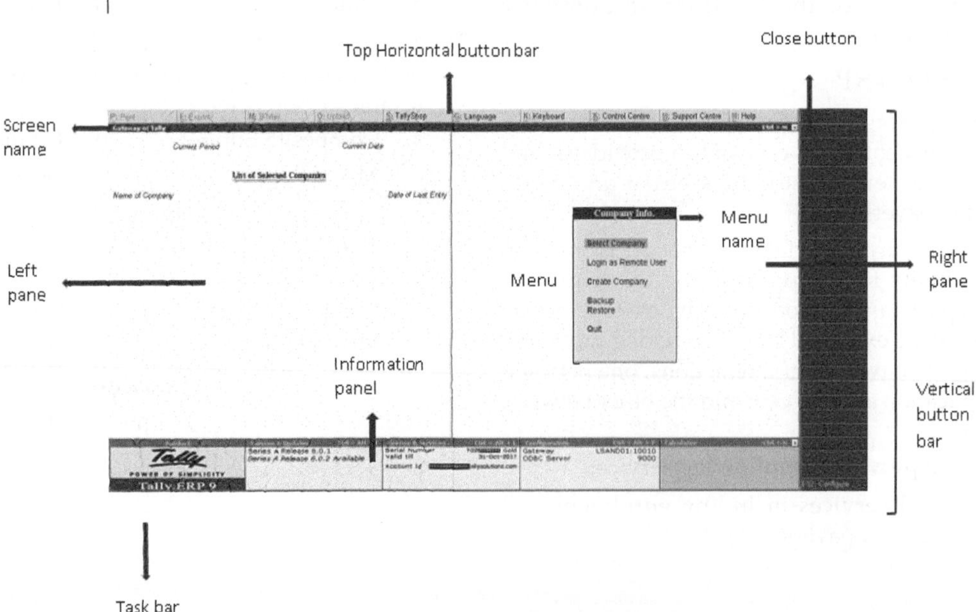


*Figure 7.1: Gateway of Tally*

The Gateway of Tally displays menus, screens, reports and options that you select. The components of a Tally.ERP 9 screen are as listed below:

- Top horizontal button bar: This is a collection of buttons that provide quick interaction, and is placed above the title bar.
- Close button: This button allows you to exit the current screen. If you are at the Gateway of Tally, clicking this button allows you to exit the application.
- Right Pane: The right part of the Gateway of Tally screen, where the menu is displayed. The shortcut key for each

menu option is a letter from the option's name, which will be highlighted in red.

- Vertical button bar: This is a collection of buttons which provide quick interaction with Tally.ERP 9, placed on the extreme right of the screen.
- Calculator Pane: This can be used for extrapolations.
- Information Panel: This displays details of Product, Version, License, and Configuration.

### 7.1.2 Mouse/Keyboard Conventions

While working with Tally.ERP 9, use the following conventions:

| Mouse/Keyboard Conventions | |
|---|---|
| Action | Particulars |
| Fn | Press the Function key |
| Fn | Press ALT + Function key |
| Fn | Press CTRL + Function key |

#### *Switching between Screen Areas*

When Tally.ERP 9 first loads, the Gateway of Tally screen will be displayed. To switch between the main screen area and the Information Panel or calculator at the bottom of the screen, press CTRL+N or CTRL+M as indicated on the screen.

### 7.1.3 Closing Tally.ERP 9

You can exit the program from any Tally.ERP 9 screen, but all screens need to be closed before it shuts down. To exit Tally.ERP 9,

- Press Esc until you see the message Quit? Yes or No? Press Enter or Y, or click Yes to exit Tally.ERP 9.
- Alternatively, to exit without confirmation, press CTRL+Q from Gateway of Tally.
- You can also press Enter when the option Quit is selected from Gateway of Tally.

## 7.2 CREATING A COMPANY IN TALLY. ERP 9

The first step towards working with Tally.ERP 9 is to create a 'company'. A 'company' in Tally.ERP 9 is a central repository where you can maintain all the financial records of your business, and from where you can extract the required financial reports and statements.

The procedure to create a company is explained below.

#### *Scenario*

**Create a company named 'Surya Traders' with the financial year beginning 1st April 2017 and book beginning 1st April 2017**

Go to Gateway of Tally > Company Info. > Create Company

The Company Creation screen appears as shown below:

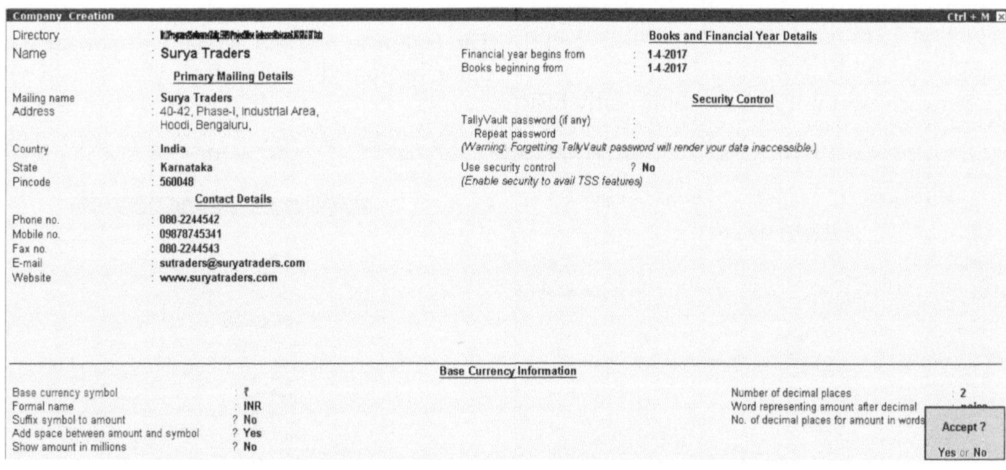


*Figure 7.2: Company Creation screen*

The message Accept? **Yes** or **No** will be displayed. Press **Y** or **Enter** to save the details.

The fields in the Company Creation screen and the information to be filled in each of them are explained below. To navigate between the fields, use the Enter/Tab/arrow keys, or mouse clicks.

- Directory: The path to the location of Tally.ERP 9 data is displayed here. By default, the path provided while installing Tally.ERP 9 will be displayed. However, you can press Backspace and specify the location in which you want the data to be stored.
- Name: Provide a name for the company that is being created. In this example, we are creating a company named National Traders.
- Primary Mailing details: The mailing name and address details of companies are picked from here for any report such as balance sheet and Statements of Accounts.
- Contact Details: We can maintain all the contact details in this section like Telephone Number, Mobile Number, Email, Website
- Books and Financial Year Details:
  - o Financial Year from: This refers to the twelve-month accounting period of the company. For Surya Traders, the financial year begins on 1-4-2017.
  - o Books beginning from: The date provided in the aforesaid field will be automatically displayed here. In the example, the date is retained. However, if you have started with maintaining your books of accounts

with Tally.ERP 9 mid-year, the required date can be set accordingly.

- Security Control:
  - o TallyVault Password (if any): Once you enter a password here, you will need it to open your company each time. The name of a company that is locked using TallyVault will be hidden with the asterisk '*' symbol. You need to provide the TallyVault password to open and access the company.
  - o Repeat Password: Here, enter the password entered in the TallyVault field, as a confirmation
  - o Use Security Control?: Setting this option to 'Yes' will allow you to define the access rights for each user who will access your company. This feature is explained in forthcoming volumes.
- Base Currency Information:
  - o Base Currency Symbol: The base currency symbol will be filled as per the country selected.
  - o Formal Name: The currency's formal name will be filled here. In this example, it is ¹ INR(Indian Rupees).
  - o Is Symbol SUFFIXED to Amounts?: For some countries, the currency symbol is specified after the amount. This option can be enabled for such countries, so that the currency symbol may be printed after the amount. However, National Traders is an Indian company and hence this option is set to 'No'.
  - o Add Space between Amount and Symbol?: Tally.ERP 9 will provide a single space between the amount and the currency symbol, if this option is set to 'Yes'. For e.g.: Rs. 5,000. Notice the space between symbol and the amount
  - o Show amounts in Millions?: If the company's financial statements need to have their values expressed in terms of millions, set this option to Yes.
  - o Number of Decimal Places: By default, the number of decimal places for the base currency is set to 2. However, you can have up to 4 decimal places. The Indian currency has 2 decimal places whereas certain other countries require 3 decimal places and so on.
  - o Word used to print decimal portion of amount: The symbol for amounts expressed in decimals will be set by de- fault. For India, it is paise.
  - o Decimal Places for printing amounts in Words: You can specify the number of decimal places for printing the amount in words. This number should be equal to or lesser than the number specified in Number of Decimal Places field. For example, if the currency has up to 3 decimal places, the value to be printed in words can be restricted to 2 decimal places.

**Note:** Base currency information is set to the default based on the country selected.

The Gateway of Tally screen will appear with the company's name displayed on the left pane as shown below:

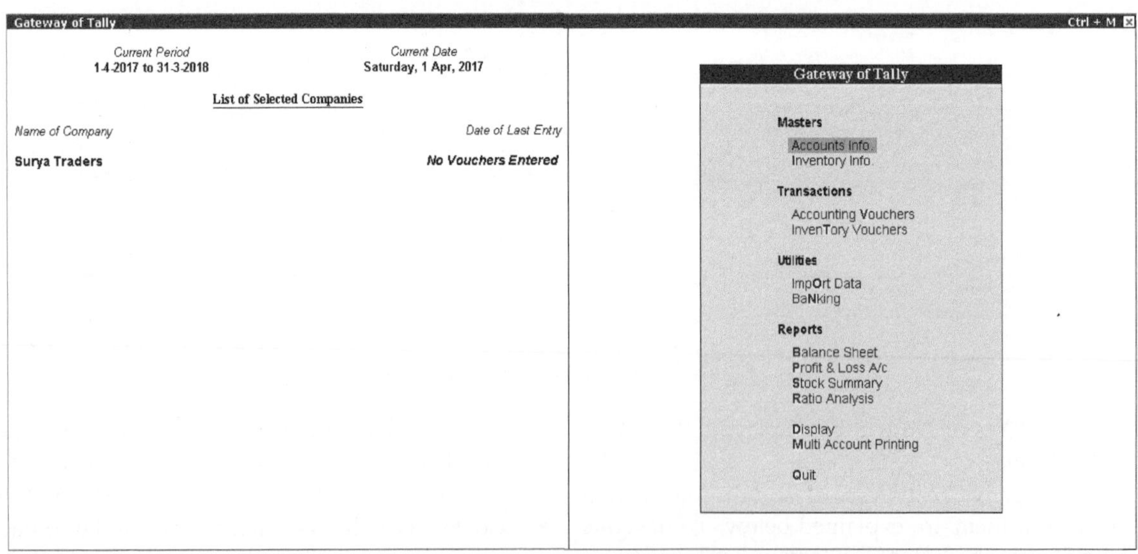


*Figure 7.3: Gateway of Tally*

This indicates that the company is currently open in Tally.ERP 9.

### *Activity*

*Create a company - Radhika Enterprises, with the financial year beginning on 1st April, 2017 and books beginning from the 1st April, 2017. You may enter the company details as required.*

### 7.2.1 Select a Company

By 'selecting' a company, you are essentially opening it in Tally.ERP 9.

1. Go to Gateway of Tally > F3 Company Info. (ALT + F3)
2. Click Select Company, or press S. Tally.ERP 9 displays the Select Company screen, with a List of Companies that are

available in the location specified. You can also press F1 to get to the Select Company screen.

### 7.2.2 Shut a Company

By 'shutting' a company, you are essentially closing a company.

1. Go to Gateway of Tally > F3 Company Info. (ALT + F3)
2. Click Shut Company. Tally.ERP 9 displays the Close Company screen, with the List of Companies that are open. You can also use ALT + F1 from the Gateway of Tally to get to this screen

### 7.2.3 Alter Company Details

By 'altering' a company, you are modifying the details which you have provided in the Company Creation screen.

1. Go to Gateway of Tally >F3 Company Info. (ALT + F3)
2. Click Alter or press A. Tally.ERP 9 displays the Select Item screen, with a List of Companies that are available in the location specified. Select the company which you need to alter and press Enter to view the Company Alteration screen. Alter the company details as required and accept the screen.

## 7.3 FEATURES AND CONFIGURATIONS

Once you have created a company in Tally.ERP 9, the next step would be to setup Tally.ERP 9's 'Features' and 'Configurations'.

The 'Features' in Tally.ERP 9 are a set of capabilities, provided as options, that enable you to maintain financial records as per your business needs. The Company Features menu can be found by clicking F11: Features on the vertical button bar. The effect of these options will be reflected only in the company for which they are enabled.

**The Company Features section in Tally.ERP 9 is divided into the following major categories:**

- Accounting Features
- Inventory Features
- Statutory & Taxation
- Audit Features
- TSS Features
- Add-On Features

You can press **F11** from any screen of Tally.ERP 9 or you may also click the **F11**: Features button available in the button bar, to enable the required features. The features are specific only to the company currently in use (for which the said feature is enabled), thereby allowing flexibility of independently enabling different features for each of the companies.

Go to **Gateway of Tally** > press **F11: Features**

The Company Features screen appears as shown below:

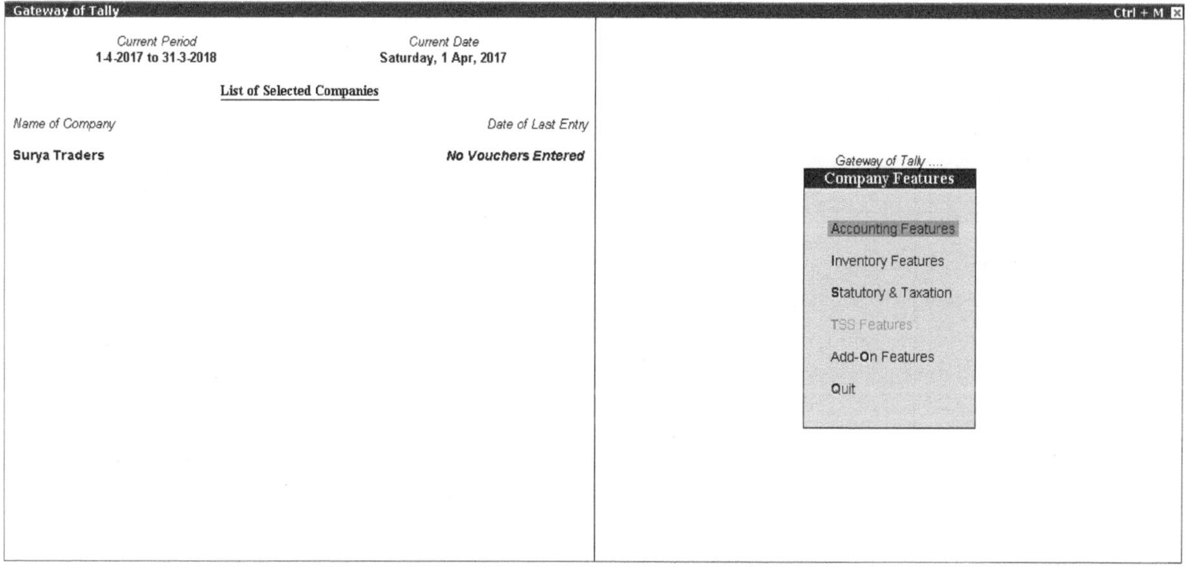


*Figure 7.4: Company Features*

**Note:** Audit Features and TSS Features appear only after activating administrator security.

The 'Configurations' in Tally.ERP 9 are options that help you modify the way a feature works. The Configuration menu can be found by clicking F12: Configure on the vertical button bar. The options when enabled, will have an effect on all the companies in the data directory.

In Tally.ERP 9, the **F12: Configurations** are provided for Accounting, Inventory & printing options and are user-definable as per the business' requirements.

The **F12: Configurations** are applicable to all the companies residing in the Tally.ERP 9 Data Directory. The **F12: Configuration** options vary depending upon the Context, i.e., if you press **F12: Configure** from Voucher entry screen, the respective **F12: Configurations** screen is displayed.

Go to **Gateway of Tally > click F12: Configure**

The **Configuration** menu appears as shown below:

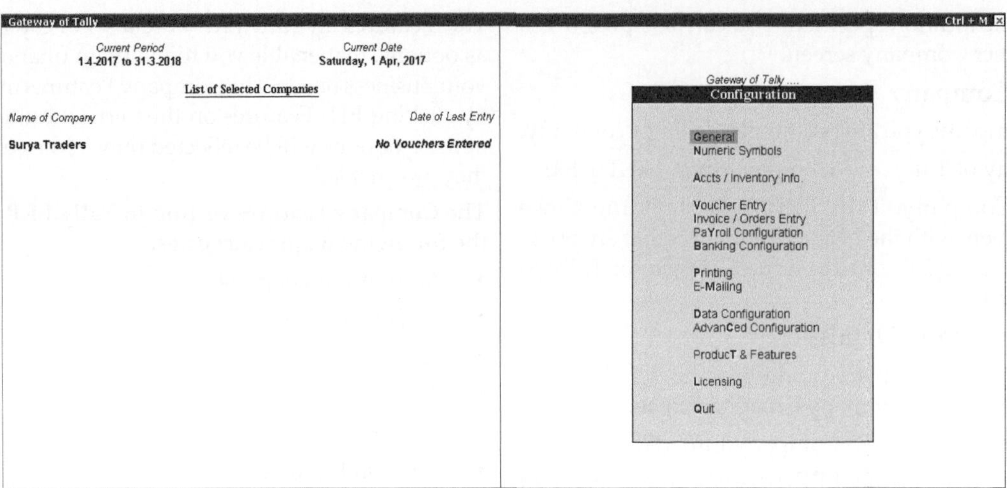


*Figure 7.5: Configuration*

There are numerous settings available under various menus in the **F12: Configuration** screen, which may be configured for any additional information required to be entered during master creations, voucher entry and printing.

## 7.4 CREATING ACCOUNTING LEDGERS AND GROUPS

### *Ledger*

A 'Ledger' is an account head. For instance, the sales account head will be called a 'Sales Ledger' in Tally.ERP 9. Similarly, a customer would be an account head, and will be called a 'party ledger'.

You can create ledgers specific to your business transactions.

For a newly created company, there are two pre-defined ledgers available in Tally.ERP 9:

1. Cash
2. Profit & Loss A/c

To view the list of ledgers, go to **Gateway of Tally > Accounts Info. > Ledgers > Display (Multiple Ledgers).**

The **Multi Ledger Display** screen appears as shown below:

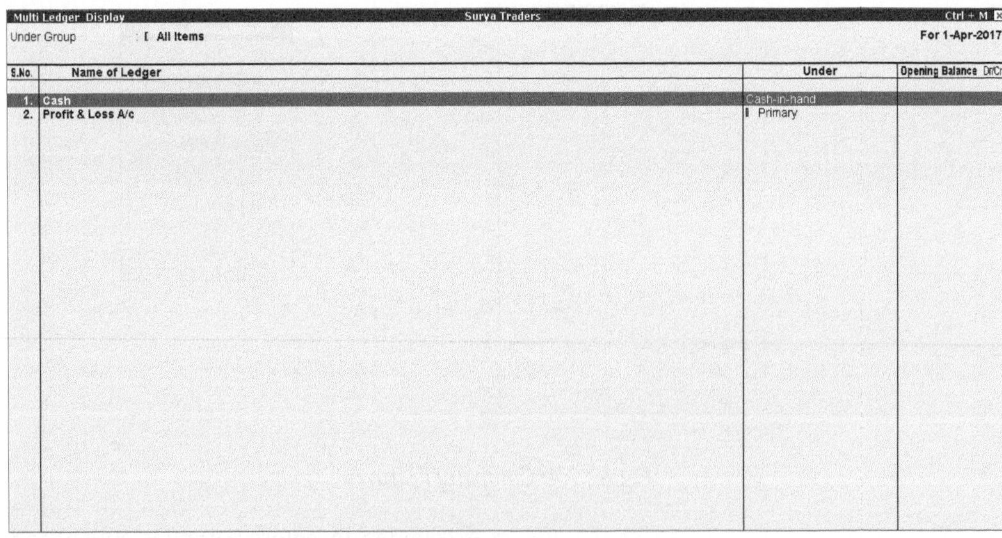


*Figure 7.6: Multi Ledger Display*

### *Group*

A 'Group' is the accounting group under which ledgers of the same nature can be classified. For instance, Tally.ERP 9 has a default Group 'Sales Accounts', under which all the sales ledgers will be classified.

There are 28 pre-defined groups in Tally.ERP 9, which feature in the Chart of Accounts of many organisations. Out of these, 15 groups are primary groups and the remaining 13 are sub-groups.

Among the 15 primary groups, 9 groups are Balance Sheet items and the remaining 6 groups are Profit & Loss A/c items. You can use these groups to build your chart of accounts, as well as create and use groups specific to your business transactions. However, you may also alter the nomenclature of these 28 groups.

To view the list of the 28 groups, known as the **List of Accounts,** go to **Gateway of Tally > Accounts Info. > Groups > Display (Multiple Groups).**

The **Multi Group Display** appears as shown below:

*Figure 7.7: Multi Group Display*

### 7.4.1 Ledger Creation

The ledgers to be created, the opening balance to be provided for them, and the groups under which they have to be classified, are specified in the table below:

### *Illustration-1*

**On 01-04-2017 Surya Traders having Capital Rs. 45,000 and Land & Building Rs. 80,000**

**Creation of Capital Account ledger**

1. Go to **Gateway of Tally > Accounts Info. > Ledgers > Create**
2. Enter **Name** as **Capital Account**
3. Select **Capital Account** from the **List of Groups**
4. Enter Rs. **45,000** in the **Opening Balance (1-Apr-2017)** field

   The completed **Ledger Creation** screen appears as shown below:

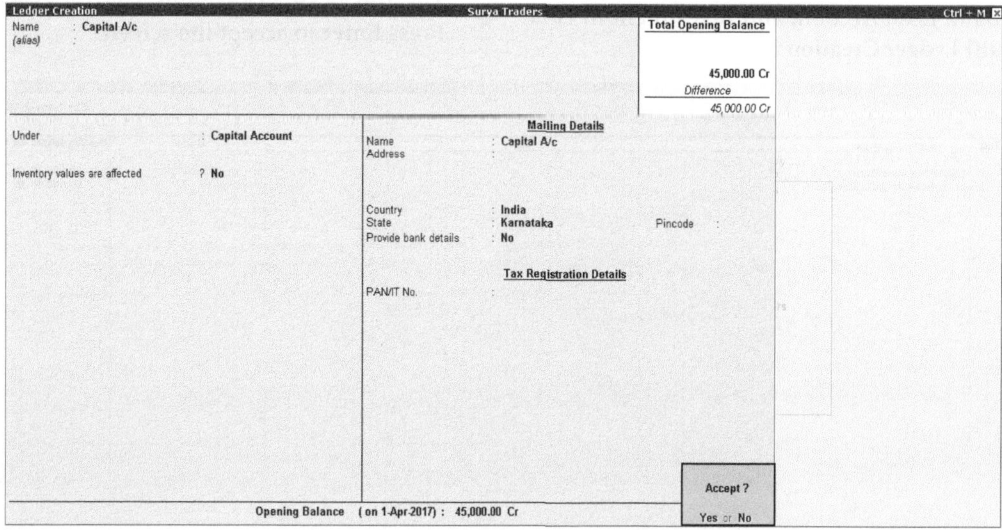


*Figure 7.8: Single Ledger Creation*

5. Press **Y** or **Enter** to accept the screen

**Creation of Land & Building ledger**

1. Go to **Gateway of Tally > Accounts Info. > Ledgers > Create**

2. Enter **Name** as **Land & Building**
3. Select **Fixed Assets** from the **List of Groups**
4. Enter Rs. **80,000** in the **Opening Balance (1-Apr-2017)** field

The **completed Ledger Creation** screen appears as shown below:

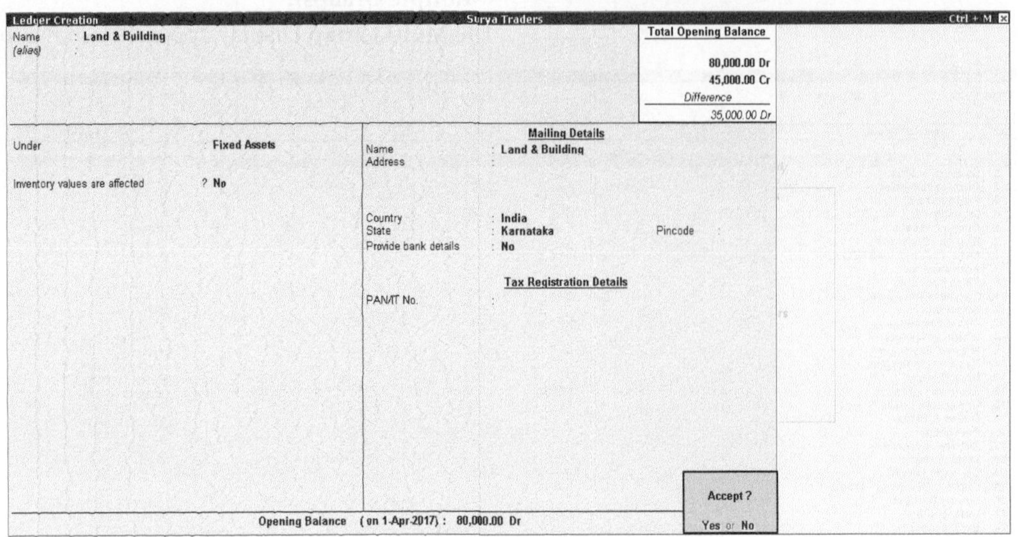


*Figure 7.9: Single Ledger Creation*

1. Press **Y** or **Enter** to accept the screen.

Tally.ERP 9 displays the total debit and credit opening balances while the ledgers are being created in the Ledger Creation screen. This is to avoid differences in the opening balance.

### 7.4.1.1 *Multi Ledger Creation*

### *Illustration-2*

**On 01-04-2017 Surya Traders having loan account in Axis Bank. Opening balance of Axis Bank Loan account is Rs. 65000. Company having investment in Gold Bond. Opening balance of Investment in Gold Bond Rs. 85,000.**

**Creation of Axis Bank Loan Account and Investment in Gold Bond through Multi Ledger Creation**

1. Go to **Gateway of Tally > Accounts Info. > Ledgers >Multi Ledger Create**
2. Select **All Items**
3. Enter name Loan from Axis Bank, select Secured Loan from Group List
4. Enter the Opening amount Rs. 65,000
5. Enter name Investment in Gold Bond, select Investment from group list
6. Enter the opening balance Rs. 85000

   The **Multi Ledger Creation** screen appears as shown below:
7. Press **Enter** to accept the screen

Multi Ledger Creation — Surya Traders — Ctrl + M

Under Group : All Items — For 1-Apr-2017

| S.No. | Name of Ledger | Under | Opening Balance Dr/Cr |
|---|---|---|---|
| 1. | Loan From Axis Bank | Secured Loans | 65,000.00 Cr |
| 2. | Investment in Gold Bond | Investments | 85,000.00 Dr |

Accept ?

Yes or No

*Figure 7.10: Multi Ledger Creation*

### *Activity*

**Create below ledgers with their opening balance in Surya Traders**

- **Raxson Ltd.** Under **Sundry Creditors,** with an opening balance of **Rs.** 95,000
- **ICICI Bank** under **Bank Accounts,** with an opening balance of **Rs.** 55,000
- **Furniture** under Fixed Assets, with an opening balance of Rs. 50,000
- **Sony Electronics** under **Sundry Debtors,** with an opening balance of Rs. 45000

### *7.4.1.2 Altering and Displaying Ledgers*

The procedures for altering and displaying ledgers are similar to those of groups. Now try this out on Surya Traders by altering the Tally.ERP 9 pre-defined ledger for Cash to Petty Cash and entering the opening balance:

1. Select **Alter** from the **Single Ledger** option.
2. Select **Cash** from the **List of Ledgers.**
3. Change the **Name** from **Cash** to **Petty Cash.**
4. Enter the **Opening Balance** of Rs. 1000.
5. Press **Y** or **Enter** to accept the screen.

If you use **Display** in **Single Ledger** now, you will see that the **List of Ledgers** shows Petty Cash instead of Cash. You can also Alter ledgers from **Accounts Info. > Ledgers > Alter (Multiple Ledgers).**

### *7.4.1.3 Deleting Ledgers*

You can delete a ledger, by pressing **Alt+D** in the **Ledger Alteration** screen.

You will not be able to delete a ledger, once the financial transactions (vouchers) have been entered (excluding the Opening Balance). If there is a need to delete a ledger with any financial transactions, all the transactions must be deleted first by pressing **Alt+D.**

## 7.4.2 Group Creation

The group to be created, and the primary group under which it has to be classified, is specified in below:

Group to be created in Surya Traders - Debtors North

Classification- Sundry Debtros

To create the group,

1. Go to **Gateway of Tally > Accounts Info. > Groups > Create**
2. Enter **Name** as **Debtors - North**
3. Against the field **Under** select **Sundry Debtors** from the **List of Groups**

   The **Group Creation** screen appears as shown below:

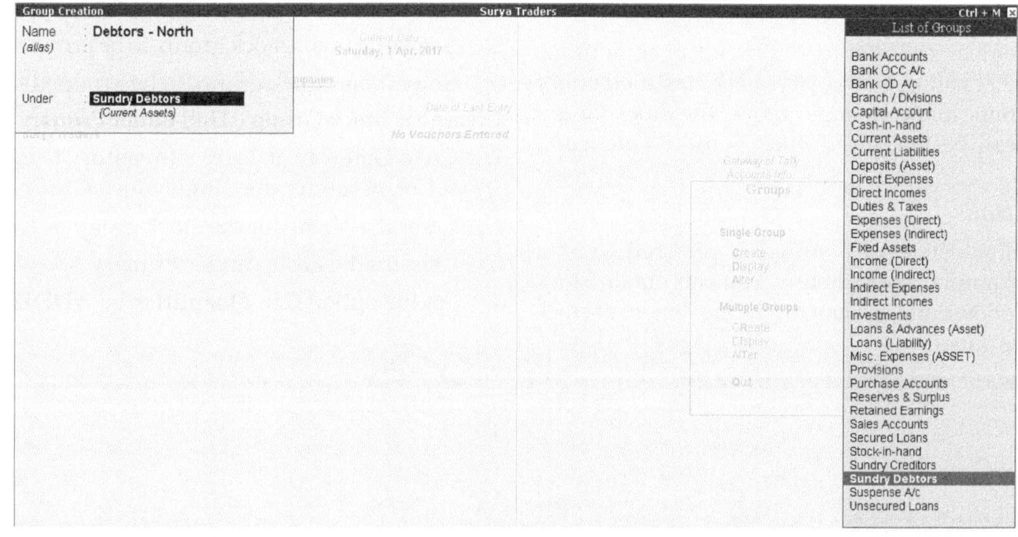


*Figure 7.11: Group Creation*

4. Press **Y** or **Enter** to accept the screen

### *Activity*

**Create the following group in Surya Traders:**

1. **Debtors – South** under **Sundry Debtors**
2. **Bengaluru Debtors** under **Debtors – South**
3. **Hyderabad Debtors** under **Debtors – South**
4. **Indore Debtors** under **Debtors – North**
5. **North Delhi Debtors** under **Debtors – North.**

Tally.ERP 9 allows you to create any number of groups under all the default groups. Two sub- groups viz. **Debtors - North** and **Debtors - South** have now been created under **Sundry Debtors.** Additionally, two sub-groups each have been created, under **Debtors - North** and **Debtors - South.**

### *7.4.2.1 Altering Groups*

Once created, groups can be altered by selecting the **Alter** option for single or multiple groups. The procedure is the same as used earlier to display groups, except that, here the data can be altered.

You can also Alter groups from **Accounts Info. > Groups > Alter (Multiple Groups).**

#### *7.4.2.2 Deleting Groups*

You can delete a group via the Group Alteration (Single Mode) screen by pressing Alt+D. However, you cannot delete Tally.ERP 9's predefined groups, or groups with sub-groups or groups containing ledgers. The lowest level must be deleted first.

## 7.5 INVENTORY MASTER CREATION

The inventory system operates in much the same way as the accounting system. In the place of accounting groups, 'Stock Groups' and 'Stock Categories' are used, and in the place of ledgers, 'Stock Items' are used.

**Inventory Masters in Tally.ERP 9**

*Stock Item*

A Stock Item is a unit of the goods that a business trades in. For instance, National Traders deal in electronic goods. 'Television' will be a 'Stock Item' for them.

*Units of Measure*

Stock items are purchased and sold on the basis of quantity. The quantity in turn is measured by units. In Tally.ERP 9, such goods are quantified using 'Units of Measurement'. Units of Measure can be 'simple' or 'compound'. Examples of simple Units of Measure are: numbers, metres, kilo- grams, pieces etc. Examples for compound Units of Measure are: a box of 10 pieces etc.

*Stock Group*

A Stock Group is similar to the Groups we create for accounting. Stock Items of similar nature, brand, etc. can be classified under a single Stock Group. In the example above, the Stock Group for 'Television' can be the brand, like 'Sony', 'Videocon', 'Philips', etc.

*Godowns/Locations*

A place where Stock Items are stored is referred to as a "Godown". For example, a warehouse. You can obtain stock reports for each Godown and account for the movement of stock between Locations/Godowns.

### 7.5.1 Creating Inventory Masters

Let us take the example of **Surya Traders** who sell **Computers and electronics devices .** Given below is the structure of items being sold:

**Main Stock Group- Dell , Samsung , Sony**

Stock Item- Dell I3, Dell I5 ( Under Dell)
Samsung I3, Samsung I5 (Under Samsung)
Sony I3, Sony I5 (Under Sony )
Pendrive 16GB (Under Sony)
CD Player (Under Samsung)

Surya Traders has two Godowns, the Shop Godown and the Warehouse Godown. The Unit of Measure will be Numbers (Nos)

To facilitate easier understanding, we have illustrated the creation of the aforesaid inventory masters for Surya Traders, in the following order:

1. Stock Groups
2. Godowns
3. Units of Measure
4. Stock Items

### 7.5.2 Creating a Stock Group

The grouping structure in Tally.ERP 9 is as follows:

1. **Dell** (main stock group, to be grouped under **Primary**)
2. **Samsung** (main stock group, to be grouped under **Primary**)
3. **Sony** (main stock group, to be grouped under **Primary**)

**Create the Stock Group – Dell under Primary in Surya Traders**

1. Go to **Gateway of Tally > Inventory Info. > Stock Groups > Create (under the Single Stock Group)**
2. Enter the **Name** for the stock group as **Dell**
3. Classify the group under **Primary**
4. Set the option **Can Quantities be ADDED** to **Yes**

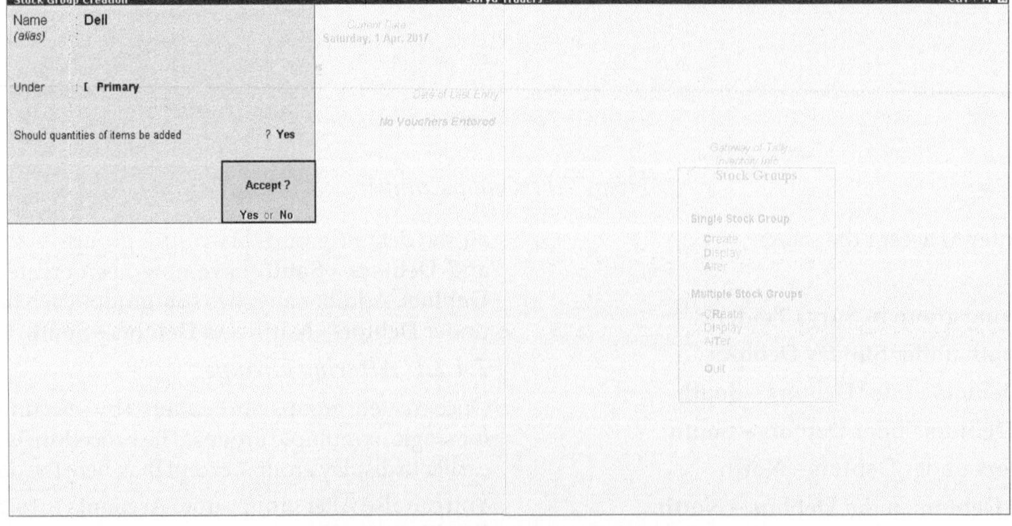


*Figure 7.12: Stock Group Creation — Dell*

5. Press **Enter** to accept the screen

## *Activity*

**Create Samsung and Sony stock group in Surya Traders**

### 7.5.3 Creating a Godown

**Locations/Godowns** are places where Stock Items are stored. You can monitor the location-wise movement of stock by creating multiple

Tally.ERP 9 has a default Godown named Main Location. You can alter Tally's default godown and create a new one. Tally.ERP 9 permits the creation of any number of godowns, under groups and subgroups to match the structure you need. You can create Locations/Godowns only if Maintain Multiple Godowns is enabled in **F11: Features > F2: Inventory Features> Storage and classification> Maintain multiple godowns to Yes.** Go to **Gateway of Tally > Inventory Info. > Godowns > Create > Shop.**

The complete Godown creation screen is given below:

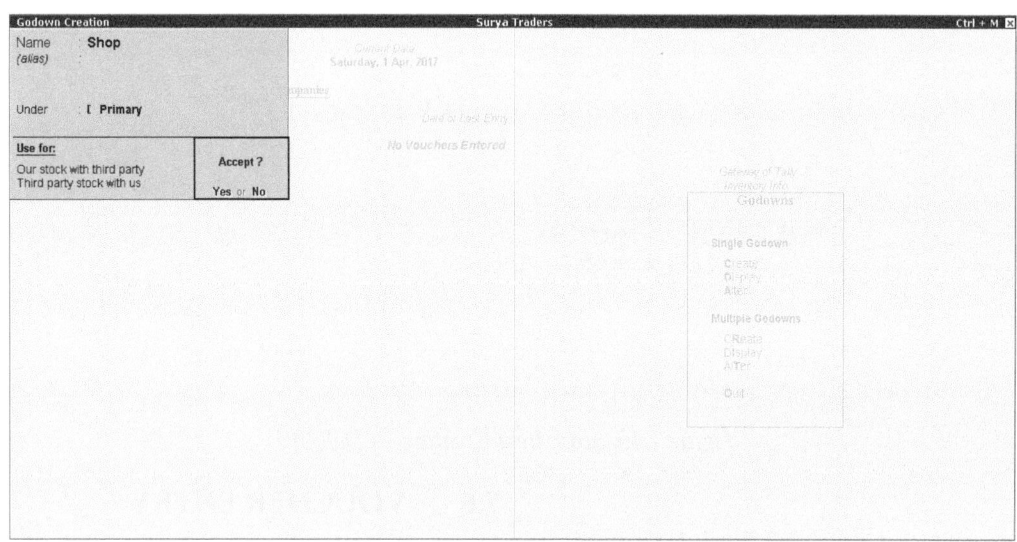


*Figure 7.13: Godown creation screen*

## *Activity*

**Create Warehouse Godown under primary in Surya Traders**

### 7.5.4 Creating a Unit of Measurement

As mentioned in the example, the **Unit of Measure** will be **Numbers (NOS)**

To create the Unit of Measure,

1. Go to **Gateway of Tally> Inventory Info.> Unit of Measure> Create**
2. Enter the Symbol to used for the Unit of Measure, that is Nos
3. Enter the Formal Name, that is Numbers
4. Specify the number of decimal places. Here, it is zero

The completed Unit Creation screen appears as shown below:

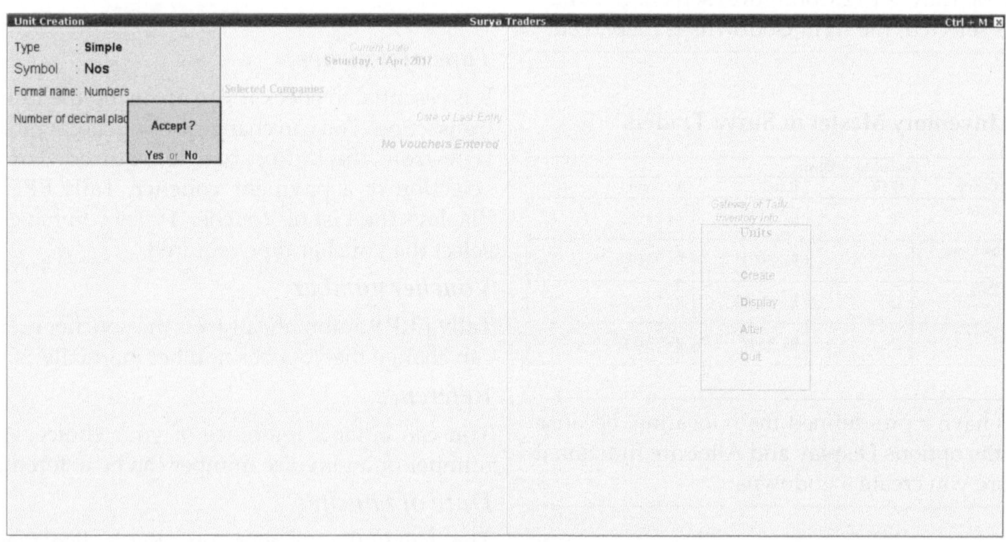


*Figure 7.14: Unit creation screen*

### 7.5.5 Creating a Stock Item

As per the example, create the Stock Item Dell I3. To create the same,

1. Go to **Gateway of Tally > Inventory Info. > Stock Items > Create**
2. Enter the **Name** for the stock item, that is Dell I3
3. Group the **stock item** under Dell
4. Select the units as **Nos**

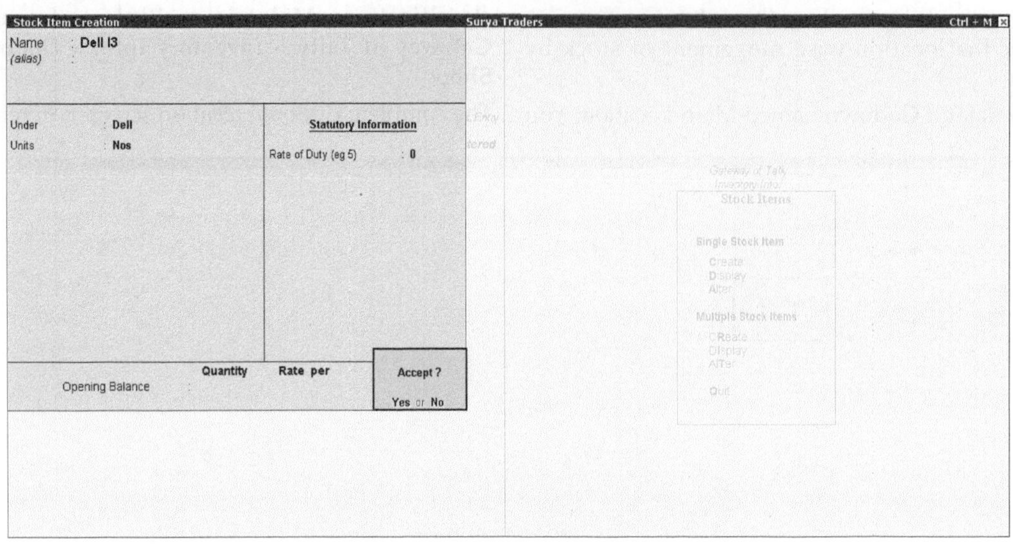


*Figure 7.15: Stock Item Creation — Dell I3*

*Activity*

**Create the following Stock Group and Stock Item in Surya Traders**

| | |
|---|---|
| Stock Group- | Hardware, Software |
| Godowon- | Onsite (Under Primary) |
| UOM- | Nos. |
| Stock Item- | CPU, RAM, Keyboard, Mouse (Under Hardware) Tally, Adobe, MS-Office (Software) |

**Note:** The term Locations is displayed in the Inventory Info. menu, if International is selected under Use Accounting Terminology in General Configuration (Gateway of Tally > F12:Configure) screen. If India/ SAARC is selected, the term Godowns is displayed.

*Activity*

**Create following Inventory Master in Surya Traders**

| Godowns – Onsite | | | | |
|---|---|---|---|---|
| Stock Item | Group | QTY | Rate | Amount |
| Samsung Galaxy Tab | Samsung | 10 | Rs. 5,500 | Rs. 55,000 |
| Samsung Smartwatch | Samsung | 20 | Rs. 2,000 | Rs. 40,000 |
| Dell Inspiron Desktops | Dell | 15 | Rs. 12,500 | Rs. 1,87,500 |
| Sony Xperia Tablet | Sony | 10 | Rs. 8,500 | Rs. 85,000 |

**Note:** Godowns have a pre-defined main location, because of which the options Display and Alter are functional even before you create a godowns

## 7.6 VOUCHER ENTRY

In accounting terms, a voucher is a document containing the details of a financial transaction. For example, a purchase invoice, a sales receipt, a petty cash docket, a bank interest statement, and so on. For every such transaction made, a voucher is used to enter the details into the ledgers to update the financial position of the company. This feature of Tally.ERP 9 will be used most often.

Tally.ERP 9 follows the Golden Rules of Accounting:

| Golden Rules of Accounting | | |
|---|---|---|
| Type of Account | Debit Aspect | Credit Aspect |
| Personal | The receiver | The giver |
| Real | What comes in | What goes out |
| Nominal | All Expenses and losses | All incomes and gains |

*Type of voucher*

It is essential to check if you are using the right voucher for the transaction. You can change the voucher type by selecting a new type from the button bar, if required. For example on the selection of a payment voucher, Tally.ERP 9 automatically displays the List of Voucher Types you have created. You can select the voucher type required.

*Voucher number*

Tally.ERP 9 automatically sets the voucher number for you. You can change the voucher number manually, if required.

*Reference*

You can enter a reference of your choice. A purchase order number or an invoice number can be entered as a reference.

*Date of voucher*

The date of the voucher you enter is displayed at the top-right of the Voucher Creation screen. The date is taken initially from the Gateway of Tally - Current Date and you may need to change it frequently to ensure that the vouchers are dated as you want.

### *Effective date*

A voucher type can be configured to allow for an Effective date. The line below the date of voucher displays the date when the **voucher will be effective.**

### *Particulars*

This is where you enter the ledger names and the debit and credit amounts. Each line displays a prompt of Dr or By for debit entries and Cr or To for credit entries.

Depending on the Voucher Type, Tally.ERP 9 selects either **'Dr'** or **'Cr'** for the first prompt, which you cannot change. Thereafter, you can change the prompt (if necessary) by typing over it with a **'D'** or a **'C'**. To select a ledger, type the first letter of its name. Tally.ERP 9 then displays a List of **Ledger Accounts** beginning with the letter highlighted. Only ledgers suitable for the voucher type are displayed. The revised current balance is shown after the amount is entered. On selecting the next ledger, Tally.ERP 9 suggests the balancing amount as the value to be entered, which may be accepted or typed over. The voucher entry cannot be completed until the debits equal the credits.

## 7.6.1 Voucher Type

Tally.ERP 9 is pre-programmed with a variety of accounting and inventory vouchers, each designed to perform a different job. The standard Accounting and Inventory Vouchers are:

### *Accounting Voucher*

- Contra Voucher (F4)
- Payment Voucher (F5)
- Receipt Voucher (F6)
- Journal Voucher (F7)
- Sales Voucher /Invoice (F8)
- Credit Note Voucher (CTRL+ F8)
- Purchase Voucher (F9)
- Debit Note Voucher (CTRL+F9)

### *Inventory Voucher*

- Purchase Order (ALT+F4)
- Sales Order (ALT+F5)
- Rejections Out (ALT+F6)
- Rejections In (CTRL+ F6)
- Stock Journal (ALT+F7)
- Delivery Note (ALT+F8)
- Receipt Note (ALT+F9)
- Physical Stock (ALT+F10)

You can alter these vouchers to suit your company, and also create new ones. Read ahead to understand the function of each Voucher Type. The following exercises are sample entries for understanding voucher entry in Tally.ERP 9.

Let us understand how to record transactions in Tally.ERP 9, with examples from the books of accounts of National Traders.

### *7.6.1.1 Contra Voucher (F4)*

A 'Contra Entry' is an entry in a business' books of accounts, indicating transfer of funds from:

- Cash account to bank account
- Bank account to cash account
- One bank account to another bank account.

### *Illustration-3*

Surya Traders withdrawn amount of Rs. 7,000 towards petty cash, from their account in ICICI Bank on 1st April, 2017.

Let us record a Contra Voucher with the details below.

| Contra Voucher Entry | | |
|---|---|---|
| **Account** | **Debit** | **Credit** |
| ICICI Bank Account | 7,000 | |
| Petty Cash | | 7,000 |

To record the transaction in Tally.ERP 9,

1. Go to **Gateway of Tally > Accounting Vouchers > F4: Contra**
2. In Voucher Creation screen, press **F12: Contra Configuration** and set the following to **Yes:**
   - **Skip the Date field in Create Mode (faster entry!)**
   - **Use Cr/Dr instead of To/By during entry**
   - **Warn on Negative Cash Balance**
   - **Show Ledger Current Balances**
   - **Show Balances as on Voucher Date**
3. Select the Bank Ledger – ICICI Bank **in Particulars** to **Credit**
4. Enter the amount as **Rs. 7,000**
5. Select the **Petty Cash** Ledger to **Debit**
6. Enter the **Amount** to be debited
7. Enter the details in the field **Narration,** if required

   The completed **Contra Voucher appears** as shown below:
8. Press **Y** or **Enter** to accept

### *7.6.1.2 Payment Voucher (F5)*

Payment entry is a transaction which is passed to record all payments made by cash or bank.

### *Illustration-4*

On 1st April, 2017, Surya Traders paid a bill raised by Raxson Ltd. By issuing a cheque for Rs. 5000. Let us record a Payment Voucher with the details below:

| Payment Voucher Entry | | |
|---|---|---|
| **Account** | **Debit** | **Credit** |
| Raxson lrd. (Sundry Creditors) | 5000 | |
| ICICI Bank | | 5000 |

To record the transaction in Tally.ERP 9,

1. Go to **Gateway of Tally > Accounting Vouchers > F5: Payment**
2. In **Voucher Creation** screen, press **F12: Payment Configuration** and set **Use Single Entry mode for Pymt/ Rcpt/ Contra** to **No**

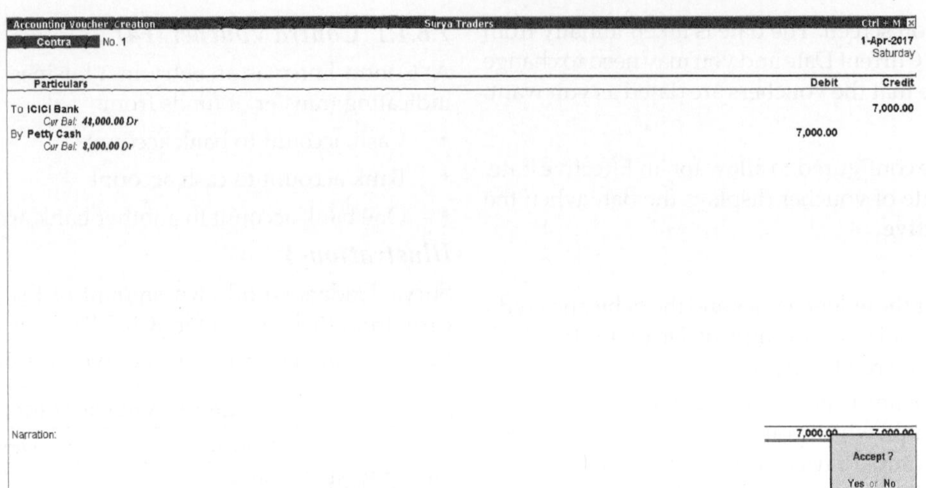


Figure 7.16: Contra Voucher

3. Select the Party **Ledger - Raxson Ltd.** in **Particulars** to **Debit**
4. Enter the amount as **Rs. 5000**
5. Select the Bank ledger – ICICI Bank to **Credit**
6. Enter the **Amount** to be credited
7. Enter the details in the field **Narration**, if required

The **completed Payment Voucher** screen appears as shown below:

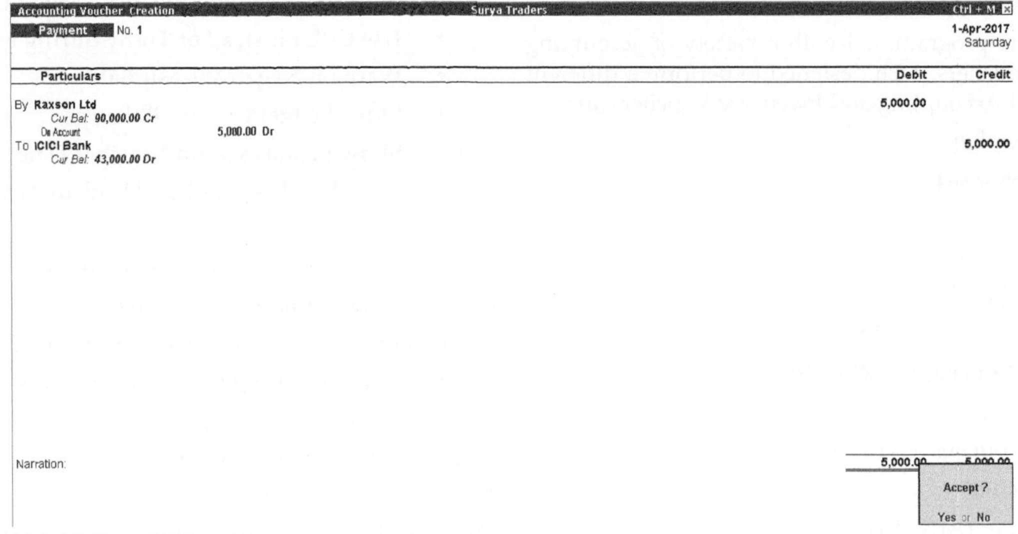


Figure 7.17 Payment Voucher

8. Press **Y** or **Enter** to accept

### *Recording a payment in Single Entry Mode*

### *Illustration-5*

On 1st April, 2017, Surya Traders paid Rs. 400 towards Stationery expenses, and Rs. 700 towards postage expenses from their Petty Cash account.

Let us record a **Payment Voucher** with the details below: To record the transaction in Tally.ERP 9,

1. Go to **Gateway of Tally > Accounting Vouchers > F5: Payment**
2. In Voucher Creation screen, press **F12: Payment Configuration** and set **Use Single Entry mode** for **Pymt/ Rcpt/ Contra** to **Yes**
3. In **Account** field select **Petty Cash**
4. Under **Particulars,** select the **Stationery Expenses** from the **List of Ledger Accounts**
5. Enter **Rs. 400** in the Amount field
6. Under Particulars, select **Postage Expenses** from the **List of Ledger Accounts**
7. Enter **Rs. 700** in the **Amount** field
8. Enter the details in the field **Narration,** if required

The completed **Payment Voucher** made in the single entry mode appears as shown below:

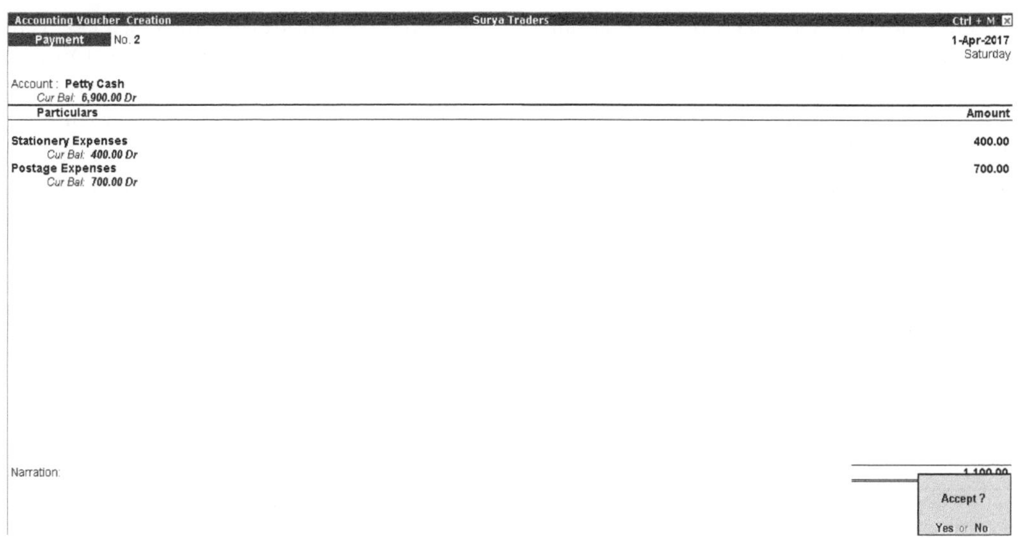

*Figure 7.18: Payment Voucher with Single Entry Mode*

9. Press **Y** or **Enter** to accept

The advantage of a single entry mode is that you can select multiple debits or credits depending on the type of entry. Similarly the transactions can be recorded in single entry mode even in Receipt and Contra vouchers.

### *7.6.1.3 Receipt Voucher (F6)*

Transactions involving receipt of cash and through bank are entered in the Receipt Voucher. For example, on 1st April, 2017, Surya Traders received interest of Rs. 1,500 on a deposit account maintained by them with ICICI.

Let us record a Receipt Voucher with the details below:

| Receipt Voucher Entry | | |
|---|---|---|
| **Account** | **Debit** | **Credit** |
| Bank Interest (Indirect Income) | 1,500 | |
| Bank Deposit Account (Deposit-Assets) | | 1,500 |

To record the transaction in Tally.ERP 9,

1. Go to **Gateway of Tally > Accounting Vouchers > F6: Receipt.**
2. In **F12: Payment Configuration**, set the option **Use Single Entry mode for Pymt/Rcpt/Contra** to **No**
3. Select the ledger **Bank Interest** in **Particulars** to **Credit**
4. Enter the amount as **Rs. 1500**
5. Select the ledger **Deposit Account** to **Debit**
6. Enter the **Amount** to be debited
7. Enter the details in the field **Narration**, if required The completed **Receipt Voucher** appears as shown below:
8. Press **Y** or **Enter** to accept

### *7.6.1.4 Journal Voucher (F7)*

In accounting and bookkeeping, a journal is a record of financial transactions in order by date. A journal is often defined as the book of original entry. The definition was more appropriate

*Figure 7.19 Receipt Voucher*

when transactions were written in a journal prior to manually posting them to the accounts in the general ledger or subsidiary ledger. Manual systems usually had a variety of journals such as a sales journal, purchases journal, cash receipts journal, cash disbursements journal, and a general journal.

With today's computerised bookkeeping and accounting, it is likely to find only a general journal in which adjusting entries and unique financial transactions are entered. In other words, accounting software has eliminated the need to first record routine transactions into a journal.

### *Illustration-6*

Surya Traders has entered some expenditure on Repair & Maintenance, amounting to Rs. 2,500, Which should have actually been posted to the Ledger Office Maintenance. To account for the correct entry, a journal voucher has to be created. First a payment voucher has to be created for the expenditure (using Petty cash) and then the Repair and Maintenance is accounted as Office Maintenance using a Journal voucher.

**Step 1:** Create Payment Voucher

1. Go to **Gateway of Tally > Accounting Vouchers > F5: Payment Voucher**
2. Record the voucher as shown below:

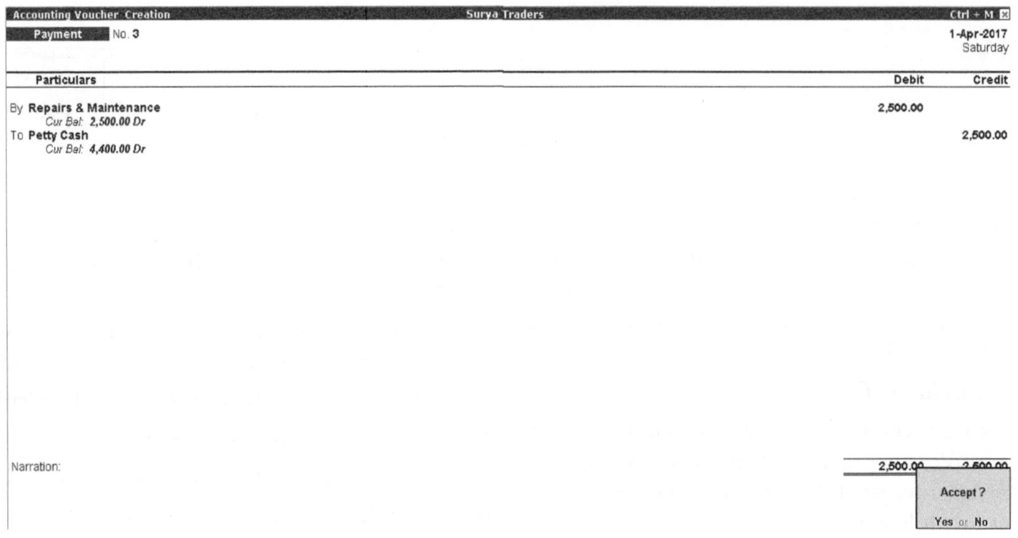


*Figure 7.20: Payment Voucher*

Let us record a Journal Voucher with the details below:

| Journal Voucher Entry | | |
|---|---|---|
| **Account** | **Debit** | **Credit** |
| Office Maintenance (Indirect Expenses) | 2,500 | |
| Repairing & Maintenance | | 2,500 |

To record the transaction in Tally.ERP 9,

1. Go to **Gateway of Tally > Accounting Vouchers > F7: Journal**
2. In **Voucher Creation** screen, press **F12: Journal Configuration** and set the following to **Yes**:
   - Skip the Date field in **Create Mode** (faster entry!)
   - Use **Cr/Dr** instead of **To/By** during entry
   - Warn on **Negative Cash Balance**
   - Show Ledger **Current Balances**
   - Show Balances as on **Voucher Date**
3. Select the **Expense Ledger – Repair and Maintenance in Particulars** to **Debit**
4. Enter the amount as **Rs. 2500**
5. Select the **Expense ledger - Office Maintenance** to **Credit**
6. Enter the **Amount** to be credited
7. Enter the details in the field **Narration**, if required

The **completed Journal Voucher** appears as shown below:

8. Press **Y** or **Enter** to accept.

### *7.6.1.5 Sales Voucher (F8)*

Sales voucher is used when the company sells some goods to the customers either by cash, cheque or on credit basis.

### *Illustration-7*

On 1st April, 2017, Surya Traders made credit sales worth Rs. 6,000 to Supriya & Co.

Let us record a Sales Voucher with the details below:

| Sales Voucher Entry | | |
|---|---|---|
| **Account** | **Debit** | **Credit** |
| Supriya & Co (Sundry Debtors) | 6,000 | |
| Local Sales (Sales Account) | | 6,000 |

To record the transaction in Tally.ERP 9,

*Figure 7.21: Journal Voucher*

1. Go to **Gateway of Tally > Accounting Vouchers > F8: Sales**
2. In **Voucher Creation** screen, press **F12: Configure** and set **Accept Supplementary Details to No**
3. Press **CTRL+V (V: As Voucher)** to enter in Voucher Mode
4. Select the Buyer's Ledger - **Supriya & Co.** in **Particulars** to **Debit**
5. Enter the **Amount** as **Rs. 6,000**
6. Select the Sales ledger - **Local Sales** to **Credit**
7. Enter the **Amount** to be credited
8. Enter the details in the field **Narration,** if required

The **completed Sales Voucher** appears as shown below:

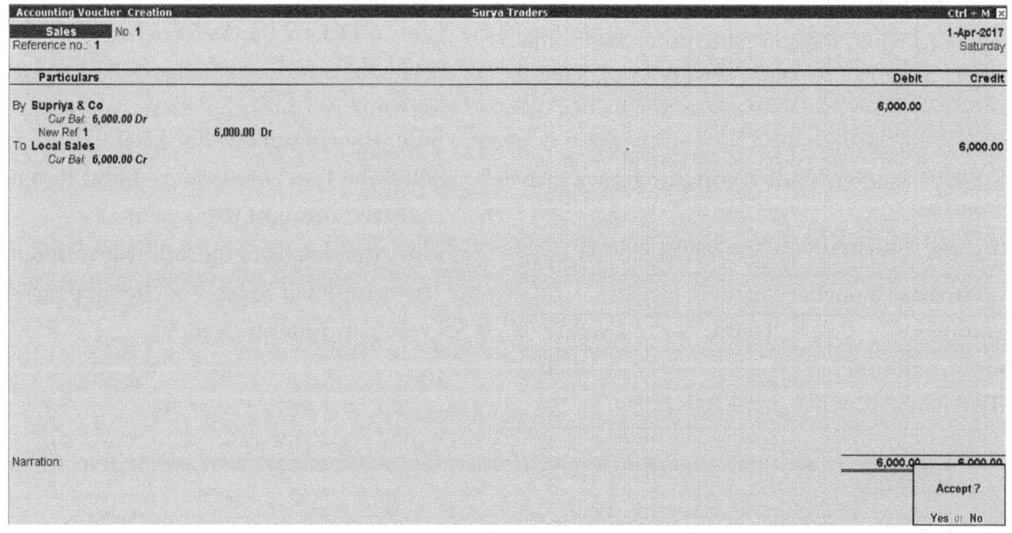


*Figure 7.22: Sales Voucher*

9. Press **Y** or **Enter** to accept

### *7.6.1.6 Credit Note Voucher (CTRL + F8)*

Credit note entry is passed to account for return of goods sold, and is generally issued by the seller to the buyer.

### *Illustration-8*

On 1st April, 2017, Supriya & Co. returned goods worth Rs. 5000.

Let us record a Credit Note with the details below:

| Credit Note Voucher Entry | | |
|---|---|---|
| Account | Debit | Credit |
| Supriya & Co. (Sundry Debtors) | 5,000 | |
| Local Sales Return (Sales Account) | | 5,000 |

This voucher type is made available when the option **Use Debit/ Credit Note** to is set to **Yes** in the **F11: Features (F1: Accounting features).**

To record the transaction in Tally.ERP 9,

1. Go to **Gateway of Tally > Accounting Vouchers > F8: Credit Note.**

2. Mention the Original Invoice No. and date of the Purchase invoice which is returned
3. Enter the **amount** as **Rs. 5000**
4. Select the Sales ledger - **Local Sale Return (Sales Account)** to **Debit**
5. Enter the **Amount** to be debited
6. Enter the details in the field **Narration,** if required

The completed **Credit Note** appears as shown below:

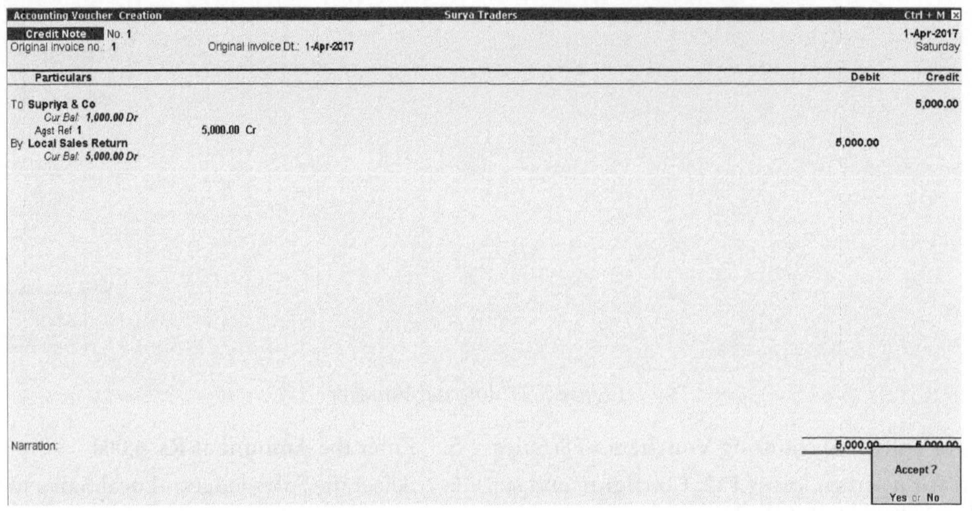


*Figure 7.23: Credit Note Voucher*

9. Press **Y** or **Enter** to accept

### *7.6.1.7 Purchase Voucher (F9)*

Purchase voucher is used when the company purchases some goods from the suppliers either by cash, cheque or on credit basis.

### *Illustration-9*

On 1st April, 2017, Surya Traders made credit purchase worth Rs. 4,500 from Jakson Ltd.

Let us record a Purchase Voucher with the details below:

| Purchase Voucher Entry | | |
|---|---|---|
| **Account** | **Debit** | **Credit** |
| Jakson Ltd. (Sundry Creditors) | | 4,500 |
| Local Purchase (Purchase Account) | 4,500 | |

1. Go to **Gateway of Tally > Accounting Vouchers > F9: Purchase**
2. Press **CTRL+V (V: As Voucher)** to enter in Voucher Mode
3. Select the Supplier's Ledger - Jakson **Ltd.** in **Particulars** to Credit
4. Enter the **Amount** as **Rs. 4,500**
5. Select the Purchase ledger - **Local Purchase** to **Debit**
6. Enter the **Amount** to be debit
7. Enter the details in the field **Narration,** if required

   The **completed Sales Voucher** appears as shown below:
8. Press Y or Enter to accept

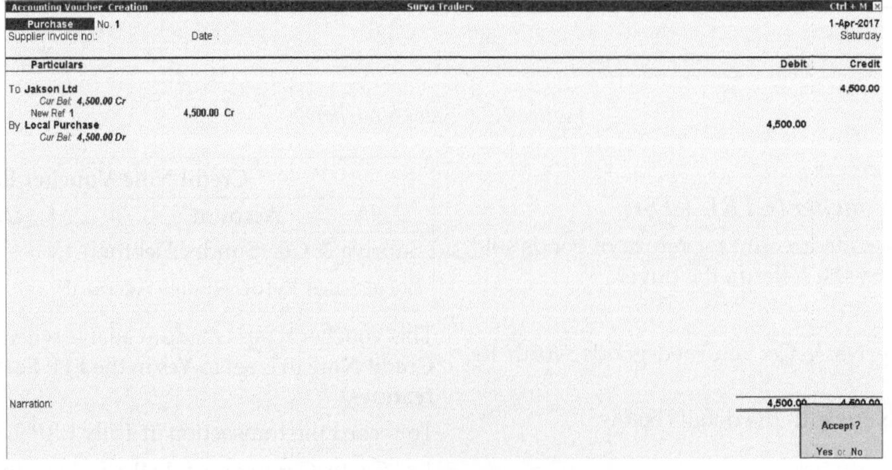


*Figure 7.24: Purchase Voucher*

### *7.6.1.8 Debit Note Voucher (CTRL + F9)*

Debit note entry is passed for purchase returns or for any change in price consideration.

### *Illustratio-10*

On 1st April, 2017, Surya Traders returned goods worth Rs. 1000 to Jakson Ltd.

Let us record a Debit Note with the details below:

| Debit Note Boucher Entry | | |
|---|---|---|
| **Account** | **Debit** | **Credit** |
| Jakson Ltd | 1,000 | |
| Local Purchase Return (Purchase Account) | | 1,000 |

This voucher type is made available when the option **Use Debit/ Credit Notes** is set to **Yes** in the **F11: Features (F1: Accounting Features).**

To record the transaction in Tally.ERP 9,

1. Go to **Gateway of Tally > Accounting Vouchers > F9: Debit Note**
2. Mention the **Original Invoice No** and **date** of the Purchase invoice which is returned
3. Select the Supplier's Ledger - **Jakson Ltd in Particulars** to **Debit**
4. Enter the amount as **Rs. 1000**
5. Select the Purchase ledger - **Local Purchases Return (Purchase Account)** to **Credit**
6. Enter the **Amount** to be credited
7. Enter the details in the field **Narration,** if required

   The completed **Debit Note** appears as shown below:

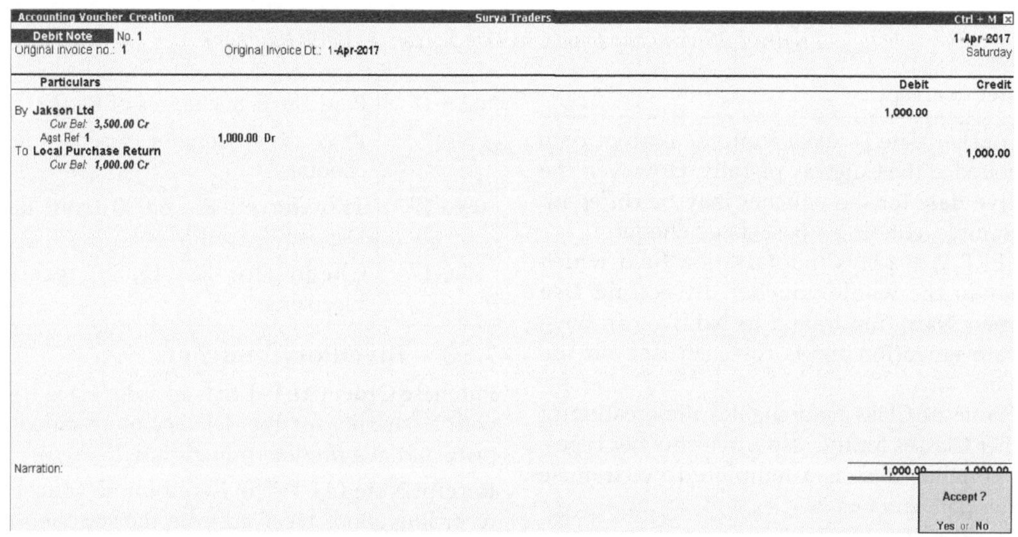


*Figure 7.25 Debit Note Voucher*

8. Press **Y** or **Enter** to accept.

## 7.6.2 Creating a New Voucher Type

**Surya Traders** wants to record bank and petty cash payments differently and needs two new voucher types to replace the pre-defined Payment voucher. In order to do this:

Create a **Bank Payment** voucher.

Go to the **Gateway of Tally > Accounts Info. > Voucher Types > Create**

1. Enter a name for the **Voucher Type**. Here, it is **Bank Payment**
2. Select the Type of Voucher whose functions the new voucher should copy. Here, it is **Payment**
3. Enter an abbreviation for the new voucher. The abbreviation will be used to denote this new voucher in reports
4. Set the Method of Voucher **Numbering** to **Automatic**

You can choose one of the following methods for numbering:

| Method of Numbering | Purpose |
|---|---|
| Automatic | For Tally.ERP 9 to automatically number the vouchers sequentially |
| Manual | This will require you to manually enter the number of the voucher |
| None | To disable numbering for this Voucher Type |

5. Set **Use Advance Configuration** to **No**
6. Set **Use EFFECTIVE Dates** for **Vouchers to No**
7. Set **Make 'Optional' as default** to **No**
8. Set **Use Common Narration** to **Yes**
9. Set **Narrations for each ledger in voucher** to **No**
10. Set **Print after saving Voucher** to **No**
11. Skip the field **Name of Class**

The completed **Voucher Type Creation** screen appears as shown below:

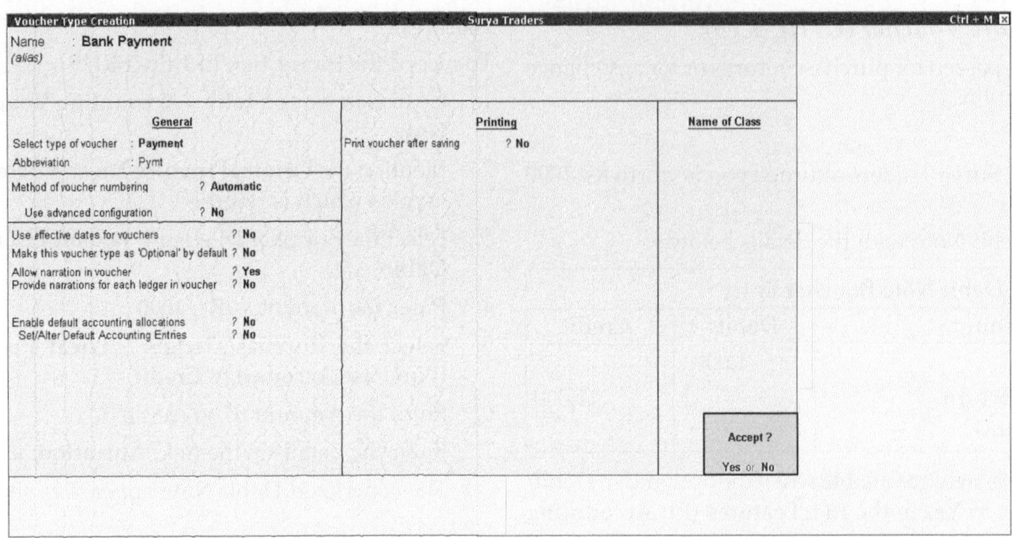


*Figure 7.26 Voucher Type Creation Screen — Bank Payment*

12. Press **Y** or **Enter** to accept

**Note:**
- The voucher date is taken from the current date mentioned at the Gateway of Tally. However, the **effective date** for the voucher may be different. For example, entering a post-dated cheque.
- Tally.ERP 9 displays the narration field which applies to the whole voucher. By setting **Use Common Narration** option to **No,** we can have separate narration fields for each line on the voucher.
- The **Name of Class** field enables the creation of Voucher Classes for the respective voucher types. (The Voucher class is a template to customise voucher data entry).

### *7.6.2.1 Displaying and Altering a Voucher Type*

Observe the menu, you will notice that you can also display and alter voucher types. Selecting these options brings up a List of Voucher Types, from which you can select the one you want to view or work on. Apart from the heading, the Voucher Type Display/Alter screens are identical to the Creation screen.

### *Activity*

Create a Payment Voucher Type for Petty Cash transaction in Surya Traders and pass following entries

| Date | Transaction details |
|---|---|
| 08-5-17 | Bank Advice received for bank interest of Rs. 800 credited to the deposit account. |
| 10-5-17 | Telephone bill for Rs. 600 received from A to Z Mobile. Paid entire amount on same day |
| 20-5-17 | Salaries of Rs. 4,500. Amount paid through Bank Account. |
| 25-5-17 | Paid commission to Suresh Rs. 1,250 through Cheque |
| 28-5-17 | Paid office maintenance Rs. 750 through petty cash |
| 02-6-17 | Paid carriage charges of Rs. 250 from Petty Cash. |
| 03-6-17 | Paid advertisement expenses Rs. 2,500 through cheque |
| 09-6-17 | Transferred Rs. 6,000 from Bank Account to Deposit Account. |
| 15-6-17 | Cheque for Rs. 45,000 received from Sony Electronics. |

### 7.6.3 Inventory Vouchers

**Purchase Order (ALT+F4):** is an order placed by a business entity with a supplier for the delivery of specified goods at a given price and at a predetermined time.

**Receipt Note (ALT+F9):** Receipt note voucher type is used for recording goods received from the supplier.

**Rejections Out (ALT+F6):** The Rejections out Voucher records goods that are rejected and returned to a supplier.

**Sales order (Alt+F5):** Sales Order is an order placed by a customer for the delivery of specified goods at a given price and at a predetermined time.

**Delivery note (Alt+F8):** This Voucher is used for recording goods delivered to a customer.

**Rejection in (Ctrl+F6):** This Voucher is used to record goods that are rejected and returned by the customer.

**To use Inventory vouchers,**

- Enable Delivery Note, Receipt Note and Rejections voucher, set Yes to Use Tracking Numbers (Delivery/Receipt Notes) and Use Rejection Inward/Outward Notes in F11: Features (F2: Inventory Features)
- Go to **Gateway of Tally > F12: Configuration > Invoice/ Orders Entry** – Set Complete Accounting Allocations in Order/Delivery Note to **Yes**
- Make sure that Inventory Values are affected? is set to **'Yes'** in all ledger accounts under the groups Sales Accounts and Purchase Accounts

Let us understand how to record inventory transactions in

Tally.ERP 9, with examples from the books of accounts of Surya Traders.

### *7.6.3.1 Stock Journal (ALT+F7)*

To record the consumption and adjustment of goods, a stock journal voucher is used. For example: the company transfers items of stock from the warehouse to the shop.

### *Illustration-11*

On 07-09-2017, Surya Traders transferred 2 Nos of Samsung Galaxy Tab to Shop from On-Site Godown.

**To record the transaction,**

1. Go to **Gateway of Tally > Inventory Vouchers > F7: Stock Journal**
2. Press **F2** and change the date to 07-09-2017.
3. Under Source (Consumption),
    - Select Name of Item
    - Select Godown from which the transfer is being made
    - Enter Quantity being transferred
    - Enter Rate. The amount will be calculated automatically
4. Under Destination (Production),
    - Select Name of Item
    - Select Godown to which the transfer is being made
    - Enter Quantity being transferred
    - Enter Rate. The amount will be calculated automatically
5. Enter **Narration**, if required

   The completed Stock Journal appears as shown below:

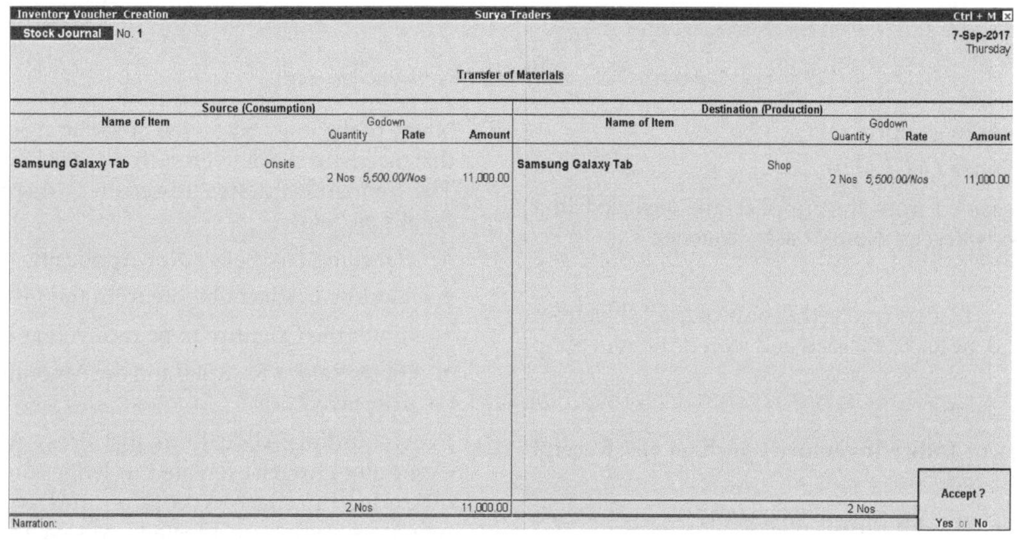


*Figure 7.27 Stock Journal*

6. Press **Y** or **Enter** to accept.

### *7.6.3.2 Delivery Note (ALT+F8)*

Goods that are being delivered to a customer are recorded in a Delivery Note voucher.

- To enable Delivery Note voucher, set Yes to Use Tracking Numbers (Delivery/Receipt Notes) in F11: Features (F2: Inventory Features).
- Ensure in F12: Configure, F12 more configuration (Delivery Note Configuration), set Complete Accounting Allocations in Order / Delivery Note to Yes.

### *Illustration-12*

On 07-09-2017, Surya Traders delivered one Samsung Galaxy Tab from their shop, to Sony Electronics

To record the transaction,

1. Go to **Gateway of Tally > Inventory Vouchers > F8: Delivery Note**
2. Press **F2** and change the date to 07-09-2017.
3. Enter the reference number SR/DN/456 in the Ref. field
4. Party's A/c Name: Select the party ledger Sony Electronics from the List of Ledger Accounts, to whom goods are delivered and press Enter to view Order Details sub-screen. Accept the default details
5. Name of the Item: Select the stock item Samsung Galaxy Tab that needs to be delivered, from the List of Stock Items. The Item Allocations sub-screen is displayed. Enter the details as shown below:
    - Tracking No: Select Not Applicable
    - Godown: Select Shop from the List of Godowns
    - Enter the Quantity to be delivered as 1
    - Enter Rate as Rs. 6,500 and the Amount is automatically displayed
6. In Accounting Allocations for: Create Computer Sales (**Under Sales Accounts and activated Inventory Values are effected**) You can create directly from Accounting Details screen with the help of ALT+C (Online Ledger Creation)

   The completed Delivery Note appears as shown below:

*Figure 7.28: Delivery Note Voucher*

7. Press **Y** or **Enter** to accept

### *7.6.3.3 Receipt Note (ALT+F9)*

Goods that are received from the supplier are recorded in a Receipt Note (Goods Receipt Note – GRN) voucher.

#### *Illustration-13*

On 08-09-2017, Surya Traders received 2 Sony Xperia Tablet from New Computer Ltd. at Rs. 8,500 each and stored them in Shop godown.

To record the transaction,

1. Go to **Gateway of Tally > Inventory Vouchers >F9: Receipt Note**
2. Press **F2** and change the date to 08-09-2017
3. Enter the reference number NCL/045/222 in Ref.. field
4. Party's A/c Name: Press Alt+C and create the party by name New Computers Ltd. under Sundry Creditors and save the ledger creation screen
5. Name of the Item: Select the Stock Item Sony Xperia Tablet that needs to be delivered, from the List of Stock Items. The Item Allocations sub-screen is displayed. Enter the details as below:
   - Tracking No: Select Not Applicable
   - Godown: Select On-Site from the List of Godowns
   - Enter the Quantity to be received as 2
   - Enter Rate as Rs. 8,200 and the Amount is automatically displayed
6. In Accounting Allocations for: Press Alt+C and create Computer Purchase (create this ledger under Purchase A/c (Under Purchase Accounts) and enable the option Inventory values are affected and save the ledger creation screen)
7. Enter the Narration, if required

   The completed Receipt Note appears as shown below.

*Figure 7.29: Receipt Note Voucher*

8. Press **Y** or **Enter** to accept

### *7.6.3.4 Rejections Out (ALT+F6)*

A Rejections Out entry is passed to record the instance of rejection of goods by the buyer, for the goods purchased. This is a pure inventory voucher..

To use this function, enable Use rejection inward and outwards notes in F11: Features (F2: Inventory Features).

#### *Illustration-14*

On 14-09-2017, Surya Traders returned one Sony Xperia Tablet to New Computers Ltd.

**To record the transaction,**

1. Go to **Gateway of Tally > Inventory Vouchers > F6: Rejections Out**
2. Press **F2** and change the date to 14-09-2017.
3. Select the New Computers Ltd. as the **party ledger**
4. Enter **Supplier's Name and Address**, if any
5. Select the **Item** as Sony Xperia Tablet.
6. Set Tracking No. to Not Applicable
7. Select the **Godown** as Onsite
8. Enter the Quantity as 1 and Rate as Rs. 8,200. The Amount gets calculated automatically
9. Enter **Narration** if required

The completed Rejections Out voucher appears as shown below:

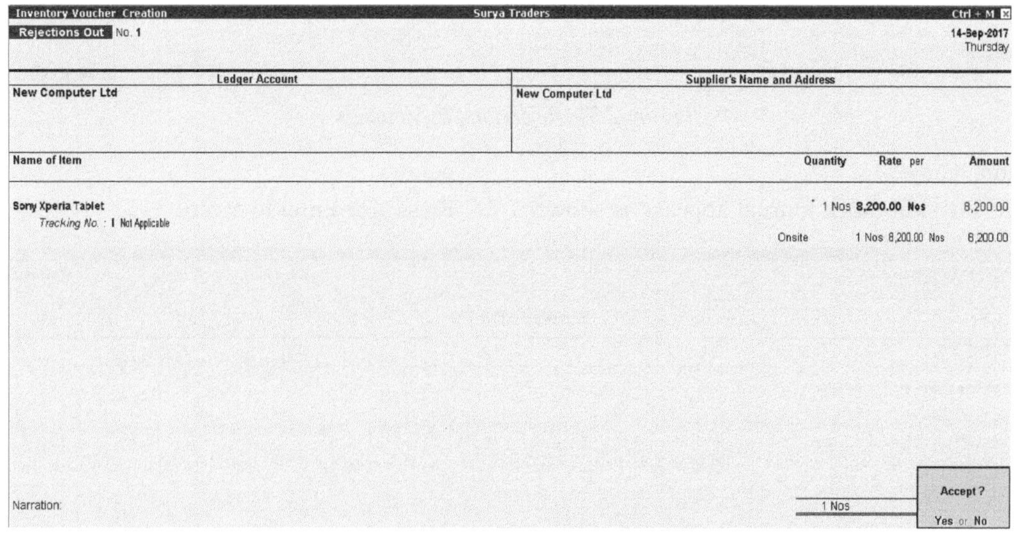


*Figure 7.30: Rejections Out Voucher*

10. Press **Y** or **Enter** to accept

### *7.6.3.5 Rejections In (CTRL+F6)*

A Rejections In entry is passed by the seller to record the instance of receipt of rejected goods. The Rejections In entry is a pure inventory voucher.

#### *Illustration-14*

On 16-09-2017, Sony Electronics returned one Nos Samsung Galaxy Tab. To record the transaction,

1. Go to **Gateway of Tally > Inventory Vouchers > F6: Rejections In**
2. Press **F2** and change the date to 16-09-2017.
3. Select Sony Electronics as the **party ledger**
4. Enter **Customer's Name and Address**, if any
5. Select the **Item** as Samsung Galaxy Tab
6. Set tracking number to Not Applicable
7. Select the **Godown** as Shop
8. Enter the Quantity as 1 and Rate as Rs. 6,500. The amount gets calculated automatically
9. Enter **Narration** if required

The completed Rejections In voucher appears as shown below.

10. Press **Y** or **Enter** to accept

### *7.6.3.6 Physical Stock Voucher (ALT+F10)*

Tally.ERP 9 considers the stock available based on the entry made in a physical stock voucher. For example, on conducting a stock-check, the company finds a discrepancy between the actual stock and the recorded stock figure. In such cases, a Physical Stock voucher can be recorded.

#### *Illustration-15*

On 17-09-2017, stock check revealed the physical stock of 19 Nos. of Samsung Smart Watch in Onsite Godown.

**To record the transaction,**

1. Go to the **Gateway of Tally > Inventory Vouchers > F10: Physical Stock**
2. Press **F2** and change the date to 17-09-2017.
3. Select the **Name** of the Item
4. Select the **Godown Onsite**
5. Enter the **Quantity**

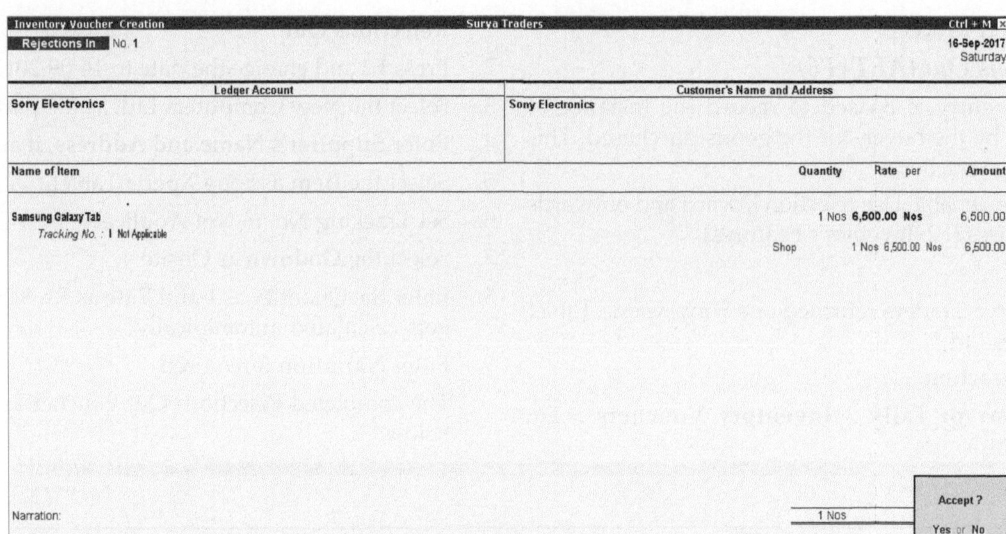


*Figure 7.31: Rejections In Voucher*

6. Enter **Narration**, if any

   The completed Physical Stock Journal appears as shown below:

7. Press **Y** or **Enter** to accept

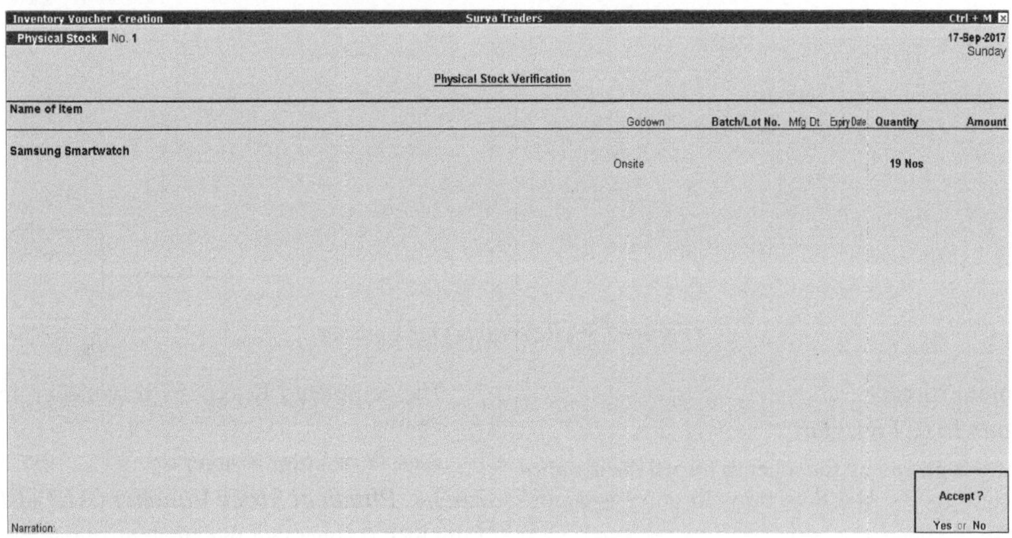


*Figure 7.32 Physical Stock Journal*

### *Activity*

Record further entries for Surya Traders

Transaction from the Books of Surya Traders

| Date | Transaction details |
|---|---|
| 10-10-2017 | Delivered 2 Nos of Samsung Smart Watch @ ₹ 2500/- from Onsite to Sony Electronics (Ref: SR/DN/2543) and for accounting allocation select Computer Sales.(Hint: Select Computer Sales.) |
| 18-10-2017 | Received 2 Nos of Dell Inspiron Desktop @ ₹ 12,300/- from Raxson Ltd. (Ref: RX/12124/056). Store it in Shop Godown and for accounting allocation select Purchase A/c. |
| 19-10-2017 | Returned 1 Nos Samsung Smart Watch @ ₹ 2500/- (damaged) by Sony Electronics. |
| 02-11-2017 | Received 4 Nos of Samsung Galaxy Tab @ ₹ 5,400/- from Smasung World Ltd. (Ref :SWL/1220/210) Store it in Onsite Godown and for accounting allocation select Purchase A/c.(Hint: Create new Ledger with the name of Samsung World Ltd. under Sundry Creditors) |
| 02-11-2017 | Delivered 2 Nos Dell Inspiron Dektop @ ₹ 12,900/- from Onsite to Disha Computers (Ref: SR/DN/021) and for accounting allocation select Computer Sales.(Hint: Select Computer Sales and Create new Ledger with the name of Disha Computers under Sundry Debtors ) |

| | |
|---|---|
| 04-11-2017 | Stock check reveals physical stock of Sony Xperia Tablet is 6 Nos. |
| 07-11-2017 | Transferred 1 Nos of Dell Inspiron Desktop from onsite to Shop. |

## 7.6.4 Entering Inventory Details in Accounting Vouchers

Assume that the inventories have to be updated at the same time as entering the accounting vouchers. This is particularly useful for organisations that send and receive goods with a bill or invoice only. In other words, they do not want to update stocks with only a delivery note, neither do they want to do this with just a Goods Receipt Note. Tally.ERP 9 permits stock movement along with invoice. Therefore, you need to select the stock items that come in or move out at the time of purchase or sales voucher entry.

Apart from the Sales and Purchase Vouchers that record the inventory movements, the following vouchers are used to record the stock movements.

- Debit Note for goods rejected and returned to supplier
- Credit Note for goods rejected and returned by customer

Tally.ERP 9 permits the entries of these vouchers in voucher mode as well as in invoice mode. In this section, you will learn how to enter them in Voucher Mode.

To record inventory details in accounting vouchers,

- Set Yes to Use Debit/Credit Notes in F11: Features (F1: Accounting Features). Do not activate the invoice mode.
- Make sure that Inventory Values are affected? is set to Yes in all ledger accounts under the groups Sales Accounts and Purchase Accounts.
- Set Use Tracking Numbers to No in F11: Features (F2: Inventory Features).
- Ensure that in F11: Features (F1: Accounting Features) Allow Invoicing is set to No.

Given below are examples of Purchase, Sales, Debit Note and Credit Note vouchers from the books of Surya Traders, with inventory details:

### *7.6.4.1 Purchase voucher*

#### *Illustration-16*

On 08-11-2017, Surya Traders purchased 6 Nos. of Keyboard at Rs. 450 from New Computer Ltd., delivered to their Onsite godown.

To record the transaction,

1. Go to **Gateway of Tally > Accounting Vouchers > F9: Purchase**
2. Press **F2** and change the date to 08-11-2017.
3. Press F12 Configuration> Show Inventory Details **No**
4. Select New Computers Ltd. from the List of **Ledger Accounts** to credit
5. Enter the amount as **Rs. 2700**
6. Select **Local Purchases** from the **List of Ledger Accounts** to **debit**
7. In the **Inventory Allocations screen**, select **Keyboard** as the item and press **Enter**
8. In the Item Allocations screen, select **Godown** as Onsite, Quantity as 6, Rate as Rs. 450 and the Amount will be calculated automatically
9. Accept the **Item Allocations** screen
10. Accept the **Inventory Allocations** screen
11. Enter **Narration** if required

The completed Purchase Voucher appears as shown below:

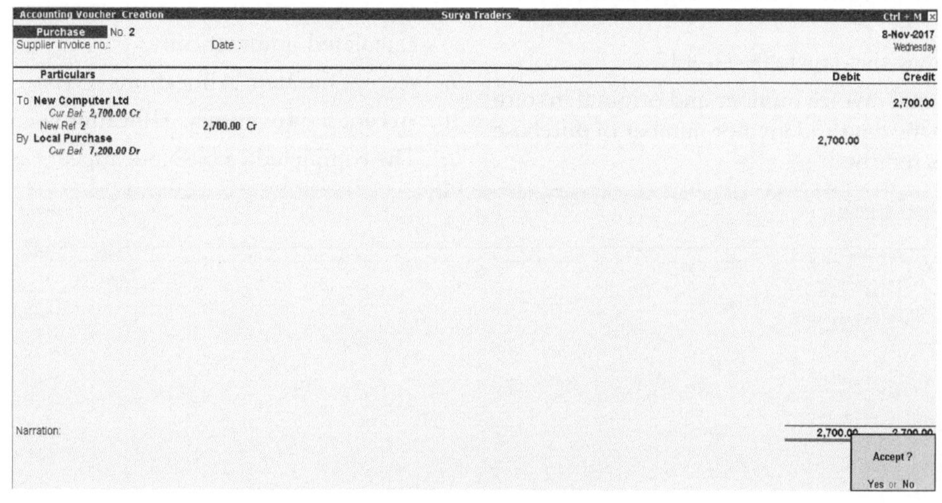


*Figure 7.33: Purchase Voucher*

12. Press **Y** or **Enter** to accept

### *7.6.4.2 Sales Voucher*

#### *Illustration-17*

On 08-11-2017, Surya Traders sold 2 Nos of Samsung Smart Watch at Rs. 2,800/Nos. to Supriya Traders, delivered from their Onsite godown.

To record the transaction,

1. Go to the **Gateway of Tally > Accounting Vouchers > F8: Sales**

2. Press **F2** and change the date to 08-11-2017
3. Select Supriya Traders from the **List of Ledger Accounts** to **debit**
4. Enter the amount as **Rs. 5600**
5. Select Local Sales from the **List of Ledger Accounts** to **credit**
6. In the **Inventory Allocations** screen, select Smart Watch as the item and press **Enter**
7. In the **Item Allocations** screen, select **Godown** as Onsite, Quantity as 2, Rate as Rs. 2,800 and the Amount will be calculated automatically
8. Accept the **Item Allocations** screen
9. Accept the **Inventory Allocations** screen
11. Enter **Narration** if required

The completed Sales Voucher appears as shown below

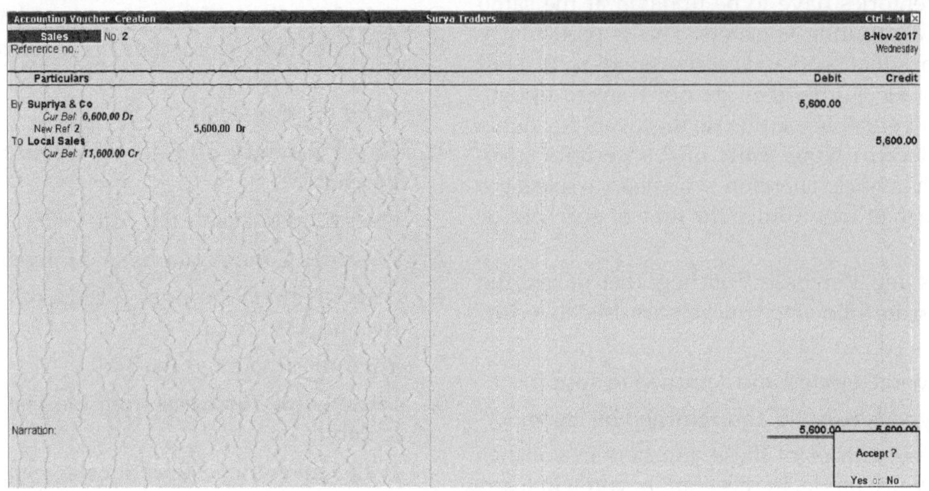

*Figure 7.34: Sales Voucher*

12. Press **Y** or **Enter** to accept

### *7.6.4.3 Debit Note*

#### *Illustration-18*

On 09-11-2017, Surya Traders returned 3 Nos. of Keyboard as they were found to be defective, to New Computers Ltd.

To record the transaction,

1. Go to the **Gateway of Tally > Accounting Vouchers > F9: Debit Note**
2. Press **F2** and change the date to 09-11-2017
3. Mention the original invoice number and original invoice date i.e. Mention the date and invoice number of purchase voucher which is returned.
4. Select New Computers Ltd. from the List of Ledger Accounts to debit
5. Enter the amount as **Rs. 1350**
6. Select Local Purchase Return Ledger
7. In the **Inventory Allocations** screen, select Keyboard as the item and press **Enter**
8. In the **Item Allocations** screen, select **Godown** as Onsite, Quantity as 3, Rate as Rs. 450 and the Amount will be calculated automatically
9. Accept the **Item Allocations** screen
10. Accept the **Inventory Allocations** screen

The completed Debit Note appears as shown below:

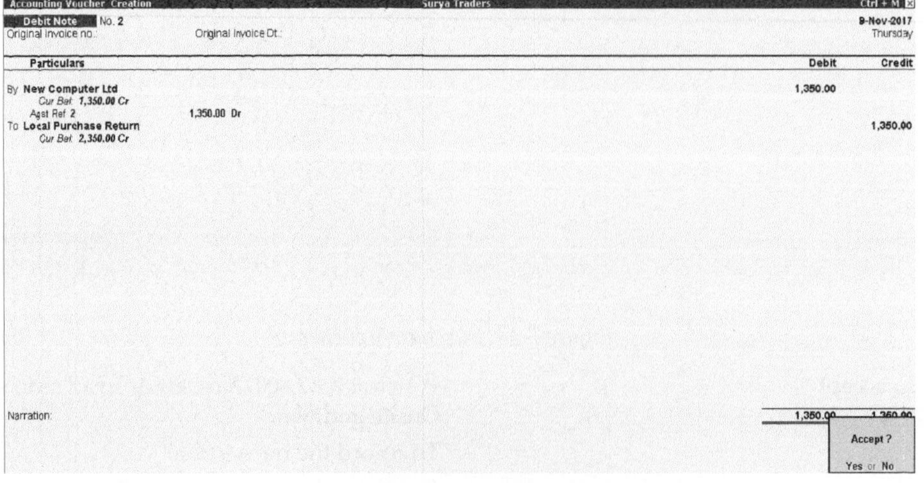

*Figure 7.35: Debit Note*

11. Press **Y** or **Enter** to accept

### *7.6.4.4 Credit Note*

#### *Illustration-19*

On 10-11-2017, Surya Traders received 1 Samsung Smart Watch from Supriya & Co., as they were found to be defective.

To record the transaction,

1. Go to the **Gateway of Tally > Accounting Vouchers > F8: Credit Note**
2. Press **F2** and change the date to 10-11-2017
3. Select Supriya & Co. from the List of Ledger Accounts to credit
4. Enter the amount as **Rs. 2,800**
5. Select Local Sales Return
6. from the **List of Ledger Accounts** to **debit**
7. In the **Inventory Allocations** screen, select Samsung Smart Watch as the item and press **Enter**
8. In the **Item Allocations** screen, select **Godown** as Onsite, Quantity as 1, Rate as Rs. 2,800 and the Amount will be calculated automatically
9. Accept the **Item Allocations** screen
10. Accept the **Inventory Allocations** screen
11. Press **Enter** to get back to the voucher entry screen

The completed Credit Note appears as shown below:

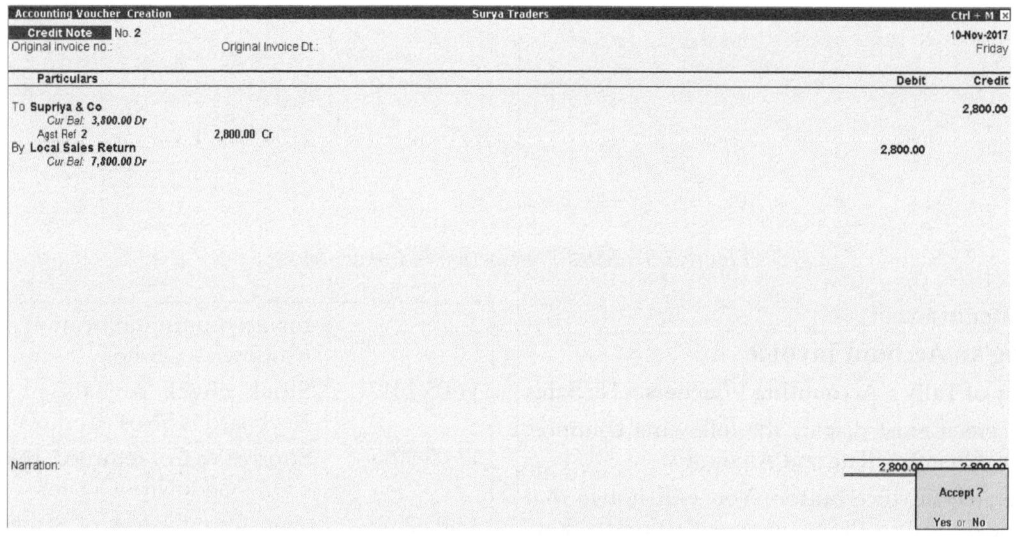


*Figure 7.36: Credit Note*

12. Press **Y** or **Enter** to accept

### 7.6.5 Item Invoice and Account Invoice

Tally.ERP 9 gives you an option called Account Invoice where you can select the ledgers instead of the stock items. An Item Invoice, on the other hand, allows you to select stock items instead of ledgers.

Businesses that require an invoice raised with the item details, can select the Item Invoice option. Businesses that want to raise invoices for services rendered, can do so by selecting the Account Invoice.

### 7.6.6 Creating an Item Invoice

Tally.ERP 9 has an in-built system to create and print sales invoices. You will now record sales and purchase invoice details, adjust accounting and inventory balances.

To enable the option of invoicing,

1. Set **'Yes'** to the following options in **F11: Features** (Accounting Features/Inventory Features).
   - Allow Invoicing,
   - Enter Purchases in Invoice Format

#### *Illustration-20*

As on 10-11-2017, Surya Traders sold 2 Nos. of Samsung Galaxy Tablet @ Rs. 6,500 to Sony Electronics. Recording sales invoice:

1. Go to the **Gateway of Tally > Accounting Vouchers > F8: Sales**
2. Ensure that the button above the Post-Dated option reads As Voucher. This button enables you to toggle between the voucher and invoice format for data entry. The button visible is the format not in use
3. Ensure that Use Common Ledger A/c for Item Allocation is set to Yes in Sales Invoice Configurations screen (F12: Configure )
4. Press **F2** and change the date to 10-11-2017
5. Select **Sony Electronics** in the **Party's A/c Name field**
6. Accept the **Party Details** screen
7. Select Sales A/c (Create using Alt+C under Sales Accounts) in the **Sales Ledger field**
8. Select the item being sold, that is Samsung Galaxy tablet
9. In the **Item Allocations** screen,

- Select Onsite as the **Godown**
- Enter Quantity being sold. Here, it is 2 Nos. The Rate and Amount will be filled automatically

10. Press **Enter** to get back to the voucher entry screen
11. Enter **Narration** if required

The completed Sales Invoice will appear as shown below:

*Figure 7.37: Sales Transaction in Invoice Mode*

13. Press **Y** or **Enter** to accept

### 7.6.7 Creating an Account Invoice

Go to the **Gateway of Tally > Accounting Vouchers > F8: Sales**

1. The invoice screen must display the following columns: Name of Item, Quantity, Rate and Amount
2. Click on the Acct Invoice button. You will notice that Tally.ERP 9 now displays the columns as Particulars, Rate and Amount
3. Select the **Party's A/c Name as Sunny Enterprises (Create Alt+C under Sundry Debtors)**
4. Press **Enter** till you reach the **Particulars** field. Press **Space bar** and Tally.ERP 9 displays the **List of Ledgers**

   *Figure 5.38: Sales Voucher in Accounting Invoice Mode*
5. Select the **Fees & Subscriptions** (create one if it is not displayed under Direct Income)
6. Specify the amount as Rs. 2,000 and press **Enter**

***Activity***

| Transaction from the books of Surya Traders | |
|---|---|
| 02-05-2017 | Purchase 10 Nos. Keyboard @Rs. 400/- from Raxson Ltd and under purchase ledger select Purchase A/c (Godown – Shop) |
| 03-05-2017 | Sold 5Nos. of Keyboard to Supriya & Co. @ Rs. 650 and under sales ledger select Purchase A/c (Godown – Shop) |
| 04-05-2017 | Received 5 Nos of Mouse @ ¹ 220/- from Jakson Ltd, and for accounting allocation select Purchase A/c (Godown – Shop) |
| 05-05-2017 | Delivered 2 Nos Samsung Smart Watch @ ¹ 2,800/- from Onsite to Sony Electronics, and for accounting allocation select Sales A/c (Godown – Onsite) |
| 11-05-2017 | Stock check reveals physical stock of Keyboard is 5Nos (Godown – Shop) |
| 12-05-2017 | Supriya & Co. returned 1Nos. keyboard @ ¹ 650/- (Godown – Onsite) |
| 13-05-2017 | Transferred 4 Nos of Samsung Smartwatch from onsite to Shop. |

## 7.7 ACCOUNTING REPORTS

Tally's display of information is designed to allow a user to get the maximum benefit out of the data of the transactions and dealings of a company. A user gets a holistic picture of the data and is also able to present information using different options. The purpose of compiling data is to present it in comprehensible accounting, inventory and Management Information System reports. On entering the vouchers, Tally.ERP 9 uses the data and provides the user with various reports in addition to all books and statements.

The display screens of Tally.ERP 9 are dynamic and interactive. Whatever a user sees on the screen can also be printed, depending on the printer's capabilities and settings.

The **Gateway of Tally** displays a few reports directly, i.e. the **Balance Sheet, Profit & Loss Account, Stock Summary** and **Ratio Analysis** as these statements are extremely critical for day-to-day business analysis. The **List of Accounts** report, a display of the Chart of Accounts of the company, is available in the Display Menu, along with all other Tally.ERP 9 report.

To view the Display Menu:

Go to **Gateway of Tally > Display**

The **Display Menu** appears as shown below:

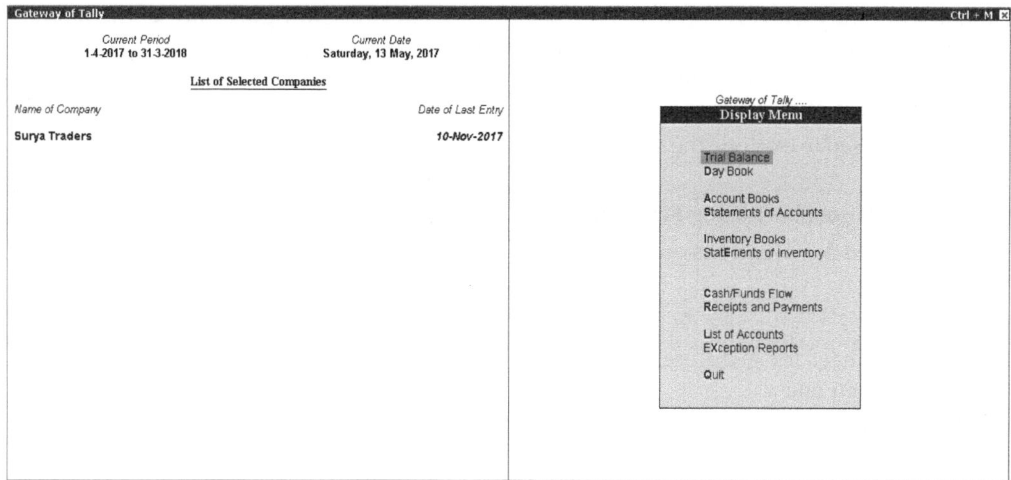


*Figure 7.39 Display Menu*

In this chapter, we will see the accounting reports which are available by default in Tally.ERP 9. However, based on the modules enabled, for example Payroll, the relevant reports for that module will also be available in the Display menu.

### 7.7.1 Basic Features of Displaying Reports

Tally.ERP 9 creates the books of accounts and the financial statements based on the vouchers entered till date. The appearance of reports can be customised as required.

For example, the user can compare different companies, periods of the financial year, groups and ledgers.

The user can also drill down to the transaction level from any report. For this, select an item in the report and press '**Enter**' to navigate to the next level. Following this process will make the user drill down, till they reach an individual voucher. To navigate back to previous levels, press '**Esc**'. The special features available for a displayed report are indicated on the button bar, which can be operated by a single-click of the mouse.

### 7.7.2 Financial Statements

Financial statements summarize the individual transactions to show totals, ratios and statistics required by users to analyse the company's financial data in a wide variety of ways. Broadly, financial statements are classified into the following major statements, which form a part of the statutory requirements in most countries:

- Balance Sheet
- Profit & Loss A/c

#### *7.7.2.1 Balance Sheet*

A Balance Sheet is a financial statement that reports a business' financial position as on a specific date. The term balance sheet implies that the report shows the balance between two figures. It shows a balance between the assets and liabilities of a business. The fundamental accounting equation is, **Assets = Liabilities + Owner's Equity**

To view the Balance Sheet,

Go to **Gateway of Tally > Balance Sheet**

The **Balance Sheet** appears as shown below:

Balance Sheet — Surya Traders — Ctrl + M

| Liabilities | Surya Traders as at 10-Nov-2017 | | Assets | Surya Traders as at 10-Nov-2017 | |
|---|---|---|---|---|---|
| **Capital Account** | | 45,000.00 | **Fixed Assets** | | 1,30,000.00 |
| *Capital A/c* | 45,000.00 | | *Furniture* | 50,000.00 | |
| **Loans (Liability)** | | 65,000.00 | *Land & Building* | 80,000.00 | |
| Secured Loans | 65,000.00 | | **Investments** | | 85,000.00 |
| **Current Liabilities** | | 98,850.00 | *Investment in Gold Bond* | 85,000.00 | |
| Sundry Creditors | 98,850.00 | | **Current Assets** | | 4,53,055.91 |
| Difference in opening balances | | 4,78,500.00 | *Closing Stock* | 3,46,155.91 | |
| | | | Sundry Debtors | 22,050.00 | |
| | | | Cash-in-hand | 2,800.00 | |
| | | | Bank Accounts | 82,050.00 | |
| | | | **Profit & Loss A/c** | | 19,294.09 |
| | | | *Opening Balance* | | |
| | | | *Current Period* | 19,294.09 | |
| **Total** | | 6,87,350.00 | **Total** | | 6,87,350.00 |

*Figure 7.40: Balance Sheet*

Balance Sheet gets updated instantly with every transaction that is recorded. The Button Bar can be used to view additional information or toggle to another report. From the options available in the **Button Bar,** a user can:

- Select **F1:Detailed/Condensed** to explode the summarized information
- Change the date of the Balance Sheet using **F2: Period**
- See the effect of different **Stock Valuations** on the Balance Sheet
- Add new columns to:
  - o Display the Balance Sheet for a different date and compare with the current one
  - o Display the Balance Sheet of another company when more than one company is open
  - o Display the Balance Sheet in a different currency
  - o Display the budget figures, if any, and analyse the variances
- Press **F12: Configure** and set the required parameters

### *7.7.2.2 Profit and Loss Account*

Profit and Loss Account or Income Statement is a periodic statement, which shows the net result of a business' operations for a specified period. All the expenses incurred and incomes earned during the reporting period are recorded in the Profit and Loss account or Income and **Expenditure** account.

The profit and loss account in Tally.ERP 9 displays the information based on the default primary groups. It is updated instantly with every transaction/voucher that is entered and saved. No special processing is required to produce a profit and loss account in Tally.ERP 9.

To view the **Profit & Loss Account,**

1. Go to **Gateway of Tally > Profit & Loss A/c**
2. Click **F1: Detailed,** to view the Profit & Loss Account in detailed format

The **Profit & Loss Account** appears as shown:

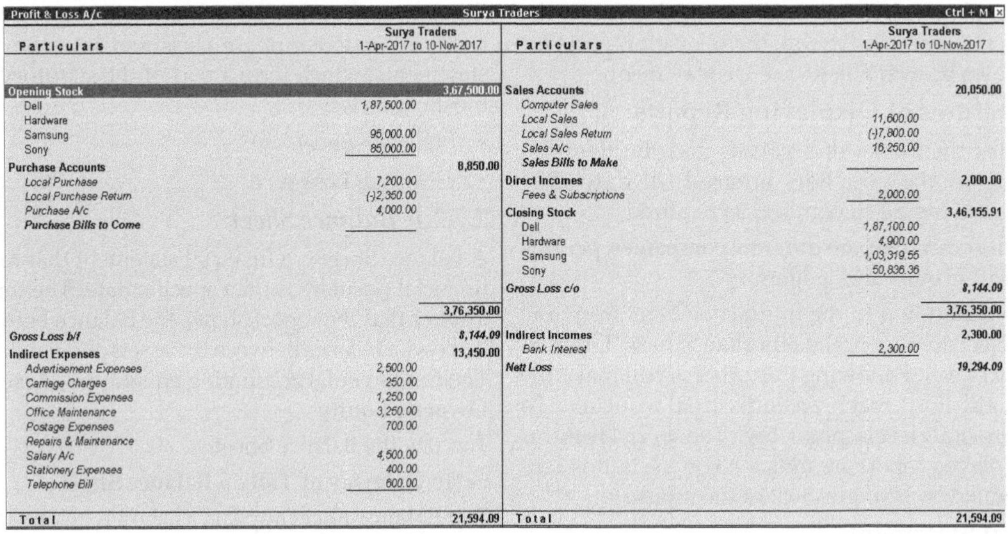

Profit & Loss A/c — Surya Traders — Ctrl + M

| Particulars | Surya Traders 1-Apr-2017 to 10-Nov-2017 | | Particulars | Surya Traders 1-Apr-2017 to 10-Nov-2017 | |
|---|---|---|---|---|---|
| **Opening Stock** | | 3,67,500.00 | **Sales Accounts** | | 20,050.00 |
| Dell | 1,87,500.00 | | *Computer Sales* | | |
| Hardware | | | *Local Sales* | 11,600.00 | |
| Samsung | 95,000.00 | | *Local Sales Return* | (-)7,800.00 | |
| Sony | 85,000.00 | | *Sales A/c* | 16,250.00 | |
| **Purchase Accounts** | | 8,850.00 | ***Sales Bills to Make*** | | |
| *Local Purchase* | 7,200.00 | | **Direct Incomes** | | 2,000.00 |
| *Local Purchase Return* | (-)2,350.00 | | *Fees & Subscriptions* | 2,000.00 | |
| *Purchase A/c* | 4,000.00 | | **Closing Stock** | | 3,46,155.91 |
| ***Purchase Bills to Come*** | | | Dell | 1,87,100.00 | |
| | | | Hardware | 4,900.00 | |
| | | | Samsung | 1,03,319.55 | |
| | | | Sony | 50,836.36 | |
| | | | ***Gross Loss c/o*** | | ***8,144.09*** |
| | | 3,76,350.00 | | | 3,76,350.00 |
| ***Gross Loss b/f*** | | ***8,144.09*** | **Indirect Incomes** | | 2,300.00 |
| **Indirect Expenses** | | 13,450.00 | *Bank Interest* | 2,300.00 | |
| *Advertisement Expenses* | 2,500.00 | | ***Nett Loss*** | | ***19,294.09*** |
| *Carriage Charges* | 250.00 | | | | |
| *Commission Expenses* | 1,250.00 | | | | |
| *Office Maintenance* | 3,250.00 | | | | |
| *Postage Expenses* | 700.00 | | | | |
| *Repairs & Maintenance* | | | | | |
| *Salary A/c* | 4,500.00 | | | | |
| *Stationery Expenses* | 400.00 | | | | |
| *Telephone Bill* | 600.00 | | | | |
| **Total** | | 21,594.09 | **Total** | | 21,594.09 |

*Figure 7.41: Profit & Loss Account*

The Profit & Loss account is generated and updated immediately from the date of opening of books till the date of last entry. It is displayed according to the configurations set in the F12: Configure menu.

## Horizontal and vertical form of Profit & Loss Account

The Profit & Loss A/c, by default is in horizontal form. However, this can be configured to display the Profit & Loss A/c in Vertical form by selecting the option in **F12: Configure.**

Some of the **Button Bar** options are:

- Select **F1: Detailed/Condensed** to display more information or see the summarized format
- Change the date of the Profit & Loss Account using **F2: Period**
- Add new columns to:
  - o Display the Profit & Loss Account for a different period to compare with the current one
  - o Display the Profit & Loss Account in a different currency
  - o Display a column with Budget figures, if any and analyse variances
  - o See the effect of different Stock Valuations on the Profit/Loss account
  - o Select and compare Profit & Loss of different companies

### *7.7.2.3 Trial Balance*

A Trial Balance is a summary report of all ledger balances to check whether the figures are correct and balanced. Considering that the journal entries are error-free and posted correctly to the general ledger, the total of all debit balances should be equal to the total credit balances.

To view the Trial Balance, go to **Gateway of Tally > Display > Trial Balance.**

The **Trial Balance** appears as shown:

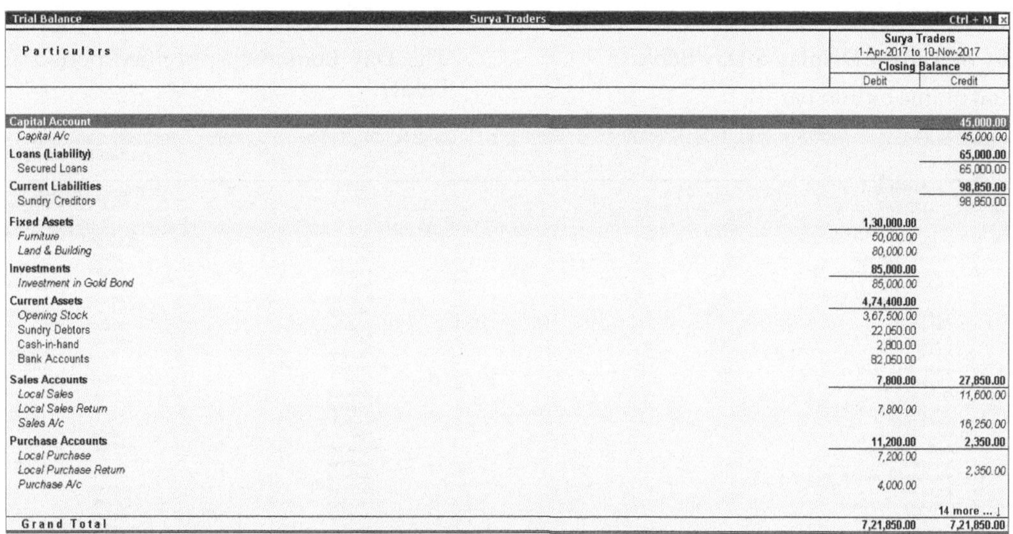

Trial Balance — Surya Traders — Ctrl + M

| Particulars | Surya Traders 1-Apr-2017 to 10-Nov-2017 Closing Balance Debit | Credit |
|---|---|---|
| **Capital Account** | | **45,000.00** |
| *Capital A/c* | | 45,000.00 |
| **Loans (Liability)** | | **65,000.00** |
| Secured Loans | | 65,000.00 |
| **Current Liabilities** | | **98,850.00** |
| Sundry Creditors | | 98,850.00 |
| **Fixed Assets** | **1,30,000.00** | |
| *Furniture* | 50,000.00 | |
| *Land & Building* | 80,000.00 | |
| **Investments** | **85,000.00** | |
| *Investment in Gold Bond* | 85,000.00 | |
| **Current Assets** | **4,74,400.00** | |
| *Opening Stock* | 3,67,500.00 | |
| Sundry Debtors | 22,050.00 | |
| Cash-in-hand | 2,800.00 | |
| Bank Accounts | 82,050.00 | |
| **Sales Accounts** | **7,800.00** | **27,850.00** |
| *Local Sales* | | 11,600.00 |
| *Local Sales Return* | 7,800.00 | |
| *Sales A/c* | | 16,250.00 |
| **Purchase Accounts** | **11,200.00** | **2,350.00** |
| *Local Purchase* | 7,200.00 | |
| *Local Purchase Return* | | 2,350.00 |
| *Purchase A/c* | 4,000.00 | |
| | | 14 more ... ↓ |
| **Grand Total** | **7,21,850.00** | **7,21,850.00** |

*Figure 7.42: Trial Balance*

### *7.7.2.4 Analysis*

The Ratio Analysis report provides a critical overview of the company's performance in the form of ratios. Not only does this report provide an instant understanding of the Working Capital, the Operating Cost percentage and the Nett and Gross Profit percentage, but also gives information about the payment performance of debtors. The return on investment percentage and the return on working capital percentage are other critical ratios available in this report.

To view the Ratio Analysis report, go to **Gateway of Tally > Ratio Analysis**

The **Ratio Analysis report** appears as shown below:

Ratio Analysis — Surya Traders — Ctrl + M

| Principal Groups | Surya Traders 1-Apr-2017 to 10 -Nov-2017 | Principal Ratios | Surya Traders 1-Apr-2017 to 10 -Nov-2017 |
|---|---|---|---|
| **Working Capital** *(Current Assets-Current Liabilities)* | 3,54,205.91 Dr | **Current Ratio** *(Current Assets : Current Liabilities)* | 4.58 : 1 |
| **Cash-in-hand** | 2,800.00 Dr | **Quick Ratio** *(Current Assets-Stock-in-hand : Current Liabilities)* | 1.08 : 1 |
| **Bank Accounts** | 82,050.00 Dr | | |
| **Bank OD A/c** | | **Debt/Equity Ratio** *(Loans (Liability) : Capital Account + Nett Profit)* | 2.53 : 1 |
| **Sundry Debtors** | 22,050.00 Dr | | |
| (due till today) | **22,050.00 Dr** | **Gross Profit %** | (-)40.62 % |
| **Sundry Creditors** | 98,850.00 Cr | **Nett Profit %** | (-)96.23 % |
| (due till today) | **98,850.00 Cr** | **Operating Cost %** *(as percentage of Sales Accounts)* | 196.23 % |
| **Sales Accounts** | 20,050.00 Cr | | |
| **Purchase Accounts** | 8,850.00 Dr | **Recv. Turnover in days** *(payment performance of Debtors)* | 165.47 days |
| **Stock-in-hand** | 3,46,155.91 Dr | | |
| **Nett Loss** | 19,294.09 Dr | **Return on Investment %** *(Nett Profit / Capital Account + Nett Profit )* | (-)75.06 % |
| **Wkg. Capital Turnover** *(Sales Accounts / Working Capital)* | 0.06 | **Return on Wkg. Capital %** *(Nett Profit / Working Capital) %* | (-)5.45 % |
| **Inventory Turnover** *(Sales Accounts / Closing Stock)* | 0.06 | | |

*Figure 7.43: Ratio Analysis*

### *7.7.2.5 Books and Registers*

In Tally.ERP 9, as soon as transactions are entered they are immediately posted to the respective ledgers, books and registers, thereby facilitating instant reporting and faster decision making.

**Books of Account** is a record of the commercial accounts of a company and consolidates the transaction details as they are entered. Although the elements of a transaction are posted to many different ledgers simultaneously, Tally.ERP 9 brings all the transactions of a particular type together into relevant books of account for viewing and printing. For example, Cash Book records all the transactions affecting cash and the Sales Book records all sales transactions.

### *7.7.2.6 Day Book*

The Day Book contains all the transactions made by a business, irrespective of the type of transaction. By default the display is set to the date of the last voucher entry made, but this can be set to list all the transactions made over a certain period. Transactions include all financial vouchers, reversing and memorandum journals as well as inventory vouchers.

To view the Day Book,

1. Go to **Gateway of Tally > Display > Day Book**
2. Click **F2: Period** on the button bar
3. Specify the required period

The **Day Book** for a specified period appears as shown below:

Day Book — Surya Traders — Ctrl + M

Day Book — 1-Apr-2017 to 10-Nov-2017

| Date | Particulars | Vch Type | Vch No. | Debit Amount / Inwards Qty | Credit Amount / Outwards Qty |
|---|---|---|---|---|---|
| 1-4-2017 | ICICI Bank | Contra | 1 | | 7,000.00 |
| 1-4-2017 | Raxson Ltd | Payment | 1 | 5,000.00 | |
| 1-4-2017 | Stationery Expenses | Payment | 2 | 400.00 | |
| 1-4-2017 | Repairs & Maintenance | Payment | 3 | 2,500.00 | |
| 1-4-2017 | Bank Interest | Receipt | 1 | | 1,500.00 |
| 1-4-2017 | Office Maintenance | Journal | 1 | 2,500.00 | |
| 1-4-2017 | Supriya & Co | Credit Note | 1 | | 5,000.00 |
| 1-4-2017 | Jakson Ltd | Debit Note | 1 | 1,000.00 | |
| 1-4-2017 | Supriya & Co | Sales | 1 | 6,000.00 | |
| 1-4-2017 | Jakson Ltd | Purchase | 1 | | 4,500.00 |
| 2-5-2017 | Raxson Ltd | Purchase | 2 | | 4,000.00 |
| 3-5-2017 | Supriya & Co | Sales | 2 | 3,250.00 | |
| 4-5-2017 | Mouse | Receipt Note | 1 | 5 Nos | |
| 5-5-2017 | Samsung Smartwatch | Delivery Note | 1 | | 2 Nos |
| 8-5-2017 | Bank Interest | Receipt | 2 | | 800.00 |
| 10-5-2017 | Telephone Bill | Petty Cash | 1 | 600.00 | |
| 11-5-2017 | Keyboard | Physical Stock | 1 | 5 Nos | |
| 12-5-2017 | Keyboard | Rejections In | 1 | | (-)1 Nos |
| 13-5-2017 | Samsung Smartwatch | Stock Journal | 1 | 4 Nos | |
| 20-5-2017 | Salary A/c | Bank Payment | 1 | 4,500.00 | |
| 25-5-2017 | Commission Expenses | Bank Payment | 2 | 1,250.00 | |
| 28-5-2017 | Office Maintenance | Petty Cash | 2 | 750.00 | |
| 2-6-2017 | Carriage Charges | Petty Cash | 3 | 250.00 | |
| 3-6-2017 | Advertisement Expenses | Bank Payment | 3 | 2,500.00 | |
| 9-6-2017 | ICICI Bank | Contra | 2 | | 6,000.00 |
| 15-6-2017 | Sony Electronics | Receipt | 3 | | 45,000.00 |
| 7-9-2017 | Samsung Galaxy Tab | Delivery Note | 2 | | 1 Nos |
| 7-9-2017 | Samsung Galaxy Tab | Stock Journal | 2 | 2 Nos | |
| 8-9-2017 | Sony Xperia Tablet | Receipt Note | 2 | 2 Nos | |
| 14-9-2017 | Sony Xperia Tablet | Rejections Out | 1 | (-)1 Nos | |

15 more ...

*Figure 7.44: Day Book*

## Purchase and Sales Registers

### *7.7.2.7 Purchase Register*

A Purchase Register displays the information about all the purchases made by a business concern. Purchase register also helps in analysing the details of movement of purchased goods to various godowns, on the basis of which the stock movement at each godown can be determined.

To view the Purchase Register,

Go to **Gateway of Tally > Display > Account Books > Purchase Register**

The **Purchase Register** for the selected period appears as shown below:

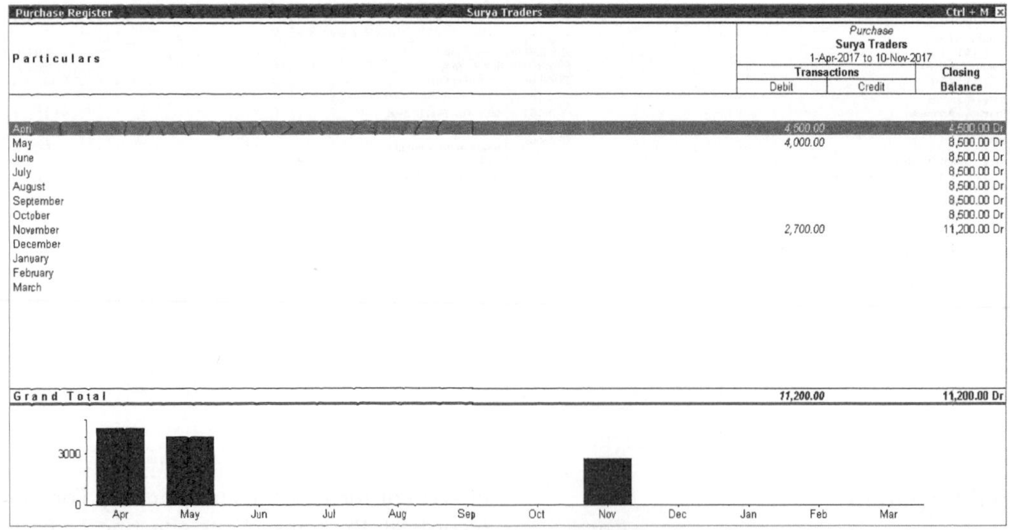

Purchase Register — Surya Traders — Ctrl + M

| Particulars | Purchase, Surya Traders, 1-Apr-2017 to 10-Nov-2017 — Transactions: Debit | Credit | Closing Balance |
|---|---|---|---|
| April | 4,500.00 | | 4,500.00 Dr |
| May | 4,000.00 | | 8,500.00 Dr |
| June | | | 8,500.00 Dr |
| July | | | 8,500.00 Dr |
| August | | | 8,500.00 Dr |
| September | | | 8,500.00 Dr |
| October | | | 8,500.00 Dr |
| November | 2,700.00 | | 11,200.00 Dr |
| December | | | |
| January | | | |
| February | | | |
| March | | | |
| Grand Total | 11,200.00 | | 11,200.00 Dr |



*Figure 7.45: Purchase Register*

### *7.7.2.8 Sales Register*

Sales Register displays the monthly summary of all sales transactions and the closing balances at the end of each month, for the selected period. The list of transactions pertaining to any month can be viewed by selecting that month and pressing '**Enter**' to view its details. Tally.ERP 9 enables change of display according to the information required.

To view the Sales Register,

Go to **Gateway of Tally > Display > Account Books > Sales Register**

The **Sales Register** for the selected period appears as shown below:

The benefits of a sales register are as follows:

- The periodic turnover can be analysed using the F2: Period button
- The periodic taxes on such turnovers can be easily computed
- Errors made while recording transactions can be easily traced
- Sales returns during the year can be analysed and timely action can be taken to remove the undesirable causes.

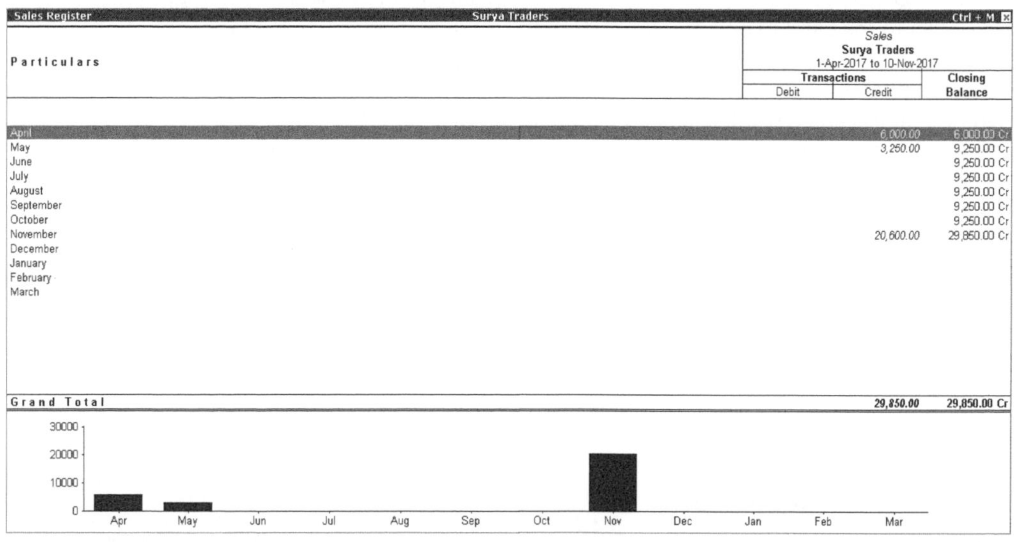

Sales Register — Surya Traders — Ctrl + M

| Particulars | Debit | Credit | Closing Balance |
|---|---|---|---|
| | Sales<br>Surya Traders<br>1-Apr-2017 to 10-Nov-2017 | | |
| April | | 6,000.00 | 6,000.00 Cr |
| May | | 3,250.00 | 9,250.00 Cr |
| June | | | 9,250.00 Cr |
| July | | | 9,250.00 Cr |
| August | | | 9,250.00 Cr |
| September | | | 9,250.00 Cr |
| October | | | 9,250.00 Cr |
| November | | 20,600.00 | 29,850.00 Cr |
| December | | | |
| January | | | |
| February | | | |
| March | | | |
| Grand Total | | 29,850.00 | 29,850.00 Cr |



*Figure 7.46: Sales Register*

## 7.7.2.9 *Statement of Accounts*

### *Statistics*

The Statistics report displays the masters created for that company and the number of vouchers entered for each type of transaction. You can drill down to the transaction level from this report.

To view the Statistics report,

Go to **Gateway of Tally > Display > Statement of Accounts > Statistics**

The **Statistics** report appears as shown below:

Statistics — Surya Traders — Ctrl + M

| Types of Vouchers | Surya Traders 1-Apr-2017 to 10-Nov-2017 | Types of Accounts | Surya Traders 1-Apr-2017 to 10-Nov-2017 |
|---|---|---|---|
| Bank Payment | 3 | Groups | 34 |
| Contra | 2 | Ledgers | 35 |
| Credit Note | 2 | Stock Groups | 5 |
| Debit Note | 2 | Stock Items | 12 |
| Delivery Note | 4 | Godowns | 4 |
| Job Work In Order | 0 | Voucher Types | 24 |
| Job Work Out Order | 0 | Units | 1 |
| Journal | 1 | Currencies | 1 |
| Material In | 0 | | |
| Material Out | 0 | | |
| Memorandum | 0 | | |
| Payment | 3 | | |
| Petty Cash | 3 | | |
| Physical Stock | 3 | | |
| Purchase | 3 | | |
| Purchase Order | 0 | | |
| Receipt | 3 | | |
| Receipt Note | 4 | | |
| Rejections In | 2 | | |
| Rejections Out | 2 | | |
| Reversing Journal | 0 | | |
| Sales | 5 | | |
| Sales Order | 0 | | |
| Stock Journal | 3 | | |
| Total | 45 | | |

*Figure 7.47: Statistics*

## 7.8 BANKING

The Banking module focuses on managing and streamlining banking transactions and activities i.e., Transactional Banking, Analytical Banking & Deposit Management. The banking feature in Tally.ERP 9 supports the requisite recording and processes essentials for effective bank accounting and recording of accounting transactions.

The features of Banking in Tally.ERP 9 are as follows:

- Cheque Printing
- Cheque Register
- Bank Reconciliation
- Deposit Slip
- Payment Advice

### 7.8.1 Cheque Printing

A cheque is a written order to the bank to pay the stated sum of money. Cheques are usually handwritten. In order to automate the entire cheque printing process, Tally.ERP 9 allows cheques to be printed directly. Cheques can be printed while printing a payment voucher. Since the cheque formats differ from bank to bank, Tally.ERP 9 facilitates a sample format and formats of various banks besides user-defined cheque dimensions.

***Activity***

**Open Radhika Enterprises and follow the below mentioned instructions**

The following illustration will demonstrate how to activate and configure Cheque Printing for a specific bank (here Axis Bank) in Tally.ERP 9. We will be creating the Bank Ledger master to configure the cheque printing.

**Step 2:** Activation of Cheque printing

1. **Press** F11: Company features > F1: Accounting Features
2. Set **Enable Cheque Printing** to **Yes**

**Step 2:** Create the Bank Account Ledger

1. Go to **Gateway of Tally > Accounts Info. > Ledger > Create**
2. Select Axis Bank in the Select Your Bank field

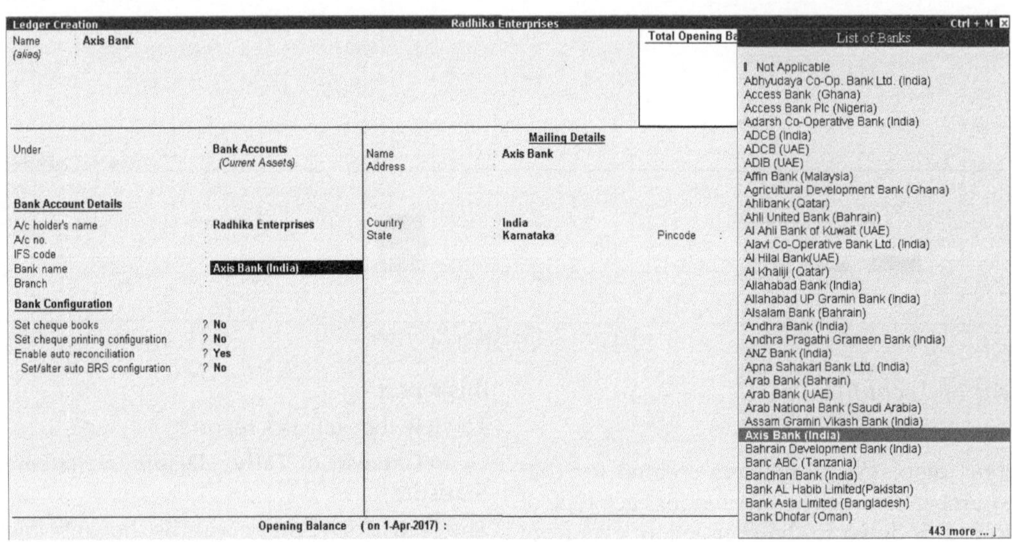


*Figure 7.48: Selecting the Bank*

5. Set cheque books to Yes.
6. Enter the From Number and To Number
7. The Number of Cheques will be filled automatically
8. Enter the Cheque Book Name.
9. Ensure that the Cheque Book Management screen is as shown below:

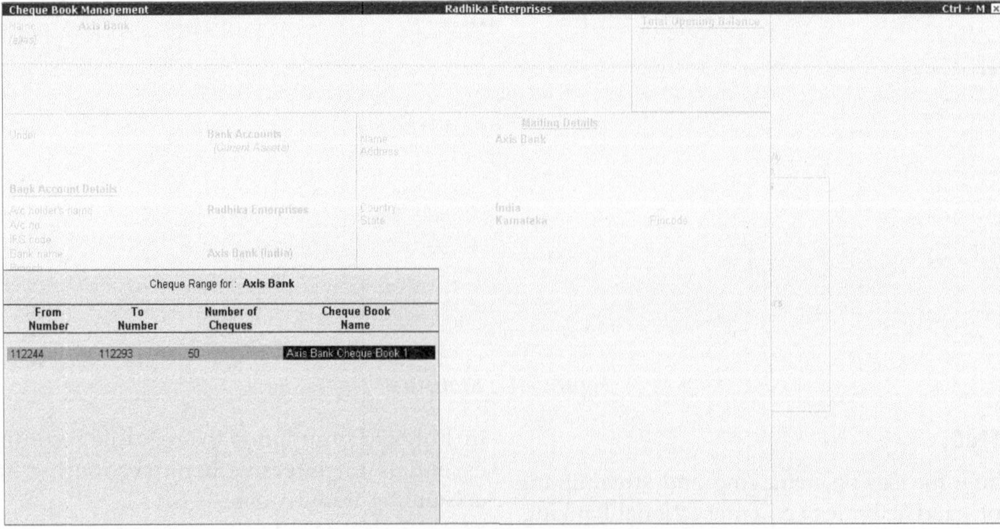


*Figure 7.49: Cheque Range screen*

10. Press **Enter** and accept the screen
    Enable **Set Cheque Printing Configuration**
11. On enabling this option, various formats of cheque of Axis Bank are displayed in the **Cheque Format Selection** screen
12. The **Cheque Format Selection** screen appears as shown below:

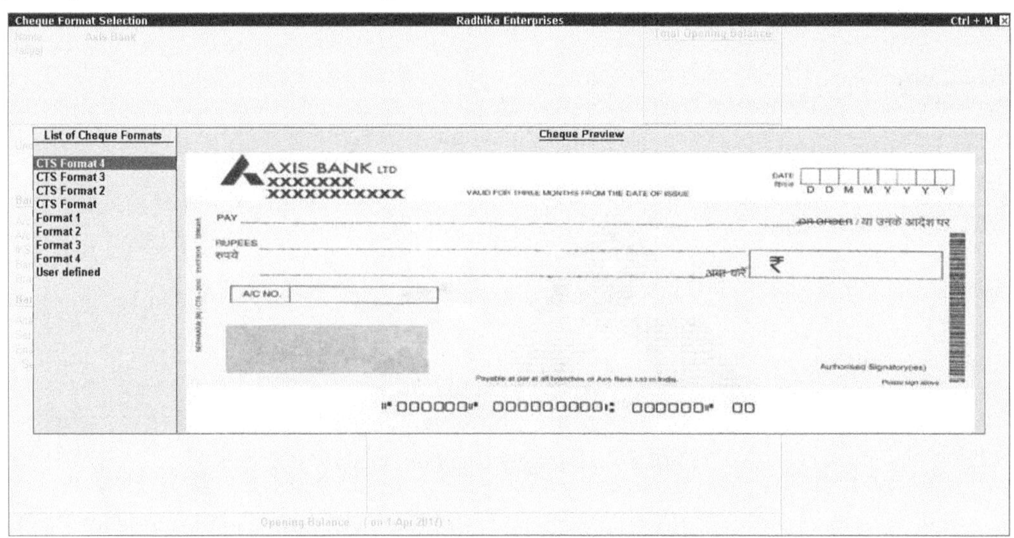


*Figure 7.50: Cheque Format Selection screen*

13. Select the required format and press **Enter**

The Cheque dimension will be auto-filled and will appear as shown below:

- To preview the setting, press ALT+P
- Press Enter to view the preview and press Esc to go out of preview screen.
- Mention the necessary details in the Bank Details screen.
- Press Enter to accept the Bank Details Screen and you will come back to Ledger creation screen.
- Mention the Mailing details if required.
- Press Enter and bring the cursor on Opening balance field and provide the opening balance of ₹ 2,50,000

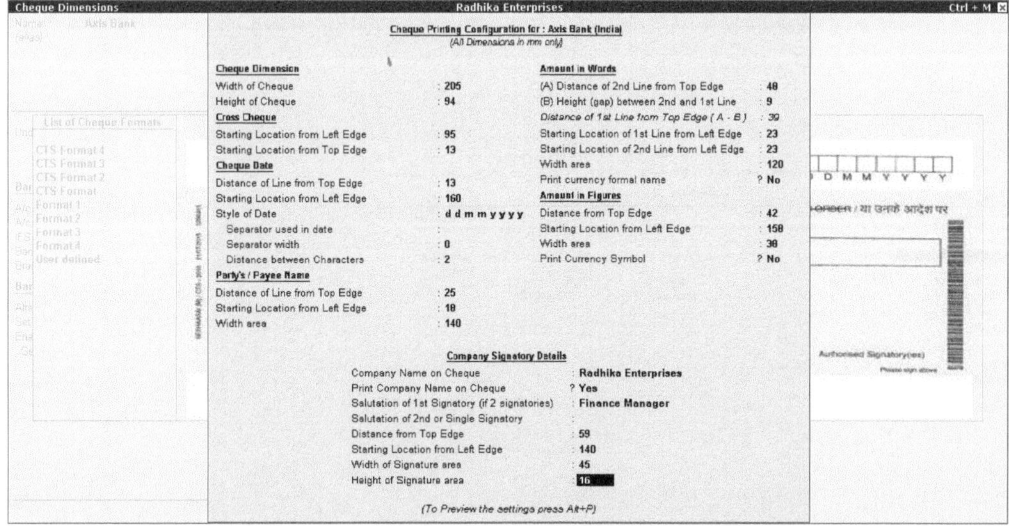


*Figure 7.51: Cheque Dimensions Pre-Filled*

> **Tip**
>
> You can compare the cheque dimensions (sample) with the actual cheque and modify accordingly to suit your requirement. Take the bank's cheque book and measure the dimensions of a cheque carefully in millimetres and fill the form. You may need to correct it after trying out a couple of cheques so that the positioning is accurate. The placing of the cheque in the printer also determines the printing. Trials could be made on photocopies of a cheque before using an actual cheque leaf.
>
> In case of a cheque with two signatories, both can be specified (Both could be the same salutation or different, e.g., the first one as Director and the second one as Secretary).

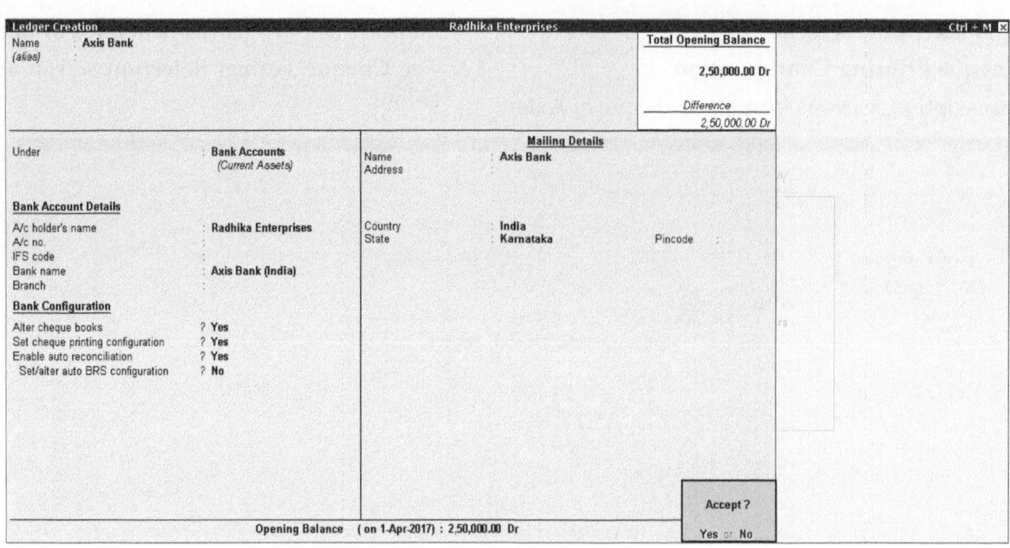


*Figure 7.52: Ledger Creation screen*

### *Activity*

Create Sudhir Enterprises Ledger account under Sundry creditors

Recording transaction of Related to Bank .

The illustration below will help you understand how these cheque ranges can be selected during voucher entry.

1. **Go to** Gateway of Tally > Accounting Voucher > F5: Payment > Select Payment Vouchers.
2. Press F12:Payment standard configuration and disable the option "Use Single entry mode for Pymt/rcpt/contra.
3. Press **F2** and change the date to 15-**04-2017**
4. In the **Debit** Field, select Sudhir Enterprises ledger and enter the **Amount** as Rs. **25000**
5. Enter the amount as **Rs. 25,000**
6. In the **Credit** field, select **Axis Bank** and accept the **Amount**
7. Press **Enter** to view the **Bank Allocations** screen
8. The **Bank Allocations** screen appears as shown below:

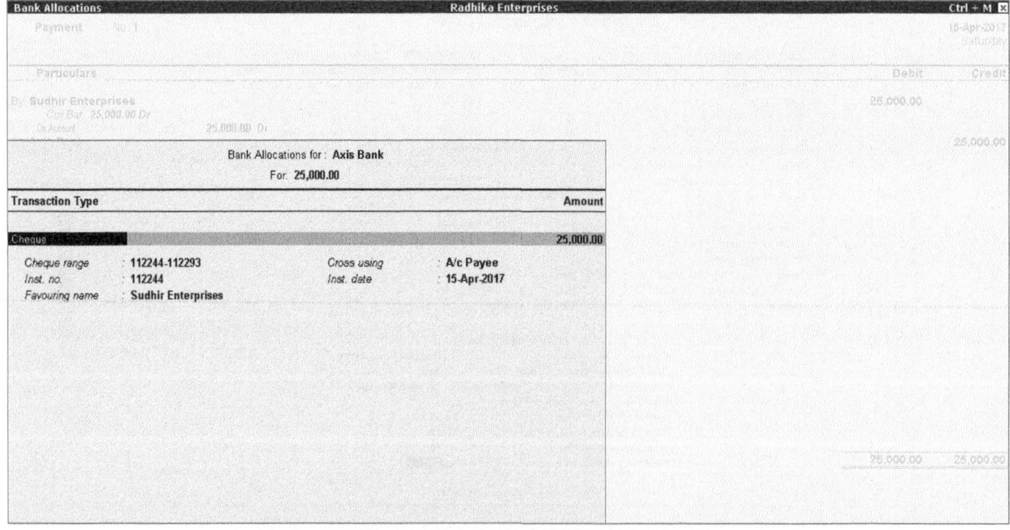


*Figure 7.53: Bank Allocations screen*

In the Bank Allocations screen, the Cheque Range and the Instrument Number are auto filled as the cheque numbers were configured earlier

9. Accept the Bank Allocations screen

   The completed Payment Voucher appears as shown below:

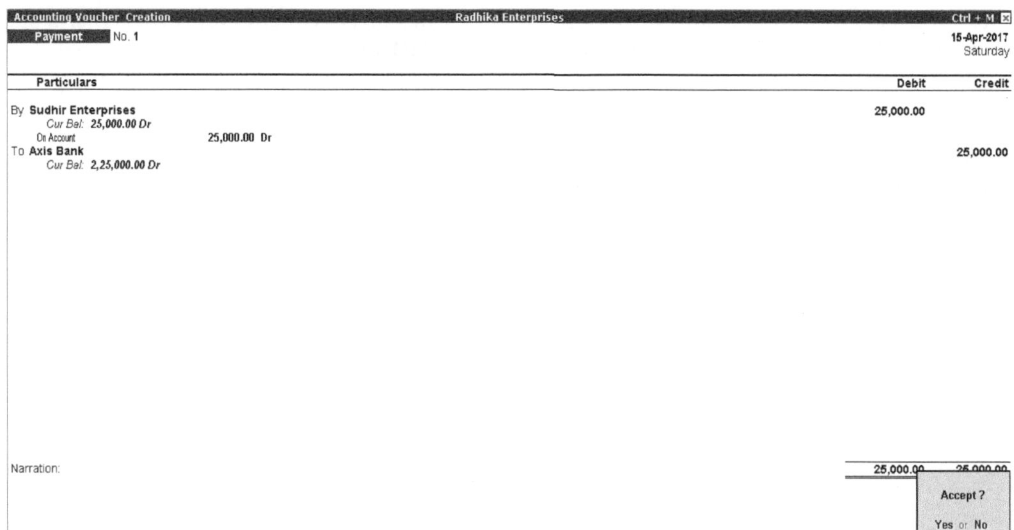


*Figure 7.54: Completed Payment Voucher*

10. Enter the **Narration** if required and accept the voucher
11. On accepting the screen, the **Cheque Printing** configuration screen appears
12. Press **Enter** to print the cheque

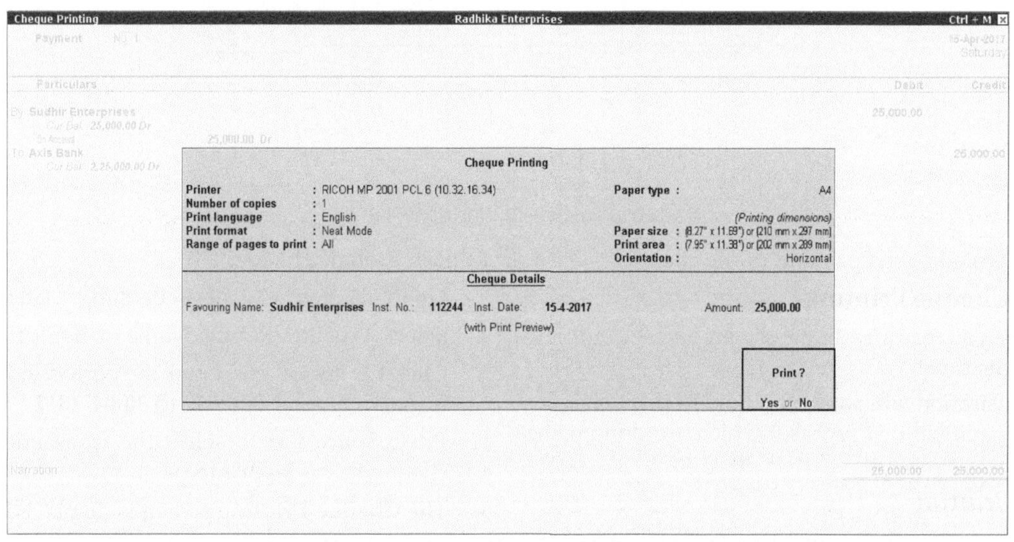


*Figure 7.55: Cheque Printing Configuration screen*

A/c Payee 1 5 0 4 2 0 1 7

Sudhir Enterprises

Twenty Five Thousand Only

**25,000.00

for Radhika Enterprises

Finance Manager

*Figure 7.56: Cheque Printing screen*

The illustration below will help you understand how to pass cash purchase entry with bank details: On 24-4-2017 Cash paid for Purchase product worth of 10,000

## *Required Ledgers Local Purchase*

Go to **Gateway of Tally > Accounts Info > Ledgers > Create Purchase A/c Under Purchase Accounts Group and enable Inventory values are affected**

Let us account the entries to print cheque.

1. **Go to** Gateway of Tally > Accounting Vouchers > F9: Purchase
2. Click on **As voucher** on vertical menu bar or you can press **CTRL+V**
3. Enter the details in the purchase invoice as per the transaction details
4. **Cr Axis Bank** Rs. 10,000
5. **Enter** to get **Bank allocation** screen
6. Select the Transaction type as Cheque
7. Dr the **Purchase A/c**
8. Enter **and** accept
9. Immediately you get the screen as:

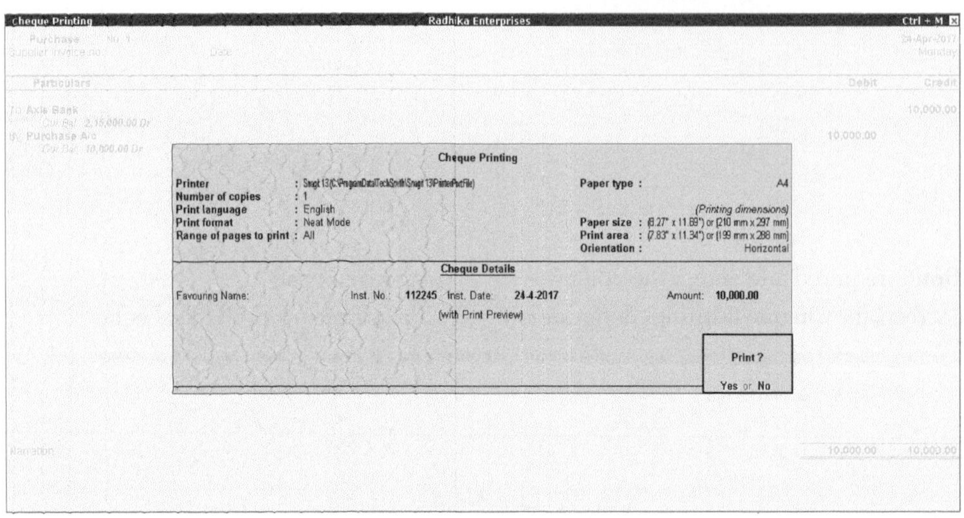


*Figure 7.57: Cheque printing screen*

9. **Say** Print **to** Yes and get a printout of the cheque.

### 7.8.2 Single Cheque Printing

Tally.ERP 9 allows you to print a single cheque and/or multiple cheques at the same time.

The following illustration will show you how to print cheques for transactions (payment or Purchase) which are done using **Bank Account.**

### *Single Cheque Printing*

To print a single cheque,

1. **Go to** Gateway of Tally > Banking > Cheque Printing
2. Select **Axis Bank** in the **Name of Bank field**
3. Click **F2: Period** and enter the period in which the cheque is dated. Enter **1-04-2017** to **30-04-2017**
4. Press **Space Bar** to select the transaction for which the cheque has to be printed
5. The **Cheque Printing** screen is displayed as shown:

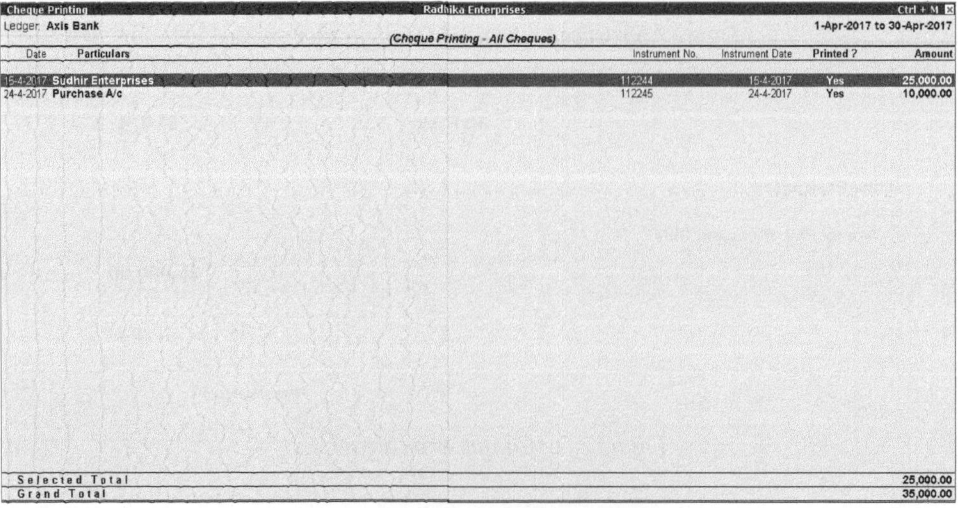


*Figure 7.58: Cheque Printing screen*

Select pressing space bar and press ALT+P

The printed cheque appears as shown below:

**A/c Payee** **1 5 0 4 2 0 1 7**

**Sudhir Enterprises**

**Twenty Five Thousand Only**

****25,000.00**

for Radhika Enterprises

Finance Manager

*Figure 7.59: Printed Cheque*

---

**Note:**
- The **Cheque Printing** facility is also available directly from the **Payment** voucher when the concerned Bank account is credited.
- After crediting the Bank account, Tally.ERP 9 asks for details of the Name on Cheque, Cheque No., and Cross Cheques explained below:
  - o **Name on the Cheque:** On selection of the Party Account, the Name on the cheque is filled with the Party's account name
  - o **Cross Cheque using:** This is filled in by the most common words used - Account payee. However, you can change it.

---

The following illustration will help you understand how to pass a cash deposit entry with bank details:

On 29-4-2017 deposited ₹ 10,000 cash in Axis Bank account

1. **Go to** Gateway of Tally > Accounting Voucher > F4: Contra > Select Bank Payment
2. Press **F2** and change the date to **29-04-2017**
3. In the Credit Field, select Cash ledger and enter the Amount asRs. 10,000
4. In the Debit field, select Axis Bank and accept the Amount
5. Press **Enter** to view the **Bank Allocations** screen
6. Press **Y** or **Enter** to accept

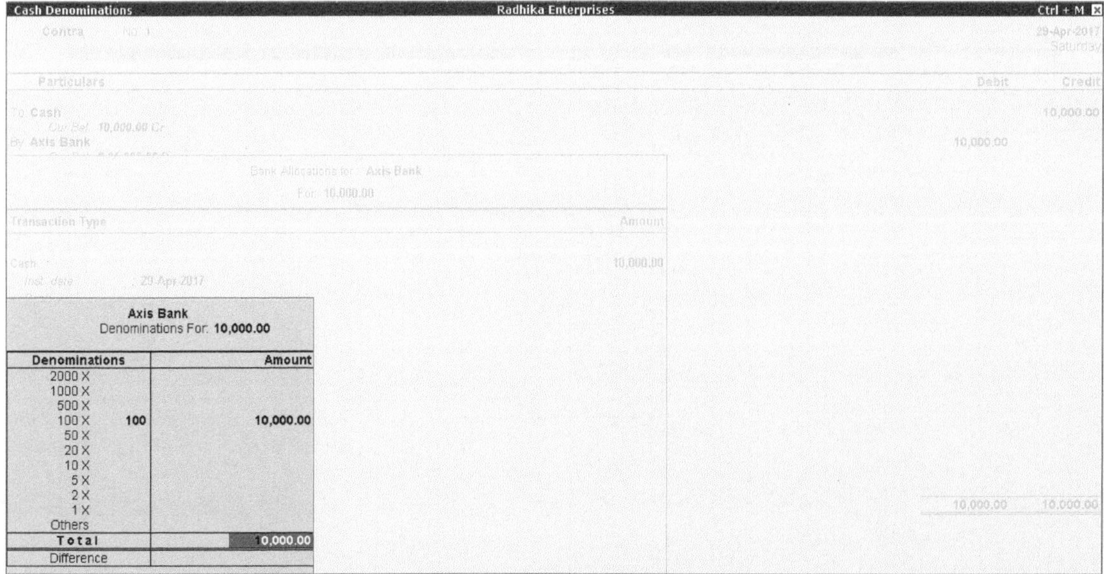


*Figure 7.60: Cash Denominations*

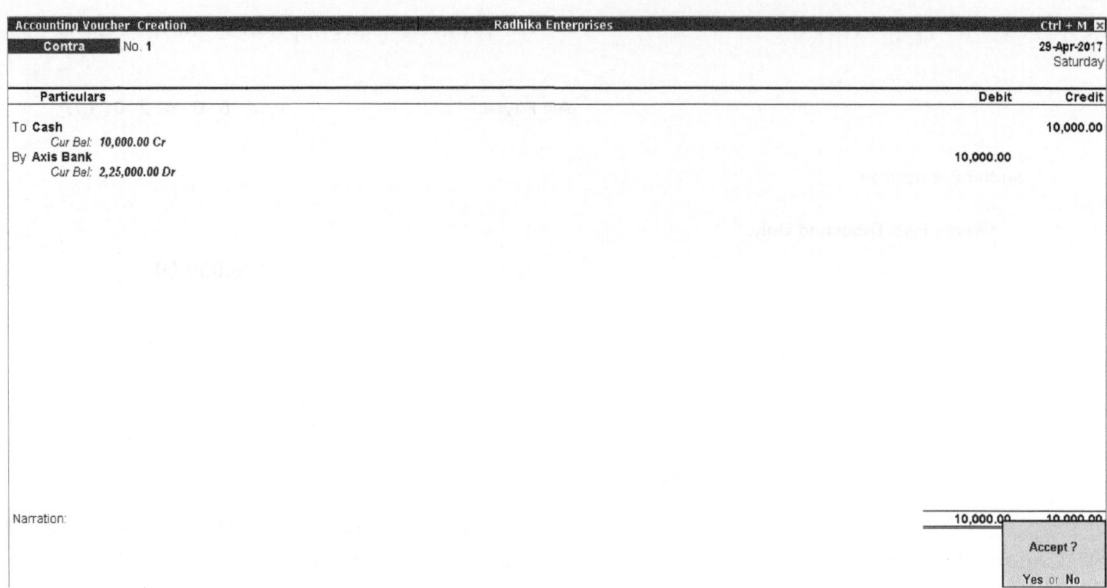


*Figure 7.61: Accounting Voucher Creation*

### 7.8.3 Cancellation of a Cheque

Tally.ERP 9 provides its users with the facility to cancel cheques. The status of an available cheque can be changed to cancelled either by cancelling a particular voucher or by cancelling a new cheque for reasons like torn cheque, lost in transit and so on.

The following illustration will demonstrate how to cancel a cheque. Radhika Enterprises cancelled the cheque numbered 112244 as it was torn. To cancel the cheque,

1. **Go to** Gateway of Tally > Banking > Cheque Register
2. Press **Enter** on **Bank Account** to view the **Cheque Range Register** screen
3. Press **Enter** on the range of cheque **112244-112293**
4. Open the transaction which you want to cancel then press ALT+X for Cancel voucher.
6. Select **Cancel Voucher** and press **Enter**
7. After cancel the voucher cheque will automatically cancel. The Voucher Cancel screen appear as shown below

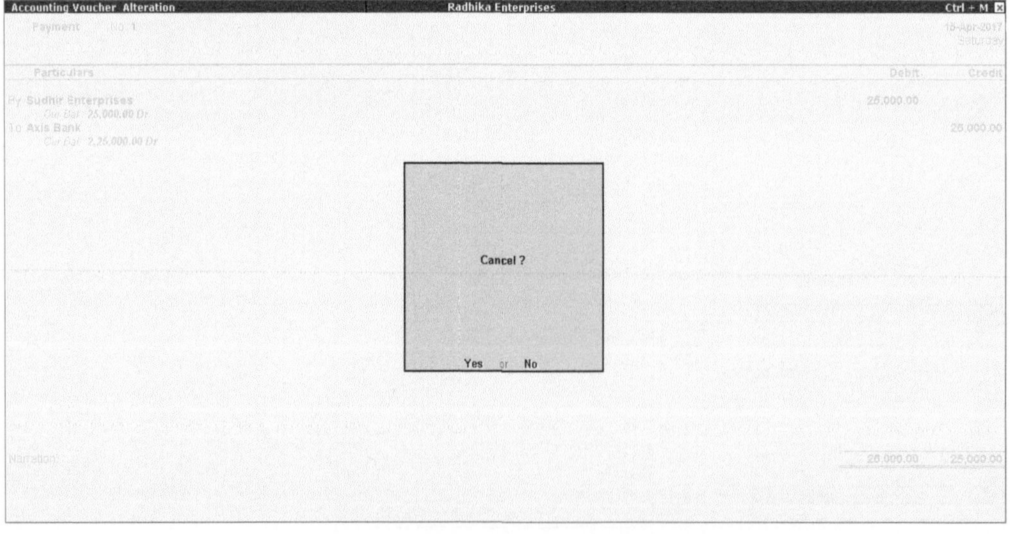


*Figure 7.62: Voucher Cancel Screen*

8. Press Y or Enter for Cancel

The completed Cancellation of Cheque Numbers screen appears as shown below:

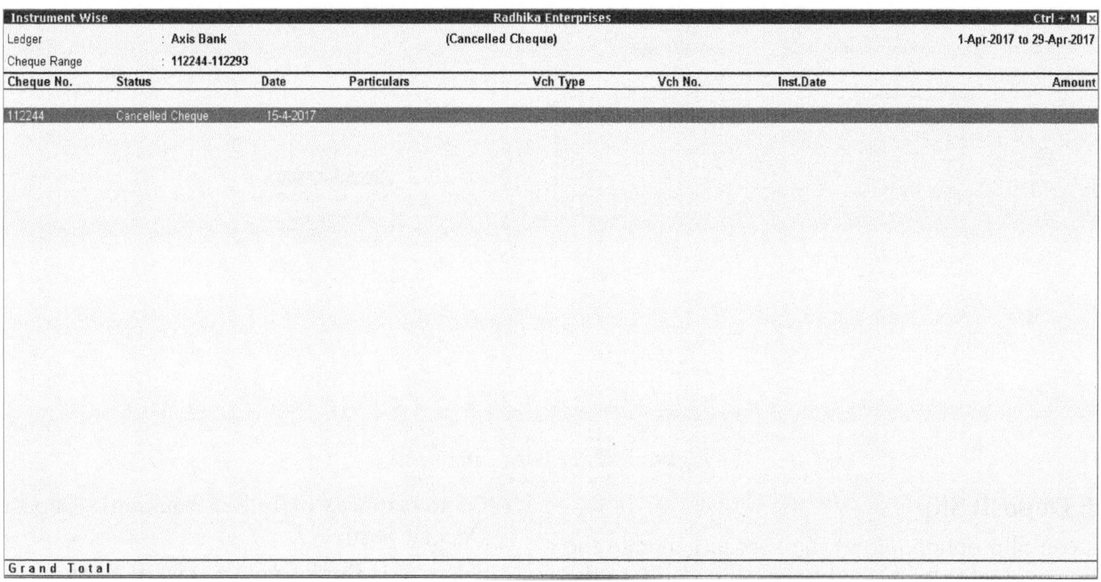

| Instrument Wise | | Radhika Enterprises | | | | | Ctrl + M |
|---|---|---|---|---|---|---|---|
| Ledger | : Axis Bank | (Cancelled Cheque) | | | | | 1-Apr-2017 to 29-Apr-2017 |
| Cheque Range | : 112244-112293 | | | | | | |
| **Cheque No.** | **Status** | **Date** | **Particulars** | **Vch Type** | **Vch No.** | **Inst.Date** | **Amount** |
| 112244 | Cancelled Cheque | 15-4-2017 | | | | | |
| Grand Total | | | | | | | |

*Figure 7.63: Cancellation of Cheque Numbers screen*

To view the Cheque Register,

1. **Go to** Gateway of Tally > Banking > Cheque Register
2. Press **ALT+F1** to obtain a detailed view

The **Cheque Register** screen appears as shown below:

Cheque Register — Radhika Enterprises — Ctrl + M

**Bank wise Register**

| Particulars | | Available Cheques | 1-Apr-2017 to 29-Apr-2017 | | | | Out of Period | Total Cheques |
|---|---|---|---|---|---|---|---|---|
| | | | Unreconciled | Reconciled | Blank | Cancelled | | |
| Axis Bank | | 48 | 1 | | | 1 | | 50 |
| *112244-112293* | (Axis Bank Cheque Book 1) | 48 | 1 | | | 1 | | 50 |
| Grand Total | | 48 | 1 | | | 1 | | 50 |

*Figure 7.64: Cheque Register screen detailed*

### 7.8.4 Deposit Slip

The Deposit Slip option in Banking enables you to generate deposit slips for cheque(s)/DD/cash that are deposited into the bank for any particular date.

To view **Deposit Slip** menu,

**Go to** Gateway of Tally > Banking > Deposit Slip

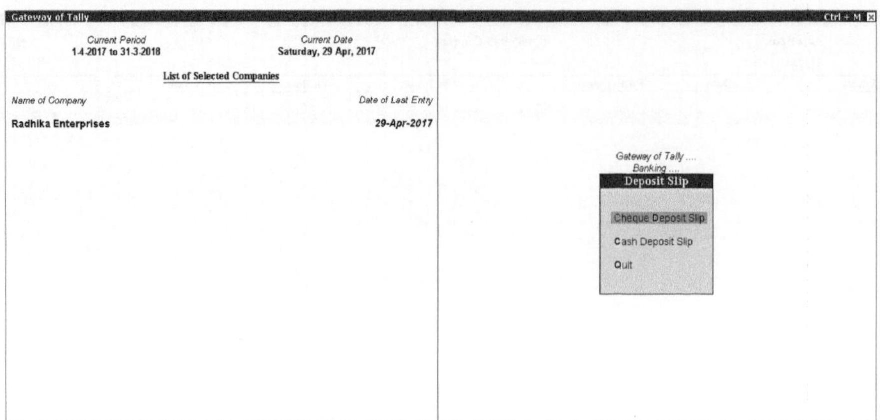


*Figure 7.65: Deposit Slip menu*

## 7.8.5 Cash Deposit Slip

The Cash Deposit Slip option allows the user to generate the deposit slip for payments which need to be deposited into the bank for any particular date.

To create a Cash Deposit slip for this,

1. **Go to** Gateway of Tally > Banking > Deposit Slip > Cash Deposit Slip
2. Select **Axis Bnak** from the **List of Bank**

   The Cash Deposit Slip screen appears as shown below:

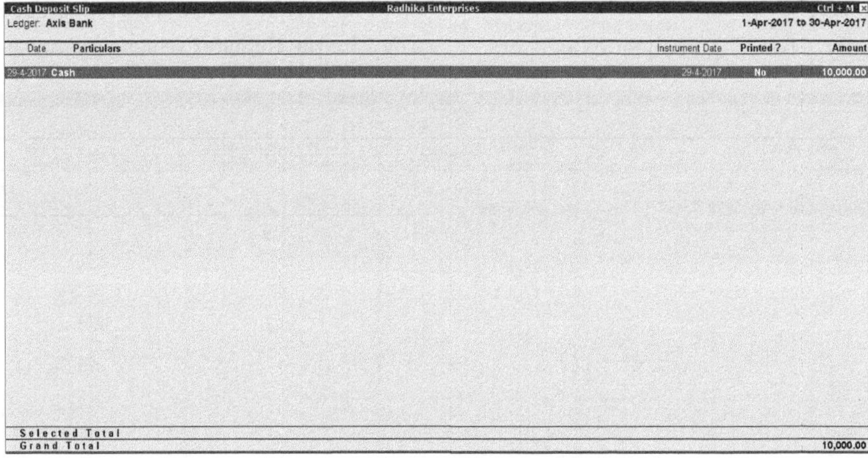


*Figure 7.66: Cash Deposit Slip*

3. Press **ALT+P** to print the deposit slip. The **Print Report** screen appears as shown below.

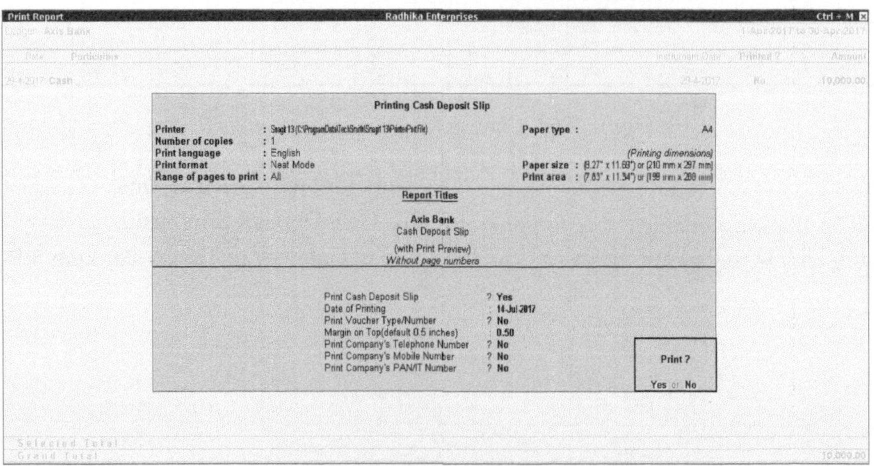


*Figure 7.67: Printing Cash Deposit Slip*

Two Copies will be generated:

(Banker's Copy)
**Cash Deposit Slip/Pay-in-Slip**

| | | | |
|---|---|---|---|
| Bank name | : **Axis Bank** | Date | : **14-Jul-2017** |
| Branch name | : | | |
| Account no. | : | | |
| Account holder name | : **Radhika Enterprises** | | |

| Denominations | | Amount |
|---|---|---|
| 2000 X | | |
| 1000 X | | |
| 500 X | | |
| 100 X | **100** | **10,000.00** |
| 50 X | | |
| 20 X | | |
| 10 X | | |
| 5 X | | |
| 2 X | | |
| 1 X | | |
| Others | | |
| **Total** | | **₹ 10,000.00** |

Amount (in words) : **INR Ten Thousand Only**

Deposited by | Received by

Signature | Signature

(Customer's Copy)
**Cash Deposit Slip/Pay-in-Slip**

| | | | |
|---|---|---|---|
| Bank name | : **Axis Bank** | Date | : **14-Jul-2017** |
| Branch name | : | | |
| Account no. | : | | |
| Account holder name | : **Radhika Enterprises** | | |

| Denominations | | Amount |
|---|---|---|
| 2000 X | | |
| 1000 X | | |
| 500 X | | |
| 100 X | **100** | **10,000.00** |
| 50 X | | |
| 20 X | | |
| 10 X | | |
| 5 X | | |
| 2 X | | |
| 1 X | | |
| Others | | |
| **Total** | | **₹ 10,000.00** |

Amount (in words) : **INR Ten Thousand Only**

Deposited by | Received by

Signature | Signature

*Figure 7.68: Printed Cash Deposit Slip*

Similarly you can generate the Cheque Deposit Slip from Banking Report

### 7.8.6 Payment Advice

The **Payment Advice** option enables the user to generate payment advice for the cheques that are issued to the suppliers and other parties.

The following illustration will demonstrate how to generate a payment advice.

Let us generate a payment advice for Payments made to Ramesh & Sons ₹ 15,000on 10-04-2017 by Bank Account. To print **Payment Advice,**

- Create Ledger by name of Ramesh & Sons under Sundry Creditor.

- Pass Payment entry Debited Ramesh & Sons & Credited Axis Bank
- **Go to** Gateway of Tally > Banking > Payment Advice
- Select the ledger to which the payment is made, from the list of ledgers. (Select **Ramesh & Sons** from the list of ledgers)
- Press **Space Bar** to select the payment vouchers recorded on **10-04-2017.**

The **Payment Advice** screen appears as shown below:

**Radhika Enterprises**

**Payment Advice**

**M/s. Ramesh & Sons** Date : **14-Jul-2017**

Karnataka -

Dear Sir/Madam,

Please find below the payment details.

| Bill Ref. | Bill Date | | Amount |
|---|---|---|---|
| On Account | | | 15,000.00 |
| | Nett Amount | | ₹ 15,000.00 |

| Payment Details | | | |
|---|---|---|---|
| Payment Mode | Instrument Details | Issued From | Amount |
| Cheque | No.: 112246<br>Dt: 10-Apr-2017 | Axis Bank | 15,000.00 |
| | | Total | ₹ 15,000.00 |

Kindly acknowledge the receipt.

Thanking You

Authorised Signatory Receiver's Signature

*Figure 7.69: Payment Advice screen*

### 7.8.7 Bank Reconciliation

Reconciling the Company's Bank Accounts with the Bank Statement is a fundamental and regular task of accounting. This process is referred to as Bank Reconciliation.

The following illustration will demonstrate how you can reconcile bank transactions.

To view and reconcile the transactions relating to Bank Account for Radhika Enterprises

1. **Go to** Gateway of Tally > Banking > Bank Reconciliation
2. Select **Axis Bank** as the Bank from the **List of Bank**
3. Set the Period as **01-04-20615** to **30-04-2017**
4. The **Bank Reconciliation** screen displays Balance as per Company Books, Amounts not reflected in Bank and Balance as per bank at the bottom of the screen

   You can see there is a difference in the Balance as per Bank and the Balance as per Company Books.

   The **Bank Reconciliation** screen appears as shown below:
5. Enter the **Bank dates** as **15-04-2017** (Once the dates are entered, you will find the **Bank Balance as per Company books** is impacted i.e., decreases/increases accordingly)

The **Bank Reconciliation** screen appears as shown below:

You can observe that the balances in the books of the company are balanced and the field **Amounts not Reflected in Bank** is blank.

This means the accounts are reconciled.

**Note:**
- The Bank Reconciliation screen can also be accessed from Gateway of Tally > Display > Accounts Books > Cash/ Bank Books > Select Bank Ledger > Select a month > F5: Reconcile.
- The Bank Date has be to be provided based on the Instrument Date and not on the Voucher Date

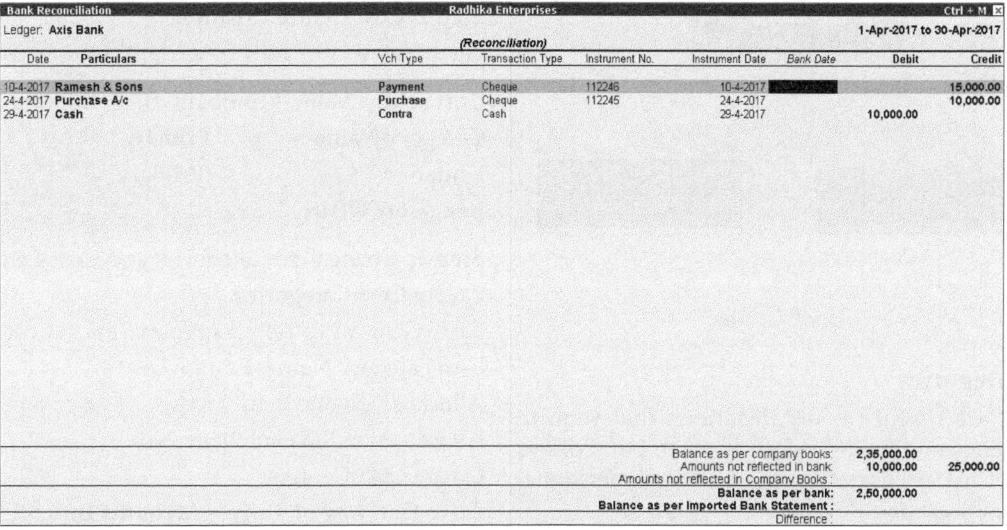

Bank Reconciliation — Radhika Enterprises — Ctrl + M

Ledger: **Axis Bank** — *(Reconciliation)* — 1-Apr-2017 to 30-Apr-2017

| Date | Particulars | Vch Type | Transaction Type | Instrument No. | Instrument Date | Bank Date | Debit | Credit |
|---|---|---|---|---|---|---|---|---|
| 10-4-2017 | Ramesh & Sons | Payment | Cheque | 112246 | 10-4-2017 | | | 15,000.00 |
| 24-4-2017 | Purchase A/c | Purchase | Cheque | 112245 | 24-4-2017 | | | 10,000.00 |
| 29-4-2017 | Cash | Contra | Cash | | 29-4-2017 | | 10,000.00 | |

| | Debit | Credit |
|---|---|---|
| Balance as per company books: | 2,35,000.00 | |
| Amounts not reflected in bank: | 10,000.00 | 25,000.00 |
| Amounts not reflected in Company Books: | | |
| **Balance as per bank:** | 2,50,000.00 | |
| **Balance as per Imported Bank Statement:** | | |
| Difference: | | |

*Figure 7.70: Bank Reconciliation screen*

Bank Reconciliation — Radhika Enterprises — Ctrl + M

Ledger: **Axis Bank** — *(Reconciliation)* — 1-Apr-2017 to 30-Apr-2017

| Date | Particulars | Vch Type | Transaction Type | Instrument No. | Instrument Date | Bank Date | Debit | Credit |
|---|---|---|---|---|---|---|---|---|
| 10-4-2017 | Ramesh & Sons | Payment | Cheque | 112246 | 10-4-2017 | 15-4-2017 | | 15,000.00 |
| 24-4-2017 | Purchase A/c | Purchase | Cheque | 112245 | 24-4-2017 | | | 10,000.00 |
| 29-4-2017 | Cash | Contra | Cash | | 29-4-2017 | | 10,000.00 | |

| | Debit |
|---|---|
| Balance as per company books: | 2,35,000.00 |
| Amounts not reflected in bank: | 10,000.0 |
| Amounts not reflected in Company Books: | |
| **Balance as per bank:** | 2,35,000.0 |
| **Balance as per Imported Bank Statement:** | |
| Difference: | |

Accept ?

Yes or No

*Figure 7.71: Bank Reconciliation screen*

**Tip**

- Press **CTRL+Enter** on the required transaction row to open the voucher in alteration mode.
- In **F12: Configuration** or in **Print Configuration**, set the option **Show Payment Favouring/Received From** to **Yes** to display the **Payment Favouring/Received From** details in the report. The **Favouring Name** column displays only those names which are different from the **Party/Ledger** account names.
- Press **C: Create Voucher** to create vouchers from the reconciliation screen itself.
- In case, if you have opening bank transactions (transactions pertaining to the last year) which are not yet credited/ debited into Bank Account, you can provide Opening BRS for such transactions by pressing **ALT+U** (**U: Opening BRS**) and provide the information in the **Unreconciled Details** for sub-screen.

## 7.9 COST CENTRE AND COST CATEGORIES

A **Cost Centre** is any unit of an organisation to which transactions (generally, revenue) can be allocated. When only costs or expenses are allocated to these units, they are referred to as Cost Centres. When profits are also allocated to these units, they become Profit Centres.

**Cost Centre:** "Tally.ERP 9's cost centres allow a dimensional analysis of financial information. Tally.ERP 9 gives you the cost centre break-up of each transaction as well as details of transactions for each cost centre."

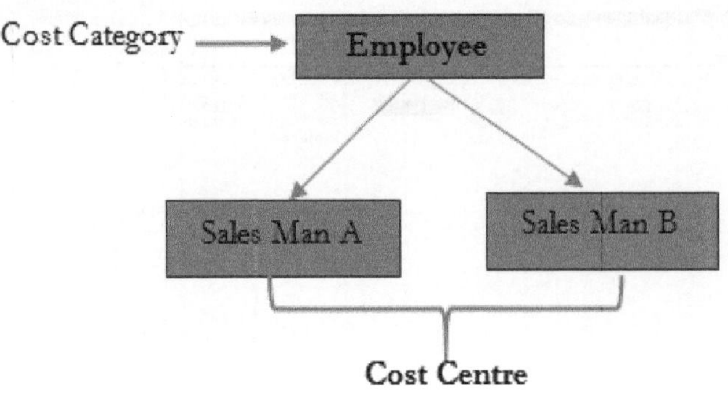


### 7.9.1 Cost Categories

Cost Categories are useful for organisations that require allocation of Revenue and Non-Revenue Items to parallel sets of Cost Centres. Cost categories facilitate third dimensional reporting of Expenditure and Revenue.

Some of the examples are:

- Region-wise or Geography-wise
- Employee-wise
- Department-wise

Let us take an example of Cost Centres and Cost Categories given above. To understand the above examples in combination of cost centre and categories given below:

***Scenario:***

**Sultan Traders** started a company as on 1-4-2017. They sell **Software.** In these process they have a different departments and many employees in the organization. In this activity business generates some expenses and income for different levels.

The objective of an organization to activate Cost Centre and Cost Category is to generate and view the reports of sources of income and expenses department-wise and employees-wise, which helps to develop and control the finance.

Let us create the Company Company Name: **Sultan Traders**

Financial year: 01-04-2017

### 7.9.2 Using Cost Category and Cost Centre in Transactions

Let us, illustrate the above Employee scenario:

As on 01-04-2017, Sultan Traders paid Rs. 60,000 towards Advertisement, out of which Rs. 30,000 was paid towards Mumbai Office and Rs. 30,000 towards Kolkata office (Use Cost Centre).

On 02-04-2017, the sales team of Sultan Traders began customer visits for giving a demo of its Software. The company provided Rs. 25,000 towards their transportation and food expenses, out of which, Rs. 15,000 is allocated for Ram (Salesman) and Rs. 10,000 to Hari (Salesman) (Use Cost Center and Cost Category).

**Step 1:** Activation

To activate Cost Centre and Cost Categories:

Enable the following options from **Gateway of Tally>F11: Company feature>F1: Accounting Feature.**

- Maintain Cost Centre set to **Yes**
- More than one Payroll/cost category set to **Yes**

**Step 2: Cost Centre Creation**

**Go to** Gateway of Tally > Accounts Info > Cost Centres > Create

**Cost centre Name-Mumbai Office, Kolkata Office**
**Category Name- Primary**
**Under- Primary**
**Bangalore Office**

**Step 3:** Create Cost Categories and Cost Centre

**Create Cost Categories**

**Go to** Gateway of Tally > Accounts Info > Cost Category > Create

Cost category Name- Employee
Allocate Revenue Item- Yes
Allocate Non Revenue Item- No

**Create Cost Centres**

Go to **Gateway of Tally > Accounts Info > Cost Centres >**

**Cost Centre Name- Ram, Hari**
**Category Name- Employee**
**Under- Primary**

**Create Ledger Master Kotak Bank**

Go to **Gateway of Tally > Accounts Info > Ledger > Create ICICI Bank under Bank Accounts give opening balance Rs. 2,50,000**

Go to **Gateway of Tally > Accounts Info > Ledger > Create Advertisement Expenses under Indirect Expenses and ensure Cost centres are applicable is set to Yes**

**Step 3:** Record Rent Payment Voucher

1. Go to **Gateway of Tally > Accounting voucher > F5: Payment**
2. To pass the entry in double entry mode **Disable the option F12 > Use single entry mode pymt/rcpt/contra= No**
3. Enter date as **01-04-2017**
4. Dr Advertisement Expenses **Rs. 60,000** next you will get the option **Cost Allocation for Screen**.

   Select Primary cost category. Then, Select Cost centre as Mumbai office Rs. 30,000 and Kolkata Office Rs. 30,000
5. Cr ICICI Bank Account and accept the Payment.

**Step 4:** Record Payment Voucher

1. Create Office Expenses Ledger under Indirect Expenses and ensure Cost centres are applicable is set to Yes
2. Go to **Gateway of Tally > Accounting voucher > F5: Payment**
3. To pass the entry in double entry mode, Disable the option **F12 > Use single entry mode pymt/rcpt/contra= No**
4. Enter date as **02-04-2017**
5. Dr **Office Expenses Rs. 25,000** next you get the option Cost of Allocation
   - Select cost category as Employees
   - Then, Select Cost centre as Ram Rs. 15000
   - Hari Rs. 10000

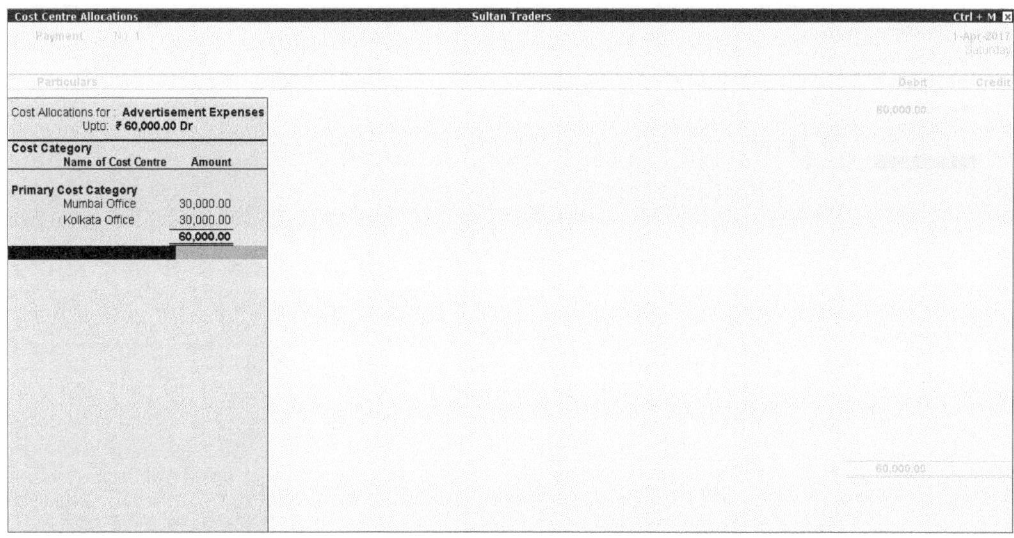


*Figure 7.72: Cost Centre Allocations*

*Figure 7.73: Cost centre allocation screen*

6. Cr ICIC Bank Account and accept the Payment

### 7.9.3 Cost Centre Classes

Cost Centre Classes are used to automate cost centre allocations in transactions. On creating a cost centre class, you need to select it in the voucher screen before making the entry. You can also use cost centre classes when Voucher Classes are being used.

This illustration helps us understand the application of cost centre classes in Item invoice mode.

On 20-4-2017, the company has pre-allocated the Training Expenses to Employee-wise ( 45% to Ram and 55% to Hari.) Company paid Rs. 10,000 for training expenses.

**Step 1:** Activate the Cost centre Class

1. Go to **Gateway of Tally > F11: Features > F1: Accounting Features**
2. Press **Enter** from the option **Use Pre-defined Cost Centre Allocations** during Entry to view the **Auto Cost Allocation** screen
3. Type **Class Name** in the **Employee Expenses**
4. Press **Enter** and specify the details
5. Select **Cost Category** as **Employees**
6. Select the **Cost centres** and enter the **percentage of allocation** as follows:
   - Ram 45%
   - Hari 55%
7. Press Enter to accept the Auto cost allocation screen and you will come back to Accounting feature screen.
8. Press Enter and save the Accounting feature screen.

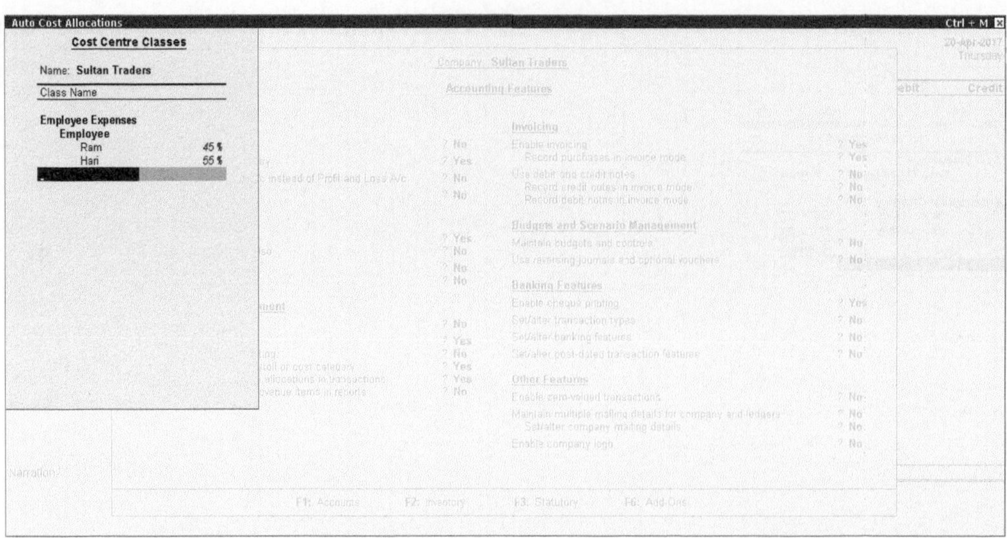


*Figure 7.74: Auto Cost Allocations screen*

**Step 2:** Create the Required Ledger

Go to **Gateway of Tally > Accounts Info > Ledger**

Create Training Expenses under Indirect Expenses and ensure Cost centres are applicable is set to Yes

1. Select the **Cost Centre/Classes**

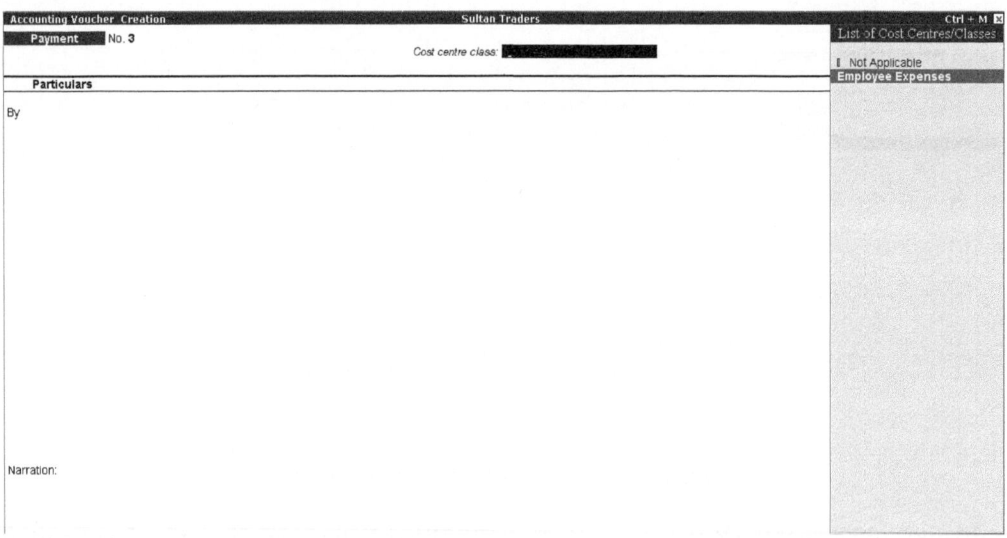


*Figure 7.75: Accounting Voucher Creation*

2. Select Training Expenses as Debit side
3. Select ICICI Bank under credit side

## 7.9.4 Cost Centre Reports

Cost centre reports are primarily performance reports. To access Cost Centre reports,

Go to **Gateway of Tally > Display > Statements of Accounts > Cost Centres**

The Cost Centres Menu comprises of the following sub menus:

- Category Summary
- Cost Centre Break-up
- Ledger Break-up
- Group Break-up

Let us discuss each report in detail.

### *7.9.4.1 Category Summary*

This report lists out all cost categories for which transactions have been allocated. Below each cost category, all the cost centres under the cost category are also listed, with the sub-cost centres, if any.

The **Cost Category Summary** report for the period 1-4-2017 to 20-04-2017 appears as shown below:

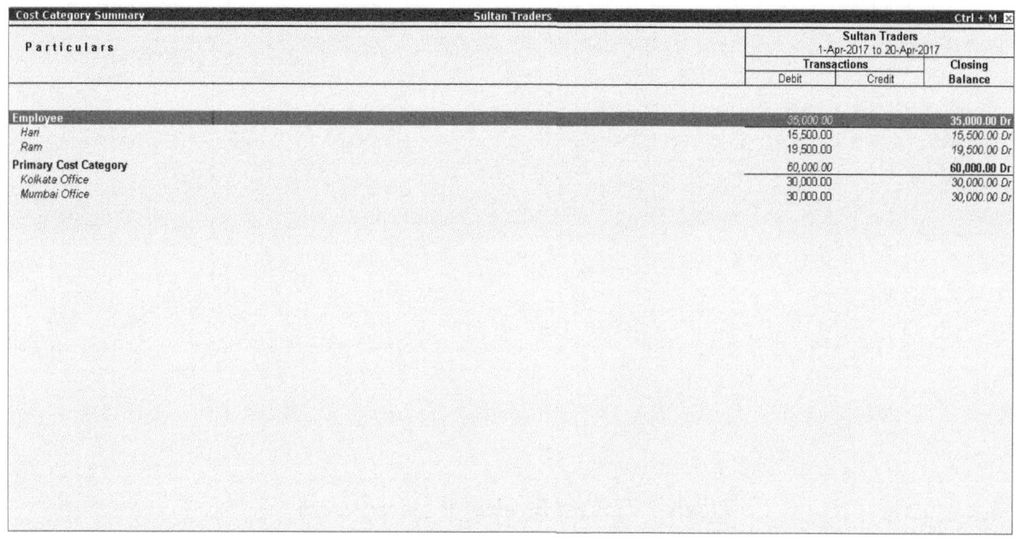

| Particulars | Sultan Traders 1-Apr-2017 to 20-Apr-2017 Transactions Debit | Credit | Closing Balance |
|---|---|---|---|
| **Employee** | 35,000.00 | | 35,000.00 Dr |
| *Hari* | 15,500.00 | | 15,500.00 Dr |
| *Ram* | 19,500.00 | | 19,500.00 Dr |
| **Primary Cost Category** | 60,000.00 | | 60,000.00 Dr |
| *Kolkata Office* | 30,000.00 | | 30,000.00 Dr |
| *Mumbai Office* | 30,000.00 | | 30,000.00 Dr |

*Figure 7.76: Cost Category Summary report*

It is possible to drill down to the transaction level from this report.

## *Cost Centre Vouchers Report*

All transactions pertaining to a cost centre will be displayed in this report.

Press Enter on the required option and you will get the Cost Centre Vouchers report

### *7.9.4.2 Cost Centre Break-up*

We noticed that transactions were allocated to cost centres. A list of all ledger accounts used in these transactions, with details of the transaction values and balance are displayed here.

Select **Cost Centre Break-up** from the **Cost Centres** menu to open it.

Select **Ram**, from the **List of Cost Centres**

Press **F2** and change the period 1-04-2017 to 20-04-2017. The **Breakup of Cost Centres** screen appears as shown below:

| Particulars | Cost Centre: Ram Sultan Traders 1-Apr-2017 to 20-Apr-2017 Transactions Debit | Credit | Closing Balance |
|---|---|---|---|
| **Indirect Expenses** | 19,500.00 | | 19,500.00 Dr |
| *Office Expenses* | 15,000.00 | | 15,000.00 Dr |
| *Training Expenses* | 4,500.00 | | 4,500.00 Dr |
| **Grand Total** | 19,500.00 | | 19,500.00 Dr |

*Figure 7.77: Breakup of Cost Centres screen*

### *7.9.4.3 Ledger Break-up*

One ledger can be allocated to different cost centres. For example, the ledger Cost of expenses is allocated to Junior and senior. We can view a comparative report of conveyance expenditures incurred by the two cost centres using the **Ledger Break-up** report.

1. From the **Cost Centres** menu, select **Ledger Break-up**
2. Select **Training Expenses**

The **Cost Breakup of Ledger** screen appears as shown below:

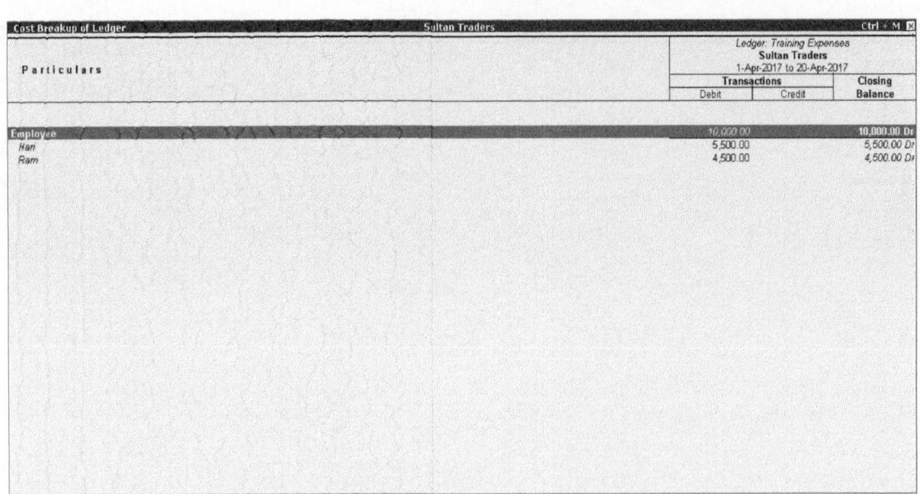


*Figure 7.78: Cost Breakup of Ledger screen*

### 7.9.4.4 *Group Break-up*

This report displays the summarised information of all Cost Centres for the selected Group. You can drill down to the list of voucher

Similar to the method that applies to Ledger Break-up, explore the Group Break-up of Cost Centres.

### *Activity*

Create a company with the name of Raghuraj Pvt. Ltd. Financial year and book beginning is 01-04-2017

1. On 01-04-2017 Company paid Commission through cheque of Kotak Bank, Rs. 15,000 to his Agent Dinesh Rs. 5,500 and Mahesh Rs. 9,500 (Hint: Create Kotak Bank with opening balance Rs. 1,50,000).
2. On 02-04-2017 Paid electricity bill of Rs. 8,000 to his Bangaluru Branch Rs. 3,500 and rest of amount for Delhi Branch through Kotak Bank.
3. Paid incentive Rs. 20,000 to Employee Raghu 20%, Nidhi 30% and Suresh 50% through Kotak Bank.

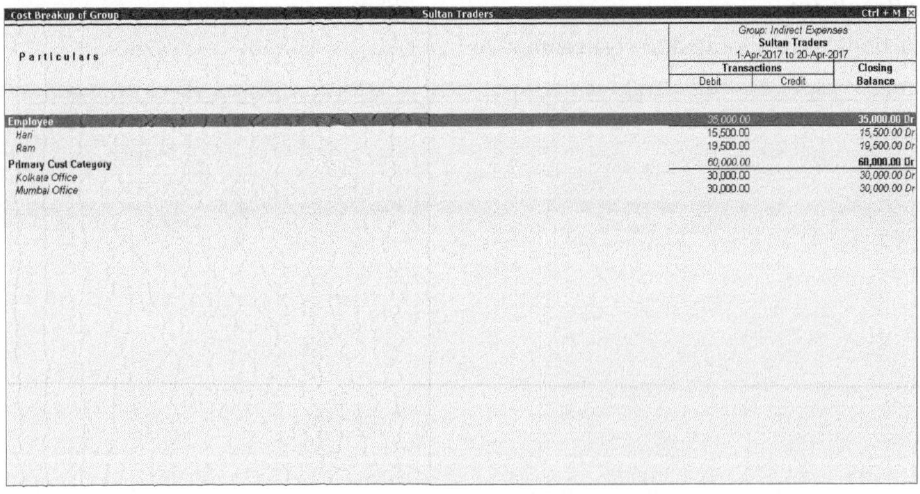


*Figure 7.79: Cost Breakup of Group screen*

## 7.10 ORDER PROCESSING

**Order Processing refers to:**

- placing purchase orders with suppliers/receiving order from customers for sale
- tracking the receipt of the goods/tracking the delivery of the goods
- paying for the goods purchased/receiving the payment for the goods sold.

**Using Order processing you can:**

- track the order position of a stock item
- know whether the goods ordered have been received or not
- know whether the orders have been delivered on time and the reasons for the delay, if any

### *Scenario*

To understand Order Processing in Tally.ERP 9, let us consider that Surya Traders placed an order for DELL Latitude Laptop from Jivan Ram & Sons and then sold it to Ridhi technologies after they received the order.

### 7.10.1 Purchase Order Processing

Let us use the same company: Surya Traders created previously. To activate Order Processing, enable the following options in the

**F11: Features (Inventory Features):** Allow Purchase Order Processing Allow Sales Order Processing Use Tracking Numbers (Delivery / Receipt Notes)

The illustration below will help you understand how to record a Purchase Order.

### *Illustration*

On 05-12-2017, raise a purchase order on Jivan Ram & Sons for 10 Nos of Dell Latitude Laptop at Rs. 25,000 each. The Laptops are due on 06-12-2017 and are to be stored in Onsite (godown).

**Step 1:** Create Required Masters Party

Party Ledger- Jivan Ram & Sons
Under- Sundry Debtros
Maintain Balance Bill-by-bill- Yes
Inventory Values are affected- No

Stock Item- Dell Latitude Laptop
Under - Dell
Unit- Nos

**Step 2:** Configure Purchase Order

1. Go to **Gateway of Tally > Order Vouchers > F4: Purc. Order**
2. Click **F12: Configure:**
   - Set **Complete Accounting Allocations in Order/ Delivery Note** to **Yes.** Enabling this option will allow you to select accounting masters (Purchase ledgers) in the order voucher
   - Set **Use Common Ledger A/c for Item Allocation** to **No**

**Step 3:** Create Purchase Order

In the Purchase Order Voucher,

1. Enter date as 05-12-2017
2. Select Jivan Ram & Sons in the Party's A/c Name field
3. The voucher number will be displayed in the Order No. field by default. This field can be changed as per requirement.

   Enter ORD-001 in this field
4. Under Name of the item, select Dell Latitude Laptop and press Enter. The Item Allocations screen appears
5. Enter 06-12-2017 in the Due on field. This is the due date for the delivery of the item. This will enable the monitoring of outstanding deliveries. The order can be split for delivery on different dates
6. Select Onsite in the Location field. (Only when the multiple Godown feature is enabled, this field will be displayed)
7. Enter 10 in the Quantity field and Rs. 25,000 in the Rate field. The Amount will be calculated automatically

   The completed Item Allocations screen appears as shown below:

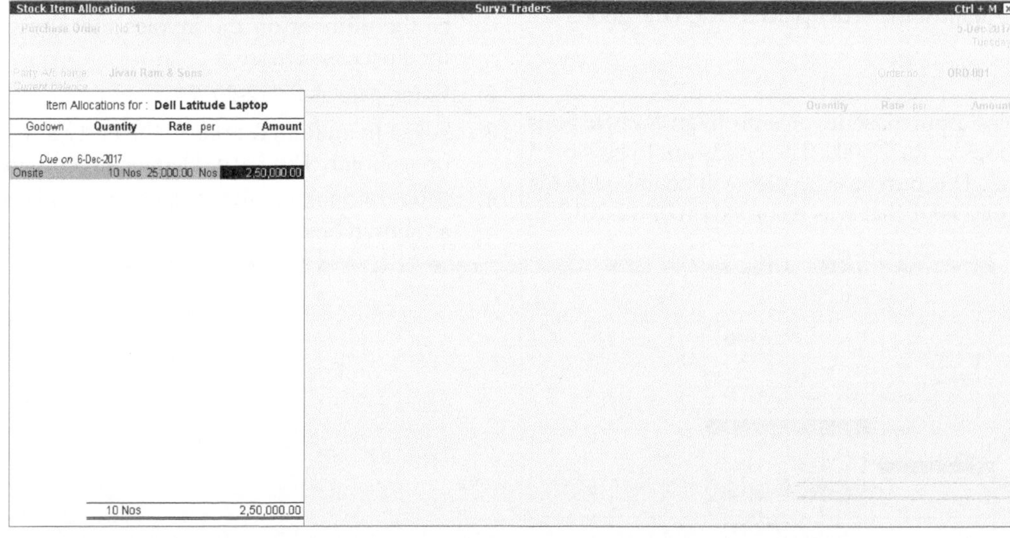


*Figure 7.80: Item Allocation for Dell Latitude Laptop*

8. Accept the **Item Allocation** screen to return to the **Purchase Order** screen
9. Press **Enter** from the **Amount** field to view the **Accounting Details** screen
10. Allocate the amount to Purchase A/c and return to the **Purchase Order** screen
11. Press **Enter** on the blank field
12. **Narration** can be entered, if required

    The completed Purchase Order screen appears as shown below:
14. Accept the Purchase Order

Figure 7.81: Purchase Order

### 7.10.1.1 *Altering a Purchase Order*

To alter a Purchase Order,

Go to **Gateway of Tally > Display > Day Book > F4: Chg Vch** and select Purchase Orders or **Go to Gateway of Tally > Display > Inventory Books > Purchase Order Book** and select the required Purchase Order to open the Order Voucher Alteration screen.

**Raising Purchase Invoices (or Delivery Notes) against Purchase Orders**

Purchase Invoice or Delivery Notes can be raised against previously recorded purchase orders.

The illustration below will help you understand how to record a purchase invoice against the order placed when the goods are received.

### *Illustration*

On 07-12-2017, raise a purchase invoice on Jivan Ram & Sons for 10 Nos of Laptops at Rs. 25,000. The goods are to be stored in Onsite (godown). This purchase invoice will be linked to the purchase order – ORD-001 that was recorded on 07-12-2017.

**Step 1:** Configure Purchase Invoice

1. Go to **Gateway of Tally > Accounting Vouchers > F9: Purchase**
2. Make sure that the **Voucher Creation screen** is in **Item Invoice mode**
3. Click **F12: Configure** button and set the following option to **Yes:**

   Accept Supplementary Details. Enabling this option will allow you to select the order number against which the purchase invoice is being raised

**Step 2:** Record Purchase Invoice

1. In the Supplier Invoice No. field enter JR-001/022. This will be the number on the invoice that the supplier raises on the Purchase Order
2. Enter date as 07-12-2017
3. Select Jivan Ram & Sons in the Party's A/c Name field and press Enter. The Party Details screen will appear
4. Select ORD-001 in the Order No(s) field under Party Details as shown below:

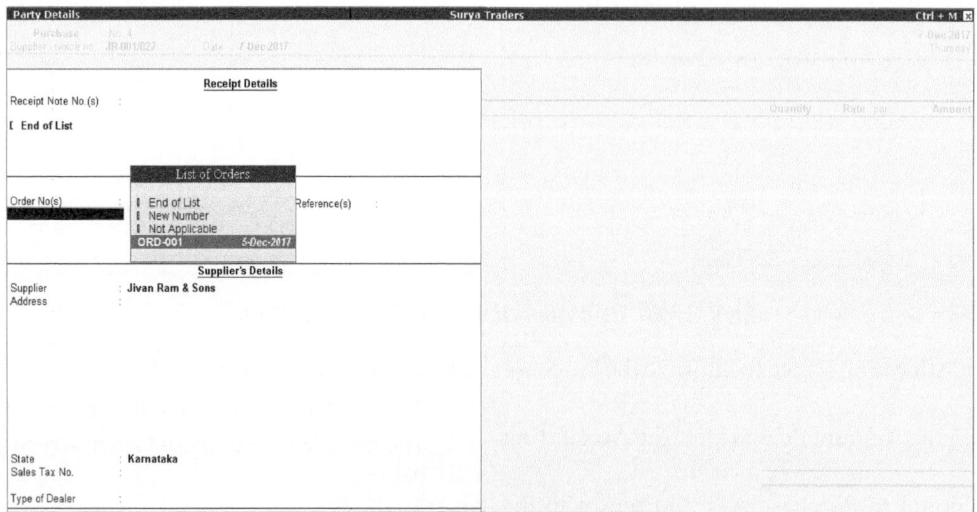


Figure 7.82: Party Details screen

5. **Accept** the screen to return to the voucher creation screen
6. The stock item Dell Latitude Laptop will appear automatically. Press **Enter** and the **Item Allocations screen** will appear with the quantity details
7. Select **Not Applicable** in the **Tracking number field** as goods are accompanying the bill
8. Select ORD-001 again in the **Order Number field** and **accept** the **Item Allocations screen**
9. Freight charges details will be automatically captured

The completed Purchase Invoice appears as shown

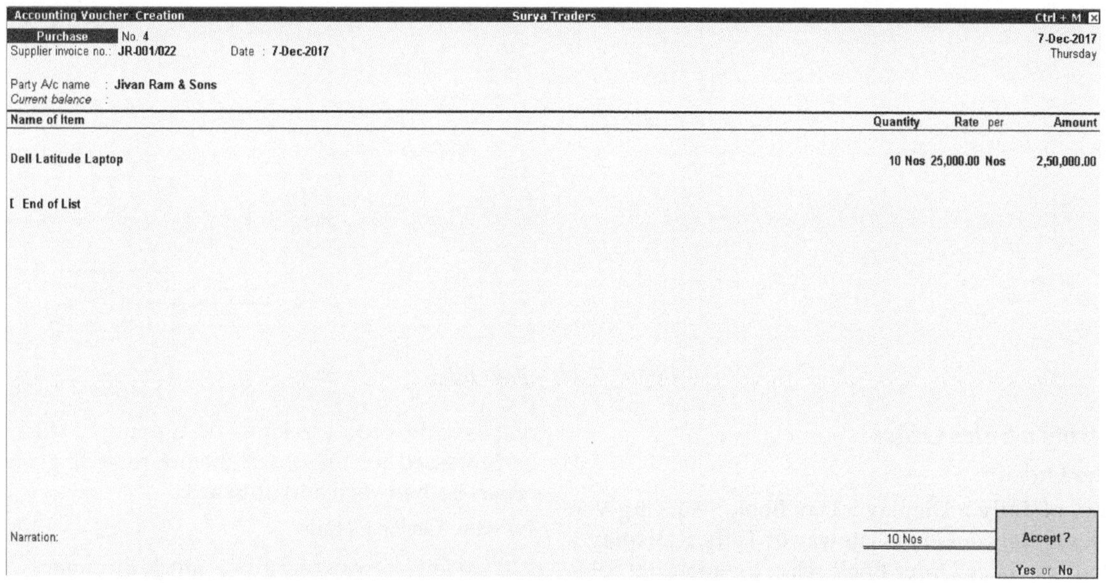


*Figure 7.83: Purchase Invoice*

10. **Accept** the Purchase Invoice

To activate Order Processing in Tally.ERP 9, enable the following options in the F11: Features (Inventory Features):

- Allow Purchase Order Processing
- Allow Sales Order Processing
- Use Tracking Numbers (Delivery / Receipt Notes)

**Note:** Use the same company- Surya Traders that was created earlier

## 7.10.2 Sales Order Processing

The illustration given below will help you understand how to record an order received for a sale. These orders are recorded in a Sales Order Voucher.

### *Illustration*

On 10-12-2017, record a sales order for the order received from Ridhi Technologies (vide Order No. SL-004) for 9 Nos of Dell Latitude Laptop at Rs. 39,000 each. The due date for delivering the Laptop is 15-12-2017.

**Step 1:** Create Required Masters

| | |
|---|---|
| Party Ledger- | Ridhi Technologies |
| Under- | Sundry Debtors |
| Maintain Balance bill-by-bill- | Yes |
| Inventory value- | No |

**Step 2:** Create Sales Order

1. Go to **Gateway of Tally > Order Vouchers > F5: Sales Order**
2. Enter the date as 10-12-2017
3. Select Ridhi Technologies in the Party's A/c Name field
4. Enter SL-004 in the Order No field. The voucher number will be displayed here by default. This field is editable as this Order No. refers to the customer's order number which is different from the voucher number
5. Under Name of the Item, select Dell Latitude Laptop and press Enter. The Item Allocations screen will appear
6. Enter 15-12-2015 in the Due on field. This is the due date for the delivering the item to the customer
7. Select Onsite in the Location field. (Only when the Multiple Godown feature is enabled, this field will be displayed)
8. Enter 9 in the Quantity field, and Rs. 39,000 in the Rate field. The Amount will be calculated automatically
9. Allocate the amount to Sales A/c and return to the Sales Order screen
10. Press Enter on the blank field
11. Type the narration if required

The completed Sales Order appears as shown below:

13. Accept the Sales Order

*Figure 7.84: Sales Order*

### *7.10.2.1Altering a Sales Order*

To alter a Sales Order,

Go to **Gateway of Tally > Display > Day Book > F4: Chg Vch** and select Sales Orders or **Go to Gateway of Tally > Display > Inventory Books > Sales Order Book** select the required Sales Order to open the Order Voucher Alteration screen

***Activity:***

**Raising Sales Invoices (or Receipt Notes) against Sales Orders**

Sales invoice or Receipt Notes can be raised against previously recorded sales orders.

### 7.10.3 Viewing Order Details

After recording purchase and sales orders, you can view the details of the orders to know the amount of stock that needs to be processed for the order, (before recording invoices for the order) both inward and outward.

To view Order Details,

1. Go to **Gateway of Tally > Stock Summary**
2. Press the **button ALT + F7**
3. Select **Sales Orders Outstanding**, and set **Use Due orders only** to **No**
4. Select Dell and drill down to the **Order Details** screen
5. In the **Sales Order Outstanding** screen, press **ALT+F1** to view the report in detailed format

The Order Details screen appears as shown below:

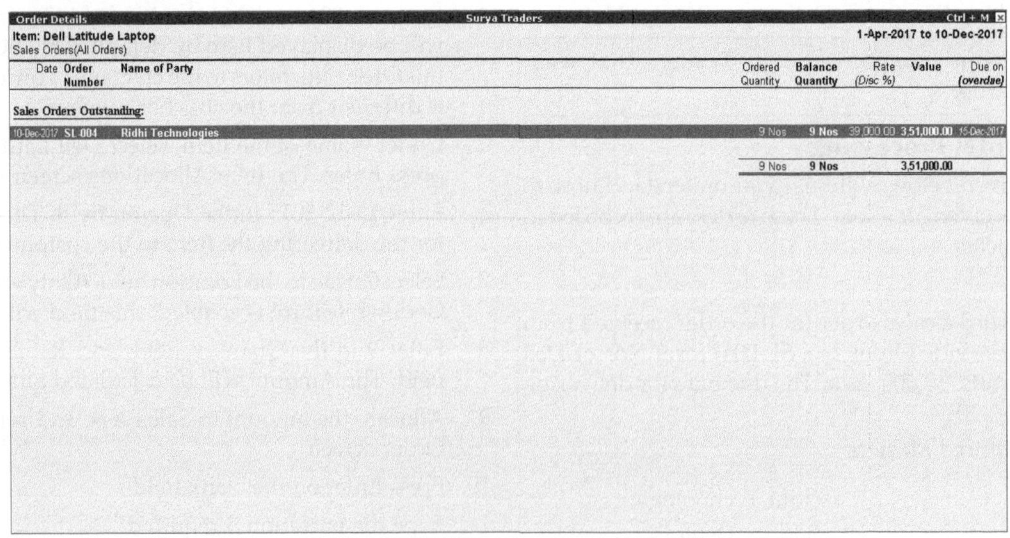

*Figure 7.85: Order Details screen*

The Order Details report is generated as on 16th December, 2017. Based on the period of the report and the due date of the order, the report will display the outstanding status of the order.

**Note:** The Sales Order Outstanding screen, by default will show the report as on last date of the voucher entry. Hence, change the period to view the report of the desired period.

6. Now, press **F2** or click F2: Period and change the period till 16-12-2017

7. Click **F12: Configure** button and set the following to Yes:
   - Show Cleared Purchase Orders

The report now shows the Outstanding positions of the Sales and Purchase Orders for the stock item Dell Latitude Laptop.

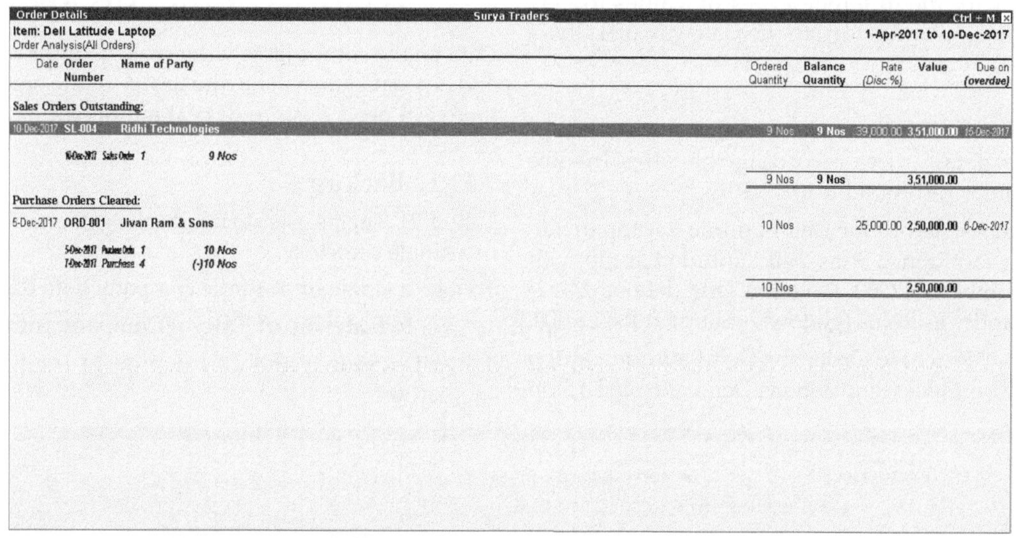

Order Details — Surya Traders — Ctrl + M

Item: Dell Latitude Laptop — 1-Apr-2017 to 10-Dec-2017

Order Analysis(All Orders)

| Date | Order Number | Name of Party | | Ordered Quantity | Balance Quantity | Rate (Disc %) | Value | Due on (overdue) |
|---|---|---|---|---|---|---|---|---|
| **Sales Orders Outstanding:** | | | | | | | | |
| 10-Dec-2017 | SL-004 | Ridhi Technologies | | 9 Nos | 9 Nos | 39,000.00 | 3,51,000.00 | 15-Dec-2017 |
| | 10-Dec-2017 Sales Order 1 | | 9 Nos | | | | | |
| | | | | 9 Nos | 9 Nos | | 3,51,000.00 | |
| **Purchase Orders Cleared:** | | | | | | | | |
| 5-Dec-2017 | ORD-001 | Jivan Ram & Sons | | 10 Nos | | 25,000.00 | 2,50,000.00 | 6-Dec-2017 |
| | 5-Dec-2017 Purchase Order 1 | | 10 Nos | | | | | |
| | 7-Dec-2017 Purchase 4 | | (-)10 Nos | | | | | |
| | | | | 10 Nos | | | 2,50,000.00 | |

*Figure 7.86: Order Details screen*

**Note:** The information changes instantly depending on the date filter you use. This is Tally.ERP 9's power of real time report generation

## 7.10.4 Display Columnar Orders & Stock Details

To view Columnar Order details, return to the Stock Summary screen:

- Click **F1: Detailed and view** the report as on 31-12-2017
- Press **ALT + N** or click Auto-Column Button, select Orders & Stock Details
- Remove Rate and Value from display, by configuring it in **F12: Configuration** (This will enable all the columns to fit in one screen)

The Sales Order Outstandings (Stock group wise) screen appears as shown below:

Stock Summary — Surya Traders — Ctrl + M

| Particulars | Dell Surya Traders 1-Apr-2017 to 10-Dec-2017 Stock details for : Our stock with us and third party | Dell Surya Traders 1-Apr-2017 to 10-Dec-2017 Sales Orders Outstanding | Dell Surya Traders 1-Apr-2017 to 10-Dec-2017 Saleable Stock | Dell Surya Traders 1-Apr-2017 to 10-Dec-2017 Purchase Orders Outstanding | Dell Surya Traders 1-Apr-2017 to 10-Dec-2017 Nett Stock |
|---|---|---|---|---|---|
| | Closing Balance Quantity | On Order Quantity | Closing Balance Quantity | On Order Quantity | Closing Balance Quantity |
| Dell Latitude Laptop | 10 Nos | 9 Nos | 1 Nos | | 1 Nos |
| Grand Total | 10 Nos | 9 Nos | 1 Nos | | 1 Nos |

*Figure 7.87: Stock Summary*

| Tip |
|---|
| • You may further drill down each column to view it in detail.<br>• In the Stock Summary screen, you can even bring up a new column using the New Column button and get more options for more details.<br>• Experiment with the different Types of Values to get familiar with them and return to the Gateway of Tally. |

### *Activity*

Perform the following actions:

1. View Orders details after recording the Sales Invoice against the Order recorded on 10-12-2017.
2. Record a Purchase Order for Dell Latitude Laptop on 20-12-2017 on Jivvan Ram & Sons Dell Latitude Laptop with the Order Number – PO02. Give the Due date as 24-12-2017 and Quantity as 5 Nos (godown - Shop) at Rs. 25,000.
3. Record another Purchase Order for Dell Latitude Laptop on 24-12-2017 on Jivvan Ram & Sons Dell Latitude Laptop with the Order Number as PO03, Due date as 28-12-2017 and Quantity as 4 Nos (godown - Onsite) at Rs. 25,000.
4. On 25-12-2017, raise Sales Order on Ridhi Technologies with Order No. as RD/007 for 5 Nosof Dell Latitude Laptop (godown - Shop) at Rs. 28,000. Give the Due date as 30-12-2017.

## 7.11 DATA BACKUP AND RESTORE

Data on the computer is vulnerable to different types of threats and any data lost will be disastrous for the organisation. Hence, there is a need to store data at a different location by taking a backup.

### 7.11.1 Backup

Tally.ERP 9 helps users to take back up of one or more companies in a single directory.

To take a single or multiple company data backup,

1. Go to **Gateway of Tally > Company Info. > Backup**
2. Enter Source and Destination of the backup as shown below:

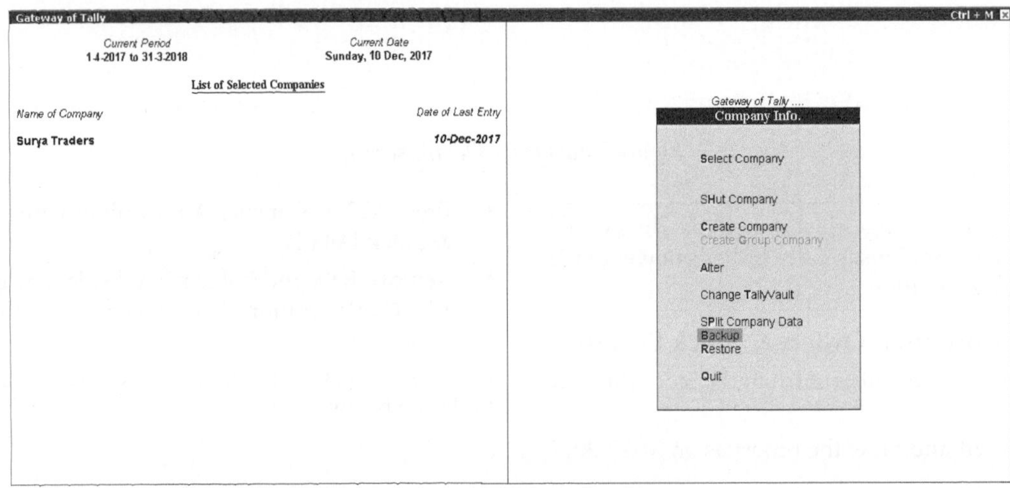


*Figure 7.88: Company Info. screen*

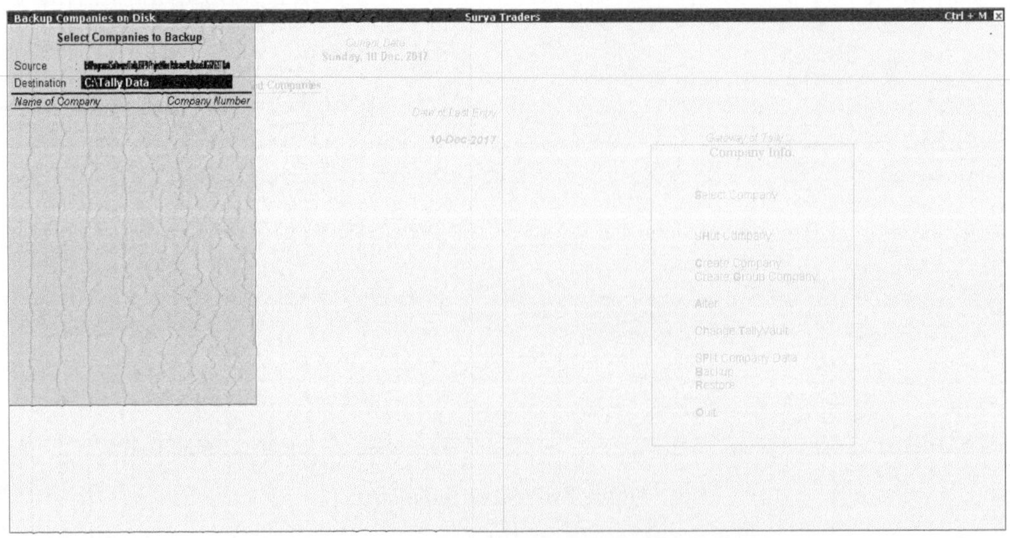


*Figure 7.89: Selecting Source and Destination for Backup*

3. Press Enter and the List of Companies available for backup will appear. Select the required companies for which data backup needs to be created, as shown below:
4. Once the required companies are selected, select End of List and accept the screen. The backup file is stored with the name TBK900.001.

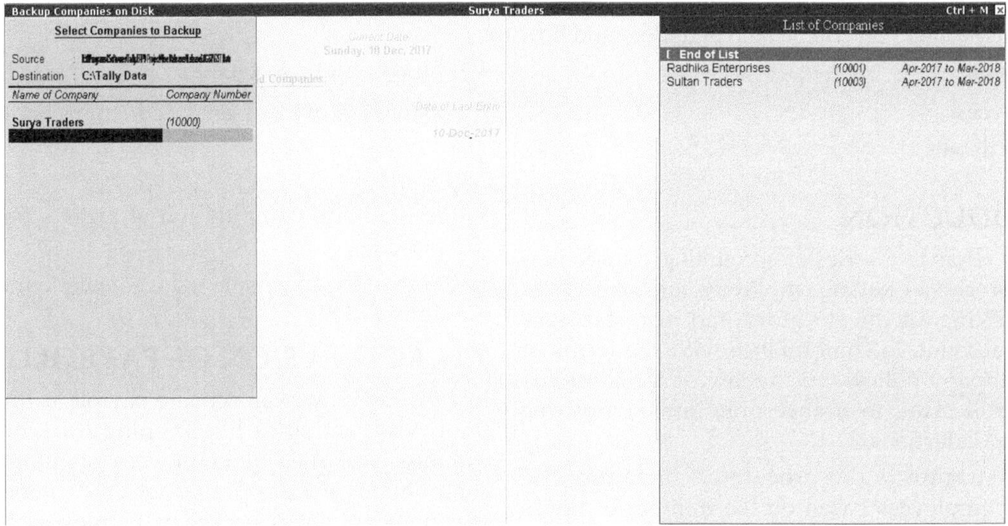


*Figure 7.90: Selecting Companies to Backup*

### 7.11.2 Restoring Data from a Backup File

The Restore functionality allows you to restore the data backup taken earlier.

While restoring the auto-back up data of multiple companies, the system displays the time of the last backup taken along with the auto-backup version. This helps in identifying the latest backup version to restore it.

1. Go to **Gateway of Tally > Company Info. > Restore**
2. Enter **Source and Destination** of the backup that needs to be restored
3. Select the required companies from the list of companies and then restore
4. Select **End of List** to complete the selection and accept the screen.

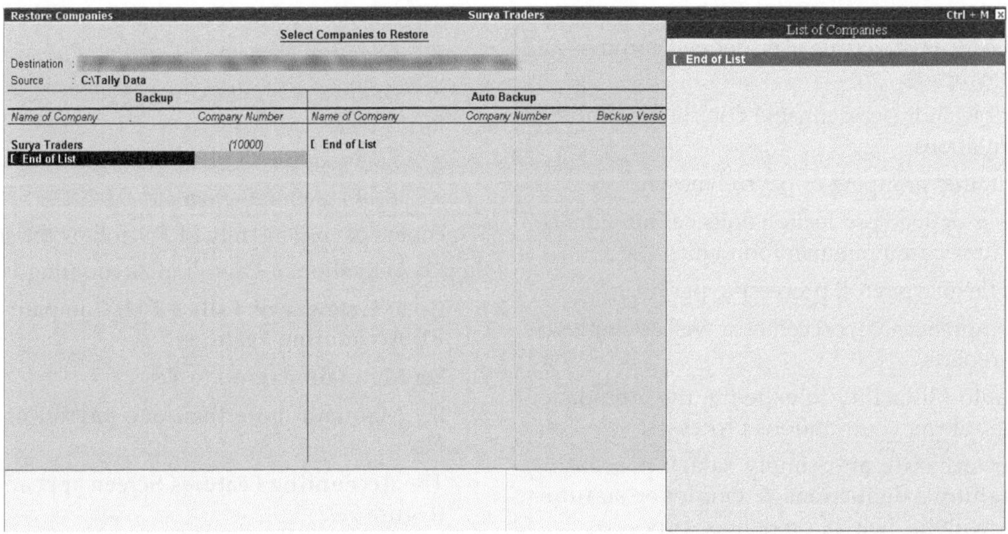


*Figure 7.91: Restores Companies on Disk*

# PAYROLL ADMINISTRATION

## LEARNING OBJECTIVES

After studying this section you will be able to understand how to:

- create pay heads
- create employees
- define salary details
- process and pay salary
- manage provident fund deductions and contribution

## 7.12 INTRODUCTION

The term payroll refers to a series of accounting transactions involved in the process of paying employees for the services rendered after taking all the statutory and non-statutory deductions into account, in conformance with the terms of employment, company policy and the law of the land i.e., payment of payroll taxes, insurance premiums, employee benefits and other deductions.

**Payroll Administration** is the process of managing the compensation of employees based on the number of hours worked by employees and it is the process of keeping the track of worked hours, commission earned by employees, statutory deductions and contributions and also it ensures that the company policies are adhering to employment laws.

## 7.13 FEATURES OF PAYROLL

- It is fully integrated with accounts to give you the benefits of simplified payroll processing and accounting.
- It has user defined classifications and sub-classifications for comprehensive reporting. This may be related to the employees, employee groups, pay components, departments etc.
- It provides the facility to create user-defined earnings and deductions pay heads.
- It allows flexible and user-definable criteria for simple or complex calculations
- It allows unlimited grouping of payroll master
- It supports user-defined production units i.e., attendance/ production/ time based remuneration units.
- It provides a flexible payroll processing period.
- It provides comprehensive cost center as well as employee-wise costing reports.
- It provides auto-fill facility to expedite the attendance, payroll and employer contributions processes.
- It ensures an accurate and timely salary processing, employee statutory deductions & employer statutory contributions with the help of predefined processes.
- It facilitates an accurate computation and deduction of ESI, EPF, professional tax, income tax, gratuity etc.
- It helps in the generation of statutory forms & challans for EPF, ESI, and income tax as prescribed.
- It allows drill-down facility to voucher level for any kind of alteration.
- It facilitates computation of arrears pertaining to prior period(s).
- Processing payments using the e-payments capability in Tally.ERP 9

## 7.14 ACTIVATION OF PAYROLL

In Tally.ERP 9, we can activate payroll feature and administer the payroll activities like keeping track of working hours, commission earned by employees, statutory deductions and contributions and also it manages the compensation based on the number of hours worked by Employees. In Tally.ERP 9, we can generate instant payroll reports like payroll statement, pay slip, pay head break up etc.

***Scenario***

**Sky Lark Pvt. Ltd**. deals in trading of Furniture's and it has expanded its business into multiple regions. To maintain proper sales process, the company has hired many sales executives and to maintain sales executive's compensation/payroll details, the company installed Tally.ERP 9 software.

To maintain payroll details in Tally.ERP 9, we need to create the company and activate Payroll feature

***Activity***: *Create the following company in Tally.ERP 9:*

- *Company Name: Sky Lark Pvt. Ltd.*
- *Address: #52, 8th Cross, Mahim Tech Park, Bengaluru-560001*
- *Financial year begins from: 01-04-2017*
- *Books beginning from : 01-04-2017*

To activate payroll in Tally ERP 9, follow the steps given below:

**Step 1:** Activation of Payroll in Accounting Features

1. Go to **Gateway of Tally > F11: Company Features** > Press **F1: Accounting Features**
2. Set **Maintain payroll** to **Yes**
3. Set **Maintain more than one payroll or cost category** to **No**

   The **Accounting Features Screen** appears as shown below (Figure 7.92)
4. Accept the screen

**Note:** The option Maintain more than one payroll or cost category is set to Yes, when separate cost categories are created to allocate employee cost. In cases, where only one cost category i.e., primary cost category is used to allocate multiple cost centres, this option may be set to No.

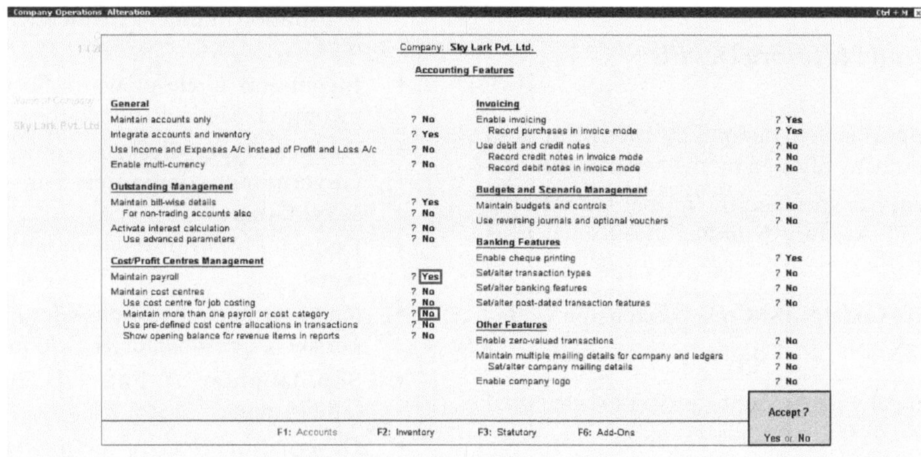


*Figure 7.92: Accounting Features Screen*

**Step 2:** Activate Payroll in Statutory & Taxation Features

1. Go to **Gateway of Tally > F11: Company Features >** Press **F3:Statutory & Taxation**
2. Set **Enable payroll statutory** to **Yes**
3. **Set/alter payroll statutory details** to **Yes**

The **Company Operations Alteration Screen** appears as shown below (Figure 7:93)

4. In the **Payroll Statutory Details** screen, enter the **Provident Fund, Employee State Insurance, National Pension Scheme and Income Tax** details of the company as shown below (Figure 7.94):

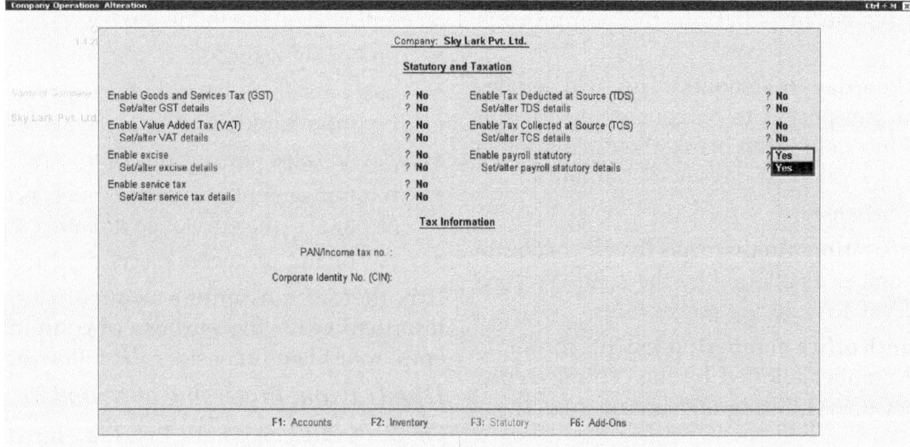


*Figure 7.93: Statutory and Taxation Screen*

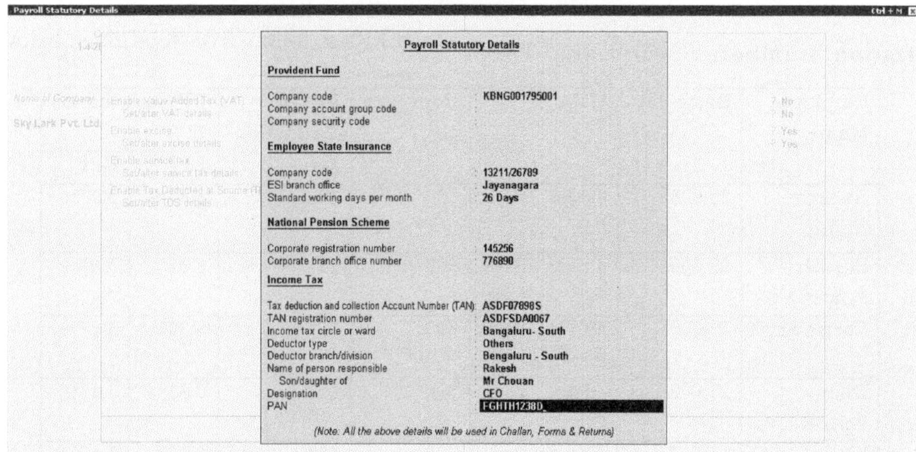


*Figure 7.94: Payroll Statutory Details Screen*

5. Accept the screen

## *Explanation of Payroll Statutory Details*

1. **Provident Fund**
   - **Company code:** This field denotes the provident fund code of the company allotted by the department.

     **PF Department** has specified the format for entering the company **PF Account Number**. The format is as shown below:

| Region Code | Office Code | Est Code | Extension Code |
|---|---|---|---|
| [KN] | [BNG] | 7 digits | 3 digits |

   **Example:** Company PF Account Number to be entered as KNBNG0001795001
   - **Company account group code:** This field denotes the provident fund group code of the company allotted by the department.
   - **Company security code:** This field denotes the security code of the company allotted by the department.
2. **Employee State Insurance**
   - **Company code:** This field denotes the ESI code of the company allotted by the department
   - **ESI branch office:** This field denotes the nearest ESI office under whose jurisdiction, the company is situated.
   - **Standard working days (per month):** This field denotes the consistent pay period to be considered for ESI calculation. If this field is left blank, the calculation is done based on the calendar days in each month
3. **National Pension Scheme**
   - **Corporate registration number:** Specify the corporate registration number as allotted by the central record keeping agency (CRA) during registration.
   - **Corporate branch office number:** Specify the corporate branch office number allotted by the central record keeping agency (CRA) during registration
4. **Income Tax**
   - **Tax deduction and collection Account Number (TAN):** Specify the 10 digit **TAN** assigned to the employer.
   - **TAN registration number:** Specify the TAN registration number provided when **TAN** is registered on **TIN**
   - **Income tax circle or ward:** Specify the name of the income tax circle, to which the employer is associated
   - **Deductor type:** Select government for **Central or State Government companies**. For all other companies, select **Others**
   - **Deductor branch/division:** Enter the branch/division name.
   - **Name of person responsible:** Enter the name of the person responsible for TDS deduction in the company
   - **Son/daughter of:** Enter the responsible person's father's name
   - **Designation:** Specify the official designation of the responsible person.
   - **PAN:** Mention the PAN number of the person

## 7.15 PROCESSING BASIC PAYROLL IN TALLY.ERP 9

Tally.ERP 9's payroll features require minimal effort for accurate payroll processing. It takes five easy steps to process payroll and generate payslip in Tally.ERP 9

Essentially, payroll involves the calculation of amounts due to an employee on the following basis.

- on hourly wages
- pay on a fixed basis such as a certain amount per week, per month and so on
- pay to sales persons on commission
- reimbursement of expenses such as travel expenses, either as paid by the employee or based on per item rate
- pay on the number of pieces produced/manufactured/sold

It is therefore essential to quantify the following payroll information for the purpose of computation of payments to employees. Let us consider the following illustration.

### *Illustration: Processing of payroll in Tally.ERP 9*

On 01-04-2017, Sky Lark Pvt. Ltd., hired 5 employees as sales executive and following is the Monthly salary structure of 5 executives, maintain the following structure in Tally.ERP 9

To maintain the above salary structure/ details of employees in Tally.ERP 9, follow five steps given below:

| Employee Name | Basic Pay | HRA | Conveyance | PF Deduction 12% | PF Contribution 12% | |
|---|---|---|---|---|---|---|
| | | | | | EPS | EPF |
| Abhinav Kumar | 20,000 | 40%of Basic Pay | 800 | 12% | 8.33% | 3.67% |
| Bhaskar Pandey | 22,000 | 40%of Basic Pay | 800 | 12% | 8.33% | 3.67% |
| Chetan Singh | 23,000 | 40%of Basic Pay | 800 | 12% | 8.33% | 3.67% |
| Dhiru Rokaya | 25,000 | 40%of Basic Pay | 800 | 12% | 8.33% | 3.67% |
| Elena D Souza | 15,000 | 40%of Basic Pay | 800 | 12% | 8.33% | 3.67% |

1. **Create Employee Master:** In this step, we will create the employee details like Name of employee, date of birth, joining date, address, bank details and statutory details etc. **For example:** In this step we create employees masters like Abhinav, Bhaskar, Chetan, Dhiru & Elena
2. **Create Payroll Units:** In this step, we will create units of measure **for example:** work can be measured based on time or quantity. Hence we will be creating the payroll unit like **hour.**
3. **Create Pay Heads:** In this step the salary components constituting an employee's pay structure i.e., Pay Head is created in Tally.ERP 9. **For Example:** Basic Pay, Conveyance, PF, HRA etc.
4. **Define Salary:** In this step, the salary details like its calculation details or formula will be defined. **For Example:** HRA should get calculated as 40% on Basic Pay, Dearness Allowance should get calculated as 30% on Basic Pay etc.
5. **Process and Pay Salary:** In this step, the payroll transactions are recorded for processing the salary. **For Example:** Recording of Attendance Voucher, Processing of Salary, Processing of PF and Making Salary Payment etc., will be recorded in Tally.ERP 9

### 7.15.1 Creation of Employee Master

The Employee master records employee information – department, date of joining, date of leaving, ID number, designation, location, function, employee bank details, statutory details, and passport & visa details and so on.

The Employee master is used to record the employee information. In Tally.ERP 9, the following employee masters can be created:

- Employee Category Master
- Employee Group Master
- Employee Master

#### *Employee Category Master*

An **Employee Category** provides an additional level to classify employees in a logical manner. This is in addition to the employee group available by default.

Employee categories option will be available only if the option **Maintain more than one payroll or cost category** is enabled in F11: Company Features>F1: Accounting Features.

#### *Employee Group Master*

Businesses with multiple departments, divisions, functions or activities may create the required employee groups and classify individual employees under a specified group.

For example, you can create the salary structure based on the department or function such as Production, Sales, and Administration soon, or by designation such as Managers, Supervisors, and Workers.

**Note:** By enabling the option "Define salary details" in the employee group creation, we can define the salary structure for the employee group. If the salary structure for the group is same then salary can be defined in employee group creation.

#### *Employee Master*

In Employee Master, we can create individual employee masters, with or without grouping them, under the employee group master.

In Tally.ERP 9, you can record all the necessary information of the employees in the employee masters Tally.ERP 9 also allows you to enter the Statutory, Expat and Contract details of the employees.

**Note:** Tally.ERP 9 allows you to configure the settings like statutory, expat & contract details from the employee creation screen, by clicking F12: Configure. You can enable "Provide passport and visa details to Yes "and "Provide contract details to Yes", to get expat details in employee creation screen.

Let us create the Employee Master by following the procedure given below:

#### *Creation of Employee Master*

- Go to **Gateway of Tally > Payroll Info. > Employees >** under **Single Employee >** Select **Create**
- Fill in the details as shown below (Figure 7.95)

  The **Completed Employee Creation Screen** appears as shown below (Figure 7.95):

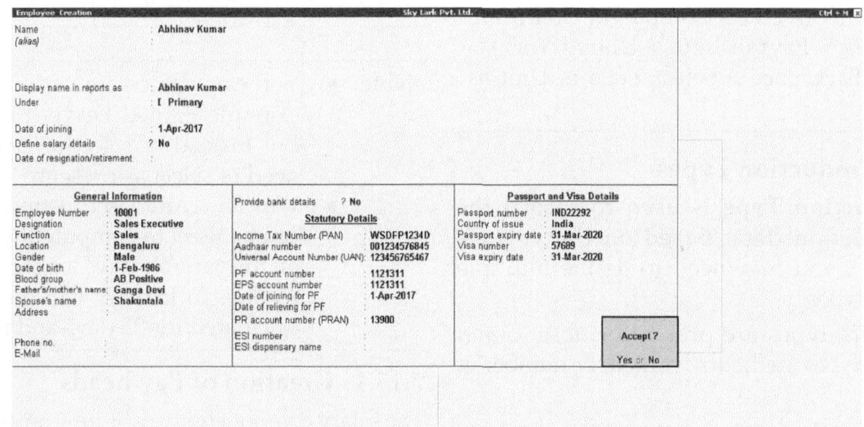


*Figure 7.95: Employee Creation Screen*

- Accept the screen

**Note:**
- The date of resignation/retirement option will be available only on the employee alteration screen. After you enter the date of resignation/retirement, you can also select a reason for leaving.
- Enable the option – Provide bank details to Yes and provide the bank information like, account number, IFS code, MICR code, bank name and branch.

***Activity:*** *Similarly create the following Employee masters under Primary and enter the Date of joining as 1-4-2017.*

- *Bhaskar Pandey*
- *Chetan Singh*
- *Dhiru Rokaya*
- *Elena D Souza*

### 7.15.2 Creation of Payroll Units

The salary paid to an employee is computed based on work done by an employee, which is measured in terms of time or quantity.

In Tally.ERP 9, work done can be quantified using the **"Payroll Unit".**

A payroll unit is similar to unit of measure used in the inventory module. You can create simple as well as compound payroll units measured on attendance/production types such as time, work or quantity.

Simple Unit Creation

Go to **Gateway of Tally > Payroll Info. > Units (Work) > Create**

| Hours | |
|---|---|
| **Against the Field** | **Actions to be Performed** |
| Type | Accept the default option, i.e., **Simple** |
| Symbol | Enter **Hrs** |
| Formal Name | Enter **Hours** |
| Number of Decimal Places Enter | **0** |

**Note:** In Tally.ERP 9, we can create Compound Unit from, Gateway of Tally > Payroll Info. > Units (Work) > Create > Press Backspace > Select Type of Unit as Compound.

### 7.15.3 Attendance/Production Types

An **Attendance/Production Type** is used to record the attendance and production data. Based on the various components (pay head), you may need to define multiple attendance/production types.

Examples for attendance types are present or absent, and examples of production types are hours worked, or number of pieces produced.

An **Attendance/Production Type** is associated with a pay head in an employee's pay structure. Attendance/Production types may also be defined in hierarchical groups whereby attendance types having a common unit are combined under logical groups.

**Example: Present Days** can have present and leave with pay as sub-groups

The Attendance/Production Type may be:

- **Attendance/Leave with Pay:** should be used to record positive attendance and leave with pay

  **For example:** Present, Sick Leave, etc.
- **Leave without Pay:** should be used to record negative attendance

  **For example:** Absent, Leave without Pay etc.
- **Production:** should be used to record the production details

  **For example:** Piece Production, Overtime Hours, etc
- **User Defined Calendar Type:** should be used to create user defined calendar which can be later used to specify the variable number of days for each month.

  **For example:** 25 days in January, 24 days in February, 26 days in March, etc

Follow the below given procedure to create attendance master

#### *Attendance Type Creation*

Go to **Gateway of Tally > Payroll Info. > Attendance/Production Types > Create**

| Present | |
|---|---|
| **Against the Field** | **Actions to be Performed** |
| Under | Select **Primary** |
| Attendance type | Select **Attendance/Leave with Pay** |
| Period Type | By Default it will take as **Days** |

| Absent | |
|---|---|
| **Against the Field** | **Actions to be Performed** |
| Under | Select **Primary** |
| Attendance type | Select **Leave without Pay** |
| Period Type | By Default it will take as **Days** |

**Note:**
- You can also create various attendance type, for example Earned Leave (EL), Casual Leave (CL). But instead of selecting primary in under field, need to select as present.
- We can create User Defined Calendar type: This can be used to compute the per day salary based on the variable days for each month. For example: 25 days in January will mean that salary will be calculated for 25 days and not for 31 days

### 7.15.4 Creation of Pay heads

The salary components constituting an employee's pay structure is called a **Pay Head**. A pay head may be an earnings for the employee, or a deduction which is recovered from his/her salary. The value of these pay heads could be either fixed or variable for each payroll period.

**For example**: **Basic Pay** is a fixed pay component, whereas variable pay, bonus, etc., are variable components.

**Pay Heads** may be broadly considered as earnings and deductions from an employee's point of view. However, these pay heads would still be expense and liability from the employer's view point.

Some examples of earnings pay heads are basic salary, dearness allowance, house rent allowance, etc. Some examples of deductions pay heads are Employees' Provident Fund (EPF), Employees' State Insurance (ESI), Professional Tax, Income Tax etc., some of the examples for contribution pay heads are EPS, EPF etc.

The essential pay heads required to be created to process the salaries of the employees of Sky Lark Pvt. Ltd., are as follows:

- **Basic Pay**
- **House Rent Allowance**
- **Conveyance**
- **Employees PF Deduction @ 12%**
- **Employers EPS Contribution @ 8.33%**
- **Employers EPF Contribution @ 3.67%**
- **EDLI & Administration charge**

Let us now see how these pay heads are created in Tally.ERP 9.

1. **Creation of Earning Pay Heads**

**Basic Pay**

- Go to **Gateway of Tally > Payroll Info. > Pay Heads > Create**

| Basic Pay | |
|---|---|
| **Against the Field** | **Actions to be Performed** |
| Pay head type | Select **Earnings for Employees** |
| Income type | Select **Fixed** |
| Under | Select **Indirect Expenses** |
| Affect net salary | Select **Yes** |
| Name to be displayed in payslip | By Default **Basic Pay** appears |
| Use for calculation of gratuity | Select **No** |
| Set/Alter Income Tax Details | Set to **No** |
| Calculation type | Select **On Attendance** |
| Attendance/leave with pay | Select **Present** |
| Calculation period | Select **Months** |
| Basis of calculation (per day) | Select **As per Calendar Period** |
| Rounding Method | Select **Normal Rounding** |
| Limit | Enter **1** |

The **Completed Basic Pay head Creation Screen** appears as shown below (Figure 7.96):

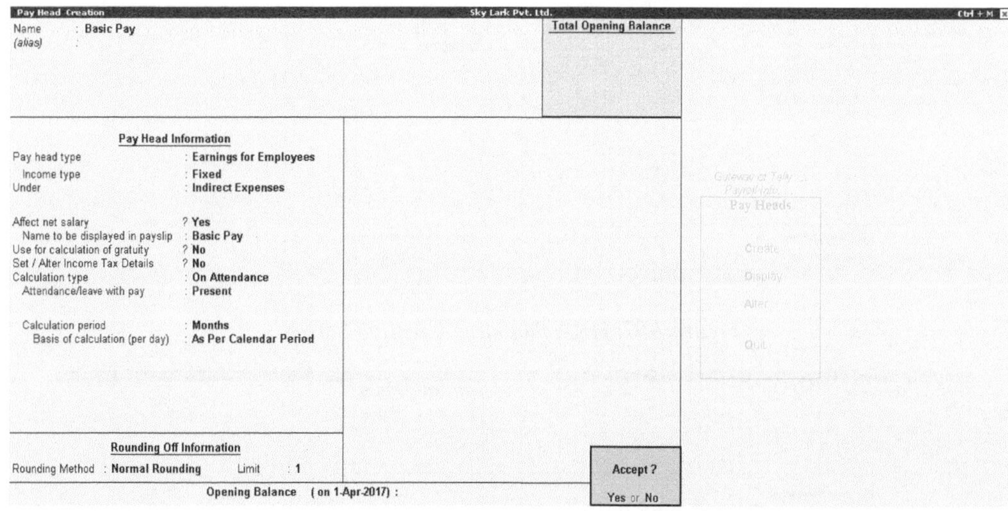


*Figure 7.96: Basic Pay Creation Screen*

- Accept the screen

**House Rent Allowance**

- Go to **Gateway of Tally > Payroll Info. > Pay Heads > Create**

| House Rent Allowance | |
|---|---|
| **Against the Field** | **Action to be Performed** |
| Pay head type | Select **Earnings for Employees** |
| Income type | Select **Fixed** |
| Under | Select **Indirect Expenses** |
| Affect Net Salary | Select **Yes** |
| Name to be displayed in payslip | Enter **HRA** |
| Use for calculation of gratuity | Select **No** |
| Set/Alter Income Tax Details | Set to **No** |

| | |
|---|---|
| Calculation type | Select **As Computed Value** |
| Calculation period | Months will be selected as default |
| Rounding Method | Select **Normal Rounding** |
| Limit | Enter **1** |
| Compute | Select **On Specified Formula** |
| **Compute on Specified Formula** | |
| Function | **Add Pay Head** appears as default |
| Pay Head | Select **Basic Pay** |
| Effective From | Enter **01-04-2017** |
| Slab Type | Select **Percentage** |
| Value Basis | Enter **40%** |

The **Completed House Rent Allowance Pay Head Creation Screen** appears as shown below (Figure 7.97):

- Accept the screen

**Conveyance**

- Go to **Gateway of Tally > Payroll Info. > Pay Heads > Create**

| **Conveyance** | |
|---|---|
| **Against the Field** | **Actions to be Performed** |
| Pay head type | Select **Earnings for Employees** |
| Income type | Select **Fixed** |
| Under | Select **Indirect Expenses** |
| Affect net salary | Select **Yes** |
| Name to be displayed in payslip | Let it be as **Conveyance** |
| Use for calculation of gratuity | Select **No** |
| Set/Alter Income Tax Details | Set to **No** |
| Calculation type | Select **Flat Rate** |
| Calculation period | Select **Months** |
| Rounding Method | Select **Normal Rounding** |
| Limit | Enter **1** |

The **Completed Conveyance Pay Head Creation Screen** appears as shown below (Figure 7.98):

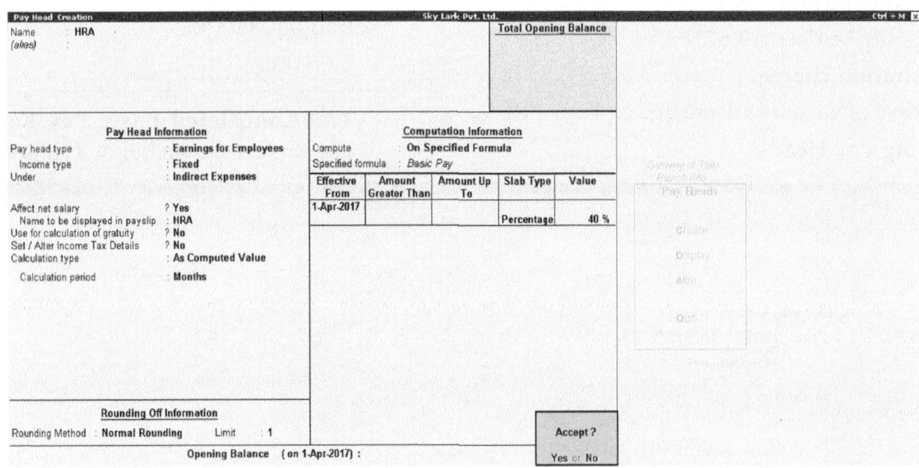


*Figure 7.97: HRA Pay Head Creation Screen*

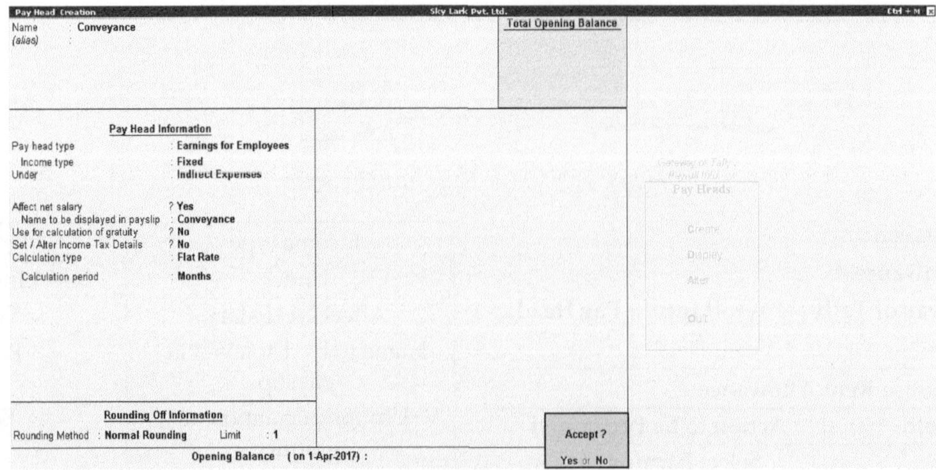


*Figure 7.98: Conveyance Pay Head Screen*

- Accept the screen

2. **Creation of Statutory Deduction Pay Head**

**Employee PF Deduction @ 12%**

- Go to **Gateway of Tally > Payroll Info. > Pay Heads > Create**

| Employees PF Deduction @ 12% | |
|---|---|
| **Against the Field** | **Actions to be Performed** |
| Pay head type | Select **Employees' Statutory Deductions** |
| Statutory pay type | Select **PF Account (A/c No. 1)** |
| Under | Select **Current Liabilities** |
| Affect net salary | Select **Yes** |
| Name to be displayed in payslip | By Default it take as **Employee's PF Deduction @ 12%** |
| Rounding Method | Select **Normal Rounding** |
| Limit | Enter **1** |
| Compute | Select **On Specified Formula** |
| **Computation on Specified Formula** | |
| Function | By Default **Add Pay Head** appears |
| Pay Head | Select **Basic Pay** |
| Effective From | Enter **01-04-2017** |
| Slab Type | Select **Percentage** |
| Value Basis | **Enter 12%** |

The **Completed Pay Head Creation Screen** for the pay head Employee's PF Deduction appears as shown below (Figure 7.99):

- Accept the screen

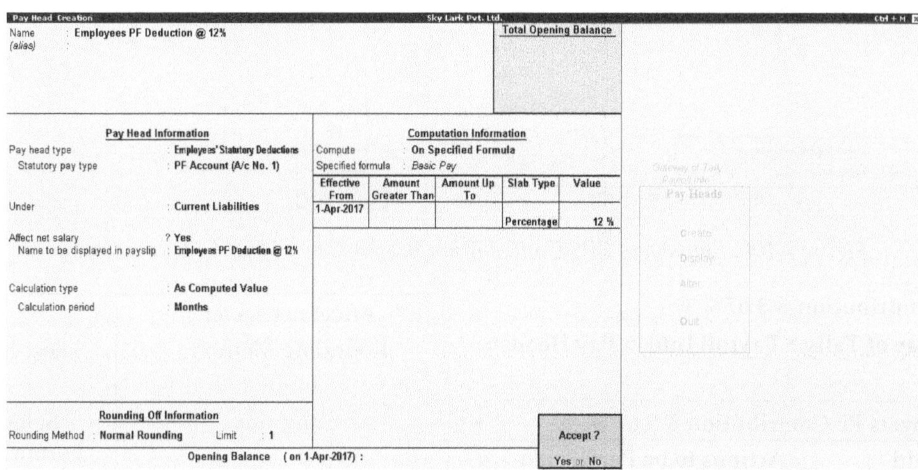


*Figure 7.99: Employee's PF Deduction@12% Pay Head*

**Note:**
- PF is a statutory deduction. It is deducted on Basic + Dearness Allowance
- DA is provided only in government departments.
- Employee's PF account number is of 7 digits which has to be provided in employee master.
- Any employee who wants to en-cash his PF amount, he can draw the total amount using of Form 10 C & Form 19

3. **Creation of Statutory Contribution Pay Heads**

**Employers EPS Contribution @ 8.33%**

- Go to **Gateway of Tally > Payroll Info. > Pay Heads > Create**

| Employers EPS Contribution @ 8.33% | |
|---|---|
| **Against the Field** | **Actions to be Performed** |
| Pay head type | Select **Employer's Statutory Contributions** |
| Statutory pay type | Select **EPS Account (A/c No. 10)** |
| Under | Select **Indirect Expenses** |
| Affect net salary | Select **No** |
| Rounding Method | Select **Normal Rounding** |
| Limit | Enter **1** |
| Compute | Select **On Specified Formula** |
| **Computation on Specified Formula** | |
| Function | By Default **Add Pay Head** appears |
| Pay Head | Select **Basic Pay** |
| Effective From | Enter **01-04-2017** |
| Amount Up To | **Enter 15,000** |
| Slab Type | Select **Percentage** |
| Value Basis | Enter **8.33%** |
| Amount greater Than | By default it will be taken as **15,000** |
| Amount Up To | **Leave it blank** |
| Slab type | Select **Value** |
| Value basis | Mention the amount as **₹ 1,250** |

The Completed **Employers EPS Contribution @ 8.33% Pay Head Creation Screen** appears as shown below (Figure 7.100):

- Accept the Screen

**Note:**
- EPS (Employee Pension Scheme) is an arrangement by which an employer and an employee pay into a fund that is invested to provide the employee with a pension on retirement.
- Employer's share to pension fund is limited to 8.33% of the workman's salary (Basic and DA) subject to a maximum of ₹ 15,000. Therefore, the monthly pension fund contribution per employee will be limited to ₹ 1,250 i.e., 8.33% of ₹ 15,000.

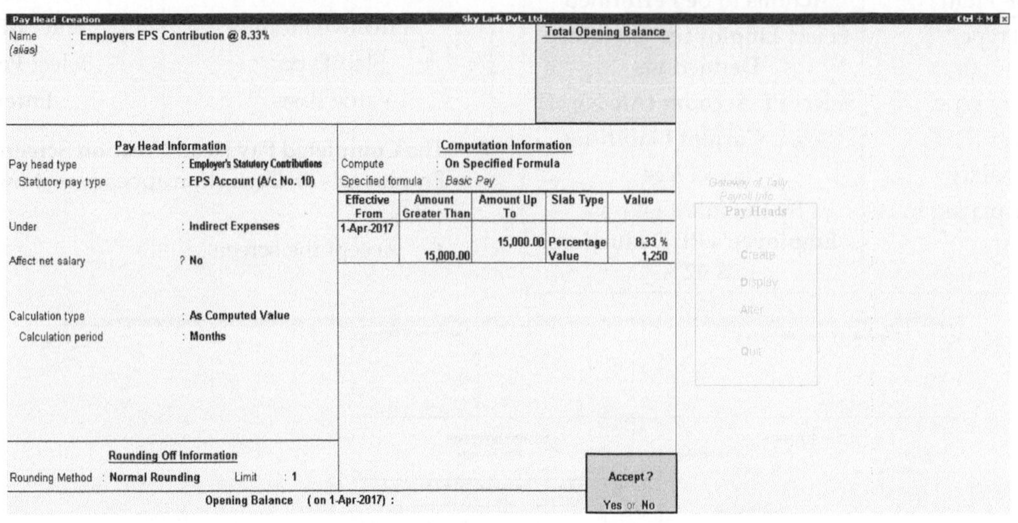


*Figure 7.100: Employers EPS Contribution @ 8.33% Pay Head Creation Screen*

**Employers PF Contribution @ 3.67%**

- Go to **Gateway of Tally > Payroll Info. > Pay Heads > Create**

| **Employers PF Contribution @ 3.67 %** | |
|---|---|
| **Against the Field** | **Actions to be Performed** |
| Pay head type | Select **Employer's Statutory Contributions** |
| Statutory pay type | Select **PF Account (A/c No. 1)** |
| Under | Select **Indirect Expenses** |
| Affect net salary | Select **No** |
| Rounding Method | Select **Normal Rounding** |
| Limit | **Enter 1** |
| Compute | **Select On Specified FormulaAdd Pay Head : Employee's PF Deduction @ 12%Subtract Pay head : Employer's EPS Contribution @ 8.33%** |

The Completed **Computation on Specified Formula Screen** appears as shown below (Figure 7.101):

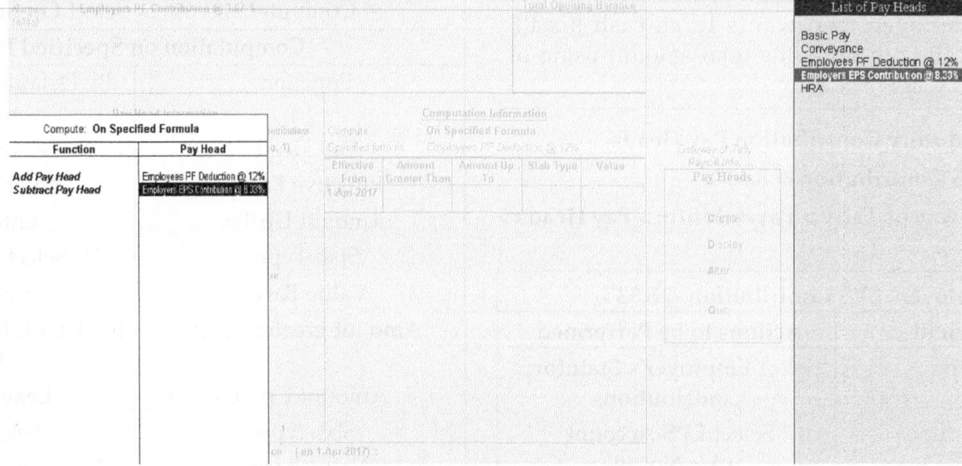


*Figure 7.101: Computation on Specified Formula Screen*

- Press **Enter** from the above screen
- In **Slab Type** field, select as **Percentage**
- In **Value field** enter as **100%**

The completed **Employers PF Contribution @ 3.67% Pay Head Creation Screen** appears as shown below (Figure 7.102):

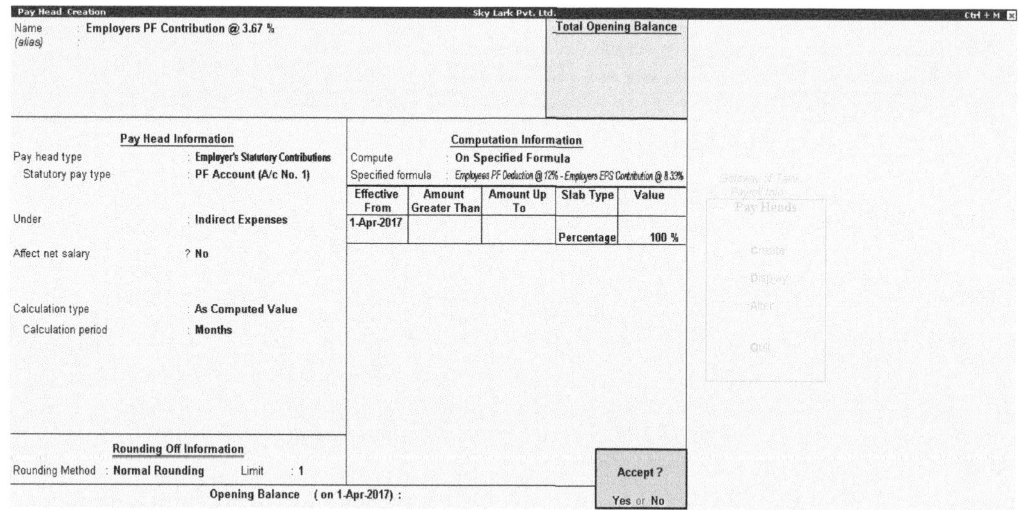

*Figure 7.102: Employer PF Contribution @ 3.67% Pay Head Creation Screen*

- Accept the screen

4. Liabilities Masters (Pay heads)
   - Go to **Gateway of Tally > Payroll Info. > Pay Heads > Create**

| Salary Payable | |
|---|---|
| **Against the Field** | **Actions to be Performed** |
| Pay head type | Select **Not Applicable** |
| Under | Select **Current Liabilities** |

The **Completed Salary Payable Pay Head Creation Screen** appears as shown below (Figure 7.103):

- Accept the screen

### 7.15.5 Defining Salary Details for an Employee

The pay structure for an employee can be defined in Tally.ERP 9 using the Salary Details option.

1. Go to **Gateway of Tally > Payroll Info. > Salary Details > Define > Select Abhinav Kumar**
2. Specify the details based on the screen shown below(Figure 7.104)

The **Completed Salary Details Screen** appears as shown below (Figure 7.104)

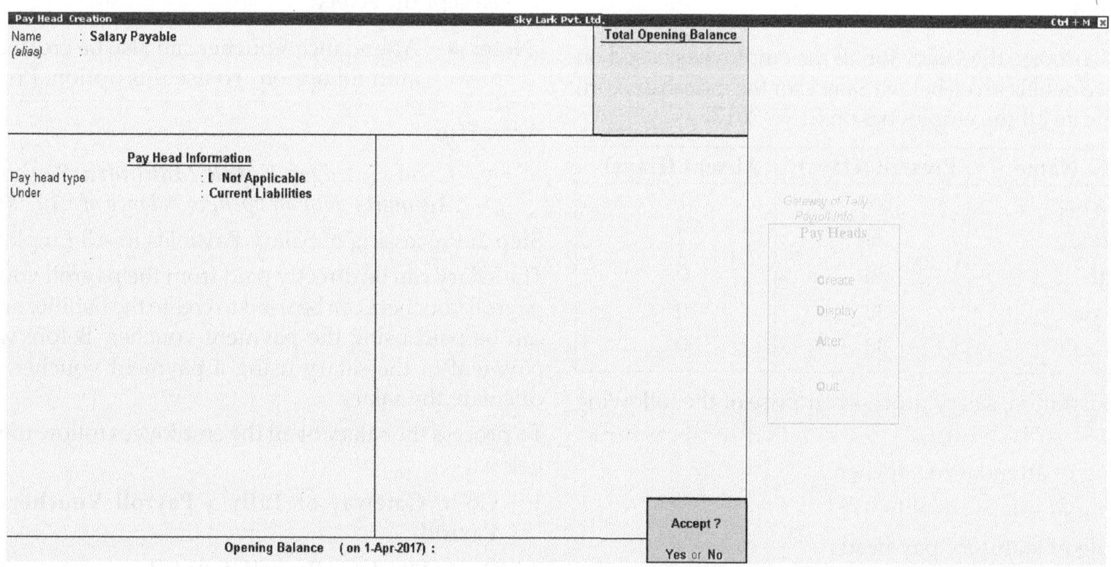

*Figure 7.103: Salary Payable*

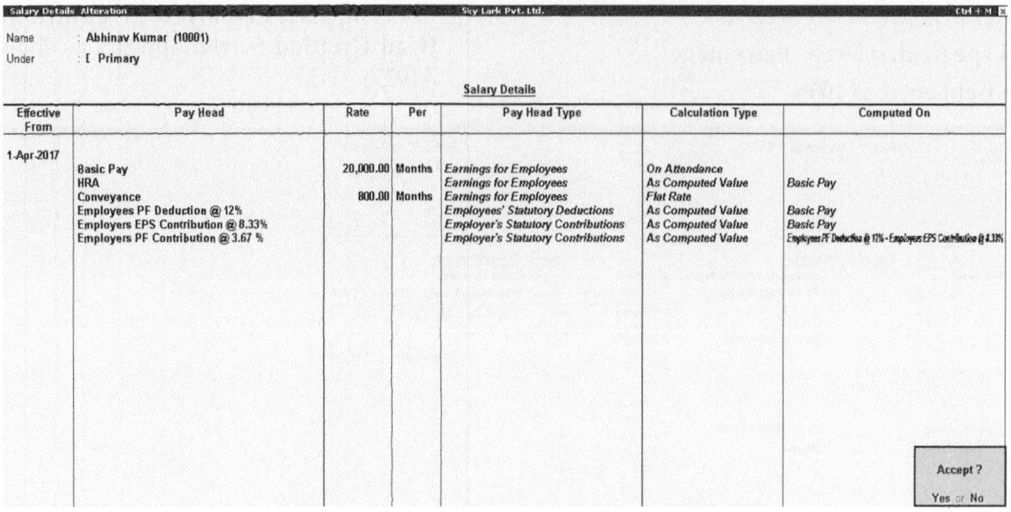

Salary Details Alteration — Sky Lark Pvt. Ltd. — Ctrl + M

Name : Abhinav Kumar (10001)
Under : [ Primary

Salary Details

| Effective From | Pay Head | Rate | Per | Pay Head Type | Calculation Type | Computed On |
|---|---|---|---|---|---|---|
| 1-Apr-2017 | | | | | | |
| | Basic Pay | 20,000.00 | Months | *Earnings for Employees* | *On Attendance* | |
| | HRA | | | *Earnings for Employees* | *As Computed Value* | *Basic Pay* |
| | Conveyance | 800.00 | Months | *Earnings for Employees* | *Flat Rate* | |
| | Employees PF Deduction @ 12% | | | *Employees' Statutory Deductions* | *As Computed Value* | *Basic Pay* |
| | Employers EPS Contribution @ 8.33% | | | *Employer's Statutory Contributions* | *As Computed Value* | *Basic Pay* |
| | Employers PF Contribution @ 3.67 % | | | *Employer's Statutory Contributions* | *As Computed Value* | Employees PF Deduction @ 12% - Employers EPS Contribution @ 8.33% |

Accept ?
Yes or No

*Figure 7.104: Salary Details-Abhinav Kumar*

3. Accept the screen

***Activity:*** *Similarly define salary details for following employees by referring to the illustration table:*

- *Bhaskar Pandey*
- *Chetan Singh*
- *Dhiru Rokaya*
- *Elena D Souza*

## 7.16 SALARY PROCESSING

Once the Salary Structures are defined for all the employees in Tally.ERP 9, then at the end of every month the company can record the payroll transactions to process the salary. Following section will explain how different types of payroll transactions are maintained in Tally.ERP 9.

***Illustration:*** *Processing of different types of payroll vouchers in Tally.ERP 9*

On 30-4-2017, process the salary for all the employees based on the Attendance details given below. Salary for the month of April should be paid to all the employees on 01-05-2017.

| Employee Name | Present (Days) | Absent (Days) |
|---|---|---|
| Abhinav Kumar | 29 | 1 |
| Bhaskar Pandey | 28 | 2 |
| Chetan Singh | 30 | 0 |
| Dhiru Rokaya | 30 | 0 |
| Elena D Souza | 30 | 0 |

As per the illustration, salary process comprise of the following Vouchers:

- Recording of attendance voucher
- Processing of salary payable
- Processing of statutory pay heads
- Processing of employers EDLI & PF admin charges
- Payment of salary to employees
- Payment of Provident Fund to PF Department

**Step 1:** Recording of Attendance Voucher

To process the salary, firstly we require to calculate the attendance of the employees. Attendance voucher allows you to enter attendance, overtime, leave or production details. You can enter separate vouchers for each day or a single voucher for a given pay period, say a month, with aggregated values.

1. Go to **Gateway of Tally > Payroll Vouchers >** Press **Ctrl+F5: Attendance**
2. Click **F2: Date** or press **F2** and change the date to **30-04-2017**
3. Record the attendance voucher for the employees

   The **Attendance Voucher Creation Screen** appears as shown below (Figure 7.105):
4. Accept the screen

**Note:** • Attendance Voucher can also be created using the auto fill option. To use this option, Press Alt + A.

***Activity:***

- *Create a ledger* ***Kotak Mahindra*** *Bank under* ***Bank Accounts*** *with an opening balance of ₹ 10, 00,000.*

**Step 2:** Processing of Salary Payables to All Employees

The salary can be directly paid from the payroll vouchers or the payroll vouchers can be used to create the liability and the salary can be paid using the payment voucher. Before we make the payment of the salary using a payment voucher, we have to calculate the salary.

To process the salary of all the employees follow the steps given below:

1. Go to **Gateway of Tally > Payroll Vouchers > Ctrl+F4: Payroll**
2. Press **Alt+A** for **Payroll Autofill**
3. In **Process for** field select as **Salary**

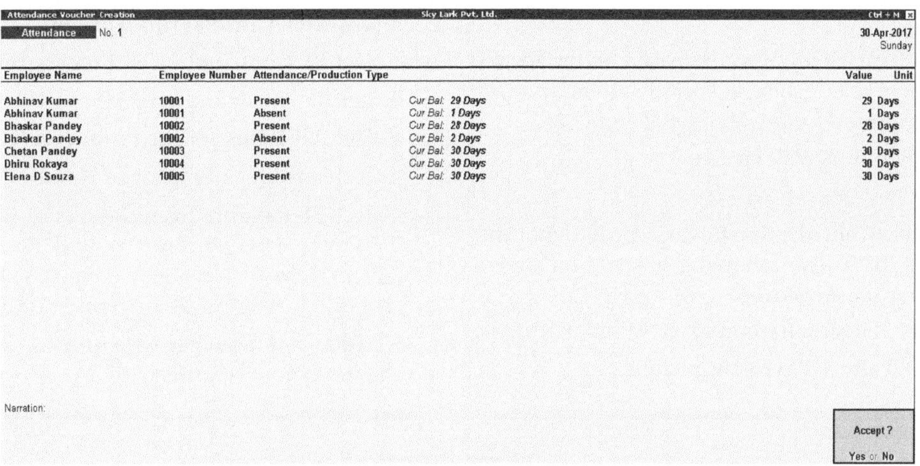


*Figure 7.105: Attendance Voucher Screen*

4. Enter the From and To dates **01-04-2017 to 30-04-2017**
5. Select **All Items** from the **List of Employees/Group** or select particular employee to process salary for one employee
6. Select Sort by as **Employee Name**
7. In Payroll/Bank/Cash Ledger field, select the **Salary Payable** ledger from the **List of Ledger Accounts** as shown below (Figure 7.106):

   The **Payroll Voucher Creation for Salary** appears as shown below (Figure 7.107)

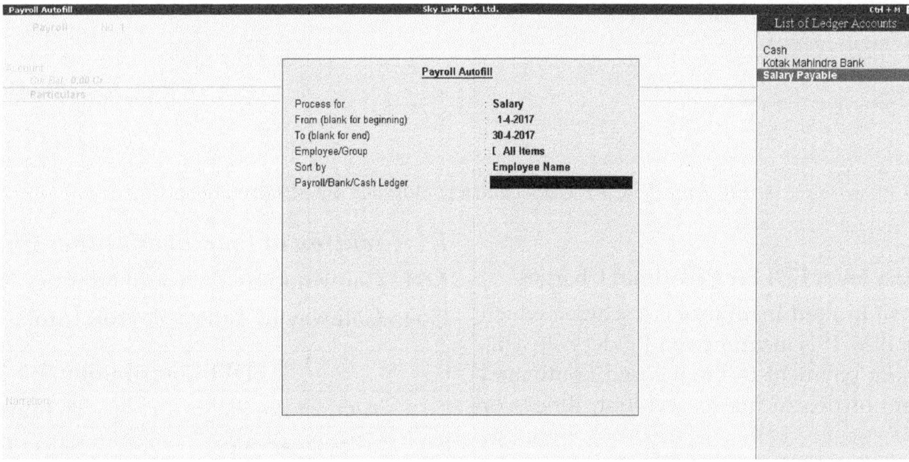


*Figure 7.106: Auto fill screen for Salary Payable*

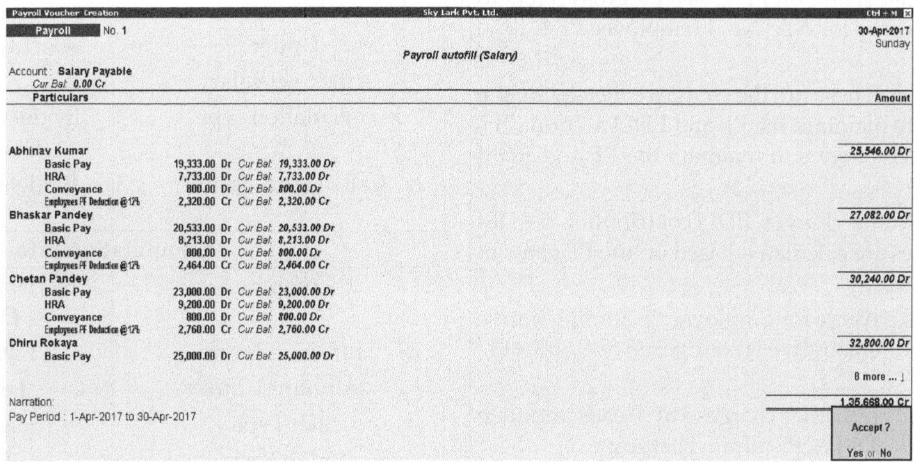


*Figure 7.107: Payroll Voucher – Salary payable*

8. Accept the screen

The salary of a month for each employee is based on the **Salary Details** defined for them and also based on the attendance for that month which is captured in the attendance voucher.

**Step 3:** Processing of Statutory Pay Heads

## *Provident Fund*

Let us see how **Employer Contribution** towards provident fund is processed in Tally.ERP 9. The following illustration shows how PF is processed for the employee

To process the Provident Fund of the employee Abhinav Kumar,

1. Go to **Gateway of Tally > Payroll Vouchers**
2. Press **Alt+A** for **Payroll Auto Fill**
3. Select PF Contribution in **Process for** field
4. Enter the From and To date as 01-04-2017 to 30-04-2017
5. Select **All Items** for the **Employee/Group**
6. Select sort by as **Employee Name**
7. Select **PF Payable** from the List of Ledger Account (If the PF Payable ledger is not created, press Alt+C from Payroll ledger field and create PF Payable ledger >Select Pay Head Type as Not Applicable > Take it under Current Liabilities)

   The **Payroll Voucher Creation for PF Payable** appears as shown below (Figure 1.108):

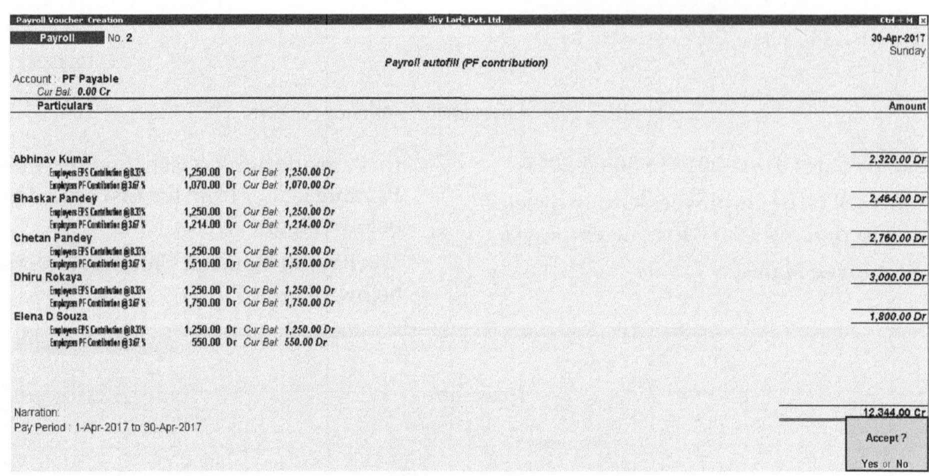


*Figure 7.108: PF Contribution Voucher Creation Screen*

8. Accept the screen

**Step 3:** Processing of Employer EDLI & PF Admin Charges

**EDLI: Employee Deposit Linked Insurance** is a scheme which is amended in the year 1976. It is insurance on PF deposit. This scheme pays a lump sum payment to the insured nominated beneficiary in the event of death due to accident, illness or accident.

All employees who join employee provident scheme are covered by EDLI Scheme and the EDLI Contribution rate is 0.5%. EDLI Contribution will be calculated on PF gross (PF gross refers to the value of pay heads used for A/c. No. 1 (employee PF @ 12%) pay head.)

**Administrative charges:** These are the charges collected by the government in order to maintain the PF and EDLI account. It's a charge paid by the employers to maintain the PF and EDLI account.

Employer PF administrative charges, EDLI contribution & EDLI Administrative charges are calculated based on the PF gross at 0.85%, 0.5% and 0.01%.

The minimum charges payable for Employer PF administrative and Employer EDLI administrative is configured as [1] 500 and [1] 200 respectively.

Let us create the employer's other charges Pay Heads and then process the employer's EDLI & PF admin charges:

## *I. Creation of Employer's other Charges Pay Heads*

**EDLI Contribution – Account Number 21**

Go to **Gateway of Tally > Payroll Info. > Pay Heads > Create**

| EDLI Contribution @ 0.50% | |
|---|---|
| Against the Field | Actions to be Performed |
| Pay head type | Select **Employer's Other Charges** |
| Statutory pay type | Select **EDLI Contribution (A/c No.21)** |
| Under | Select **Current Liabilities** |
| Affect net salary | Select **No** |
| Calculation type | By default it will take **As Computed Value** |
| Calculation Period | By default it will take as **Months** |
| **Computation Info** | |
| Compute | By default it will take as **On PF Gross.** |
| Effective From | Enter **01-04-2017** |
| Amount Upto | **Leave it Blank** |
| Slab Type | Select **Percentage** |
| Value Basis | Enter **0.50%** |

**Creation of EDLI Admin charges- Account Number 22**

| EDLI Admin Charges @ 0.01% | |
|---|---|
| **Against the Field** | **Actions to be Performed** |
| Pay head type | Select **Employer's Other Charges** |
| Statutory pay type | Select **EDLI Admin Charges (A/c No.22)** |
| Minimum Rs 2/Employee? | Set to **No** |
| Under | Select **Current Liabilities** |
| Affect net salary | Select **No** |
| Calculation type | By default it will take **As Computed Value** |
| Calculation Period | By default it will take as **Months** |
| **Computation Info** | |
| Compute | By default it will take as **On PF Gross.** |
| Effective From | Enter **01-04-2017** |
| Amount Up To | Leave it **Blank** |
| Slab Type | Select **Percentage** |
| Value Basis | Enter **0.01%** |

**Note:**
- When the option minimum ₹ 2/employee is set to Yes, the EDLI Admin Charges for each employee will be minimum ₹ 2.
- The minimum charges payable for Employer PF Administrative and Employer EDLI Administrative is configured as ₹ 500 and ₹ 200 respectively

**Creation of PF Admin charges – Account number 2**

| PF Admin Charges @0.85% | |
|---|---|
| Pay head type | Select **Employer's Other Charges** |
| Statutory pay type | Select **Admin Charges (A/c No.2)** |
| Under | Select **Current Liabilities** |
| Affect net salary | Select **No** |
| Calculation type | By default it will take **As Computed Value** |
| Calculation Period | By default it will take as **Months** |
| **Computation Info** | |
| Compute | By default it will take as **On PF Gross.** |
| Effective From | Enter **01-04-2017** |
| Amount Up To | Leave it **Blank** |
| Slab Type | Select **Percentage** |
| Value Basis | Enter **0.85%** |

**Note:** Employer's Other Charges pay heads will not be included in the salary details for the employees as this is an employer related expenses and needs to be handled separately.

### *Create Expense Ledger*

Go to **Gateway of Tally > Accounts Info > Ledgers > Create**

| PF Admin Expenses | |
|---|---|
| Against the Field Name | Action to be Performed |
| Under | Select **Indirect Expenses** |
| Inventory values are affected | Set **No** |

## *II. Process the PF Admin Charges*

To process the Employer PF Admin Charges follow the steps given below:

1. Go to **Gateway of Tally > Accounting Vouchers >Press F7: Journal**
2. Press **F2** to change the Date to **30-04-2017**
3. Press **Ctrl+O** for **Other Charges Auto Fill**
4. In the **Other Charges Auto Fill** screen, enter the From and To date as **01-04-2017 to 30-04-2017**
5. Select Employee group **All Items** for the **Employee/Group**
6. Select **PF Admin Expense**s in the **Expense Ledger** field
7. In **Admin Charges (A/c No.2)**, select **PF Admin Charges @0.85%**
8. In **EDLI Contribution (A/c No.21**), select **EDLI Contribution @ 0.50%**
9. In **EDLI Admin Charges (A/c No.22**), select **EDLI Admin Charges @ 0.01%**

   The **Other Charges Auto Fill** screen appears as shown below (Figure 7.109):
10. The **Admin Charges** will be calculated for all the employees automatically.

    The completed **Journal Voucher** appears as shown below (Figure 7.110):

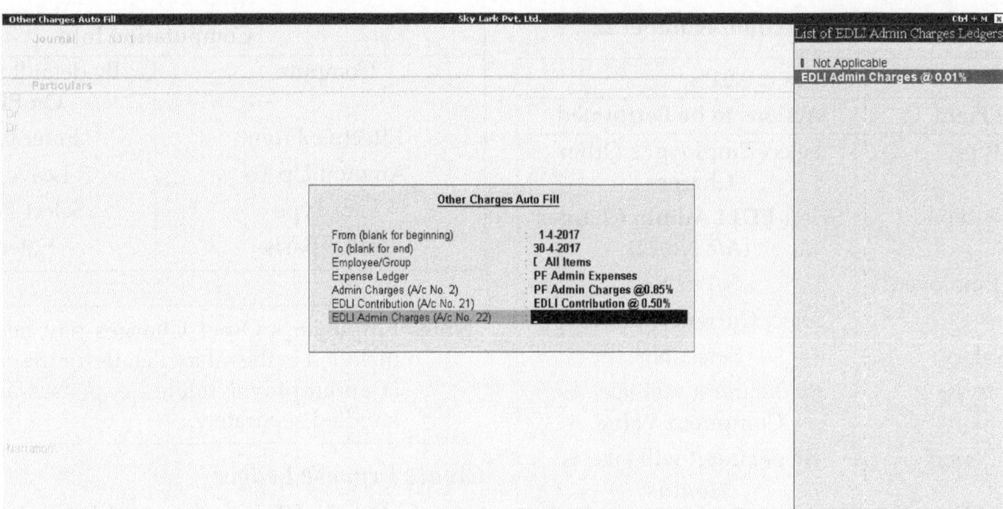


*Figure 7.109: Other Charges Auto Fill Screen*

Accounting Voucher Creation — Sky Lark Pvt. Ltd. — Ctrl + M

Journal No. 1 — 30-Apr-2017, Sunday

*Payroll autofill (Other charges)*

Account : **PF Admin Expenses**
*Cur Bal: 1,590.00 Dr*

| Particulars | | Amount |
|---|---|---|
| **PF Admin Charges @0.85%** | | 875.00 |
| *Cur Bal: 875.00 Cr* | | |
| Abhinav Kumar | 164.33 Cr | |
| Bhaskar Pandey | 174.53 Cr | |
| Chetan Pandey | 195.50 Cr | |
| Dhiru Rokaya | 212.50 Cr | |
| Elena D Souza | 128.14 Cr | |
| **EDLI Contribution @ 0.50%** | | 515.00 |
| *Cur Bal: 515.00 Cr* | | |
| Abhinav Kumar | 96.67 Cr | |
| Bhaskar Pandey | 102.67 Cr | |
| Chetan Pandey | 115.00 Cr | |
| Dhiru Rokaya | 125.00 Cr | |
| Elena D Souza | 75.66 Cr | |
| **EDLI Admin Charges @ 0.01%** | | 200.00 |
| *Cur Bal: 200.00 Cr* | | |
| Abhinav Kumar | 39.73 Cr | |
| Bhaskar Pandey | 39.85 Cr | |
| Chetan Pandey | 40.10 Cr | |
| | | 2 more ... |
| | | 1,590.00 |

Narration:
Pay Period : 1-Apr-2017 to 30-Apr-2017

*Figure 7.110: Journal Voucher-Other Charges*

11. Accept the screen

**Note:**
- PF Admin Charges, EDLI Contribution and EDLI Admin Charges is calculated as per latest change and it is calculated on PF Gross as defined
- In the above case the total PF Admin charges calculation is above ₹ 500. If PF Admin charges were below ₹ 500, then the employer have to remit minimum of ₹ 500. For example: if the total admin charges come up to ₹ 480, then it will take as ₹ 500

**Step 4:** Record Salary Payment

To make the Salary Payment, follow the steps given below:

1. Go to **Gateway of Tally > Accounting Vouchers** >Press **F5:Payment**
2. Press **F2** to change the Date to **01-05-2017**
3. Press **Alt+A** for **Payment Autofill**
4. **Process for** select as **Salary Payment**
5. Enter the From and To date **01-04-2017 to 30-04-2017**
6. Enter the **Voucher Date** as **01-05-2017**
7. Select **All Items** from the **List of Employees/Group**
8. Select **Payroll Ledger** as **Salary Payable**
9. Select **Kotak Mahindra Bank** ledger from the List of Ledger Accounts
10. Set the option **"Use Mode of Payment/Transaction Type"** to **No**
11. Accept the **Bank Allocations** screen

    The **Completed Accounting Voucher Creation Screen** for Salary Payment appears as shown below (Figure 7.111)
12. Accept the screen

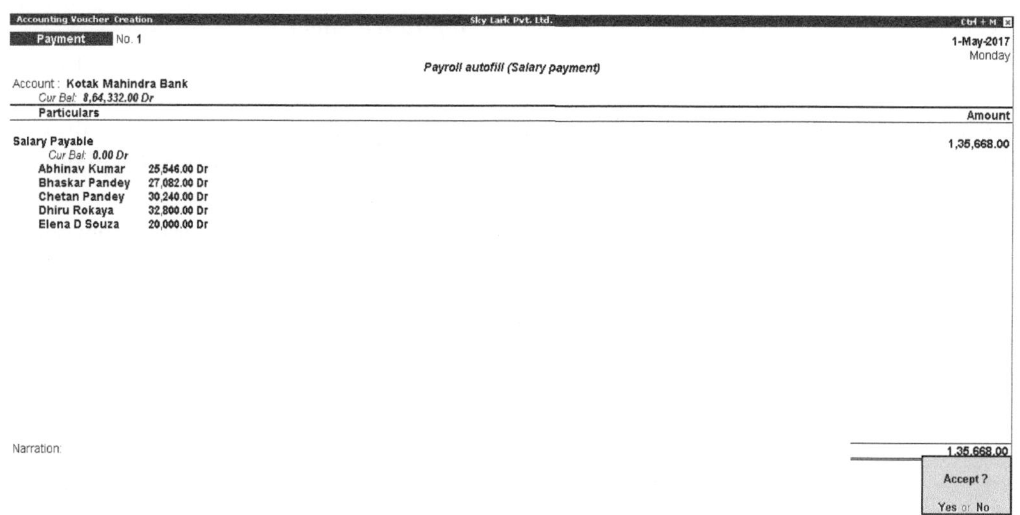

Accounting Voucher Creation — Sky Lark Pvt. Ltd. — Ctrl + M

Payment No. 1 — 1-May-2017 Monday

Payroll autofill (Salary payment)

Account: Kotak Mahindra Bank
Cur Bal: 8,64,332.00 Dr

| Particulars | | Amount |
|---|---|---|
| Salary Payable | | 1,35,668.00 |
| Cur Bal: 0.00 Dr | | |
| Abhinav Kumar | 25,546.00 Dr | |
| Bhaskar Pandey | 27,082.00 Dr | |
| Chetan Pandey | 30,240.00 Dr | |
| Dhiru Rokaya | 32,800.00 Dr | |
| Elena D Souza | 20,000.00 Dr | |

Narration: 1,35,668.00

Accept? Yes or No

*Figure 7.111: Salary Payment*

This completes the processing of payroll in Tally.ERP 9. In this section we have learnt how different salary structure of all the employees is defined by creating employee master, earning pay head, deduction pay head and contribution pay head.

## 7.17 PAYROLL REPORTS

In Tally.ERP 9, we can generate reports instantly once the salary is processed, we can generate following reports like:

- Statement of Payroll:
- Attendance Sheet
- Attendance Register
- Expat Reports
- Statutory Reports

### 7.17.1 Generating Pay Slip in Tally.ERP 9

A **Pay Slip** is a document issued to an employee that lists each component of earnings and deductions, and the net amount paid to an employee for a given pay period. It provides details on how the net amount has been arrived at.

The **Pay Slip** option in Tally.ERP 9 facilitates the users to view the pay slip for individual employees, configure the content and appearance based on the requirement and then print or e-mail the pay slip. To view the pay slip, follow the steps given below:

1. Go to **Gateway of Tally > Display > Payroll Reports > Statements of Payroll > Pay Slip > Single Pay Slip**
2. Select **Abhinav Kumar**
3. Press **F2:Period** and enter the period as 01-04-2017 to 30-04-2017

The **Pay Slip Screen** appears as shown below (Figure 7.112):

In the above pay slip you are getting the earnings and deduction details, to get contribution details in the pay slip, press **F12: Configure** from the above screen (Figure 7.112) and enable the option **Show Employers Contribution.** In F12: Configure, we can enable many options like vertical pay slip, employees details, attendance details etc.

Pay Slip — Sky Lark Pvt. Ltd. — Ctrl + M

Pay Slip for April-2017

Abhinav Kumar

| | | | |
|---|---|---|---|
| Employee Number | : 10001 | Income Tax Number (PAN) | : WSDFP1234D |
| Function | : Sales | Universal Account Number (UAN) | : 123456765467 |
| Designation | : Sales Executive | PF account number | : 1121311 |
| Location | : Bengaluru | ESI Number | : |
| Bank Details | : | PR Account Number (PRAN) | : 13900 |
| Date of joining | : 1-Apr-2017 | Passport Details | : IND22292 |
| | | Visa expiry date | : 31-Mar-2020 |

| Attendance Details | Value |
|---|---|
| Absent | 1 Days |
| Present | 29 Days |

| Earnings | Amount | Gross Salary | Deductions | Amount | Gross Salary |
|---|---|---|---|---|---|
| Basic Pay | 19,333.00 | 20,000.00 | Employees PF Deduction @ 12% | 2,320.00 | 2,400.00 |
| HRA | 7,733.00 | 8,000.00 | | | |
| Conveyance | 800.00 | 800.00 | | | |
| Total Earnings | 27,866.00 | 28,800.00 | Total Deductions | 2,320.00 | 2,400.00 |
| | | | Net Amount | ₹ 25,546.00 | ₹ 26,400.00 |

*Figure 7.112: Pay Slip*

Similarly, we can generate Pay sheet, Payroll statement, Payroll register, employee profile, employee head count etc. from statement of payroll option.

## 7.17.2 Generating Attendance Sheet in Tally.ERP 9

The following Attendance/Production related reports can be generated in Tally.ERP 9:

- Attendance Sheet
- Attendance Register

### *Attendance Sheet*

The Attendance Sheet report is similar to pay sheet report, and displays a pre-formatted report with columns, related to your attendance/production data. To view the attendance sheet,

1. Go to **Gateway of Tally > Display > Payroll Reports > Attendance Sheet**
2. Press **F2:Period** and enter the from date as **01-04-2017** and **to** date as **30-04-2017**

The **Attendance Sheet** appears as shown below (Figure 7.113):

Attendance Sheet — Sky Lark Pvt. Ltd. — Ctrl + M

For all employees — 1-Apr-2017 to 30-Apr-2017

| Particulars | Absent | Present |
|---|---|---|
| Abhinav Kumar | 1 Days | 29 Days |
| Bhaskar Pandey | 2 Days | 28 Days |
| Chetan Pandey | | 30 Days |
| Dhiru Rokaya | | 30 Days |
| Elena D Souza | | 30 Days |

*Figure 7.113: Attendance Sheet*

In the above report (Figure 7.113), we will get the details of attendance of all the employees with present and absent details.

**Note:** Similarly, we can generate the following reports:

- Attendance Register: it displays the summary report of the attendance voucher
- Expat Reports: it displays the passport and visa expiry details.

## 7.17.3 Generating Payroll Statutory Summary Report in Tally.ERP 9

In Tally.ERP 9, we can generate Statutory Reports like Summary, Provident Fund, Employee State Insurance, and Professional Tax, National Pension Scheme, Gratuity and Income Tax details.

To generate payroll statutory summary report, follow the steps given below:

1. Go to **Gateway of Tally > Display > Payroll Reports > Statutory Reports > Summary**
2. Press **F2:Period** and enter the from date as **01-04-2017** and to date as **30-04-2017**

The **Payroll Statutory Summary Report Screen** appears as shown in below (Figure 7.114)

Payroll Statutory Summary — Sky Lark Pvt. Ltd. — Ctrl + M

Payroll Statutory Computation — 1-Apr-2017 to 30-Apr-2017

| Particulars | Payable Amount | Paid Amount |
|---|---|---|
| **Provident Fund** | | |
| Employees' Statutory Deductions | 12,344.00 | |
| Employer's Statutory Contributions | 12,344.00 | |
| Employer's Other Charges | 1,590.00 | |
| **Employee State Insurance** | | |
| Employees' Statutory Deductions | | |
| Employer's Statutory Contributions | | |
| **National Pension Scheme** | | |
| Employees' Statutory Deductions | | |
| Employer's Statutory Contributions | | |
| **Professional Tax** | | |
| Employees' Statutory Deductions | | |
| **Income Tax** | | |
| Employees' Statutory Deductions | | |
| Grand Total | 26,278.00 | |

*Figure 7.114: Payroll Statutory Summary Report Screen*

In the above report (Figure 7.114), we can view the details of Provident Fund, because we have defined the details of PF deduction and contribution in the salary details of employees. Further drill down to get the details of employee wise PF Deduction and contribution details.

In the same report, we can view the detail summary of Employee State Insurance, National Pension Scheme, Professional Tax & Income Tax details. If the same is defined in the salary details of employees. In this case we have defined only the provident fund details, hence we are getting on PF details.

# PRACTICE EXERCISE

## Section A: Review Questions

1. Define Payroll
2. What are the steps to implement Payroll in Tally.ERP 9?

## Section B: Objective Questions

1. From where can we activate payroll features?
   a. F11>F1 b. F11>F2
   c. F11>F1&F2 d. F11>F1&F3
2. PF is calculated on?
   a. Basic b. Basic & HRA
   c. Basic & DA d. Basic, DA & HRA
3. EDLI contribution is:
   a. Earnings for employee
   b. Employee's statutory deduction
   c. Employer's statutory deduction
   d. Employer's others charges
4. What is the rate of percentage for PF Calculation?
   a. 12% b. 12.5%
   c. 15% d. 15.5%
5. EPS contribution rate is?
   a. 8.33% b. 3.67
   c. 8.67% d. 3.33%

# PART B: STATUTORY FEATURES AND ADVANCED FEATURES

# GETTING STARTED WITH TAX DEDUCTED AT SOURCE (TDS)

## OBJECTIVES:

After studying this section, you will be able to understand how to:

- Configure Tax Deducted at Source in Tally.ERP 9
- Record simple TDS transactions
- View TDS reports

## 7.18 INTRODUCTION

**TDS** stands for **Tax Deducted at Source**. The concept of TDS was introduced in the Income Tax Act, 1961, with the objective of deducting the tax on an income, at the source of the income. It is one of the methods of collecting Income Tax, which ensures regular flow of revenue to the Government.

## 7.19 BASIC CONCEPTS OF TDS

It is important to understand some of the terminologies & concepts of TDS:

### *Scope and Applicability*

At present, incomes from several sources are subjected to TDS. Some of the incomes which are subject to TDS are:

- Salary
- Interest on securities, debentures
- Deemed Dividend
- Interest other than interest on securities
- Winnings from lottery or crossword puzzles
- Winnings from horse races
- Payment to contractors (Advertisement contractors)
- Payment to contractors (Other than advertisement)
- Payment to sub-contractors
- Payment to non-residents
- Payment to non-resident sportsmen or sports association
- Payment in respect of deposit under NSS
- Payment on account of re-purchase of units by Mutual Fund or UTI
- Payment in respect of units to an offshore fund
- Payment of compensation on acquisition of immovable property
- Insurance commission
- Commission etc., on sale of lottery tickets
- Commission, brokerage etc.
- Rent of land, building or furniture
- Rent of plant, machinery or equipment
- Royalty agreement made on or after June 1, 2005
- Short-term capital gains U/s 111A
- Fees for professional or technical services
- Fees for tech. services agreement made on or after June 1, 2005
- Income in respect of units of non-residents
- Income from foreign currency bonds or shares of Indian company
- Income of foreign institutional investors from securities
- Income from foreign exchange assets payable to an Indian citizen
- Income by way of long term capital gains referred to in Section 115E
- Any other interest on securities
- Interest on 8% Savings (Taxable) Bonds, 2003

### *What is TAN?*

TAN is the Tax deduction Account Number issued by the Income Tax Department to all persons deducting tax at source. TAN has to be quoted in all relevant challans, tax deduction certificates, TDS returns and other notified documents. To obtain TAN, the person or organisation is required to apply in Form 49B to the TAN Facilitation Centres of NSDL.

### Who has to deduct the tax?

Any person making the payments to third parties as specified in the scope and applicability section mentioned above are required

To deduct tax at source.

### *Who is a Deductee?*

A Deductee is a third party that provides services and bills to the buyer (deductor) and the buyer will then deduct the tax at source at a prescribed rate, before paying the bill amount.

Deductees may belong to any of the following categories:

- Individual
- Hindu undivided Family (HUF)
- Body of Individual (BOI)
- Association of persons (AOP)
- Co-Operative society
- Local Authority
- Partnership firm
- Domestic Company (Indian company)
- Foreign Company
- Artificial Judicial Person

## 7.20 TDS IN TALLY.ERP 9

The TDS module in Tally.ERP 9 is integrated with financial accounts and takes care of all the TDS and e-TDS requirements of your business, right from voucher entry to report generation. Tally.ERP 9 completely automates your TDS management - accurately computes tax to be deducted at source & TDS payable amount, and generates TDS payment challans, TDS Certificates, Statutory Returns and other related MIS reports.

Its e-TDS features further assist you to file your mandatory tax returns in electronic format as specified by the Income Tax Department. It helps in minimizing error-prone entry of information, incorrect remittances and also provides accounting for interest & penalties (if any) for smooth and effective functioning of your business.

### *Features of TDS compliant Tally.ERP 9*

Tally.ERP 9 comprises of comprehensive features to ensure accurate and automatic computation of Tax Deductible at Source for non-salaried deductees according to the provisions stipulated in the Income Tax Act.

The TDS functionality in Tally.ERP 9 encompasses the following salient features:

- Simple & user friendly
- Easy & quick to set up and implement
- Maintains complete tracking of each transaction from booking deduction till payment
- Allows deduction of TDS at the time of booking expenses in the same voucher or separately at a later date
- Allows deduction of TDS at lower/zero rate
- Allows deduction of TDS on multiple expenses of single nature of payment type in a single voucher.
- Allows computation of TDS on expenses partly subject to tax
- Allows TDS calculation on advance payments
- Provides facility to compute TDS with/without considering Surcharge Exemption Limits for parties
- Provides retrospective surcharge calculations for prior/ current period
- Allows partial/full payment of TDS
- Provides automatic computation of TDS amount for each nature of payment
- Generates TDS payment Challan ITNS 283 (for Corporate & Non-Corporate)
- Generates TDS Certificates, TDS Outstanding report and various other TDS related MIS Reports
- Facilitates automatic generation of quarterly as well as annual e-TDS returns in both physical and e-Returns formats
- Provides challan reconciliation facility to keep track of issue of TDS certificates and remittance through challans
- Comprises of all required provisions for TDS as specified by Income Tax Department
- Also generates consolidated TDS Certificates, Challan and Annual Returns for statutory and tax audit purpose

## 7.21 SETUP

### *Scenario:*

Prathap Trading Co started a business of customer care service center in different locations and different products for which it has to pay the Rent. Since the rent amount crosses the exemption limit, Prathap Trading co as to pay TDS duty on Rent to Government.

**Let us create a company for Prathap Trading Co.**

The completed **Company Creation** screen appears as shown below:

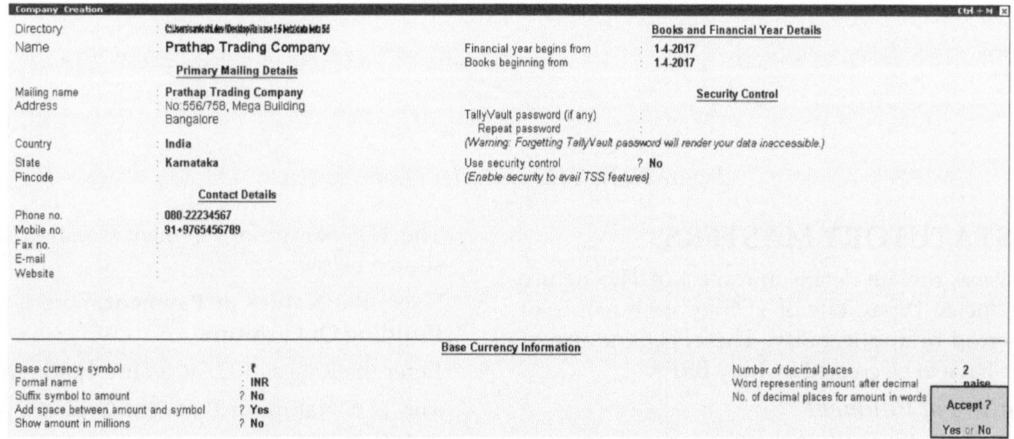


*Figure 7.115: Completed Company Creation screen*

### 7.21.1 Activation

To configure TDS in Tally.ERP 9, follow the steps given below:

1. **Go to** Gateway of Tally > F11: Features > Statutory and Taxation
2. In the **Company Operations Alteration** screen, set **Enable Tax Deducted at Source (TDS)** to **Yes**
3. Enable the option **Set/alter TDS details**

   The Company Operations Alteration screen appears as shown below:

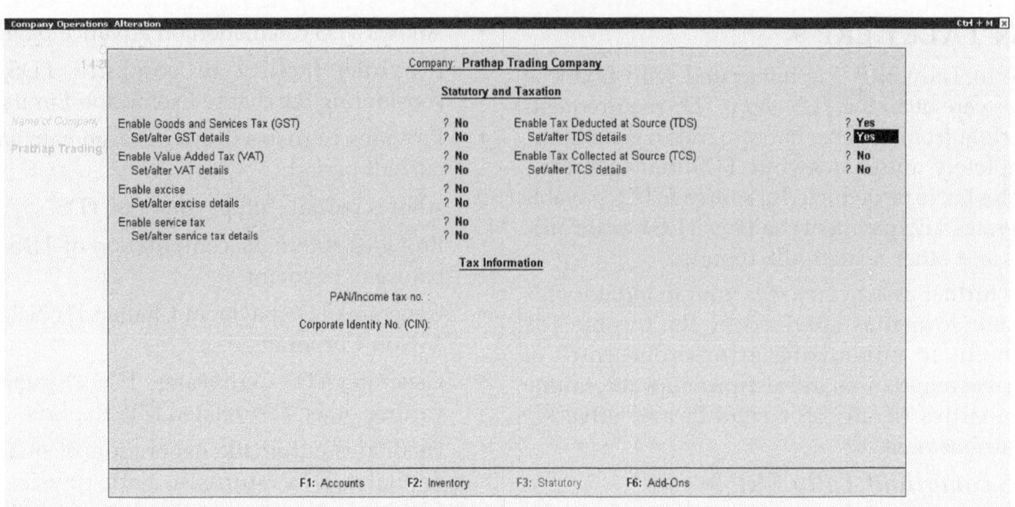


*Figure 7.116: Company Operations Alteration screen*

4. Press **Enter**.
5. Fill in the TDS Details as shown in the screen given below:

   The TDS Deductor Details screen appears as shown below:

- Press Enter
- Press **Ctrl + A** to save the details

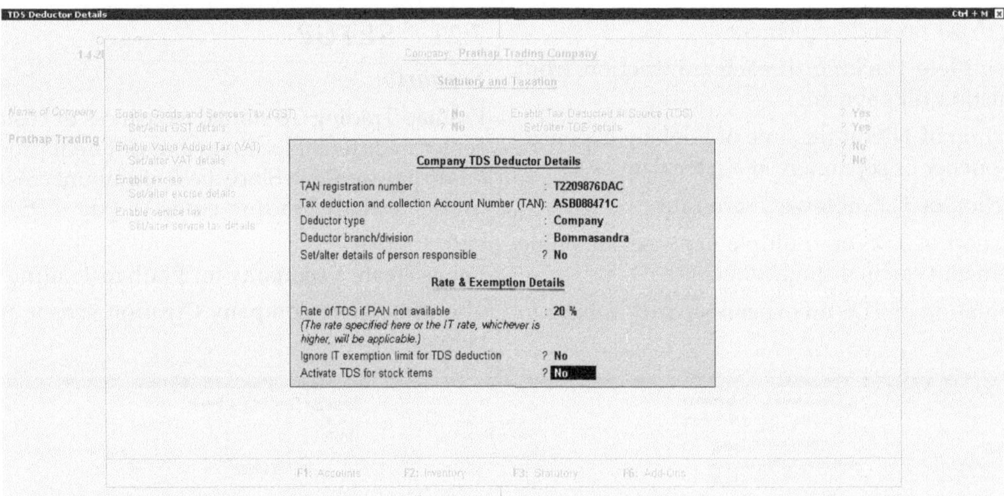


*Figure 7.117: TDS Deductor Details screen*

## 7.22 TDS STATUTORY MASTERS

The statutory masters contain details in respect of TDS nature of payments, Deductee Types, rate of TDS for each nature of payment and period of applicability. These TDS nature of payment masters have to be created in Tally.ERP9.

### *Create TDS Nature of Payment*

1. Go to **Gateway of Tally > Accounts Info. > Statutory Info. > TDS Nature of Pymts > Create**
2. Press **Ctrl+C: Helper**

   The TDS Nature of Payment Creation screen appears as shown below:

3. Select the **Nature of Payment**, here it is **Rent of Land, Building Or Furniture**
4. Enter the Rate as 10% and Threshold limit as 1,80,000

   The TDS Nature of Payment Creation screen appears as shown below:

5. Press **Enter** to save the details

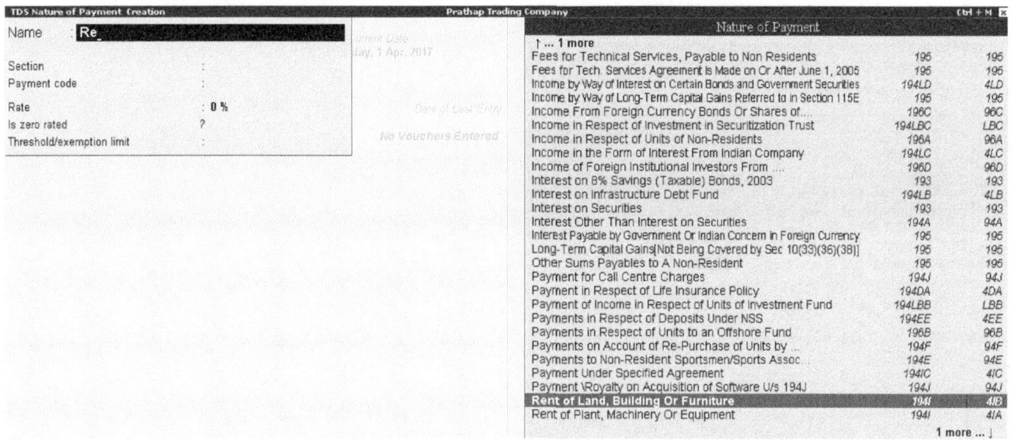


*Figure 7.118: displaying complete list of Nature of Payment*

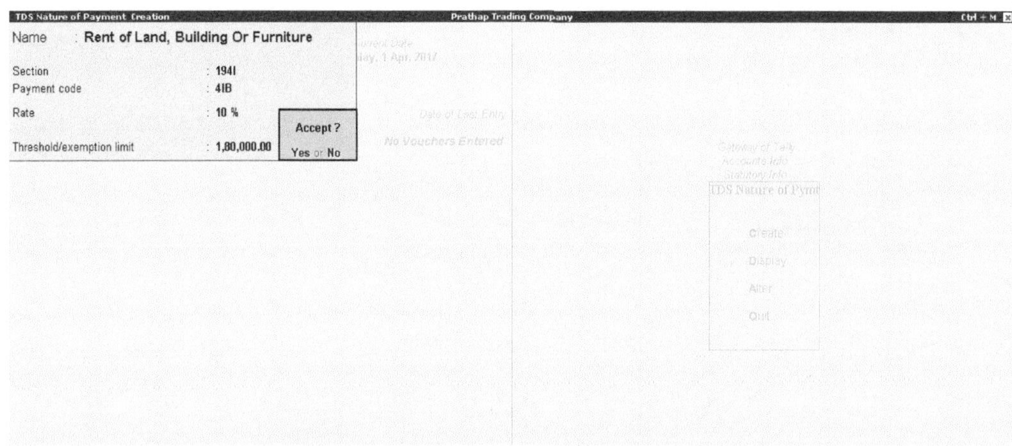


*Figure 7.119: TDS Nature of Payment Creation screen*

## 7.23 CONFIGURING TDS AT GROUP LEVEL

The illustration below will demonstrate how to account various expenses of same nature of payment.

Prathap Trading Co has various expenses on rent like Rent on Building, Rent on machinery.

On 30-6-2017, Prathap Trading generated the liability for Rent on Building of ¹ 2,00,000. Since the liable amount is exceeding the exemption limit, Prathap Trading company has decided to deduct the TDS on the same bill and pay the remaining to Guru Agencies. Let us account the same in Tally.ERP 9.

**Step:** I Create Required Accounting Masters Group Ledger

Go to **Gateway of Tally > Accounts Info > Group > Create**

1. Create party ledger – **Guru Agencies**
   - Group under **Sundry Creditors**
   - Maintain balances bill by bill, select as **YES**
   - Default credit period as **Blank**
   - Check for credit days during voucher entry, select as **No**
   - Inventory values are affected, select as **No**
   - Is TDS Deductable, select as **Yes**
   - Deductee Type select **Company-Resident**
   - Deduct TDS in Same Voucher, set to **Yes**
   - Provide PAN details, set to **Yes**
   - Select Available in **PAN Status**
   - Accept the screen
2. Create a Expense Group as **Rent Expenses**
   - Group under **Indirect Expenses**
   - Keep all the option as it is and follow next step
   - Set/Alter TDS Details, Set to **Yes**

   The Group Creation screen appears as shown below:
   - Select Nature of Payment as **Rent of Land, building or Furniture**
   - Press Enter to save
3. Create Ledger as **Rent on Building**
   - Group under **Rent Expenses**
   - Inventory values are affected, select as **No**
   - Is TDS is Applicable, Select **Applicable**
   - Nature of Payment as **Undefined**

The **Ledger Creation** screen appears as shown below:

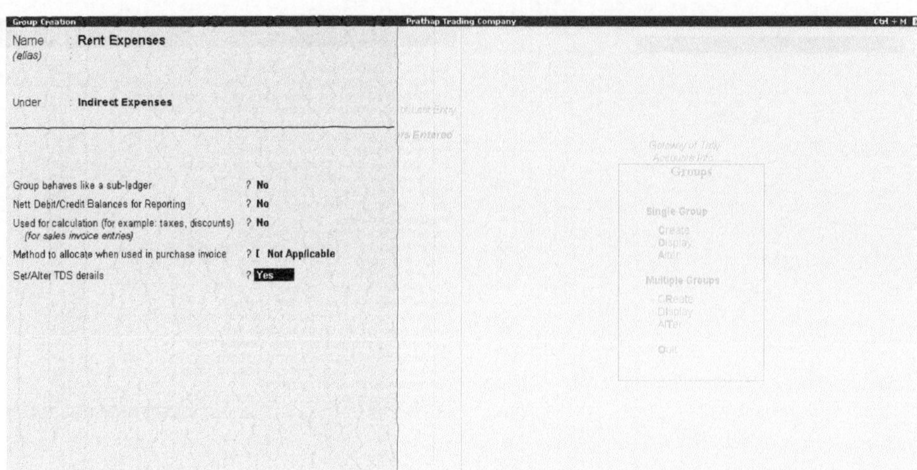


*Figure 7.120: Group Creation*

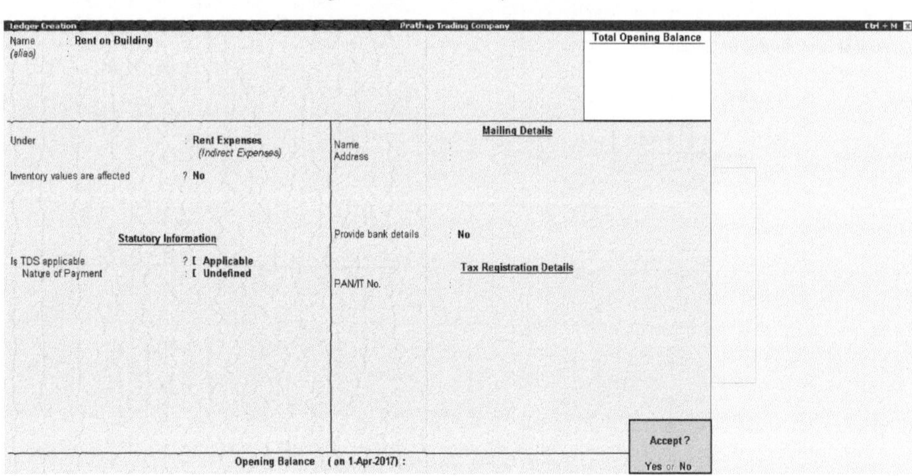


*Figure 7.121: Completed Ledger Creation screen*

***Activity:*** *Similarly, create Rent on Machinery ledger by following the instructions given for Rent on Building ledger creation.*

4. Create Tax/Duty Ledger as **TDS Duty on Rent**

1. Go to **Gateway of Tally > Accounts Info. > Ledgers > Create**
2. Type **TDS Duty on Rent** in the **Name** field
3. Select **Duties & Taxes** group in the **Under** field
4. Select **TDS** from the list in the **Type of Duty/Tax** field
5. Select **Rent of Land, Building Or Furniture** from the list, in the **Nature of Payment** Field as shown below:

   The Ledger Creation screen – duty ledger appears as shown below:

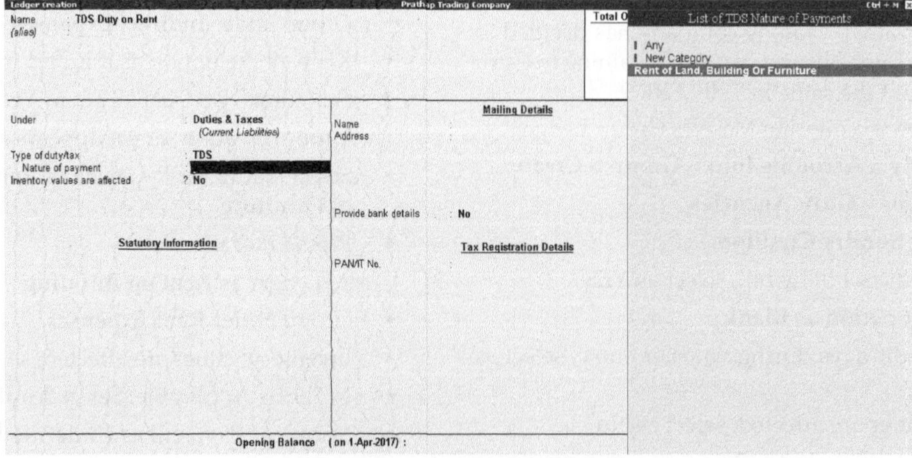


*Figure 7.122: Ledger Creation screen*

6. Set **No** in the **Inventory values are affected** field
7. Press **Enter** to accept

### 7.23.1 Recording Transactions

As discussed earlier, tax deducted at source on incomes specified by income tax department is affected at source when income arises/accrues or paid whichever is earlier.

The applicable income tax rates for payment of '**Rent of Land Building Or Furniture** to '**Company Resident Deductee**' Type is given below:

| Particulars | Rate |
|---|---|
| TDS | 10% |
| Surcharge | - |
| Education Cess | - |
| Secondary Education Cess | - |

**Step 1:** Create journal voucher to book the expenses and deduct TDS

1. Go to **Gateway of Tally** > **Accounting Voucher** > **F7: Journal**
2. Click **F2: Date** to change the date to 30-6-2017
3. Debit the **Rent on Building** expense ledger
4. Enter ₹ **2,00,000** in the amount field
5. Credit **Guru Agencies**. The amount after TDS deduction will appear in the **Amount** field automatically
6. Press **Enter**
7. Enter the **Bill-wise Details**, as required
8. Press **Enter**
9. Credit the TDS Duty on Rent ledger. The TDS amount will automatically get filled in the **Amount** field
10. Press **Enter**
11. Enter **Narration**, if required

The **Journal** voucher appears as shown below:

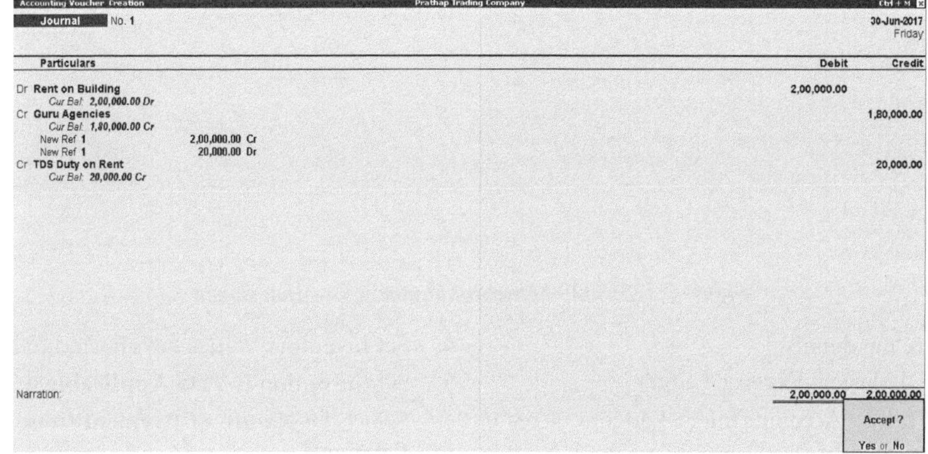


*Figure 7.123: Journal Voucher screen*

12. Press **Ctrl + A** to save the voucher

**Step 2:** Making payment to party after deducting TDS

1. Create a bank ledger as Kotak Bank under Bank Accounts and enter the opening balance as ₹ 2,00,000
2. Go to Gateway of Tally > Accounting Voucher > F5: Payment
3. Make the payment entry as per the screen shown below:

The **Payment Voucher** appears as shown in the figure

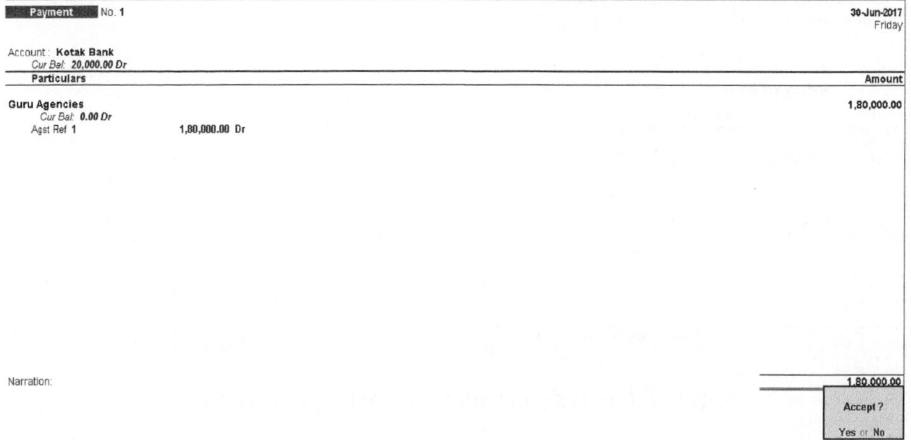


*Figure 7.124: Payment Voucher screen*

***Activity:*** *Similarly, book the following expenses in journal voucher and deduct the TDS.*

On 30-6-2017, Prathap Trading Co has booked rent expenses on Machinery. Since the **Rent on Machinery** expenses is of ¹ 1, 90,000 & deduct the TDS on the same and make the payment to Guru **Agencies.**

## 7.24 CONFIGURING TDS AT LEDGER LEVEL

If there is a single expense pertaining to any particular Nature of Payment, e.g. Commission expenses, it is advisable to maintain the TDS detail at the ledger level itself.

The below given illustration will demonstrate how to configure TDS in the ledger for a single expense pertaining to a particular Nature of Payment.

On 30-06-2017, Prathap Trading Co. has incurred a commission expenses of ₹ 1, 20,000 for the service taken from Ravi Consultancy.

**Step 1:** To Create TDS Nature of Payment

1. Go to **Gateway of Tally > Accounts Info. > Statutory Info. > TDS Nature of Pymts > Create**

   The **TDS Nature of Payment Creation** screen appears as shown below:

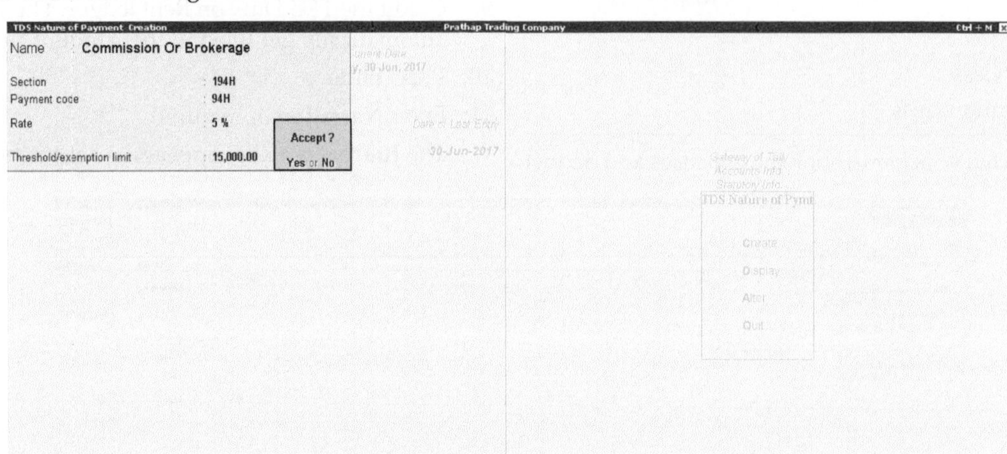


*Figure 7.125: TDS Nature of Payment Creation screen*

2. Press **Enter** to save the details

**Step 2:** Create Required Masters Expense Ledger

1. Go to Gateway of Tally > Accounts Info. > Ledgers > Create
2. Enter the Name **Commission**
3. Select **Indirect Expenses** as the group name in the **Under** field
4. Set Inventory values are affected to No
5. Set the option **Is TDS Applicable** to **Applicable**
6. Select the **Nature of Payment** from the **List of Nature of Payments**

   The **Ledger Creation** screen appears as shown below:

Ledger Creation — Prathap Trading Company — Ctrl + M

Name : Commission
(alias) :

Total Opening Balance: 2,00,000.00 Dr
Difference: 2,00,000.00 Dr

Under : Indirect Expenses
Inventory values are affected ? No

Statutory Information
Is TDS applicable ? [ Applicable
Nature of Payment : Commission Or Brokerage

Mailing Details
Name :
Address :
Provide bank details : No

Tax Registration Details
PAN/IT No. :

Opening Balance ( on 1-Apr-2017) :

Accept ?
Yes or No

*Figure 7.126: Ledger creation screen (Expense Ledger)*

## *Party Ledger*

Go to **Gateway of Tally > Accounts Info > Ledgers > Create**

1. Create party ledger –**Ravi Consultancy**
   - Group under **Sundry Creditors**
   - Maintain balances bill by bill, select as **YES**
   - Default credit period as **Blank**
   - Inventory values are affected, select as **No**
   - Is TDS Deductable, select as **Yes**
   - Deductee Type select **Company-Resident**
   - Deduct TDS in Same Voucher, Set to **Yes**
   - Update the PAN no as XYZPQ1234K
   - Accept the screen

The Ledger Creation party ledger appears as shown below:

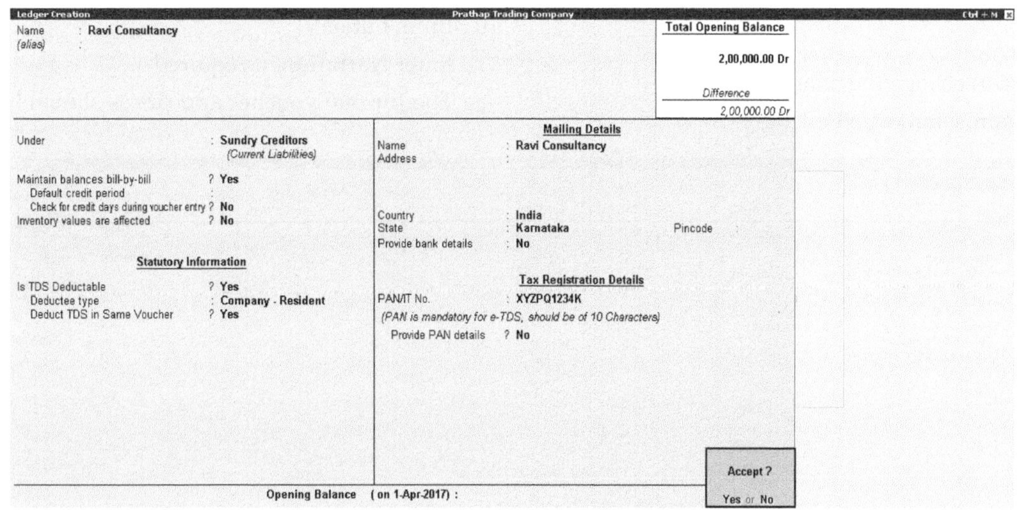

*Figure 7.127: Ledger creation screen (Party Ledger)*

## *TDS Duty Ledger*

1. Go to **Gateway of Tally > Accounts Info. > Ledgers > Create**
2. Type **TDS duty on Commission** in the **Name** field
3. Select **Duties & Taxes** group in the **Under** field
4. Select **TDS** from the list in the **Type of Duty/Tax** field
5. Select **Commission & Brokerage** from the list, in the **Nature of Payment** field, as shown below:

   The Ledger Creation – TDS Duty ledger appears as shown below:

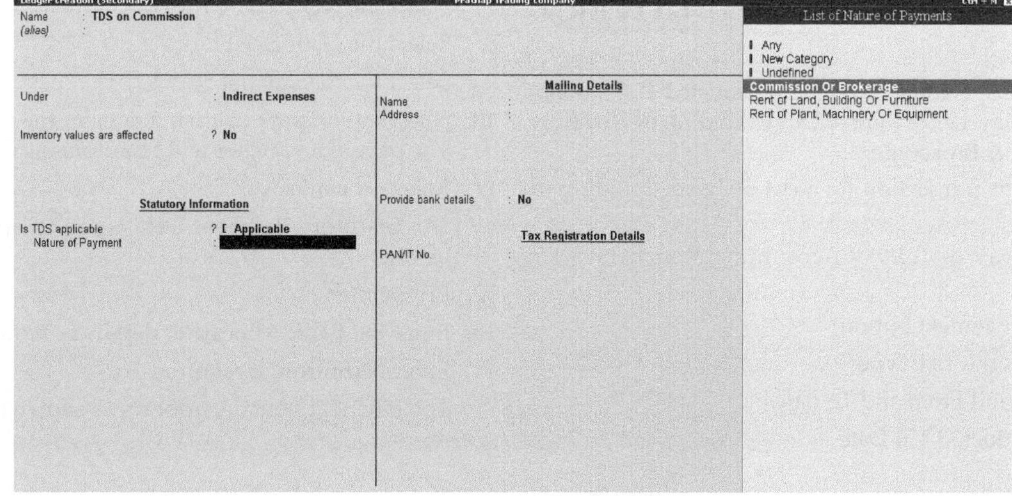

*Figure 7.128: Ledger Creation screen*

6. Set **No** in the **Inventory values are affected** field
7. Press **Enter** to accept

The applicable income tax rates for payment of 'Commission & Brokerage to 'Company Resident Deductee' Type is given below:

| Particulars | Rate |
|---|---|
| TDS | 5% |
| Surcharge | - |
| Education Cess | - |
| Secondary Education Cess | - |

**Step 2:** Create Journal Voucher to book the expenses and deduct TDS

1. Go to **Gateway of Tally > Accounting Voucher > F7: Journal**
2. Click **F2: Date** to change the date to 30-6-2017
3. Debit the **Commission** expense ledger
4. Enter ₹ **1,20,000** in the amount field
5. Credit **Ravi Consultancy.** The amount after TDS deduction will appear in the **Amount** field automatically
6. Press **Enter**
7. Enter the **Bill-wise Details,** as required
8. Press **Enter**
9. Credit the TDS tax ledger. The TDS amount will get filled automatically in the **Amount** field
10. Press **Enter**
11. Enter **Narration,** if required

The **Journal** voucher appears as shown below:

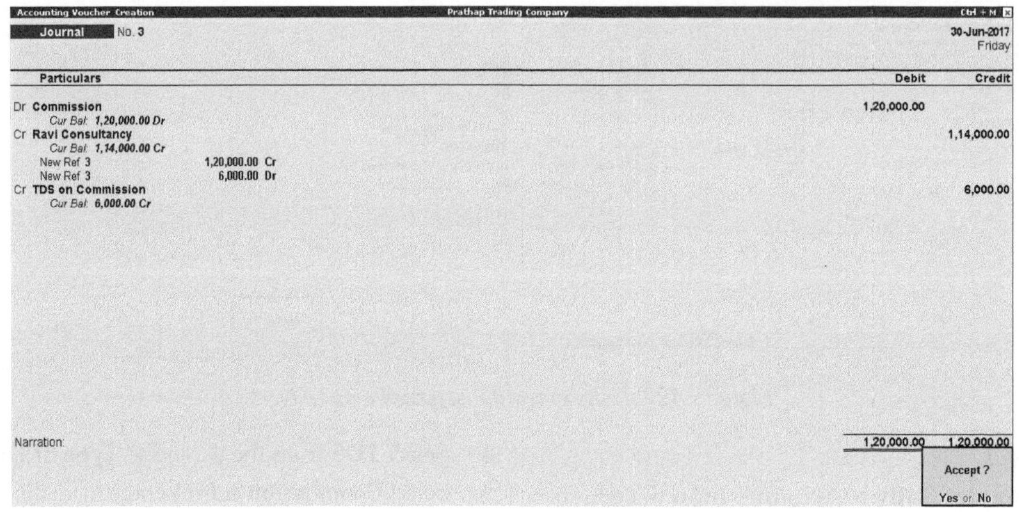


*Figure 7.129: Journal Voucher Creation screen*

12. Press **Ctrl + A** to save the voucher.

## 7.25 MAKING PAYMENT TO GOVERNMENT

On 30-6-2017, Global Trading Co. paid the deducted TDS amount in the month of May. i.e., of Rent of Land, Building or Furniture and Commission & Brokerage.

Record a payment transaction for Rent of Land, Building or Furniture:

1. Go to Gateway of Tally > Accounting Vouchers > F5: Payment
2. Click S: Stat Payment button
3. Select TDS as the Tax Type
4. Enter the Period From and To dates
5. Enter the Deducted Till Date
6. Select the Section from the List of Section
7. Select the required Nature of Payment
8. Select the Deductee Status
9. Select the Residential Status
10. Select either bank or cash ledger in the Cash/Bank field. The payment voucher will be automatically filled with the
11. Relevant values

The **Statutory Payment** Details screen appears as shown below:

12. Press **Enter**
13. Enter the **Bank Allocation details** as required
14. Enter **Narration,** if required

The Payment voucher appears as shown below:

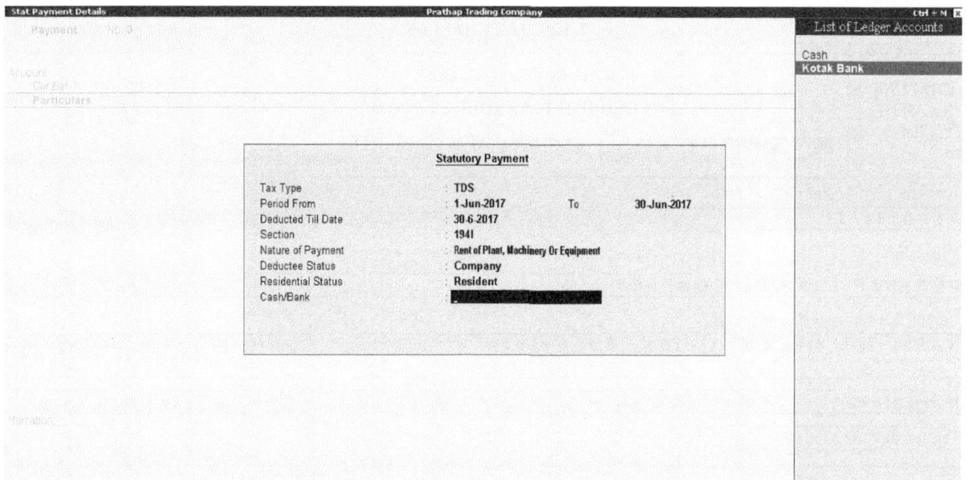


*Figure 7.130: Statutory Payment Details*

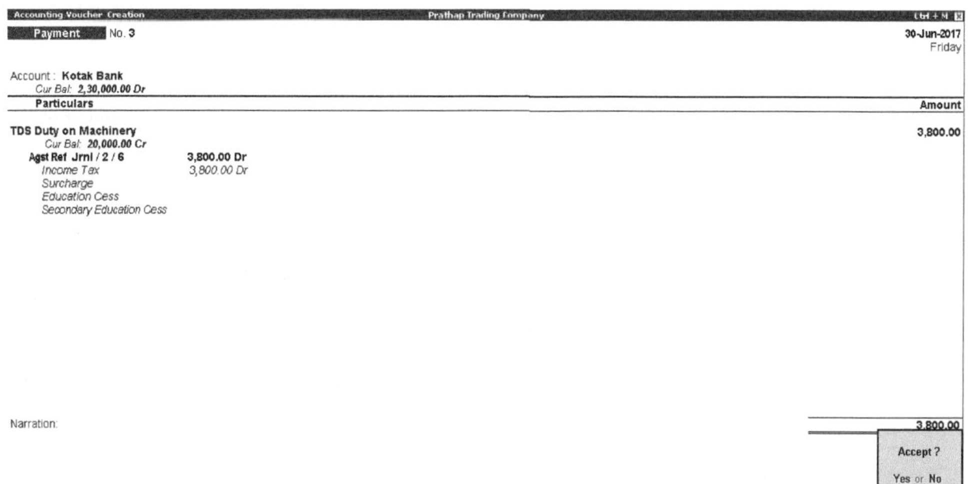


*Figure 7.131: Payment Voucher Creation screen*

15. Press Ctrl+A to save the voucher

    To print ITNS 281 Challan, Open the Payment made to Government > Press Alt+P

16. Press Enter.

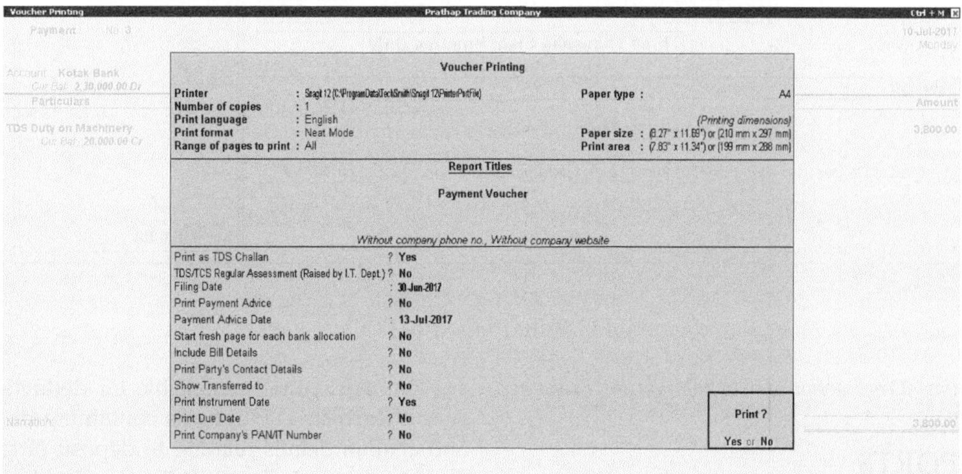


*Figure 7.132 Voucher Printing Screen*

**T.D.S. TAX CHALLAN** Single Copy (to be sent to ZAO)

| CHALLAN No./ ITNS 281 | Tax Applicable (Tick one)* TAX DEDUCTED AT SOURCE FROM (0020) COMPANY DEDUCTEES ☑ (0021) NON-COMPANY DEDUCTEES ☐ | Assessment Year 2018-19 |
|---|---|---|

Tax Deduction Account No. (T.A.N.) ASB088471C

Full Name: PRATHAP TRADING COMPANY

Complete Address with City & State: No556/768, Mega Building, Bangalore

Karnataka

Tel. No. 080-22235645 Pin

**Type of Payment** Code * 4IA

TDS Payable by Taxpayer (200) ☑

TDS Regular Assessment (Raised by I.T. Deptt.) (400) ☐

FOR USE IN RECEIVING BANK

Debit to A/c / Cheque credited on

DD MM YY

SPACE FOR BANK SEAL

Rs. 3,800.00

**DETAILS OF PAYMENTS**

| | Amount (in Rs. Only) |
|---|---|
| Income Tax | 3,800.00 |
| Fee under sec. 234E | |
| Surcharge | |
| Education Cess | |
| Interest | |
| Penalty | |
| Total | 3,800.00 |

Total (in words):

| CRORES | LACS | THOUSANDS | HUNDREDS | TENS | UNITS |
|---|---|---|---|---|---|
| Zero | Zero | Three | Eight | Zero | Zero |

Paid in Cash/ Debit to A/c /Cheque No. 123456 Dated 10-Jul-2017

Drawn on -

(Name of the Bank and Branch)

**Date: 30-Jun-2017** **Signature of person making payment**

Tear Here

**Taxpayers Counterfoil** (To be filled up by taxpayer)

TAN ASB088471C

Received from PRATHAP TRADING COMPANY (Name)

Cash/ Debit to A/c /Cheque No. 123456 For Rs. 3,800

Rs. (in words) Three Thousand Eight Hundred Only.

Drawn on -

(Name of the Bank and Branch)

Company(0020) Deductees

on account of Tax Deducted at Source (TDS) from 4IA for the Assessment Year 2018-19

SPACE FOR BANK SEAL

Rs. 3,800.00

*Figure 7.133 Print Preview of ITNS challan*

***Activity:*** *Record a payment transaction for Commission and Brokerage and generate the Challan.*

## 7.26 TDS REPORTS

As per the Income Tax Act, 1961, every corporate and government entity responsible for deduction of tax at source should furnish TDS returns containing details of deductee(s) and challan details relating to deposit of tax with the Income Tax Department. Form 26Q is the Quarterly return of TDS in respect of all payments other than salaries. This is applicable for Resident and the due date for Government entities is July 31st, October 31st, January 31st and May 15th; for non-government entities the due dates for filing returns are July 15th, October 15th, January 15th and May 15th.

The Form 26Q report in Tally.ERP 9 assists you in generating accurate the returns to be filed.

### *To Generate Form 26Q*

1. Go to Gateway of Tally > Display > Reports > Statutory Reports > TDS Reports > Form 26Q
2. Press Alt+F2 to change the period

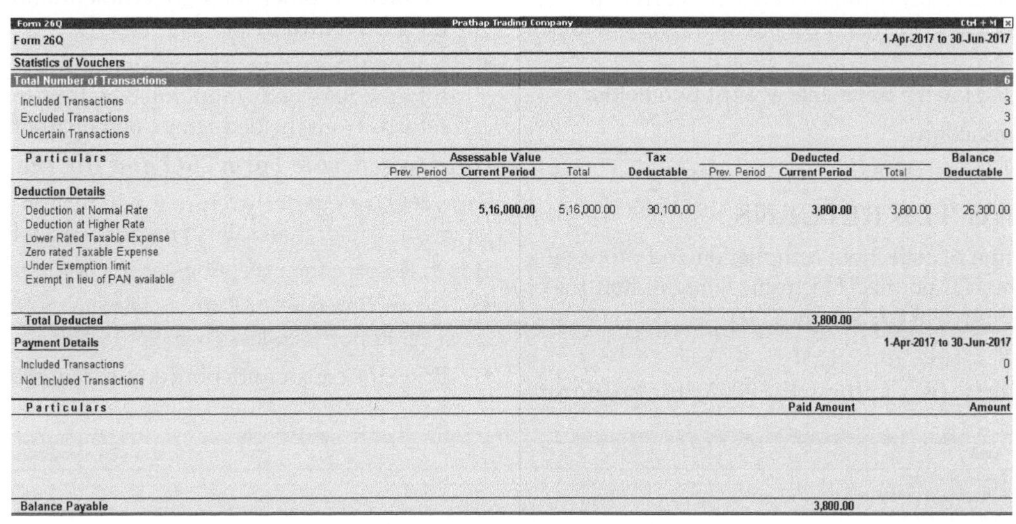

Form 26Q — Prathap Trading Company — Ctrl + M

Form 26Q — 1-Apr-2017 to 30-Jun-2017

**Statistics of Vouchers**

| Total Number of Transactions | 6 |
|---|---|
| Included Transactions | 3 |
| Excluded Transactions | 3 |
| Uncertain Transactions | 0 |

| Particulars | Assessable Value | | | Tax | Deducted | | | Balance |
|---|---|---|---|---|---|---|---|---|
| | Prev. Period | Current Period | Total | Deductable | Prev. Period | Current Period | Total | Deductable |
| **Deduction Details** | | | | | | | | |
| Deduction at Normal Rate | | **5,16,000.00** | 5,16,000.00 | 30,100.00 | | **3,800.00** | 3,800.00 | 26,300.00 |
| Deduction at Higher Rate | | | | | | | | |
| Lower Rated Taxable Expense | | | | | | | | |
| Zero rated Taxable Expense | | | | | | | | |
| Under Exemption limit | | | | | | | | |
| Exempt in lieu of PAN available | | | | | | | | |
| **Total Deducted** | | | | | | **3,800.00** | | |

**Payment Details** — 1-Apr-2017 to 30-Jun-2017

| Included Transactions | 0 |
|---|---|
| Not Included Transactions | 1 |

| Particulars | Paid Amount | Amount |
|---|---|---|
| **Balance Payable** | **3,800.00** | |

*Figure 7.134: Form 26Q*

The Form 26Q report has the following sections:

**Note:** To move the tax payment entry made to government, we need to reconcile the challan from challan reconciliation screen. Once the payment entry is reconciled the same will move to Included transactions field

### *Statistics of Vouchers*

All transactions, whether recorded correctly, incorrectly, or inadequately will be captured and categorized in the Form 26Q report as follows:

### *Included Transactions*

These are transactions that will be a part of Form 26Q. Transactions that will be considered as Included for generating Form 26Q are:

- Booking entries, with or without TDS deduction
- TDS deduction entries
- Advance payments made to parties
- TDS adjustment entries (in the case of government entities)
- Entries accounting for TDS reversals and TDS deduction with respect to escalations and de-escalations

### *Excluded Transactions*

These are transactions that do not carry the TDS details that are requisite to generate Form 26Q, and hence will be excluded while generating the form. Transactions that will be considered as Excluded for generating Form 26Q:

- All entries where TDS is not applied
- Entries recorded using any of the following Voucher Types:
  - o Payment
  - o Contra
  - o Inventory Vouchers
  - o Sales Order
  - o Purchase Order
  - o Debit Note (recorded for purchases with no TDS implications)
  - o Credit Note (entries with no TDS implications)
  - o Vouchers marked as Optional
  - o Payroll Vouchers

### *Uncertain Transactions*

These are transactions that do not fulfill the criteria of the Included and Excluded categories. A voucher will be listed as Uncertain when there is insufficient information entered in:

- Masters
- Transactions

### *Deduction Details*

This section denotes the type of deduction under which each of the Included transaction is grouped.

Deduction details are classified into:

- Deduction at Normal Rate
- Deduction at Higher Rate
- Lower Rated Taxable Expense
- Zero Rated Taxable Expense
- Under Exemption Limit
- Exempt in lieu of PAN Available

The assessable value, tax deductible, and the tax deducted for transactions grouped in the above categories are displayed here.

### *Payment Details*

This will contain the statistics of all TDS payments (deemed or actual) that exist in the data till date. This will not contain any of the payment entries that are not related to the current period. Any payment entries other that TDS payment entry will not appear here.

The section will display the payments against two fields:

- Included Transactions
- Not Included Transactions

## 7.27 E-FILING TDS RETURNS

With the automation of collection, compilation and processing of TDS returns, the ITD notified Electronic Filing of Returns of Tax Deducted at Source in the Scheme 2003.

Under this scheme,

- It is mandatory (w.e.f. June 1st, 2003) for corporate deductors to furnish their TDS returns in electronic form (e-TDS return)
- From F.Y. 2004-2005 onwards furnishing TDS returns in electronic form is also mandatory for government deductors in addition to corporate deductors
- Deductors (other than government and corporates) may file TDS return in
- National Securities Depository Ltd. (NSDL) is the e-TDS Intermediary body (appointed by ITD) to receive the e-TDS returns from the deductors, on behalf of ITD

### *How to generate Form 26Q and file the E-Return.*

Form 26Q is a quarterly return for deduction of tax in respect of payments (other than salary) made to residents.

Step 1: Resolve the exceptions or uncertain transactions

- Go to Gateway of Tally > Display > Statutory Report > TDS Report > Select Form 26Q
- Bring the cursor under uncertain transaction and press nter.

Form 26Q — Prathap Trading Company — Ctrl + M

Form 26Q — 1-Apr-2017 to 30-Jun-2017

| Statistics of Vouchers | |
|---|---|
| **Total Number of Transactions** | 6 |
| Included Transactions | 3 |
| Excluded Transactions | 3 |
| Uncertain Transactions | 0 |

| Particulars | Assessable Value | | | Tax | Deducted | | | Balance |
|---|---|---|---|---|---|---|---|---|
| | Prev. Period | Current Period | Total | Deductable | Prev. Period | Current Period | Total | Deductable |
| **Deduction Details** | | | | | | | | |
| Deduction at Normal Rate | | **5,16,000.00** | 5,16,000.00 | 30,100.00 | | **3,800.00** | 3,800.00 | 26,300.00 |
| Deduction at Higher Rate | | | | | | | | |
| Lower Rated Taxable Expense | | | | | | | | |
| Zero rated Taxable Expense | | | | | | | | |
| Under Exemption limit | | | | | | | | |
| Exempt in lieu of PAN available | | | | | | | | |
| **Total Deducted** | | | | | | **3,800.00** | | |

| Payment Details | 1-Apr-2017 to 30-Jun-2017 |
|---|---|
| Included Transactions | 1 |
| Not Included Transactions | 0 |

| Particulars | Paid Amount | Amount |
|---|---|---|
| Rent of Plant, Machinery Or Equipment | 3,800.00 | |
| **Total Paid** | **3,800.00** | |
| **Balance Payable** | | |

*Figure 7.135: Resolving Uncertain Transactions in Form 26Q*

---

**Note:** In the above given screen we don't have the uncertain transactions. Hence no need to rectify the transactions.

---

**Step 2:** Saving Form 26Q

After resolving the required exceptions, the changes made can be saved.

### *To save the Form 26Q*

1. Click F6: Save button from the Form 26Q Report

If all the exceptions are resolved, and the count of uncertain transactions is zero, then a message prompt appears as shown below:

The Form 26Q screen appears as shown below:

2. Set as Yes and save the Return
3. The saved return will be available in the Return Transaction book

The Return Transaction Book screen appears is given below:

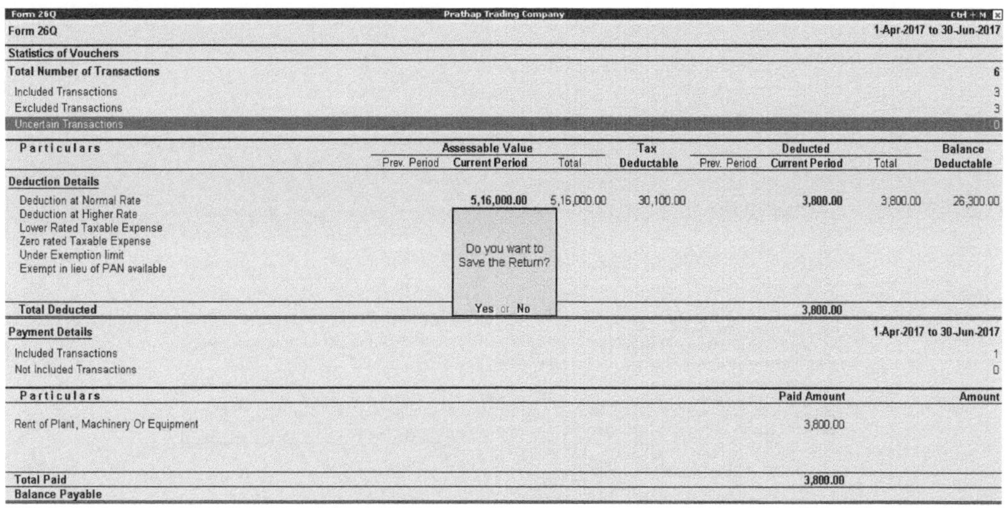


*Figure 7.136: Saving Form 26Q*

Return Transaction Book — Prathap Trading Company — Ctrl + M

Return Transaction Book — 1-Apr-2017 to 30-Jun-2017

| Date | From Date | To Date | Tax Type | Is Modified | Form Type |
|---|---|---|---|---|---|
| 30-Jun-2017 | 1-Apr-2017 | 30-Jun-2017 | TDS | No | 26Q |

*Figure 7.137: Return Transaction Book*

**Note:** Once after saving the return, if you make any changes in the TDS voucher then the return will come for reconciliation can either overwrite the previous return with the existing one or save a revised one.

The saved return will be available in the return transaction book where you will get the details of return along modification details.

**Step 3:** Exporting the Form

On saving the modifications, e-filing of the returns can be done from Form 26Q.

## *To export Form 26Q*

1. Go to Gateway of Tally > Display > Statutory Report > TDS Report > Select Form 26Q

   The Form 26Q screen appears as shown below:

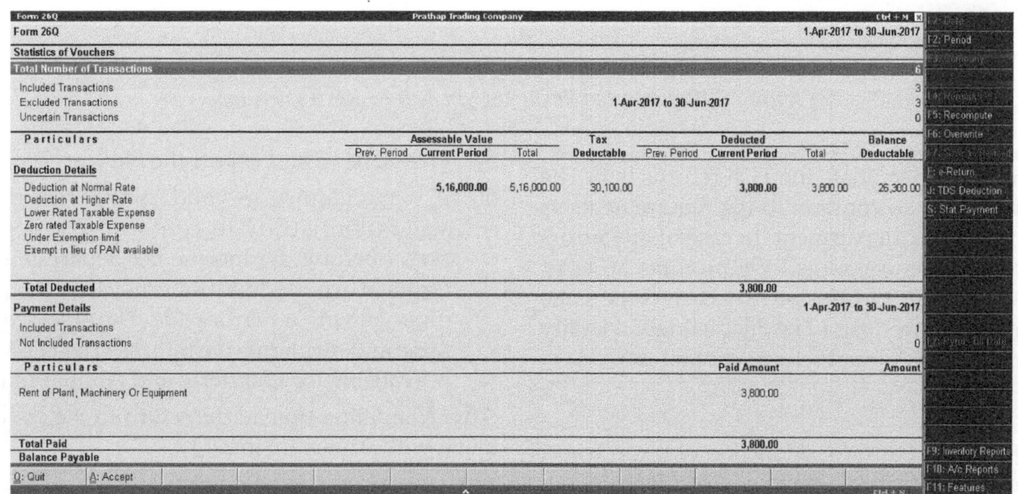


*Figure 7.138: Form 26Q*

**Note:** From the Form 26Q/27Q, you can record the Journal voucher to deduct the TDS and also you can make a payment of TDS to the government

2. Press Ctrl+E, you will get the following screen

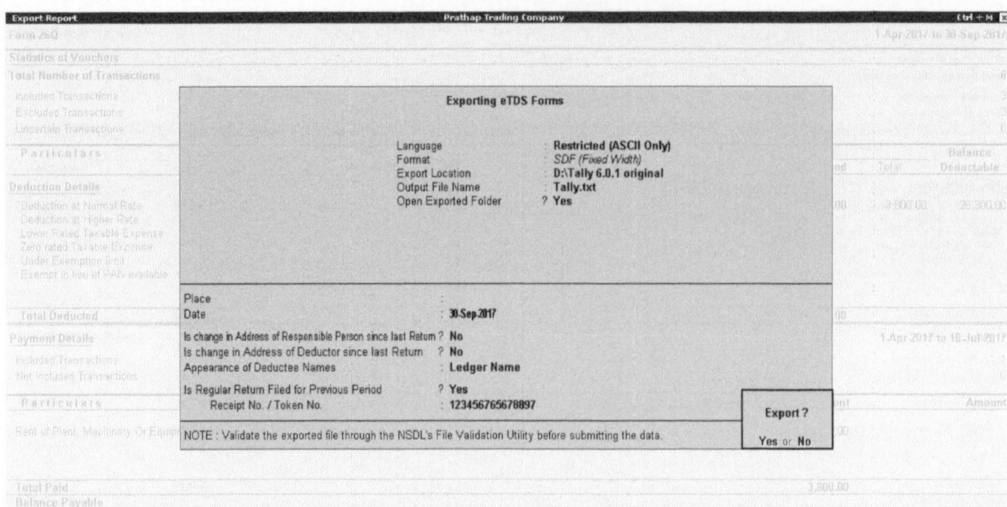

*Figure 7.139: Exporting e-TDS Forms*

3. Press Enter to export the data in the selected format

   The exported file is placed in the Tally.ERP 9 Directory with the specified file name as shown below:

The exported file (Form 26Q) is required to be validated with the File Validation Utility (a freely downloadable utility from NSDL website) and after validation, the returns should be submitted to the department in a CD along with the Form 27A in physical format.

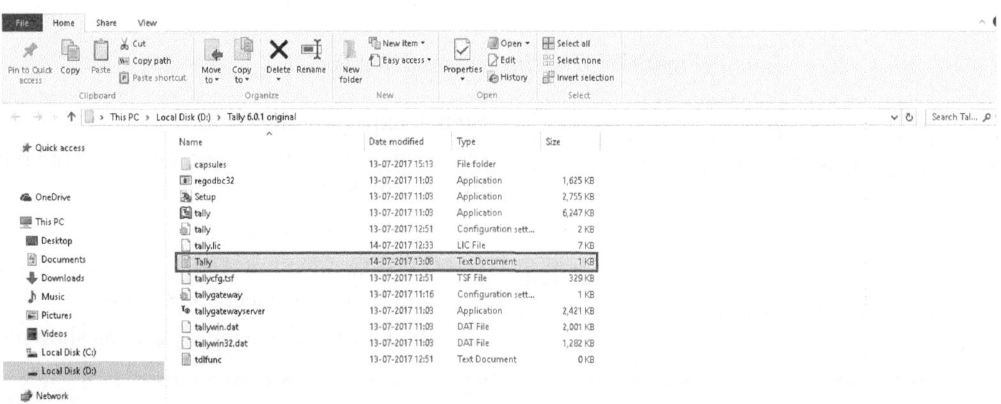

*Figure 7.140: Exported Form 26Q in Tally.ERP 9 Directory*

**Note:** It is mandatory to validate the TDS returns with File Validation Utility to conform to the requirements as by the Income Tax department. In case of any errors in exported file(returns), the FVU prompts an error with an error code. The assesse may correct the same and revalidate the returns ( The File Validation Utility for Quarterly and Annual returns separately)

## *Form 27 Q*

Form 27Q is a Quarterly return for deduction of tax in respect of payments made (other than salary) to non-residents.

### *To print Form 27Q,*

3. Go to Gateway of Tally > Display > Statutory Reports > TDS Reports > Form 27Q
4. Save the return by pressing F6
5. Press Ctrl+E and export the file
6. It is mandatory to validate the TDS returns with File Validation Utility to conform to the requirements as prescribed by the Income tax department. In case of any errors in exported file (Returns), the FVU prompts an error message with an error code. The assessee may correct the same and revalidate the returns (The File Validation Utility is available for Quarterly and Annual returns separately)

After Validating upload the return to the government website along with Annexure to 27Q

# PRACTICE EXERCISE

## Section A: Review Questions

1. Explain TDS.
2. Create the following company and configure TDS.
   - Company name: Mahesh Enterprises.

## Section B: Objective Questions

1. TDS is ___________tax.
   - a. Direct Tax
   - b. Indirect Tax
   - c. Tax on Tax
   - d. Entry Tax
2. TDS is deducted and then the payment is made to the party.
   - a. True
   - b. False
3. National Securities Depository Ltd. (NSDL) is the e-TDS Intermediary body (appointed by ITD) to receive the e-TDS returns from the deductors, on behalf of ITD.
   - a. True
   - b. False
4. ___________is a quarterly return for deduction of tax in respect of payments (other than salary) made to residents.
   - a. Form 26 Q
   - b. Form 27Q
   - c. Form 25 Q
   - d. Form 30 Q
5. ___________is a quarterly return for deduction of tax in respect of payments (other than salary) made to non-residents.
   - a. Form 26 Q
   - b. Form 27Q
   - c. Form 25 Q
   - d. Form 30 Q

# ADVANCED FEATURES OF TALLY.ERP 9

## OBJECTIVES

After studying this section, you will understand:

- E-mailing capabilities in Tally.ERP 9
- How to send reports, invoices etc., by e-mail in Tally.ERP 9
- How to Export and import data in Tally.ERP 9

## 7.28 E-MAILING IN TALLY.ERP 9

Using the e-mail facility provided in Tally.ERP 9, you can e-mail reports like outstanding statements and documents such as invoices, purchase orders, reminder letters to customers.

## 7.29 E-MAILING A REPORT

To e-mail a report,

1. Go to **Gateway of Tally > Display > Statement of Accounts > Outstanding > Ledger** (or any report)
2. Select the required ledger
3. Click **M: E-Mail** or press **Alt+M**
4. Specify the required configurations and details such as the e-mail IDs of the sender and the recipient. Tally.ERP 9 also allows sending it to multiple email addresses
   - To specify only one e-mail address in the **To** field, select one of the e-mail addresses that appears by default (e-mail addresses specified in the ledger master) or select **New Address** option and specify the new e-mail address
   - To specify more than one e-mail address in the **To** field, select the option **Multiple Address**

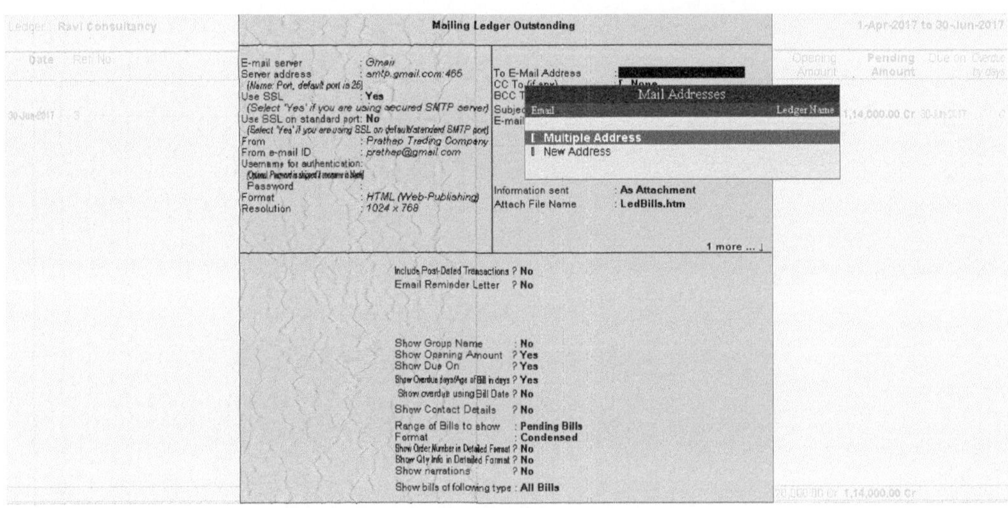


*Figure 7.141: E-mail Report*

5. On selecting **Multiple Address**, in the **To E-mail Address** field appears in the **Multiple E-mail Ids Selection** screen,

**Note:** Select **New Address** to add an e-mail address that is not displayed in the list or select other e-mail addresses that are displayed by default.

The completed **Multiple E-mail Ids Selection** screen appears as shown below:

6. Press **Enter** to accept and navigate back to the **E-Mail Report** screen
7. Specify an e-mail address or multiple e-mail addresses in the **CC or BCC To (if Any)** field to send a copy of the same mail to other recipients
8. By default, the **Subject** line is pre-filled with the respective line for each report. Alter the message, if required. In the
9. **E-mail message (if any)** field, type a message to the recipient which will precede the report in the mail, if required
10. In the **Information Sent** field, select the required **Mail Sending** type i.e., as an attachment or direct view in mail (Applicable only for HTML format)
11. In the **Attach File Name** field, the report name is displayed by default. Alter the attachment name, if required
12. Set **Include Post-Dated Transactions?** to **Yes** to include post-dated transactions
13. Set **E-mail reminder letter to?** to **Yes** to e-mail reminder letter to the customers
14. **Designation of Signing Authority,** enter the signing authority designation or postion
15. Set **Show Due on** to **yes** to mail the details of due on date

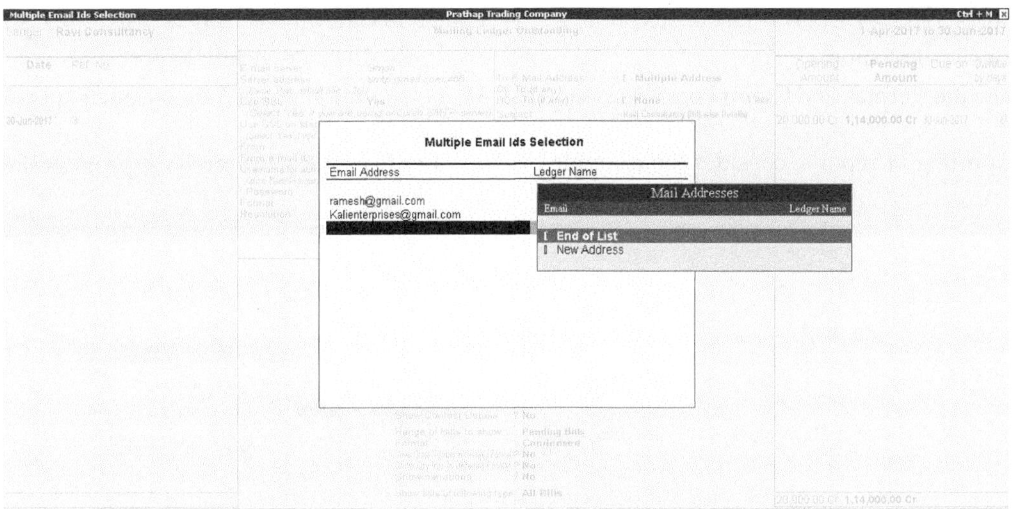


*Figure 7.142: Multiple Email Ids Selection screen*

16. Set **Show overdue using Bill Date?** option to **Yes** to mail the ageing days based on bill date
17. For example: If the **Bill date** is **01-06-2017** and **Due date** is on **10-07-2013**, and the option **'Show overdue using Bill Date'** is set to **Yes**, then the **'Age of Bill in Days'** will be calculated from the **Bill date** and not from the **Due date**
18. Set the option **Show Contact Details** to **Yes** to mail the ledger contact details as mentioned in the ledger master

    The Mailing Ledger Outstanding screen appears as shown below:

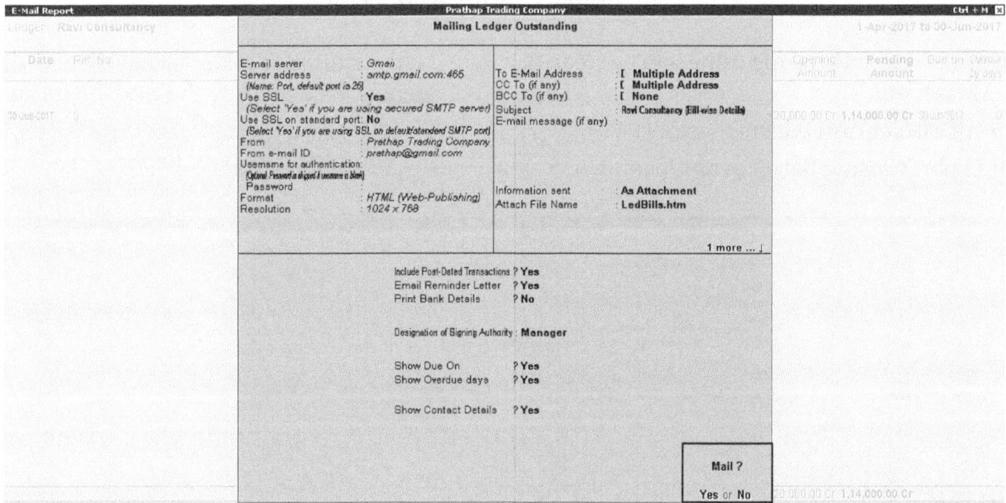


*Figure 7.143: Mailing Ledger Outstanding*

19. Accept the screen to mail the ledger account details to the client

**Note:** Tally.ERP 9 contains pre-defined server address for 3 email servers namely. Gmail, Yahoo and Hotmail. Select user defined to enter the same for any other service provider

The options shown in the bottom part of e-mailing screen belong to the report being e-mailed and hence vary accordingly.

## 7.30 BENEFITS

- The need for an external e-mailing software for mailing reports generated using Tally.ERP 9, is eliminated
- A convenient and time saving option to disburse information and report

## 7.31 EXPORT AND IMPORT OF DATA

Tally.ERP 9 allows import and export of data in different formats for e.g., ASCII, Excel, HTML, JPEG,PDF, and XML.

***Exporting the data in XML format:***

XML Format is used to export and import the data from one company to another which is maintained in Tally.

### 7.31.1 Exporting Data

To understand exporting of reports, consider the example of List of Ledgers

1. Go to Gateway of Tally > Display > List of Accounts
2. Press **Alt+E** or click **E: Export**
3. Select the **Language**, **Format**, and **Export** Location as shown below:

To understand exporting of reports, consider the example of List of Ledgers

1. Go to Gateway of Tally > Display > List of Accounts
2. Press Alt+E or click E: Export
3. Select the Language, Format, and Export Location as shown below:

The Export Report screen appears as shown below:

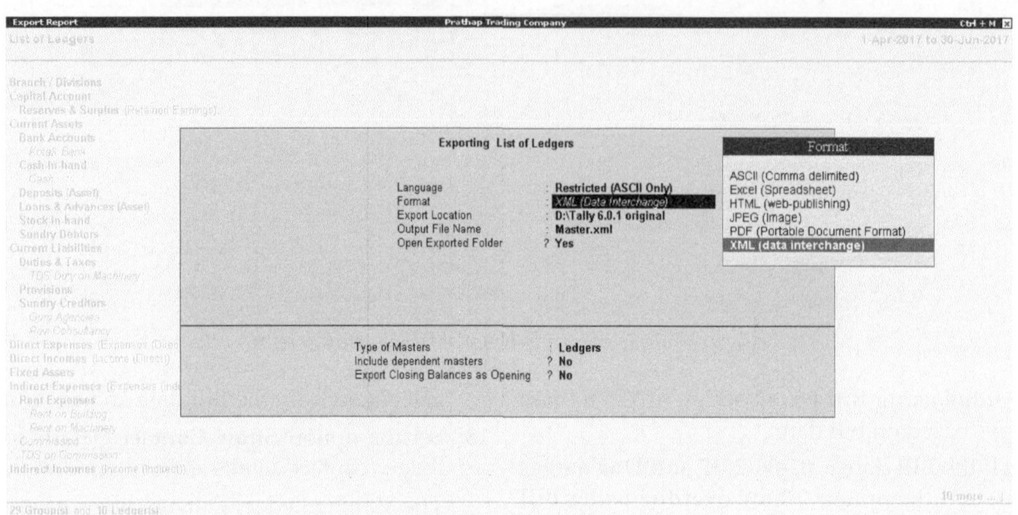


*Figure 7.144: Export Report screen*

4. Based on the Format selected, the file name will be created. For example, Master.xml
5. Select the Type of Masters as Ledgers to export
6. Set the option Export Closing Balances as Opening to Yes if it is required to take closing balances of all the ledgers as opening balances for the next financial year. Otherwise, set it to No

The completed Export Report screen appears as shown below:

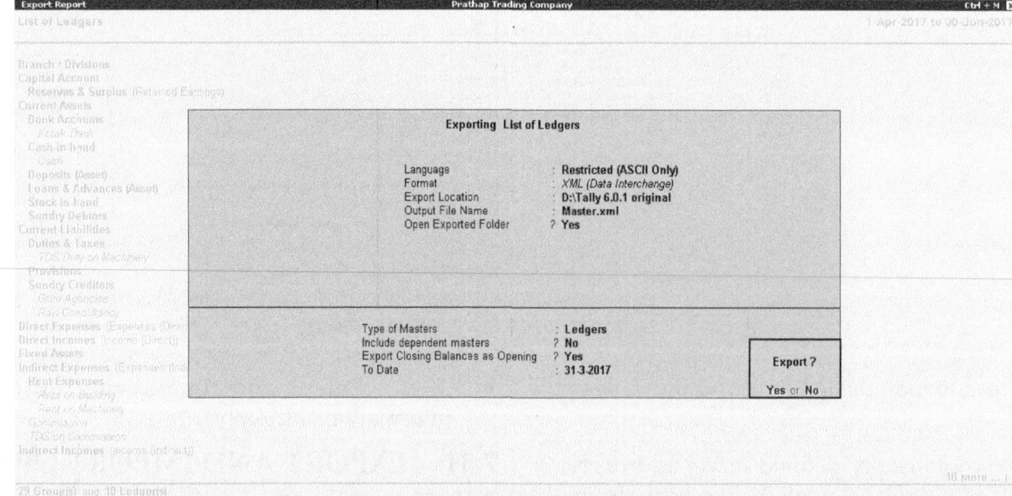


*Figure 7.145: Exporting List of Ledge*

7. Accept the screen

## 7.31.2 Importing Data

To import the data go to,

1. **Gateway of Tally > Import of Data > Select Masters**

The Import Data menu appears as shown in the figure 7.146

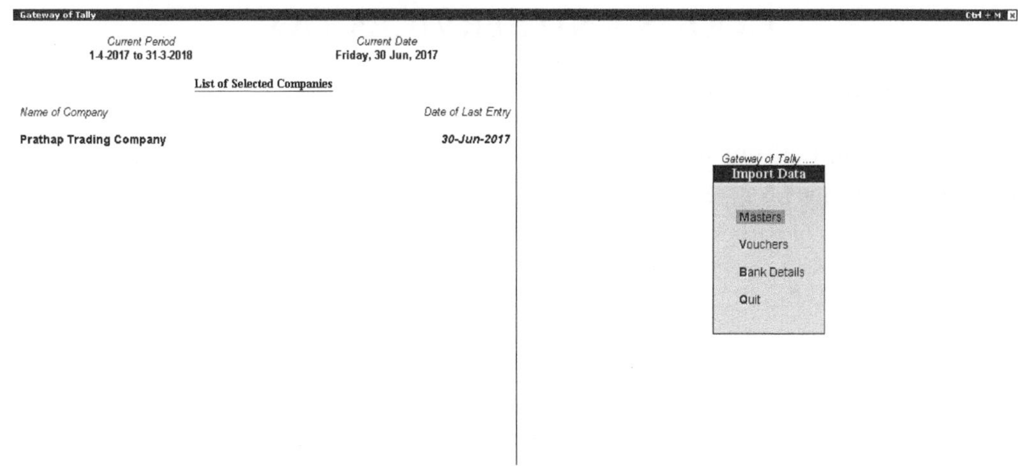


*Figure 7.146: Import Data Menu*

2. Enter the path of the file with its name and extension in Import File Name (XML)
3. Select the required behavior for the Treatment of entries already existing

The Import of Data screen appears as shown below:

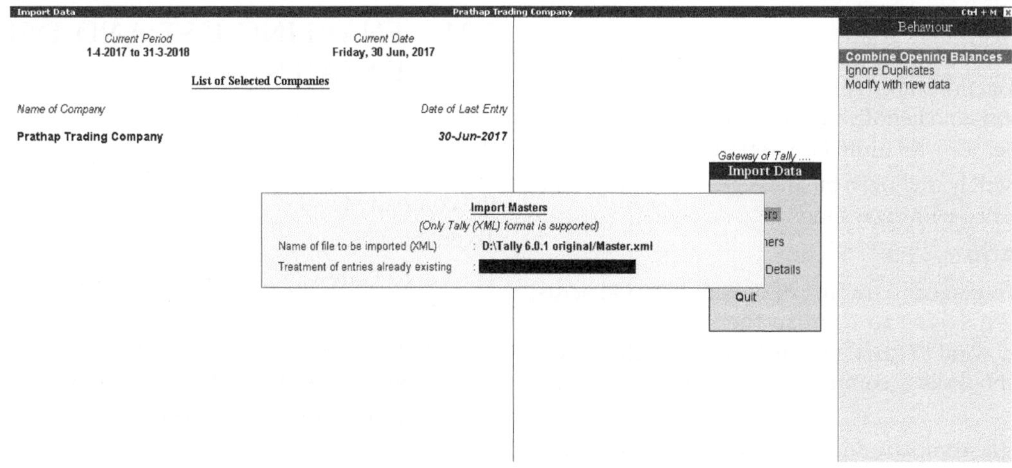


*Figure 7.147: Import of Data*

## 7.32 BENEFITS

- Exporting company data helps in transfer of data to another location in a secure manner
- Data can be transferred to other applications
- No additional steps are required when migrating data from an older version of Tally to a newer one

***Activity:*** *Export the transactions from one company to another.*

# GOODS AND SERVICES TAX

## LEARNING OBJECTIVES

- Activate GST for a company in Tally.ERP 9
- Maintain GST registration details for the company
- Record GST registration details of parties
- Transferring of VAT/excise/service tax, input tax credit to GST
- Record the following transactions:
    - Intrastate Supplies - Inward
    - Intrastate Supplies - Outward
    - Intrastate Supplies - Inward
    - Intrastate Supplies – Outward
    - Supply of Services – Outward
- Record goods return transactions
- Adjustment of input tax credit against tax liability
- GST tax payment
- Return Filing

## 7.33 INTRODUCTION

From the time a company is registered for GST, Tally.ERP 9 enables the business to maintain the company's registration details. With GST maintaining complete details of a business's suppliers and customers also becomes critical. Availing input tax credit is solely dependent on furnishing all the necessary details at an invoice level, which can be easily stored and retrieved using Tally.ERP 9.

Generating GST compliant invoices is so simple no matter how complex the transactions are. Tally.ERP 9 intuitively handles all business scenarios and handles all forms of supplies, resulting in seamlessly generating accurate GST reports.

In this lesson we will learn how a business gets up and running with GST compliance within no time.

### Business Scenario

Raheja Traders is engaged in trading of Badam Hair Oil across the country. They decide to digitise their business using Tally.ERP 9. They want to carry forward the tax credit to GST, and maintain the books of accounts as per the requirements for GST compliance

Let us now create the company and set up GST details for Raheja Traders in Tally.ERP 9.

### *Activity:*

*Create a company in Tally.ERP 9 with the following details:*

*Company Name: Raheja Traders*

*Address: No. 310, 20th Cross, unity building, Karnataka 560030*

*Financial Year: 01-04-2017*

## 7.34 ENABLING GST AND DEFINING TAX DETAILS

We will now enable GST for this company and record the registration details. The company deals with stock items of one GST rate, 18%. Therefore, Raheja Traders define tax details at the company level.

To enable GST,

1. Go to **Gateway of Tally** > Click **F11: Feature** > Click **F3: Statutory**.
2. Set the options **Enable Goods and Services Tax (GST)** to **Yes** and **Set/alter GST details** to **Yes.**

   The **Statutory and Taxation** sub-screen appears as shown in figure 7.148:

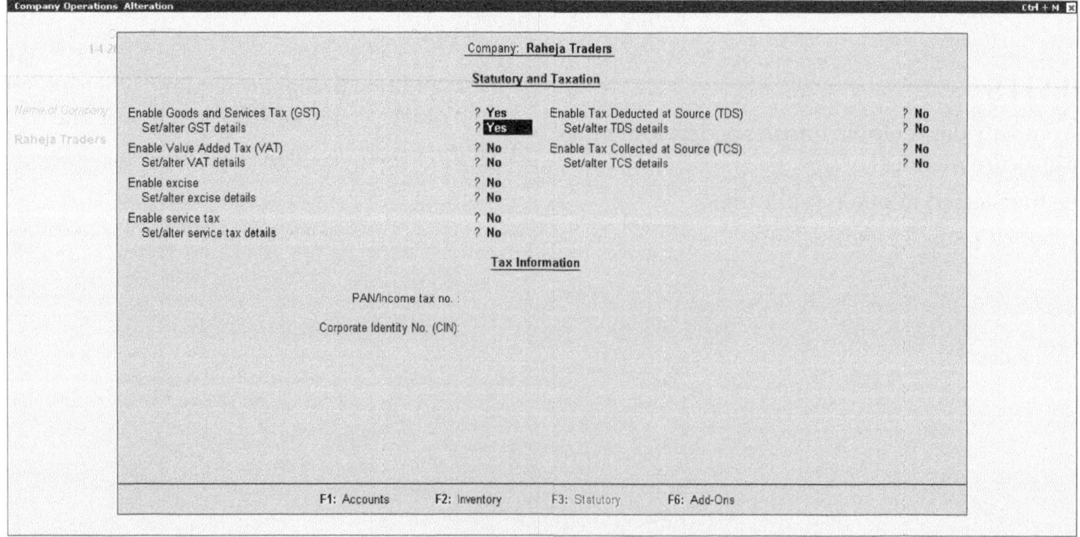


*Figure 7.148: Statutory and Taxation*

3. Press **Enter** to view the **Company GST Details** screen and enter the following details:
   - **State:** Karnataka
   - **Registration type**: Regular (By default **Regular** is selected as the **Registration type**)
   - **GSTIN/UIN:** 29BBBBB1234B1Z5

**Note**: Currently the only Registration Type supported in Tally.ERP 9 is **Regular**, and this is pre-filled by default.

   - **Applicable from**: 1-Jul-2017 (By default the date of GST implementation will be captured here)
   - **Set/alter GST rate details**: Yes (Enabling this option will allow you to define tax details at the company level.

The **Company GST Details** screen appears as shown in figure 7.149:

4. Press **Enter** to view the **GST Details** screen.
5. Click **F12: Configure** to display more options.

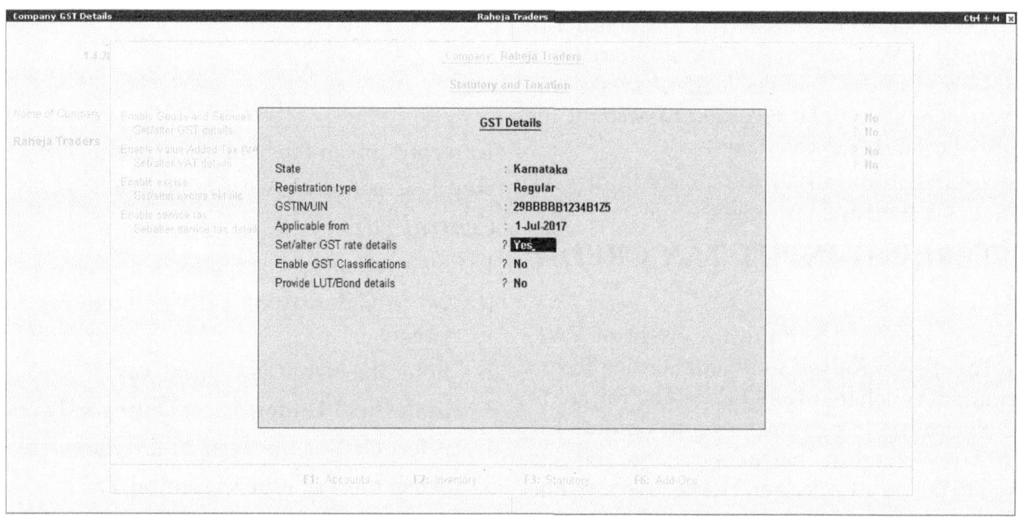


*Figure 7.149: Company GST Details screen*

6. Enable the options **Allow HSN/SAC details** and **Show all GST Tax Types**.
7. Enter the GST details as specified.

| Against the Field | Action to be Performed |
|---|---|
| Description | Enter **Hair Oil** |
| HSN/SAC | Enter **33011100** |
| Taxability | Select **Taxable** |
| Integrated Tax | Enter **18%** |
| Central Tax | Gets auto-filled based on the value of **Integrated Tax**. Press **Enter**. |
| State Tax | Gets auto-filled based on the value of Integrated Tax. Press **Enter**. |

The **Tax Rate Details** sub-screen appears as shown in figure 7.150:

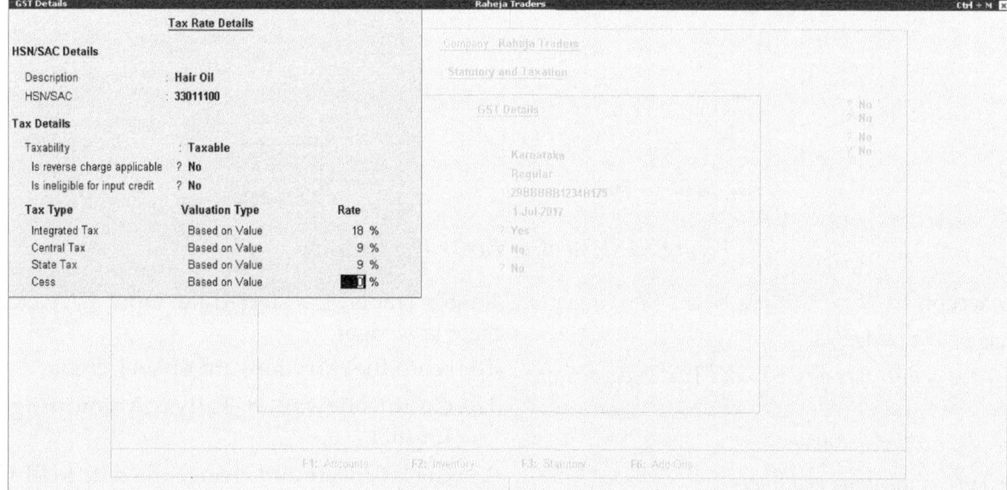


*Figure 7.150: Tax Rate Details*

6. Press **Enter** to go to the **Company GST Details** screen.
7. Press **Ctrl+A** to go to the **Statutory and Taxation** sub-screen.
8. Press **Ctrl+A** to accept.

We have enabled GST for Raheja Traders. Now, we can transfer the closing balance, and continue recording day-to-day transactions for the company in Tally.ERP 9.

In Tally.ERP 9, we can transfer the input tax credit of VAT, CENVAT, Service Tax, Krishi Kalyan Cess and Service Tax to GST by recording journal voucher in Tally.ERP 9. The Tax credit of Service tax and Excise has to be transferred to Central Tax ledger and the tax credit of VAT, additional tax, surcharge and cess has to be transferred to the state tax ledger. Hence, two separate journal vouchers have to be recorded to account for the opening balance of central and state taxes.

In this section we will learn to transfer the tax credit of VAT and CENVAT to state tax & central tax ledger.

## 7.35 TRANSFERRING INPUT TAX CREDIT TO GST

In Tally.ERP 9, we can transfer the input tax credit of VAT, CENVAT, Service Tax, Krishi Kalyan Cess and Service Tax to GST by recording journal voucher in Tally.ERP 9. The Tax credit of Service tax and Excise has to be transferred to Central Tax ledger. The tax credit of VAT, additional tax, surcharge and cess has to be transferred to the state tax ledger. Hence, two separate journal vouchers have to be recorded to account for the opening balance of central and state taxes.

In this section we will learn how to transfer credit of VAT and CENVAT to state tax and central tax ledgers.

***Illustration 1:*** *Transfer of closing balance of input tax credit to GST*

| Date | Particulars |
|---|---|
| 01-07-2017 | **Voucher: Journal**Raheja Trader, transferred the input VAT credit of 10,000 to state tax ledger. |
| 01-07-2017 | **Voucher: Journal**Raheja Traders, transferred the CENVAT credit of 2,000 to central tax ledger.<br>***Note:*** *As per GST, a dealer can claim CENVAT on the purchase.* |

To record this in the books of accounts,

**Step 1:** Creation of Accounting Masters

### *Central Tax*

To create a Central Tax ledger,

1. Go to **Gateway of Tally** > **Accounts Info.** > **Ledgers** > **Create.**
2. Enter the **Name** as **Central Tax.**
3. In the field **Under**, select **Duties & Taxes.**
4. Select **GST** as the **Type of duty/tax.**
5. Select the **Tax type** as **Central Tax.**
6. Press **Enter.**

   The central tax ledger appears as shown in the figure 7.151.

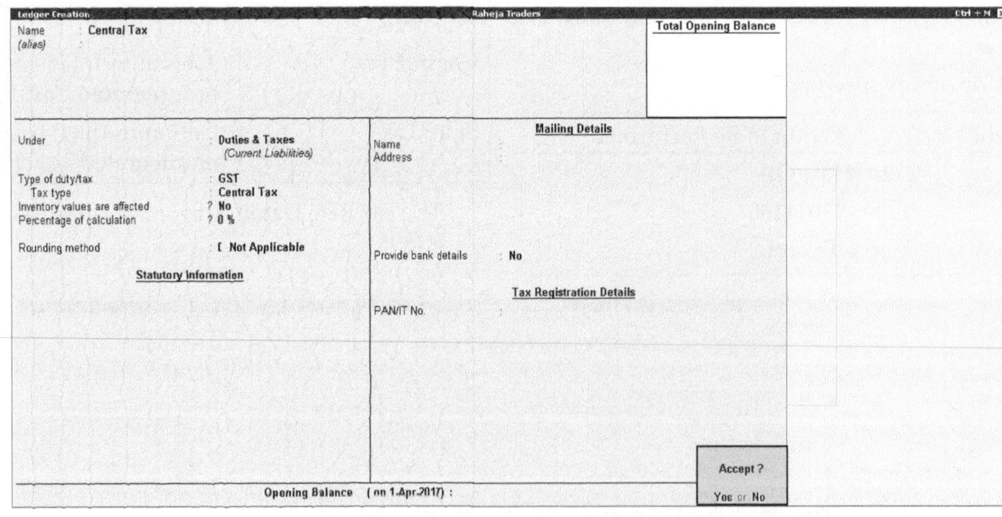


*Figure 7.151: Central Tax Ledger Creation*

7. Press **Enter** to accept.

***Activity:*** *Create the following ledgers:*

*State Tax with Type of duty/tax as GST, and Tax Type as State Tax.*

***VAT*** *with Type of duty/tax as Others*

***CENVAT*** *with Type of duty/tax as Others.*

**Step 2**: Recording Journal Transactions

Raheja Trader, transferred the input VAT credit of 10,000 to state tax ledger.

To record the carry forward of VAT credit,

1. Go to **Gateway of Tally** > **Accounting Vouchers** > **F7: Journal.**
2. Click **F2:Date** and change the date to 01-07-2017
3. Click **J: Stat Adjustment.**

4. In the **Stat Adjustment Details** screen, select the details as shown in figure 7.152:

   The **Stat Adjustment Details** screen appears as shown in the figure 7.152:

5. Press **Enter**.

6. Debit the **State Tax** ledger and enter the amount as **10,000.**

7. Credit the **VAT** ledger and the amount will get captured automatically.

   The completed journal transaction appears as shown in the figure 7.153:

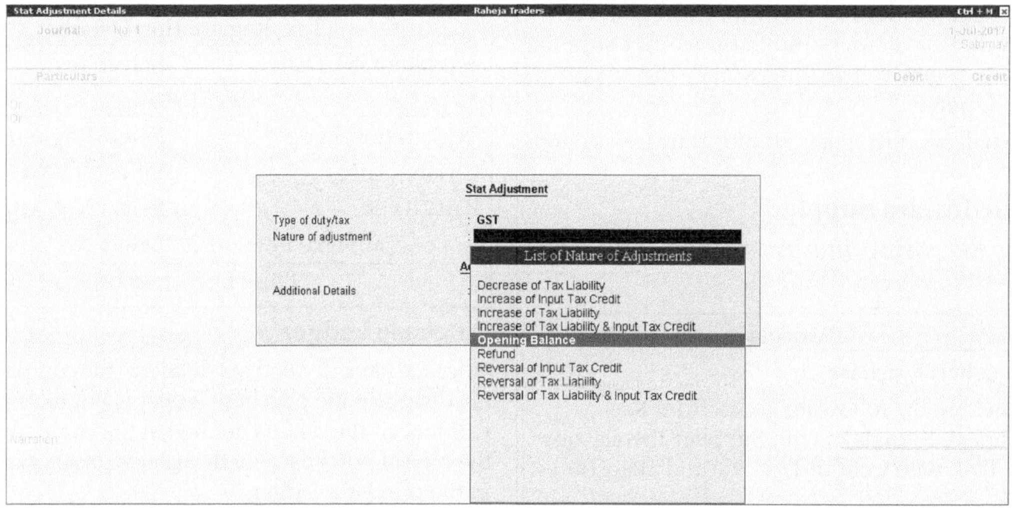


*Figure 7.152: Stat Adjustment for Opening Balance*

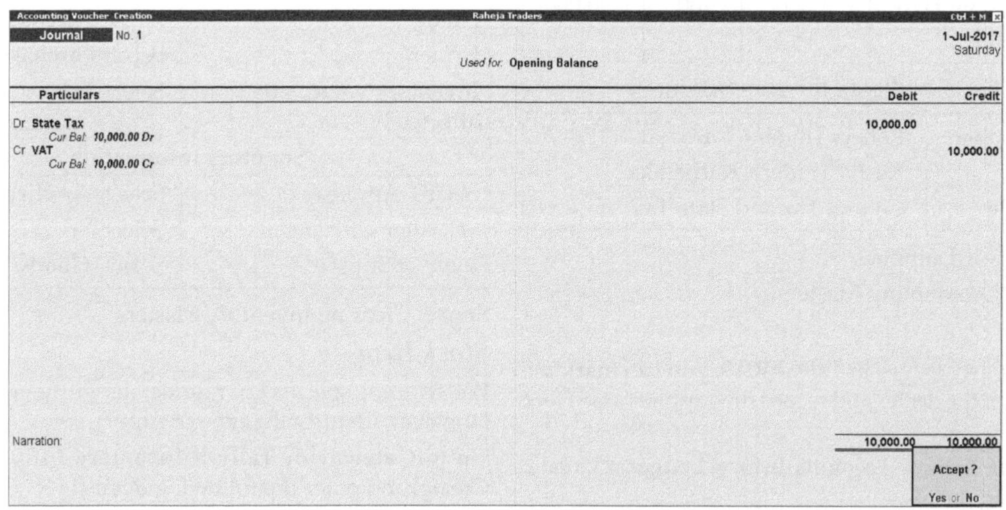


*Figure 7.153: Transferring Opening Balance – VAT*

8. Press **Enter** to accept.

**Note:** The opening balance entered for central tax and state tax in ledger master or journal voucher is a book entry maintained for matching purpose and it will not reflect in the statutory reports because, in the latest GST taxation system the liability and input tax credit information will be pulled from GSTN network. Hence it will not reflect in the statutory report.

The Journal voucher can be recorded from GSTR-1 and GSTR2 report in Tally.ERP 9.

***Activity:*** *Record the following entry:*

| ***01-07-2017*** | ***Voucher: Journal*** |
|---|---|
| | *Raheja Traders, transferred the CENVAT credit of 2,000 to central tax ledger.* <br> ***Note:*** *As per GST, a dealer can claim CENVAT on the purchase.* |

***Hint:*** *While recording the journal voucher debit the Central Tax ledger and credit the CENVAT ledger.*

## 7.36 INTRASTATE SUPPLY OF GOODS

We know taxability depends on the place of supply. Determining the place of supply is critical to identify the taxability.

Intrastate supply is a transaction where the location of supplier, and the place of supply are the same.

For example, Raheja Traders is a company registered in Karnataka. When Raheja Traders purchase from a supplier whose company is registered in Karnataka, the supply is intrastate inward supply.

In this section we will see how to record intrastate transactions using Tally.ERP 9.

### 7.36.1 Intrastate Inward Supply

***Illustration 2:*** *Recording inward supply of goods in Tally.ERP 9.*

| Date | Particulars | | | |
|---|---|---|---|---|
| 01-07-2017 | **Voucher: Purchase**<br>Purchase the following goods from Kesha Traders, Karnataka with Supplier Invoice no.: PUR/1, with Central Tax - 9% and State Tax – 9%. | | | |
| | **Name of Item** | **Quantity /Btl.** | **Rate /Btl.** | **Amount** |
| | **Badam Hair Oil** | 1,000 | 400 | 4,00,000 |

Let us determine the taxability of this transaction:

| | |
|---|---|
| **Location of Supplier** | Raheja Traders, Karnataka |
| **Place of Supply** | Kesha Traders, Karnataka |
| **Taxes Applicable** | Central Tax and State Tax |

To account for inward supplies

**Step 1:** Recording Accounting Masters

#### *Party ledger*

When creating a party ledger in Tally.ERP 9, you can mark the Registration type of the dealer and record the supplier's GSTIN/UIN in the master.

**Go to Gateway of Tally > Accounts Info. > Ledger > Create.** Enter the following details:

| Kesha Traders | |
|---|---|
| **Against the field** | **Action to be performed** |
| Name | **Enter Kesha Traders** |
| Under | **Select Sundry Creditors** |
| Maintain balances bill-by-bill | **Select Yes** |
| Default credit period | **Press Enter** |
| Check for credit days during | **Select No** |
| Inventory values are affected | **This field will be skipped** |

| Mailing Details | |
|---|---|
| Address | **No. 92, Twin Tower** |
| Country | **Select India** |
| State | **Select Karnataka** |
| Pincode | **Enter 560029** |
| **Tax Registration Details** | |
| Set/alter GST Details | **Select Yes** |
| **GST Details** | |
| Registration Type | **Select Regular** |
| GSTIN/ UIN | **Enter 29AAAAA1252A1Z9** |
| Party Type | **Select Not Applicable** |
| Is a e-Commerce operator? | **Select No** |
| Press Enter to accept | |

#### Purchase Ledger

Since we have defined tax details at the company level, defining tax details in the purchase ledger is not required. Transactions will inherit the details defined at the company level. However, the type of purchase whether goods or services can be identified in the purchase ledger.

| Purchases | |
|---|---|
| **Against the Field** | **Action to be Performed** |
| Name | Enter **Purchases** |
| Under | Select **Purchase Accounts** |
| Inventory values are affected? | Select **Yes** |
| **Statutory Information** | |
| Is GST Applicable? | Select **Applicable** |
| Set/alter GST Details? | Select **No** |
| Type of Supply | Select **Goods** |

**Step 2:** Creating Inventory Masters

#### *Stock Item*

We will not specify tax rate details in the stock item as well. However, identify the type of supply.

**Go to Gateway of Tally > Inventory Info. > Stock Items > Create**, and enter the following details:

| Badam Hair Oil | |
|---|---|
| **Against the Field** | **Action to be Performed** |
| **Name** | Enter **Badam Hair Oil** |
| **Under** | Select **Primary** |
| Units | Press **Alt+C and create the unit Btl.** |
| GST Applicable? | Select **Applicable** |
| Set/Alter GST Details? | Select **No** |
| Type of Supply | Select **Goods** |
| Press **Enter** to accept | |

Since this is an intrastate supply, this transaction attracts central tax and state tax. We will now see how the transaction is recorded in Tally.ERP 9.

**Step 3:** Recording Intrastate Inward Supplies

To record intrastate inward supply of goods,

1. Go to **Gateway of Tally > Accounting Vouchers > F9: Purchase.**
2. Ensure the purchase voucher is in **Item Invoice** mode.
3. Click **F12: Configure** and set the option **Use common ledger account for item allocation** to **Yes**.
4. Press **Ctrl+A**.
5. Enter the **Supplier invoice no** as **P/01**, the **Date** field will be automatically filled same as **voucher date.**
6. Select **Kesha Traders** in the **Party A/c name** field, press **Enter** to get **Party Details** screen.

**Note**: The GSTIN/UIN as entered in the supplier ledger is displayed here.

7. Select **Regular** as the **Type of Dealer**.

The **Party Details** screen appears as shown in the figure 7.154:

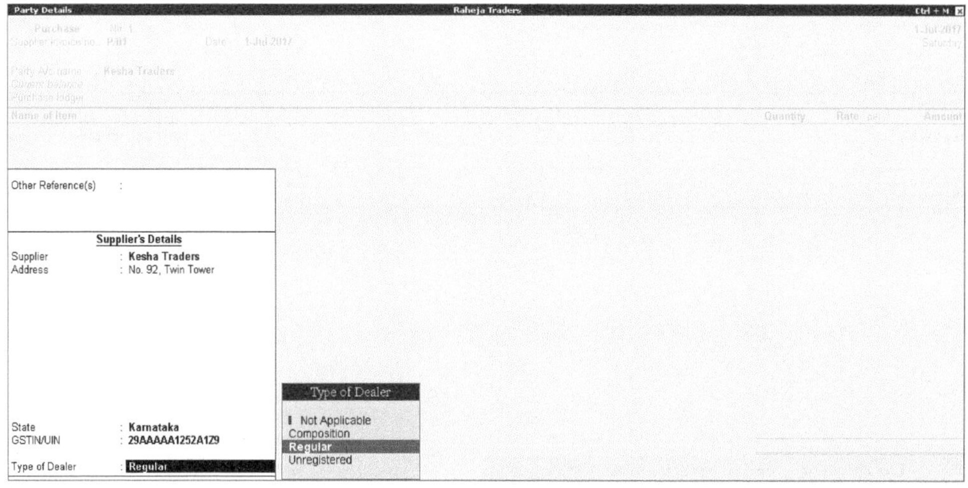


*Figure 7.154: Party Details*

8. Select **Purchases** in **Purchase ledger** field
9. In the **Name of Item** field, select **Badam Hair Oil** from **List of Stock Items.**
10. Enter **Quantity** as **1,000 Btl.** and Rate as **400/Btl.**, the amount will be calculated automatically.
11. Press **Enter** twice to select the GST duty ledgers.
12. Select **Central Tax** ledger, the tax amount will get captured automatically.
13. Select the **State Tax** ledger, the tax amount will get captured automatically.
14. Click A: **Tax Analysis** to view the tax implication in this transaction.
15. Click **F1: Detailed.**

The **Tax Analysis** screen appears as shown in the figure 7.155:

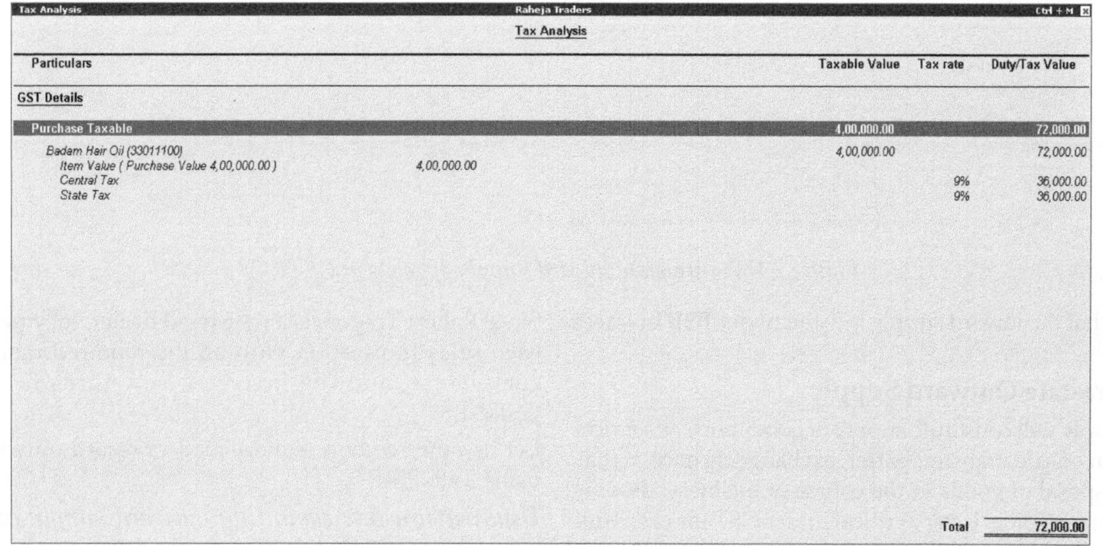


*Figure 7.155: Tax Analysis*

***Observation:*** *We can see that State tax and Centre tax have been calculated at 18% each. This is based on the integrated tax rate defined for the company.*

12. Press **Esc** to go to the voucher creation screen.
13. Accept the **Bill wise Details** screen as it is

The intrastate inward supply appears as shown in the figure 7.156

12. Enter the **Narration**, if required.
13. Press **Enter**.

Since this transaction is an inward supply, the tax implication of this transaction can be viewed in **GSTR – 2**.

To view **GSTR-2**,

Go to **Gateway of Tally > Display > Statutory Reports > GST > GSTR-2.**

The **GSTR-2** report appears as shown in the figure 7.157:

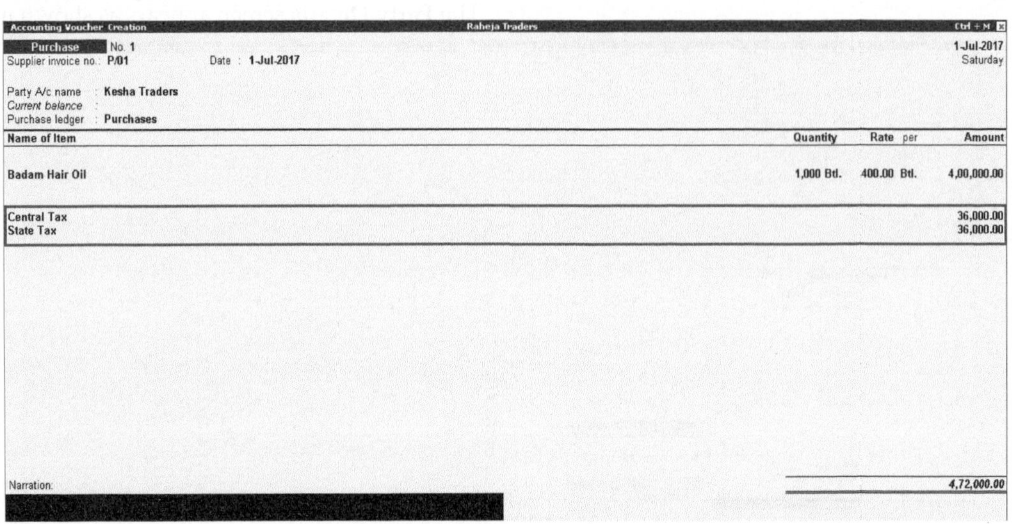

*Figure 7.156: Intrastate Inward Supply*

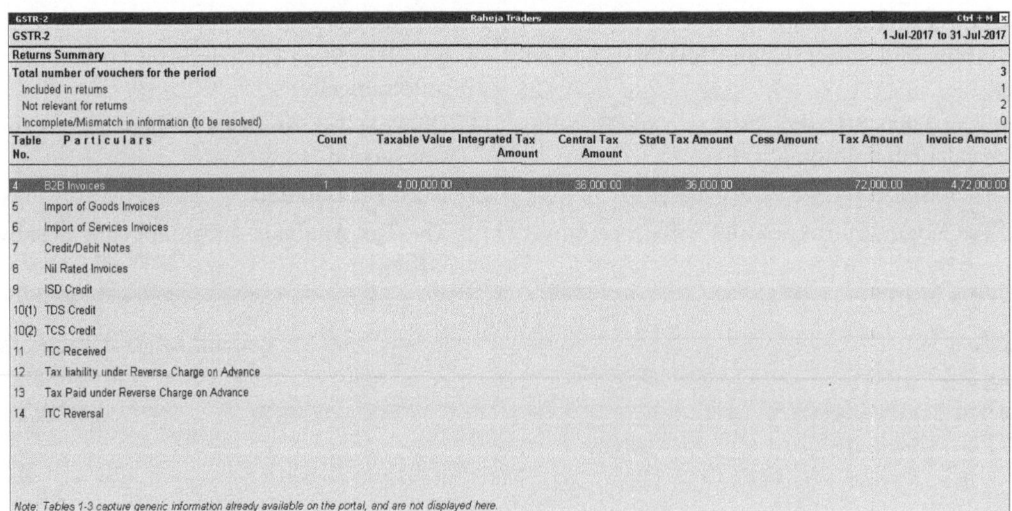

*Figure 7.157: Intrastate Inward Supply of goods in GSTR-2*

You can see that the inward supply is listed under **B2B Invoices** of **GSTR-2**.

## 7.36.2 Intrastate Outward Supply

Outward supply will constitute supply of goods and/or services of transaction of sale, transfer, barter, exchange, licence, rental, lease and disposal of goods in the course of business. Issuing GST compliant invoices is very critical under GST for error-free return filing.

Since Raheja Traders is a registered dealer, they need to record each sales transaction with all the required details for GST compliance, and file invoice-wise returns in the form of GSTR-1.

Let us now see how Raheja Traders record outward supplies using Tally.ERP 9.

***Illustration 3:*** *Accounting outward supply of goods and generating of GST invoice in Tally.ERP*

| Date | Particulars | | | |
|---|---|---|---|---|
| 03-07-2017 | **Voucher: Sales**<br>Sold the following goods to TK Traders, Karnataka with Reference no.:1/RT, with Central Tax - 9% and State Tax – 9% | | | |
| | **Name of Item** | **Quantity /Btl.** | **Rate /Btl.** | **Amount** |
| | **Badam Hair Oil** | 100 | 70 | 70,000 |
| | **Packing Charge = 5,000**<br>**Discount Allowed @ 1%** | | | |

Let us determine the taxability of this transaction:

| | |
|---|---|
| **Location of Supplier** | Raheja Traders, Karnataka |
| **Place of Supply** | TK Traders, Karnataka' |
| **Taxes Applicable** | Central Tax and State Tax |

To account for outward supplies,

**Step 1:** Creation of Accounting Masters

## *Party Ledger*

Go to **Gateway of Tally > Accounts Info. > Ledgers > Create,** and enter the following details:

| TK Traders | |
|---|---|
| **Against the field** | **Action to be performed** |
| Name | **Enter TK Traders** |
| Under | **Select Sundry Debtors** |
| Maintain balances bill-by-bill | **Select Yes** |
| Default credit period | **Press Enter** |
| Check for credit days during | **Select No** |
| Inventory values are affected | **Select No** |
| **Mailing Details** | |
| Address | |
| Country | **Select India** |
| State | **Select Karnataka** |
| Pincode | **Enter 560030** |
| **Tax Registration Details** | |
| Set/alter GST Details | **Select Yes** |
| **GST Details** | |
| Registration Type | **Select Regular** |
| GSTIN/ UIN | **Enter 29SSSSS1234S1Z1** |
| Is a e-Commerce operator? | **Select No** |
| Press Enter to accept. | |

**Note:** Tax is calculated based on state and registration type. Ensure these fields are defined appropriately.

## *Expense Ledgers*

Expenses like packing charges, freight charges, etc have to be included in the transaction value on which GST will be calculated. To include the value of expenses, the option **Include in assessable value for has** to be enabled.

| Packing Charges | |
|---|---|
| Against the Field | **Action to be Performed** |
| **Name** | Enter **Packing Charges** |
| **Under** | Select **Indirect Expenses** |
| **Inventory values are affected?** | Select **No** |
| **Statutory Information** | |
| **Is GST Applicable?** | Select **Not Applicable** |
| **Set/alter GST Details?** | This field will be skipped by default |
| **Include in assessable value calculation for** | Select **GST** |
| **Appropriate to** | Select **Goods** |
| **Method of Calculation** | Select **Based on Value** |
| **Press** Enter **to accept.** | |

**Note:** The option **Include in assessable value calculation?** will be available only if the option **Is GST Applicable?** Is set to **Not Applicable.**

| Discount Allowed | |
|---|---|
| Against the Field | **Action to be Performed** |
| **Name** | Enter **Discount Allowed** |
| **Under** | Select **Indirect Expenses** |
| **Inventory values are affected?** | Select **No** |
| **Statutory Information** | |
| **Is GST Applicable?** | Select **Not Applicable** |
| **Set/alter GST Details?** | This field will be skipped by default |
| **Include in assessable value calculation for** | Select **GST** |
| **Appropriate to** | Select **Goods** |
| **Method of Calculation** | Select **Based on Value** |
| **Press** Enter **to accept.** | |

**Note:** The option **Include in assessable value calculation?** will be available only if the option **Is GST Applicable?** is set to **Not Applicable.**

*Sales Ledger*

| Sales | |
|---|---|
| Against the Field | **Action to be Performed** |
| **Name** | Enter **Sales** |
| **Under** | Select **Sales Accounts** |
| **Inventory values are affected?** | Select **Yes** |
| **Statutory Information** | |
| **Is GST Applicable?** | Select as **Applicable** |
| **Set/alter GST Details?** | Select **No** |
| **Type of Supply** | Select as **Goods** |

**Step 2:** Recording Intrastate Outward Supply

To record intrastate outward supply,

1. Go to **Gateway of Tally > Accounting Vouchers > F8: Sales.**
2. Ensure **Sales Voucher** is in **Item Invoice mode**.
3. Click **F2: Date** and change the date to **03-07-2017**.
4. Enter **Reference no.:** as **1/RT.**
5. Select **TK Traders** in the **Party A/c name** field.
7. In the **Party Details** screen, make sure the **State, GSTIN/ UIN,** and **Type of dealer** is selected.
7. Select **Sales** in **Sales ledger** field.
8. In the **Name of Item** field select **Badam Hair Oil** from **List of Stock Items.**
9. Enter the **Quantity as 100/Btl.** and **Rate as ₹ 700/Btl.**, the amount will be calculated automatically. Press **Enter** twice to select the additional ledgers.
10. Select **Packing Charges** ledger and enter the amount as ₹ **5,000.**
11. Select **Discount Allowed** ledger, enter rate as **-1%**, the discount value will get calculated automatically.
12. Select **Central Tax** ledger, the tax amount will get captured automatically.
13. Select the **State Tax** ledger, the tax amount will get captured automatically.
14. Press **Alt+A** to view **Tax Analysis** screen, press **Alt+F1,** to view in **Detailed** mode.

The **Tax Analysis** screen appears as shown in figure 7.158.

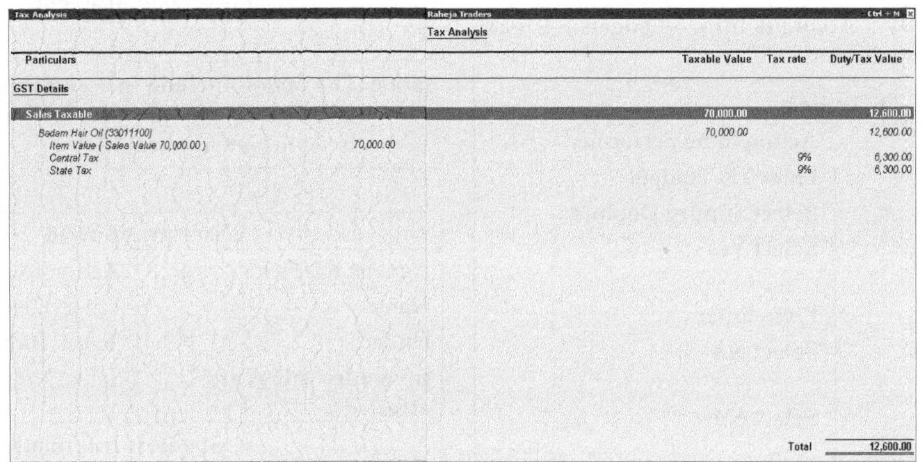


*Figure 7.158: Tax Analysis*

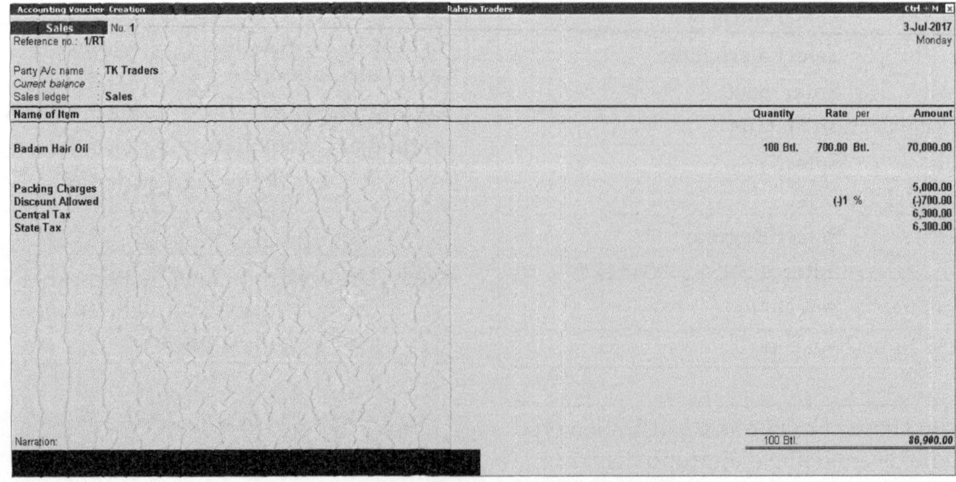


*Figure 7.159: Intrastate Outward Supply*

***Observation:*** *The assessable value is calculated by including the value of packing charge and deducting the discount allowed. Central and State taxes are calculated on the assessable value after this computation.*

11. Press **Esc** from the **Tax Analysis** screen, you will come back to sales voucher creation screen.

    The **intrastate outward supply** appears as shown in figure 7.159:

11. In the **Bill-wise details for: TK Traders** sub-screen, select **New Ref** as the **Type of Ref** and enter the Name as **1/RT**.
12. Enter the **Narration**, if required.
13. Accept the screen.

Since this transaction is an outward supply, the tax implication of this transaction can be viewed in **GSTR – 1**.

To view **GSTR-1**,

Go to **Gateway of Tally > Display > Statutory Reports > GST > GSTR-1.**

The **GSTR-1** report appears as shown in the figure 7.160:

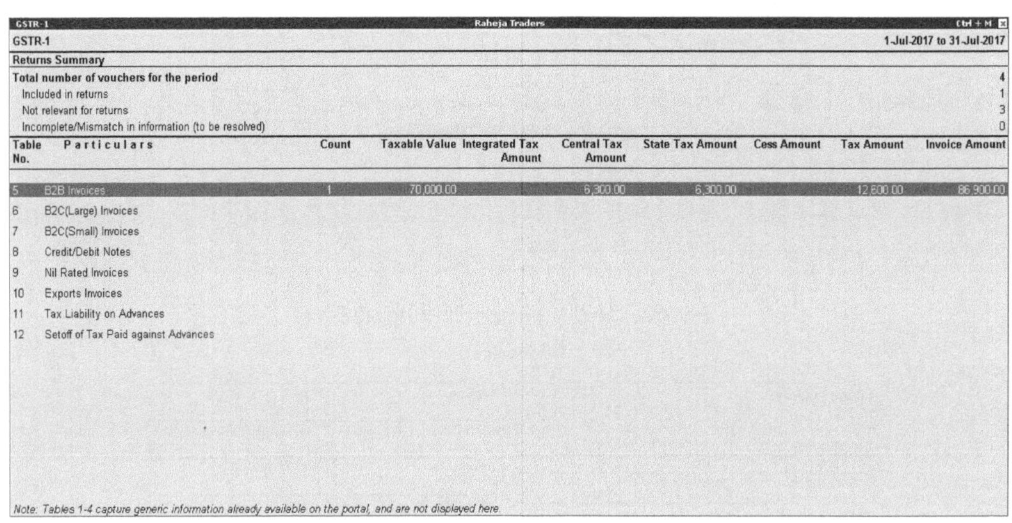


| Table No. | Particulars | Count | Taxable Value | Integrated Tax Amount | Central Tax Amount | State Tax Amount | Cess Amount | Tax Amount | Invoice Amount |
|---|---|---|---|---|---|---|---|---|---|
| 5 | B2B Invoices | 1 | 70,000.00 | | 6,300.00 | 6,300.00 | | 12,600.00 | 86,900.00 |
| 6 | B2C(Large) Invoices | | | | | | | | |
| 7 | B2C(Small) Invoices | | | | | | | | |
| 8 | Credit/Debit Notes | | | | | | | | |
| 9 | Nil Rated Invoices | | | | | | | | |
| 10 | Exports Invoices | | | | | | | | |
| 11 | Tax Liability on Advances | | | | | | | | |
| 12 | Setoff of Tax Paid against Advances | | | | | | | | |

*Figure 7.160: Intrastate Outward Supply is GSTR-2*

You can see that the outward supply is listed under **B2B Invoices** of **GSTR-2**.

**Step 3:** Generating of GST Tax Invoice

Since Raheja Traders are registered dealers, supplying taxable goods, to another registered dealer, they will have to issue a tax invoice to Tara Traders.

To generate GST Invoice in Tally.ERP 9,

1. Go to **Gateway of Tally > Accounting Vouchers > F8: Sales.**
2. Press **Pg up** until you open the outward supply invoice in alteration mode.
3. Click **P: Print**.
4. Click **F12: Configure** and enable the options as shown in figure 7.161.

   The **Invoice Print Configuration** screen appears as shown in the figure 7.161:

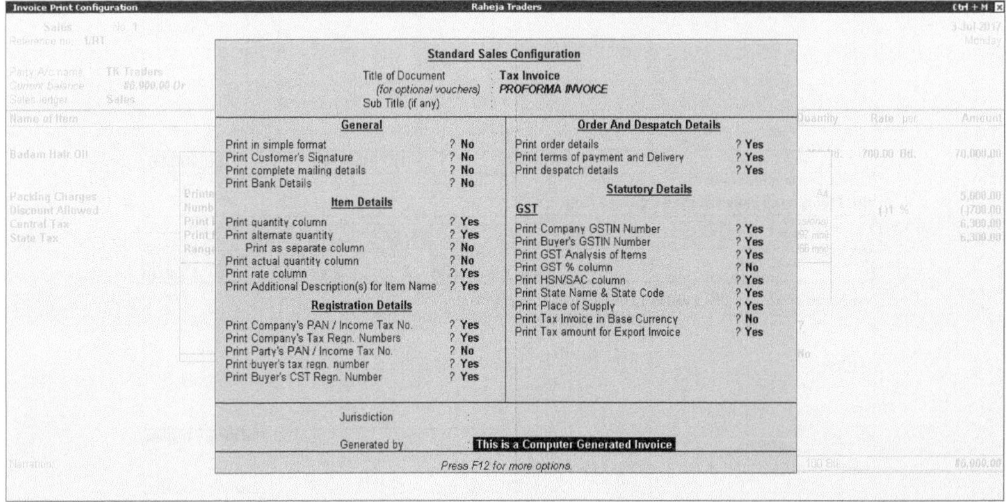


*Figure 7.161: Sales invoice configuration*

5. Press **Enter** to go to the sales invoice.

   The **Voucher Printing** screen appears as shown in the figure 7.162:

6. Press **Enter**.

   The **Tax Invoice** screen in preview mode appears as shown in the figure 7.163:

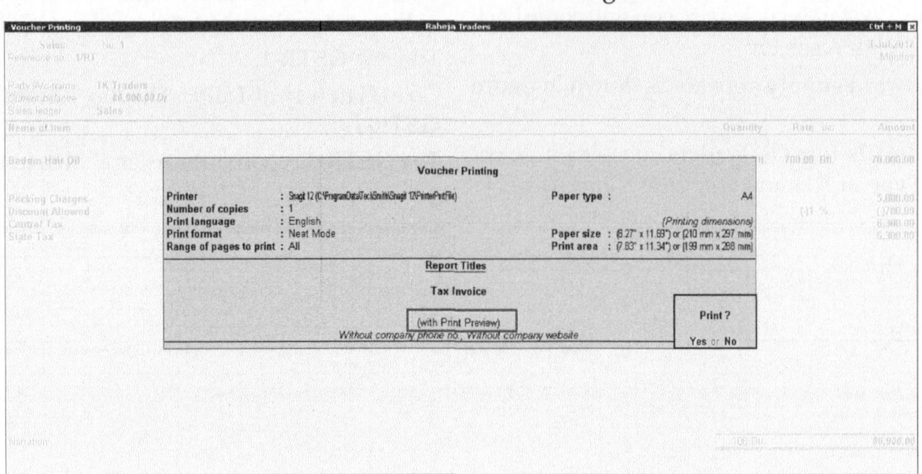


*Figure 7.162: Voucher Printing screen*

**Tax Invoice**

| Raheja Traders<br>No.310<br>20th Cross<br>Unity Building<br>GSTIN/UIN: 29BBBBB1234B1Z5<br>E-Mail : Rajehatraders@gmail.com | Invoice No.<br>**1** | Dated<br>**3-Jul-2017** |
|---|---|---|
| | Delivery Note | Mode/Terms of Payment |
| | Supplier's Ref.<br>**1/RT** | Other Reference(s) |
| Buyer<br>**TK Traders**<br>Karnataka, Code : 29<br>GSTIN/UIN:29SSSSS1234S1Z1<br>Place of Supply : Karnataka | Buyer's Order No. | Dated |
| | Despatch Document No. | Delivery Note Date |
| | Despatched through | Destination |
| | Terms of Delivery | |

| Sl No. | Description of Goods | HSN/SAC | Quantity | Rate | per | Amount |
|---|---|---|---|---|---|---|
| 1 | **Badam Hair Oil** | 33011100 | **100 Btl.** | 700.00 | Btl. | **70,000.00** |
| | *Packing Charges* | | | | | **5,000.00** |
| | *Less :* *Discount Allowed* | | | (-)1 | % | **(-)700.00** |
| | *Central Tax* | | | | | **6,300.00** |
| | *State Tax* | | | | | **6,300.00** |
| | Total | | **100 Btl.** | | | **₹ 86,900.00** |

Amount Chargeable (in words) *E. & O.E*

**INR Eighty Six Thousand Nine Hundred Only**

| HSN/SAC | Taxable Value | Central Tax Rate | Central Tax Amount | State Tax Rate | State Tax Amount |
|---|---|---|---|---|---|
| 33011100 | 70,000.00 | 9% | 6,300.00 | 9% | 6,300.00 |
| **Total** | **70,000.00** | | **6,300.00** | | **6,300.00** |

Tax Amount (in words) : **INR Twelve Thousand Six Hundred Only**

Declaration
We declare that this invoice shows the actual price of the goods described and that all particulars are true and correct.

**for Raheja Traders**

Authorised Signatory

This is a Computer Generated Invoice

*Figure 7.163: Tax invoice in preview mode*

## 7.37 INTERSTATE SUPPLY

Interstate supply is a transaction where the location of supplier is different from the, place of supply.

For example, Raheja Traders is a company registered in Karnataka. When Raheja Traders purchase from a supplier whose company is registered in Pune, Maharashtra, the supply is intrastate inward supply.

Interstate transactions attract Integrated Tax.

In this section we will see how to record intrastate transactions using Tally.ERP 9.

### 7.37.1 Interstate Inward Supply

Illustration 4: Accounting of interstate purchase of goods in Tally.ERP 9.

| Date | Particulars | | | |
|---|---|---|---|---|
| 04-07-2017 | **Voucher: Purchase**<br>Purchased the following goods from Palani Traders, Tamil Nadu with Reference no.: PUR/ 2, with integrated GST 18%. | | | |
| | **Name of Item** | **Quantity /Btl.** | **Rate /Btl.** | **Amount** |
| | **Badam Hair Oil** | 100 | 400 | 40,000 |

Let us determine the taxability of this transaction:

| | |
|---|---|
| **Location of Supplier** | Raheja Traders, Karnataka |
| **Place of Supply** | Palani Traders, Tamil Nadu' |
| **Taxes Applicable** | Integrated Tax |

To account for inward supplies,

**Step 1:** Recording Accounting Masters

*Party ledger*

**Go to Gateway of Tally > Accounts Info. > Ledgers > Create,** and enter the following details:

| Palani Traders | |
|---|---|
| **Against the field** | **Action to be performed** |
| **Name** | Enter **Pillai Traders** |
| **Under** | Select **Sundry Creditors** |
| **Maintain balances bill-by-bill** | Select **Yes** |
| **Default credit period** | Press **Enter** |
| **Check for credit days during** | Select **No** |
| **Inventory values are affected** | Select **No** |
| **Mailing Details** | |
| Address | |
| **Country** | Select **India** |
| **State** | Select **Tamil Nadu** |
| **Pincode** | Enter **600018** |

| Tax Registration Details | |
|---|---|
| **Set/alter GST Details** | Select **Yes** |
| **GST Details** | |
| **Registration Type** | Select **Regular** |
| **GSTIN/ UIN** | Enter **33UUUUU1252U1Z9** |
| **Is a e-Commerce operator?** | Select **No** |
| **Press** Enter **to accept.** | |

*Purchase Ledger*

| Interstate Purchases | |
|---|---|
| **Against the Field** | **Action to be Performed** |
| **Name** | Enter **Interstate Purchases** |
| **Under** | Select **Purchase Accounts** |
| **Inventory values are affected?** | Select **Yes** |
| **Statutory Information** | |
| **Is GST Applicable?** | Select **Applicable** |
| **Set/alter GST Details?** | Select **No** |
| **Type of Supply** | Select as **Goods** |
| **Press Enter to accept** | |

*Duties and Taxes Ledger*

| Integrated Tax | |
|---|---|
| **Against the Field** | **Action to be Performed** |
| **Name** | Enter **Integrated Tax** |
| **Under** | Select **Duties & Taxes** |
| **Type of duty/tax** | Select **GST** |
| **Tax type** | Select **Integrated Tax** |
| **Inventory values are affected?** | Select **No** |
| **Percentage of calculation?** | Press **Enter** to skip this field. |
| **Press Enter to accept** | |

**Step 2:** Recording Interstate Inward Supply

To record interstate inward supply of goods,

1. Go to **Gateway of Tally > Accounting Vouchers > F9: Purchase.**
2. Press **F2: Date** and change the date to **04-07-2017**.
3. Enter the **Supplier invoice no** as **P/02**, the **Date** field will be automatically filled same as **voucher date.**
4. Select **Palani Traders** in the **Party A/c name** field, press **Enter** to get **Party Details** screen.
5. State and GSTIN/UIN number will get captured from party ledger. Select the **Type of Dealer** as **Regular**.
6. Select the ledger, **Interstate Purchases.**
7. In the **Name of Item** field, select **Badam Hair Oil** from **List of Stock Items.**
8. Enter **Quantity** as **100 Btl.** and Rate as [1] **400/Btl.**, the amount will be calculated automatically.
9. Press **Enter** twice to select the GST duty ledgers.

10. Select the ledger **Integrated Tax**. The amount is calculated automatically.
11. Click **A: Tax Analysis** to view the tax implication in this transaction.
12. Click **F1: Detailed.**

The **Tax Analysis** screen appears as shown in the figure 7.164:

*Observation: We can see that integrated tax is 18% of the value of the transaction.*

12. Press **Esc** to go to the voucher creation screen.
13. Accept the **Bill wise Details** screen as it is.

The interstate inward supply appears as shown in the figure 7.165:

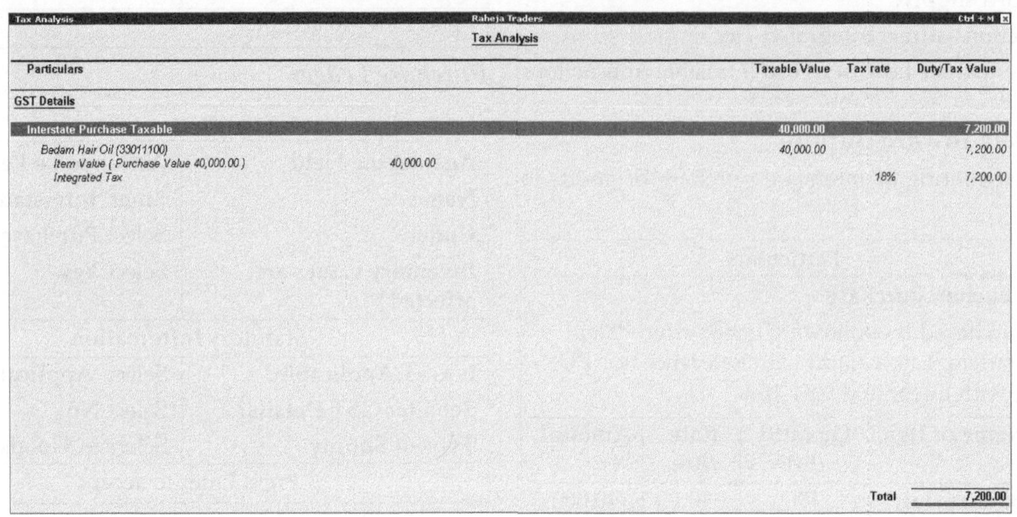


*Figure 7.164: Tax Analysis*

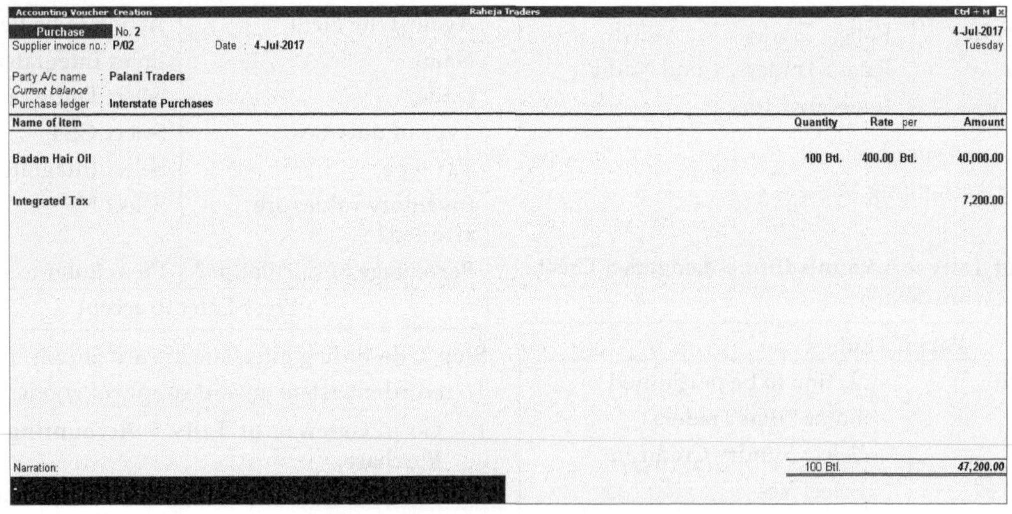


*Figure 7.165: Intrastate Inward Supply*

12. Enter the **Narration**, if required.
13. Press **Enter**.

Since this transaction is an inward supply, the tax implication of this transaction can be viewed in **GSTR – 2**.

To view **GSTR-2**,

1. Go to **Gateway of Tally > Display > Statutory Reports > GST > GSTR-2.**
2. Press **Enter** on **B2B Invoices**.
3. The GSTR – 2 report appears as shown in figure 7.166.

The GSTR-2 appears as shown in the figure 7.166:

In figure 7.166, we observe that the integrated tax column captures the tax amount of ₹ 7,200. This report provides the information of suppliers GSTIN/UIN number, Voucher Type, GST tax bifurcation etc. This report is updated instantly once the transaction are recorded with required GST configuration.

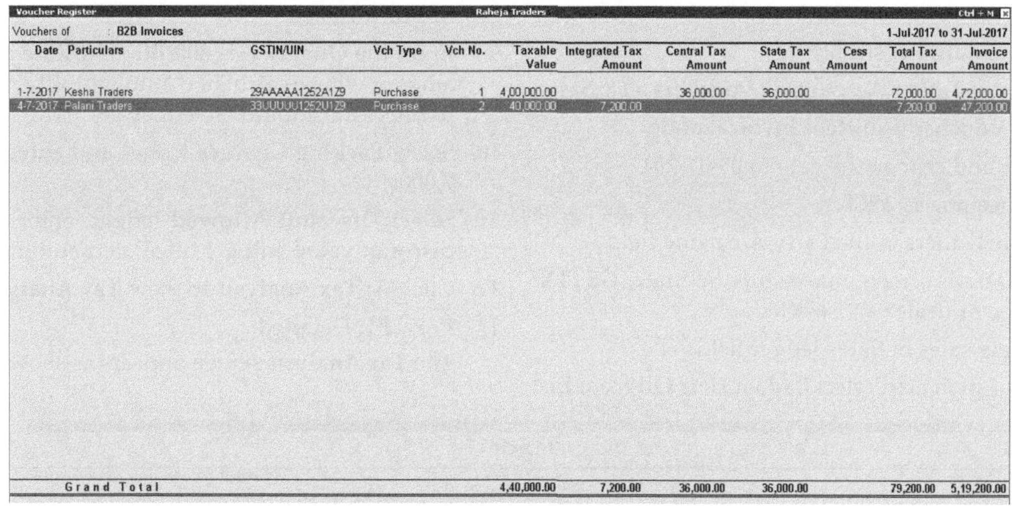

Voucher Register — Raheja Traders — Ctrl + M

Vouchers of : B2B Invoices — 1-Jul-2017 to 31-Jul-2017

| Date | Particulars | GSTIN/UIN | Vch Type | Vch No. | Taxable Value | Integrated Tax Amount | Central Tax Amount | State Tax Amount | Cess Amount | Total Tax Amount | Invoice Amount |
|---|---|---|---|---|---|---|---|---|---|---|---|
| 1-7-2017 | Kesha Traders | 29AAAAA1252A1Z9 | Purchase | 1 | 4,00,000.00 | | 36,000.00 | 36,000.00 | | 72,000.00 | 4,72,000.00 |
| 4-7-2017 | Palani Traders | 33UUUUU1252U1Z9 | Purchase | 2 | 40,000.00 | 7,200.00 | | | | 7,200.00 | 47,200.00 |
| | Grand Total | | | | 4,40,000.00 | 7,200.00 | 36,000.00 | 36,000.00 | | 79,200.00 | 5,19,200.00 |

*Figure 7.166: Voucher Register screen*

### 7.37.2 Interstate Outward Supply

In this section, we will learn to record interstate outward supplies when the place of supply and location of supplier are different, under GST tax regime,

***Illustration 5:*** *Accounting of interstate sales of goods in Tally.ERP 9.*

<table>
<tr><th>Date</th><th colspan="4">Particulars</th></tr>
<tr><td rowspan="4">05-07-2017</td><td colspan="4">Voucher: Sales<br>Sold the following goods to Mahesh Traders, Tamil Nadu with Reference no.:2/RT, with Integrated Tax – 18%</td></tr>
<tr><td>Name of Item</td><td>Quantity /Btl.</td><td>Rate /Btl.</td><td>Amount</td></tr>
<tr><td>Badam Hair Oil</td><td>800</td><td>700</td><td>5,60,000</td></tr>
<tr><td colspan="4">Packing Charge = 7,000<br>Discount Allowed @ 1%</td></tr>
</table>

Let us determine the taxability of this transaction:

| | |
|---|---|
| **Location of Supplier** | Raheja Traders, Karnataka |
| **Place of Supply** | Mahesh Traders, Tamil Nadu' |
| **Taxes Applicable** | Integrated tax |

To account for outward supplies,

**Step 1:** Creation of Accounting Masters

### *Party Ledger*

Go to **Gateway of Tally > Accounts Info. > Ledgers > Create,** and enter the following details:

| Mahesh Traders | |
|---|---|
| **Against the field** | **Action to be performed** |
| **Name** | Enter **Mahesh Traders** |
| **Under** | Select **Sundry Debtors** |
| **Maintain balances** | Select **Yes** |
| **bill-by-bill** | |
| **Default credit period** | Press **Enter** |
| **Check for credit days during** | Select **No** |
| **Inventory values are affected** | Select **No** |
| **Mailing Details** | |
| Address | |
| **Country** | Select **India** |
| **State** | Select **Tamil Nadu** |
| **Pincode** | Enter **600018** |
| **Tax Registration Details** | |
| Set/alter GST Details | Select Yes |
| **GST Details** | |
| **Registration Type** | Select **Regular** |
| **GSTIN/ UIN** | Enter **33PPPPP1234P1Z9** |
| **Is a e-Commerce operator?** | Select **No** |
| Press Enter to accept. | |

### *Sales Ledger*

| Interstate Sales | |
|---|---|
| Against the Field | **Action to be Performed** |
| **Name** | Enter **Interstate Sales** |
| **Under** | Select **Sales Accounts** |
| **Inventory values are affected?** | Select **Yes** |
| **Statutory Information** | |
| **Is GST Applicable?** | Select **Applicable** |
| **Set/alter GST Details?** | Select **No** |
| **Type of Supply** | Select as **Goods** |
| Press Enter to accept | |

**Step 2:** Recording Interstate Outward Supply

To record intrastate outward supply,

1. Go to **Gateway of Tally > Accounting Vouchers > F8: Sales.**
2. Ensure **Sales Voucher** is in **Item Invoice mode.**
3. Click **F2: Date** and change the date to **05-07-2017**.
4. Enter **Reference no.:** as **2/RT.**
5. Select **Mahesh Traders** in the **Party A/c name** field.
6. In the **Party Details** screen, make sure the **State, GSTIN/ UIN,** and **Type of dealer** are selected.
7. Select **Interstate sales** in **Sales ledger** field.
8. In the **Name of Item** field select **Badam Hair Oil** from **List of Stock Items.**
9. Enter the **Quantity** as **800/Btl.** and **Rate as ₹ 700/Btl.**, the amount will be calculated automatically. Press **Enter** twice to select the additional ledgers.
10. Select **Packing Charges** ledger and enter the amount as ₹ **7,000**.
11. Select **Discount Allowed** ledger, enter rate as **-1%**, the discount value will get calculated automatically.
12. Click **A: Tax Analysis** to view **Tax Analysis** screen.
13. Press **F1: Detailed**.

    The **Tax Analysis** screen appears as shown in figure 7.167.

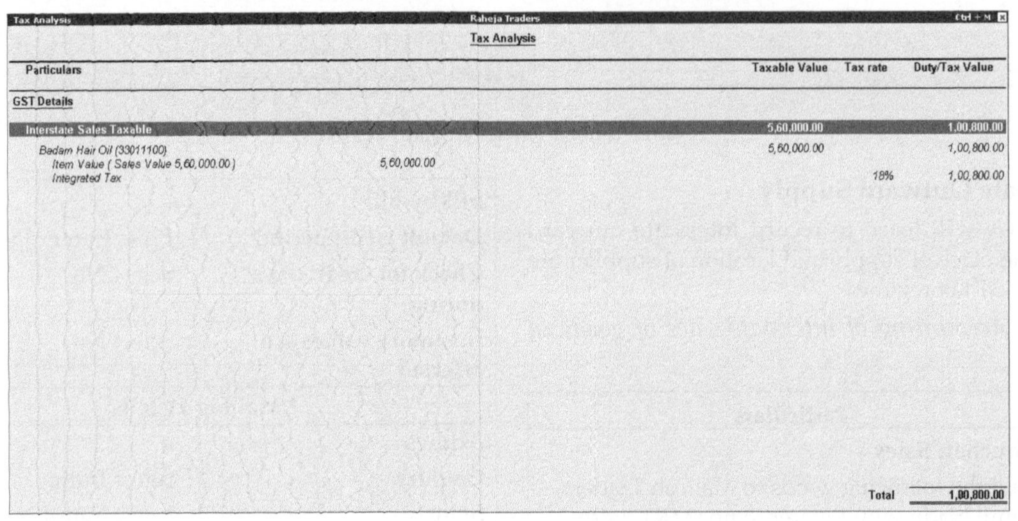

Tax Analysis — Raheja Traders

| Particulars | | Taxable Value | Tax rate | Duty/Tax Value |
|---|---|---|---|---|
| GST Details | | | | |
| Interstate Sales Taxable | | 5,60,000.00 | | 1,00,800.00 |
| Badam Hair Oil (33011100) | | 5,60,000.00 | | 1,00,800.00 |
| Item Value ( Sales Value 5,60,000.00 ) | 5,60,000.00 | | | |
| Integrated Tax | | | 18% | 1,00,800.00 |
| | | | Total | 1,00,800.00 |

Figure 7.167: Tax Analysis

***Observation:*** *The assessable value is calculated by including the value of packing charge and deducting the discount allowed. Central and State taxes are calculated on the assessable value after this computation.*

14. Press **Esc** from the **Tax Analysis** screen, you will come back to sales voucher creation screen.
15. In the **Bill-wise details for: Mahesh Traders** sub-screen, select **New Ref** as the **Type of Ref** and enter the Name as **2/RT**.
16. Enter the **Narration**, if required.
17. Press **Enter** to accept.

Since this transaction is an outward supply, the tax implication of this transaction can be viewed in **GSTR – 1**.

Voucher Register — Raheja Traders

Vouchers of : B2B Invoices — 1-Jul-2017 to 31-Jul-2017

| Date | Particulars | GSTIN/UIN | Vch Type | Vch No. | Taxable Value | Integrated Tax Amount | Central Tax Amount | State Tax Amount | Cess Amount | Total Tax Amount | Invoice Amount |
|---|---|---|---|---|---|---|---|---|---|---|---|
| 3-7-2017 | TK Traders | 29SSSSS1234S1Z1 | Sales | 1 | 70,000.00 | | 6,300.00 | 6,300.00 | | 12,600.00 | 86,900.00 |
| 5-7-2017 | Mahesh Traders | 33PPPPP1234P1Z9 | Sales | 2 | 5,60,000.00 | 1,00,800.00 | | | | 1,00,800.00 | 6,62,200.00 |
| | Grand Total | | | | 6,30,000.00 | 1,00,800.00 | 6,300.00 | 6,300.00 | | 1,13,400.00 | 7,49,100.00 |

Figure 6.168: voucher register

To view **GSTR-1**,

Go to **Gateway of Tally > Display > Statutory Reports > GST > GSTR-1.**

The **GSTR-1** report appears as shown in the figure 7.168:

1. Go to **Gateway of Tally > Display > Statutory Reports > GST > GSTR-1.**
2. Press **Enter** on **B2B Invoices**, you will get the voucher register screen.

The **Voucher Register** screen appears as shown in the figure 7168:

Raheja Traders can print the invoice from the alteration mode of the transaction, when required.

## 7.38 RETURN OF GOODS

It is common that goods purchased are sometimes returned to the supplier due to various reasons. Similarly, goods sold may be returned by the customers. In this section we will discuss in brief the provisions for handling tax liability under GST, and how return of supplies is recorded in Tally.ERP 9.

Under GST law, when goods are received as an inward supply, as returns by the recipient within six months from the date of invoice, the tax payable will be equal to the input tax credit availed on the inward supply. However, if the goods are returned beyond six months, the rate of tax will be as on the date of return.

Purchase returns will be recorded in debit notes and sales returns in credit notes. Let us activate debit notes and credit notes for Raheja Traders.

To activate debit notes and credit notes,

1. Go to **Gateway of Tally** > Click **F11: Features** > Click **F1: Accounts.**
2. Set the following options to **Yes.**
   - Use debit and credit notes.
   - Record credit notes in invoice mode.
   - Record debit notes in invoice mode.
3. Press **Ctrl+A** to accept the **Accounting Features** sub-screen.

Credit Notes and Debit notes are now available for Raheja Traders.

### 7.38.1 Purchase Returns

***Illustration 6:*** *Accounting of Purchase Returns using debit note voucher in Tally.ERP 9.*

| Date | Particulars | | | |
|---|---|---|---|---|
| 05-07-2017 | **Voucher: Purchase**<br>Purchase the following goods from SRK Traders, Karnataka with supplier Invoice no.: P/03, with Central Tax - 9% and State Tax – 9%. | | | |
| | **Name of Item** | **Quantity /Btl.** | **Rate /Btl.** | **Amount** |
| | **Badam Hair Oil** | 100 | 400 | 40,000 |
| 06-07-2017 | **Voucher: Debit Note**<br>Returned the following damaged goods to SRK Traders against the supplier invoice no.: P/03, dated 05-07-2017, with Central Tax - 9% and State Tax – 9%. | | | |
| | **Name of Item** | **Quantity /Btl.** | **Rate /Btl.** | **Amount** |
| | **Badam Hair Oil** | 50 | 400 | 20,000 |

To record purchase returns, create the required ledgers in the activity below:

### *Activity*

- ***Create the party SRK Traders.***
- ***Record the purchase entry on 05-07-2017.***
- ***View the tax implication of this transaction in GSTR-2.***

**Step 3:** Recording Purchase Returns

To record the debit note,

1. Go to **Gateway of Tally > Accounting Vouchers >** Click **F9: Debit Note.**
2. Click **F2: Date** and change the date as **06-07-2017.**
3. Enter the **Original Invoice no.:** as **P/03.** (Enter the purchase invoice no. against which the returns are made).
4. Enter the **Original Invoice Dt**.: as **05-07-2017**(Enter the purchase invoice date against which the returns are made).
5. Select **SRK Traders** in the **Party A/c name** field.
6. Press **Enter.**
7. State and GSTIN/UIN number will get captured from party ledger. Select the **Type of Dealer** as **Regular.**
8. In the **Name of Item** field, select **Badam Hair Oil** from **List of Stock Items.**
9. Enter **Quantity** as **50 Btl.** and Rate as ¹ **400/Btl.**, the amount will be calculated automatically.
10. Press **Enter** twice to select the GST duty ledgers.
3. Select **Central Tax** ledger, the tax amount will get captured automatically.
4. Select **State Tax** ledger, the tax amount will get captured automatically.
5. Enable the option **Provide GST details** to **Yes.**
6. Enter **Supplier's Debit/Credit No.** and **Date.**
7. In the **Bill wise Details** screen, enter the following details:
   - Select **Agst Ref** as the **Type of Ref.**
   - Select **P/03** as the bill **Name** from the list of **Pending Bills.**
   - The amount will get captured automatically.
   - Press **Enter** to accept.

The **Debit Note Voucher** appears as shown in the below given figure 7.169:

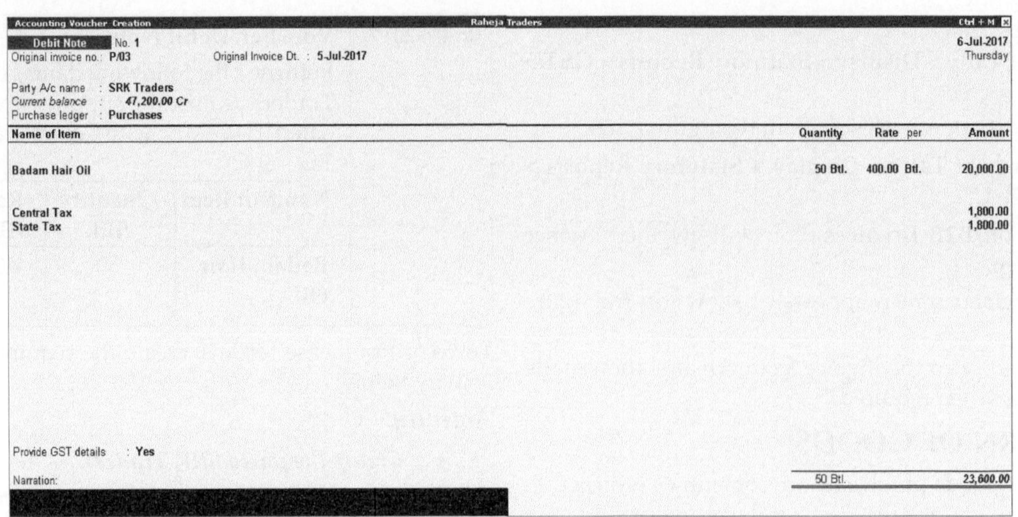


*Figure 7.169: Debit Note Voucher*

8. Enter the **Narration**, if required.
9. Press **Ctrl+A** to accept.

The tax implication of this transaction can be viewed in **GSTR – 2.**

To view **GSTR-2,**

Go to **Gateway of Tally > Display > Statutory Reports > GST > GSTR-2.**

The **GSTR – 2** report appears as shown in figure 7.170:

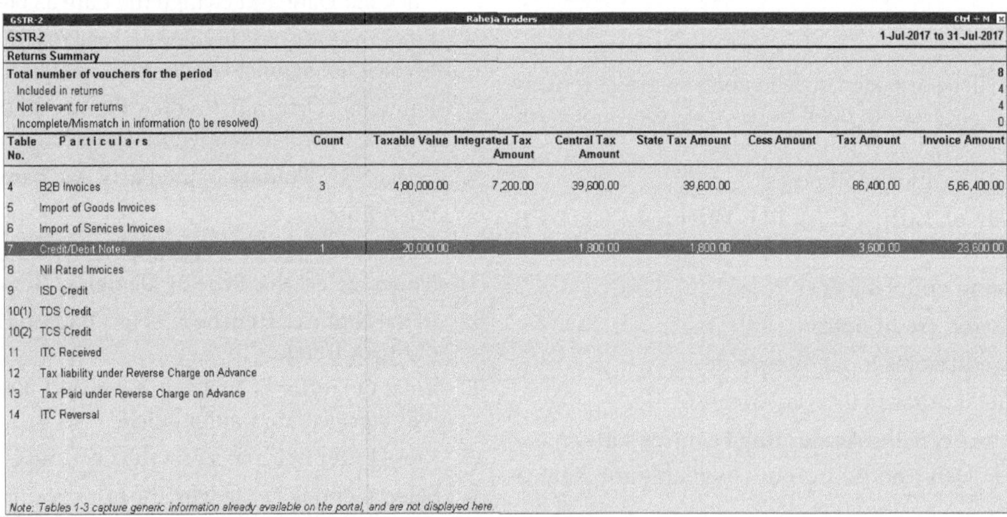


*Figure 7.170: GSTR-2*

The purchase return transaction is listed under **Credit/Debit Notes** of **GSTR-2.**

## 7.38.2 Sales Returns

***Illustration 7:*** *Accounting of sales returns using credit note voucher in Tally.ERP 9.*

| Date | Particulars | | | |
|---|---|---|---|---|
| 06-07-2017 | **Voucher: Sales**<br>Sold the following goods to Mi-Tech Traders, Karnataka with Reference no.: 3/RT, with Central Tax - 9% and State Tax – 9%. | | | |
| | **Name of Item** | **Quantity /Btl.** | **Rate /Btl.** | **Amount** |
| | **Badam Hair Oil** | 100 | 700 | 70,000 |
| 07-07-2017 | **Voucher: Credit Note**<br>Mi-Tech Traders returned the following goods against the sales reference no.: 3/RT, dated 06-07-2017, with Central Tax - 9% and State Tax – 9%. | | | |
| | **Name of Item** | **Quantity /Btl.** | **Rate /Btl.** | **Amount** |
| | **Badam Hair Oil** | 10 | 700 | 7,000 |

To record the above transactions in the books of account, first ensure that the required ledgers are created in Tally.ERP 9.

### *Activity*

- ***Create the Mi-Tech Traders with GSTIN/ UIN as*** 29PPPPP1234P1Z4.
- ***Record the sales and credit note transaction displayed in illustration 7 table***
- ***View the tax implication of this transaction in GSTR-1.***

## 7.39 OUTWARD SUPPLY OF SERVICES

After enabling GST in the company, you can record inward and outward supply of services using purchase voucher and sale of services using sales voucher respectively.

We know taxability depends on the place of supply. Determining the place of supply is critical to identify the taxability.

A supply of services shall be an intrastate supply if the service provider and the service recipient are located in the same State.

In this section, we will learn to record outward supply of services using Tally.ERP 9

**Note:** Similarly, a supply of services shall be an interstate supply if the service provider and the service recipient are located in different States.

### Business Scenario

Raheja Traders, diversified its business and entered in providing advertising services to different customers in and around the state.

***Illustration 8:*** *Recording transaction for intrastate inward supply of service with GST and checking tax analysis details.*

| Date | Particulars |
|---|---|
| 10-07-2017 | **Voucher: Sales**<br>Raheja Traders provided Advertising Services of worth ₹ 4, 00,000 to AZ Pvt. Ltd. Bengaluru, Karnataka. Additionally, GST@18% is charged on the invoice with reference number:4/RT. |

Let us determine the taxability of this supply

| | |
|---|---|
| **Location of Supplier** | Raheja Traders, Bengaluru, Karnataka |
| **Place of Supply** | AZ Pvt. Ltd, Bengaluru, Karnataka |
| **Taxes Applicable** | Central Tax and State Tax |

To record inward supplies,

**Step 1:** Create Accounting Masters

### *Party Ledger*

| AZ Pvt. Ltd. | |
|---|---|
| **Against the field** | **Action to be performed** |
| **Name** | Enter **AZ Pvt. Ltd.** |
| **Under** | Select **Sundry Debtors** |
| **Maintain balances bill-by-bill** | Select **Yes** |
| **Default credit period** | Press **Enter** |
| **Check for credit days during** | Select **No** |
| **Inventory values are affected** | Select **No** |
| **Mailing Details** | |
| **Country** | Select **India** |
| **State** | Select **Karnataka** |
| **Pincode** | Enter **560018** |
| **Tax Registration Details** | |
| Set/alter GST Details | Select Yes |
| **GST Details** | |
| **Registration Type** | Select **Regular** |
| **GSTIN/ UIN** | Enter **29MMMMM1234P1Z9** |
| **Is a e-Commerce operator?** | Select **No** |
| Press Enter to accept. | |

### *Service Income Ledger*

| Advertising Services | |
|---|---|
| Against the field | **Action to be performed** |
| Name | Enter **Advertising Services** |
| Under | Select **Indirect Incomes** |
| Inventory values are affected | Select **No** |
| Is GST Applicable | Select **Applicable** |
| Set/alter GST details | Select **No** |
| Type of Supply | Select **Services.** |
| **Press** Enter **to accept.** | |

**Note: Set/alter GST details** is set to **No** in the ledger because, GST is configured in the company level.

**Step 2:** Recording Outward Supply of Services

To record intrastate inward supply of services,

1. Go to **Gateway of Tally > Accounting Vouchers > F8: Sales**
2. Click **F2:Date** and set the date to **10-07-2017**
3. Enter the **Reference no. as 4/RT**.
4. In the **Party A/c name** field select **AZ Pvt. Ltd.** The **Party Details** screen is displayed.

**Note:** The **GSTIN/UIN** as entered in the supplier ledger is displayed.

5. Select **Regular** as the **Type of Dealer.**
6. Under the **Particulars** field select the **Advertising Services** ledger
7. **Enter** the amount as ₹ **4, 00,000** and press **Enter.**
8. Select the **State Tax ledger**. The amount is filled in automatically.
9. Select the ledger **Central Tax** Ledger. The amount is filled in automatically.

10. In the **Bill-wise Details** screen, select **New Ref** with Name **4/RT** and accept the details.
11. Click **A: Tax Analysis** to view the **Tax Analysis**.
12. Click **F1: Detailed**.

The **Tax Analysis** screen appears as shown in the figure 7.171:

13. Press **Esc**.
14. Enter the **Narration**, if required.

The Sales Invoice appears as shown in the figure 7.172:

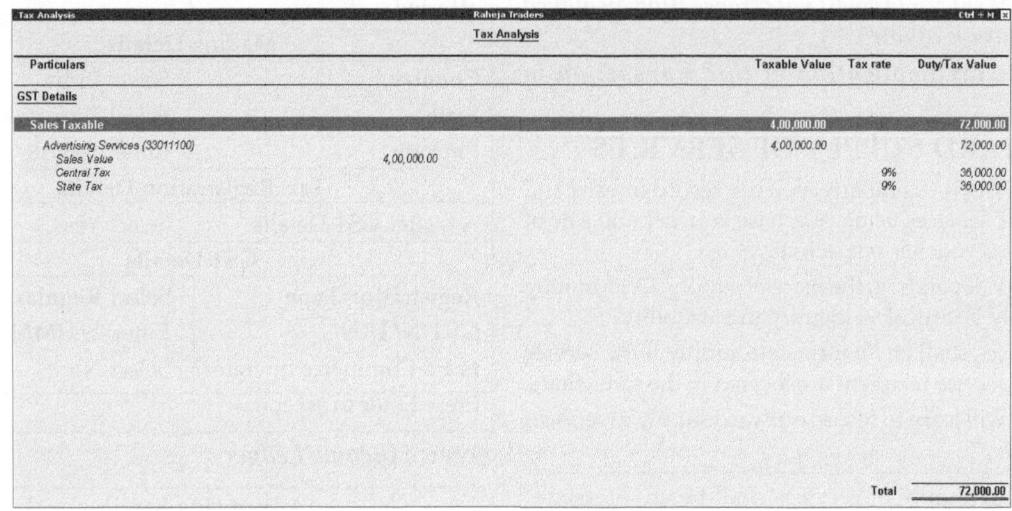


*Figure 7.171: Tax Analysis screen*

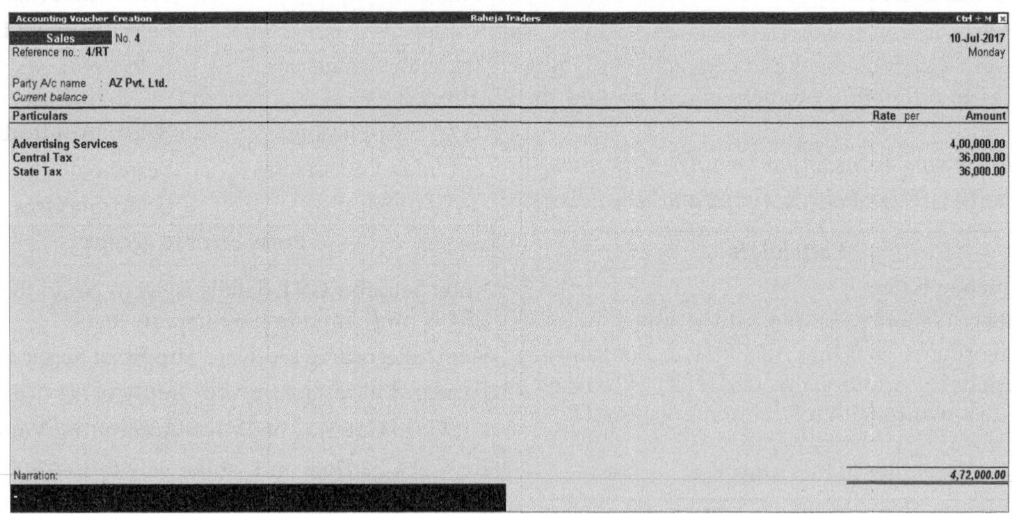


*Figure 7.172: outward supply of services*

15. Press **Enter** to accept.

Since this is an ouward supply, the tax implication of this transaction can be viewed in **GSTR – 1**.

To view **GSTR-1**,

Go to **Gateway of Tally > Display > Statutory Reports > GST > GSTR-1.**

The transaction is captured under B2B invoices. The taxable value is ₹ . 4, 00,000, Central Tax value is ₹ . 36,000, and State Tax value is ₹ . 36,000. Total Tax amount is ₹ . 72,000.

## 7.40 GST REPORTS

In this section, we will learn to generate GST reports like GSTR-1 and GSTR-2 details from Tally.ER P. By now we are aware that GSTR-1 contains the details of outward supplies and GSTR-2 contains the details of inward supplies. Now let us explore the other information available in these reports.

### 7.40.1 Generating GSTR-1 Report in Tally.ERP 9

GSTR-1 is the monthly return which include the details of all outward supplies and it has to be filed by taxable person registered under GST. GSTR-1 format is standardised format prescribed by  department, GSTR-1 return form is divided into multiple tables, each table is used for a different type of outward supply. In Tally.ERP 9, GSTR-1 can be viewed in a report format with tax computation details.

In Tally.ERP 9, we can check the details of all outward supplies along with the capability to resolve the exception before exporting the GSTR-1 return. The report also enables you to update the status of each transaction in the return based on the acceptance and reconciliation status of the transaction on GSTN portal using the **Status Reconciliation** option.

To generate the **GSTR-1** report, follow the steps given below:

1. Go to **Gateway of Tally > Display > Statutory Reports > GST.**
2. Select **GSTR-1.**
3. Click **Alt+V: Default View,** you will get the following screen.

The **GSTR-1** screen appears as shown in the figure 7.173:

GSTR-1 Raheja Traders Ctrl + M

GSTR-1 1-Jul-2017 to 31-Jul-2017

Returns Summary

| Total number of vouchers for the period | 11 |
|---|---|
| Included in returns | 5 |
| Not relevant for returns | 6 |
| Incomplete/Mismatch in information (to be resolved) | 0 |

| Table No. | Particulars | Count | Taxable Value | Integrated Tax Amount | Central Tax Amount | State Tax Amount | Cess Amount | Tax Amount | Invoice Amount |
|---|---|---|---|---|---|---|---|---|---|
| 5 | B2B Invoices | 4 | 11,00,000.00 | 1,00,800.00 | 48,600.00 | 48,600.00 | | 1,98,000.00 | 13,03,700.00 |
| 6 | B2C(Large) Invoices | | | | | | | | |
| 7 | B2C(Small) Invoices | | | | | | | | |
| 8 | Credit/Debit Notes | 1 | 7,000.00 | | 630.00 | 630.00 | | 1,260.00 | 8,260.00 |
| 9 | Nil Rated Invoices | | | | | | | | |
| 10 | Exports Invoices | | | | | | | | |
| 11 | Tax Liability on Advances | | | | | | | | |
| 12 | Setoff of Tax Paid against Advances | | | | | | | | |

*Note: Tables 1-4 capture generic information already available on the portal, and are not displayed here.*

*Figure 7.173: GSTR-1 Screen*

**Return Summary:** Return Summary will display the Total number of vouchers for the period, vouchers included in returns, vouchers not relevant for returns, incomplete/mismatch in information(to be resolved).

**Particulars:** It will display the details of the the taxable value and tax amount from outward supplies considered in the returns. Drill down from any part to display detailed information at the subsequent levels.

In Tally.ERP 9, from GSTR-1 report, we can perform the following activities:

- Click **V: Table-wise View** - To view the GSTR-1 report in table format. In this format we will get the details of B2B, B2C, Nil Rated, Export, Advances etc. The table-wise report is structured in line with the GSTR-1 format given by the department.
- Click **J: Stat Adjustment -** To record the stat adjustment entry in journal voucher.
- Click **U: Status Reconciliation** – To mark the status of each transaction based on the online status. This will allow you to track the status of all the transactions uploaded in GST portal without having to login to the portal.
- Click **E: Return** – To export the GSTR-1 return in the required excel format for any given period All the transactions that are displayed under Included in returns section in GSTR-1 report will be exported. The MS excel file created on export of GSTR-1 is in line with the format prescribed by the department. The file can be imported to the utility tool. This tool then creates the .json file that can be uploaded on the GST portal.
- Click **N: HSN/SAC Summary** – It displays the summary of HSN/SAC code of all the stock item.
- Click **A: View Accepted as is -** It displays the details of the screen list of vouchers accepted as is, while solving the exception.

### 7.40.2 Generating GSTR-2 Report in Tally.ERP 9

GSTR-2 displays the details of inward supplies. GSTR-2 format is standardised format prescribed by department, GSTR-2 form is divided into multiple tables, and each table is used for a different type of inward supply. In Tally.ERP 9, GSTR-2 can be viewed in a report format with tax computation details.

In Tally.ERP 9, we can check the details of all inward supplies along with the capability to resolve the exception before exporting the GSTR-2 return. The report also enables you to update the status of each transaction in the return based on the acceptance and reconciliation status of the transaction on GSTN portal using the **Status Reconciliation** option.

To generate the **GSTR-2** report, follow the steps given below:

4. Go to **Gateway of Tally > Display > Statutory Reports > GST.**
5. Select **GSTR-2.**
6. Click **Alt+V: Default View,** you will get the following screen.

The **GSTR-2** screen appears as shown in the figure 7.174:

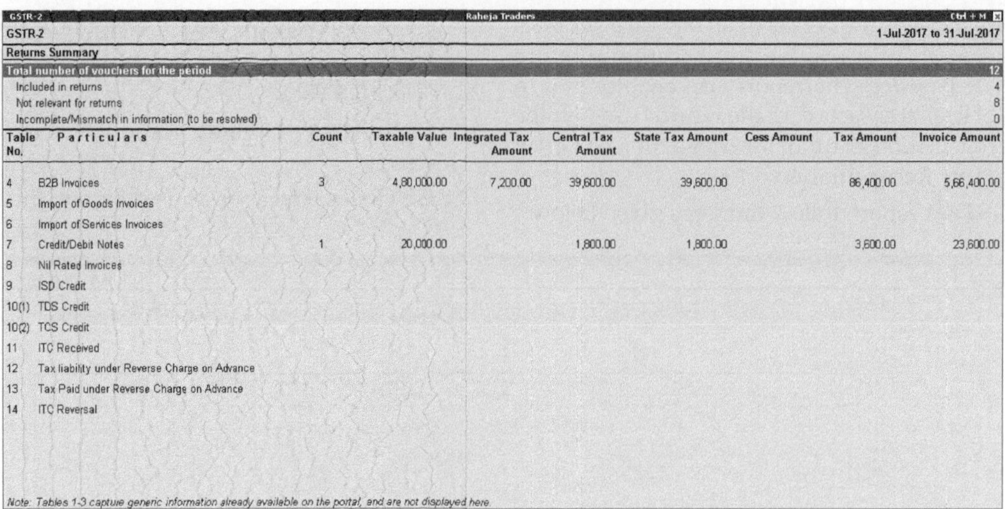

GSTR-2 | Raheja Traders | Ctrl + M

GSTR-2 | 1-Jul-2017 to 31-Jul-2017

Returns Summary

| Returns Summary | |
|---|---|
| Total number of vouchers for the period | 12 |
| Included in returns | 4 |
| Not relevant for returns | 8 |
| Incomplete/Mismatch in information (to be resolved) | 0 |

| Table No. | Particulars | Count | Taxable Value | Integrated Tax Amount | Central Tax Amount | State Tax Amount | Cess Amount | Tax Amount | Invoice Amount |
|---|---|---|---|---|---|---|---|---|---|
| 4 | B2B Invoices | 3 | 4,80,000.00 | 7,200.00 | 39,600.00 | 39,600.00 | | 86,400.00 | 5,66,400.00 |
| 5 | Import of Goods Invoices | | | | | | | | |
| 6 | Import of Services Invoices | | | | | | | | |
| 7 | Credit/Debit Notes | 1 | 20,000.00 | | 1,800.00 | 1,800.00 | | 3,600.00 | 23,600.00 |
| 8 | Nil Rated Invoices | | | | | | | | |
| 9 | ISD Credit | | | | | | | | |
| 10(1) | TDS Credit | | | | | | | | |
| 10(2) | TCS Credit | | | | | | | | |
| 11 | ITC Received | | | | | | | | |
| 12 | Tax liability under Reverse Charge on Advance | | | | | | | | |
| 13 | Tax Paid under Reverse Charge on Advance | | | | | | | | |
| 14 | ITC Reversal | | | | | | | | |

*Note: Tables 1-3 capture generic information already available on the portal, and are not displayed here*

*Figure 7.174: GSTR-2 Screen*

**Return Summary:** Return Summary will display the Total number of vouchers for the period, vouchers included in returns, vouchers not relevant for returns, incomplete/mismatch in information (to be resolved).

**Particulars:** It will display the details of the the taxable value and tax amount from inward supplies considered in the returns. Drill down from any part to display detailed information at the subsequent levels.

## 7.41 INPUT TAX CREDIT SET OFF

On every transaction within a state, a component of Central Tax and State Tax will be applicable.

Integrated Tax will be applicable on interstate transactions. A registered dealer's liability to pay can be set off against the input tax credit that he/she is entitled to avail. Let us understand how to set off the input credit against each of these components in the order as prescribed by the GST Law.

Refer the below given table:

| Input Tax Credit | Set off Against Liability |
|---|---|
| Central Tax | Central Tax and Integrated Tax (in that order) |
| State Tax/UT Tax | State/UT Tax and integrated Tax (in that order) |
| Integrated Tax | Central, State and Integrated Tax (in that order) |

If the input credit tax amount is less than the liability then we need to pay tax to the government and if the input credit tax amount is more than liability, then the credit will get carry forward to the next period.

**Note:** Integrated tax credit can be set off against integrated, central, state and UT tax.

### *Illustration 9: Adjusting of input tax credit against tax liability*

<table>
<tr><th>Date</th><th colspan="2">Particulars</th></tr>
<tr><td rowspan="5">20-07-2017</td><td colspan="2">Adjust the following input credit against available tax liability.</td></tr>
<tr><td>Input Tax Credit</td><td>Liability Amount</td></tr>
<tr><td>Central Tax – 37,800</td><td>Central Tax -47,970</td></tr>
<tr><td>State Tax – 37,800</td><td>State Tax – 47,970</td></tr>
<tr><td>Integrated Tax – 7,200</td><td>Integrated Tax – 1,00,800</td></tr>
</table>

To record the above transactions in the books of account, first ensure that all exceptions are resolved in GSTR-1 and GSTR-2 report in Tally.ERP 9.

Before recording input credit adjustment entry, payment of tax entry or exporting the return, one must resolve all exceptions falling under the head **Incomplete/Mismatch in information (to be resolved)** field in GSTR-1 and GSTR-2 report.

**Step 1:** Resolving the Exceptions

For this company there are no transactions which is falling under the head **Incomplete/Mismatch in information (to be resolved)** field in GSTR-1 and GSTR-2 report. Hence this step can be skipped.

**Step 2:** Setting of Central Tax Input Credit against Central Tax Liability

1. Go to **Gateway of Tally > Accounting Vouchers > Click F7: Journal.**
2. Click **F2:Date,** to change the date as 20-07-2017
3. Press **Alt+J**
4. Enter the following details in **Stat Adjustment Details** screen.
   - **Type of duty/tax:** GST.
   - **Nature of Adjustment:** Decrease of Tax Liability.
   - **Additional Details:** Select Adjustment Against Credit.

   The completed **Stat Adjustment Details** screen appears as shown in figure 7.175:

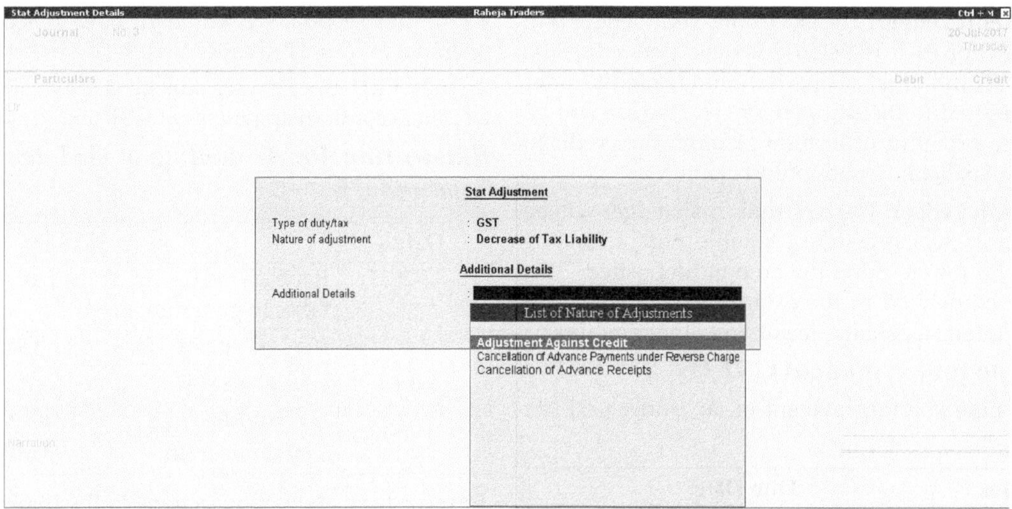


*Figure 7.175: Stat Adjustment Details Screen*

5. Press **Enter** to go back to the journal voucher.
6. **Debit** the Central Tax ledger and enter the amount to the extent of credit available. i.e., 1, 39,800.
7. **Credit** the Central Tax ledger to set-off the payable amount against the available credit.

   The completed **Journal Voucher** appears as shown in the figure 7.176:

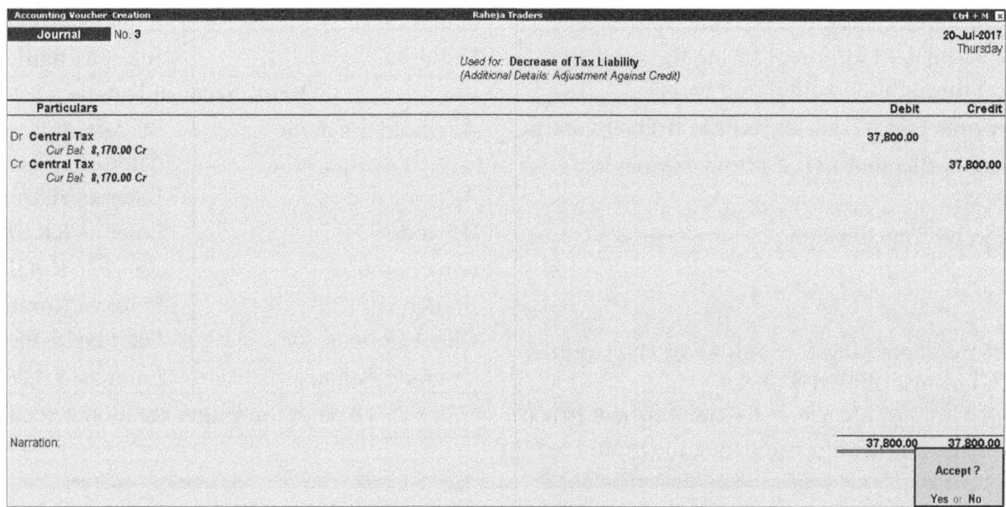


*Figure 7.176: Journal Voucher*

***Observation:*** *In the figure 7.176, we can observe that the balance of Central Tax ledger is appearing as 8,170. This value is appearing from the following calculation:*

*Central Tax Input Credit Value = 37,800*

*Opening Input Credit Balance provided = 2,000*

*Central Tax Liability = 47,970*

*47,970 - 37,800 - 2,000 = 8,170*

*Therefore in Tally.ERP 9, the input credit opening balance transferred will automatically get deducted from the tax liability.*

8. Press **Enter** to accept.

### *Activity*

*Similarly adjust the state tax and integrated tax input credit against their respective liability.*

## 7.42 GST TAX PAYMENT

The liability of tax, input tax credit and deposits of every registered taxable person is maintained and administered on a common portal under the following accounts:

- **Electronic Tax Liability Register:** All the amount payable by a taxable person will be debited (added) to an electronic tax liability register. The electronic tax liability registered will be credited to the extent of the payment made by utilizing the input tax credit or by depositing the amount to the said register be e-filed. The details of each form are listed below along with details of applicability and periodicity.

- **Electronic Credit Ledger:** The electronic credit ledger will be maintained for each registered taxable person on the common portal and every claim of input tax credit under it shall be credited to the said ledger. The ledger will be debited to the extent of utilization of input tax credit to discharge the tax liability and refund claim.
- **Electronic Cash Ledger:** The electronic cash ledger will be maintained for each registered taxable person on the common portal for crediting the amount deposited. This account will be debited to the extent of payment made towards tax, interest, penalty, fee or any other amount.

### 7.42.1 Time line for payment of GST tax

Following is the time line for payment of tax under GST tax regime:

| Type of Dealer | Due Date |
|---|---|
| Regular | 20th of the subsequent month |
| Composition Dealer | 18th of the subsequent quarter |

### 7.42.2 Modes of Payment

We can make a payment of tax and other dues in online mode or offline mode and the details are explained below:

**Online Mode:**

- Internet banking through authorized banks
- Credit card or Debit card after registering the same in the common portal through the authorized bank
- National Electronic Fund Transfer (NEFT) from any bank
- Real Time Gross Settlement (RTGS) from any bank

**Offline Mode:**

Offline payment can be done through:

- Cash
- Cheque
- Demand draft by depositing through Over the Counter Payment (OTC) from authorized banks.

Offline payment can be done only if the payment is up to ₹ 10,000 per challan per tax period. Once after adjusting the Input credit within this section, we will learn how to account the GST tax payment entry in Tally.ERP 9.

In Tally.ERP 9, once after adjusting the available input credit we can account the payment of GST tax.

***Illustration 10:** Accounting of GST tax payment to the department.*

| Date | Particulars | |
|---|---|---|
| 20-07-2017 | Raheja Traders, made the payment of following taxes to government. | |
| | **Type of Tax** | **Tax Amount (₹)** |
| | Central Tax | 8,170 |
| | State Tax | 170I |
| | ntegrated Tax | 93,600 |

To record the above transactions in the books of account, first ensure that all the necessary masters are created in Tally.ERP 9

**Step 1:** Creation of Accounting Masters

Go to **Gateway of Tally > Accounts Info. > Ledgers > Create**, enter the following details.

| Kotak Bank A/c | |
|---|---|
| Against the field | Action to be performed |
| Name | Enter as **Kotak Bank A/c** |
| Under | Select as **Bank Accounts** |
| **Bank Account Details** | |
| A/c holder's name | By default it will take company name |
| A/c no. | Enter as **908765677899009** |
| IFS code | Enter as **KKBK0000424** |
| Bank name | Select as **Kotak Bank** |
| Branch | Enter as **Koramangala** |
| Client Code | Let it be blank |
| Opening Balance | Enter as **₹ 1,00,000** |
| Accept the ledger creation screen | |

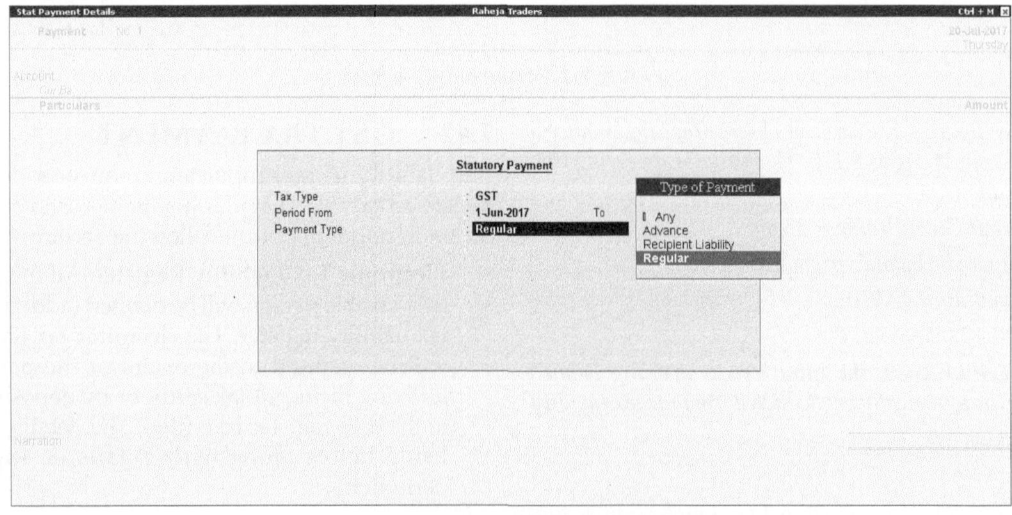


*Figure 7.177: Stat Payment Details Screen*

**Step 2:** Recording of GST tax payment Transaction

To record the payment entry, follow the steps given below:

1. **Go to Gateway of Tally > Accounting Vouchers > Click F5: Payment.**
2. Click **F2: Date** and change the date to 20-07-2017.
3. Click **Alt+S: Stat Payment,** to get the **Stat Payment Details** screen.
4. Enter the following details:
   - **Tax Type – GST.**
   - **Period from – 01-07-2017 to 31-07-2017** (enter the period for which you are making the payment).
   - **Payment Type – Regular.**

   The **Stat Payment Details** screen appears as shown in the figure 7.177:
5. Press **Enter** to accept **Stat Payment Details** screen.
6. In the Account field select Kotak Bank
7. Under Particulars select Central Tax and State Tax ledger and enter the amount as shown in figure 7.178:

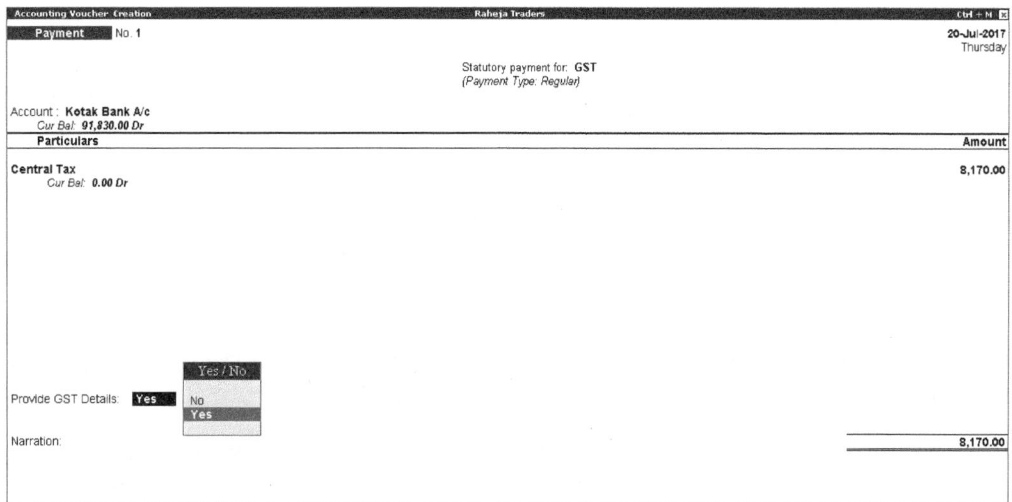


*Figure 7.178: Payment Voucher*

The **Payment Voucher** appears as shown in the figure 7.178:

8. Set the option **Provide GST Details** to **Yes,** to select the mode of payment.

   The **Provide GST Details** screen appears as shown in the figure 7.179:
9. Enter the necessary details as shown in the figure 7.179 and accept the screen.
10. In the **Bank allocation details** enter the necessary details like Transaction Type, Account Number, IFS Code, Bank etc. and save the screen.

    The completed **Payment Voucher** appears as shown in the figure 7.180:
11. Press Enter to accept voucher.

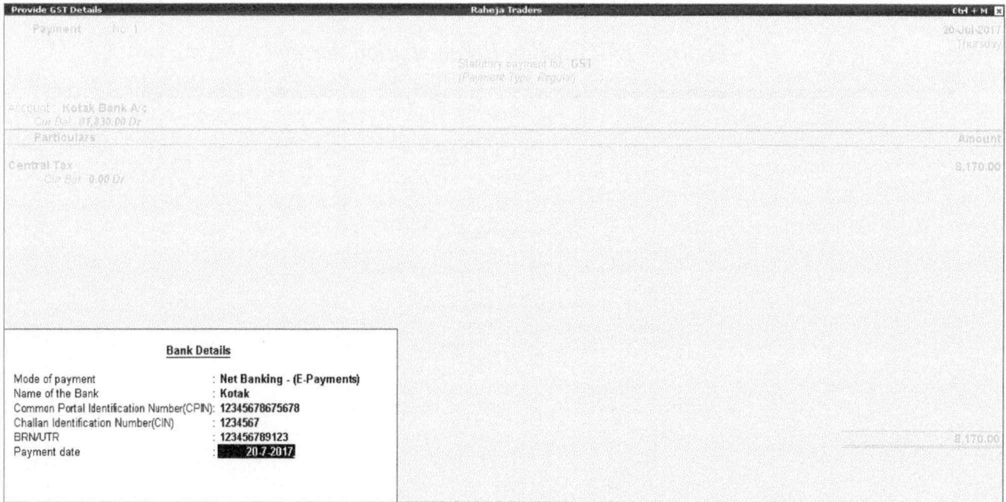


*Figure 7.179: Provide GST Details Screen*

*Figure 7.180: Payment Voucher*

### 7.42.3 Challan Reconciliation

In challan reconciliation we can define the details payment details, in case if any details are left while recording the payment voucher, the same can be set in this screen.

To reconcile challan, follow the steps given below:

1. Go to **Gateway of Tally > Display > Statutory Reports > GST.**
2. Select **Challan Reconciliation.**

   The **Challan Reconciliation** screen appears as shown in the figure 7.181:
3. Click **Alt+S: Set Details.**

   The **Stat Payment Details** screen appears as shown in the figure 7.182:

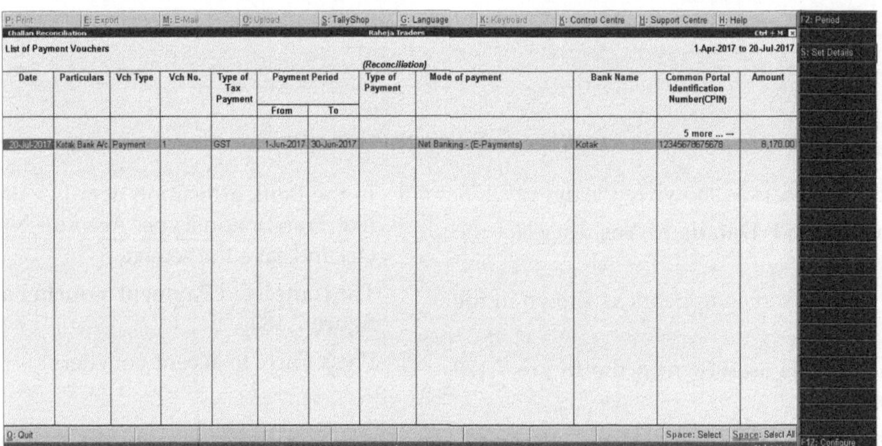


*Figure 7.181: Challan Reconciliation Screen*

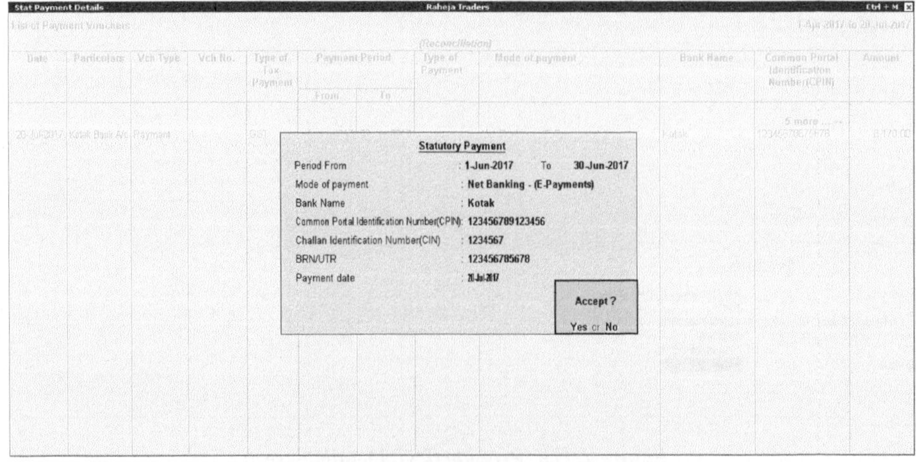


*Figure 7.182: Stat Payment Details Screen*

4. Press **Enter** to accept the screen.

**Note:** Any details like period, mode of payment, payment date etc. is missed at the time of recording tax payment enter, then the same can be defined in the screen shown in figure 7.182.

## 7.43 EXPORTING GSTR-1 RETURN AND UPLOADING IN GST PORTAL

To export GSTR1 return make sure all the exceptions falling under the head **Incomplete/Mismatch in information (to be solved),** to be resolved. GSTR-1 return can be exported in the required excel format for any given period. All the transactions that are displayed under Included in returns section in GSTR-1 report will be exported.

To export the GSTR-1, return in the required excel format, follow the steps given below:

1. Go to **Gateway of Tally > Display > Statutory Reports > GST.**
2. Click **F2: Period** and change the period to 01-07-2017 to 31-07-2017.
3. Click **Alt+V: Table View.**

   The **GSTR-1** screen appears as shown in the figure 7.183:

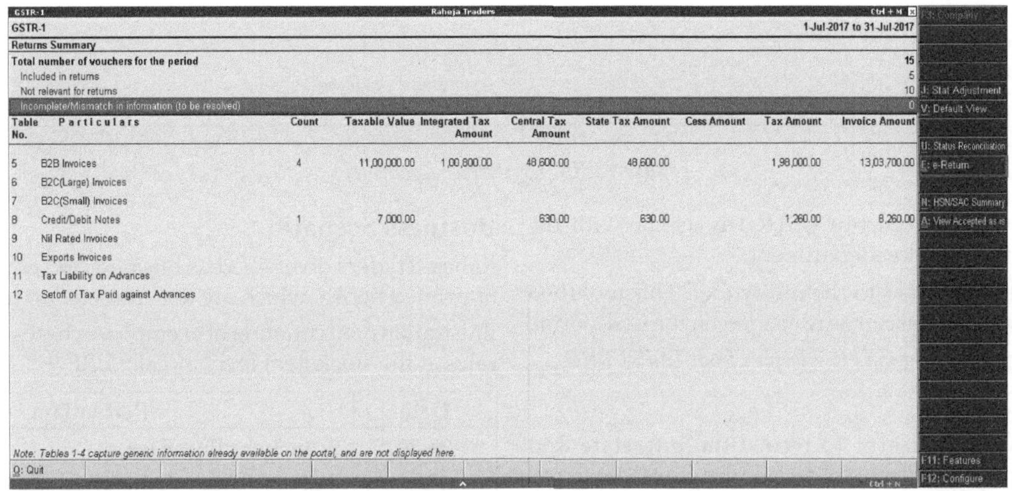

*Figure 7.183: GSTR-1 Screen*

***Observation:** Observe that there no exception under the head **Incomplete/Mismatch in information (to be solved).** Hence it is not required to solve the exception. Solving exception is explained in next lesson*

4. Click **Ctrl+E: e-Return.**

   The **Export Report** screen appears as shown in the figure 7.184:

5. Enter the details as shown in the figure 7.184.
6. Press **Enter** to accept the screen.

   The **Exported Excel Sheet** appears as shown in the figure 7.184:

7. In the figure 7.185, we will get all the outward supplies transaction details falling under different head like B2B, B2C, Export invoices etc.

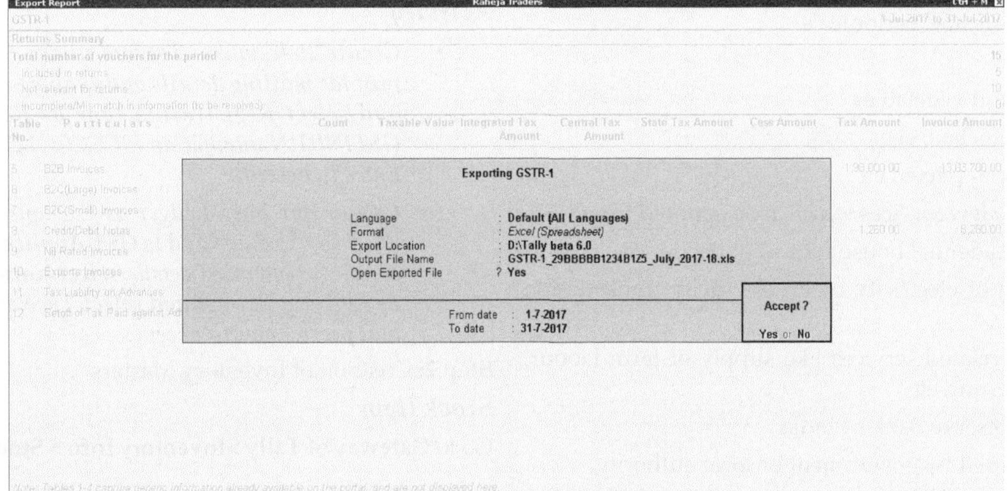

*Figure 7.184: Export Report Screen*

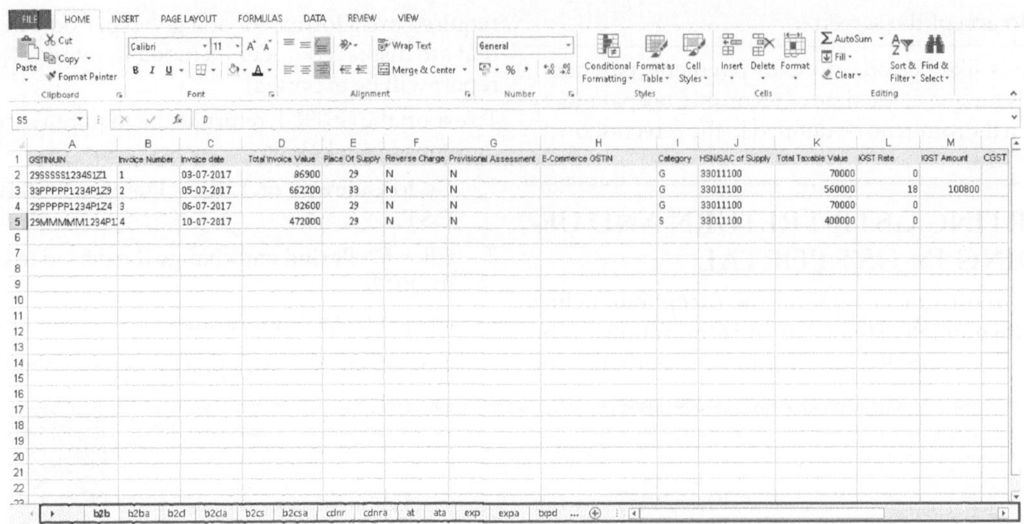


*Figure 7.185: Exported Excel Sheet*

8. The file created on export of GSTR-1 is in line with the format prescribed by the department.
9. The file can be imported to the utility tool. This tool then creates the .json file that can be uploaded on the GST portal.

***Activity:*** *Similarly export the GSTR-2 Report from Tally.ERP 9*

## CONCLUSION

In this lesson, we have learnt to record the intrastate and interstate transactions, inclusive of tax, return transaction and transferring of Input tax credit of VAT and Excise to State and Central Tax. We have learnt the complete procedure to make tax payment, adjust input credit against available liability and generated GSTR-1 in excel format to upload the same in GST portal.

## 7.44 EXEMPTED GOODS/SERVICES

Exempted goods are the goods which are not subjected to tax. The local or interstate purchases of goods exempted from GST can be recorded in Tally.ERP 9.

The following are few goods which are exempted from GST.

- Books, Journals and periodicals
- Newspaper
- Fresh fruits and vegetables
- Fresh meat, chicken, eggs, milk
- Stamps, judicial papers etc.

The Following are few services which are exempted from GST.

- Renting of residential house for use of residence.
- Transmission of electricity by an electricity transmission utility.
- Agricultural related services like supply of farm labour, cutting harvesting etc.
- Services by Reserve Bank of India
- Service provided by government or local authority.

Let us check how to record the exempted goods/services transaction in Tally.ERP 9.

### Business Scenario

Raheja Traders diversified its business and entered into trading of printed books, which are not subjected to tax.

Illustration 6: Accounting of exempt purchases and defining GST rates at the stock item level in Tally.ERP 9

<table>
<tr><th>Date</th><th colspan="4">Particulars</th></tr>
<tr><td rowspan="3">01-08-2017</td><td colspan="4">Voucher : Purchase<br>Raheja Traders purchased the following exempted goods from Indramukhi Traders, Bengaluru with supplier invoice number P/04</td></tr>
<tr><td>Particulars</td><td>Quantity /Nos.</td><td>Rate /Nos.</td><td>Amount (₹)</td></tr>
<tr><td>Printed Books</td><td>1,000</td><td>500</td><td>5,00,000</td></tr>
</table>

To record the exempt purchases in Tally. ERP 9, follow the steps given below:

**Step 1:** Creation of Accounting Masters

### *Activity*

- ***Create*** *Indramukhi Traders* ***under*** *Sundry Creditors,* ***provide mailing details and enable*** *Set/alter GST details* ***and select Registration type as*** *Regular,* ***and enter GSTIN/UIN number as*** *29CCCCC1234C1Z6* ***and press*** *Enter* ***to accept.***
- ***Create Purchase Ledger as*** *Exempted Purchase* ***under*** *Purchase Accounts* ***and Is GST Applicable as*** *Applicable,* ***enable*** *Set/alter GST details,* ***select Nature of transaction as*** *Purchase Exempt* ***and select*** *Type of Supply* ***as*** *Goods* ***and press*** *Enter* ***to accept.***

**Step 2:** Creation of Inventory Masters

### *Stock Item*

Go to **Gateway of Tally >Inventory Info > Stock items > Create**

| Printed Books | |
|---|---|
| **Against the Field** | **Action to be Performed** |
| Name | Enter as **Printed Books** |
| Under | Select as **Primary** |
| Units | Select as **Nos** |
| **Statutory Information** | |
| GST Applicable | Select **Applicable** |
| Set/alter GST details | Select as **Yes** |
| **Tax Rate Details** | |
| **HSN/SAC Details** | |
| Description | Enter as **Printed Books** |
| HSN/SAC | Enter as **49011010** |
| **Tax Details** | |
| Calculation Type | Select **On value** |
| Taxability | Select as **Exempt** |
| Type of Supply | Select as **Goods** |

The **Tax Rate Details** sub-screen defined at the stock item level appears as shown in the figure 7.186:

After defining the GST Rate at the stock item level, save the stock item creation screen.

**Note:** In order to enter the **HSN/SAC Details** press **F12 from Tax Rate Details** sub screen and enable **Allow HSN/SAC details** and accept the screen

**Step 2:** Recording exempt purchases in Tally.ERP 9

To record the exempt purchases in the books of account, follow the steps given below:

1. Go to **Gateway of Tally > Accounting Vouchers > F9: Purchase.**
2. Click **F2: Date** and change the date to **01-08-2017**.
3. Enter the **Supplier invoice no** as **P/04**, the **Date** field will be automatically filled same as **voucher date.**
4. Select **Indramukhi Traders** in the **Party A/c name** field, press **Enter** to get **Party Details** screen.

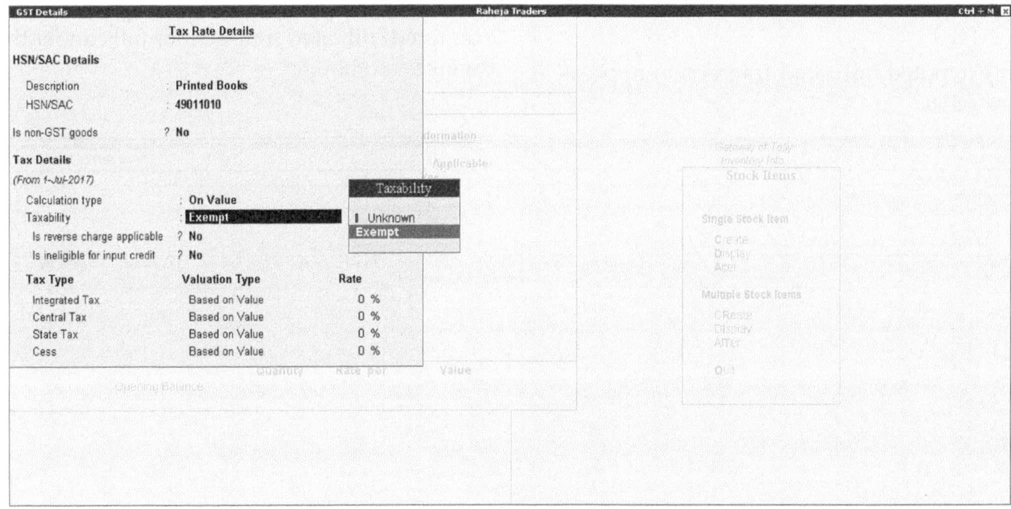


*Figure 7.186: Tax Rate Details Sub-screen*

5. State and GSTIN/UIN number will get captured from party ledger. Select the **Type of Dealer** as **Regular**.
6. Select the ledger, **Exempted Purchase**
7. In the **Name of Item** field, select **Printed Books** from **List of Stock Items.**
8. Enter **Quantity** as **1,000 Nos** and Rate as **₹ 500/Nos**, the amount will be calculated automatically.
9. Click A: **Tax Analysis** to view the details of tax calculation, observe that the tax is not getting calculated because it is exempted goods. Press **Esc** from **Tax Analysis** screen, to go back to the voucher creation screen.
10. Accept the **Bill wise Details** screen as it is

The **Purchase Voucher** appears as shown in the figure 7.187:

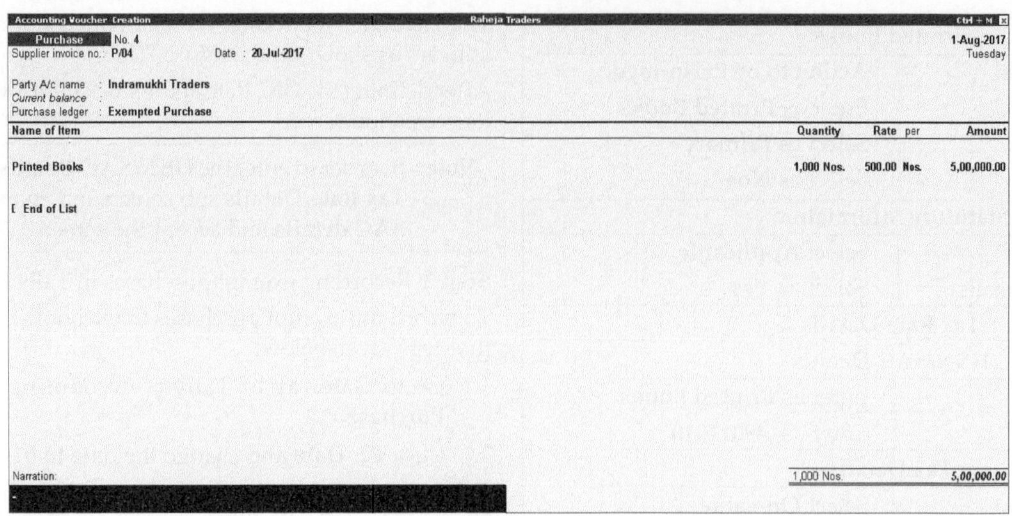
Accounting Voucher Creation — Raheja Traders — Ctrl + M

Purchase No. 4 — 1-Aug-2017, Tuesday
Supplier invoice no.: P/04 Date : 20-Jul-2017

Party A/c name : Indramukhi Traders
Current balance :
Purchase ledger : Exempted Purchase

| Name of Item | Quantity | Rate per | Amount |
|---|---|---|---|
| Printed Books | 1,000 Nos. | 500.00 Nos. | 5,00,000.00 |
| End of List | | | |
| | 1,000 Nos. | | 5,00,000.00 |

Narration:

*Figure 7.187: Purchase Voucher Screen*

Once after recording the exempted purchase transaction, to check the report go to Gateway of Tally > Display > Statutory Reports > GST > GSTR-2

The **GSTR-2** with exempted/nil rated transaction appears as shown in the figure 7.188:

In the figure 7.188, we can observe that the tax is not getting calculated as the same is exempted from the tax and the exempted/nil rated transactions falls under the head **Nil Rated Invoices** as shown.

GSTR-2 — Raheja Traders — Ctrl + M

GSTR-2 — 1-Aug-2017 to 31-Aug-2017

Returns Summary

| Total number of vouchers for the period | 1 |
|---|---|
| Included in returns | 1 |
| Not relevant for returns | 0 |
| Incomplete/Mismatch in information (to be resolved) | 0 |

| Table No. | Particulars | Count | Taxable Value | Integrated Tax Amount | Central Tax Amount | State Tax Amount | Cess Amount | Tax Amount | Invoice Amount |
|---|---|---|---|---|---|---|---|---|---|
| 4 | B2B Invoices | | | | | | | | |
| 5 | Import of Goods Invoices | | | | | | | | |
| 6 | Import of Services Invoices | | | | | | | | |
| 7 | Credit/Debit Notes | | | | | | | | |
| 8 | Nil Rated Invoices | 1 | 5,00,000.00 | | | | | | 5,00,000.00 |
| 9 | ISD Credit | | | | | | | | |
| 10(1) | TDS Credit | | | | | | | | |
| 10(2) | TCS Credit | | | | | | | | |
| 11 | ITC Received | | | | | | | | |
| 12 | Tax liability under Reverse Charge on Advance | | | | | | | | |
| 13 | Tax Paid under Reverse Charge on Advance | | | | | | | | |
| 14 | ITC Reversal | | | | | | | | |

*Note: Tables 1-3 capture generic information already available on the portal, and are not displayed here.*

*Figure 7.188: GSTR-2*

***Activity:*** *Record the following Transaction:*

<table>
<tr><th>Date</th><th colspan="4">Particulars</th></tr>
<tr><td rowspan="3">8-08-2017</td><td colspan="4">Voucher : Sales<br>Raheja Traders sold the following exempted goods to Hima Traders, a registered dealer in Bengaluru.</td></tr>
<tr><th>Particulars</th><th>Quantity</th><th>Rate (₹)</th><th>Amount (₹)</th></tr>
<tr><td>Printed Books</td><td>500</td><td>600</td><td>3,00,000</td></tr>
</table>

**Note:** Similarly, we can record the transactions which involve exempted services. While creating the exempted service ledger, we need to enable **Set/alter GST Details** to **Yes** and select the **Taxability** as **Exempted** and record the transaction.

The following figure 7.189 displays the details of services exempted from GST configuration at ledger level.

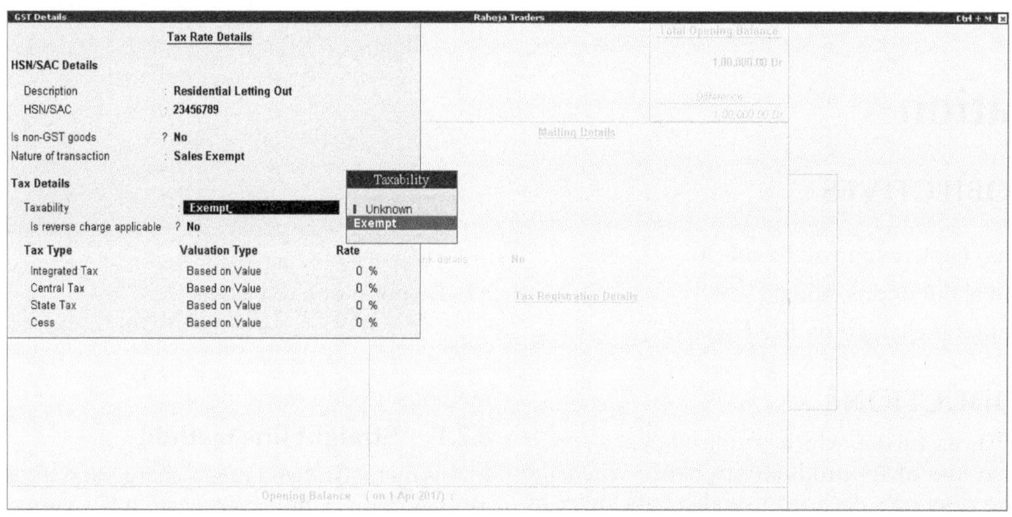


*Figure 7.189: Ledger Creation Screen – Exempt*

# PRACTICE EXERCISE

## Section A: Review Question

1. What is GST?
2. Explain Central Tax, State Tax and Integrated Tax.

## Section B: Objective Question

1. Which among the following taxes are subsumed under Central tax of GST?
   a. VAT b. Central Sales Tax
   c. Service Tax d. TDS
2. Which among the following Tax is charged for Interstate transactions under GST?
   a. Central Tax b. State Tax
   c. UT Tax d. Integrated Tax
3. In GSTR-2 report which details will be captured?
   a. Inward Supply b. Outward Supply
   c. Export d. SEZ Sales
4. GSTR-1 is a yearly return.
   a. True b. False
5. GSTR-2 is a monthly return.
   a. True b. False

# Chapter 8

# Depreciation

## LEARNING OBJECTIVES

After studying this chapter, you will be able to:

- You will learn about depreciation
- How deprecation is charged on fixed assets
- Disposal of fixed assets

## 8.1 INTRODUCTION

Every fixed asset has useful life, which is utilized over a period of time, this cause loss of its productivity hence when the productivity of the asset gets declined its value gets lower by lower, this reduction in the value of asset is called depreciation. Finally when the asset becomes useless it is disposed after charging depreciation.

### *Factors to remember*

**Cost** – This is the total value of asset which includes purchase price of asset, transportation, installation, maintenance and any other additional expenses.

**Estimated life of Asset** – This is the expected life during the course of business.

**Residue** – This is the value of an unproductive asset which remains after charging depreciation to the cost of asset.

**Disposal of Asset** – The unproductive asset is sold as scrap is called as disposal of asset

**Note:** The land is the only fixed asset which is not depreciated.

## 8.2 DEPRECIATION METHODS

There are various methods to compute depreciation on fixed asset out of which we would understand the most important methods used for accounting.

### 8.2.1 Straight line method

In this method a fixed rate is charged on the original cost of the asset as depreciation every year. It is a very easy and simple to calculate.

$$\text{Depreciation} = \frac{\text{Original Cost value of Fixed Asset} - \text{Residual Value}}{\text{Estimated life of the Asset}}$$

#### *8.2.1.1 Illustration*

In the books of **Bismill Traders** - Financial Year 16-17, On 1-4-2012, The company purchased Machinery worth Rs. 4,00,000, payment made through bank and company estimates to use that asset is for 5 years, which means the effective rate of depreciation will be @ 20% and 5 Years later machinery can be disposed after recovering Rs. 25000 by selling it as scrap. Company sold the machinery for Rs. 63750/- on 31-08-2016 after charging the deprecation which was credited in the bank account.

- Let's make **Working Note**
- Pass the necessary **Journal Entries**
- Prepare **Deprecation A/c**

Depreciation = (400000-25000) = 375000 X 10%
= 37500 fixed for each year.

**Working Note**

| Date | Particulars | Periods | Depr | Amount |
|---|---|---|---|---|
| 01-04-12 | Original Cost of Machinery | | | 400000 |
| 31-03-13 | Depreciation for the effective financial period | 12 months | 75000 | |
| 31-03-14 | Depreciation for the effective financial period | 12 months | 75000 | |
| 31-03-15 | Depreciation for the effective financial period | 12 months | 75000 | |
| 31-03-16 | Depreciation for the effective financial period | 12 months | 75000 | |
| 31-08-16 | Depreciation for the effective financial period 37500 X 5 / 12 | 5 months | 31250 | |
| 31-08-16 | Total Deprecation | | 331250 | |
| 31-08-16 | Value of asset after Depreciation Original Cost of Machinery – Total Deprecation | | | 68750 |
| 31-08-16 | Sale of Machinery | | | 63750 |
| 31-08-16 | Loss on Sale of Machinery | | | 5000 |

### Journal Entries in the book of Bismill Traders

| Date | Particulars | | Debit | Credit |
|---|---|---|---|---|
| 01-04-12 | Machinery A/c | Dr | 400000 | |
| | To Bank A/c | Cr | | 400000 |
| 31-03-13 | Depreciation A/c | Dr | 75000 | |
| | To Machinery A/c | Cr | | 75000 |
| 31-03-14 | Depreciation A/c | Dr | 75000 | |
| | To Machinery A/c | Cr | | 75000 |
| 31-03-15 | Depreciation A/c | Dr | 75000 | |
| | To Machinery A/c | Cr | | 75000 |
| 31-03-16 | Depreciation A/c | Dr | 75000 | |
| | To Machinery A/c | Cr | | 75000 |
| 31-08-16 | Depreciation A/c | Dr | 31250 | |
| | To Machinery A/c | Cr | | 31250 |
| 31-08-16 | Bank A/c | Dr | 63750 | |
| | Loss on Sale A/c | Dr | 5000 | |
| | To Sale of Machinery A/c | Cr | | 68750 |

### In the books of Bismill Traders

| Depreciation A/c | | | | | |
|---|---|---|---|---|---|
| Date | Particulars | Amount | Date | Particulars | Amount |
| 31-03-13 | To Machinery A/c | 75000 | 31-03-13 | By Profit & Loss A/c | 75000 |
| 31-03-14 | To Machinery A/c | 75000 | 31-03-14 | By Profit & Loss A/c | 75000 |
| 31-03-15 | To Machinery A/c | 75000 | 31-03-15 | By Profit & Loss A/c | 75000 |
| 31-03-16 | To Machinery A/c | 75000 | 31-03-16 | By Profit & Loss A/c | 75000 |
| 31-08-16 | To Machinery A/c | 31250 | 31-08-16 | By Profit & Loss A/c | 31250 |
| | | 331250 | | | 331250 |

### 8.2.2 Diminishing balance method

Under this method, a fixed rate of depreciation is charged on asset instead of fixed amount of deprecation. Which means if the value of fixed assets get changed the rate of depreciation charged on fixed asset will be constant. Hence, when the value of fixed asset get reduced, the following deprecation will be charged on written down value of the fixed asset. Thus amount of depreciation is high at initial period and lowers in later periods

**Deprecation** = Fixed Rate is charged on cost value for the first year and further on declining book value of the asset.

Under this method the book value remaining at the closing of the year of the asset is considered as salvage value of the asset.

### Computation of Depreciation

| Years | Book value at beginning of year | Rate | Depreciation for the Year | Declined book value of asset |
|---|---|---|---|---|
| 1st | | | | |
| 2nd | | | | |

#### *8.2.2.1 Illustration*

In the books of **Bhugan Enterprises** - Financial Year 16-17, On 1-4-2010, The company purchased Machinery worth Rs. 5,00,000, payment made through bank and company estimates to use that asset is for 7 years, company decided to charge depreciation @ 20% and later machinery can be disposed as scrap.

Company sold the machinery for Rs. 115000/- on 31-08-2016 after charging the deprecation which was credited in the bank account.

- Let's make **Working Note**
- Pass the necessary **Journal Entries**
- Prepare **Deprecation A/c and Machinery (Asset) A/c**

**Depreciation Computation**

| Year | Book value at beginning of year | Rate | Depreciation for the Year | (Written Down) Book value of asset after Depreciation |
|---|---|---|---|---|
| 1 | 500000 | 20% | 100000 | 400000 |
| 2 | 400000 | 20% | 80000 | 320000 |
| 3 | 320000 | 20% | 64000 | 256000 |
| 4 | 256000 | 20% | 51200 | 204800 |
| 5 | 204800 | 20% | 40960 | 163840 |
| 6 | 163840 | 20% | 32768 | 131072 |
| **7** | **131072** | **20%** | **(For 5months) 10923** | **120149** |

**Note:** The deprecation of asset, in the year which is sold would also be taken into consideration

**Written Down/ Book value** after deprecation (–) **Scrap sales** value Here it is the 7th year, hence the calculation is 120149 – 1150000 = **5149**

Calculations are as follows

**Working Note**

| Date | Particulars | Periods | Depr | Amount |
|---|---|---|---|---|
| 01-04-10 | Original Cost of Machinery | | | 500000 |
| 31-03-11 | Depreciation for the effective financial period | 12 months | 100000 | |
| 31-03-12 | Depreciation for the effective financial period | 12 months | 80000 | |
| 31-03-13 | Depreciation for the effective financial period | 12 months | 64000 | |
| 31-03-14 | Depreciation for the effective financial period | 12 months | 51200 | |
| 31-03-15 | Depreciation for the effective financial period | 12 months | 40960 | |
| 31-03-16 | Depreciation for the effective financial period | 12 months | 32768 | |
| **31-08-16** | **Depreciation for the effective financial period (difference in scrap value and last diminished book value is considered)** | **5 months** | **10923** | |
| | Total Deprecation | | | 379851 |
| 31-08-16 | Value of asset after Depreciation (Original Cost of Machinery – Total Deprecation) | | | 120149 |
| 31-08-16 | Sale of Machinery | | | 115000 |
| 31-08-16 | Loss on sale of Machinery | | | 5149 |

**Journal Entries in the book of Bhugan Enterprises**

| Date | Particulars | | Debit | Credit |
|---|---|---|---|---|
| 01-04-10 | Machinery A/c | Dr | 500000 | |
| | To Bank A/c | Cr | | 500000 |
| 31-03-11 | Depreciation A/c | Dr | 100000 | |
| | To Machinery A/c | Cr | | 100000 |
| 31-03-12 | Depreciation A/c | Dr | 80000 | |
| | To Machinery A/c | Cr | | 80000 |
| 31-03-13 | Depreciation A/c | Dr | 64000 | |
| | To Machinery A/c | Cr | | 64000 |
| 31-03-14 | Depreciation A/c | Dr | 51200 | |
| | To Machinery A/c | Cr | | 51200 |
| 31-03-15 | Depreciation A/c | Dr | 40960 | |
| | To Machinery A/c | Cr | | 40960 |
| 31-03-16 | Depreciation A/c | Dr | 32768 | |
| | To Machinery A/c | Cr | | 32768 |
| 31-08-16 | Depreciation A/c | Dr | **10923** | |
| | To Machinery A/c | Cr | | **10923** |
| 31-08-16 | Bank A/c | Dr | 115000 | |
| | Loss on Sale of Machinery A/c | Dr | 5149 | |
| | To Sale of Machinery A/c | Cr | | 120149 |

**In the books of Bhugan Enterprises**

| Depreciation A/c | | | | | |
|---|---|---|---|---|---|
| Date | Particulars | Amount | Date | Particulars | Amount |
| 31-03-11 | To Machinery A/c | 100000 | 31-03-11 | By Profit & Loss A/c | 100000 |
| 31-03-12 | To Machinery A/c | 80000 | 31-03-12 | By Profit & Loss A/c | 80000 |
| 31-03-13 | To Machinery A/c | 64000 | 31-03-13 | By Profit & Loss A/c | 64000 |
| 31-03-14 | To Machinery A/c | 51200 | 31-03-14 | By Profit & Loss A/c | 51200 |
| 31-03-15 | To Machinery A/c | 40960 | 31-03-15 | By Profit & Loss A/c | 40960 |
| 31-03-16 | To Machinery A/c | 32768 | 31-03-16 | By Profit & Loss A/c | 32768 |
| **31-08-16** | To Machinery A/c | **10923** | **31-08-16** | By Profit & Loss A/c | **10923** |
| | | **379851** | | | **379851** |

**In the books of Bhugan Enterprises**

| Machinery A/c | | | | | |
|---|---|---|---|---|---|
| Date | Particulars | Amount | Date | Particulars | Amount |
| 31-03-11 | To Bank A/c | 500000 | 31-03-11 | By Depreciation A/c | 100000 |
| | | | 31-03-12 | By Depreciation A/c | 80000 |
| | | | 31-03-13 | By Depreciation A/c | 64000 |
| | | | 31-03-14 | By Depreciation A/c | 51200 |
| | | | 31-03-15 | By Depreciation A/c | 40960 |
| | | | 31-03-16 | By Depreciation A/c | 32768 |
| | | | 31-08-16 | By Depreciation A/c | 10923 |
| | | | 31-08-16 | By Bank A/c | 115000 |
| | | | 31-08-16 | By Loss on Sales | 5149 |
| | | **500000** | | | **500000** |

## PRACTICE EXERCISE

1. In the books of **Long-Life Enterprises** - Financial Year 16-17, On 1-4-2013, The company purchased Machinery worth Rs. 10,00,000, payment made through bank and company estimates to use that asset is for 5 years, which means the effective rate of deprecation will be @ 20% and 5 Years later machinery can be disposed after recovering Rs. 50000 by selling it as scrap. Company sold the machinery for Rs. 3,33,900/- on 30-09-2016 after charging the deprecation which was credited in the bank account.
   - Prepare **Working Note**
   - Pass the necessary **Journal Entries**
   - Prepare **Deprecation A/c and Machinery (Asset) A/c**

   **Solve the above question using Straight Line Method**

2. In the books of **Sampro Tech** - Financial Year 16-17, On 1-4-2012, The company purchased Machinery worth Rs 4,00,000, payment made through bank and company estimates to use that asset is for 20 years, company decided to charge depreciation @ 45% and later machinery can be disposed as scrap.

   Company sold the machinery for Rs. 28,000/- on 30-09-2016 after charging the deprecation which was credited in the bank account.

   Depreciation for the 5$^{th}$ year by 30$^{th}$ September 2016 is – Rs 8236/-

   Loss on sale of machinery – Rs. 367/-
   - Prepare **Working Note**
   - Pass the necessary **Journal Entries**
   - Prepare **Deprecation A/c and Machinery (Asset) A/c**

   **Solve the above question using Diminishing Balance Method**

Chapter 9

# Accounting for Joint Venture

## LEARNING OBJECTIVES

After studying this chapter, you will understand:

- The Meaning of Joint Venture
- The Difference Between Joint Venture and Consignment
- The Different Methods of Maintaining Joint Venture Accounting Records
- The Preparation of Different Accounts Relating to Joint Venture

## 9.1 JOINT VENTURE

Joint Venture is a business activity in which two parties combine their resources to complete a specific business project or task and once the project is completed the parties share the profit and loss equally or share the same as per the agreement.

**For Example:** Shyam and Ram decided to combine their resources for completion of specific project i.e., Construction of Commercial Building for ₹ 5,00,000 and the profit and loss will be shared equally between the parties. Once the project/ transaction is completed the venture will be over between two parties.

When two parties joint to complete a specific job (It can be construction, purchase of property or any other business activity), it is termed as Joint Venture and both the parties will be termed co-venturer.

## 9.2 IMPORTANT FEATURES OF JOINT VENTURE

1. **Agreement between the parties:** Agreement is made between two or more parties who are joining together to complete a Venture.
2. **Agreement for Execution of Venture:** Agreement is prepared for the completion of the Venture.
3. **Sharing of Profit and Loss:** If the agreement is not available then the profit and loss will shared equally, if the agreement is available, then the profit and loss will be shared as per the agreed ratio.
4. **Closure of Venture:** Once the Business project or any activity undertaken by the parties is completed, then the venture is closed automatically.

## 9.3 DIFFERENCE BETWEEN JOINT VENTURE AND CONSIGNMENT

The Difference between the Joint Venture and Consignment is given below:

| | Joint Venture | Consignment |
|---|---|---|
| **Meaning** | Joint Venture is a business activity in which two parties combine their resources to complete a specific business project or task and once the project is completed the parties share the profit and loss equally and the project is closed on its completion. | In Consignment the goods are sent to another party/consignee for further sale. |
| **Fund Contribution** | In case of Joint Venture the fund is provided by the co-venturers. | In case of Consignment the funds is provided by the consignor not consignee. |
| **Profit Sharing** | Profit is shared by the joint venture equally or it is shared based on the agreed ration. | Profit is not shared between consignor and consignee, but the commission is provided to consignee for the sales made by him. |
| **Loss/Risk Sharing** | Risk factor will be on all co-venturers | Risk factor will be on consignor. |
| **Rights** | Co-Venturers have equal rights to make payments, sell, and buy on account of joint venture. | Here, consignee need to work based on the instructions given by the consignor/principal. |

## 9.4 ACCOUNTING TREATMENT

In Joint Venture accounting records can be maintained in the following ways:

1. **Maintenance of Separate Accounting Book:** This method is followed when the size of the venture is huge.
2. **Maintenance of Accounting Book by One Venturer:** In this method books of account are maintained by one venturer and the other venturers will contribute their part of share.
3. **Maintenance of Accounting Book by all Venturers:** This method is followed when the size of the venture is small and in this methods all the venturers will keep the accounting of transactions related to them.

### 9.4.1 Maintenance of Separate Accounting Book

As explained earlier, this method is followed when the size of the venture is huge. In this method first the contribution of fund is made by all the venturers to joint funds in the joint bank account and any payments will be made from Joint Bank Account and then Joint Venture Account is maintained and the nature of this account is same as Trading and Profit & Loss Account and it is debited for purchases made and for expenses incurred. Personal Accounts of all the venturers are opened and it is credited when funds are contributed towards joint venture and it is debited with loss. The following accounts are maintained under this method:

a. Joint Venture Account

b. Joint Bank Account

c. Personal Accounts of all Venturers

Following are the list of Journal Entries recorded in case of Maintenance of Separate Accounting Books:

| Journal Entries | | | | |
|---|---|---|---|---|
| S. No. | Transactions | Particulars | Debit (₹) | Credit (₹) |
| 1. | Contribution of cash by joint venturers to joint funds. | Joint Bank A/c Dr. (Enter the total amount of all venturers) | xxx | |
| | | To Venturer' s A/c (Enter the individual contribution amount) | | xxx |
| | | Dr. | xxx | |
| 2. | Expenses incurred or purchases made for venture. | Joint Venture A/c | | xxx |
| | | To Joint Bank A/c | | |
| | | | | |
| 3. | Expenses paid by any venturers. | Joint Venture A/c Dr. | xxx | |
| | | To Venturer' s A/c | | xxx |
| | | | | |
| 4. | Cash Sales | Joint Bank A/c Dr. | xxx | |
| | | To Joint Venture A/c | | xxx |
| | | | | |
| 5. | Credit Sales | Sundry Debtor's A/c Dr. | xxx | |
| | | To Joint Venture A/c | | xxx |
| | | | | |
| 6. | Stock lying unsold. | Joint Venture Stock A/c Dr. | xxx | |
| | | To Joint Venture A/c | | xxx |
| | | | | |
| 7. | Stock taken by a venturer | Venturer' s A/c Dr. | xxx | |
| | | To Joint Venture A/c | | xxx |
| | | | | |
| 8. | Balance of joint venture account showing profit. | Joint Venture A/c Dr. | xxx | |
| | | To Venturer' s A/c | | xxx |
| | | | | |
| 9 | Balance of joint venture account showing loss. | Venturer' s A/c Dr. | xxx | |
| | | To Joint Venture A/c | | xxx |
| | | | | |

The following illustration will demonstrate about the maintenance of separate accounting book for a venture.

***Illustration 1:*** *Pratap Enterprises and Mohan Enterprises agreed to import machineries from Japan to India on 1st August 2016, both the parties opened a joint bank account with ₹ 1, 00,000 out of which Pratap Enterprises contributed 50,000 and remaining amount was contributed by Mohan Enterprises, both the parties agreed to share profit and loss based on their cash contribution. They remitted ₹92,000 to their agent to pay for the machinery purchased and later remitted ₹5,000 and settled his account. Dock charges, Fright Charges and insurance charges amounted to ₹5,000. On 1st December, 2016, the sales amounted to ₹ 1, 10,000 and the venture was closed and Mohan Enterprises decided to take over the unsold machinery for ₹ 2,000. Prepare the joint venture account showing profit and loss and prepare the accounts of Pratap Enterprises and Mohan Enterprises.*

***Solution:***

| Joint Venture Account | | | |
|---|---|---|---|
| Particulars | ₹ | Particulars | ₹ |
| To Joint Bank A/c | 1,00,000 | By Joint Bank A/c | 1,10,000 |
| To Joint Bank A/c (Commission paid to agent) | 5,000 | By Mohan A/c | 10,000 |
| To Joint Bank Account (Freight insurance) | 5,000 | | |
| To Profit transferred to: | | | |
| Pratap Enterprises- 50% of profit (10,000*50%) | 5,000 | | |
| Mohan Enterprise50% of profit (10,000*50%) | 5,000 | | |
| | **1,20,000** | | **1,20,000** |

| Joint Bank Account | | | |
|---|---|---|---|
| To Pratap Enterprises A/c | 50,000 | By Joint Venture A/c | 92,000 |
| To Mohan Enterprises A/c | 50,000 | By Joint Venture A/c | 5,000 |
| To Joint Venture A/c | 1,10,000 | By Joint Venture A/c | 5,000 |
| | | By Pratap Enterprises A/c (contribution amount + Profit share i.e., 50,000 + 5,000) | 55,000 |
| | | By Mohan Enterprises A/c (50,000 + 3000), 3000 is the amount got after removing the unsold stock value of 2000 from profit. | 53,000 |
| | **2,10,000** | | **2,10,000** |

| Pratap Enterprises | | | |
|---|---|---|---|
| To Joint Bank A/c | 55,000 | By Joint Bank A/c | 50,000 |
| | | By Joint Venture A/c | 5,000 |
| | **55,000** | | **55,000** |
| | | | |

| Mohan Enterprises | | | |
|---|---|---|---|
| To Joint Bank A/c | 53,000 | By Joint Bank A/c | 50,000 |
| To Joint Venture A/c | 2,000 | By Joint Venture A/c | 5,000 |
| | **55,000** | | **55,000** |

### 9.4.2 Maintenance of Accounting Books by One Venturer

In this method of accounting the books of accounts are maintained by one of the co-venturers and he will be paid extra for the services rendered from profit earned. Following are the accounts maintained by the co-venturer.

a. **Joint Venturer Account:** This account is will show the profit and loss earned on the venture.

b. **Personal Account:** This account will record the accounting details of all the co-venturers.

Following are the list of Journal Entries recorded in case of Maintenance of Separate Accounting Book by One Venturer:

| Journal Entries | | | | | |
|---|---|---|---|---|---|
| **S. No.** | **Transactions** | **Particulars** | | **Debit (₹)** | **Credit (₹)** |
| 1. | Receiving of share of investment by the working partner from other co-venturers. | Cash/Bank A/c | Dr. | xxx | |
| | | To Venture's A/c | | | xxx |
| | | | | | |
| | | | Dr. | xxx | |
| 2. | Purchase of goods | Joint Venture A/c | | | xxx |
| | | To Cash/Creditors A/c | | | |
| | | | | | |
| 3. | Expenses incurred for venture | Joint Venture A/c | Dr. | xxx | |
| | | To Cash A/c | | | xxx |
| | | | | | |
| 4. | Goods are sold on cash. | Cash A/c | Dr. | xxx | |
| | | To Joint Venture A/c | | | xxx |
| | | | | | |
| 5. | Goods are sold on credit. | Sundry Debtor's A/c | Dr. | xxx | |
| | | To Joint Venture A/c | | | xxx |
| | | | | | |
| 6. | Working partner is allowed an extra commission for the services rendered by him. | Joint Venture A/c | Dr. | xxx | |
| | | To Commission A/c (Later the same is transferred to working partner P&L A/c) | | | xxx |
| | | | | | |
| 7. | Distribution of profit or loss earned on the venture | | | | |
| | i. Working partner profit will be transferred his P&L A/c | Joint Venture A/c | Dr. | xxx | |
| | | To P&L A/c | | | xxx |
| | | | | | |
| | ii. Profit of all others co-venturers will be transferred to their accounts. iii. Then the venturers account will show the due amount in respect of profit or loss and their investment. | Joint Venture A/c | Dr. | xxx | |
| | | To Individual A/c (Accounts of co-venturers) | | | xxx |

The following illustration will demonstrate about the maintenance of accounting books by one venturer.

***Illustration 2:*** *Shakti Traders and Mukta Traders entered into a joint venture and agreed to share the profit and losses in the ratio of 2:1. Shakti Traders sent the goods to Mukta Traders for ₹ 70,000 and incurred expenses of ₹ 3,000 for packing, freight and insurance charges. While transferring the goods, few goods of ₹ 6,000 were damaged for which insurance was claimed for ₹ 3,000. As reported by Mukta Traders that 90% of the remaining goods were sold at a profit of 35% of their original cost. At the closure of venture due to fire remaining goods were damaged and the damaged goods were not insured and Mukta Traders agreed to compensate Shakti Traders by paying the cash 80% of aggregate of the original cost of such goods with proportionate expenses incurred by Shakti Traders. Apart from joint venture profit Mukta Traders is also entitled of 5% commission on net profit of joint venture and after charging commission total selling Expenses incurred by Mukta Traders is ₹ 2,000. Mukta Traders earlier remitted an advance of ₹ 11,000, he duly paid the balance due to Shakti Traders by draft. Prepare the Joint Venture Account and Mukta Traders Account in the books of Shakti Traders.*

***Solution:***

| Accounting Books of Shakti Traders Joint Venture Account | | | |
|---|---|---|---|
| **Particulars** | **₹** | **Particulars** | **₹** |
| To Purchases (Cost of goods sent) | 70,000 | By Bank (Insurance Claim) | 3,000 |
| To Bank (Expenses) | 3,000 | By Sales (Mukta Traders) **(Refer Calculation 2)** | 77,760 |
| To Mukta Traders Expenses | 2,000 | By Mukta Traders (agreed value for damaged goods) **(Refer Calculation 3)** | 5,339 |
| To Mukta Traders Commission **(5% on 11,099)** | 555 | | |
| To Profit Transferred to: | | | |
| P&L A/c **(10,544 * 2/3)** | 7,030 | | |
| Mukta Traders **(10,544 * 1/3)** | 3,514 | | |
| | **86,099** | | **86,099** |

| Mukta Traders Account | | | |
|---|---|---|---|
| To Joint Venture A/c (sales) | 77,790 | By Bank (Advance) | 11,000 |
| To Joint Venture A/c (claim portion) | 5,339 | By Joint Venture A/c (Expenses incurred by Mukta) | 2,000 |
| | | By Joint Venture A/c (Commission) | 555 |
| | | By Joint Venture A/c (Profit share of Mukta) | 3,514 |
| | | By Bank (Balance received) | 66,060 |
| | **83,129** | | **83,129** |

***Calculations:***

| **2. Calculation of Sales** | |
|---|---|
| Cost of goods sent | 70,000 |
| *Less: Cost of damaged goods* | 6,000 |
| | **64,000** |
| Cost of unsold stock (64,000*10%) | 6,400 |
| Cost of goods sold (64,000* 90%) | **57,600** |
| Profit of 35% | 20,160 |
| Sales | **77,760** |

| **3. Claim calculation for loss of goods by fire admitted by Mukta Traders** | |
|---|---|
| Cost of Goods | 6,400 |
| *Add: Proportionate Expenses (3,000 * 6,400)/70,000)* | 274 |
| | **6,674** |
| *Less:20%* | 1,335 |
| **Amount to be claimed** | 5,339 |

1. Assume that the goods damaged during transit have no residual value.

### 9.4.3 Maintenance of Accounting Book by all Venturers:

Under this method all the venturers will keep the accounting records. Under this method they are two ways to keep the books of accounts as given below:

1. When co-ventures inform each other regarding the transactions made by them on account of joint venture on regular interval of time.
2. When co-venturers furnish the information on the completion of the venture. This is also known as Memorandum Method.

### 9.4.3.1 *Each venturer gets the complete information from other venture on regular interval*

In the above method following accounts are maintained by all the co-venturers.

a. **Joint Venture Account:** This account is similar to profit and loss account and this account is debited with Purchases and expenses, it is credited with sales account and stock in hand amount. The balanced amount will profit or loss.

b. **Personal Account:** In this we will maintain co-venturers account, this account is written as Joint Venture with ....Account. This is done to distinguish it from other personal accounts of main business. This account is closed after settlement of the balance.

Following are the list of Journal Entries recorded in case of Maintenance of Accounting Book by all Venturers:

| Journal Entries | | | | |
|---|---|---|---|---|
| **S. No.** | **Transactions** | **Particulars** | **Debit (₹)** | **Credit (₹)** |
| 1. | When goods are purchased or Money is paid on joint venture by him. | Joint Venture A/c Dr. | xxx | |
| | | To Seller's /Bank A/c | | xxx |
| | | Dr. | xxx | |
| 2. | When he receives a report that his co-venture has purchases the goods and paid money on the joint venture. | Joint Venture A/c | | xxx |
| | | To Co-Venturers Personal A/c | | |
| | | | | |
| 3. | When goods are sold by him on joint venture. | Cash/Purchasers A/c Dr. | xxx | |
| | | To Joint Venture A/c | | xxx |
| | | | | |
| 4. | When he receives a report that his co-venture has sold the goods on Joint Venture A/c | Co-Venturers A/c Dr. | xxx | |
| | | To Joint Venture A/c | | xxx |
| | | | | |
| 7. | Distribution of profit or loss earned on the venture | | | |
| | i. Share of profit to be taken by him | Joint Venture A/c Dr. | xxx | |
| | | To P&L A/c | | xxx |
| | | | | |
| | ii. Share of profit to his co-venturers **(In case of loss entries will be reversed)**<br>iii. When co-venturers accounts are balanced, it will show the amount due to him or amount due from him | Joint Venture A/c Dr. | xxx | |
| | | To Individual A/c (Accounts of co-venturers) | | xxx |

The following illustration will demonstrate about the maintenance of accounting books by all venturer, if venturer gets accounting information on regular basis.

***Illustration 3:*** *Akash Traders and Biswas Traders entered into an agreement of joint venture and decided to share the profit and losses in the ratio of 60 per cent and 40 per cent. Akash Traders purchased goods for ₹ 4,00,000 and the goods were sent to Biswas Traders. Akash Traders paid ₹ 30,000 in the process and Biswas reported stating that he had sold the goods for ₹ 4, 20,000 and few goods were left unsold. Akash and Biswas Traders decided to send the goods on consignment basis to KK & Co., he agreed to sell the goods on commission basis, all expenses incurred by him on consignment and 5% commission need to be paid to him. KK sent the details of sales made by him along with the cheque of ₹ 40,000 to Biswas Traders (KK & Co., deducted expenses of ₹ 5,000 and 5% commission) and the unsold stock were sent to Biswas Traders and he purchased the goods for ₹ 25,000 and prepared a statement of account to Akash Traders and reported that he spent ₹ 15,000 on this joint venture and both of then agreed to settle their account on completion of venture. Prepare the required ledger accounts in the books of Akash Traders and Biswas Traders and show the final settlement of accounts.*

***Solution:***

| Books of Akash Joint Venture Account | | | |
|---|---|---|---|
| **Particulars** | **₹** | **Particulars** | **₹** |
| To Bank A/c (Purchase of goods) | 4,00,000 | By Biswas Traders | 4,20,000 |
| To Bank A/c (Expenses) | 30,000 | By Biswas Traders (through consignment) | 40,000 |
| To Biswas Traders (Expenses) | 15,000 | By Biswas Traders (Stock) | 25,000 |
| To Profit and Loss A/c **((Profit = 40,000) 40,000 * 60/100 = 24,000)** | 24,000 | | |
| To Biswas Traders **(40,000 * 40/100 = 16,000)** | 16,000 | | |
| | **4,85,000** | | **4,85,000** |

| Biswas Account | | | |
|---|---|---|---|
| **Particulars** | **₹** | **Particulars** | **₹** |
| To Joint Venture A/c (Sales made) | 4,20,000 | By Joint Venture A/c (Expenses) | 15,000 |
| To Joint Venture A/c (Consignment sales) | 40,000 | By Joint Venture A/c (Profit) | 16,000 |
| To Joint Venture A/c (Stock purchased) | 25,000 | By Bank A/c | 4,54,000 |
| | **4,85,000** | | **4,85,000** |

| Books of Biswas Joint Venture Account | | | |
|---|---|---|---|
| **Particulars** | **₹** | **Particulars** | **₹** |
| To Akash A/c (Goods sent) | 4,00,000 | By Cash (Sales) | 4,20,000 |
| To Akash (Expenses) | 30,000 | By Cash (Consignment sales) | 40,000 |
| To Cash (Expenses) | 15,000 | By Purchases (Stock) | 25,000 |
| To Profit & Loss A/c **((Profit = 40,000) 40,000 * 40/100 = 16,000)** | 16,000 | | |
| To Akash Traders **(40,000 * 40/100 = 16,000)** | 24,000 | | |
| | **4,85,000** | | **4,85,000** |

| Akash Account | | | |
|---|---|---|---|
| **Particulars** | **₹** | **Particulars** | **₹** |
| To Bank A/c | 4,54,000 | By Joint Venture A/c (Goods) | 4,00,000 |
| | | By Joint Venture A/c (Expenses) | 30,000 |
| | | By Joint Venture (Profit) | 24,000 |
| | **4,54,000** | | **4,54,000** |

### 9.4.3.2 *Memorandum Joint Venture Method of Accounting*

In this method the all the accounting information is reported on completion of the venture, following are the important features of Memorandum Joint Venture Method.

1. **Maintenance of Only One Personal Account:** Under Memorandum Method only one personal account needs to be maintained by every venturer. For example XYZ enter into Joint venture, and X will maintain only one personal joint account for Y and Z, similarly Y will maintain only one personal joint account for X and Z.
2. **Recording of Transactions by Co-Venturer:** Each venturer will account only those transactions recorded by him on joint venture. For example suppose X is purchasing some goods, then this entry will be accounted in the books of X not in the books of Y and Z.
3. **Opening of Memorandum Account:** To find the profit and loss made on the venture memorandum account is prepared. All the personal accounts are combined and presented in memorandum account i.e., all the debit side balance of personal accounts are debited in the memorandum account and the credit side balances are credited in the account. Any transaction which will not affect the profit and loss, then the same is not accounted.

The following illustration will demonstrate about the maintenance of accounting books by all venturer under memorandum joint venture method.

***Illustration 4:*** *Arun and Bikram came together for dealing in land and started the venture from 1st August 2016, Arun purchased plot of land measuring 10,000 square yard on the advanced money for ₹1, 00,000. Both the venturer decided to sell the land in smaller plots and prepared a plan at a cost of ₹1,000, which was paid by Bikram. Plot was planned in such a way that 1/3 of the total area of land was left for roads and the remaining land were divided into 5 plots of equal size. On 1st November 2016, 3 plots were sold at ₹40 per square yard, the buyer of the plot deducted ₹1,100 for stamp duty and he agreed to pay the registration expenses by himself. On 1st December 2016, remaining 2 plots were sold at net price of ₹30 per square yard. Arun received all the sales money. After charging interest at 5% p.a. on the investment of A and allowing 1% on the net sale value of plots as commission to Bikram, then the net profit or loss made on venture needs to be shared in proportion of 3/4 and 1/4 to Bikram. Prepare the memorandum joint venture account and personal accounts of venturer and show the balance payable to one another and Joint venture was completed on 1st December 2016,*

## *Solutions:*

| Akash Books Joint Venture with Bikram | | | | |
|---|---|---|---|---|
| **Particulars** | **₹** | **Particulars** | | **₹** |
| To Bank A/c (Advance) | 1,00,000 | By Bank (Sales) (3,999*40 = 1,59,960) | *1,59,960* | |
| To Interest **(Refer below given calculation-2)** | 1,013 | *Less: Stamp duty per plot i.e., 1,100 per plot(1,100 * 3 = 3,300)* | *3,300* | 1,56,660 |
| To P & L A/c **( Profit share of Arun) (Refer below given calculation- 3)** | 99,196 | By Bank (Sales) 2,666*30 | | 79,980 |
| To Bank (Final Settlement) **(Refer below given calculation-4)** | 36,431 | | | |
| | **2,36,640** | | | **2,36,640** |

| Bikram Books Joint Venture with Arun | | | |
|---|---|---|---|
| **Particulars** | **₹** | **Particulars** | **₹** |
| To Bank (Expense) | 1,000 | By Bank (Final Settlement) | 36,431 |
| To Commission | 2,366 | | |
| To P & L A/c (Share of profit) | 33,065 | | |
| | | | |
| | **36,431** | | **36,431** |

| Memorandum Joint Venture Account | | | |
|---|---|---|---|
| **Particulars** | **₹** | **Particulars** | **₹** |
| To Purchases (Arun) | 1,00,000 | By Sales | 2,36,640 |
| To Interest (Arun) | 1,013 | | |
| To Expenses (Bikram) | 1,000 | | |
| To Commission (Bikram) | 2,366 | | |
| To Profit: | | | |
| Akash 99,196 | | | |
| Bikram 33,065 | 1,32,261 | | |
| | **2,36,640** | | **2,36,640** |

## *Calculations:*

1. **Area used for roads** = 1/3 of total plot i.e., ( 1/3 * 10,000 = 3,334)

   **Remaining area of land** = Total Plot – Area used for road i.e. (10,000 – 3,334 = 6,666)

   Distribution of remaining area of land in 5 equal plots i.e. (6,666/5 = 1,333), hence per plot = 1,333 square yards.
2. Interest Receivable by Arun = Advance amount * Interest rate * Period (1st August 2016 to 1st December 2016)

   = 1, 00,000 * 5/100*4/12

   = 1,666

   Interest Payable by Arun = Sales amount * Interest rate * Period (1st November 2016 to 1st December 2016)

   = 1, 56,660 * 5/100*1/12

   = 653

   **Net Interest Receivable by Arun** = Interest Receivable – Interest Payable

   = 1,666 – 653

   = 1,013
3. **Profit share of Arun** = Profit – Expenses incurred by Bikram – Commission payable to Bikram*3/4

   = (Profit = 2, 36,640 – 1, 01,013) – (1000) – (1% on 2, 36,640)* (3/4)

   = (1, 35,627) – (1,000) – (2,366) * (0.75)

= 1, 32,261*0.75

= 99,196

4. **Profit share of Bikram** = (1,32,261 * 1/4) + 1,000 + 2,366

= (33,065) + 1,000 + 2,366

= 36,431

## KEY TAKEAWAYS

- Joint Venture is a business activity in which two parties combine their resources to complete a specific business project
- Person who will join the joint venture will be termed as Venturer

## PRACTISE EXERCISES

### Section A: Review Questions

1. What is Joint Venture?
2. Who is a Venturer?

### Section B: Multiple Choice Questions

Select the most appropriate answer from the choices given below:

1. The person who will join a joint venture is termed as?

| a. Joint Venturer | b. Consignee |
|---|---|
| c. Bank | d. Consignor |

2. In joint venture fund is contributed by __________.

| a. Consignee | b. Joint Venturer |
|---|---|
| c. Consignor | d. Bank |

### Section C: Practical Questions

1. Akash Enterprises and Suresh Enterprises agreed to import machineries from Japan to India on 1st May 2016, both the parties opened a joint bank account with ₹ 2, 00,000 out of which Akash Enterprises contributed 1, 00,000 and remaining amount was contributed by Suresh Enterprises, both the parties agreed to share profit and loss based on their cash contribution. They remitted ₹ 1, 00,000 to their agent to pay for the machinery purchased and later remitted ₹ 10,000 and settled his account. Dock charges, Fright Charges and insurance charges amounted to ₹ 15,000. On 1st August, 2016, the sales amounted to ₹ 2, 50,000 and the venture was closed and Suresh Enterprises decided to take over the unsold machinery for ₹ 5,000. Prepare the joint venture account showing profit and loss and prepare the accounts of Akash Enterprises and Suresh Enterprises.

2. Surya Traders and Mukhi Traders entered into a joint venture and agreed to share the profit and losses in the ratio of 2:1. Surya Traders sent the goods to Mukhi Traders for ₹ 1, 00,000 and incurred expenses of ₹ 4,000 for packing freight and insurance charges. While transferring the goods, few goods of ₹ 7,000 were damaged for which insurance was claimed for ₹ 4,000. As reported by Mukhi Traders that 90% of the remaining goods were sold at a profit of 30% of their original cost. At the closure of venture due to fire remaining goods were damaged and the damaged goods were not insured and Mukhi Traders agreed to compensate Surya Traders by paying the cash 80% of aggregate of the original cost of such goods with proportionate expenses incurred by Surya Traders. Apart from joint venture profit Mukhi Traders is also entitled of 5% commission on net profit of joint venture and after charging commission total selling Expenses incurred by Mukhi Traders is ₹ 3,000. Mukhi Traders earlier remitted an advance of ₹ 15,000, he duly paid the balance due to Surya Traders by draft. Prepare the Joint Venture Account and Mukhi Traders Account in the books of Surya Traders

3. A & S Traders and B & C Traders entered into an agreement of joint venture and decided to share the profit and losses in the ratio of 70 per cent and 30 per cent. A & S Traders purchased goods for $^{1}$ 5, 00,000 and the goods were sent to B & C Traders. A & S Traders paid $^{1}$ 50,000 in the process and B & C reported stating that he had sold the goods for $^{1}$ 5, 50,000 and few goods were left unsold. A & S and B & C Traders decided to send the goods on consignment basis to KK & Co., he agreed to sell the goods on commission basis, all expenses incurred by him on consignment and 5% commission need to be paid to him. KK sent the details of sales made by him along with the cheque of $^{1}$ 50,000 to B & C Traders (KK & Co., deducted expenses of $^{1}$ 6,000 and 5% commission) and the unsold stock were sent to B & C Traders and he purchased the goods for $^{1}$ 35,000 and prepared a statement of account to A & S Traders and reported that he spent $^{1}$ 25,000 on this joint venture and both of then agreed to settle their account on completion of venture. Prepare the required ledger accounts in the books of A & S Traders and B & C Traders and show the final settlement of accounts.

Chapter 10

# Accounting for Consignment

## LEARNING OBJECTIVES

After studying this chapter, you will be able to:

- Explain the Concept of Consignment
- Prepare consignment Accounts

## 10.1 ACCOUNTING FOR CONSIGNMENT

In the present business environment, where success of a business is directly related to the ability of the manufacturers or dealers to quickly respond to market demand for goods, distance between suppliers and customers could prove to be a big challenge. It is this challenge that has given rise to the concept of consignment, wherein a dealer (or manufacturer) enters into a trading agreement with a reliable local trader to sell goods on his behalf (as an agent), at an agreed amount of commission. In such an arrangement, the dealer, called the Consigner remains the owner (title holder) of the goods until they are paid for in full and, after a certain period, takes back the unsold goods from the local trader called the Consignee. The goods sent by the consignor to the consignee are called 'Goods sent on Consignment'.

For example, if Ram of Tamil Nadu sends 500 television sets to Shyam in Bihar, to sell the television on his behalf and risk (Ram's risk), the transaction between the two will be a consignment transaction with Ram being the 'consignor', Shyam being the 'consignee' and the cell phones being the 'goods on consignment'. Under the arrangement, Ram will be liable to pay Shyam only as and when the goods (televisions) are sold; the payment will include the reimbursement of expenses incurred by Shyam for obtaining, storing and selling the goods, in addition to the commission as agreed upon. At the end of the consignment period, Shyam will have to return the unsold televisions back to Ram.

**Note:** Originally, the term consignment was associated with despatch or shipping of goods to an agent in a foreign country for sale on commission basis. However, over time, the term came to be used for despatch of goods to an agent in different parts of the same country.

### 10.1.1 Features of Consignment

The key features of a consignment transaction are:

**Principal and Agent:** The relationship between the consignor and consignee is that of a Principal and Agent (not seller and buyer).

**Transfer of Possession:** A consignment arrangement involves the transfer of possession of goods (not title of goods like in a sale).

**Consignor's Risk:** The risk of goods sent on consignment is borne by the consigner. Therefore, in case of any loss or destruction of goods, the loss will be borne by the consignor and not the consignee.

**Remuneration for Consignee:** The consignee will be eligible to receive remuneration that includes the reimbursement of expenses incurred in obtaining, storing and selling the goods, in addition to the commission as agreed upon. The sale proceeds belong to the consignor.

### 10.1.2 Differences between a Sale and a Consignment

The main differences between a consignment and sales are as shown in the following table:

| Terms of Agreement | Sale | Consignment |
|---|---|---|
| *Nature of Relationship* | Buyer and Seller; in case of credit sales, or a Debtor and a Creditor between the two persons | Consignor (Principal) and Consignee (Agent) |
| *Transfer of Ownership* | Ownership transferred from seller to buyer | Ownership remains with consignor till goods are sold by the consignee (only possession is transferred to consignee) |
| *Risk* | Transfer of risk from seller to buyer | Consignor bears risk till goods are sold by the consignee |
| *Return of Goods* | Goods sold cannot be returned, unless the seller agrees to take them back | Unsold goods are returned to the consignor |
| *Expenses (freight, storage, insurance, etc.)* | Borne by the purchaser unless specified in the agreement | Borne by the consignor |

### 10.1.3 Important Terms in a Consignment Transaction

Some of the terms associated with consignment transactions accounting are explained below:

**Proforma Invoice:** A Proforma Invoice is a statement prepared by the consignor containing information regarding quantity, quality and price of the goods at which the consignee ought to sell the goods being despatched. It is sent to the consignee along with the goods despatched.

**Note:** Proforma Invoice and an Invoice are not the same. An invoice is prepared by a seller, and implies that a sale has taken place. It contains information regarding the goods sold and the amount due by the buyer to the seller.

**Account Sales:** An Account Sales is a periodic statement prepared and sent by the consignee to the consignor, stating the sales and expenses incurred, commission earned and the consequent net amount due from the consignee after deducting the advances, if any, to the consignor.

***Account Sales - Specimen:***

Account Sales of 50 cell phone sets sold by M/s A. Das & Co., Kolkata on account and risk of M/s Malabar & Co., Kerala, India.

| M/s A. Das & Co., Kolkata | | | |
|---|---|---|---|
| **Particulars** | **(₹)** | **(₹)** | **(₹)** |
| 80 cell phones @ 7,000 | | 5,60,000 | |
| 20 cell phones @ 12,000 | | 2,40,000 | 8,00,000 |
| *Less:* Charges | | | |
| Freight | 6,000 | | |
| Warehouse Rent | 5,000 | 11,000 | |
| Commission @ 5% | | 40,000 | 51,000 |
| | | | 7,49,000 |
| Less: Draft accepted | | | 25,000 |
| Balance due, Bank draft enclosed | | | 7,24,000 |
| E & O.E.<br>Kolkata, the 30th June, 2016 | For M/s A. Das & Co., Kolkata<br>(Sd) Virat Kumar<br>Manager | | |

**Commission (Consignee's Remuneration):** Commission is the remuneration payable to the consignee at a fixed rate on the proceeds of the goods sold by him, for his services. Apart from the commission, the consignee is reimbursed all expenses incurred by him in connection with the consignment sales. These expenses could be dock charges, custom duties, freight, storage rent, insurance of goods in possession, etc.

Commission can be classified into 3 types, namely, Simple, Overriding and Del-credere.

i. **Simple Commission:** The simple commission is usually calculated as a fixed percentage on total sales.

ii. **Over-riding Commission:** The arrangement wherein a consignee is given an additional commission over and above the smple commission when sales exceeds a certain limit is called the over-riding commission. It is also calculated as a percentage on total sales, and is usually used as an additional incentive to motivate the consignee to increase sales.

iii. **Del-credere Commission:** Under a consignment agreement, consignees are required to sell on cash-basis, as bad or doubtful debts resulting from credit sales are required to be borne by the consignor. However, at times an arrangement is made in a consignment agreement wherein the consignee guarantees payment and undertakes responsibility for bad debts (i.e, the consignee agrees to pay the consignor, even if does not receive payment from the purchaser/s). For taking on this risk, the consignee is given an additional commission on the total sales, called del-credere commission.

### *Illustration 10.1.1*

Hero Appliances Private Ltd., Bangalore sent 1000 Flasks costing 1 80 each for sale on consignment basis to Griha Sukh, Mysore, on the following consignee remuneration terms:

i. Selling price per flask: ₹ 100

ii. Consignee's Commission:

   a. Simple Commission: 5 percent on normal selling price;

   b. Over-riding Commission: 2 percent if selling price is higher than normal selling price; and

   c. Del-credere Commission: 1 percent on total sales for guaranteeing payment on credit sales.

The sales reported by Griha Sukh were:

| | |
|---|---|
| **Cash Sales:** | **₹** |
| 400 Flasks @ ₹ 100 | 40,000 |
| 100 Flasks @ ₹ 120 | 12,000 |
| **Credit Sales:** | 26,000 |
| 200 Flasks @ ₹ 130 | |
| 50 Flasks @ ₹ 140 | 7,000 |
| Total | 85,000 |

Ascertain the commission due to the consignee, Griha Sukh, Mysore.

### *Solution:*

Statement of Commission due to Griha Sukh, Mysore

| Statement of Commission due to Griha Sukh, Mysore | |
|---|---|
| **Particulars** | **₹** |
| Simple Commission: 400*100*5/100 | 2,000 |
| Over-riding Commission: (12,000+26,000+7,000)*2/100 | 900 |
| Del-credere Commission: 85,000*1/100 | 850 |
| | 3,750 |

**Direct Expenses:** All expenses incurred till the goods reach the consignee's godown, such as freight, carriage, loading and unloading charges, insurance, etc., are considered as part of direct expenses. These expenses are generally of a non-recurring nature.

**Indirect Expenses:** All expenses incurred after the goods reach the consignee's godown such as warehousing charges, advertising expense, salesmen's salaries, etc., form part of indirect expenses. These expenses are of a recurring nature.

**Advance:** The amount deposited by the consignee with the consignor as a security deposit for the goods being sent by the consignor to him is considered as an advance. The advance is usually a percentage of the value of goods sent as consignment. For example, if goods of ₹ 100,000 are goods, then the advance amount will be ₹ 10,000.

**Pricing of Goods Sent on Consignment:** The pricing of goods sent on consignment can either be (a) at Cost or (b) at Invoice Price

a. **At Cost Pricing:** As the name suggests, under this pricing method, the goods sent on consignment are charged at cost price to the consignor. So the Proforma invoice will also be prepared at the cost price of goods. For example, if Nirmal of

   Delhi, purchases goods at a cost ₹ 50,000 and s a consignee, Rajesh in Mumbai, the proforma invoice will show the value of goods as ₹ 25,000. The consignee will be instructed to sell the goods at a certain price.

b. **At Invoice Price:** Under this pricing method, the goods are charged to the consignment at a price above the cost price. The proforma invoice is prepared accordingly, with goods being priced above the cost price. For example, if in the above case, the goods are consigned at a 25 percent on the cost price, the proforma invoice will be prepared for ₹ 31,250 (i.e, 25,000 + 6,250).

## 10.1.4 Accounting Treatment – Consignor's Books of Account

To maintain a proper record of transactions relating to each consignment, the consignor usually maintains three accounts, as discussed below:

i. **Consignment Account:** Considered a special Trading and Profit & Loss account, it is prepared to arrive at the profit or loss made on a particular consignment. A consignment account is a nominal account.

ii. **Consignee's Account:** It helps in evaluating the position of the consignee with regard to remittances on sales to the consignor. Since the consignee's account's is a personal account, if all payments are made in full to the consignor, he will be a debtor and if he has not paid all the balance due by him he will be a creditor.

iii. **Goods Sent on Consignment:** This real account is closed by transferring its balance to the Purchases account.

The following table gives details of the accounting entries to be passed in the books of a Consignor:

Book of Consignor

Journal

| Sl. No. | Transaction | Debit | Credit |
|---|---|---|---|
| 1 | **When goods are sent on consignment:** | | |
| (a) | at Cost price | Consignment A/c | Goods sent on Consignment A/c (cost price) |
| (b) | at Invoice Price | (i) Consignment A/c | Goods sent on Consignment A/c (invoice price) |
| | Adjustment entry to bring cost of goods sent on consignment to cost - with difference between invoice price and cost price) | (ii) Goods sent on Consignment A/c | Consignment A/c |
| | | | |
| 2 | Security deposit is sought | Bank or Cash A/c | Consignee's A/c |
| | | | |
| 3 | Expenses incurred (by consignor) | Consignment A/c | Cash A/c |
| | | | |
| 4 | **On receipt of Account Sales from consignee:** | | |
| (a) | for sales made by consignee | Consignee's A/c | Consignment A/c |
| (b) | for expenses incurred by consignee | Consignment A/c | Consignee's A/c |
| (c) | for commission | Consignment A/c | Consignee's A/c |
| | | | |
| 5 | In case of bad debts (consignee is not del credere agent) | Consignment A/c | Consignee's A/c |
| | | | |
| 6 | **For stock in hand with Consignee:** | | |
| (a) | Goods sent at cost price | Stock on Consignment A/c | Consignment A/c |
| (b) | Goods sent at invoice price | (i) Stock on Consignment A/c | Consignment A/c |
| | Adjustment entry to write-off unrealised profit on stock (with difference between invoice price and cost price) | (ii) Consignment A/c | Stock Reserve A/c |
| | | | |
| 7 | **Settlement of Accounts with the Consignee:** | | |
| (a) | If the consignee pays the amount owed in cash or through bank to consignor | Bank or Cash A/c | Consignee's A/c |
| (b) | If the consignor pays the amount owed in cash or through bank to consignee | Consignee's A/c | Bank or Cash A/c |
| | | | |
| 8 | Transfer of profit or loss to Profit & Loss A/c | | |
| (a) | Profit | Consignment A/c | Profit & Loss A/c |
| (b) | Loss | Profit & Loss A/c | Consignment A/c |
| | | | |
| 9 | Closure of Goods sent on Consignment A/c by transfering balance to Purchases or trading A/c | Goods sent on Consignment A/c | Purchases or Trading A/c |

### *Illustration 10.1.2*

On 1st June, 2016, Anirudh Textiles Private Limited, Mumbai, consigned 1000 pieces of dress material costing ₹ 20,000 to Vinayak Fabrics, Kerala. The consignee, Vinayak fabrics is entitled to a commission of 5% on total sales.

Anirudh Textiles incurred the following expenses: ₹

| | ₹ |
|---|---|
| Insurance | 200 |
| Carriage | 500 |
| Freight | 300 |

Anirudh Textiles issued a cheque of ¹ 5,000 in favour of Vinayak Fabrics, which was accepted by them.

On 31st July, 2016, Vinayak Fabrics sent the Account Sales with the following details:

| | ₹ |
|---|---|
| Goods sold | 25,000 |
| Expenses incurred | 400 |
| Stock in hand | 5,000 |

Vinayak Textiles enclosed a demand draft for the net amount due to Anirudh Textiles, along with the Account Sales.

Pass the journal entries and ledger accounts in the books of the consignor.

### *Solution*

Journal

| Date 2016 | Particulars | | L.F | Dr. | Cr. |
|---|---|---|---|---|---|
| June | Consignment to Kerala A/c | Dr. | | 20,000 | |
| | To Goods sent on Consignment A/c | | | | 20,000 |
| | (Being 1000 pieces of dress materials consigned to Vinayak Fabrics, Kerala) | | | | |
| | | | | | |
| | Consignment to Mumbai A/c | Dr. | | 1,000 | |
| | To Cash A/c | | | | 1,000 |
| | (Being expenses incurred: Insurance ₹200, Carriage ₹500 and Freight ₹300) | | | | |
| | | | | | |
| | Bank A/c | Dr. | | 5,000 | |
| | To Vinayak Fabrics, Kerala A/c | | | | 50,00 |
| | (Being cheque received from Vinayak Fabrics, Kerala) | | | | |
| | | | | | |
| | Consignment to Kerala A/c | Dr. | | 400 | |
| | To Vinayak Fabrics, Kerala | | | | 400 |
| | (Being expenses incurred by the consignee with respect to the consignment) | | | | |
| | | | | | |
| | Consignment to Kerala A/c | Dr. | | 1,250 | |
| | Vinayak Fabrics, Kerala A/c | | | | 1,250 |
| | (Being the 5% commission due to the consignee) | | | | |
| | | | | | |
| | Vinayak Fabrics, Kerala A/c | Dr. | | 25,000 | |
| | To Consignment to Kerala A/c | | | | 25,000 |
| | (Being sales made) | | | | |
| | | | | | |

| | | | | | |
|---|---|---|---|---|---|
| | Stock on Consignment A/c | Dr. | | 5,000 | |
| | To Consignment to Kerala A/c | | | | 5,000 |
| | (Being the remaining stock with the consignee) | | | | |
| | | | | | |
| Jul-31 | Goods sent on Consignment A/c | Dr. | | 20,000 | |
| | To Trading A/c | | | | 20,000 |
| | (Being transfer of goods sent on consignment to Trading A/c) | | | | |
| | | | | | |
| | Bills Receivable A/c | Dr. | | 18,350 | |
| | To Vinayak Fabrics A/c | | | | 18,350 |
| | (Being B/R rceeived as net amount due) | | | | |
| | | | | | |
| | Consignment to Kerala A/c | Dr. | | 7,350 | |
| | To Profit & Loss A/c | | | | 7,350 |
| | (Being transfer of profit to P&L A/c) | | | | |

**Ledger Accounts**

Dr. **Consignment to Kerala A/c** Cr.

| Date 2016 | Particulars | ₹ | Date 2016 | Particulars | ₹ |
|---|---|---|---|---|---|
| June 01 | To Goods sent on Consignment | 20,000 | July 31 | By Vinayak Fabrics, Kerala | 25,000 |
| | To Cash (expenses) | 1,000 | | By Stock on Consignment | 5,000 |
| | To Vinayak Fabrics (expenses) | 400 | | | |
| July 31 | To Vinayak Fabrics (commission) | 1,250 | | | |
| | To Profit & Loss A/c | 7,350 | | | |
| | | 30,000 | | | 30,000 |

Dr. **Good sent on Consignment A/c** Cr.

| Date 2016 | Particulars | ₹ | Date 2016 | Particulars | ₹ |
|---|---|---|---|---|---|
| July 31 | To Trading A/c (sales) | 20,000 | June 01 | By Consignment to Kerala A/c | 20,000 |

### *10.1.4.1 Valuation of Unsold Stock*

If all stocks sent on consignment are not sold, the remaining unsold stocks have to be valued, like closing stock in case of a trading account. The valuation of unsold stock includes:

i. Proportionate cost price, and

ii. Proportionate direct expenses, i.e., expenses incurred by both the consignor and consignee till the goods reach the consignee's godown

Further, as is the practice with regard to valuation of stock, stock should be valued at cost or market price, whichever is lower.

### *Illustration 10.1.3*

Chethan Enterprise, Goa, consigns 40 iron boxes of ₹ 1000 to Niranjan Electricals.

Chethan Enterprises bears the following expenses with regard to the consignment: ₹

| | |
|---|---|
| Insurance | 200 |
| Carriage | 300 |
| Freight | 500 |

Niranjan Electricals bears the following expenses till the goods reach his godown:

| | |
|---|---|
| Customs Duty | 1500 |
| Dock Dues | 400 |
| Warehouse rent | 300 |
| Office rent | 500 |

By the end of the year Niranjan Enterprise had managed to sell 30 transistors. The market value of the remaining iron boxes was ₹ 1,050 per piece.

Calculate the value of unsold stock with the consignee.

### *Solution:*

**Statement showing Value of Unsold Stock with Consignee**

| Particulars | (₹) | (₹) |
|---|---|---|
| Cost of 10 iron boxes @ 1,000 | | 10,000 |
| Direct Expense (in proportion of 10/40) | | |
| Insurance | 50 | |
| Carriage | 75 | |
| Freight | 125 | |
| Customs Duty | 375 | |
| Dock Dues | 100 | 725 |
| | | 10,725 |

Market value of unsold stock = 10 x 1,050 = 10,500

Market value being less than the cost, the 10 iron boxes should be valued at **₹ 10,500**

### *10.1.4.2 Loss of Stock*

In a consignment transaction, loss of stock can occur due to several reasons; these could occur during transit or after the goods sent on consignment reaches the consignee's godown. The treatment of loss of stock depends on the type and place of loss of goods. Loss can be of two types, namely, normal loss or abnormal loss.

i. **Normal Loss:** Loss due to the inherent nature of goods, that leads to loss due to causes like evaporation, sublimation, leakage or drying up of goods is called normal loss. These losses are uncontrollable and unavoidable. Normal loss is not shown in a consignment account and there is no need to pass any entry in the books of account. It is used in arriving at the value of closing stock wherein the loss on account of normal loss is included in the value of good units. Thus,

**Value of Closing Stock =**

$$\frac{\textit{Total Value of Goods Sent} * \textit{Units of Closing Stock}}{\textit{Units actually received by the Consignee}}$$

ii. **Abnormal Loss:** Loss due to accidental causes is called an abnormal loss. Destruction of goods due to fire or floods, theft, etc., are examples of abnormal loss. It is unexpected loss and beyond human control. Abnormal loss is debited to Abnormal Loss Account and credited to Consignment Account. The Abnormal Loss Account may be closed after transferring the amount to the Profit & Loss Account.

The valuation of stock lost due to abnormal losses is on the same lines as the valuation of stock on consignment, viz., proportionate cost price in addition to proportionate direct expenses incurred up to the date of loss.

Value of Abnormal Loss =

$$\frac{\textit{Total Cost*Units of Abnormal Loss}}{\textit{Total units to be received by the Consignee}}$$

**Note:** The stage or phase of loss of goods is important in case of abnormal loss. i.e, if the loss is during transit to consignee or after reaching the consignee's godown, as illustrated below.

### *Illustration 10.1.4*

Vivek of Chennai consigned 100 kgs of goods @ ₹ 60 per kg to Amit of Delhi. Freight and Cartage paid by the consignor was ₹ 3,000. Amit received only 95 kgs of goods. Heincurred unloading charges of ₹ 500. At the end of the consignment period, Amit was left with 20 kgs of unsold goods.

You are required to calculate:

(i) Value of closing stock, considering the loss to be a normal loss due to leakage

(ii) Value of abnormal loss due to theft during transit from Chennai to Delhi; Value of closing stock in case of abnormal loss

(iii) Value of abnormal loss due to theft from the consignee's godown, instead of the theft durinh transit

### *Solution*

(i) **Value of Closing Stock - Normal Loss**

| | |
|---|---|
| Cost price of 100 kgs of goods @ ₹ 60 per kg | 60,000 |
| Freight and Cartage paid by the consignor | 3,000 |
| Unloading charges paid by consignee | 500 |
| Cost of 95 kgs = | 63,500 |

**Cost of Closing Stock** = (Total Value of Goods Sent*Units of Closing Stock)/(Units actually received by the Consignee)

= (63,500 x 20)/95 **₹ 13,368**

(ii-a) **Value of Abnormal Loss:**

| | |
|---|---|
| Cost price of 100 kgs of goods @ ₹ 60 per kg | 60,000 |
| Freight and Cartage paid by the consignor | 3,000 |
| Total Cost of Goods | 63,000 |

Value of Abnormal Loss = (Total Cost*Units of Abnormal Loss)/Total Units to be received by the Consignee

= (63,000*5)/100= **3,150**

(ii-b) **Value of Closing Stock - Abnormal Loss during Transit**

| | |
|---|---|
| Cost price of 100 kgs of goods @ ₹ 60 per kg | 60,000 |
| Freight and Cartage paid by the consignor | 3,000 |
| Total Cost of Goods | 63,000 |

Cost of 20 kgs of closing stock = (63,000/100)*20

= 12,600

*Add:* Proportionate expenses incurred by consignee = (500*20)/95= 105 = **12,705**

(iii-a) **Value of Abnormal Loss at Consignee's Godown**

| | |
|---|---|
| Cost price of 100 kgs of goods @ ₹ 60 per kg | 60,000 |
| Freight and Cartage paid by the consignor | 3,000 |
| Unloading expenses incurred by the consignee | 500 |
| Total Cost of Goods | 63,500 |

Value of Abnormal Loss = (Total Cost*Units of Abnormal Loss)/Total Units to be received by the Consignee (63,500*5)/100= **3,175**

(iii-b) **Value of Closing Stock - Abnormal Loss from Consignee's Godown**

| | |
|---|---|
| Cost price of 100 kgs of goods @ ₹ 60 per kg | 60,000 |
| Freight and Cartage paid by the consignor | 3,000 |
| Unloading expenses incurred by the consignee | 500 |
| Total Cost of Goods | 63,500 |
| Value of Closing Stock (20 units)=(63,500*20)/100 | **12,700** |

Often businessmen take an insurance policy in respect of the goods being sent or received on consignment. Such policies are available only in respect of abnormal losses. In such cases the amount of claim admitted by the insurer should be debited to the insurer and balance of the loss amount may be debited to the Profit and Loss Account.

## 10.2 ACCOUNTING TREATMENT – CONSIGNEE'S BOOKS OF ACCOUNT

In the consignee's books of account, only those transactions that affect him directly are entered.

**Book of Consignee**

**Journal**

| Sl. No. | Transaction | Debit |
|---|---|---|
| 1 | On payment of advance (security deposit) | |
| | Consignor's A/c | Dr. |
| | To Bank or B/P | |
| | (amount of security deposit) | |
| | | |
| 2 | On receipt of stock - No entry (entry in stock register) | |
| | | |
| 3 | For expenses incurred for receipt of goods | |
| | Consignor's A/c | Dr. |
| | To Bank (or Creditor's) A/c | |
| | (amount of expenses incurred) | |
| | | |
| 4 | On Sales made | |
| | Bank (or Debtor's) A/c | Dr. |
| | To Consignor's A/c | |
| | (sales amount) | |
| | | |
| 5 | For Commission earned | |
| | Consignor's A/c | Dr. |
| | to Commission A/c | |
| | (commission amount) | |
| | Note: Del-credere commission has to be credited to Del-credere Commission A/c and bad debts debited from it. Balance has to be transferred to Profit & Loss A/c | |

### *Illustration 10.2.1*

Anand of Vijayawada sent a consignment of goods to Roop Kumar of Bihar at an invoice price of ₹ 15,000 and incurred the following expenses:

- Freight: ₹ 800
- Cartage: ₹ 300
- Insurance: ₹ 500

The consignee sold the goods at charges of from the consignee in settlement of the dues.
was ₹ 22,000paid a ndsimple commission of 5 percent, storage The ₹ 150coansignordsellingreceivexpensesda3 ofmonths₹ 600 .bill of exchange
Pass the necessary journal entries and prepare the necessary accounts on the books of the consignee.

| Journal | | | | |
|---|---|---|---|---|
| Sl. No. | Particulars | | Dr. (₹) | Cr. (₹) |
| 1 | Anand, Vijayawada A/c | Dr. | 750 | |
| | To Bank A/c | | | 750 |
| | (Being expenses incurred with receipt of goods on consignment - storage and selling expenses) | | | |
| | | | | |
| 2 | Bank A/c | Dr. | 22,000 | |
| | To Anand, Vijayawada A/c | | | 22,000 |
| | (Being credit of sale proceeds to Anand) | | | |
| | | | | |
| 3 | Anand, Vijayawada A/c | Dr. | 1,100 | |
| | To Commission A/c | | | 1,100 |
| | (Being commission earned) | | | |
| | | | | |
| 4 | Anand, Vijayawada A/c | Dr. | 20,150 | |
| | To Bills Payable A/c | | | 20,150 |
| | (Being the bill of exchange accepted in settlement of account) | | | |
| | | | | |
| 5 | Bills Payable A/c | Dr. | 20,150 | |
| | To Bank A/c | | | 20,150 |
| | (Being payment made on maturity of B/E) | | | |

## KEY TAKEAWAYS

In a consignment transaction, a dealer (or manufacturer) enters into a trading agreement with a reliable local trader to sell goods on his behalf (as an agent), at an agreed amount of commission.

In a consignment transaction, ownership of goods remains with consignor till the goods are sold by the consignee.

The pricing of goods sent on consignment can either be (a) at Cost or (b) at Invoice Price.

The treatment of loss of stock depends on the type and place of loss of goods.

Loss in consignment can be of two types, namely, normal loss or abnormal loss.

## PRACTICE EXERCISES

### Section A: Review Questions

1. Explain the term 'consignment' in your own words.
2. Differentiate between the terms direct expenses and indirect expenses in connection with consignment transactions.
3. Discuss any three differences between a sale and a consignment transaction.

### Section B: Multiple Choice Questions

1. Kiran Cements, Andhra Pradesh sent 50 tonnes of cemen to Ravikanth Cements in Bihar, to sell the cement on thei behalf. Kiran Cements has two partners in Telengana Vishal Cements and Vishal Hardware. In the abov consignment agreement, who is the consignee?
   a. Kiran Cements b. Ravikanth Cements
   c. Vishal Cements d. Vishal Hardware
2. Which of the following is an example of a normal loss o goods in a consignment transaction?
   a. Loss due to fire b. Theft
   c. Evaporation d. Mob violence

### Section C: Practical Questions

1. Naveen Sports Private Ltd., Gurgaon consigned 20( carrom-boards costing ₹ 1,200 each for sale on consignmen basis to Nita Sports Center, Odisha, on the followin consignee remuneration terms:
   i. Selling price per carrom board: ` 1,500
   ii. Consignee's Commission:
      a. Simple Commission: 5 percent on normal sellin price;
      b. Over-riding Commission: 1.5 percent if sellin price is higher than normal selling price; and
      c. Del-credere Commission: 1 percent on total sale for guaranteeing payment on credit sales.

   The sales reported by Griha Sukh were:

   **Cash Sales:**

   50 carrom boards @ ₹ 1,500

   20 carrom boards @ ₹ 1,800

   **Credit Sales:**

   30 carrom boards @ ₹ 1,750
2. Visha, Delhi, consigns 100 goods of ₹ 20,000 to Ariji Electricals. The consignor bears the following expense with regard to the consignment:

   | | ₹ |
   |---|---|
   | Insurance | 2,000 |
   | Carriage | 900 |
   | Freight | 10,00 |

   The consignee bears the following expenses till the good reach his godown:

   | | |
   |---|---|
   | Customs Duty | 10,500 |
   | Dock Dues | 600 |
   | Warehouse rent | 600 |
   | Office rent | 700 |

   By the end of the year the consignee had managed to sel 80 goods. The market value of the remaining goods was 22,000 per piece.

   Calculate the value of unsold stock with the consignee.

Chapter 11

# Hire Purchase and Instalment

## LEARNING OBJECTIVES

- You will learn about hire purchase price
- How to calculate and preparing interest table
- How journal entries are recorded in both hire purchaser and seller
- How various ledger accounts are maintained

## 11.1 INTRODUCTION

### *Hire Purchase System*

It is a business activity, when a **buyer** obtain goods from the **seller** on an agreement, stating to repay the price of goods on instalment basis, which include the interest and does not allows the **ownership** of the goods until the last instalment is paid by the buyer.

In the activity of **hire purchase** the buyer gets the full possession of the goods immediately and can use the goods, the ownership of goods is transferred to the buyer once he pays all the instalments. But, if the buyer fails to makes the payment of instalments, the seller has the right to take back the possession of goods.

The seller may ask for a certain amount of money, from the buyer to commence the hire purchase activity as a down payment, and the remaining amount is collected by the seller with interest on instalment basis. The instalment are fixed and can be collected by seller on monthly, quarterly, half yearly or on yearly basis.

In this business activity the seller get the scope to increase the sales straightaway and collect the payments on instalments which includes **interest**. This system thus benefits both the parties and seller is assured and reserves the repossession of goods in case of any default in payment by the buyer.

### *Instalment System*

In this system, when the buyer acquire goods from the seller, the ownership of the goods is transferred immediately by the seller regardless the payment procurement is on instalment basis. The buyer hold full possession and can start using the goods and the buyer promise to repay the price of goods on instalment basis. The buyer is not under any legal obligation and may evade the last instalment.

The instalment paid by the buyer is treated as repayment of principal with interest hence the relation between both the parties are similar to debtor and creditor.

If the buyer default to make payment, the seller cannot repossess the goods since the ownership of goods is already transferred to the buyer. The buyer is responsible for maintaining goods in fine condition and the buyer may also sell the goods to other party as he is the owner of the goods.

## 11.2 INSIGHTS

- **Hire purchase begin with an agreement between two parties**
  - o Supplier is termed as **Hire Seller**
  - o Purchaser is termed as **Hire Purchaser**
- **Instalment System begin with promise between two parties**
  - o Supplier is termed as **Seller**
  - o Purchaser is termed as **Buyer**
- **Cash Price** - The price at which the goods can be purchased from the market at full payment
- **Instalment** – The payment which is done in parts, at a definite interval instead paying it full, is called instalment. The instalment includes the principle amount with interest.
- **Down payment** – The sum of the amount demanded by the hire seller for commencement of the hire purchase is called down payment.

**Note:** The downpayment is not subjected to any interest.

## 11.3 AGREEMENT TERMS AND CONTENTS

It is a written statement which states that the goods are lent on hire and the hire purchaser can get the ownership of goods, only when the entire payments are made in definite periodic instalments by the hire purchaser.

The hire purchaser can obtain full possession of goods and use it as an when the agreement is applied.

### 11.3.1 Aspects

- **Hire Seller** delivers the goods to the buyer on **terms and conditions** of the agreement.
- **Hire purchaser** (buyer) can possesses the goods and can use it immediately but must keep the goods in **fine condition**.
- The hire purchaser have to make the payments to hire seller on fixed instalments and provide **down payment** if demanded, for commencement of the hire purchase activity.
- The instalment and the down payment paid by the hire purchaser is considered as hire charge for using the asset, hence it is not treated as the repayment price and the excess of total payment over the cash price is accounted as interest.
- If hire purchaser fails to make any of the instalments the seller reserves the right to **repossession** of the goods.
- Once the **last instalment** is paid by the hire purchaser the hire purchase activity becomes **complete purchase**.

**Following points are emphasised**

- Date of hire purchase agreement
- Value of goods on cash price
- Value of goods on hire purchase

- Interest Column
- Instalment Amount
- Total Number of Instalments and date of Instalment
- Instalment payment method
- Details of property in goods and warranties
- Other Terms and Conditions

## 11.4 DEPRECIATION CHARGE ON ASSETS PURCHASED ON HIRE PURCHASE

In the hire purchase system, the assets in form of goods are also charged depreciation, in this business activity the deprecation to be charged on asset, is allowed to hire purchaser. The reason that the hire purchaser is allowed to charge deprecation on asset, is the hire purchaser possess and uses the asset for the business purposes. The hire purchaser is believed and deemed to be the owner of the asset once the entire instalments are paid therefore the hire seller is not allowed to charge deprecation.

## 11.5 COMPUTATION OF HIRE PURCHASE PRICE

It is very necessary to understand the exact hire purchase price, since it is the absolute payable amount by the hire purchaser, in order to complete the purchase or acquire the asset.

| Hire Purchase Price | | |
|---|---|---|
| **If the case of downpayment** | Down Payment + Total Instalments | Cash Price + Total Interest |
| | | |
| **If the case of no downpayment** | Total Instalments | Not Applicable |

## 11.6 INTEREST CALCULATION ON HIRE PURCHASE GOODS

The seller in the hire purchase or instalment system charge higher for goods beside the **cash price** of goods present at **market**. Hence, the excess of the cash price over the hire purchase price of the goods is the total amount of interest. Interest will be calculated on cash price if there is no downpayment and in the case of downpayment paid, then interest must be calculated on **net cash price** i.e. cash price less downpayment paid.

**(Net Cash Price = Cash Price – Downpayment)**

### 11.6.1 Computation of Interest and Closing Balance without knowing principal factor

A. **Interest Calculation based on Rate of Interest Only**

1. **If the case of downpayment**
   - First Period = Net Cash Price x Rate of Interest
   - Subsequently = Closing Balance x Rate of Interest
2. **If the case of no downpayment**
   - First Period = Cash Price x Rate of Interest
   - Subsequently = Closing Balance x Rate of Interest

B. Closing Balance

- Closing Balance = Payable - Instalment

*Interest Table Format*

| Hire Purchase Interest Calculation Method 1 | | | |
|---|---|---|---|
| **Periods** | **Effect** | **Particular** | **Amount** |
| | | Cash Price of Goods | |
| | Less | Down Payment | |
| | | Net Cash Price | |
| | Add | Interest @ due | |
| | | Payable | |
| | Less | 1st Instalment | |
| | | Closing Balance O/s | |
| | Add | Interest @ due | |
| | | Payable | |
| | Less | **Following** or Last Instalment | |

#### 11.6.1.1 *Illustration*

A. **Interest Calculation based on Rate of Interest Only**

S Ltd purchased machinery from E Ltd on hire purchase based on the following details lets calculate the interest.

- Cash Price – Rs. 300000/-
- Down Payment – Rs. 100000/-
- Instalment – Rs. 56400 for 4 Years
- Rate of Interest Per annum – 5%
- Last Instalment Interest must be rounded off by Rs. 10.20/-

*Interest Table*

| Hire Purchase Interest Calculation Method 1 | | | |
|---|---|---|---|
| **Periods** | **Effect** | **Particular** | **Amount** |
| 01/04/2011 | | Cash Price of Goods | 300000 |
| | Less | Down Payment | 100000 |
| | | Closing Balance O/s | 200000 |
| | Add | Interest @ 10% | 10000 |
| | | Payable | 210000 |
| | Less | 1st Instalment | 56400 |
| | | Closing Balance O/s | 153600 |
| | Add | Interest @ 10% | 7680 |
| | | Payable | 161280 |
| | Less | 2nd Instalment | 56400 |
| | | Closing Balance O/s | 104880 |
| | Add | Interest @ 10% | 5244 |
| | | Payable | 110124 |
| | Less | 3rd Instalment | 56400 |
| | | Closing Balance O/s | 53724 |
| | Add | **Interest Rounded Off** | **2676** |
| | | Payable | 56400 |
| | Less | 4th Instalment | 56400 |

**Note: Closing Balance** = Payable - Instalment

### 11.6.2 Computation of Interest and Closing Balance with knowing principal factor

A. **Interest Calculation based on Rate of Interest with Principal Factor**

1. **If the case of downpayment**
   - First Period = Net Cash Price x Rate of Interest
   - Subsequently = Opening Balance x Rate of Interest
2. **If the case of no downpayment**
   - First Period = Cash Price x Rate of Interest
   - Subsequently = Opening Balance x Rate of Interest

i. Principal Factor

i. Principal Not Given

o Principal = Instalment – Interest

ii. **Principal Given but Instalment unavailable and unequal**

o Instalment = Principal + Interest

B. **Closing Balance Calculation**

- Opening Balance – Principal

### *Interest Table Format*

| Hire Purchase Interest Calculation Method 2 | | | | | |
|---|---|---|---|---|---|
| Period(s) | Opening Balance O/s | Interest Portion | Principal Portion | (Instalment) | Closing Balance O/s |
| 1 | (a) | (b) | (c) | (d) | (e) |
| Following/ Final Years | | | | | |

**The Opening Balance Column contains the following**

- **Cash Price** at Beginning
- Subsequently the **Closing Balance** is carry forwarded in this column

**Note:** Interest of the last instalment must be rounded off if **principal** is **fixed or unavailable**.

### *11.6.2.1 Illustration*

A. Interest Calculation based on Rate of Interest with Principal Factor

i. Principal Not Given

**E Ltd** purchased **machinery** from **T Ltd** on hire purchase based on the following details lets calculate the interest.

- Cash Price – Rs. 550000/-
- Down Payment – Rs. 100000/-
- Instalment – Rs. 141900 for 4 Years
- Rate of Interest Per annum – 10%
- Last Instalment Interest must be rounded off by Rs. 287.10/-

### *Interest Table*

| Hire Purchase Interest Calculation Method 2 | | | | | |
|---|---|---|---|---|---|
| Period(s) | Opening Balance O/s | Interest Portion | DP/Principal Portion | (Instalment) | Closing Balance O/s |
| 1 | 550000 | | 100000 | | 450000 |
| 1 | 450000 | 45000 | 96900 | 141900 | 353100 |
| 2 | 353100 | 35310 | 106590 | 141900 | 246510 |
| 3 | 246510 | 24651 | 117249 | 141900 | 129261 |
| 4 | 129261 | 12639 | 129261 | 141900 | 0 |

**Note: Closing Balance Calculation** = Opening Balance – Principal

i. Principal Given but Instalment unavailable and unequal

**Z Ltd** purchased **equipment** from **A Ltd** on hire purchase based on the following details lets calculate the interest.

- Cash Price – Rs. 350000/-
- Down Payment – Rs. 50000/-
- Principal – Rs. 60000 for 5 Years
- Rate of Interest Per annum – 5%

### *Interest Table*

| Hire Purchase Interest Calculation Method 2 | | | | | |
|---|---|---|---|---|---|
| Period(s) | Opening Balance O/s | Interest Portion | DP/Principal Portion | (Instalment) | Closing Balance O/s |
| 1 | 350000 | | 50000 | | 300000 |
| 1 | 300000 | 15000 | 60000 | 75000 | 240000 |
| 2 | 240000 | 12000 | 60000 | 72000 | 180000 |
| 3 | 180000 | 9000 | 60000 | 69000 | 120000 |
| 4 | 120000 | 6000 | 60000 | 66000 | 60000 |
| 5 | 60000 | 3000 | 60000 | 63000 | 0 |

**Note: Closing Balance Calculation** = Opening Balance – Principal

## 11.7 FULL CASH PRICE METHOD

In this method, the hire purchaser of goods is considered as the owner of the asset. Hence in this method, the asset purchased by the hire purchaser is recorded at full cash price, which is legally incorrect however, this is the most practical method used for accounting hire purchase or instalment

Now let us understand the accounting of hire purchase system using full cash price method following by the illustration

### 11.7.1 Accounting Journal Entries

| Transactions | In the Books of Hire Purchaser | | In the Books of Hire Seller | |
|---|---|---|---|---|
| Purchase of Goods | Asset A/c<br>To Hire Seller | Dr<br>Cr | Not Applicable | |
| (Note: Entry of asset must always be recorded on cash price) | | | | |
| Sales of Goods | Not Applicable | | Hire Purchaser A/c<br>To Hire Sales A/c | Dr<br>Cr |
| (Note: Entry of asset must always be recorded on cash price) | | | | |
| Down Payment | Hire Seller A/c<br>To Cash/ Bank A/c | Dr<br>Cr | Cash/ Bank A/c<br>To Hire Purchaser A/c | Dr<br>Cr |
| Interest Due | Interest A/c Dr<br>To Hire Seller A/c | Dr<br>Cr | Hire Purchaser A/c<br>To Interest A/c | Dr<br>Cr |
| Transfer of Interest to P & L Account | P & L A/c<br>To Interest A/c | Dr<br>Cr | Interest A/c<br>To P & L A/c | Dr<br>Cr |
| Instalment Payment | Hire Seller A/c<br>To Cash/ Bank A/c | Dr<br>Cr | Cash/ Bank A/c<br>To Hire Purchaser | Dr<br>Cr |
| Depreciation | Depreciation A/c<br>To Asset A/c | Dr<br>Cr | Not Applicable | |
| Depreciation Transfer to P & L A/c | P & L A/c<br>To Depreciation A/c | Dr<br>Cr | Not Applicable | |

**Disclosure in Balance Sheet Using Full Cash Price Method**

| In the Books of Hire Purchaser Balance Sheet as at | | | In the Books of Hire Seller Balance Sheet as at | | |
|---|---|---|---|---|---|
| Liabilities | Assets | Rs | Liabilities | Assets | Rs |
| | Fixed Assets | | | Current Assets | |
| | HP Asset at Full Price | | | Sundry Debtors | |
| | (-) Depreciation | | | Hire Purchaser | |
| | (-) Balance in Hire Seller A/c | | | | |

## 11.8 ILLUSTRATION

On 1st April, 2012. **Anil International Pvt Ltd** purchased machinery from **HIVE Machines & Instruments Ltd** on hire purchase systems, the details of the transactions are as follows.

- The **Cash Price** of the Machinery in the Market is Rs. 15,00,000/-
- The **Down Payment** mentioned was Rs. 2,00,000/-
- The **Instalment** amount is fixed to Rs. 4,10,000/- at each interval and paid on 31st March of Following Year. The deal would complete in **4 years**
- The **Rate of Interest is 10%** per annum
- **Anil International Pvt Ltd** charge **deprecation** the fixed asset @ 5% using straight line method.
- The Last instalment interest would be **rounding off** at the difference of Rs. 520/-

**Let us calculate the interest**

## *Interest Table*

| Hire Purchase Interest Calculation Method 1 | | | |
|---|---|---|---|
| Periods | Effect | Particular | Amount |
| 01/04/2011 | | Cash Price of Goods | 1500000 |
| | Less | Down Payment | 200000 |
| | | Closing Balance O/s | 1300000 |
| | Add | Interest @ 10% | 130000 |
| | | Payable | 1430000 |
| | Less | 1st Instalment | 410000 |
| | | Closing Balance O/s | 1020000 |
| | Add | Interest @ 10% | 102000 |
| | | Payable | 1122000 |
| | Less | 2nd Instalment | 410000 |
| | | Closing Balance O/s | 712000 |
| | Add | Interest @ 10% | 71200 |
| | | Payable | 783200 |
| | Less | 3rd Instalment | 410000 |
| | | Closing Balance O/s | 373200 |
| | Add | **Interest Rounded Off** | **36800** |
| | | Payable | 410000 |
| | Less | 4th Instalment | 410000 |

**Total Interest = 340000/-**

Let us take the same above illustration and use the alternative method for interest calculation.

On 1st April, 2012. **Anil International Pvt Ltd** purchased machinery from **HIVE Machines & Instruments Ltd** on hire purchase systems, the details of the transactions are as follows.

- The **Cash Price** of the Machinery in the Market is Rs. 15,00,000/-
- The **Down Payment** mentioned was Rs. 2,00,000/-
- The **Instalment** amount is fixed to Rs. 4,10,000/- at each interval and paid on 31st March of Following Year. The deal would complete in **4 years**
- The **Rate of Interest is 10%** per annum
- **Anil International Pvt Ltd** charge **deprecation** the fixed asset @ 10% using straight line method.
- The Last instalment interest would be **rounding off** at the difference of Rs. 520/-

## *Interest Table*

| Hire Purchase Interest Calculation Method 2 | | | | | |
|---|---|---|---|---|---|
| Period(s) | Opening Balance O/s | Interest Portion | DP/Principal Portion | (Instalment) | Closing Balance O/s |
| 1 | 1500000 | | 200000 | | 1300000 |
| 1 | 1300000 | 130000 | 280000 | 410000 | 975000 |
| 2 | 975000 | 102000 | 308000 | 410000 | 650000 |
| 3 | 650000 | 71200 | 338800 | 410000 | 325000 |
| 4 | 325000 | **36800** | **373200** | 410000 | 0 |

**Total Interest = 340000/-**

## *Principal Calculation*

- Principal = Instalment – Interest

## *Closing Balance Calculation*

- Opening Balance – Principal

## *Journal Entries*

**In the books of Hire Purchaser (Anil International Pvt Ltd)**

| Date | Particulars | | LF | Dr. | Cr. |
|---|---|---|---|---|---|
| 01-04-12 | Machinery A/c | Dr | | 1500000 | |
| | To Hive Machines & Equipment Ltd A/c | Cr | | | 1500000 |
| | (Being goods bought on hire purchase basis) | | | | |
| 01-04-12 | Hive Machines & Equipment Ltd A/c | Dr | | 200000 | |
| | To Bank A/c | Cr | | | 200000 |
| | (Being downpayment made) | | | | |
| 31-03-13 | Interest A/c | Dr | | 130000 | |
| | To Hive Machines & Equipment Ltd A/c | Cr | | | 130000 |
| | (Made the interest due) | | | | |
| 31-03-13 | Hive Machines & Equipment Ltd A/c | Dr | | 410000 | |
| | To Bank A/c | Cr | | | 410000 |
| | (Being 1st Instalment paid) | | | | |
| 31-03-13 | Depreciation A/c | Dr | | 150000 | |
| | To Machinery A/c | Cr | | | 150000 |
| | (Being depreciation charged on fixed asset) | | | | |
| 31-03-13 | Profit & Loss A/c | Dr | | 150000 | |
| | To Depreciation A/c | Cr | | | 150000 |
| | (Being depreciation transferred to P&L A/c) | | | | |
| 31-03-14 | Interest A/c | Dr | | 102000 | |
| | To Hive Machines & Equipment Ltd A/c | Cr | | | 102000 |
| | (Made the interest due) | | | | |
| 31-03-14 | Hive Machines & Equipment Ltd A/c | Dr | | 410000 | |
| | To Bank A/c | Cr | | | 410000 |
| | (Being 2nd Instalment paid) | | | | |
| 31-03-14 | Depreciation A/c | Dr | | 150000 | |
| | To Machinery A/c | Cr | | | 150000 |
| | (Being depreciation charged on fixed asset) | | | | |
| 31-03-14 | Profit & Loss A/c | Dr | | 150000 | |
| | To Depreciation A/c | Cr | | | 150000 |
| | (Being depreciation transferred to P&L A/c) | | | | |
| 31-03-15 | Interest A/c | Dr | | 71200 | |
| | To Hive Machines & Equipment Ltd A/c | Cr | | | 71200 |
| | (Made the interest due) | | | | |
| 31-03-15 | Hive Machines & Equipment Ltd A/c | Dr | | 410000 | |
| | To Bank A/c | Cr | | | 410000 |
| | (Being 3rd Instalment paid) | | | | |
| 31-03-15 | Depreciation A/c | Dr | | 150000 | |
| | To Machinery A/c | Cr | | | 150000 |
| | (Being depreciation charged on fixed asset) | | | | |
| 31-03-15 | Profit & Loss A/c | Dr | | 150000 | |
| | To Depreciation A/c | Cr | | | 150000 |
| | (Being depreciation transferred to P&L A/c) | | | | |
| 31-03-16 | Interest A/c | Dr | L.F | 36800 | |
| | To Hive Machines & Equipment Ltd A/c | Cr | | | 36800 |
| | (Made the interest due) | | | | |
| 31-03-16 | Hive Machines & Equipment Ltd A/c | Dr | | 410000 | |
| | To Bank A/c | Cr | | | 410000 |
| | (Being 4th Instalment paid) | | | | |
| 31-03-16 | Depreciation A/c | Dr | | 150000 | |
| | To Machinery A/c | Cr | | | 150000 |
| | (Being depreciation charged on fixed asset) | | | | |
| 31-03-16 | Profit & Loss A/c | Dr | | 150000 | |
| | To Depreciation A/c | Cr | | | 150000 |
| | (Being depreciation transferred to P&L A/c) | | | | |

**In the books of Hire Purchaser (Anil International Pvt Ltd)**

## *Vendor Account*

| Hive Machines & Equipment Ltd A/c | | | | | |
|---|---|---|---|---|---|
| Date | Particulars | Amount | Date | Particulars | Amount |
| 01-04-12 | To Bank A/c | 200000 | 01-04-12 | By Machinery A/c | 1500000 |
| 31-03-13 | To Bank A/c | 410000 | 31-03-13 | By Interest A/c | 130000 |
| 31-03-14 | To Bank A/c | 410000 | 31-03-14 | By Interest A/c | 102000 |
| 31-03-15 | To Bank A/c | 410000 | 31-03-15 | By Interest A/c | 71200 |
| 31-03-16 | To Bank A/c | 410000 | 31-03-16 | By Interest A/c | 36800 |
| | | 1840000 | | | 1840000 |

| Machinery A/c | | | | | |
|---|---|---|---|---|---|
| Date | Particulars | Amount | Date | Particulars | Amount |
| 01-04-12 | To Hive Machines & Equipment Ltd A/c | 1500000 | 31-03-13 | By Depreciation A/c | 150000 |
| | | | 31-03-14 | By Depreciation A/c | 150000 |
| | | | 31-03-15 | By Depreciation A/c | 150000 |
| | | | 31-03-16 | By Depreciation A/c | 150000 |
| | | | 31-03-16 | By Balance b/d | 900000 |
| | | 1500000 | | | 1500000 |

| Depreciation A/c | | | | | |
|---|---|---|---|---|---|
| Date | Particulars | Amount | Date | Particulars | Amount |
| 31-03-13 | To Machinery A/c | 150000 | 31-03-13 | By Profit & Loss A/c | 150000 |
| 31-03-14 | To Machinery A/c | 150000 | 31-03-14 | By Profit & Loss A/c | 150000 |
| 31-03-15 | To Machinery A/c | 150000 | 31-03-15 | By Profit & Loss A/c | 150000 |
| 31-03-16 | To Machinery A/c | 150000 | 31-03-16 | By Profit & Loss A/c | 150000 |
| | | 600000 | | | 600000 |

### *Journal Entries*

**In the books of Hire Seller (Hive Machines & Equipment Ltd)**

| Date | Particulars | | L.F | Dr. | Cr. |
|---|---|---|---|---|---|
| 01-04-12 | Anil International Pvt Ltd A/c<br>To Sales of Machinery A/c<br>(Being goods sold on hire purchase basis) | Dr<br>Cr | | 1500000 | <br>1500000 |
| 01-04-12 | Bank A/c<br>To Anil International Pvt Ltd A/c<br>(Being downpayment received) | Dr<br>Cr | | 200000 | <br>200000 |
| 31-03-13 | Anil International Pvt Ltd A/c<br>To Interest A/c<br>(Interest receive due) | Dr<br>Cr | | 130000 | <br>130000 |
| 31-03-13 | Interest A/c<br>To Profit & Loss A/c<br>(Being Interest transferred to P&L A/c) | Dr<br>Cr | | 130000 | <br>130000 |
| 31-03-13 | Bank A/c<br>To Anil International Pvt Ltd A/c<br>(Being 1st Instalment received) | Dr<br>Cr | | 410000 | <br>410000 |
| 31-03-14 | Anil International Pvt Ltd A/c<br>To Interest A/c<br>(Interest receive due) | Dr<br>Cr | | 102000 | <br>102000 |
| 31-03-14 | Interest A/c<br>To Profit & Loss A/c<br>(Being Interest transferred to P&L A/c) | Dr<br>Cr | | 102000 | <br>102000 |
| 31-03-14 | Bank A/c<br>To Anil International Pvt Ltd A/c<br>(Being 2nd Instalment received) | Dr<br>Cr | | 410000 | <br>410000 |
| 31-03-15 | Anil International Pvt Ltd A/c<br>To Interest A/c<br>(Interest receive due) | Dr<br>Cr | | 71200 | <br>71200 |
| 31-03-15 | Interest A/c<br>To Profit & Loss A/c<br>(Being Interest transferred to P&L A/c) | Dr<br>Cr | | 71200 | <br>71200 |
| 31-03-15 | Bank A/c<br>To Anil International Pvt Ltd A/c<br>(Being 3rd Instalment received) | Dr<br>Cr | | 410000 | <br>410000 |
| 31-03-16 | Anil International Pvt Ltd A/c<br>To Interest A/c<br>(Interest receive due) | Dr<br>Cr | | 36800 | <br>36800 |
| 31-03-16 | Interest A/c<br>To Profit & Loss A/c<br>(Being Interest transferred to P&L A/c) | Dr<br>Cr | | 36800 | <br>36800 |
| 31-03-16 | Bank A/c<br>To Anil International Pvt Ltd A/c<br>(Being 4th Instalment received) | Dr<br>Cr | | 410000 | <br>410000 |

**In the books of Hire Seller (Hive Machines & Equipment Ltd)**

### *Customer Account*

| Anil International Pvt Ltd A/c | | | | | |
|---|---|---|---|---|---|
| Date | Particulars | Amount | Date | Particulars | Amount |
| 01-04-12 | To Machinery A/c | 1500000 | 01-04-12 | By Bank A/c | 200000 |
| 31-03-13 | To Interest A/c | 130000 | 31-03-13 | By Bank A/c | 410000 |
| 31-03-14 | To Interest A/c | 102000 | 31-03-14 | By Bank A/c | 410000 |
| 31-03-15 | To Interest A/c | 71200 | 31-03-15 | By Bank A/c | 410000 |
| 31-03-16 | To Interest A/c | 36800 | 31-03-16 | By Bank A/c | 410000 |
| | | 1840000 | | | 1840000 |

| Interest A/c | | | | | |
|---|---|---|---|---|---|
| Date | Particulars | Amount | Date | Particulars | Amount |
| 31-03-13 | To Profit & Loss A/c | 1500000 | 31-03-13 | By Anil International Pvt Ltd A/c | 130000 |
| 31-03-14 | To Profit & Loss A/c | 130000 | 31-03-14 | By Anil International Pvt Ltd A/c | 102000 |
| 31-03-15 | To Profit & Loss A/c | 102000 | 31-03-15 | By Anil International Pvt Ltd A/c | 71200 |
| 31-03-16 | To Profit & Loss A/c | 71200 | 31-03-16 | By Anil International Pvt Ltd A/c | 36800 |
| | | 340000 | | | 340000 |

## 11.9 DEFAULT AND REPOSSESSION

In the hire purchase system, the agreement made between the hire seller and purchaser, state that if the hire purchaser makes default in the payment of instalments, the hire seller has the right to repossess the goods sold.

The purpose of hire purchase transaction is to transfer the ownership of goods to hire purchaser, only once the last payment is made. But if the hire purchaser default in making payment of instalment, the hire purchaser has to forfeit the earlier paid instalments, and the hire seller repossesses the goods either in full or partially.

The repossession of goods in full is known as **complete repossession** and if part of goods are repossessed then it is called as **partial repossession**.

In the partial repossession of goods by the hire seller are calculated at agreed price, hence the calculation of **agreed price** is based on the following points.

- Repossession of goods may be calculated on the basis of depreciation, the hire seller can charge rate of depreciation higher than normal rate applied by hire purchaser.

**Note:** Depreciation calculated by hire seller is only for calculation of partial repossession of good, hence the journal entries of depreciation must not be recorded in the books of hire seller since the advantage of depreciation of asset is already taken by hire purchaser.

- The agreed value may calculated on cash price or hire purchase price at certain rate.
- Any other agreed amount determined by mutual agreement between hire purchaser and hire seller.

**Note:** In the partial repossession both the parties, the hire seller as well as hire purchaser, does not close the account of each other in their respective books.

### 11.9.1 Accounting Treatment for repossession

**In the books of Hire Seller**

| | | |
|---|---|---|
| All the entries to be recorded as usual until the date of default | Regular Journal Entries | |
| Even at the period of default - **Interest** on goods as applicable | Hire Purchaser A/c<br>To Interest A/c | Dr<br>Cr |
| **Transfer of Interest** to P&L A/c | Interest A/c<br>To Profit & Loss A/c | Dr<br>Cr |
| In the event of default – **Depreciation** on **Partial Repossessed Goods** | Depreciation A/c<br>To Repossessed Goods A/c | Dr<br>Cr |
| The period of default. – If **loss** incurred in Goods Repossession. | Profit & Loss A/c<br>To Hire Purchaser A/c | Dr<br>Cr |
| The period of default. – If **profit** incurred in Goods Repossession | Hire Purchaser A/c<br>To Profit & Loss A/c | Dr<br>Cr |

| | | |
|---|---|---|
| The period of default. – **Repossession of Goods & Closing of Purchaser A/c** | Repossessed Goods A/c<br>To Hire Purchaser A/c | Dr<br>Cr |
| Any **expenses** made towards goods after repossession. | Expense for Goods A/c<br>To Bank A/c | Dr<br>Cr |
| **Transfer of expense** to goods account | Repossessed Goods A/c<br>To Expense for Goods A/c | Dr<br>Cr |
| **Sale** of Repossessed Goods | Bank A/c<br>To Repossessed Goods A/c | Dr<br>Cr |
| **Profit** on Sale of Repossessed Goods | Repossessed Goods A/c<br>To Profit & Loss A/c | Dr<br>Cr |
| **Loss** on Sale of Repossessed Goods | Profit & Loss A/c<br>To Repossessed Goods A/c | Dr<br>Cr |

### In the books of Hire Purchaser

| | | |
|---|---|---|
| All the entries to be recorded as usual until the date of default | Regular Journal Entries | |
| Even at the period of default - **Interest** on goods as applicable | Interest A/c<br>Hire Seller A/c | Dr<br>Cr |
| Even at the period of default – **Depreciation** charged on Asset | Depreciation A/c<br>To Fixed Asset | Dr<br>Cr |
| **Transfer of depreciation** to P&L A/c | Profit & Loss A/c<br>To Depreciation A/c | Dr<br>Cr |
| If **loss** incurred in Submission of Goods. | Profit & Loss A/c<br>To Asset A/c | Dr<br>Cr |
| If **profit** incurred in Submission of Goods. | Asset A/c<br>To Profit & Loss A/c | Dr<br>Cr |
| The period of default – **Submission of Goods & Closing of Seller A/c** | Hire Seller A/c<br>To Fixed Asset A/c | Dr<br>Cr |

## 11.9.2 Illustration – Complete Repossession

On 1st April. 2014, **Octogems Pvt Ltd** purchased Equipment from **Rantan Steel Ltd** on hire purchase systems, the details of the transactions are as follows

- The **Cash Price** of the Machinery in the Market is Rs. 4,00,000/-
- The **Down Payment** paid was Rs. 1,00,000/-
- The **Principal** amount is fixed to 1,00,000/- at each interval and instalment is paid on 31st March of Following Year. The deal would complete in **3 years**
- The **Rate of Interest is 5%** per annum
- **Octogems Pvt Ltd** charge deprecation the fixed asset @ 20% using **Straight Line Method.**

**Octogems Pvt Ltd** paid the first year instalment but unable to pay further instalments, Rantan steel Ltd took over the possession of equipment. On 31st March 2016, **Maintenance** of Rs. 6000 were incurred on equipment and thereafter on the same date, the equipment were sold for Rs. 2,20,000/-

Let us prepare interest calculation table, pass the necessary journal entries and prepare respective ledger accounts.

### *Interest Table*

| Hire Purchase Interest Calculation Method 2 | | | | | |
|---|---|---|---|---|---|
| **Period(s)** | **Opening Balance O/s** | **Interest Portion** | **DP/Principal Portion** | **(Instalment)** | **Closing Balance O/s** |
| 1 | 400000 | | 100000 | | 300000 |
| 1 | 300000 | 15000 | 100000 | 115000 | 200000 |
| 2 | 200000 | 10000 | 100000 | 110000 | 100000 |
| 3 | 100000 | 5000 | 100000 | 105000 | 0 |

**Total Interest = 30000/-**

### *Journal Entries*

#### In the books of Hire Seller (Rantan Steel Ltd)

| Date | Particulars | | L.F | Debit | Credit |
|---|---|---|---|---|---|
| 01-04-14 | Octogems Pvt Ltd A/c<br>To Sales of Equipment A/c<br>(Being goods sold on hire purchase basis) | Dr<br>Cr | | 400000 | 400000 |
| 01-04-14 | Bank A/c<br>To Octogems Pvt Ltd A/c<br>(Being downpayment received) | Dr<br>Cr | | 100000 | 100000 |
| 31-03-15 | Octogems Pvt Ltd A/c<br>To Interest A/c<br>(Interest receive due) | Dr<br>Cr | | 15000 | 15000 |
| 31-03-15 | Interest A/c<br>To Profit & Loss A/c<br>(Being Interest transferred to P&L A/c) | Dr<br>Cr | | 15000 | 15000 |
| 31-03-15 | Bank A/c<br>To Octogems Pvt Ltd A/c<br>(Being 1st Instalment received) | Dr<br>Cr | | 115000 | 115000 |
| | **Year of Default** | | | | |
| 31-03-16 | Octogems Pvt Ltd A/c<br>To Interest A/c<br>(Interest receive due) | Dr<br>Cr | | 10000 | 10000 |
| 31-03-16 | Interest A/c<br>To Profit & Loss A/c<br>(Being Interest transferred to P&L A/c) | Dr<br>Cr | | 10000 | 10000 |
| 31-03-16 | Repossession of Goods A/c<br>To Octogems Pvt Ltd A/c<br>(Being goods repossessed) | Dr<br>Cr | | 210000 | 210000 |
| 31-03-16 | Maintenance of Equipments A/c<br>To Bank A/c<br>(Maintenance expenses incurred on the equipment) | Dr<br>Cr | | 6000 | 6000 |
| 31-03-16 | Repossession of Goods A/c<br>To Maintenance of Equipments A/c<br>(Being equipment expenses added to the goods) | Dr<br>Cr | | 6000 | 6000 |
| 31-03-16 | Bank A/c<br>To Repossession of Goods A/c<br>(Being profit on sale of repossessed goods acknowledge) | Dr<br>Cr | | 220000 | 220000 |
| 31-03-16 | Repossession of Goods A/c<br>To Profit & Loss A/c<br>(Being profit on sale of repossessed goods acknowledge) | Dr<br>Cr | | 4000 | 4000 |

### *Customer Account*

| Octogems Pvt Ltd A/c | | | | | |
|---|---|---|---|---|---|
| **Date** | **Particulars** | **Amount** | **Date** | **Particulars** | **Amount** |
| 01-04-14 | To Equipment A/c | 400000 | 01-04-14 | By Bank A/c | 100000 |
| 31-03-15 | To Interest A/c | 15000 | 31-03-15 | By Bank A/c | 115000 |
| | | | 31-03-15 | By Balance c/d | 200000 |
| | | 415000 | | | 415000 |
| | | **Year of Default** | | | |
| 01-04-16 | To Balance b/d | 200000 | 31-03-16 | By Repossessed Goods A/c | 210000 |
| 31-03-16 | To Interest A/c | 10000 | | | |
| | | 210000 | | | 210000 |

### *Stock Account*

| Repossessed Goods A/c | | | | | |
|---|---|---|---|---|---|
| **Date** | **Particulars** | **Amount** | **Date** | **Particulars** | **Amount** |
| 31-03-16 | To Octogems Pvt Ltd A/c | 210000 | 31-03-16 | By Bank A/c | 220000 |
| 31-03-16 | To Maintenance of Equipments A/c | 6000 | | | |
| 31-03-16 | To Profit & Loss A/c (Profit on Sales) | 4000 | | | |
| | | 220000 | | | 220000 |

### *Journal Entries*

#### In the books of Hire Purchaser (Octogems Pvt Ltd)

| Date | Particulars | | L.F | Debit | Credit |
|---|---|---|---|---|---|
| 01-04-14 | Equipment A/c<br>To Rantan Steel Ltd A/c<br>(Being goods bought on hire purchase basis) | Dr<br>Cr | | 400000 | 400000 |
| 01-04-14 | Rantan Steel Ltd A/c<br>To Bank A/c<br>(Being downpayment made) | Dr<br>Cr | | 100000 | 100000 |
| 31-03-15 | Interest A/c<br>To Rantan Steel Ltd A/c<br>(Made the interest due) | Dr<br>Cr | | 15000 | 15000 |

| | | | | |
|---|---|---|---|---|
| 31-03-15 | Rantan Steel Ltd A/c<br>To Bank A/c<br>(Being 1st Instalment paid) | Dr<br>Cr | 115000 | 115000 |
| 31-03-15 | Depreciation A/c<br>To Machinery A/c<br>(Being depreciation charged on fixed asset) | Dr<br>Cr | 80000 | 80000 |
| 31-03-15 | Profit & Loss A/c<br>To Depreciation A/c<br>(Being depreciation transferred to P&L A/c) | Dr<br>Cr | 80000 | 80000 |
| | **Year of Default** | | | |
| 31-03-16 | Interest A/c<br>To Rantan Steel Ltd A/c<br>(Made the interest due) | Dr<br>Cr | 10000 | 10000 |
| 31-03-16 | Depreciation A/c<br>To Machinery A/c<br>(Being depreciation charged on fixed asset) | Dr<br>Cr | 80000 | 80000 |
| 31-03-16 | Profit & Loss A/c<br>To Depreciation A/c<br>(Being depreciation transferred to P&L A/c) | Dr<br>Cr | 80000 | 80000 |
| 31-03-16 | Rantan Steel Ltd A/c<br>To Equipment A/c<br>(Being goods submitted) | Dr<br>Cr | 210000 | 210000 |
| 31-03-16 | Equipment A/c<br>To Profit & Loss A/c<br>(Being loss incurred on submitting the goods) | Dr<br>Cr | 30000 | 30000 |

*Vendor Account*

| Rantan Steel Ltd A/c | | | | | |
|---|---|---|---|---|---|
| **Date** | **Particulars** | **Amount** | **Date** | **Particulars** | **Amount** |
| 01-04-14 | To Bank A/c | 100000 | 01-04-14 | By Equipment A/c | 400000 |
| 31-03-15 | To Bank A/c | 115000 | 31-03-15 | By Interest A/c | 15000 |
| 31-03-15 | To Balance c/d | 200000 | | | |
| | | 415000 | | | 415000 |
| | | **Year of Default** | | | |
| 31-03-16 | To Equipment A/c | 210000 | 01-04-16 | To Balance c/d | 200000 |
| | | | 31-03-15 | By Interest A/c | 10000 |
| | | 210000 | | | 210000 |

*Fixed Asset Account*

| Equipment A/c | | | | | |
|---|---|---|---|---|---|
| **Date** | **Particulars** | **Amount** | **Date** | **Particulars** | **Amount** |
| 01-04-14 | To Rantan Steel Ltd A/c | 400000 | 31-03-15 | By Depreciation A/c | 80000 |
| | | | 31-03-15 | By Balance c/d | 320000 |
| | | 400000 | | | 400000 |
| 01-04-16 | To Balance b/d | 320000 | 31-03-16 | By Depreciation A/c | 80000 |
| | | | 31-03-16 | By Rantan Steel Ltd A/c | 210000 |
| | | | | By Profit & Loss A/c (Loss on Submitting) | 30000 |
| | | 320000 | | | 320000 |

## 11.9.3 Illustration – Partial Repossession

On 1st April. 2014, **Moon Gold Enterprises** purchased Instruments from **Laser & Torrent Ltd** on hire purchase systems, the details of the transactions are as follows

- The **Cash Price** of the Machinery in the Market is Rs. 6,00,000/-
- The **Down Payment** paid was Rs. 1,75,000/-
- The **Instalment** amount is fixed to 1,34,000/- at each interval and instalment is paid on 31st March of Following Year. The deal would complete in **4 years**
- The **Rate of Interest is 10%** per annum
- **Moon Gold Enterprises** charge deprecation the fixed asset **@ 20%** using straight line method.
- The Last instalment interest would be **rounding off** at the difference of Rs. **348.50**/-

**Moon Gold Enterprises** paid the first year instalment but unable to pay further instalments, **Laser & Torrent Ltd** agreed to leave some instruments and partially took over possession of remaining instruments.

**Laser & Torrent Ltd**, taken over **60%** of the instruments after assessing it **on the basis of depreciation** and the **rate of depreciation** charged on instruments is **@ 30%** on annual basis using **Reducing Balance Method.**

Let us prepare interest calculation table, asset calculation table, pass the necessary journal entries in both, the books of hire purchaser and seller and prepare respective ledger accounts.

*Interest Table*

| Hire Purchase Interest Calculation Method 2 | | | | | |
|---|---|---|---|---|---|
| **Period(s)** | **Opening Balance O/s** | **Interest Portion** | **DP/Principal Portion** | **(Instalment)** | **Closing Balance O/s** |
| 1 | 600000 | | 175000 | | 425000 |
| 1 | 425000 | 42500 | 91500 | 134000 | 333500 |
| 2 | 333500 | 33350 | 100650 | 134000 | 232850 |
| 3 | 232850 | 23285 | 110715 | 134000 | 122135 |
| 4 | 122135 | 11865 | 122135 | 134000 | 0 |

Below is the calculation table of Asset Possessed by Seller and Retained by Purchaser and the difference in Net Asset on partial repossession

**Hire Seller** Valued the **Asset Possessed** – Rs. 600000/-

| In the Books of Hire Seller | | | |
|---|---|---|---|
| **Year** | **Possession on Total Asset @ 60%** | **Depreciation @ 30%** | **Net Asset** |
| 1st Year | 360000 | 108000 | 252000 |
| 2nd Year | 252000 | 75600 | **176400** |

**Difference in Net Asset on Partial Repossession** – Rs. 600000/-

| In the Books of Hire Purchaser | | | |
|---|---|---|---|
| **Year** | **Holding on Total Asset @ 60%** | **Depreciation @ 20%** | **Net Asset** |
| 1st Year | 360000 | 72000 | 288000 |
| 2nd Year | 288000 | 57600 | **230400** |

**Hire Purchaser** Valued the **Asset Retained** – Rs. 600000/-

| In the Books of Hire Purchaser | | | |
|---|---|---|---|
| **Year** | **Holding on Total Asset @ 40%** | **Depreciation @ 20%** | **Net Asset** |
| 1st Year | 240000 | 48000 | 192000 |
| 2nd Year | 192000 | 38400 | **153600** |

*Journal Entries*

**In the books of Hire Purchaser (Moon Gold Enterprises)**

| Date | Particulars | | L.F | Debit | Credit |
|---|---|---|---|---|---|
| 01-04-14 | Instruments A/c<br>To Laser & Torrent Ltd A/c<br>(Being goods bought on hire purchase basis) | Dr<br>Cr | | 600000 | 600000 |
| 01-04-14 | Laser & Torrent Ltd A/c<br>To Bank A/c<br>(Being downpayment made) | Dr<br>Cr | | 175000 | 175000 |
| 31-03-15 | Interest A/c<br>To Laser & Torrent Ltd A/c<br>(Made the interest due) | Dr<br>Cr | | 42500 | 42500 |
| 31-03-15 | Laser & Torrent Ltd A/c<br>To Bank A/c<br>(Being 1st Instalment paid) | Dr<br>Cr | | 134000 | 134000 |
| 31-03-15 | Depreciation A/c<br>To Instruments A/c<br>(Being depreciation charged on fixed asset) | Dr<br>Cr | | 120000 | 120000 |
| 31-03-15 | Profit & Loss A/c<br>To Depreciation A/c<br>(Being depreciation transferred to P&L A/c) | Dr<br>Cr | | 120000 | 120000 |

| Year of Default | | | | | |
|---|---|---|---|---|---|
| 31-03-16 | Interest A/c<br>To Laser & Torrent Ltd A/c<br>(Made the interest due) | Dr<br>Cr | | 33350 | 33350 |
| 31-03-16 | Depreciation A/c<br>To Instruments A/c<br>(Being depreciation charged on fixed asset) | Dr<br>Cr | | 96000 | 96000 |
| 31-03-16 | Profit & Loss A/c<br>To Depreciation A/c<br>(Being depreciation transferred to P&L A/c) | Dr<br>Cr | | 96000 | 96000 |
| 31-03-16 | Laser & Torrent Ltd A/c<br>To Instruments A/c<br>(Being goods submitted) | Dr<br>Cr | | 176400 | 176400 |
| 31-03-16 | Profit & Loss A/c<br>To Instruments A/c<br>(Being loss incurred on submitting the goods) | Dr<br>Cr | | 54000 | 54000 |

**Laser & Torrent Ltd A/c**

| Date | Particulars | Amount | Date | Particulars | Amount |
|---|---|---|---|---|---|
| 01-04-14 | To Bank A/c | 175000 | 01-04-14 | By Instruments A/c | 600000 |
| 31-03-15 | To Bank A/c | 134000 | 31-03-15 | By Interest A/c | 42500 |
| 31-03-15 | To Balance c/d | 333500 | | | |
| | | 642500 | | | 642500 |
| | | Year of Default | | | |
| 31-03-16 | To Instruments A/c | 176400 | 01-04-16 | To Balance c/d | 333500 |
| 31-03-16 | To Balance c/d | 190450 | 31-03-16 | By Interest A/c | 33350 |
| | | 366850 | | | 366850 |

**Instruments A/c**

| Date | Particulars | Amount | Date | Particulars | Amount |
|---|---|---|---|---|---|
| 01-04-14 | To Laser & Torrent Ltd A/c | 600000 | 31-03-15 | By Depreciation A/c | 120000 |
| | | | 31-03-15 | By Balance c/d | 480000 |
| | | 600000 | | | 600000 |
| | | Year of Default | | | |
| 01-04-16 | To Balance b/d | 480000 | 31-03-16 | By Depreciation A/c | 96000 |
| | | | 31-03-16 | By Rantan Steel Ltd A/c | 176400 |
| | | | 31-03-16 | By Profit & Loss A/c (Loss on Submitting) | 54000 |
| | | | 31-03-16 | By Balance c/d | 153600 |
| | | 480000 | | | 480000 |

## *Journal Entries*

**In the books of Hire Seller (Laser & Torrent Ltd)**

| Date | Particulars | | L.F | Dr. | Cr. |
|---|---|---|---|---|---|
| 01-04-14 | Moon Gold Enterprises A/c<br>To Sales of Instruments A/c<br>(Being goods sold on hire purchase basis) | Dr<br>Cr | | 600000 | 600000 |
| 01-04-14 | Bank A/c<br>To Moon Gold Enterprises A/c<br>(Being downpayment received) | Dr<br>Cr | | 175000 | 175000 |
| 31-03-15 | Moon Gold Enterprises A/c<br>To Interest A/c<br>(Interest receive due) | Dr<br>Cr | | 42500 | 42500 |
| 31-03-15 | Interest A/c<br>To Profit & Loss A/c<br>(Being Interest transferred to P&L A/c) | Dr<br>Cr | | 42500 | 42500 |
| 31-03-15 | Bank A/c<br>To Moon Gold Enterprises A/c<br>(Being 1st Instalment received) | Dr<br>Cr | | 134000 | 134000 |
| | Year of Default | | | | |
| 31-03-16 | Moon Gold Enterprises A/c<br>To Interest A/c<br>(Interest receive due) | Dr<br>Cr | | 33350 | 33350 |
| 31-03-16 | Interest A/c<br>To Profit & Loss A/c<br>(Being Interest transferred to P&L A/c) | Dr<br>Cr | | 33350 | 33350 |
| 31-03-16 | Repossession of Goods A/c<br>To Moon Gold Enterprises A/c<br>(Being 60% partial goods repossessed) | Dr<br>Cr | | 176400 | 176400 |

**Moon Gold Enterprises A/c**

| Date | Particulars | Amount | Date | Particulars | Amount |
|---|---|---|---|---|---|
| 01-04-14 | To Instruments A/c | 600000 | 01-04-14 | By Bank A/c | 175000 |
| 31-03-15 | To Interest A/c | 42500 | 31-03-15 | By Bank A/c | 134000 |
| | | | 31-03-15 | By Balance c/d | 333500 |
| | | 642500 | | | 642500 |
| | | Year of Default | | | |
| 01-04-16 | To Balance b/d | 333500 | 31-03-16 | By Repossessed Goods A/c | 176400 |
| 31-03-16 | To Interest A/c | 33350 | 31-03-16 | By Balance c/d | 190450 |
| | | 366850 | | | 366850 |

**Repossessed Goods A/c**

| Date | Particulars | Amount | Date | Particulars | Amount |
|---|---|---|---|---|---|
| | | | | | |
| | | Year of Default | | | |
| 31-03-16 | To Moon Gold Enterprises A/c | 176400 | 31-03-16 | By Balance c/d | 176400 |
| | | 176400 | | | 176400 |

## PRACTICE EXERCISE

**Q1. On 1st April. 2012, Soham Int Pvt Ltd purchased machinery from Titan Machines & Instruments Ltd on hire purchase systems, the details of the transactions are as follows.**

- The Cash Price of the Machinery in the Market is Rs. 5,00,000/-
- The down payment mentioned was Rs. 1,00,000/-
- The Instalment is Rs. 1,26,000/- and paid on 31st March of Following Year.
- The Rate of Interest is 10% per annum
- The deal would complete in 4 years
- Soham Enterprises charge deprecation the fixed asset @ 20% using straight line method.
- The Last instalment interest would be rounding at the difference of Rs. 874/-

Pass the journal entries in the book of Hire Purchaser (**Soham Enterprises**), and prepare the **interest calculation** table and the following ledger accounts.

**Vendors Ledger Account**

**Fixed Asset Account**

**Depreciation Account**

Pass the journal entries in the book of Hire Seller (**Titan Machines & Instruments Ltd**), and prepare the interest calculation table and the following ledger accounts.

**Customer Ledger Account**

**Interest Account**

**Q2. On 1st April. 2014, Fly Kite Enterprises purchased machine from Birglass Tools Ltd on hire purchase systems, the details of the transactions are as follows**

- The Cash Price of the Machinery in the Market is Rs. 2,50,000/-
- The down payment paid was Rs. 50,000/-
- The Principal amount is fixed to 50,000/- and instalment is paid on 31st March of Following Year.

- The Rate of Interest is 5% per annum
- The deal would complete in 4 years
- Octogems Pvt Ltd charge deprecation the fixed asset @ 20% using straight line method.

**Fly Kite Enterprises** paid the first year instalment but unable to pay further instalments, **Birglass Tools Ltd** took over the possession of **machine**. On 31st March 2016, Maintenance of Rs. 5000 were incurred on machine and thereafter on the same date, the equipment were sold for Rs. 1,65,000/-

Pass the journal entries in the book of Hire Seller (**Birglass Tools Ltd**), and prepare the **interest calculation** table and the following ledger accounts.

**Customer Ledger Account**

**Repossessed Goods Account**

**Q3. On 1st April. 2014, Desert Sultan Pvt Ltd purchased Equipments from Toyo Steel Ltd on hire purchase systems, the details of the transactions are as follows**

- The **Cash Price** of the Machinery in the Market is Rs. 5,00,000/-
- The **Down Payment** paid was Rs. 1,25,000/-
- The **Instalment** amount is fixed to 1,18,300/- at each interval and instalment is paid on 31st March of Following Year. The deal would complete in **4 years**
- The **Rate of Interest is 10%** per annum
- **Desert Sultan Pvt Ltd** charge deprecation the fixed asset @ **20%** using straight line method.
- The Last instalment interest would be **rounding off** at the difference of Rs. **7.20**/-

**Desert Sultan Pvt Ltd** paid the first year instalment but unable to pay further instalments, **Toyo Steel Ltd** agreed to leave partial equipment with the purchaser and took over possession of remaining Equipments.

**Toyo Steel Ltd**, taken over **60%** of the **Equipments** after assessing it **on the basis of depreciation** and the **rate of depreciation** charged on instruments is **@ 30%** on annual basis using **Straight Line Method**.

**Prepare interest calculation table, asset calculation table, pass the necessary journal entries in both, the books of hire purchaser and seller and prepare respective ledger accounts.**

## Multiple Choice Questions

1. What is the buyer in the hire purchase system called as ________
   a. Dealer Purchaser b. Broker
   c. Agent Buyer d. **Hire Purchaser**
2. The excess of hire price over the cash price is called as
   a. Commission b. **Interest**
   c. Brokerage d. Penalty
3. The instalment amount paid is sum of ________ + __________
   a. **Principal + Interest**
   b. Principal + Closing Balance
   c. Interest + Penalty
   d. Cash Price + Hire Purchase Price
4. The price at which the goods can be purchased from the market at full payment
   a. Hire Purchase Price b. Interest Price
   c. **Cash Price** d. Instalments
5. Who reserves the right to repossess the goods at the event of default.
   a. Hire Purchaser b. **Hire Seller**
   c. Government of India d. Local Government

## Review Questions

1. Once the last instalment is made by the hire purchaser, what would happen
   a. **Hire purchaser get the ownership of the goods**
   b. Hire seller take back the goods
   c. Hire seller depreciate the goods for the final time
2. Ever Instalment paid by the hire purchaser is treated as
   a. Loss to the company
   b. Profit to the company
   c. **Hire charge**
3. In the event of non-payment of instalment by the hire purchaser
   a. Hire purchaser would destroy goods and claim the amount from the insurance
   b. Hire purchaser would depreciate the assets at 100%
   c. **Hire seller would repossess the goods**

Chapter 12

# Accounting for Inland Branches

## LEARNING OBJECTIVES

After studying this chapter, you will understand:

- Different Types of Branches
- Systems of Accounting
- Recording Transaction in the Book of Dependent Branches
- Recording Transactions in the Bok of Independent Branches
- How to Prepare the Consolidated Profit & Loss Account
- How to Prepare the Consolidated Balance Sheet

## 12.1 INTRODUCTION

In order to increase sales or market their products in different locations, a business should make its products available to large territories or split the business in different parts or locations.

Numerous division of the business are located in different locations either in the same place or different place i.e., a business can be located in different part of the city like kormangala, Jayanagar and Indranagar in Bangalore city or different part of the country like Karnataka, Delhi, Kolkata, Assam or different countries like India, United Kingdom, Japan, U.S.A. These are known as branches and head office controls the activities of many branches.

Inland Branches are the branches located within the Country, Inland branches are also called as Home Branch or Domestic Branch.

## 12.2 PURPOSE OF BRANCH ACCOUNTING

The purpose of maintaining Branch accounts depends on the type of business and the requirement of the business concern which differ from business to business, the overall purpose of branch accounting in case of any business are given below:

1. **Profit or Loss**: Branch Accounts are maintained to know the profit or loss of the branch separately.
2. **Estimate the Progress and Performance:** By keeping the track of accounting details of Branch office, we can estimate the progress and performance of different branch offices and take the right business decision.
3. **Find out the Financial Position:** We can find out the financial position of branch at any given date.
4. **Auditing:** All Branch companies should maintained the accounting details for auditing purpose.
5. **Expansion of Business:** It helps in taking the decision whether the business has to be expanded or not.

## 12.3 TYPES OF BRANCHES

They are two types of branches in which the business transactions are recorded in the Books of accounts:

1. Dependent Branches: Dependent
2. Independent Branches
   a. Home Branch
   b. Foreign Branch

### 12.3.1 Dependent Branches

Dependent Branches doesn't maintains its books of accounts, they are maintained by its Head office.

Following are the main features of Dependent branch is given below:

1. **Full System of Accounting is Not Maintained:** As explained earlier in case of Dependent branches the books of accounts are maintained by the head office, but branch maintains details of Debtors Ledger and Stock Ledger. When the branch have permission to sell the goods on credit, then Debtors ledger are maintained to know the payable amount from Debtors and also a Stock Ledger is maintained to track the movement of goods from head office to branch office like goods received from head office and the balance of goods/stock in hand.
2. **Sometimes Branch Office are Permitted to Make Purchases:** Head office will supply the goods to Branch office on regular bases, sometimes the head office will allow the branch office to make purchases from local supplier and the payments for the purchases made by branch office will be made by head office.
3. **Remittance of Cash Collected by Branch Office to Head Office:** Cash collected from the cash sales or debtors are transferred to head office through local bank.
4. **Branch Expenses are Maintained by the Head Office:** Expenses incurred by the branch office like salary, rent, promotion expense etc., are paid by the head office through cheque for a particular period.
5. **Petty Cash is provided to Branch by Head Office:** Petty cash is provided to branch office by head office in order to meet their petty expenses and branch maintains the Petty cash book.

### 12.3.2 System of Accounting for dependent Branches

Head office will maintains the books of accounts of branch office. Based on the nature of business, size of business, volume of transactions etc., the head office will opt for any one of the following method to maintain the books of accounts of dependent branches.

I. Debtors System

II. Stock and Debtors System

III. Final Accounts System

IV. Wholesale Branch System

Let us understand how books of accounts of dependent branches are maintained in Debtors System.

### *12.3.2.1Debtors System*

This method is followed when the size of the branch is small. In this a branch account is maintained by the Head office and it is a nominal account and is prepared to calculate profit & loss for each branch. This method is also known as One Account System and is maintained as per the following simple system:

a. Branch account is debited with the opening balance or whatever the branch has in the beginning of accounting period like stock, debtors, petty cash, furniture, goods sent to branch account less returns etc.

b. Branch is debited, when head office send anything to branch during the accounting period like head office my send the cash to branch for the purchases made or for the expenses incurred by the branch.

c. Branch account is credited when head office receives anything from branch office like goods returned by the branch, cash remitted by branch etc.

d. Branch account is credited with the closing balance or whatever the branch has at the end of the accounting period like stock, debtors, petty cash etc.

The following are the Branch transactions which are recorded in the books of head office:

**Accounting of Branch Transactions in the books of Head Office**

| S.No | Branch Transactions | Particulars | L.F | Dr. | Cr. |
|---|---|---|---|---|---|
| 1 | Goods supplied to branch office from head office | Branch A/c Dr. | | xxx | |
| | | To Goods sent to Branch A/c | | | xxx |
| | | (Being goods sent to branch) | | | |
| | | | | | |
| 2 | Goods returned by branch office to head office | Goods sent to Branch A/c Dr. | | xxx | |
| | | To Branch A/c | | | xxx |
| | | (Being goods returned by branch) | | | |
| | | | | | |
| 3 | Goods sent by branch to another branch with head office permission | Goods sent to Branch A/c Dr. | | xxx | |
| | | To Branch A/c | | | xxx |
| | | (Being goods returned by branch) | | | |
| | | | | | |
| 4 | Cheque or draft is received from the branch | Bank A/c Dr. | | xxx | |
| | | To Branch A/c | | | xxx |
| | | (Being remittance received from Branch) | | | |
| | | | | | |
| 5 | Expenses incurred by the branch office are paid by Head office | Branch A/c Dr. | | xxx | |
| | | To Bank A/c | | | xxx |
| | | (Being branch office expenses met by head office) | | | |
| | | | | | |
| 6 | Goods returned by branch debtors to head office directly. | Goods sent to Branch A/c Dr. | | xxx | |
| | | To Branch A/c | | | xxx |
| | | (Being goods returned by branch debtors) | | | |
| | | | | | |
| 7 | Transfer of balance in goods sent to branch A/c | Goods sent to Branch A/c Dr. | | xxx | |
| | | To Purchase A/c | | | xxx |
| | | (Being transfer of balance in goods sent to branch) | | | |
| | | | | | |
| 8 | Branch asset at the end of accounting period | Branch Asset A/c Dr. | | xxx | |
| | | To Branch A/c | | | xxx |
| | | (Being adjustment entry for branch closing assets) | | | |
| | | | | | |
| 9 | Branch liabilities at the end of the accounting period | Branch A/c Dr. | | xxx | |
| | | To Branch Liabilities A/c | | | xxx |
| | | (Being adjustment entry for branch closing liability) | | | |
| | | | | | |
| 10 | **For profit or loss** | | | | |
| | Profit at branch transferred to profit & loss account | Branch A/c Dr. | | xxx | |
| | | To General Proft & Loss A/c | | | xxx |
| | | (Being branch profit transferred to P & L A/c) | | | |
| | | | | | |
| | Loss at branch transferred to profit & loss account | General Proft & Loss A/c Dr. | | xxx | |
| | | To Branch A/c | | | xxx |
| | | (Being branch Loss transferred to P & L A/c) | | | |
| | | | | | |
| 11 | **At the end of the accounting year the assets and liabilities will appear in the balance sheet of head office and it has to be transferred to branch office in the beginning of the next accounting year.** | | | | |
| | Transfer of Branch assets | Branch A/c Dr. | | xxx | |
| | | To Branch Asset A/c | | | xxx |
| | | (Being branch opening assets transferred to branch) | | | |
| | | | | | |
| | Transfer of Branch Liabilities | Branch Liabilities Dr. | | xxx | |
| | | To Branch A/c | | | xxx |
| | | (Being branch liabilities transferred to branch) | | | |
| | | | | xxx | xxx |

The Sample Branch Account format is given below:

**Branch Account**

| Date 2016 | Particulars | | ₹ | Date 2016 | Particulars | | ₹ |
|---|---|---|---|---|---|---|---|
| | To Opening Balances | | | | By Opening Balances | | |
| | Stock | xxxx | | | Outstanding Expenses | xxxx | |
| | Debtors | xxxx | | | Creditors | xxxx | xxxx |
| | Furniture | xxxx | | | By Bank | | |
| | Petty Cash | xxxx | | | Collections from Debtors | xxxx | |
| | Pre-paid Expenses | xxxx | xxxx | | Cash Sales (remittance) | xxxx | xxxx |
| | To Goods sent to Branch A/c | | xxxx | | By Goods sent to Branch A/c (Goods returned to head office or returned by branch debtors or transferred to other branch) | | xxxx |
| | To Bank (for payments made by head office on behalf of branch) | | xxxx | | By Closing Balances | | |
| | To Closing Balances | | | | Petty Cash | xxxx | |
| | Outstanding expenses | xxxx | | | Furniture (at depreciation value) | xxxx | |
| | Creditors | xxxx | xxxx | | Debtors | xxxx | |

| To Profit (Transfer to general profit & loss account) | | | Pre-paid Expenses | xxxx | xxxx |
|---|---|---|---|---|---|
| | | | By Loss (Transfer to general profit & loss account) | | xxxx |
| | | | | | |

**Note:** If the debit side is more than the credit side then the branch office is under loss, if debit side is less than the credit side then the branch office is in profit.

Points need to be considered while recording the transactions in the Branch Account.

1. Head office should not record the following transactions in branch account.
   a. Surplus and shortage of stock
   b. Credit sales made by Branch
   c. Sales return made by branch debtors to branch ( if the goods are return by branch debtors to head office then the entry should be recorded)
   d. Bad Debts, Discounts etc.
2. **Sale of fixed assets**: Brach can sell the fixed asset assets on cash and remit the amount to head office. In case of the branch sell the fixed assets on credit then the amount due will be shown as debtors at the branch at the end of accounting period. The net asset amount is shown at the end of accounting period and it is derived as shown below:

   Opening Balance + Purchase of Fixes Assets – Amount Realized on Account of Sale of Fixed Assets.

   No need of recording the separate entry for profit or loss made by the sale of fixed assets as it is taken automatically when the closing and opening balances are accounted in the branch account.
3. **Depreciation:** Depreciation of fixed assets is not shown in the Branch account but branch account is debited with the fixed assets value in the beginning of the accounting period and it is credited in the end of the accounting period and the difference that is depreciation is charged automatically.

   *For Example:*

   Fixed assets value in the beginning of the accounting period = 20,000

   Depreciation charged p.a 20%

   Now, in the beginning of the accounting period the branch account is debited with fixed asset value 20,000 and it is credited at the end of accounting period with fixed asset value as 18,000 and 2,000 is automatically charged as depreciation.
4. **Insurance claimed:** Amount received from the insurance company on account of damages incurred by the branch office will be remitted to head office.
5. **Petty Expenses:** Petty expenses incurred by the branch office is not recorded. The branch account is debited with petty cash opening balance and cash sent by head office to branch for meeting petty expenses and it is credited with petty cash closing balance. Thus the petty cash expenses are automatically charged to the branch account.

   ***For example:***

   Petty cash balance with branch account in the beginning of accounting period = 10,000

   Petty Cash sent by head office to branch office to meet their petty expenses = 15,000

   Petty expenses incurred by branch office = 20,000

   Now, in the beginning of the accounting period the petty cash is debited with the value 25,000 (Opening balance + cash sent by head office) and it will be credited with the value 5,000 at the end of the accounting period.

***Illustration 1:** T&T Enterprises have its head office at Delhi and branch office at Karnataka, following are the transactions with head office at branch for the year ended 31st August, 2016*

| Date 2016 | Transactions |
|---|---|
| Sep. 1 | Stock at branch ₹ 40,000 |
| | Debtors at branch ₹20,000 |
| | Petty Cash ₹ 5,000 |
| | Goods supplied to branch office for ₹ 1,60,000 |
| | Cash sales remittance from branch ₹ 11,000 |
| | Realization of debtors ₹ 1,60,000 |
| | Salary of ₹ 20,000 sent to branch |
| | Rent of ₹10,000 sent to branch |
| | Petty cash of ₹ 10,000 sent to branch |
| Aug. 31 | Stock at branch ₹20,000 |
| | Debtors at branch ₹ 10,000 |
| | Petty Cash ₹ 10,000 |

Record the above transaction in the journal and prepare the Branch Account.

***Solution:***

In the book of the T&T Head Office
Journal Entries

| Date (2016) | Particulars | | L.F | Dr. | Cr. |
|---|---|---|---|---|---|
| Sep. 1 | Karnataka Branch A/c | Dr. | | 65,000 | |
| | To Branch Stock A/c | | | | 40,000 |
| | To Branch Debtors A/c | | | | 20,000 |
| | To Petty Cash A/c | | | | 5,000 |
| | (Being Branch opening assets transferred to Branch A/c) | | | | |
| | | | | | |
| Jan. 1 to Aug. 31 | Karnataka Branch A/c | Dr. | | 1,60,000 | |
| | To Goods sent to branch A/c | | | | 1,60,000 |
| | (Being goods sent to branch) | | | | |
| Jan. 1 to Aug. 31 | Bank A/c | Dr. | | 11,000 | |
| | To Karnataka Branch A/c | | | | 11,000 |
| | (Being remittance received from branch) | | | | |
| Jan. 1 to Aug. 31 | Bank A/c | Dr. | | 1,60,000 | |

| Date | Particulars | L.F. | Dr. ₹ | Cr. ₹ |
|---|---|---|---|---|
| | (Being realization of Debtors) | | | |
| | | | | |
| Jan. 1 to Aug. 31 | Karnataka Branch A/c Dr. | | 20,000 | |
| | To Salary A/c | | | 20,000 |
| | (Being salary sent to branch) | | | |
| | | | | |
| Jan. 1 to Aug. 31 | Karnataka Branch A/c Dr. | | 10,000 | |
| | To Rent A/c | | | 10,000 |
| | (Being Rent sent to branch) | | | |
| | | | | |
| Jan. 1 to Aug. 31 | Karnataka Branch A/c Dr. | | 10,000 | |
| | To Petty Cash A/c | | | 10,000 |
| | (Being Petty Cash sent to branch) | | | |
| | | | | |
| Aug. 31 | Branch Stock A/c Dr. | | 20,000 | |
| | Branch Debtors A/c Dr. | | 10,000 | |
| | Petty Cash A/c Dr. | | 10,000 | |
| | To Karnataka Branch A/c | | | 40,000 |
| | (Being Adjustment entry with branch closing assets) | | | |
| | | | **4,76,000** | **4,76,000** |

The following is the branch account in the books of head office.

| Karnataka Branch Account | | | | | | | |
|---|---|---|---|---|---|---|---|
| **Date (2016)** | **Particulars** | | **₹** | **Date (2016)** | **Particulars** | | **₹** |
| Sep. 1 | To Opening Balances b/d | | | Aug. 31 | By Closing Balances c/d | | |
| | Branch Stock A/c | 40,000 | | | Branch Stock A/c | 20,000 | |
| | Branch Debtors A/c | 20,000 | | | Branch Debtors A/c | 10,000 | |
| | Petty Cash A/c | 5,000 | **65,000** | | Petty Cash A/c | 10,000 | **40,000** |
| | To Goods sent to Branch A/c | | 1,60,000 | Sep. 1 | By Bank A/c | | |
| | To Salaries A/c | | 20,000 | | Cash Sales | 11,000 | |
| | To Rent A/c | | 10,000 | | Debtors | 1,60,000 | **1,71,000** |
| | To Petty Cash | | 10,000 | | By Loss transferred to general profit & loss A/c | | 54,000 |
| | | | **2,65,000** | | | | **265000** |

**Note:** In the above illustration debit balance is more than credit balance, hence the Karnataka branch account is showing loss.

***Illustration 2:*** *KK Enterprises have its head office at Mumbai and branch office at Kolkata, following are the transactions with head office at branch for the year ended 31st October, 2016, prepare branch account in the books of head office.*

| Date 2016 | Transactions |
|---|---|
| Nov. 1 | Stock at branch ₹ 12,000 |
| | Debtors at branch ₹ 6,000 |
| | Debtors at branch ₹ 6,900 as on Oct. 31 |
| | Furniture at branch ₹ 2,200 |
| | Petty Cash ₹ 700 |
| | Salaries outstanding at branch ₹300 |
| | Pre-paid fire insurance ₹ 3509 |
| | Cash sales during the year ₹ 1,50,000 |
| | Goods supplied to branch office for ₹ 1,00,000 |
| | Cash sales remittance from branch ₹ 11,000 |
| | Credit sales during the year ₹ 60,000 |
| | Cash received from debtors ₹ 55,000 |
| | Cash paid by branch office directly to head office ₹ 4,000 |
| | Discount allowed to debtors ₹ 300 |
| | Cash sent for the expenses incurred by branch office |
| | • Rent ₹ 4,000 |
| | • Salaries ₹ 4,,400 |
| | • Petty Cash ₹ 3,000 |
| | Goods Return by Debtors ₹4,000 |
| | Goods returned by branch ₹ 3,000 |
| | Stock as on Oct. 31 ₹ 7,000 |
| | Petty Expenses at Branch ₹ 1,050 |
| | Provide depreciation on furniture 10% p.a |
| | Goods costing 1,400 destroyed in accident and claimed ₹ 1,200 from insurance company. |

## *Solution:*

| Kolkata Branch Account | | | | | |
|---|---|---|---|---|---|
| **Particulars** | | **₹** | **Particulars** | | **₹** |
| To Opening Balances: | | | By Opening Balances: | | |
| Branch Stock A/c | 12,000 | | Outstanding Salaries A/c | | 300 |
| Branch Debtors A/c | 6,000 | | By Remittance | | |
| Furniture A/c | 2,200 | | Cash Sales | 1,50,000 | |
| Petty Cash A/c | 700 | | Cash Received from Debtors A/c | 55,000 | |
| Pre-paid Insurance A/c | 350 | **21,250** | Cash paid by debtors directly to H.O | 4,000 | |
| To Goods supplied to branch A/c | | 1,00,000 | Received from Insurance Company | 1,400 | **2,10,400** |
| To Bank A/c | | | By Good sent to branch A/c (Return of goods by branch) | | 3,000 |
| Rent A/c | 4,000 | | By Closing Balances: | | |
| Salary A/c | 4,400 | | Branch Stock A/c | 7,000 | |
| Petty Cash A/c | 3,000 | | Branch Debtors A/c | 6,900 | |
| Insurance A/c | 800 | **12,200** | Furniture A/c | 1,980 | |
| To Net Profit | | 98,780 | Petty Cash A/c | 2,650 | **18,530** |
| | | **2,32,230** | | | **2,32,230** |

**Note:** At the end Petty Cash Balance is calculated based on the information given below:

| | |
|---|---|
| Petty Cash Opening balance is | 700 |
| *Add: Petty Cash received from head office* | 3,000 |
| Total Petty cash | **3,700** |
| *Less: Petty Cash spent by Branch office* | 1,050 |
| Petty Cash Closing Balance | **2,65** |

## *Invoice Price Method:*

- **Recording of Adjustment Entry Required in Head Office**

When the goods are sent to branch office by head office at Invoice price or selling price (Cost plus some profit percentage) and the branch should sell the goods at invoice price only.

In order to know the profit or loss made by the branch office, head office needs to record the adjustment entries as shown below:

| Adjustment entries in the books of Head office | | |
|---|---|---|
| **Adjusting excess price of opening stock at branch** | | |
| Stock Reserve A/c | xxx | |
| To Branch A/c | | xxx |
| (Being adjusted excess price of opening stock) | | |
| | | |
| **Adjusting excess price of closing stock of branch or stock in transit at branch** | | |
| Branch A/c | xxx | |
| To Stock Reserve A/c | | xxx |
| (Being excess of closing stock of branch adjusted) | | |

Based on the conservatism principle, no profit should be anticipated and all losses should be provided. Therefore it is mandatory to make a provision for the profit included in the unsold goods, because it will not earn any profit until sold.

| Adjustment of excess price of goods sent to branch less returns made to head office | | |
|---|---|---|
| Branch A/c | xxx | |
| To Stock Reserve A/c | | xxx |
| (Being excess of closing stock of branch adjusted) | | |

- **Calculation of Loading or Excess Price**

  For calculation of Loading or Excess Price or Markup, the following procedure needs to be followed.

  Suppose the goods are supplied at Invoice price i.e. cost plus 20% profit. Consider cost is ₹ 100, profit is ₹ 25, selling price is 125 and the ratio of profit to selling price is 100/125. For the excess price value between invoice price and the cost price adjustments will be made based on the profit ratio 100/125 or 1/5 of the invoice price.

  If the sales price is given with the percentage i.e., the percentage is given on sale price as 25%, then if the sales price is ₹ 100, profit will ₹ 25 and the cost will be ₹ 75 and the percentage on cost will be 1/3 of the cost or 25/75*100

### *12.3.2.2Stock and Debtors System*

This method is followed when the branch turnover is huge and also in this method more than one accounts are opened for various transactions at branch i.e., Head office should maintain a separate ledger accounts. For example Branch Stock, Branch Debtors, Goods supplied to Branch, Expenses incurred by Branch, Branch Assets and liabilities etc. Explanation about the each account is given below:

a. **Branch Stock Account:** In this account the transactions details like Goods received from head office, goods sold by branch office, goods returned to head office, goods returned by customers to the branch office etc. are recorded. It also provide the information regarding shortage of goods, excess of goods and closing stock.

b. **Branch Fixed Assets Account:** In this account transactions relating to fixed assets are recorded.

c. **Branch Expense Account:** In this account transaction relating to branch expenses are recorded i.e., summary of expenses incurred by branch like Discount, Bad debts etc.

d. **Branch Adjustment Account:** In this account transactions relating to goods sent to the branch, shortage or surplus at branch, opening and closing of stocks etc.., are recorded. This account is maintained to find out the gross profit.

e. **Branch Cash Account:** In this account all cash transactions of the branch is recorded.

f. **Branch Debtors Account:** In this account all transactions relating to debtors are recorded.

g. **Goods sent to Branch Account:** In this account transactions relating to goods movement to branch is recorded for example it will account the details of goods supplied to the branch and the goods returned by the branch to head office.

h. **Branch Profit & Loss Account:** This account is prepared in order to find out the profit and loss made by the branch office. Gross profit or loss is transferred to this account from branch adjustment account. This account is debited with all the expenses & loses and it is credited with all incomes and profit and the balanced amount will be the net profit or loss.

In case of Stock and Debtors System the following journal entries are recorded in the books of head office.

**Accounting of Branch Transactions in the books of Head Office as per Stock and Debtors System**

| S.No | Branch Transactions | Particulars | L.F | Dr. | Cr. |
|---|---|---|---|---|---|
| 1 | Goods supplied to branch office from head office (at invoice price) | Branch Stock A/c Dr. | | xxx | |
| | | To Goods sent to Branch A/c | | | xxx |
| | | (Being goods sent to branch at invoice price) | | | |
| | | | | | |
| 2 | Goods returned by branch office to head office(at invoice price) | Goods sent to Branch A/c Dr. | | xxx | |
| | | To Branch Stock A/c | | | xxx |
| | | (Being goods returned by branch at invoice price) | | | |
| | | | | | |
| 3 | Goods sent by branch to another branch with head office permission (This entry will be recorded as if branch has sent the goods to head office and from there it is transferred to another branch office)<br>a. Branch A sent the goods to branch B | Goods sent to A Branch A/c | Dr. | xxx | |
| | | To A Branch Stock A/c | | | xxx |
| | | | | | |
| | | Branch Stock A/c | Dr. | xxx | |
| | | To goods sent to B Branch A/c | | | xxx |
| | | (Being goods sent to other branch) | | | |
| | | | | | |
| 4 | For Discounts, Bad Debts etc. | Branch Expenses A/c Dr. | | xxx | |

| | | | | | |
|---|---|---|---|---|---|
| | | To Branch Debtors A/c | | | xxx |
| | | (Being expenses incurred) | | | |
| 5 | Expenses incurred by the branch office | Branch Expenses A/c | Dr. | xxx | |
| | | To Bank A/c | | | xxx |
| | | (Being branch office expenses) | | | |
| 6 | For abnormal losses or pilferage | Branch Adjustment A/c (enter amount of loading) | Dr. | xxx | |
| | | Branch Profit & Loss A/c (enter shortage at cost) | | xxx | |
| | | To Branch Stock A/c (enter shortage at invoice price) | | | xxx |
| | | (Being abnormal losses incurred) | | | |
| **Note:** Reverse entry is recorded for surplus at branch and no entry should be accounted for normal loss of stock. | | | | | |
| 7 | Amount received from insurance company for abnormal loss | Branch Cash A/c | Dr. | xxx | |
| | | To Branch Profit & Loss A/c | | | xxx |
| | | (Being amount received from insurance company) | | | |
| 8 | Branch sold the goods on credit (at invoice price) | Branch Debtors A/c | Dr. | xxx | |
| | | To Branch Stock A/c | | | xxx |
| | | (Being sales made on credit by branch office) | | | |
| 9 | Branch sold goods on cash (at invoice price) | Cash A/c | Dr. | xxx | |
| | | To Branch Debtors A/c | | | xxx |
| | | (Being goods sold on cash) | | | |
| 10 | Goods returned by branch debtors to branch office (at invoice price) | Branch Stock A/c | Dr. | xxx | |
| | | To Branch Debtors A/c | | | xxx |
| | | (Being goods return by branch debtors to branch office) | | | |
| 11 | Goods returned by Branch Debtors to head office directly (at invoice price) | Goods sent to Branch A/c | Dr. | xxx | |
| | | To Branch Debtors A/c | | | xxx |
| | | (Being goods returned by branch debtors to head office) | | | |
| 12 | Transfer of Branch Expenses to branch profit & loss account | Branch Profit & Loss A/c | Dr. | xxx | |
| | | To Branch Expenses A/c | | | xxx |
| | | (Being branch expenses transferred) | | | |
| 13 | Adjustment of loading in the opening stock | Stock Reserve A/c | Dr. | xxx | |
| | | To Branch Adjustment A/c | | | xxx |
| | | (Being adjusted loading of opening stock) | | | |
| 14 | Adjustment of loading in the closing stock | Branch Adjustment A/c | Dr. | xxx | |
| | | To Stock reserve A/C | | | xxx |
| | | (Being adjusted loading of closing stock) | | | |
| 15 | Transfer of net profit at the branch | Branch Profit & Loss A/c | Dr. | xxx | |
| | | To General Profit & Loss A/c | | | xxx |
| | | (Being transfer of net profit at the branch) | | | |
| | | | | xxx | xxx |

***Illustration 3:*** *Suraj Industries, Pune, has a Branch at Karnataka to which goods are sent at cost plus 25%. Branch makes credit and cash sales. Branch has to remit all cash received into the Head Office Bank Account at Karnataka and expenses incurred by head office are paid by the head office. From the following details prepare the accounts in the head office and find out the branch profits.*

| | |
|---|---|
| Stock at Karnataka Branch on 1st August, 2016. | 10,000 |
| Sundry Debtors at Karnataka on August, 2016. | 8,200 |
| Stock at branch on 31st July, 2016. | 12,000 |
| Goods received from head office at invoice price. | 70,000 |
| Return of goods to head office at invoice price. | 2,200 |
| Cash Sales. | 25,000 |
| Credit Sales. | 37,000 |
| Cash received from Sundry Debtors. | 33,000 |
| Discount allowed to Sundry Debtors. | 700 |
| Sales Return at Karnataka Branch. | 1,000 |
| Rent at Karnataka Branch. | 2,000 |
| Salaries at Karnataka Branch. | 7,000 |
| Office Expenses. | 700 |
| Bad Debts | 500 |

## *Solution:*

**Karnataka Branch Stock Account in the books of Suraj Industries**

| Particulars | ₹ | Particulars | ₹ |
|---|---|---|---|
| To Balance b/d (Opening Stock) | 3,000 | By Cash Sales (Bank) | 25,000 |
| To Goods sent to Branch A/c | 70,000 | By Branch Debtors A/c (Credit Sales) | 37,000 |
| To Branch Debtors A/c (Returns) | 1,000 | By Goods sent to Branch A/c (Returns) | 2,200 |
| To Branch Profit & Loss A/c (Surplus) | 2,200 | By Balance c/d (Closing Stock) | 12,000 |
| | **76,200** | | **76,200** |

**Karnataka Branch Debtors Account**

| Particulars | ₹ | Particulars | ₹ |
|---|---|---|---|
| To Balance b/d (Sundry Debtors) | 8,200 | By Bank A/c | 33,000 |
| To Branch Stock Account (Sales) | 37,000 | By Branch Profit & Loss A/c | |
| | | Bad Debts 500 | |
| | | Discounts 700 | 1,200 |
| | | By Branch Stock Account (Returns) | 1,000 |
| | | By Balance c/d | 10,000 |
| | **45,200** | | **45,200** |

**Karnataka Branch Adjustment Account**

| Particulars | ₹ | Particulars | ₹ |
|---|---|---|---|
| To Goods sent to branch A/c (Load on returns to H.O) **(Refer Below given calculation-1)** | 440 | By Balance b/d (Load in opening stock) | 2,000 |
| To Branch c/d (Load on closing stock) **(Refer calculation 2)** | 2,400 | By Goods Sent to Branch A/c (Load on goods sent) | 14,000 |
| To Branch Profit & Loss A/c | 13,160 | | |
| | **16,000** | | **16,000** |

**Karnataka Branch Expense Account**

| Particulars | ₹ | Particulars | ₹ |
|---|---|---|---|
| To Bank A/c | | By Profit & Loss A/c | 9,000 |
| Rent | 2,000 | | |
| Salaries | 7,000 | | |
| Office Expenses | 7,00 | | |
| | **9,000** | | **9,000** |

| Karnataka Branch Profit & Loss Account | | | |
|---|---|---|---|
| **Particulars** | **₹** | **Particulars** | **₹** |
| To Branch Expense A/c | 9,000 | By Branch Adjustment A/c | 13,160 |
| To Branch Debtors A/c (Discount) | 7,00 | By Branch Stock A/c | 2,200 |
| To Branch Debtors A/c (Bad Debts) | 5,00 | | |
| To General Profit & Loss A/c | 6,360 | | |
| | **15,360** | | **15,360** |

| Goods Sent to Karnataka Branch Account | | | |
|---|---|---|---|
| **Particulars** | **₹** | **Particulars** | **₹** |
| To Branch Adjustment A/c | 14,000 | By Karnataka Branch Stock A/c | 70,000 |
| To Branch Stock A/c | 2,200 | By Branch Adjustment A/c | 440 |
| To Purchase A/c | 54,240 | | |
| | **70,440** | | **70,440** |

## *Calculations:*

1. **Load on return to Head office** = Return of goods to head office * 1/5

   = 2,200 * 1/5

   = 440

2. **Load on Closing Stock** = Closing Stock * 1/5

   = 12,000 * 1/5

   = 2,400

### *12.3.2.3Final Accounts System*

In this method profit and loss made by branches are found out by preparing the Branch Trading and Profit & Loss Account is prepared at cost price (i.e., cost of goods sent to the branch). Branch Trading and profit & Loss account is considered as memorandum account and will not form as a part of accounting system. Head Office may prepare the branch account and the nature of this account will be personal account as different from the branch account prepared by head office in case of Debtors System which is Nominal in nature. Hence the balances at the end of the accounting period represents the net assets at the branch (Assets – Liabilities at Branch)

***Illustration 4:*** *TIM Traders started branches at Chennai and Kerala as on 1st April, 2016. All goods are transferred by head office to branch office at cost plus 25 per cent. Head office pays all expenses incurred by the branch office. Cash collected by the branches are remitted to head office on daily bases. Each branch maintains its own sales ledger and sends the weekly statements to head office. The following are the details extracted from the weekly statements, sent by the different branches to head office for the half yearly period ended 30th September, 2016.*

| Particulars | Chennai (₹) | Kerala(₹) |
|---|---|---|
| Cash Sales made by branch | 80,600 | 84,200 |
| Credit Sales made by branch | 127,200 | 1,12,000 |
| Sundry Debtors | 36,500 | 25,600 |
| Sales Return | 4,300 | 3,200 |
| Rent and Rates | 5,200 | 6,500 |
| Bad debts | 8,000 | -- |
| Salaries paid | 18,000 | 20,000 |
| General expenses incurred | 4,600 | 3,500 |
| Goods received from head office | 1,52,000 | 1,27,000 |
| Advertisement | 9,500 | 7,200 |
| Stock on 30th September, 2016 | 47,000 | 37,000 |

Prepare the branch accounts in the books of head office, showing the profit or loss for the accounting period and then prepare the Trading and Profit & Loss Account separately for each branch

## *Solution:*

| TIM Traders Branch Trading and Profit & Loss Account as on 30th September, 2016 | | | | | |
|---|---|---|---|---|---|
| **Particulars** | **Chennai (₹)** | **Kerala (₹)** | **Particulars** | **Chennai (₹)** | **Kerala (₹)** |
| To Goods sent to Branch (at cost prise) | 1,21,600 | 1,01,600 | By Cash Sales | 80,600 | 84,200 |
| To Bad Debts | 8,000 | | By Credit Sales | 1,27,200 | 1,12,000 |
| To Rent and Rates | 5,200 | 6,500 | *Less: Returns* | 4,300 | 3,200 |
| To Salaries paid | 18,000 | 20,000 | | **2,03,500** | **1,93,000** |
| To Advertisement | 9,500 | 7,200 | By Closing Stock (at cost price) | 37,600 | 29,600 |
| To General Expenses Incurred | 4,600 | 3,500 | | | |
| To Net profit to General Profit & Loss Account | 74,200 | 83,800 | | | |
| | **2,41,100** | **2,22,600** | | **2,41,100** | **2,22,600** |

**Calculation:** To find out the cost price of goods sent to branch follow the below given procedure.

Goods transferred to branch by head office is cost + 25%

Assume that the gods are invoiced at cost price 100 plus 25%

If the cost price is 100

Profit percentage is 25% of ₹ 100 i.e., ₹ 25

Selling price is 125 (100+25)

The ratio of profit to selling price is 25/125 Or 1/5

Therefore to find out the cost price for the above illustration take the ration 1/5

Invoice price = 1, 52,000

Profit = 30,400 (1, 52, 000 * 1/5)

Cost price = 1, 21,600 (1, 52,000 – 30,400)

| Branch Accounts | | | | | |
|---|---|---|---|---|---|
| **Particulars** | **Chennai (₹)** | **Kolkata (₹)** | **Particulars** | **Chennai (₹)** | **Kolkata (₹)** |
| To Goods Sent to branch account | 1,52,000 | 1,27,000 | By Cash Sales | 80,600 | 84,200 |
| To Salaries | 18,000 | 20,000 | By Collection from debtors **(Refer calculation 3)** | 78,400 | 83,200 |
| To Rent and Rates | 5,200 | 6,500 | By Goods Set to Branch A/c (Loading/Mark up) **(Refer calculation 2)** | 30,400 | 25,400 |
| To Advertisement | 9,500 | 7,200 | By Balance c/d (Debtors & Stock) | 83,500 | 62,600 |
| To General Expenses | 4,600 | 3,500 | | | |
| To Stock Reserve **(Refer calculation 1)** | 9,400 | 7,400 | | | |
| To Profit and Loss Account (Profit) | 74,200 | 83,800 | | | |
| | **2,72,900** | **2,55,400** | | **2,72,900** | **2,55,400** |

## *Calculations:*

1. Calculation of stock reserve

   Stock Reserve of Chennai = 47,000 * 1/5 = 9,400 (Closing stock * 1/5)

   Similarly calculate stock reserve for Kolkata

2. Calculation of Goods sent to Branch A/c (Loading or mark up or excess price)

Loading = 1,52,000 * 1/5 = 30,400 (Goods sent to Branch office * 1/5)

3. Collection from debtors = Credit Sales - Sales Return - Sundry Debtors -Bad Debts

= 1,27,200 - 4,300 - 36,500 - 8,000

= 78,400

### 12.3.2.4 Wholesale Branch System

Manufacturers may sell the goods to the consumers through approved dealers or wholesalers or through their own branches. If manufacturers sells the goods directly to its branch office then it can earn more profit.

**For example:** Cost price of an item is ₹ 100 to a Manufacturer and he sells the same item at ₹ 130 to a wholesalers and then the goods are sold to consumers by retailers at ₹ 180, in this case the manufacturer will be able to earn only ₹ 30 as profit and wholesaler and other middlemen will take ₹ 50 as profit.

In case if the manufacturer sells the goods to its own branch then the overall profit will be earned by him i.e., ₹ 80 will be earned by Manufacturers.

If branch expenditure is less than the profit earned, then manufacturer will not earn any profit i.e., if the branch expenditure exceeds ₹ 50, then selling of goods through branch will not earn any profit, if the branch expenditure is less than ₹ 50, then the selling of goods through branch will be in profit. Take the above example, if the branch expenditure come to ₹ 60, then the profit earned by manufacturer will be ₹ 20, then in this case manufacturer is earning less profit by selling the goods to its own branch. Head office prepares the branch account on this basis i.e., Invoice price is the cost price to the branch office instead of cost price to the head office, Hence the profit of the branch is found out on invoice price basis. If all the goods available in branch office are sold then there is no problem, if some of the goods remain unsold in the branch office, then these unsold goods should be priced at cost price by creating a stock reserve for unrealised profit (Difference between invoice price and cost price). The System of finding out the profit or loss at branch is known as Wholesale Branch System.

The following illustration will demonstrate Wholesale Branch System of accounting.

***Illustration 5:*** *T&T Bros. head office is located in New Delhi and branch office is located in Mumbai. The goods are sent to branch at 20% less than the Invoice Price which is cost plus 100%. Find out the profit made by the branch and head office based on the wholesale branch system.*

| Particulars | Head Office (₹) | Branch Office (₹) |
|---|---|---|
| Opening Stock (Cost/ Invoice Price) | 30,000 | 15,000 |
| Branch Expenses | 30,000 | 6,000 |
| Purchases | 3,00,000 | -- |
| Good destroyed by accident (Invoice Price) | -- | 2,000 |
| Sales at List Price | 1,70,000 | 90,000 |
| Goods sent to branch (Invoice price) | 90,000 | 90,000 |

***Solution:***

**Branch Stock Account**

| Particulars | ₹ | Particulars | ₹ |
|---|---|---|---|
| To Balance b/d (Opening stock) | 15,000 | By Sales (Cash/Debtors) | 80,000 |
| To Goods sent to Branch A/c | 80,000 | By Profit & Loss A/c (Goods Destroyed) | 2,000 |
| To Gross Profit c/d | 18,000 | By Balance c/d (Closing stock at invoice price) (refer below given calculation) | 31,000 |
| | **1,13,000** | | **1,13,000** |

***Calculations:***

If cost price = 100

List price = Cost + 100% = 100 + 100 = 200

Then Invoice price = 160 (200-40)

Cost of goods sold = 90,000*160/200 = 72,000

**Calculation of Closing stock at branch (at invoice price**

Closing Stock = Opening Stock + Goods from Head office - Cost of Goods Sold - Stock Destroyed

= 15,000 + 90,000 - 72,000 - 2,000

= 31,000

**Branch Profit & Loss Account**

| Particulars | ₹ | Particulars | ₹ |
|---|---|---|---|
| To Goods Destroyed A/c | 2,000 | By Gross Profit b/d | 16,000 |
| To Branch Expenses A/c | 6,000 | | |
| To Net Profit | 8,000 | | |
| | **16,000** | | **16,000** |

**Branch Profit & Loss Account**

| Particulars | ₹ | Particulars | ₹ |
|---|---|---|---|
| To Trading A/c | 80,000 | By Branch Stock A/c | 80,000 |
| | **80,000** | | **80,000** |

**General Trading and Profit and Loss Account of Head Office**

| Particulars | ₹ | Particulars | ₹ |
|---|---|---|---|
| To Opening Stock | 30,000 | By Sales | 1,70,000 |
| To Purchases | 3,00,000 | By Goods sent to Branch | 90,000 |
| To Gross profit | 1,18,750 | By Closing Stock at cost price( Refer below given calculation) | 1,88,750 |
| | **4,48,750** | | **4,48,750** |
| To Expenses | 30,000 | By Gross Profit b/d | 1,18,750 |
| To Stock Reserve ( Refer below given calculation-2) | 11,250 | By Branch P&L A/c | 8,000 |
| To Net Profit taken to balance sheet | 91,125 | By Stock Reserve( Refer below given calculation-1) | 5,625 |
| | **1,32,375** | | **1,32,375** |

***Calculations:***

**Closing stock at cost price (at head office) = Opening Stock + Purchases - Cost of Goods Sold - Cost of Goods sent to Branch**

= 30,000 + 3, 00,000 – (1, 70,000 * 100/200) – (90,000 * 100/ 600)

= 30,000 + 3, 00,000 – 85,000 – 56,250

= 1, 88,750

**Stock Reserve adjustment Calculation: Closing and Opening Stock at branch office are appearing at Invoice price, now the head office have to adjust the unrealised profits**

1. Stock Reserve (Opening Stock at Branch) = 15,000 * 60/160 = 5,625

2. Stock Reserve ( Closing Stock at Branch) = 30,000 * 60/160 = 11,250

### 12.3.3 Independent Branches

Independent branches maintains its own books of accounts under double entry system and also it follows its own sales terms and policies. Apart from receiving the goods from head office, these branches can purchase the goods from suppliers or from market in short independent branches will maintain all the accounting transactions.

These branches prepare their own reports like Trial Balance, Profit & Loss Account and Balance Sheet and also it opens head office account in their books and it is debited whenever branch sends goods and cash to head office and also when the payments are made by the branch office (like payments made for purchase of assets and for losses of head office) on behalf of head office. Head Office is credited when branch office receives cash and goods from head office and also it is credited while recording for depreciation of branch fixed assets, profit earned by branch and charges made by the head office for providing services.

Similarly, the branch account will be maintained by the head office and the transactions will be maintained in the same way but it will be in reverse side.

**Steps involved in preparation of independent branch accounts are as follows**

1. Reconciliation Entries
2. Adjustment Entries
3. Incorporation/Consolidation of Branch Trial Balance in Head Office Book

#### *12.3.3.1 Reconciliation Entries*

Balance of head office account in branch books may not match with the balance of branch office account in the head office books. Following are the reasons for difference along with the accounting entry for reconciliation.

1. **Cash-in-transit:** Wile transferring the cash from head office to branch office and branch office to head office, they are chances that, at the end of the accounting period the cash may not have been received by the head office or branch office as the case may be, by this the balance of head office account will not match with the balance of branch office account. For reconciling the difference in balance a reconciliation entry can be recorded in the books of Head office or Branch office, but we cannot record the reconciliation entry in both the books.

**Reconciliation entry in the books of Head Office**

| Particulars | | Debit | Credit |
|---|---|---|---|
| Cash-in-transit A/c | Dr. | xxxx | |
| To Branch Office A/c | | | xxxx |

**Reconciliation entry in the books of Branch Office**

| Particulars | | Debit | Credit |
|---|---|---|---|
| Cash-in-transit A/c | Dr. | xxxx | |
| To Head Office A/c | | | xxxx |

2. **Goods-in -transit:** Wile transferring the goods from head office to branch office and branch office to head office, they are chances that, at the end of the accounting period the goods may not have been received by the head office or branch office as the case may be, by this the balance of head office account will not match with the balance of branch office account. For reconciling the difference in balance a reconciliation entry can be recorded in the books of Head office or Branch office, but we cannot record the reconciliation entry in both the books.

**Reconciliation entry in the Books of Head Office**

| Particulars | | Debit | Credit |
|---|---|---|---|
| Goods-in-transit A/c | Dr. | xxxx | |
| To Branch Office A/c | | | xxxx |

**Reconciliation entry in the Books of Branch Office**

| Particulars | | Debit | Credit |
|---|---|---|---|
| Goods-in-transit A/c | Dr. | xxxx | |
| To Head Office A/c | | | xxxx |

**Note:** Reconciliation entry cannot be recorded in both the books (Head Office Books and Branch Office books)

***Illustration 6:*** *Record the journal entries for reconciling the balances of head office and branch office from the following Trail Balance of head office and branch office.*

| Trial Balance | | | | |
|---|---|---|---|---|
| Particulars | Head Office | | Branch Office | |
| | Debit (₹) | Credit (₹) | Debit (₹) | Credit (₹) |
| Current Accounts | 1,00,000 | | | 70,000 |
| Goods Received by/Sent to Branch | | 1,50,000 | 1,25,000 | |

### *Solution:*

In the above illustration current account shows the different balances in head office and branch office and the difference amount is ₹ 30,000 (1, 00,000 - 70,000).

Goods received or sent account also shown the different balances in head office and branch office and the difference amount is ₹ 25,000 (1, 50,000 – 1, 25,000), by this we will come to know that out of ₹ 30,000, ₹ 25,000 is the difference in goods-in-transit and remaining amount of ₹ 5,000 is the difference in cash-in-transit. Now the following entries need to be recorded in the books of Head office or Branch office but not in both the books.

**Reconciliation entry in the Books of Head Office**

| Particulars | | Debit | Credit |
|---|---|---|---|
| Goods-in-transit A/c | Dr. | 25,000 | |
| Cash-in-transit A/c | Dr. | 5,000 | |
| To Branch Office A/c | | | 30,000 |

**Reconciliation entry in the Books of Branch Office**

| Particulars | | Debit | Credit |
|---|---|---|---|
| Goods-in-transit A/c | Dr. | 25,000 | |
| Cash-in-transit A/c | Dr. | 5,000 | |
| To Head Office A/c | | | 30,000 |

### *12.3.3.2 Adjustment Entries*

Adjustment entries needs to be recorded at the end of the accounting year for few transactions like Depreciation account of branch office maintained by the head office and the expenses borne by the head office for the branch office, these transactions will take place between head office and branch office and adjustment entries has to be recorded for such transactions as shown below:

1. **Expenses borne by the head office for the branch:** Head office will provide services to branch office on regular bases and head office will charge for these services. **For example** head office will render administrative services to branch office and will charge sum of ₹ 10,000 to branch.

**Adjustment entry in the Books of Head Office**

| Particulars | | Debit | Credit |
|---|---|---|---|
| Branch A/c | Dr. | xxxx | |
| To Expenses (Administrative) A/c | | | xxxx |

**Adjustment entry in the Books of Branch Office**

| Particulars | | Debit | Credit |
|---|---|---|---|
| Expenses Incurred by Head Office A/c | Dr. | xxxx | |
| To Head Office A/c | | | xxxx |

2. **Depreciation account of branch maintained by head office:** When head office maintains the fixed asset account of branch office, then the following adjustment entries are required for depreciation on fixed assets:

**Adjustment entry in the Books of Head Office**

| Particulars | | Debit | Credit |
|---|---|---|---|
| Branch A/c | Dr. | xxxx | |
| To Branch Fixed Asset A/c | | | xxxx |

**Adjustment entry in the Books of Branch Office**

| Particulars | | Debit | Credit |
|---|---|---|---|
| Depreciation A/c | Dr. | xxxx | |
| To Head Office A/c | | | xxxx |

The following Illustration will demonstrate about the Adjustment Entries.

***Illustration 7:*** *Suka Enterprises have two branch one in Kolkata and other one is in Karnataka. Record the following transactions in the books of Head office (Suka Enterprises) and pass the necessary adjustment entries.*

1. Kolkata Branch transferred goods to Karnataka Branch for ₹ 10,000
2. Depreciation of fixed assets (Branch) account are maintained by head office-Karnataka Branch ₹ 40,000 and Kolkata Branch ₹ 50,000
3. On 1st January 2016, Head Office sent the goods to Kolkata Branch for ₹ 20,000, but Kolkata Branch received the goods on 1st February 2016.
4. Head office charged ₹ 30,000 to Karnataka Branch for providing administrative services.
5. On 5th January 2016, Karnataka Branch remitted ₹ 50,000 to Head Office, but Head Office received the amount on 5th February 2016.

***Solution:***

**Journal Entries in the Books of Head Office**

| | Particulars | | Debit | Credit |
|---|---|---|---|---|
| 1 | Karnataka Branch A/c | Dr. | 10,000 | |
| | To Kolkata Branch A/c | | | 10,000 |
| | (Being goods transferred from Kolkata branch to Karnataka branch) | | | |
| | | | | |
| 2 | Karnataka Branch A/c | Dr | 40,000 | |
| | Kolkata Branch A/c | Dr | 50,000 | |
| | To Karnataka Fixed Asset A/c | | | 40,000 |
| | To Kolkata Fixed Asset A/c | | | 50,000 |
| | (Being fixed asset adjustment entry recorded for both the branches) | | | |
| | | | | |
| 3 | Goods-In-Transit A/c | Dr. | 20,000 | |
| | To Kolkata Branch A/c | | | 20,000 |
| | (Being goods in transit) | | | |
| | | | | |
| 4 | Karnataka Branch A/c | Dr. | 30,000 | |
| | To Administrative Expenses A/c | | | 30,000 |
| | (Being administrative expense charged to branch office) | | | |
| | | | | |
| 5 | Cash-In-Transit A/c | Dr. | 50,000 | |
| | To Karnataka Branch A/c | | | 50,000 |
| | (Being cash in transit) | | | |

### *12.3.3.3 Incorporation/Consolidation of Branch Trial Balance in Head Office Book*

It is mandatory for the head office to prepare the consolidated Balance sheet at the end of the accounting period, because all the branches fall under one organization and shareholders and vendors will be interested in knowing the overall performance and position of the organisation, for this purpose it is necessary to consolidate the balances of different branches with head office. The process of preparing the consolidated Balance Sheet of the organisation is called as Incorporation of Branch Trial Balance in Head Office Book.

**They are two ways to incorporate the branch Trial Balance in head office book as shown below**

I. **Detailed Incorporation:** In this method all items of trading and profit & loss account are incorporated in the head office books and also Assets and Liabilities are incorporated. To prepare the consolidated Balance sheet the following entries are passed.

| Detailed Incorporation | | | | | |
|---|---|---|---|---|---|
| S.No | Transactions | Explanation | Particulars | Dr. | Cr. |
| 1 | For incorporating the items showing under debit side of the Trading Account. | This transaction is recorded with the total value of items which are debited in Trading Account like Opening Stock, Net Purchases and Direct expenses (Wages, manufacturing expenses etc.). | Branch Trading A/c Dr. | xxx | |
| | | | To Branch A/c | | xxx |
| 2 | For incorporating the items showing under credit side of the Trading Account. | This transaction is recorded with the total value of items which are credited in Trading Account like Net Sales and Closing Stock etc. | Branch A/c Dr. | xxx | |
| | | | To Branch Trading A/c | | xxx |
| 3. | For transferring gross profit to branch profit and loss account. | This entry is recorded in order to transfer the gross profit to P. & L. A/c | Branch Trading A/c Dr. | xxx | |
| | | | To Branch P. & L. A/c | | xxx |
| 4. | For transferring gross loss to branch profit and loss account. | This entry is recorded in order to transfer the gross loss to P. & L. A/c | Branch P. & L. A/c Dr. | xxx | |
| | | | To Branch Trading A/c | | xxx |
| 5 | For incorporating the items showing under debit side of the Branch P & L Account. | This transaction is recorded with the total value of items which are debited in Branch Profit and Loss Account like Rent, Commission, Salary, Depreciation, Bad Debts etc. | Branch P. & L. A/c Dr. | xxx | |
| | | | To Branch A/c | | xxx |
| 6 | For incorporating the items showing under credit side of the Branch P & L Account. | This transaction is recorded with the total value of items which are credited in Branch Profit and Loss Account like Commission earned, Discount Received etc. | Branch A/c Dr. | xxx | |
| | | | To Branch P. & L. A/c | | xxx |
| 7 | For transferring net profit to general profit and loss account of head office. | This entry is recorded in order to transfer the net profit to General or Head office P.& L.A/c | Branch P. & L. A/c Dr. | xxx | |
| | | | To General or Head Office P. & L. A/c | | xxx |
| 8 | For transferring net loss to branch profit and loss account. | This entry is recorded in order to transfer the net loss to P & L A/c | General or Head Office P.& L.A/c Dr. | xxx | |
| | | | To Branch P. & L. A/c | | xxx |
| 9 | For incorporating assets of branch after adjustments, if any. | While recording this entry each asset need to be debited individually | Branch Asset (Individually) A/c Dr. | xxx | |
| | | | To Branch A/c | | xxx |
| 10 | For incorporating liabilities of branch after adjustments, if any. | While recording this entry each liability need to be credited individually | Branch A/c Dr. | xxx | |
| | | | To Branch Liabilities (Individually) A/c | | xxx |

The branch accounts will be closed in the head office books because of these incorporation entries, then in the beginning of next accounting year, the assets and liabilities will be transferred to the branch.

The following entries are recorded for transferring the assets and liabilities to the branch.

Transferring Assets and Liabilities to Branch Office

| Transferring Assets and Liabilities to Branch Office | | | | | |
|---|---|---|---|---|---|
| S.No | Transactions | Explanation | Particulars | Dr. | Cr. |
| 1 | Transferring of branch assets to branch. | This entry is recorded to transfer the branch assets to branch at the beginning of accounting year. | Branch A/c Dr. | xxx | |
| | | | To Branch Assets A/c | | xxx |
| | | | (Being transfer of branch assets to branch) | | |
| 2 | Transferring of branch liabilities to branch. | This entry is recorded to transfer the branch liabilities to branch at the beginning of accounting year. | Branch Liabilities A/c Dr. | xxx | |
| | | | To Branch A/c | | xxx |
| | | | (Being transfer of branch assets to branch) | | |

The following illustration will demonstrate how the branch accounts are incorporated in the head office books of account.

***Illustration 8:*** *Following is the Trial Balance of Karnataka branch office as on 31st March, 2016. Incorporate the Karnataka branch account with head office by giving the journal entries, after incorporating assets and liabilities show the branch account in head office books.*

| Trial Balance as on 31st March, 2016 | | |
|---|---|---|
| **Particulars** | **Debit (₹)** | **Credit (₹)** |
| Opening Stock | 40,000 | |
| Manufacturing Expenses | 20,000 | |
| Wages | 50,000 | |
| Purchases | 90,000 | |
| Rent | 14,000 | |
| Salaries | 20,000 | |
| General Expenses | 15,000 | |
| Cash-In-Hand | 12,000 | |
| Goods Received from Head Office | 25,000 | |
| Purchase Returns | | 2,000 |
| Sales | | 1,60,000 |
| Discount Earned | | 2,000 |
| Debtors | 25,000 | |
| Creditors | | 15,000 |
| Head Office Account | | 1,23,000 |
| **Total** | **3,11,000** | **3,11,000** |

Rent Outstanding is ₹ 1,000 and Closing Stock at Branch is ₹ 40,000, Depreciation of 15% to be provided on Branch furniture of ₹ 10,000 and 20 % on Branch Machinery of ₹ 60,000.

***Solution:***

| Journal Entries in the Books of Head Office | | | | |
|---|---|---|---|---|
| **Date (2016)** | **Particulars** | **L.F** | **Dr.** | **Cr.** |
| Mar. 31 | Karnataka Branch A/c Dr. | | 13,500 | |
| | To Branch Furniture A/c | | | 1,500 |
| | To Branch Machinery A/c | | | 12,000 |
| | (Being depreciation charged to branch) | | | |
| | | | | |
| Mar. 31 | Karnataka Branch Trading A/c Dr. | | 2,14,000 | |
| | To Karnataka Branch A/c | | | 2,14,000 |
| | (Being the total of stock, wages, goods received from H.O, manufacturing expenses and wages debited to branch trading A/c) | | | |
| | | | | |
| Mar. 31 | Karnataka Branch A/c Dr. | | 2,00,000 | |
| | To Karnataka Branch Trading A/c | | | 2,00,000 |
| | (Being the total of Branch Stock-40,000 and Sales-1,60,000 credited to branch trading A/c) | | | |
| | | | | |
| Mar. 31 | Karnataka Branch P. & L. A/c Dr. | | 23,000 | |
| | To Karnataka Branch Trading A/c **(Refer the below given calculation-1)** | | | 23,000 |
| | (Being gross loss transferred) | | | |
| | | | | |
| Mar. 31 | Karnataka Branch P. & L. A/c Dr. | | 63,500 | |
| | To Karnataka Branch A/c **(Refer below given calculation-2)** | | | 63,500 |
| | (Being total of branch expenses transferred to branch P. & L. A/c) | | | |
| | | | | |
| Mar. 31 | Karnataka Branch A/c Dr. | | 2,000 | |
| | To Karnataka Branch P. & L. A/c | | | 2,000 |
| | (Being discount earned credited to Branch P. & L. A/c) | | | |
| | | | | |
| Mar. 31 | General Profit & Loss A/c Dr. | | 84,500 | |
| | To Karnataka Branch P. & L. A/c ( **Refer below given calculation- 3)** | | | 84,500 |
| | (Being net loss transferred to head office profit and loss account) | | | |
| | | | | |
| Mar. 31 | Karnataka Cash A/c Dr. | | 12,000 | |
| | Karnataka Stock A/c Dr. | | 40,000 | |
| | Karnataka Debtors A/c Dr. | | 25,000 | |
| | To Karnataka Branch A/c | | | 77,000 |
| | (Being transfer of all branch assets to head office) | | | |
| | | | | |
| Mar. 31 | Karnataka Branch A/c Dr. | | 16,000 | |
| | To Branch Creditors A/c | | | 15,000 |
| | To Branch Outstanding (Expenses) A/c | | | 1,000 |
| | (Being transfer of all liabilities to head office books) | | | |

***Calculations:***

1. Gross Profit/Loss = Sales – Cost of goods sold (Cost of goods sold = Beginning Inventory + Direct Expenses + Purchases – Ending Inventory).

   = 1, 60,000 – (40,000 + 95,000 + 88,000 – 40,000)

   = 1, 60,000 – 1, 83,000

   = 23,000 (It is a loss because revenue is less than the cost)

2. Branch Expenses as per the above illustration = Salaries + Depreciation + General Expenses + Rent

   = 20,000 + 13,500 + 15,000 + 15,000

   = 63,500

3. Net Profit or Loss = Gross Loss + Indirect expenses – Income ( Discount earned)

   = 23,000 +63,500 – 2,000

   = 84,500 (It is a loss because expenses are more than incomes)

| Karnataka Branch Account in Head Office Books | | | | | |
|---|---|---|---|---|---|
| **Date (2016)** | **Particulars** | **₹** | **Date (2016)** | **Particulars** | **₹** |
| Mar. 31 | To Balance b/d | 1,23,000 | Mar. 31 | By Karnataka Branch Trading A/c | 2,14,000 |
| Mar. 31 | To Branch Furniture A/c (Depreciation) | 1,500 | Mar. 31 | By Karnataka Branch P. & L. A/c (total branch expenses) | 63,500 |
| Mar. 31 | To Branch Machinery A/c (Depreciation) | 12,000 | Mar. 31 | By Branch Assets | 77,000 |
| Mar. 31 | To Karnataka Trading A/c (Stock + Sales) | 2,00,000 | | | |
| Mar. 31 | To Karnataka Branch P. & .L A/c | 2000 | | | |
| Mar. 31 | To Branch Liabilities | 16,000 | | | |
| | | **3,54,500** | | | **3,54,500** |

II. **Abridged Method:** In this method a Memorandum Account is prepared i.e., Branch Trading and Profit & Loss Account is prepared as a Memorandum account and the entries are recorded to transfer the net profit or loss in the head office books. Head Office will not record any transaction for incorporating branch assets and liabilities because branch account in books of head office will show the balance equal to net worth.

The following illustration will demonstrate, how to prepare the Branch Trading and Profit & Loss Account

***Illustration 9:*** *Saha Group of companies opens a new branch in Karnataka and it trades independently. The following are the transactions of the branch for the year ended 31st March, 2016. Prepare the Branch Trading and Profit & Loss Account and branch account in the books of head office.*

| Transactions | |
|---|---|
| **Transactions** | **₹** |
| Goods received from Head office. | 22,000 |
| Purchases from Market. | 20,500 |
| • On Credit - ₹ 16,500 | |
| • On Cash - ₹ 4,000 | |
| Sales to Customers. | 31,600 |
| • On Credit – ₹ 26,000 | |
| • On Cash - ₹ 5,600 | |
| Cash paid to Creditors. | 16,200 |
| Cash received from Customers. | 32,400 |
| Expenses Paid by Branch. | 10,950 |
| Credit purchase of machinery by branch. | 5,500 |
| Cash received from head office in the beginning. | 7,000 |
| Remittance to head office. | 13,000 |

After incorporation of branch Trial Balance, we have taken the following into consideration.

i. Branch fixed assets accounts are maintained in Head Office Books.

ii. Branch Closing stock is ₹ 14,000

iii. Write off depreciation on machinery at 7 per cent per annum

iv. A remittance of ₹ 4,000 from branch to the head office is in transit.

## *Solutions:*

| Karnataka Branch Trading and Profit and loss account in the books of H.O as on 31st March, 2016 | | | |
|---|---|---|---|
| **Particulars** | **₹** | **Particulars** | **₹** |
| To Goods Received from Head Office | 22,000 | By Credit Sales | 26,000 |
| To Credit Purchases | 16,500 | By Cash Sales | 5,600 |
| To Cash Purchases | 4,000 | By Closing Stock | 14,000 |
| To Gross profit c/d | 3,100 | | |
| | **45,600** | | **45,600** |
| To Expenses | 10,950 | By Gross profit b/d | 3,100 |
| To Depreciation on machinery (5500*7% = 385) | 385 | By Net Loss Transferred to General (H.O) P. & L. A/c | 8,235 |
| | **11,335** | | **11,335** |

| Karnataka Branch Account | | | | |
|---|---|---|---|---|
| **Particulars** | **₹** | **Particulars** | | **₹** |
| To Cash | 7,000 | By Machinery | | 5,500 |
| To Goods supplied to branch | 22,000 | By Remittance | 13,000 | |
| To Branch Machinery (Depreciation) | 385 | *Less: Cash-in- Transit* | 4,000 | |
| | | | | **9,000** |
| | | By General (H.O) Profit & Loss A/c | | 8,235 |
| | | By Balance c/d (Assets - Liabilities) **(Refer below given calculation-1)** | | 6,650 |
| | **29,385** | | | **29,385** |

## *Calculation for Assets - Liabilities*

1. Assets = Closing Stock + Cash in Hand + Cash in Transit

   = 14,000 + (7,000 + 5,600 + 32,400 – 16,200 – 10,950 – 4,000 – 13,000) + 4,000

   = 14,000 + 850 + 4,000

   = 18,850

   Liabilities = Creditors for Machinery +Advance from Debtors + Sundry Creditors

   = (5,500) + (32,400 – 26,000) + (16,500 - 16,200)

   = 5,500 + 6,400 + 300

   = 12,200

   **Now:** Assets – Liability = 6,650

***Illustration 10:*** *Khan Group of Companies started a business on 01-04-2016 with head office at Karnataka and a branch office at Mumbai. Complete purchases were handled by head office were the goods were processed before sale and there are no loss or wastages in processing. Branch will handled only the processed goods received from head office and the goods were sent to branch at processed cost plus 10%.All sales made by head office or branch office were at same gross profit of 25% on their respective cost.*

| Trial Balance as on 31st March, 2016 | | | | |
|---|---|---|---|---|
| **Particulars** | **Head Office** | | **Branch Office** | |
| | **Debit (₹)** | **Credit(₹)** | **Debit (₹)** | **Credit(₹)** |
| Capital | | 3,20,000 | | |
| Drawings | 65,000 | | | |
| Purchases | 19,79,500 | | | |
| Cost of Processing | 51,500 | | | |
| Goods Sent to Branch | | 9,25,000 | | |
| Sales | | 12,81,000 | | 8,20,000 |
| Administrative Expenses | 1,40,000 | | 15,000 | |
| Selling Expenses | 51,000 | | 7,200 | |
| Branch Current Assets | 3,90,800 | | | |
| Debtors | 3,10,600 | | 1,14,600 | |
| Creditors | | 6,08,900 | | 21,800 |
| Bank Balance | 1,53,000 | | 78,000 | |
| Head Office Current Account | | | | 2,62,500 |
| Goods Received From Head Office | | | 8,81,000 | |
| | **31,41,400** | **31,34,900** | **10,95,800** | **11,04,300** |

Additional Information is given below:

1. As on 01-03-2016, Head Office sent the goods to branch office for ₹ 45,000, but branch office did not received the goods till 01-04-2016.
2. As on 01-03-2016, Branch office sent the remittance of ₹ 85,300 Head office, which was not received till 01-04-2016
3. Branch disclosed the shortage of ₹ 21,000 (at selling price to the branch)
4. As on 31-03-2016, head office showed the cost of unprocessed goods for ₹ 1,01,000

   Prepare the columnar Trading and profit & loss account with combined form and also prepare the consolidated Balance sheet of the business as on 31-03-2016.

## Solution:

**Trading and Profit & Loss Account of Khan Group of Companies as on 31st March, 2016**

| Particulars | Head Office | Branch | Total | Particulars | Head Office | Branch | Total |
|---|---|---|---|---|---|---|---|
| To Purchase | 19,79,500 | | 19,79,500 | By Sales | 12,81,000 | 8,20,000 | 21,01,000 |
| To Cost of Processing | 51,500 | | 51,500 | By Goods sent to branch A/c | 9,25,000 | | |
| To Goods Received from Head Office | | 8,81,000 | | By Stock Shortage ( at selling price) i.e., 21,000*1/5 | | 16,800 | 16,800 |
| To Gross Profit c/d | 3,40,291 | 1,64,000 | 6,86,471 | By Goods in Transit | | | 45,000 |
| | | | | By Closing Stock Processed Goods **(Refer calculation 1 a & b)** | 64,291 | 2,08,200 | 2,72,491 |
| | | | | Unprocessed Goods | 1,01,000 | | 1,01,000 |
| | **23,71,291** | **10,45,000** | **27,17,471** | | **23,71,291** | **10,45,000** | **25,36,291** |
| To Administrative Expenses | 1,40,000 | 15,000 | 1,55,000 | By Gross Profit b/d | 3,40,291 | 1,64,000 | 6,86,471 |
| To Selling Expenses | 51,000 | 7,200 | 58,200 | | | | |
| To Stock Shortage | | 16,800 | 16,800 | | | | |
| To Stock Reserve **(Refer calculation 2)** | 24,910 | | 24,910 | | | | |
| To Net Profit | 1,24,381 | 1,25,000 | 2,49,381 | | | | |
| | **3,40,291** | **1,64,000** | **5,04,291** | | **3,40,291** | **1,64,000** | **6,86,471** |

**Consolidated Balance Sheet of Khan Group of Companies as on 31st March,2016**

| Liabilities | | ₹ | Assets | | ₹ |
|---|---|---|---|---|---|
| Capital | 3,20,000 | | Closing Stock: | | |
| *Add: Net Profit* | 2,49,381 | | Processed Stock: | | |
| | **5,69,381** | | Head Office | 64,291 | |
| *Less: Drawings* | 65,000 | | Branch Office | 2,08,200 | |
| | | **5,04,381** | | **2,72,491** | |
| Creditors: | | | *Less: Stock Reserve (Refer calculation 2)* | 20,820 | **2,51,671** |
| Head Office | 6,08,900 | | Unprocessed Goods | | 1,01,000 |
| Branch Office | 21,800 | | Bank Balance: Head Office | 1,53,000 | |
| | | **6,30,700** | Branch Office | 78,000 | **2,31,000** |
| | | | Goods in Transit ( 45,000 - 4,090) (Refer Calculation 2) | | 40,910 |
| | | | Cash-in-Transit | | 85,300 |
| | | | Debtors: | | |
| | | | Head Office | 3,10,600 | |
| | | | Branch Office | 1,14,600 | **4,25,200** |
| | | **11,35,081** | | | **11,35,081** |

## Calculations:

| | | |
|---|---|---|
| **1. Closing Stock Calculation:** | | |
| a) Stock at head office (19,79,500 + 51,500 - 1,01,000 ) = | | 19,30,000 |
| *Less: Cost of goods sold at branch ₹ 9, 25,000 * 100/110 =* | 8,40,909 | |
| *Cost of goods sold = 12, 81,000 * 100/125 =* | 10,24,800 | 18,65,709 |
| Processed stock at head office = | | **64,291** |
| b) Stock at Branch office: | | |
| Goods received from head office = | | 8, 81,000 |
| *Less: Invoice value of goods sold (8, 20,000 * 100/125) =* | 6, 56,000 | |
| *Invoice value of shortage of stock (21,000 * 100/125)=* | 16,800 | 6,72,800 |
| Stock Branch (at invoice price) | | **2,08,200** |
| *Less: Stock Reserve (2,08,200 * 10/110)* | | 20,820 |
| Processed stock at Branch office at cost = | | **1,87,380** |
| | | |
| **2. Stock Reserve Calculation:** | | |
| Branch stock unrealised profit (2,08,000 * 10/110) | | 20,820 |
| Goods-in-Transit unrealised profit (45,000 * 10/110) | | 4,090 |
| | | **24,910** |

## KEY TAKEAWAYS

- Inland Branches are the branches located within the Country, Inland branches are also called as Home Branch or Domestic Branch.
- Depended Branch and Independent Brach are the two types of branch in which books of accounts are maintained.
- Dependent Branches doesn't maintains its books of accounts, they are maintained by its Head office.
- Independent branches maintains its own books of accounts under double entry system.

## PRACTISE EXERCISES

### Section A: Review Questions

1. What is Branch Accounting?
2. Explain the purpose of Branch Accounting?
3. What is dependent Branch?
4. What is Independent Branch?
5. What does Goods-In-Transit mean?
6. What does Cash-In-Transit mean?

### Section B: Multiple Choice Questions

Select the most appropriate answer from the choices given below:

1. ____________ maintains its own book of accounts and sales policies.
   a. Dependent Branch  b. Independent Branch
   c. Domestic Branch  d. Head Office
2. ____________ doesn't maintains its books of accounts.
   a. Dependent Branch  b. Independent Branch
   c. Domestic Branch  d. Head Office

3. Debtor's System is one of the system of accounting for ____________.
   a. Dependent Branch  b. Independent Branch
   c. Domestic Branch  d. Head Office
4. How many types of systems of accounting available for dependent branches?
   a. 3  b. 2
   c. 4  d. 1

## Section C: Practical Questions

1. Mukta Enterprises have its head office at Karnataka and branch office at Mumbai, following are the transactions with head office at branch for the year ended 31st August, 2016.

| Date 2016 | Transactions |
|---|---|
| Sep. 1 | Stock at branch ₹ 50,000 |
| | Debtors at branch ₹30,000 |
| | Petty Cash ₹ 15,000 |
| | Goods supplied to branch office for ₹ 1,70,000 |
| | Cash sales remittance from branch ₹ 21,000 |
| | Realization of debtors ₹ 1,70,000 |
| | Salary of ₹ 30,000 sent to branch |
| | Rent of ₹20,000 sent to branch |
| | Petty cash of ₹ 20,000 sent to branch |
| Aug. 31 | Stock at branch ₹30,000 |
| | Debtors at branch ₹ 20,000 |
| | Petty Cash ₹ 20,000 |

Record the above transaction in the journal and prepare the Branch Account under Debtor's System of Accounting.

2. SUK Traders started branches at Delhi and Kolkata as on 1st April, 2016. All goods are transferred by head office to branch office at cost plus 25 per cent. Head office pays all expenses incurred by the branch office. Cash collected by the branches are remitted to head office on daily bases. Each branch maintains its own sales ledger and sends the weekly statements to head office. The following are the details extracted from the weekly statements, sent by the different branches to head office for the half yearly period ended 30th September, 2016.

| Particulars | Chennai (₹) | Kerala(₹) |
|---|---|---|
| Cash Sales made by branch | 90,600 | 94,200 |
| Credit Sales made by branch | 137,200 | 1,22,000 |
| Sundry Debtors | 46,500 | 35,600 |
| Sales Return | 14,300 | 13,200 |
| Rent and Rates | 15,200 | 16,500 |
| Bad debts | 18,000 | -- |
| Salaries paid | 28,000 | 30,000 |
| General expenses incurred | 14,600 | 13,500 |
| Goods received from head office | 1,62,000 | 1,37,000 |
| Advertisement | 19,500 | 17,200 |
| Stock on 30th September, 2016 | 57,000 | 47,000 |

Prepare the branch accounts in the books of head office showing the profit or loss for the accounting period and then prepare the Trading and Profit & Loss Account separately for each branch as per Final Accounts Systems.

3. Ashok Bros. head office is located in New Delhi and branch office is located in Kolkata. The goods are sent to branch at 20% less than the Invoice Price which is cost plus 100%. Find out the profit made by the branch and head office based on the wholesale branch system.

| Particulars | Head Office (₹) | Branch Office (₹) |
|---|---|---|
| Opening Stock (Cost/ Invoice Price) | 30,000 | 15,000 |
| Branch Expenses | 30,000 | 6,000 |
| Purchases | 3,00,000 | -- |
| Good destroyed by accident (Invoice Price) | -- | 2,000 |
| Sales at List Price | 1,70,000 | 90,000 |
| Goods sent to branch (Invoice price) | 90,000 | 90,000 |

4. Record the journal entries for reconciling the balances of head office and branch office from the following Trial Balance of head office and branch office.

| Particulars | Head Office Debit (₹) | Head Office Credit (₹) | Branch Office Debit (₹) | Branch Office Credit (₹) |
|---|---|---|---|---|
| Current Accounts | 1,10,000 | | | 80,000 |
| Goods Received by/Sent to Branch | | 1,60,000 | 1,35,000 | |

5. TK Enterprises have two branch one in Mumbai and other one is in Delhi. Record the following transactions in the books of Head office (TK Enterprises) and pass the necessary adjustment entries.
   a. Mumbai Branch transferred goods to Delhi Branch for ₹ 10,000
   b. Depreciation of fixed assets (Branch) account are maintained by head office-Delhi Branch ₹ 40,000 and Mumbai Branch ₹ 50,000
   c. On 1st January 2016, Head Office sent the goods to Mumbai Branch for ₹ 20,000, but Mumbai Branch received the goods on 1st February 2016.
   d. Head office charged ₹ 30,000 to Delhi Branch for providing administrative services.

   On 5th January 2016, Delhi Branch remitted ₹ 50,000 to Head Office, but Head Office received the amount on 5th February 2016.

## Chapter 13

# Other Features

## 13.1 INTEREST CALCULATION

Interest is a legitimate return on money invested and chargeable in the business world on loans and also on delayed payments. Interest can be calculated on the basis of simple interest or compound interest.

- **Simple Interest:** Simple Interest is a quick method of calculating the interest charged on a loan. It will be fixed throughout the period.
- **Compound Interest:** Compound Interest is the interest on interest.

In Tally.ERP 9 you can calculate interest in two ways.

- Simple Mode
- Advanced Mode

**Simple Mode:** Simple mode is used when the rate of interest is fixed.

**Advance Mode:** This mode is used when the rate of interest is fluctuating.

Let us learn how the interest is calculated on the day to day credit transactions in Tally.ERP 9.

***Activity:*** *Create the following Company*

**Company Name:** Sara Traders

***Address:*** *No. 198, 6th Cross, Vinayakanagar*

*Bengaluru 560078*

***State:*** *Karnataka*

***Financial Year:*** *01-04-2017 to 31-03-2018*

### 13.1.1 Activating Interest Calculation

To activate Interest Calculation follow the steps given below:

1. Go to **Gateway of Tally** > Press **F11: Company Features > F1: Accounting Features**
2. Set the option **Activate interest calculation** to **Yes**
3. Set the option **Use advanced parameters** to **Yes,** by enabling this option we can define the fluctuating interest rates
4. Press **Ctrl+A** to save the **Accounting Features** screen

### 13.1.2 Calculation of Simple Interest in Tally.ERP 9 using Simple Mode

In Tally.ERP 9, you can calculate interest on outstanding balance amounts and on outstanding bills/invoices/transactions (receivables and payables) and also on outstanding balances.

In this section we will learn to calculate interest if the customers are delayed in making payments against the credit purchases made by them.

***Illustration:*** *Calculation of Interest on delayed payments.*

On 01-07-2017, Sara Traders sold 10 Nos of HD Television at ₹ 20,000 each to Raichand Traders on credit. If the customer is not paying the total amount within 30 days of invoice then 5% interest is collected on the total invoice amount.

**Step 1:** Creation of Masters

***Activity:*** *Create the following Masters*

- *Sales A/c under Sales ledger*
- *HD Television – while creating this stock item, enter the opening balance quantity as 100Nos.*
- *Create the Party Ledger by referring the below given figure 13.1:*

**Note:** While creating party ledger it is mandatory to enable the option **Activate Interest Calculation** to **Yes,** and define the interest rate details, if not the interest will not get calculated.

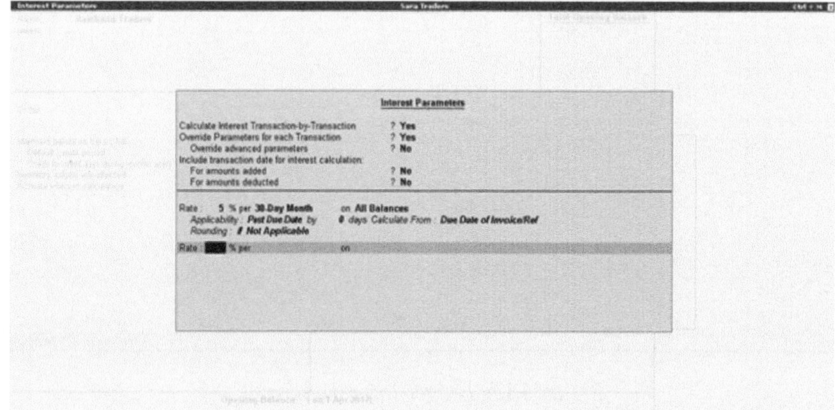


*Figure 13.1: Ledger Creation Screen*

**Step 2:** Recording Sales Transaction

1. Go to **Gateway of Tally > Accounting Vouchers >** Press **F8: Sales Voucher,** enter the details as shown in figure 13.2:

**Note:** While recording the sales invoice make sure to enter the correct due date or else the interest will get calculated from the wrong period.

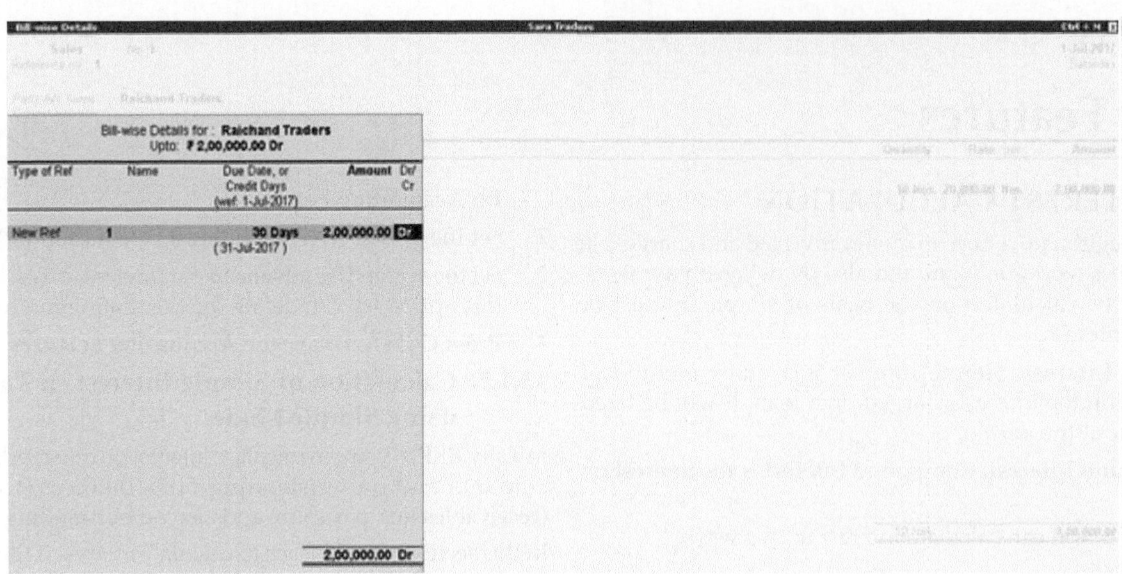


*Figure 13.2: Bill-wise Details Screen*

2. Press **Ctrl+A** twice to save the sales invoice.

Consider that the party has not made payment within 30 days of credit period, then the interest rate 5% should get calculated. Let us check how the interest gets calculated in Tally.ERP 9.

### 13.1.3 Interest Receivable Report

In Tally. ERP 9, we can check the details of interest receivable for any given period and also the interest amount reflecting in this report will not impact the books of account. In order to bring the interest amount to our books of account then the following entry needs to be recorded.

To bring Interest Receivable amount,

1. Go to **Gateway of Tally > Display > Statements of Accounts > Interest Calculations > Interest Receivable**
2. Press **F2:Period** and enter the period as 01-08-2017 to 31-08-2017
3. Press **Enter** till you get the **Ledger Interest** report
4. Press **Alt+F1: Detailed**

The **Ledger Interest** screen appears as shown in the figure 13.3:

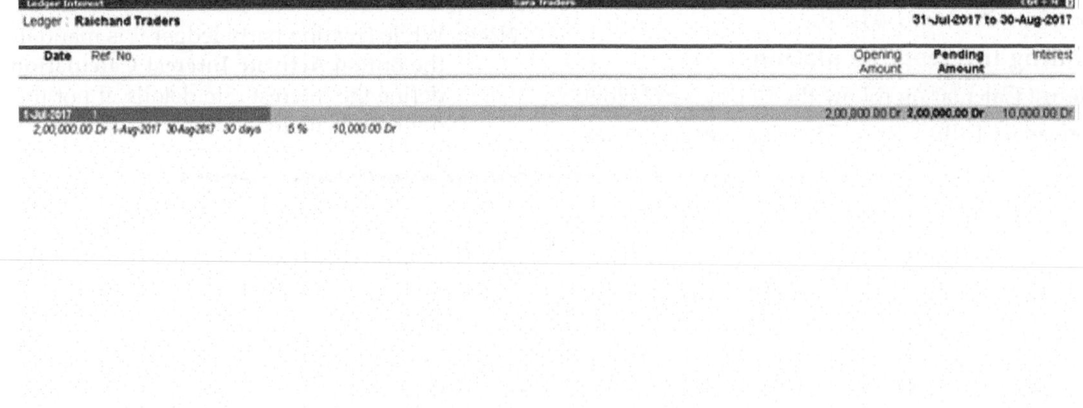


*Figure 13.3: Ledger Interest Screen*

The interest amount of ₹ 10,000 which is reflected in figure 13.3 does not impact the books of account. In order to bring the interest amount in the books of account we need to record the debit or credit note with configured voucher class.

Let us now bring the interest receivable amount in the books of account by recording debit note with configured voucher class.

### 13.1.4 Bringing Interest Amount in the Books of Account

In this section we will learn to bring the interest amount from interest receivable report to books of account. To do so, we need to follow the below given steps:

1. Create a Voucher Class based on the interest calculation type i.e. Simple Interest or Compound Interest.
2. Record the Debit Note with voucher class.

**Step 1:** Create a Voucher Class based on the interest calculation type i.e. Simple Interest or Compound Interest.

1. Go to **Gateway of Tally > Accounts Info > Voucher Type > Alter**
2. Select **Debit Note** from the **List of Voucher Types**
3. Bring the cursor under **Name of Class** field and type **Simple Interest Class** and press **Enter**
4. Enable the option **Use Class for Interest Accounting** to **Yes**

   The **Voucher Type Class** screen appears as shown in the figure 13.4:

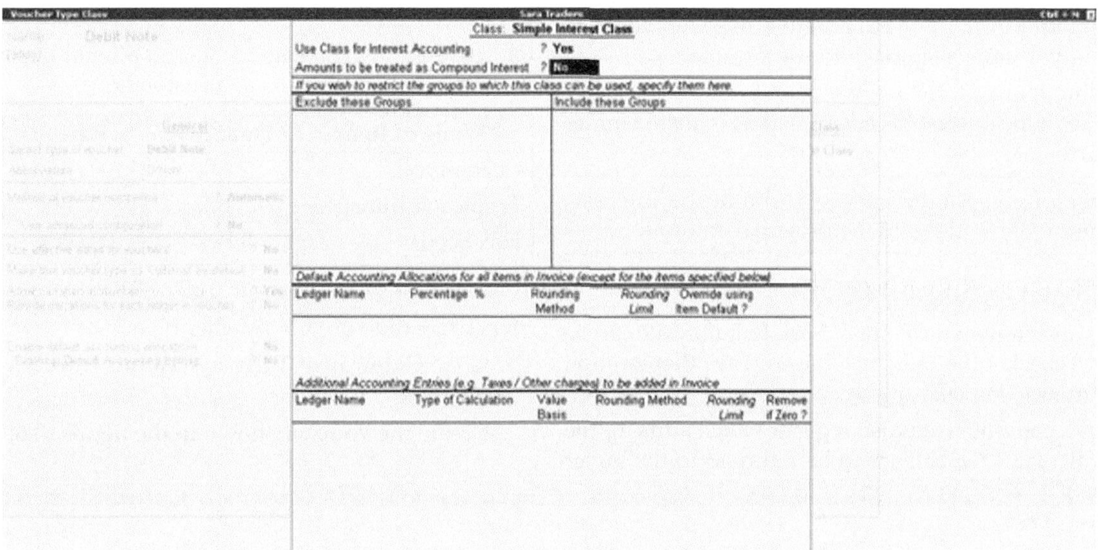


*Figure 13.4: Voucher Type Class Screen*

   Based on our requirement, we can enable the option **Amounts to be treated as Compound Interest** to **Yes** or **No**. Let this option be **Yes**, because we want the interest to be calculates based on Simple Interest Formula.

5. Press **Ctrl+A** twice to save the voucher class

***Activity:** Press **F11 > F1** and enable the following option to Yes*

- *Use debit and credit note*
- *Record debit note in invoice mode*

**Step 2:** Recording of debit note with voucher class

1. Go to **Gateway of Tally > Accounting Voucher > F9:Debit Note**
2. Select the **class** which is created from **Voucher Class List**
3. Press **F2:Date** and enter the date as 30-08-2017
4. Debit the **Raichand Traders**
5. Select the bill from **List of Interest Bill** as shown in figure 13.5:

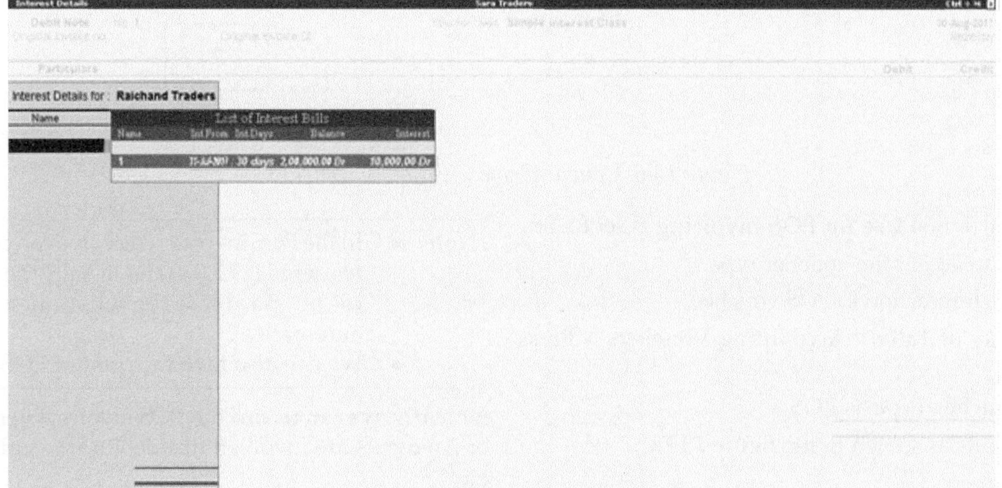


*Figure 13.5: Interest Details Screen*

6. Credit interest received ledger (If the ledger is not created press Alt+C and create the ledger under indirect incomes)
7. Press **Ctrl+A** to save the debit note voucher

Once after recording the entry check the balance sheet report and press enter on current liabilities head > again press enter on sundry creditors head, observe the debit amount is reflecting as ₹ 2,10,000

The interest amount of ₹ 10,000 is added up to the principal amount. We need to record the journal voucher in order to move the interest amount from principal amount, this step needs to be followed only in case of simple interest formula.

While recording journal voucher, we need to Debit the Party Ledger and Credit the Interest Receivable ledger (Created under the group Current Assets).

**Note:** In case of compound interest formula the interest amount will be added to the principal amount.

## 13.2 POINT OF SALES (POS)

POS or PoS is an acronym for Point of Sale. Point of Sale can be a retail outlet, a checkout counter in a shop, or any other location where a sale transaction takes place.

POS system is a computerised cash register which adds up the sales totals, calculates the balance to be returned to the buyer and automatically adjusts the inventory levels to reflect the quantity sold. The equipment required for POS to work effectively are cash registers, card readers, bar-code scanners etc.

Tally.ERP 9's point of sale application can search your inventory database not only on item description or SKU but also by alias name, part number, keywords and so on. Stock summary reports can be used for viewing group-wise, category-wise, location-wise, batch-wise and supplier-wise details of the stock items.

Let us record POS transaction in Tally.ERP 9.

On 30-08-2017, Sara Traders started a retail business and sold the following stock items to a customer.

| Name of Item | Quantity | Rate | Amount |
|---|---|---|---|
| Coconut oil | 2 Btl. | 100/Btl. | 200 |
| Tropicana Juice | 3 Btl. | 150/Btl. | 450 |
| Flax Seed | 5 Pck | 100/Pck | 500 |

To record the POS invoice in Tally.ERP 9,

**Step 1:** Creation of POS voucher type

1. Go to **Gateway of Tally > Accounts Info. > Voucher Type > Create**
2. Create the voucher shown in the figure 13.6:

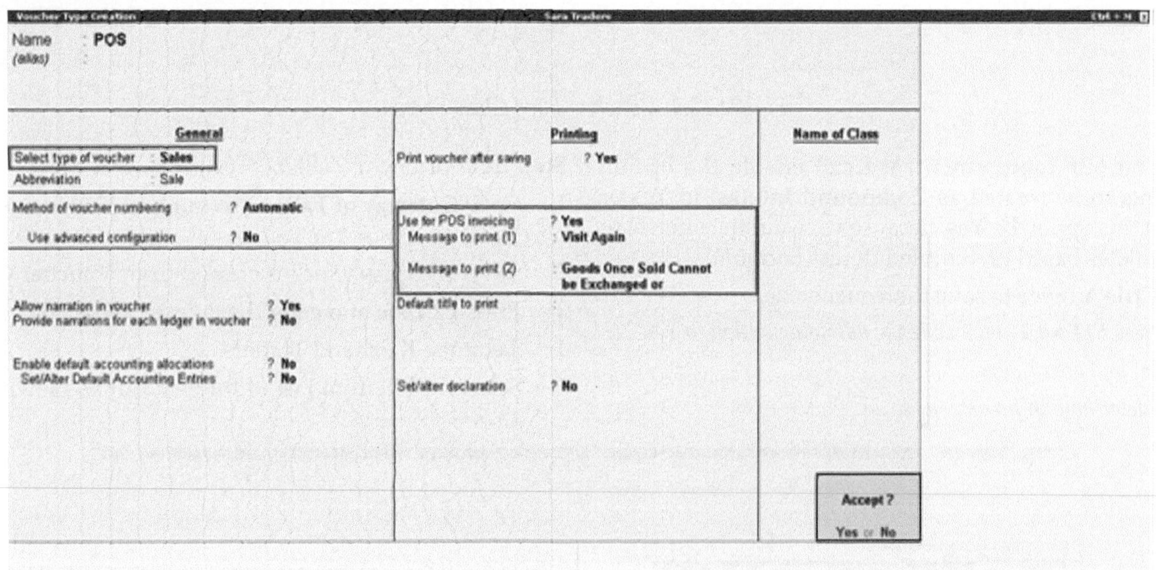


*Figure 13.6: Voucher Type Creation Screen-POS*

3. Make sure the option **Use for POS invoicing** is set to **Yes**
4. Press **Ctrl+A** to accept the voucher type.

**Step 2:** Record the transaction in POS voucher.

1. Go to **Gateway of Tally > Accounting Vouchers > Press F8:Sales**
2. Select the **Voucher Type** as **POS**
3. Fill in the details as shown in the figure 13.7:
4. Accept the screen

**Note:**
- In the POS invoice screen, we can observe that cash tendered is ₹2,000 and in Tally the balance amount to be paid to the customer is calculated automatically.
- We can also take the print of POS invoice

Similarly, we can record the POS invoice when multiple modes of payments are involved like debit card, sudexo, gift voucher etc.

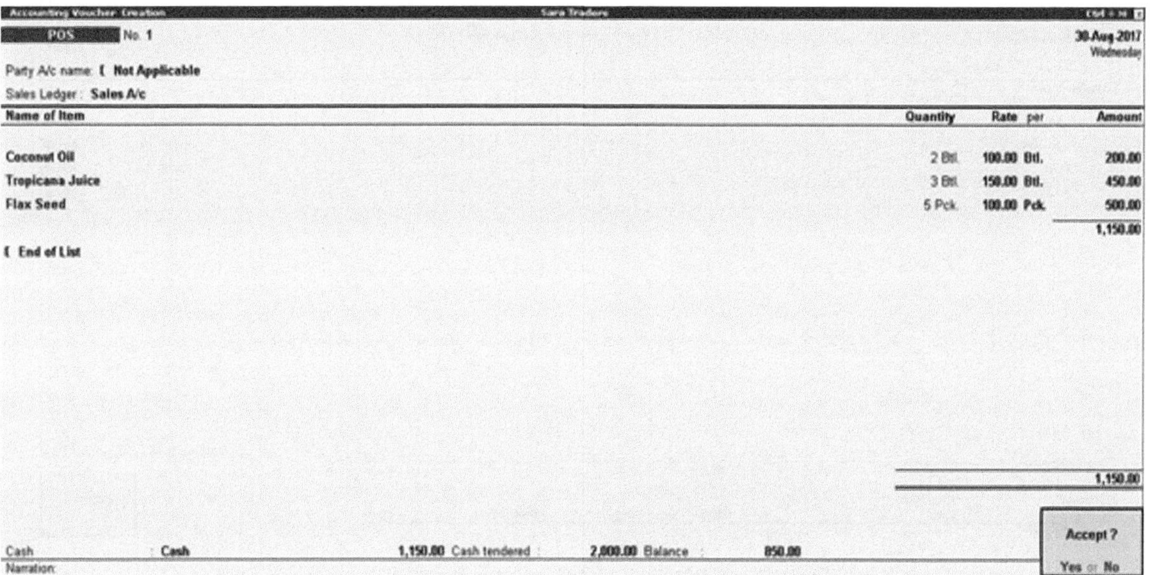


Figure 13.7: POS Invoice Screen

To record the multiple modes of payments details in POS,

**Step 1:** Create the POS voucher Class

1. Go to **Gateway of Tally > Accounts Info. > Voucher Types > Alter**
2. Fill in the details in **Voucher Type Class** as shown in figure 13.8:
3. Press **Ctrl+A** twice to accept the voucher type

**Step 2:** Record POS Invoice with Multiple Modes of Payments in Tally.ERP 9

1. Go to **Gateway of Tally > Accounting Vouchers > Press F8:Sales**

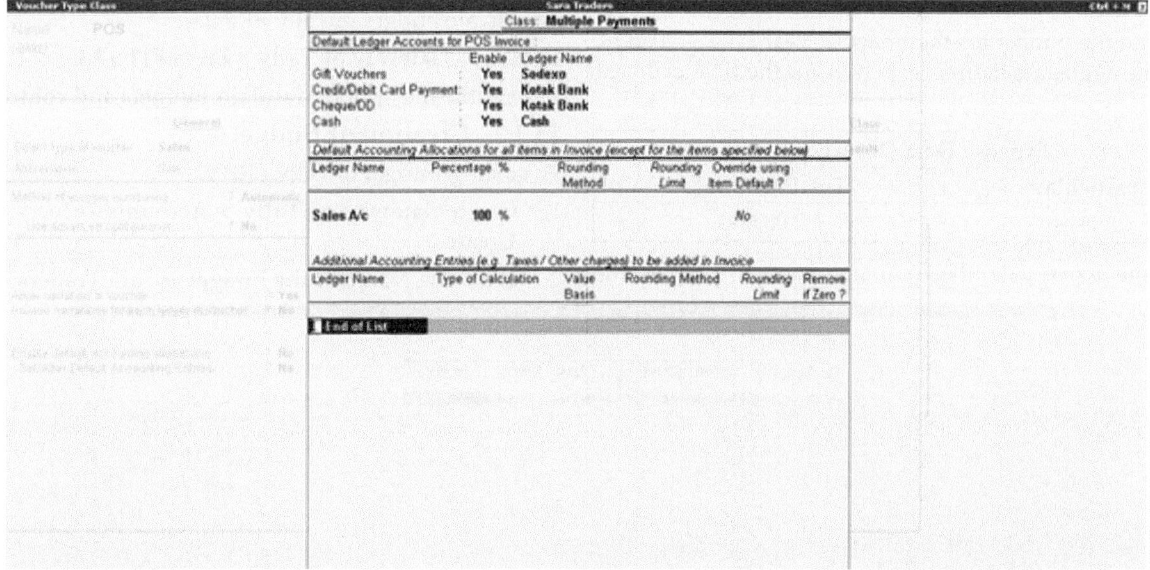


Figure 13.8: Voucher Type Class Screen - POS

2. Select **Voucher Type** as Sales and select the created voucher class
3. Fill in the details as shown in the figure 13.9:
4. Accept the voucher

Once after recording the POS transaction, the details will reflect in POS register, to view go to **Gateway of Tally > Display > Account Books > Ledger > POS Register**

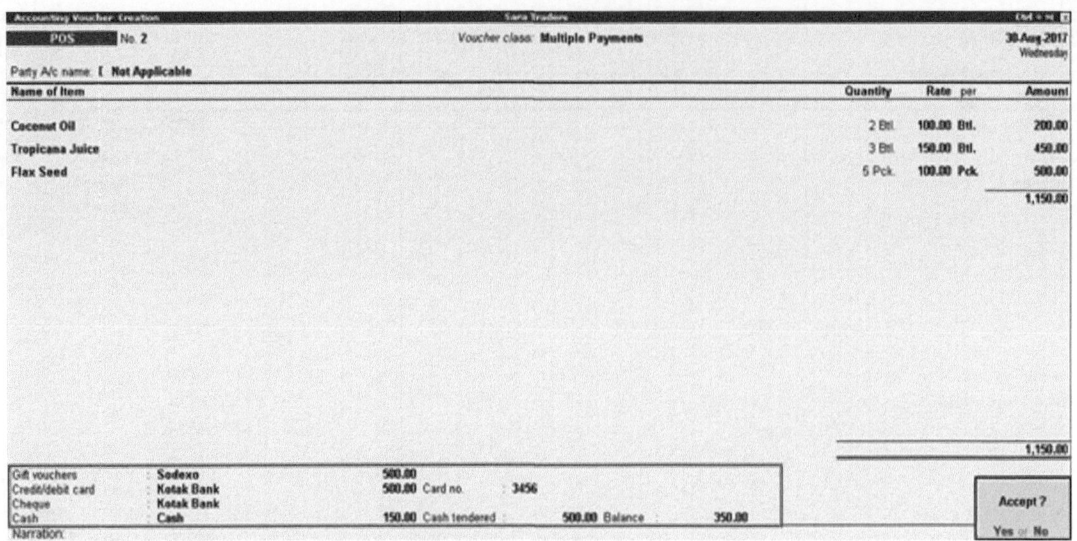


*Figure 13.9: POS with Multiple Modes of Payments*

## 13.3 BUDGET

A budget is a plan prepared for the flow of funds in an organisation. It contains financial projections, and helps to refine goals and use funds efficiently. It provides accurate information for evaluation of financial activities, aids in decision making and provides a reference for planning.

Tally.ERP 9 allows you to create multiple budgets and also maintain budgets for specific purposes, e.g. for the Bank, for the Head Office, Marketing Budget, Finance Budget etc.

Let us create the budget for the financial year 2017 – 2018 by referring the aggregate indirect expenses for the financial year 2016-2017.

| Expense Data (2016-17) | |
|---|---|
| **Particulars** | **Total Amount** |
| Indirect Expenses | ₹ 2,00,000 |

Based on the above data, the company wants to prepare the **budget** for the financial year **2017-18** to analyse the **expenses to ensure that capital is not wasted.**

**Prepare the following budget for the financial year (2017-18)**

| Sara Traders Annual Budget (2017-18) | |
|---|---|
| **Particulars** | **Total Amount** |
| Indirect Expenses | ₹ 2,50,000 |

### 13.3.1 Activation of Budget in Tally.ERP 9

To activate budget in Tally.ERP 9,

1. Go to **Gateway of Tally > Press F11 > F1**
2. Enable the option **Maintain budgets and controls** to **Yes**

### 13.3.2 Creation of Budget

To create a budget in Tally.ERP 9,

1. Go to **Gateway of Tally > Accounts Info. > Budgets > Create**
2. Enter the **Name of the budget** as Sara Traders (2017-18)

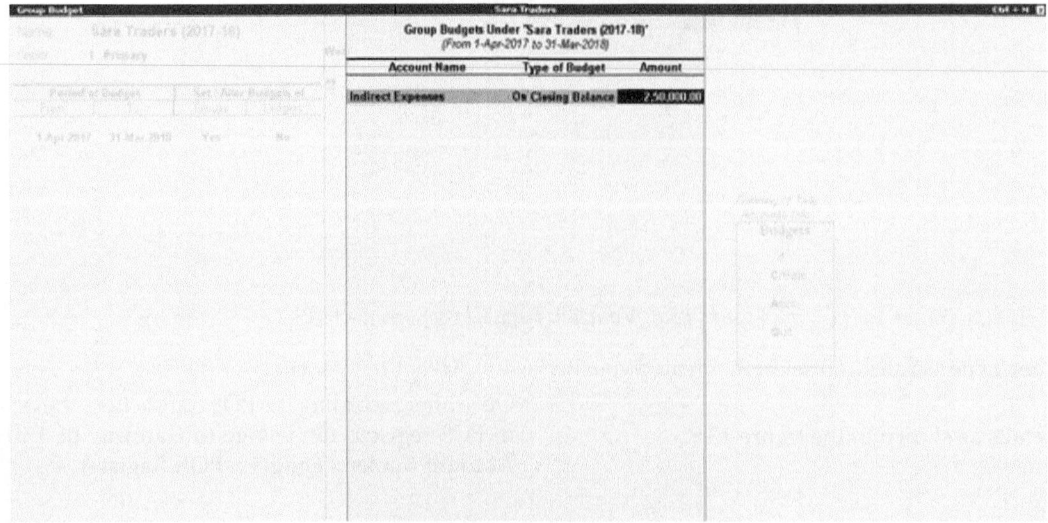


*Figure 13.10: Group Budget Creation Screen*

3. In the field **Under**, select **Primary** from the **List of Budgets** displayed
4. Specify the period of the budget from 01-04-2017 to 31-03-2018 (The period could be a Month, a Year or any required period starting from one date to another)
5. To set **budgets for Groups**, set **Yes** under **Groups**, this will lead to the **Group Budgets** screen, enter the details as shown in figure 13.10:
6. Press **Ctrl+A** twice to accept the budget creation screen

Once after creating the budget, whenever we are recording the voucher with indirect expenses ledger, then the expense amount will get deducted from the set budget.

**Note:** Similarly, budgets can be set for a ledger by setting Ledgers to "Yes" in the Budget Creation screen.

Once after recording the transaction which involves expenses ledger. In Tally.ERP 9 **Budget Variance** reports can be checked from **Trial Balance** report and **Group Summary** report.

## 13.4 BILL OF MATERIALS (BOM)

A **Bill of Materials** is a list of constituent items along with quantity details that can be allotted for the manufacture of a certain product, by-product or likewise. This facilitates immediate reduction in stock of the item automatically. This process of listing the items that make up another item is made possible in Tally by enabling the Bill of Materials facility.

**Bill of Materials (BoM)** is created only for those items that are being assembled in-house or manufactured. Therefore, you need to specify a BoM at the time of creating a Stock Item or while altering the stock item. For trading items it is not required to create a BoM.

TK Manufacturers are involved in assembling of Computer and the following is the list of stock items required to manufacture 1 unit of computer.

| **List of stock items required to manufacture Computer** | |
|---|---|
| **Name of stock item** | **Quantity required (to manufacture one unit of Computer)** |
| Display | 1 Nos |
| Keyboard | 1 Nos |
| Mouse | 1 Nos |
| CPU | 1 Nos |
| Battery | 1 Nos |

### *Activity:*

- *Create the company TK Manufacturers.*
- *Create the stock items displayed in the above list under Component stock group*

### 13.4.1 Defining BoM in Finished Goods

Once after creating the stock items (components), next step is to define the BoM for finished goods (Computer).

To define BoM in Finished goods,

1. From Stock Item Creation screen, press **F12: Configure** and set the option **Enable component list details (Bill of Materials)** to **Yes** and save the configuration screen.
2. Set the option **Set components** to **Yes**
3. Enter the details as shown in the figure 13.11:

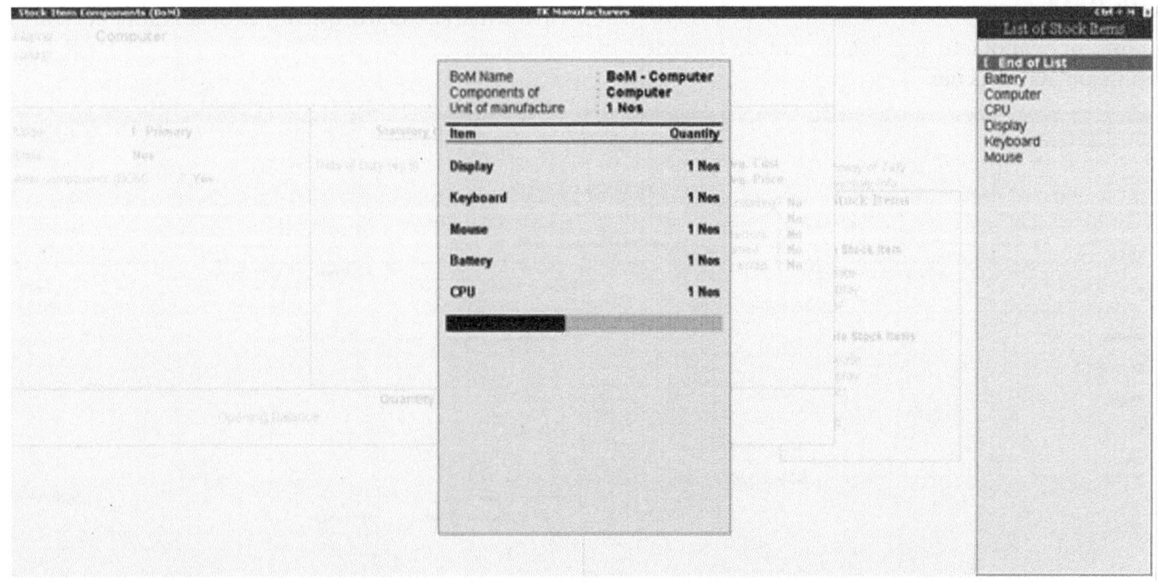


*Figure 13.11: Stock Item Components (BoM) Screen*

4. Press **Ctrl+A** twice to save the stock item

**Note:** We need to define the BoM, only for the finished goods.

### 13.4.2 Create the Manufacturing Journal Voucher

Manufacturing Journal is not a default Voucher Type in Tally.ERP 9. A new voucher type has to be created for this.

To create Manufacturing journal voucher,

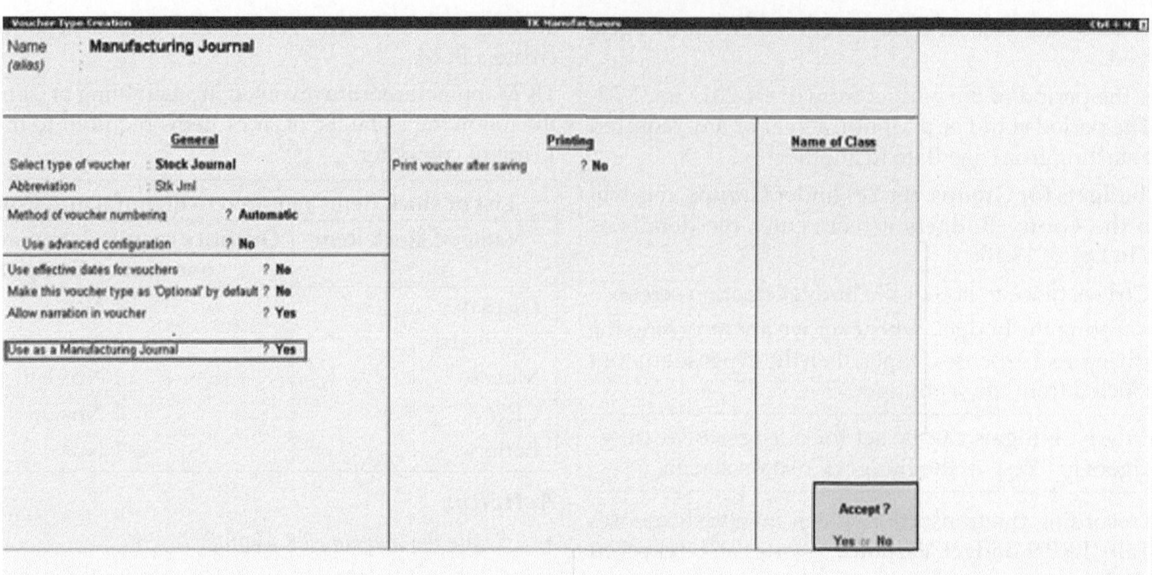


*Figure 13.12: Manufacturing Journal Voucher*

1. Go to **Gateway of Tally > Accounts Info > Voucher Type > Create**
2. Create the Manufacturing Journal Voucher by following the figure 13.12:
3. Make sure to enable the option **Use as a Manufacturing Journal**.
4. Accept the screen.

### 13.4.3 Recording Manufacturing Journal Voucher with BoM

The assembling or manufacturing details can be recorded in manufacturing journal voucher.

On 01-07-2018, TK Manufacturers, manufactured 100 Nos. of Computers.

To record Manufacturing Journal Voucher.

1. Go to **Gateway of Tally > Inventory Info. > Press Alt+F7**
2. Select **Manufacturing Journal** as Voucher Type
3. Enter the details as shown in the figure 13.13:
4. Press **Ctrl+A** to accept

Once after defining the Quantity as 100 in the above figure 13.13 (In the marked field), quantities of components will get captured automatically.

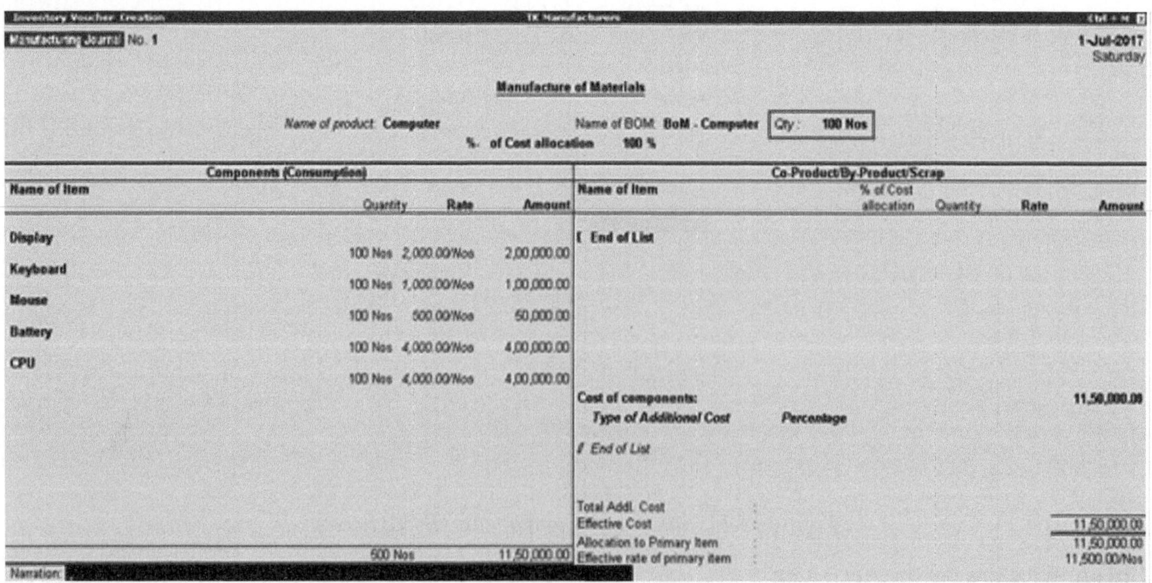


*Figure 13.13: Manufacturing Journal Voucher*

## 13.5 MEMORANDUM VOUCHER

Memorandum is a separate voucher type which is a non-accounting voucher. The entries made using it will not affect Company's Books of Accounts. Tally.ERP 9 posts entries recorded using Memorandum Vouchers in a separate Memo Register. You can alter and convert a Memo voucher into a regular voucher type when you decide to record an entry in your books. However, if you wish to include any entries temporarily for reporting purposes, then you can do so by creating scenarios in Tally.ERP 9.

To activate Memorandum Voucher in Tally.ERP 9.

1. Go to Gateway of Tally > Press F11 > F1
2. Activate the option **Use reversing journals and optional vouchers** to **Yes**

To record Memorandum Voucher in Tally.ERP 9

1. Go to **Gateway of Tally > Accounting Voucher >** Press **Ctrl+F10: Memos,** in this voucher we can record any transaction, but the same will not impact the books of account.
2. Once after recording if required the memo voucher can be converted to required accounting voucher.

## 13.6 REVERSING JOURNAL

A Reversing Journal is a separate voucher similar to a Journal, it is used to record an adjustment entry, but unlike a Journal it reverses its effect in the reports after the specified date.

By default, Reversing Journal entries don't affect the Books of Accounts. They are non-accounting vouchers. Tally. ERP 9 does not post these entries into ledgers. It stores them in a separate register called Reversing Journal Register.

For example, making a provision for depreciation. Depreciation is usually provided at the end of the year, however for monthly reporting, including it would give a more accurate status.

To activate Reversing Journal in Tally.ERP 9.

1. Go to Gateway of Tally > Press F11 > F1
2. Activate the option **Use reversing journals and optional vouchers** to **Yes**

To record Reversing Journal in Tally.ERP 9

1. Go to **Gateway of Tally > Accounting Voucher >** Press **F10: Reversing journal.**
2. In this journal we can define the Applicable Upto date and the transaction will impact the report till the date defined in **Applicable Upto** field.

## 13.7 TAX COLLECTED AT SOURCE (TCS)

Tax Collected at Source (TCS) is tax collected from the source (transaction) by the seller (collector) from the buyer (collectee/ payee), for goods traded u/s 206C (1) of the Income Tax Act, 1961. It is collected when accrued or when paid, whichever occurs earlier. It is prescribed for any business or trade dealing with alcoholic drinks, forest produce, scrap, etc. It also includes lease, license or contract related to parking lots, toll plaza, mines and quarry, etc., as defined in Section 206C of the Income Tax Act, 1961.

**Scenario:** PK Timber Traders deals with timber that is obtained from forest lease. This is subject to TCS 2.5%. Let us create a company in Tally.ERP 9 to maintain the books of account

### 13.7.1 Activation of TCS in Tally.ERP 9

Tally.ERP 9's simple yet powerful TCS feature enables you to record transactions related to Tax Collection at Source with ease. It also helps you generate the necessary reports and returns such as Form 27D, e-TCS Forms (Form 27E, Form 27EQ) and Form 27B.

***Activity:*** *Create the following Company*

*Company Name : PK Timber*

*Financial Year – 2017-18*

To Activate,

1. Go to **Gateway of Tally > Press F11 > F3**
2. Set the option **Enable Tax Collected at Source (TCS)** to **Yes**
3. **Set/alter TCS details** to **Yes**
4. Enter the necessary details in Company TCS as shown in figure 13.14:

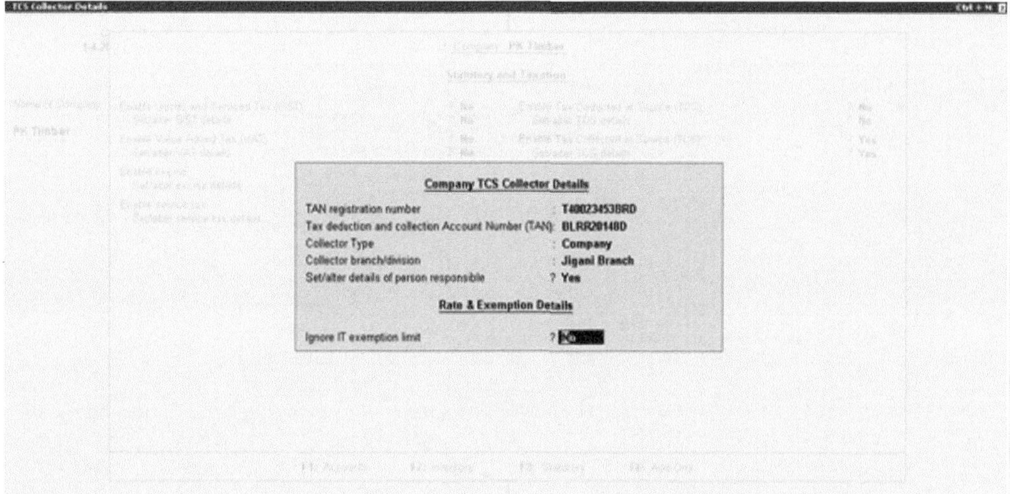


*Figure 13.14: TCS Collector Details Screen*

5. Press **Ctrl+A** twice to accept the Statutory and Taxation screen

On 1-7-2017, PK Timbers, sold 2000 Metric ton (MT) at ₹ 9000/ MT of timber to Mohan Traders.

To record the above transaction follow the steps given below:

**Step 1:** Creation OF TCS Nature of Goods

1. Go to **Gateway of Tally > Accounts Info. > Statutory Info. > TCS Nature of Goods > Create**
2. Enter the details as shown in figure 13.15:

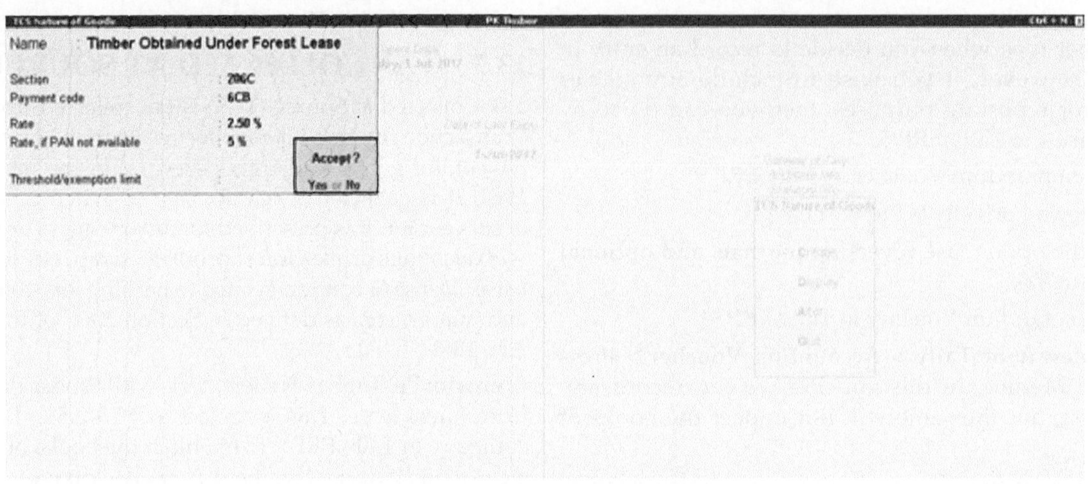


*Figure 13.15: TCS Nature of Goods*

**Note:** If PAN is not available, then the rate will be higher of double the TCS rate or 5%.

3. Accept the screen

**Step 2:** Creation of Accounting Masters

***Activity:*** *Create the following ledgers*

| *Name of Ledger* | *Under* | *Configuration* |
|---|---|---|
| *Mohan Traders* | *Sundry Debtors* | • *Is TCS Applicable to Yes*<br>• *Buyer/Lessee type as Company-Resident*<br>• *PAN/IT No. as ASDFG1234D* |
| *Sales A/c* | *Sales Accounts* | • *Is TCS Applicable to Yes*<br>• *Nature of Goods – Select Timber Obtained Under Forest Lease* |
| *TCS Duty* | *Duties and Taxes* | • *Type of duty/tax as TCS*<br>• *Nature of goods/contract/ license/lease as Timber Obtained Under Forest Lease* |

**Step 3:** Creation of Stock Item

1. Go to Gateway of Tally > Inventory Info > Create
2. Refer figure 13.16 and create the stock item

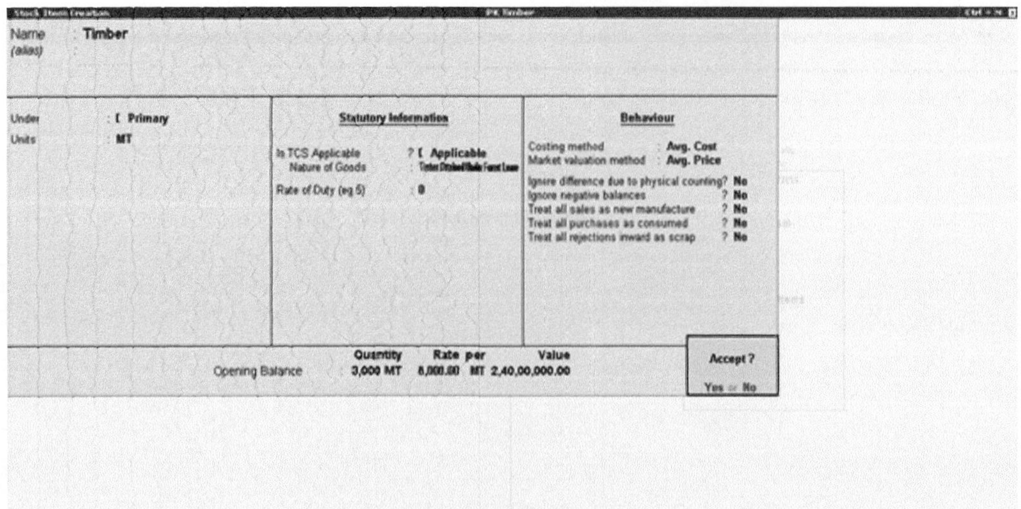


*Figure 13.16: Stock Item Creation Screen*

*Figure 13.17: Sales Voucher Creation*

3. Accept the screen

**Step 4:** Recording Sales Transaction with TCS.

1. Go to **Gateway of Tally > Accounting Vouchers > Create**
2. Enter the details as shown in the figure 13.17:
3. Accept the Screen

## 13.7.2 TCS Reports

TCS reports in Tally.ERP 9 are extensive. Statutory reports are integrated, making it convenient to print and file reports in government prescribed formats. Additionally, a wide range of reports such as reconciliation reports and display reports are available. These reports provide information at a glance and help in managing TCS issues with ease.

### *13.7.2.1Form 27 EQ*

As per the Income Tax Act, 1961, every corporate and government entity responsible for collection of tax at source should furnish TCS returns containing details of collectee(s) and challan details relating to deposit of tax with the Income Tax Department. Form 27EQ is the quarterly return statement for TCS. The due dates for filing returns are July 15th, October 15th, January 15th, and for the last quarter, April 30th.

The Form 27EQ report in Tally.ERP 9 assists you in generating accurate returns to be filed.

The report can be drilled down to the voucher entry level to display complete information of each transaction.

To generate the Form 27EQ,

1. Go to **Gateway of Tally > Display > Statutory Reports > TCS Reports > Form 27EQ**
2. Click **F1: Detailed**

The **Form 27EQ** report appears as shown in figure 13.18:

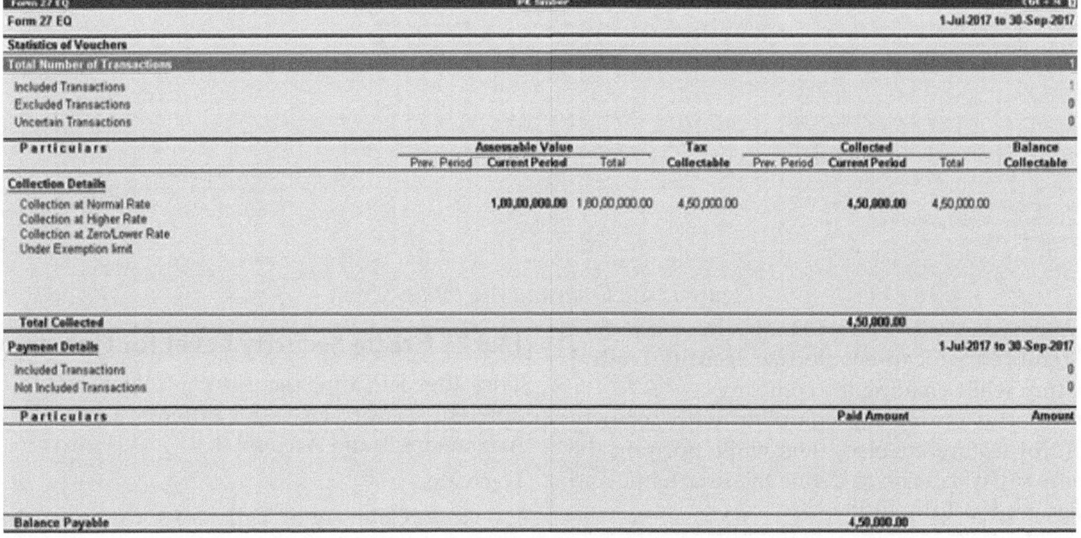


*Figure 13.18: Form 27EQ*

The above report will display the details of Included, excluded and uncertain transactions. It also displays the Collection Details with assessable value, tax collected and balance collectable. This report also displays the details of TCS Payment made to government.

From the above report we are getting the details of details of the Balance Payable, his is the amount of TCS tax which we need to pay to the government.

## 13.8 SECURITY CONTROL

Security Control is used to protect the data by providing the password and creating different user level rights to each account.

This is mainly used in multiple environment configuration. Generally, in multi user scenario, Tally data is accessed by multiple users wherein there are many activities done by each and every user. In such cases there will be chances of misuse of data, wrong entries and lack of knowledge which will render the data tampered. To avoid all these complications, security control helps to secure the data in high standards.

Security controls need to be defined based on the work profile of an employee. Typically, in an organisation the administrator will have the full access rights to the system, whereas the employees are given access based on their work profile demonstrating segregation of duties.

In Tally.ERP 9, by default, there are two levels of security - namely Owner and Data Entry.

**Owner:** The owner has full access rights which will enable him to work with all the features of Tally.ERP 9, except for Tally Audit and company alteration, which are reserved for the administrator. Based on pre-defined security levels the administrator can create other security levels and assign or restrict access based on the requirement.

**Data Entry:** Data Entry has restricted access but the administrator can assign or restrict the access based on the requirement.

**For Example:** PK Timbers appointed three accountants to maintain its books of accounts. Accountant 1 is authorised to record only purchase and sales transactions, Accountant 2 is authorised to record only payments and receipts transactions and Accountant 3 is authorised to check and generate the financial reports. This shows that all three accountants have different work profiles and it is not required to give the full control to these three accountants.

This shows the requirement to create the different user levels for these three accountants and authorise each accountant with their respective work profile.

### 13.8.1 Activation of Security Control

In order to keep the data secure and also to assign the rights based on the work profile of the company, we need to activate security control feature in Tally.ERP 9.

To activate,

1. Go to **Gateway of Tally > Press Alt+F3 > Alter**
2. Select the company in which security control needs to be activated.
3. Entre the details as shown in figure 13.19:
4. Accept the screen

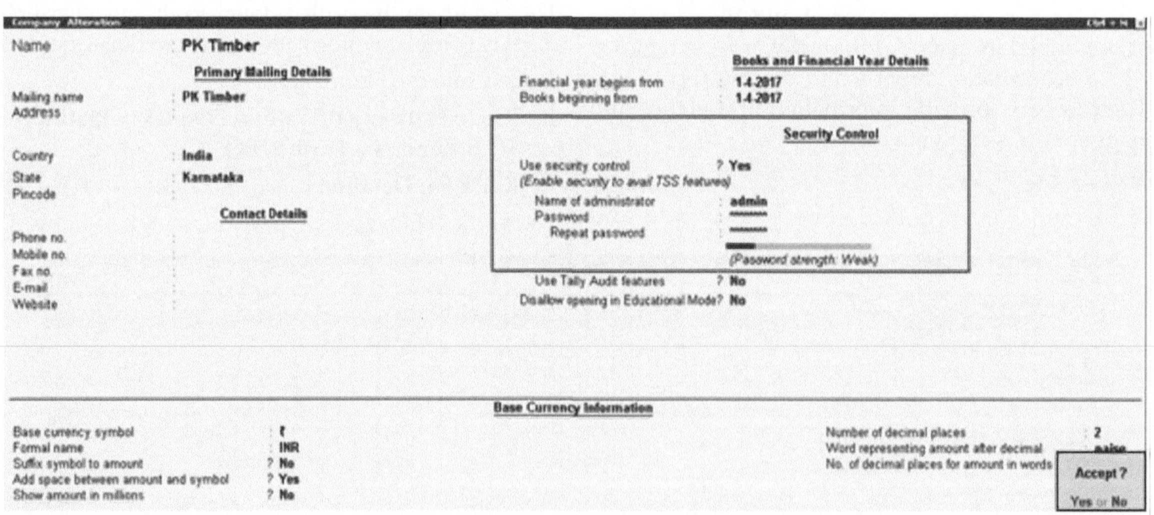


*Figure 13.19: Company Alteration Screen*

**Note:**
- If required we can enable Use security control feature while creating the company.
- Once after saving the company with security control feature enabled, then while opening the company it will ask to define the user name and password in Tally.ERP 9.

### 13.8.2 Create Security Level for Company

Once after activating security control feature, we can also create different security levels for different users like Accountant 1, Accountant 2, and Account 3.

To create,

1. Go to **Gateway of Tally > F3: Company Info > Security Control > Types of Security**

2. The **Security Levels** screen displays the **List of Security Levels**
3. Enter the details as shown in Figure 13.20:
4. Press **Ctrl+A** twice to save

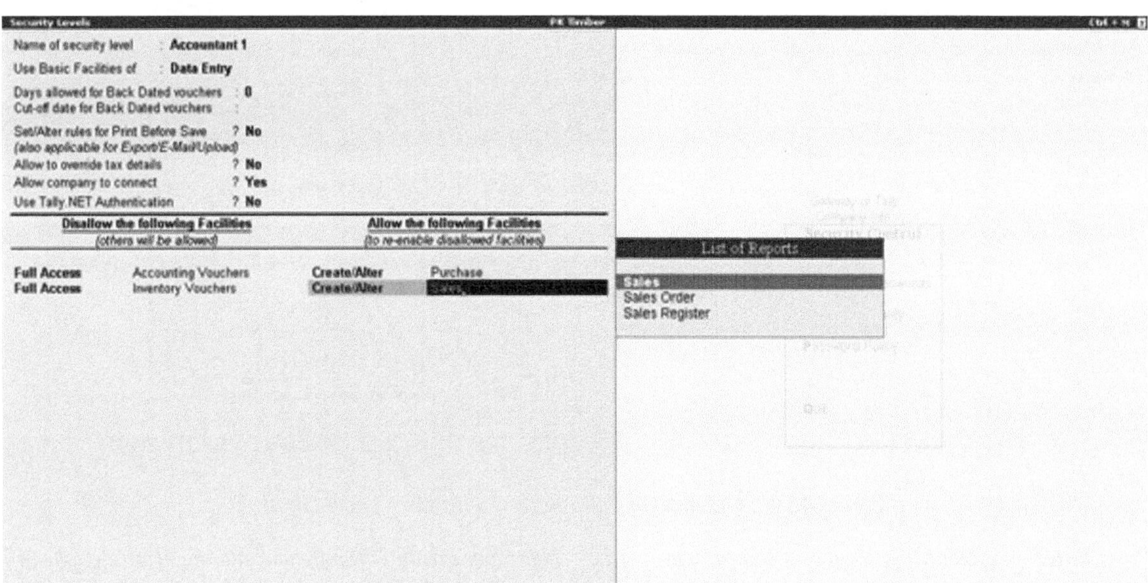

*Figure 13.20: Security Levels Screen*

***Activity:*** *Similarly create one more security level by name* ***Accountant 2*** *and use* ***Basic Facilities of Data Entry*** *selecting the following rights:*

1. Disallow the following facilities: Give **Full Access** to Inventory Vouchers.
2. Allow the following facilities: Give **Create/Alter** access to Payment and Receipt

### 13.8.3 Create Users and Passwords

1. Go to Gateway of Tally > F3: Company Info > Security Control > Select Users and Passwords
2. In **Security Level** field select the Accountant 1 from the **Security List**
3. Enter the details as shown in Figure 13.21

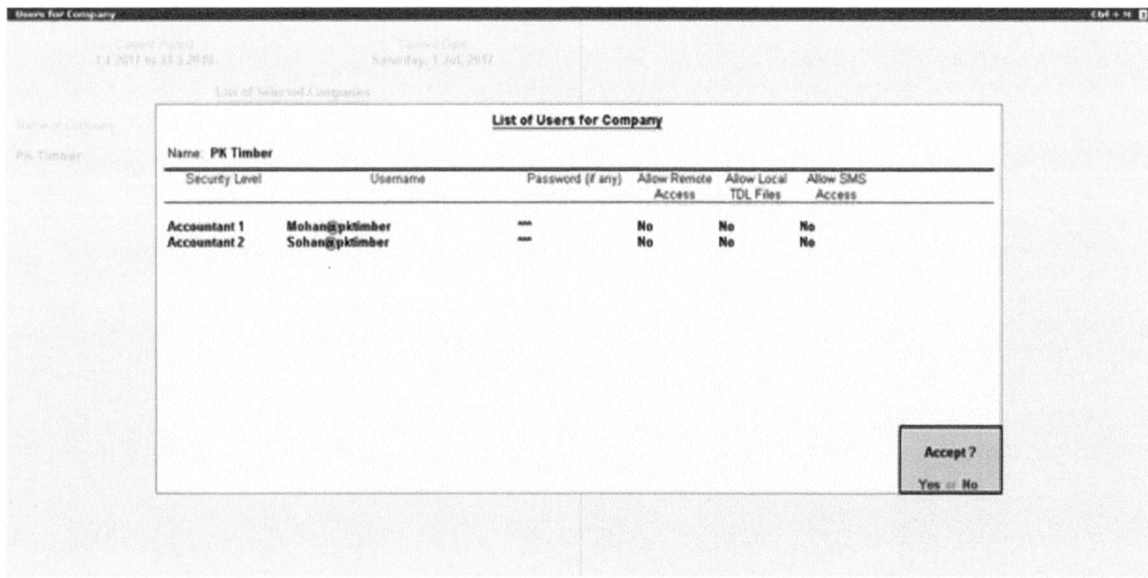

*Figure 13.21: User Creation Screen*

4. Accept the screen

Once after creating users, we can access the PK Timbers company with user level I.D and Password, to do so logout the company with admin rights. Then open the same company with user level I.D and password.

The **Gateway of Tally** screen with user level screen appears as shown in figure 13.22:

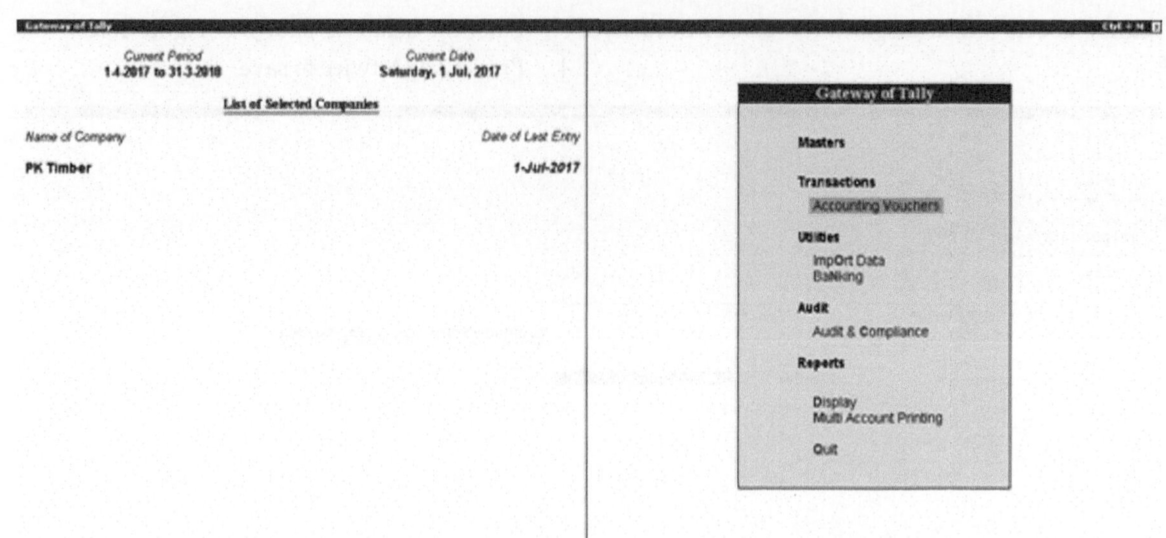


*Figure 13.22: Gateway of Tally Screen with User Level Login*

***Activity:*** *Press* ***Enter*** *on Accounting Vouchers screen, you will be able to record only the purchase and sales transactions in Tally.ERP 9.*

Chapter 14

# Tally.ERP Release 6.1 Features

## 14.1 UNIT QUANTITY CODE (UQC) FOR GST INVOICE

As per GST rule a tax invoice issued by a regular dealer should contain the unit quantity code details. UQC is a uniform measuring unit used by the department for measuring quantity in the returns filed. UQCs are used to maintain consistency and prevent variations in quantities in the returns filed by different businesses. This requires the businesses to measure the quantities of items using the UQC from the list given by the department

In this section we will learn to define the UQC while creating the unit of measure in Tally.ERP 9.

If the unit of measure are is not mapped with UQC, then the transactions recorded will not reflect in the return. Hence it is mandatory to define the UQC while creating the unit of measure or we can define the same from **Map UoM – UQC** option available in **GST Reports** menu.

To define UQC while creating the unit of measure in Tally.ERP 9

1. Go to **Gateway of Tally > Inventory Info. > Unit of Measure > Create**
2. Enter the **Symbol** as Nos.
3. Enter the **Formal name** as Numbers

   The **Unit Creation** screen appears as shown in the figure 14.1:

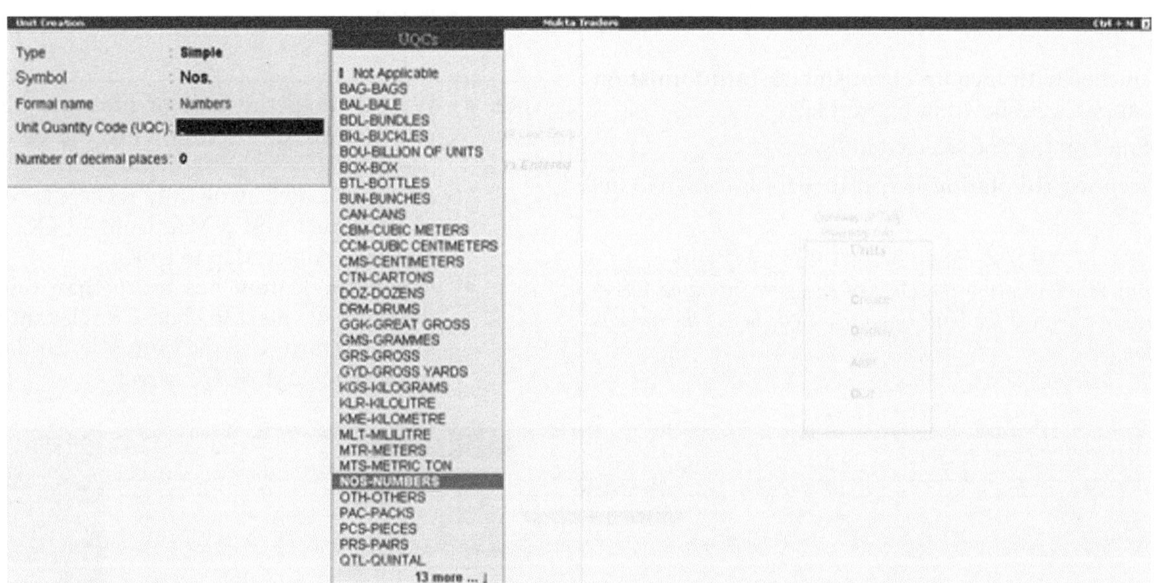


*Figure 14.1: Unit Creation Screen*

4. From the **Unit Creation** screen, select the relevant UQC from UQCs list.
5. Press **Enter** and accept the unit creation screen.
6. The same unit of measure can be selected while creating the stock item.

**Note:** If the UQCs are not mapped while creating the Unit of Measure, then the transactions recorded using these units of measure will not be relevant for GST return.

### *Activity:*

- *Similarly create the following unit of measure by name Pcs and do not define the Unit Quantity Code (UQC).*
- *Create the following*
  - o *Cups and select the Unit as Pcs.*
  - o *Computers and select the Units as Nos.*
- *Record the following Sales transactions:*

| Date | Particulars | | | |
|---|---|---|---|---|
| 31-07-2017 | Sold the following stock items to Mohan & Sons on Cash (GST Applicable) | | | |
| | Name of Item | Quantity/Nos. | Rate/Nos. | Amount |
| | Computer | 10 | 11,000 | 1,10,000 |
| 31-07-2017 | Sold the following stock items to Mohan & Sons on Cash (GST Applicable) | | | |
| | Name of Item | Quantity/Nos. | Rate/Nos. | Amount |
| | Cups | 100 | 2,000 | 2,00,000 |

Once after recording the transaction check the GSTR-1 report.

1. Go to **Gateway of Tally > Display > Statutory Reports > GST > GSTR–1.**
2. Press Enter on **Incomplete/Mismatch in information (to be resolved field).**

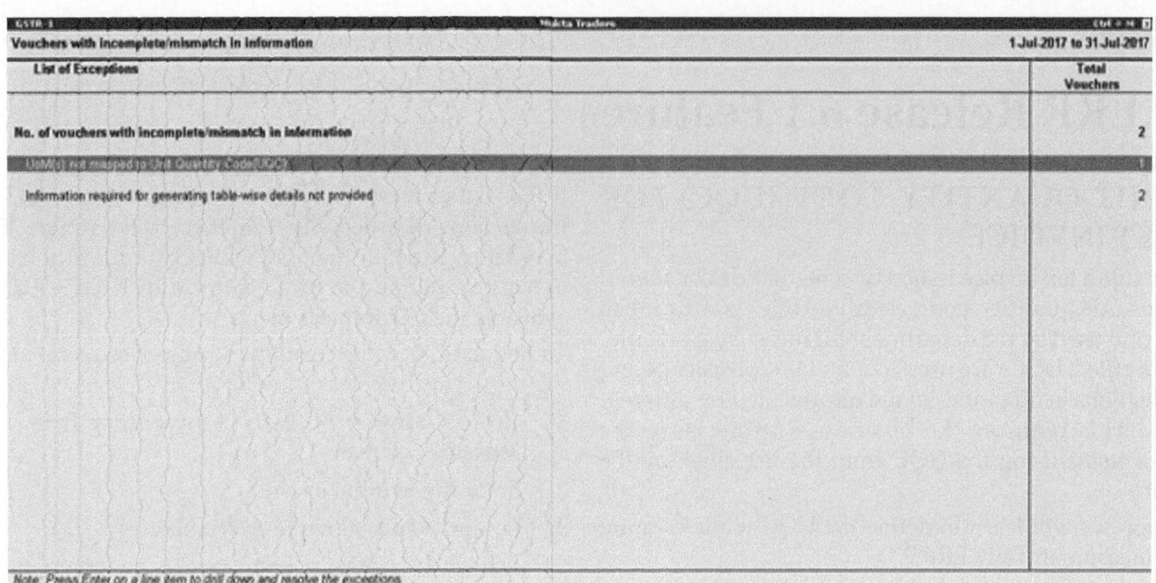


*Figure 14.2: Voucher with Incomplete/Mismatch in Information Screen*

The **Voucher with incomplete/mismatch in information** screen appears as shown in figure 14.2:

3. Press Enter on the line selected in figure 14.2.

   The **Exception Resolution** screen appears as shown in the figure 14.3:

4. Map the relevant UQC against the unit of measure.

***Observation:*** *While creating the Unit of Measure by name Pieces (Pcs) we have not defined the Unit Quantity Code hence the same is appearing here.*

**Note:**
- We can map the unit of measure against its relevant UQCs by following the below given procedure:
  - o Go to Gateway of Tally > Display > Statutory Reports > GST > Map UoM – UQC.
  - o Press Alt+S: Map to UQC.
- When stock item has more than one unit of measure, we need to choose a relevant to export in GST return. Use the button U: Update RUQC from Map UoM – UQC screen

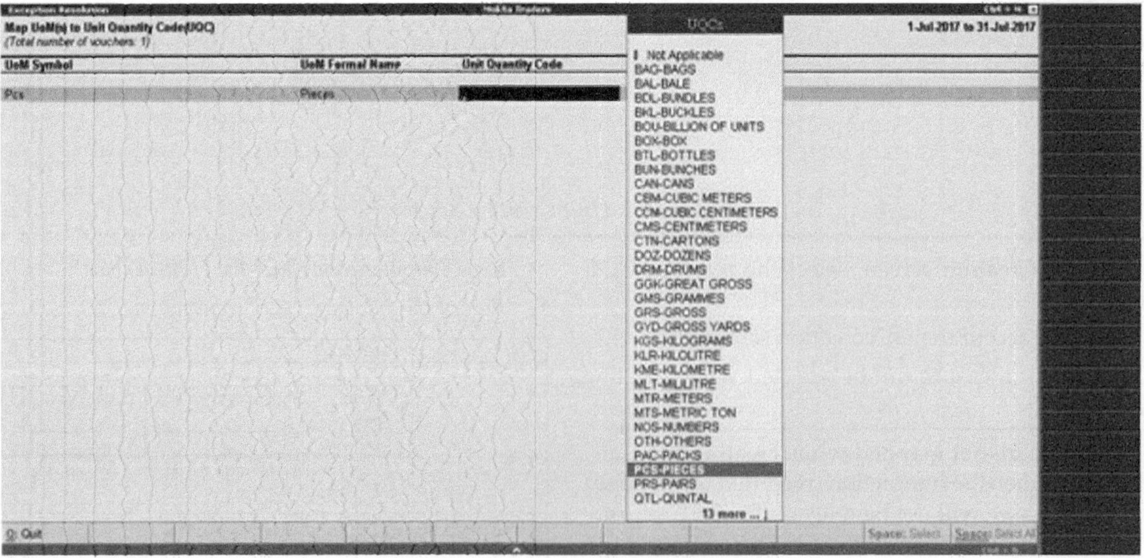


*Figure 14.3: Exception Resolution Screen*

## 14.2 DEFINING MRP DETAILS

In Tally.ERP 9 we can define the MRP details while creating the stock item. To do so follow the steps given below:

1. Go to Gateway of Tally > Inventory Info. > Stock Items > Create.
2. Press **F12: Configure** and enable the option **"Allow MRP/**

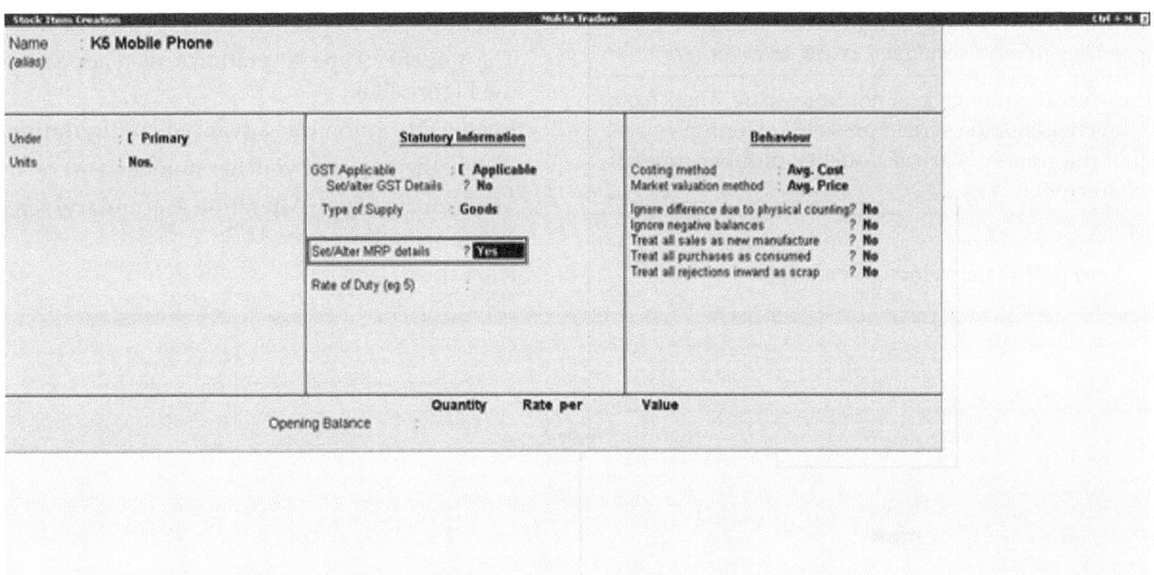


*Figure 14.4: Stock Item Creation with MRP details*

**Marginal for stock items"** to **Yes,** to get the option **Set/ Alter MRP details** in stock item creation screen.

The **Stock Item Creation** screen with MRP details appears as shown in the figure 14.4:

3. Enable the option **Set/Alter MRP details** to **Yes** to define the MRP details.
4. Once after defining the MRP details the transaction can be recoded in Tally.ERP 9.

## 14.3 DEFINING 16 CHARACTERS INVOICE NUMBER IN TALLY.ERP 9.

As per GST rule invoice numbering should be within 16 digit. If it is more than 16 digit then the transaction will not be relevant for the return. In Tally.ERP 9, we can predefine the 16 digit in the sales voucher type and also we will get a warning message if the invoice number exceeds 16 digit.

Let us check what happens when we try to give invoice number more than 16 digit in Tally.ERP 9.

1. Create a Tax Invoice Voucher Type. While creating in **Select Type of Voucher field** select as **Sales.**
2. In **Method of voucher numbering** select as **Manual** and save the Voucher Creation screen.
3. Record the Sales Voucher and in Invoice number field enter as **123456789112345678,** you will get the following **Warning** message because the voucher number exceeds 16 character.

The **Sales Voucher Creation** screen with warning message appears as shown in the figure 14.5:

*Figure 14.5: Sales Voucher Creation Screen with Warning Message*

***Observation:** We are getting the warning message because as per the GST rule the voucher number should not exceed 16 characters.*

---

**Note:** If the warning message is not appearing, then from the voucher creation screen press F12: Configure and enable the option Warn if voucher number exceeds 16 characters to Yes

---

In Tally.ERP 9, we can predefine the 16 characters voucher number. To do so follow the below given steps:

1. Alter the Tax Invoice Voucher.

   The **Voucher Type Alteration** screen appears as shown in the Figure 14.6:

2. Enable the option **Use advanced configuration** to **Yes**
3. Define the required voucher number as shown below:

   The **Voucher Type Alteration (Secondary)** screen appears as shown in the figure 14.7:

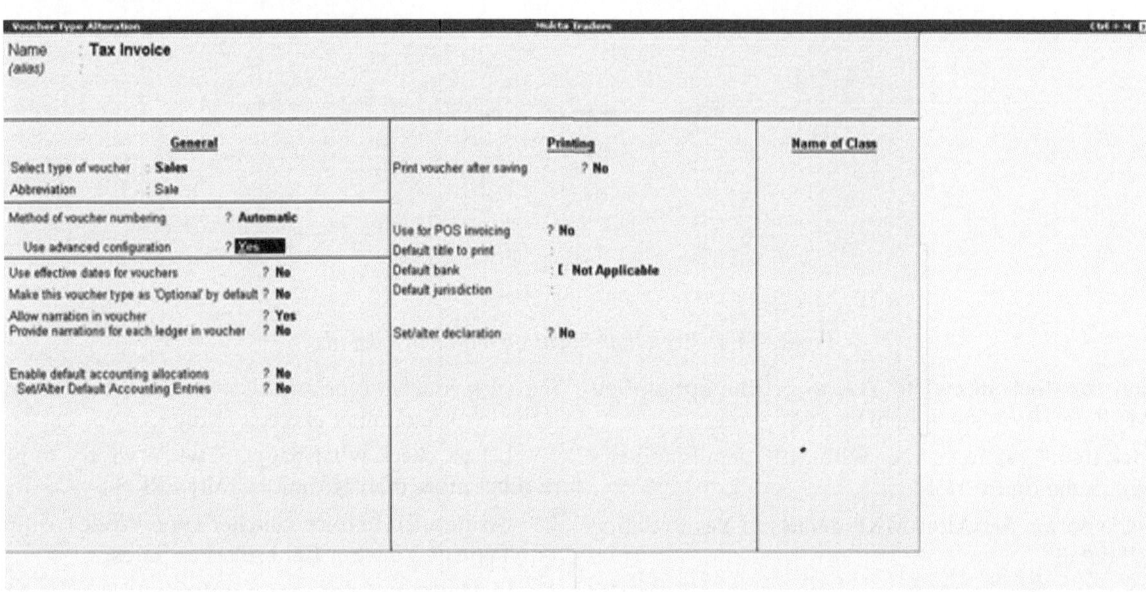


*Figure 14.6: Voucher Type Alteration Screen*

Voucher Type Alteration (Secondary) — Mukta Traders

Starting Number ? 1
Width of Numerical Part 5
Prefill with zero ? Yes

| Restart Numbering | | | Prefix Details | | Suffix Details | |
|---|---|---|---|---|---|---|
| Applicable From | Starting Number | Particulars | Applicable From | Particulars | Applicable From | Particulars |
| 1-Jul-2017 | 1 | Yearly | 1-Jul-2017 | MT | 1-Jul-2017 | 12345678 |

*Figure 14.7: Voucher Type Alteration (Secondary)*

4. Once after defining the voucher number details accept the screen.
5. Press **Ctrl+A** to save the voucher.
6. While recording the sales voucher in Tally.ERP 9, the invoice number will be captured automatically in Tally ERP 9:

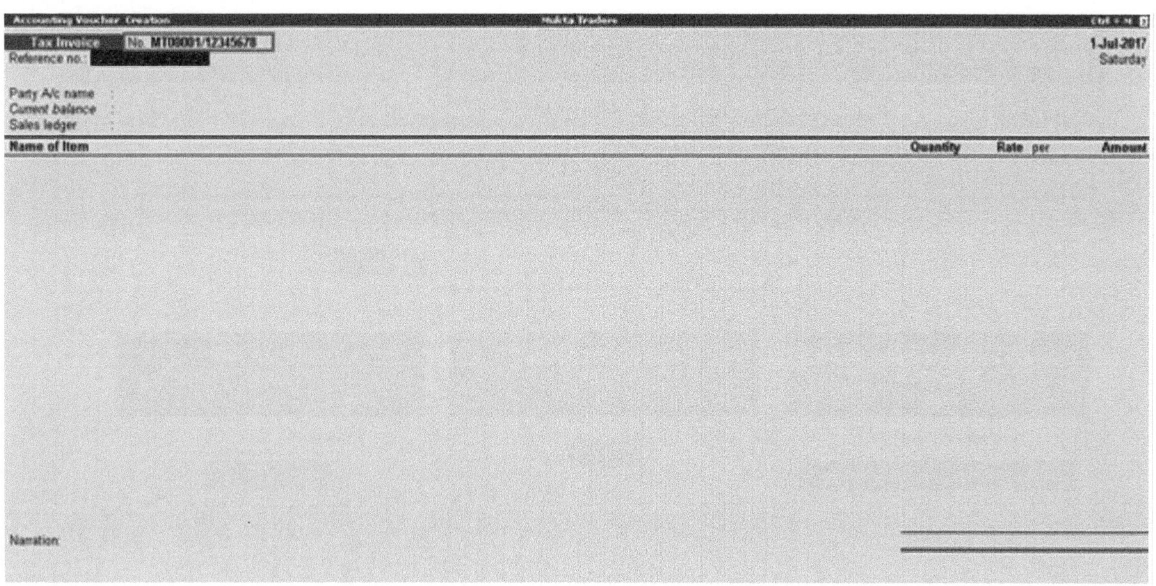


*Figure 14.8: Sales Voucher Creation Screen*

The **Sales Voucher Creation** screen appears as shown in the figure 14.8:

This time it was not required to define the invoice number manually in Tally.ERP 9.

## 14.4 VOUCHERS

### 14.4.1 Filing GSTR-3B and making Payments

**To file GSTR-3B returns**

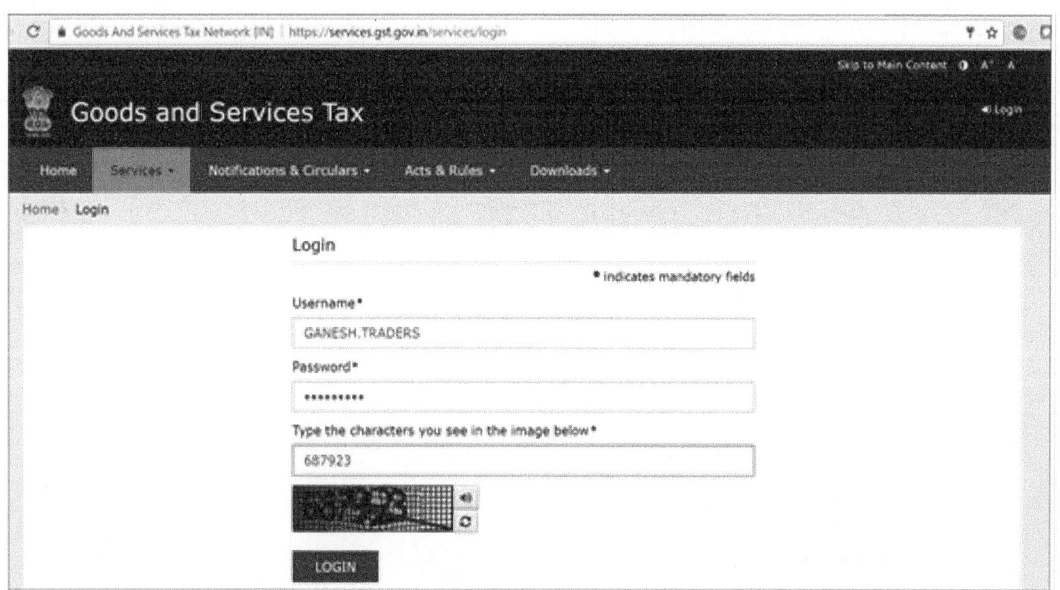


*Figure 14.9: GST Portal*

1. Log in to the GST Portal.
2. Go to **Services** > **Returns** > **Returns Dashboard**.
3. Select the **Return Filing Period**, and click **Search**. Now **GSTR1, GSTR2A**, and **GSTR-3B** will appear.
4. Under **Monthly Return GSTR-3B**, click **Prepare Online**.
5. Select the required section.
6. Enter the necessary details. We can either copy GSTR-3B details generated from Tally.ERP 9 in the MS Word format, or we can manually fill the details by referring to the printout.

**Note:** The procedure to generate GSTR-3B is provided in the section by name Filing Returns.

7. Click **Confirm**.

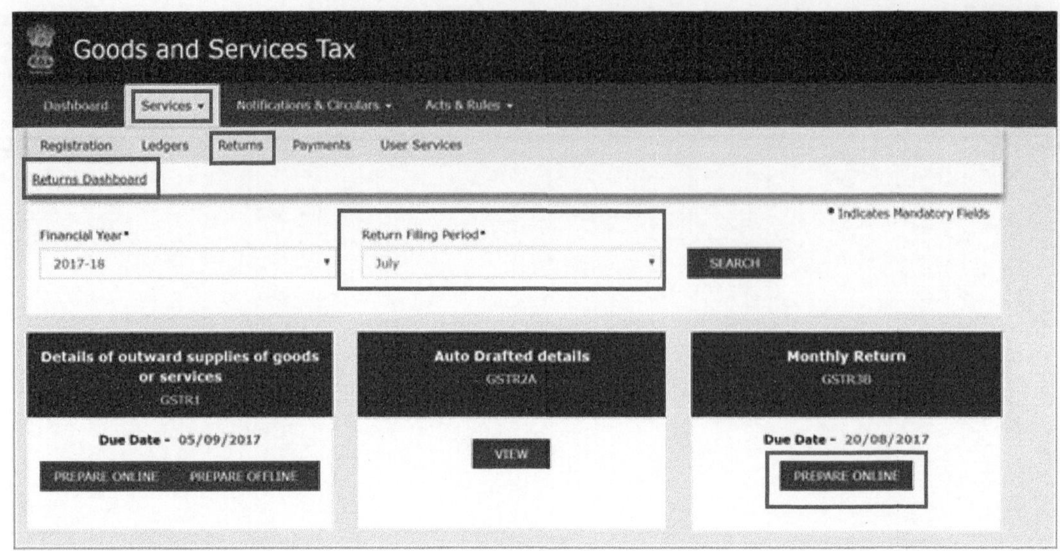


*Figure 14.10: Returns Dashboard*

*Figure 14.11: Section selection*

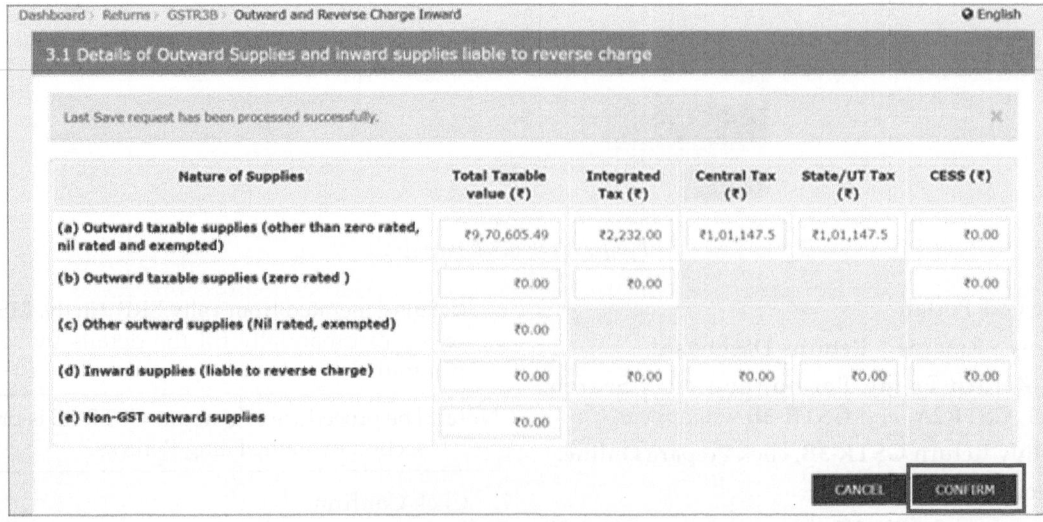


*Figure 14.12: Outward and Reverse Charge Inward*

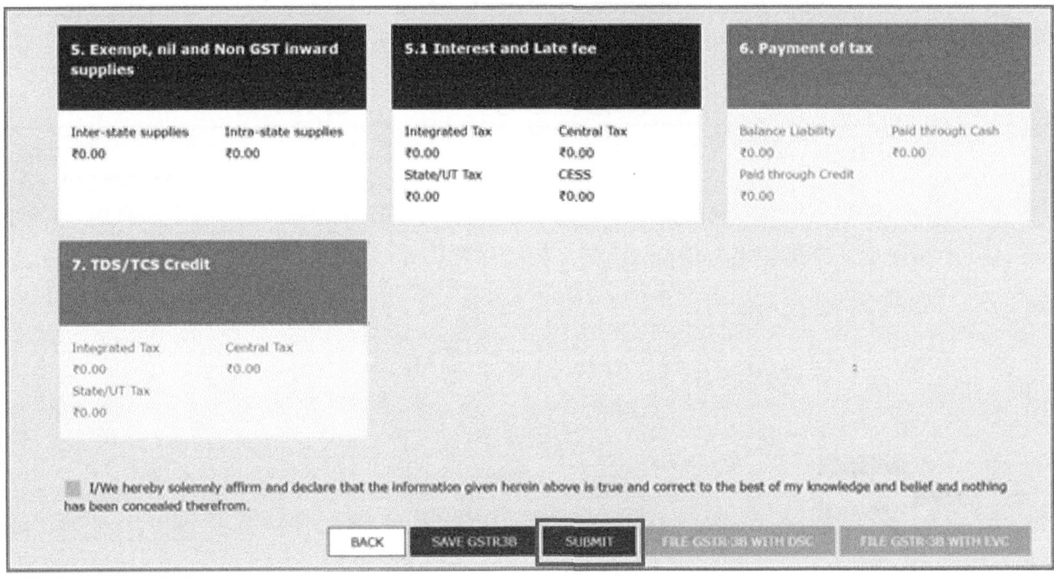


*Figure 14.13 Submit Screen*

**Note:** The above tax values are used only for illustration purpose.

8. Verify the details, and click **Submit**. To file GSTR-3B returns, we have to make payments towards GSTR-3B.

**Note:** Once we click **the Submit** button, GSTR-3B cannot be revised.

After successfully filing GSTR-3B, you can easily make payments to GST by creating a challan.

**To make payments towards GSTR-3B**

1. Log in to the GST portal.
2. Go to **Services** > **Payments** > **Create Challan**.
3. Under **Tax Liability**, enter the required values.
4. Under **Payment Modes**, select the required method of payment. If you have chosen NEFT/RTGS as the mode of payment, you also have to select your preferred **Remitting Bank**.
5. Click **Generate Challan**
6. The **Beneficiary Details** appear according to the **Remitting Bank** selected.
7. Click **DOWNLOAD** to generate the challan. You can make the payment from your bank using this challan.

## 14.5 E-SUGAM NUMBER FOR KARNATAKA UNDER GST

The Commercial Taxes Department of Karnataka has introduced e-Sugam to upload the transportation details of notified goods before the movement of such goods. Under GST e-Sugam feature is provided for Karnataka. When you obtain the e-Sugam number for a transaction, you can enter it in the invoice or in the **e-Sugam** report. The **e-Sugam** number can also be printed in the invoice.

***Illustration 1:*** *Recording Sales Invoice with e-sugam number*

| Date | Particulars | | | |
|---|---|---|---|---|
| 31-07-2017 | **Voucher: Sales** | | | |
| | Sold the following goods to Tara Traders, Karnataka with Reference no.:8/MT, with Central Tax - 9% and State Tax – 9% | | | |
| | **Name of Item** | **Quantity/Nos.** | **Rate/Nos.** | **Amount** |
| | Computer | 50 | 11,000 | 5,50,000 |

To record sales invoice with e-sugam number, follow the steps given below:

1. Go to **Gateway of Tally** > **Accounting Vouchers** > **F8: Sales.**
2. Enter the details as shown in the figure 14.14.

The Sales Invoice screen appears as shown in figure 14.14:

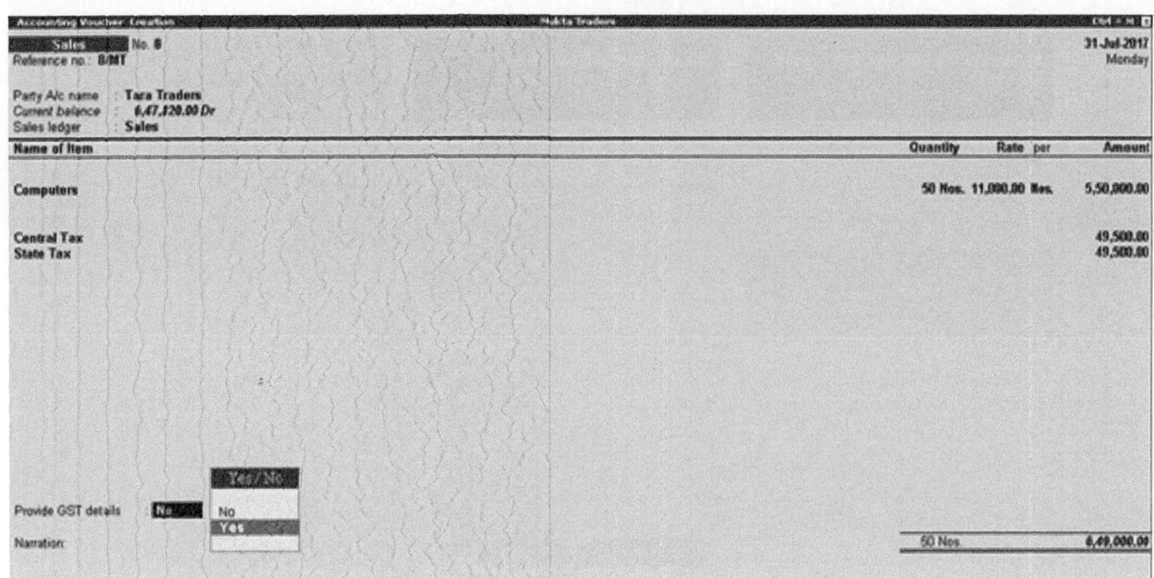


*Figure 14.14: Sales Voucher Creation Screen*

**Note:** All the GST Sales Invoice screen used in TallyACE/PRO/GURU book will have the option **Provide GST details.**

3. Set the option **Provide GST details** to **Yes** and enter the transport details as shown in figure 14.15:

   The **Statutory Details** screen appears as shown in figure 14.15:

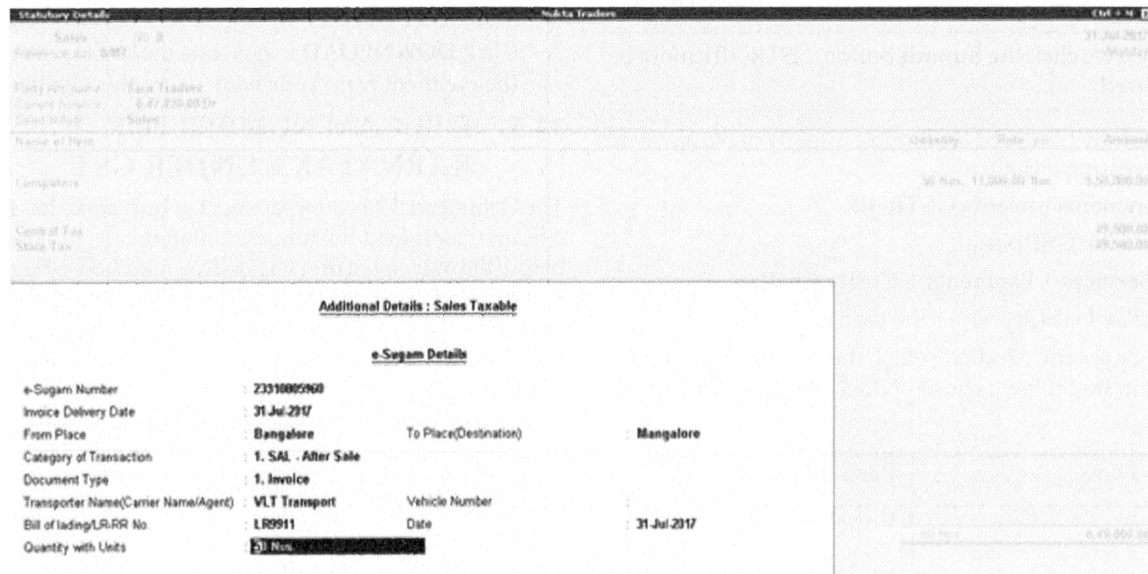


*Figure 14.15: Statutory Details Screen*

4. Press **Ctrl+A** to accept the screen.
5. Press **Alt+P** to get the **Voucher Printing** screen.

**Note:** Make sure in the Voucher Printing screen the option **with Print Preview** is appearing, if not press **Alt+I: With Preview.**

6. Press Enter from Voucher Printing screen to get the printing of tax invoice as shown in figure 14.16:

The **Tax Invoice** print appears as shown in the figure 14.16:

**Note:**
- e-Sugam detail is captured in the Tax Invoice.
- Vehicle number and LR/RR number is captured in Tax Invoice.
- Make sure that Print E-sugam No.? is set to Yes in the Invoice Print Configuration screen.
- The tax invoice used in TallyACE/PRO/GURU will appear as shown here.

**Tax Invoice**

| **Mukta Traders**<br>No. 209, 19th Cross<br>Twin Tower, Karnataka 560029<br>GSTIN/UIN: 29AAAAA1234A1Z5 | Invoice No.<br>**8** | e-Sugam No.<br>**23310805960** | Dated<br>**31-Jul-2017** |
|---|---|---|---|
| | Delivery Note | | Mode/Terms of Payment |
| | Supplier's Ref.<br>**8/MT** | | Other Reference(s) |
| Buyer<br>**Tara Traders**<br><br>State Name : Karnataka, Code : 29<br>GSTIN/UIN : 29RRRRR1234R1Z1<br>Place of Supply : Karnataka | Buyer's Order No. | | Dated |
| | Despatch Document No. | | Delivery Note Date |
| | Despatched through | | Destination<br>**Mangalore** |
| | Bill of Lading/LR-RR No.<br>**LR9911 dt. 31-Jul-2017** | | Motor Vehicle No. |
| | Terms of Delivery | | |

| Sl No. | Description of Goods | HSN/SAC | Quantity | Rate | per | Amount |
|---|---|---|---|---|---|---|
| 1 | **Computers** | 84713010 | **50 Nos.** | 11,000.00 | Nos | **5,50,000.00** |
| | ***Central Tax*** | | | | | **49,500.00** |
| | ***State Tax*** | | | | | **49,500.00** |
| | Total | | **50 Nos.** | | | **₹ 6,49,000.00** |

Amount Chargeable (in words) *E. & O.E*

**INR Six Lakh Forty Nine Thousand Only**

| HSN/SAC | Taxable Value | Central Tax | | State Tax | | Total Tax Amount |
|---|---|---|---|---|---|---|
| | | Rate | Amount | Rate | Amount | |
| 84713010 | 5,50,000.00 | 9% | 49,500.00 | 9% | 49,500.00 | 99,000.00 |
| **Total** | **5,50,000.00** | | **49,500.00** | | **49,500.00** | **99,000.00** |

Tax Amount (in words) : **INR Ninety Nine Thousand Only**

Declaration
We declare that this invoice shows the actual price of the goods described and that all particulars are true and correct.

**for Mukta Traders**

Authorised Signatory

This is a Computer Generated Invoice

*Figure 14.16 Tax Invoice*

7. Once after checking the preview.
8. Save the sales voucher.

Once after recording the sales invoice with e-Sugam number, the same can be checked in the e-Sugam report available in Tally.ERP 9.

**To view e-Sugam details**

1. Go to **Gateway of Tally** > **Display** > **Statutory Reports** > **GST** > **e-Sugam**.

2. Select the period using **F2: Period.**
3. Select the required voucher, and click **S: Set e-Suga No** to enter the e-Sugam number.

The **e-Sugam Vouchers** screen appears as shown in th figure 14.17:

4. Press **Alt+S: Set e-SUGAM No.** in order to modify or ente the e-Sugam number.

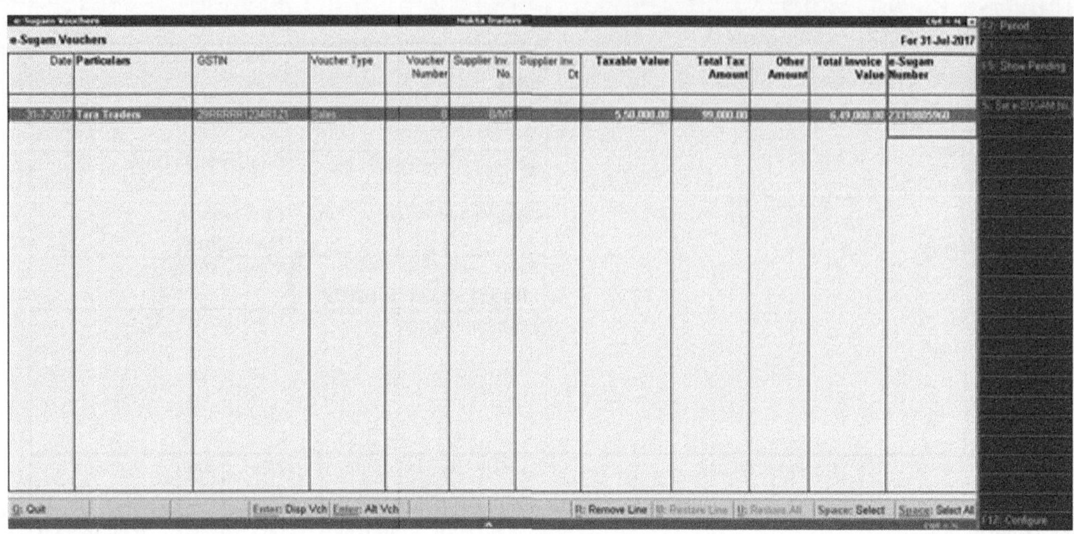

*Figure 14.17: e-Sugam Voucher*

5. Press **Enter** to accept.

**Note:** As per e-Sugam rules, sales transactions of ₹ 50,000 and above are displayed in the **e-Sugam Vouchers** report. To capture transactions of values below ¹ 50,000, click **F12: Configure** and set the transaction limit.

The **Configuration** screen appears as shown in figure 14.18:

- Set the option **Show tax types in separate columns?** to **Ye** to view the breakup of taxes and cess.
- Based on the transaction limit set in the **Configuratio** screen, the sales transactions will appear in the **e-Sugan Vouchers** report.

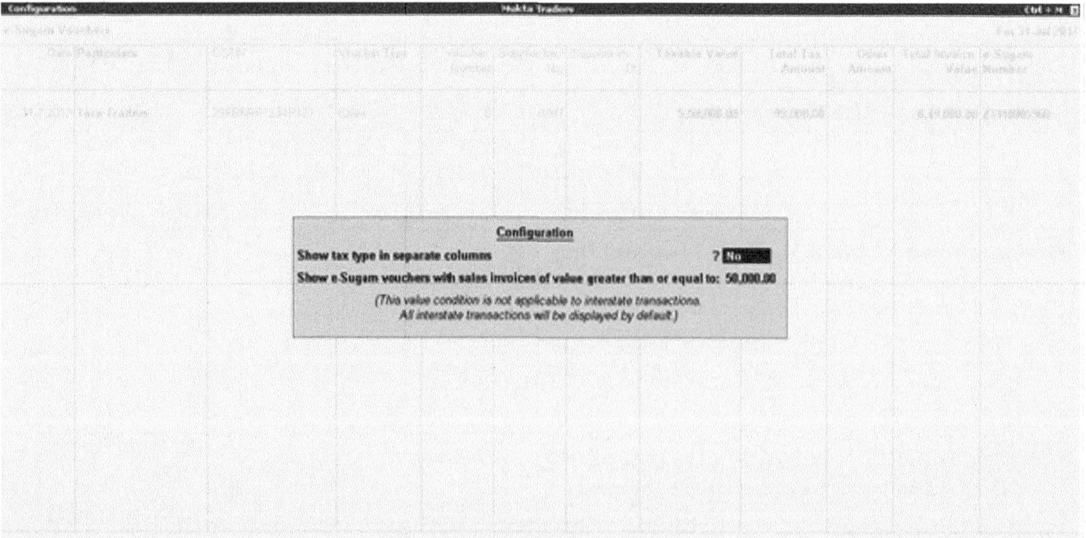


*Figure 14.18: Configuration screen*

## 14.6 ACCOUNTING OF ADVANCE RECEIPTS AND BOOKING OF TAX LIABILITY

We have learnt to record the transactions which involves advance receipts and how GST rates are accounted in Tally. ERP 9.

As per GST rule, for any advance received for goods or services if the corresponding sales invoice is not raised in the sam month, the dealer who has received the advance has to pay th GST for that particular month.

In this section we will learn to record advance receipts and mak partial sales against the advance and check the details of the same in the **Advance Receipts Summary** report.

***Illustration:*** *Recording of Sales Invoice against the advance receipts.*

<table>
<tr><th>Date</th><th colspan="4">Particulars</th></tr>
<tr><td>01-08-2017</td><td colspan="4">Voucher: Receipts<br>Received an advance of ₹ 1,18,000 from DD Traders, Karnataka<br>Hint: While recording the receipt entry use the key Alt+V: Advance Receipts.</td></tr>
<tr><td rowspan="3">15-08- 2017</td><td colspan="4">Voucher: Sales<br>Sold the following goods to DD Traders, Karnataka with GST 18%</td></tr>
<tr><td>Name of Item</td><td>Quantity</td><td>Rate</td><td>Amount</td></tr>
<tr><td>Computer</td><td>5</td><td>10,000</td><td>50,000</td></tr>
</table>

## *Activity:*

- *Create the following Masters:*
  - o *Party ledger – DD Traders under Sundry Debtors, enter the GSTIN number as 29AAAAA1234S1ZA*
  - o *Create a Sales Ledger.*
  - o *Create the stock item and enter the GST details at the item level.*
  - o *Create the GST duty ledgers*
- *Record the advance receipt voucher in Tally.ERP 9.*

Once after recording the advance receipt voucher check the GSTR-1 report.

1. Go to **Gateway of Tally > Display > Statutory Reports > GST > GSTR-1**

The **GSTR-1** report screen appears as shown in the figure 14.19:

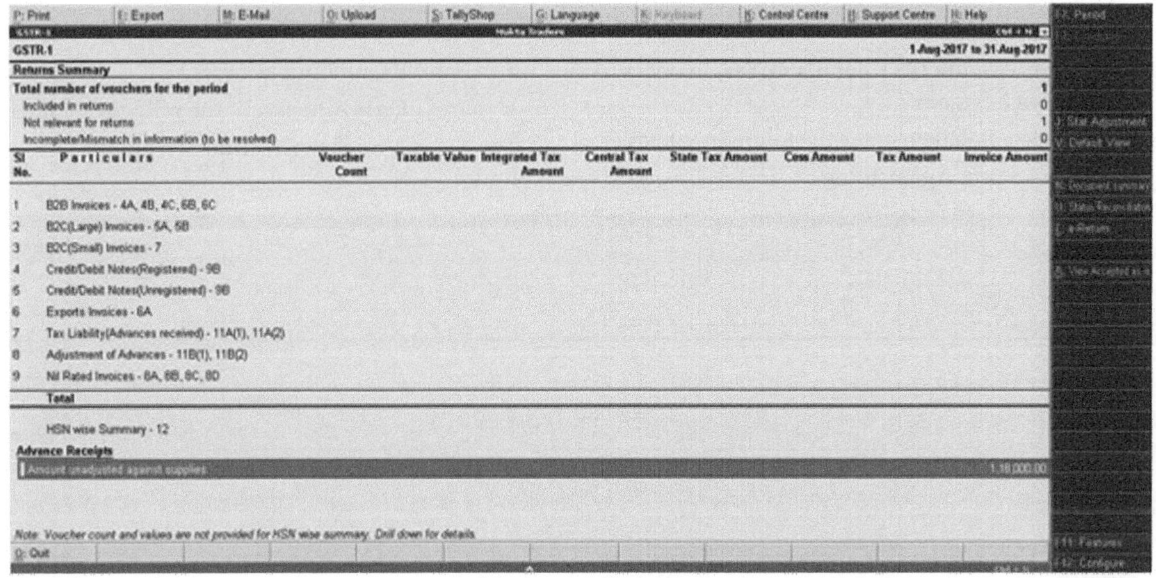


*Figure 14.19: GSTR-1*

**Note:** From the above screen press Alt+N: Document Summary, to view the details like voucher number from and to details, total voucher details, cancelled voucher details etc.

2. Press **Enter** on the field **Amount unadjusted against supplies**

The **Advance Receipts Summary** screen appears as shown in the figure 14.20:

## *Observation:*

- *In the advance receipts summary report, we will get the details of Unadjusted Advanced and Advance Received.*
- *In the Advance Receipts Summary, we will get the state wise details of advance receipts.*

Recording of sales voucher against the advance receipts.

1. Go to **Gateway of Tally > Accounting Vouchers > Press F8:Sales**
2. Click **F2: Date** and change the date to 15-08-2017
3. Enter the **Reference no**
4. Select **DD Traders** in the **Party A/c name** field
5. Accept the **Party Details** screen as it is
6. Select Sales ledger in the **Sales ledger** field
7. Under the field **Name of Item**, select HK Printer
8. Enter **Quantity** as 5 Nos
9. Enter the **Rate** as [1] 10,000 and the amount will get captured automaticallyFigure 1.20: Advance Receipts Summary Screen

*Figure 14.20: Advance Receipts Summary Screen*

10. Select the GST duty ledgers
11. Enable the option **Provide GST details** to **Yes,** in order to enter the details of e-Sugam.
12. In the Bill wise details screen enter the following details:
    - Type of Ref – Select Against Ref
    - Name – Select the pending bill ADV/01
    - Enter the amount as 59,000
    - Press **Ctrl+A** to accept the bill wise details screen

The **Sales Voucher Creation** screen appears as shown in figure 14.21:

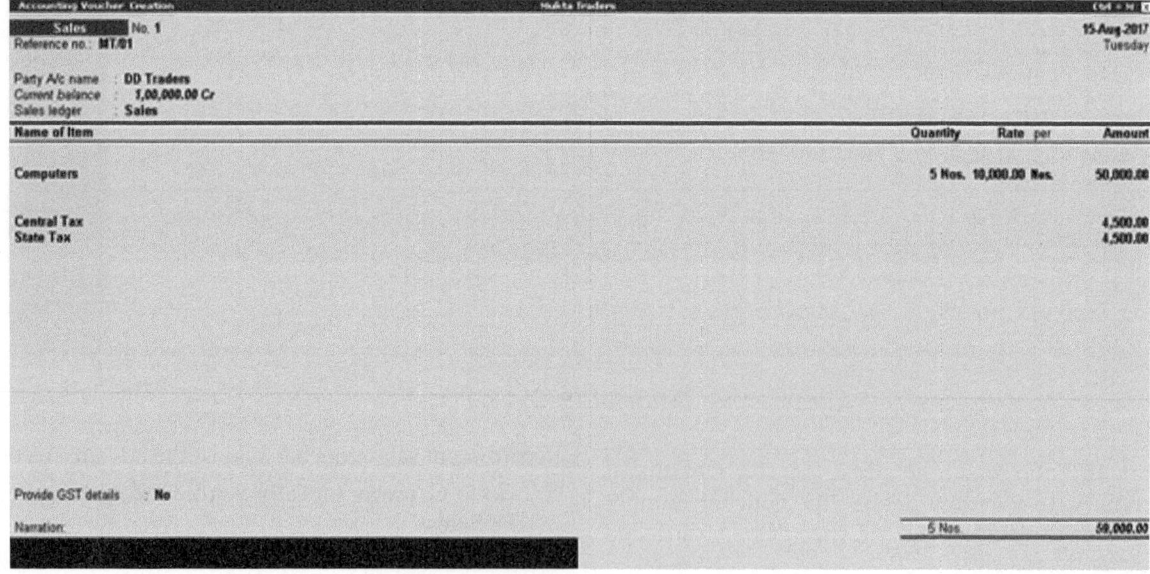

*Figure 14.21: Purchase Voucher Creation*

13. Press **Ctrl+A** to accept

Once after recording the sales entry in Tally.ERP 9, check the Advance Receipt Summary:

1. Go to **Gateway of Tally > Display > Statutory Reports > GST > GSTR-1**
2. Press **Enter** on **Amount unadjusted against supplies.**
3. Press **Enter** on Place of Supply field (State name will appear, press Enter on the state) – In this field we will get the state wise advance receipts details.
4. Press **Alt+F1:Detailed**

The **Advance Receipt-Tax Liability** screen appears as shown in the figure 14.22:

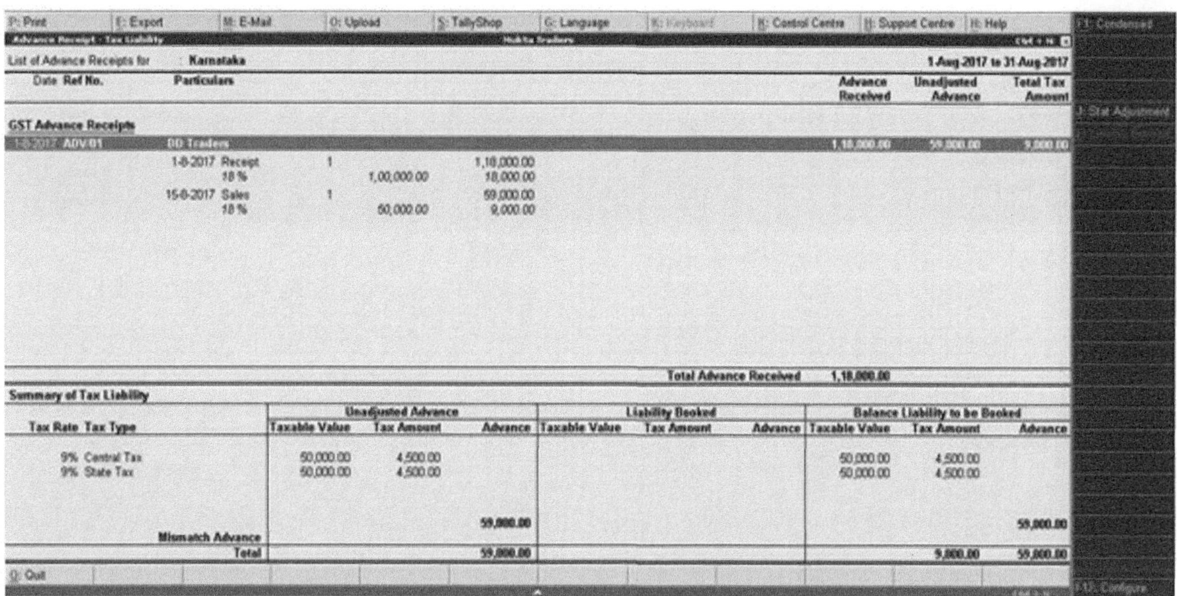

*Figure 14.22: Advance Receipt-Tax Liability*

In the **Advance Receipt – Tax Liability** screen we are getting the details of:

- **Advance Received** - This column displays the details of total advance we have received for the period.
- **Unadjusted Advance** - This column displays the details of advance receipt against which we have not recorded the sales invoice.
- **Total Tax Amount** - This column displays the details of tax amount which is adjusted.
- **Summary of Tax Liability** – This field will display the details of the following:
  - o **Unadjusted Advance** – This column displays the details of advance receipt against which we have not recorded the sales invoice.
  - o **Liability Booked** – This column displays the details of amount against which liability is booked. (Usually when a sales invoice is not recorded in the same month against the advance received, then we must raise a liability against the advance. Once we raise the liability against the advance receipt, the details will capture in this field)
  - o **Balance Liability to be Booked** – This column displays the details of amount against which the liability needs to be raised

**Note:**
- From the Advance Receipt-Tax Liability press F12: Configure and enable the option Show fully adjusted advance receipt also to Yes, to get the details of advance receipts adjusted fully.
- From the same screen we can book a tax liability by using the key Alt+J

Booking the Liability against the Advance Receipt

1. To book go to, **Advance Receipt-Tax Liability** screen and press **Alt+J: Stat Adjustment**
2. Enter the following details in **Stat Adjustment** screen:
   - Type of duty/tax – By default it will be selected as **GST**
   - Nature of adjustment – By default it will be selected as **Increase of Tax Liability**
   - Additional Details – Select as **On Account of Advance Receipts**
   - Press Enter to save the **Stat Adjustment** screen
3. **Debit** the **Tax on Advance** ledger (If the ledger is not created then press Alt+C and group it under current assets) and enter the amount as 4500
4. **Credit** the **Central Tax** ledger, in the GST details screen enter the rate and taxable value (As per this illustration the taxable value is 50,000 and the rate is 9%)
5. **Credit** the **State Tax** ledger, in the GST details screen enter the rate and taxable value
6. Enable the option **Provide GST Details** to **Yes,** to enter the details like **Ledger Name, GSTIN/UIN, Place of Supply, Registration type and Party type**

   The **Journal Voucher Creation** appears as shown in the figure 14.23
7. Press **Ctrl+A** to accept

Once after recording the entry check the **Advance Receipt – Tax Liability** report as shown in figure 14.24:

***Observation:*** *Once after recording the Journal Voucher – Adjustment entry. The liability amount is moved from* ***Balance Liability to be booked*** *column to Liability Booked.*

*Figure 14.23: Journal Voucher Creation*

Advance Receipt - Tax Liability — Mukta Traders

List of Advance Receipts for : Karnataka — 1-Aug-2017 to 31-Aug-2017

| Date | Ref No. | Particulars | | | | Advance Received | Unadjusted Advance | Total Tax Amount |
|---|---|---|---|---|---|---|---|---|
| **GST Advance Receipts** | | | | | | | | |
| 1-8-2017 | ADV/01 | DD Traders | | | | 1,18,000.00 | 59,000.00 | 9,000.00 |
| | | 1-8-2017 Receipt | 1 | | 1,18,000.00 | | | |
| | | 18 % | | 1,00,000.00 | 18,000.00 | | | |
| | | 15-8-2017 Sales | 1 | | 59,000.00 | | | |
| | | 18 % | | 50,000.00 | 9,000.00 | | | |
| | | | | | Total Advance Received | 1,18,000.00 | | |

Summary of Tax Liability

| Tax Rate | Tax Type | Unadjusted Advance | | | Liability Booked | | | Balance Liability to be Booked | | |
|---|---|---|---|---|---|---|---|---|---|---|
| | | Taxable Value | Tax Amount | Advance | Taxable Value | Tax Amount | Advance | Taxable Value | Tax Amount | Advance |
| 9% | Central Tax | 50,000.00 | 4,500.00 | | 50,000.00 | 4,500.00 | | | | |
| 9% | State Tax | 50,000.00 | 4,500.00 | | 50,000.00 | 4,500.00 | | | | |
| | | | | 59,000.00 | | | 59,000.00 | | | 0.00 |
| | Mismatch Advance | | | | | | | | | |
| | Total | | | 59,000.00 | | | 59,000.00 | | | |

*Figure 14.24: Advance Receipt – Tax Liability*

**Note:**
- In Tally.ERP 9, while recording Advance Receipt entry, if we select Not Applicable under the field Particulars in Advance Receipt details screen, then the receipt entry will fall under the head GST Advance Receipt - Mismatch as shown in the figure 14.25,entry no 2:
- To rectify the mismatch due to not providing the details in Advance Receipt details screen , we need to alter the receipt voucher and entry the stock and tax rate details in the Advance Receipt details screen
- In Tally.ERP 9,when there is a mismatch in the tax rate defined at the time of recording advance receipt and sales invoice, then the entry will fall under the head GST Advance Receipts as shown in figure 14.25, entry no 3.
- To rectify the mismatch due to not providing the same tax rate, we must alter the sales or journal voucher and enter the correct tax rate.

## 14.7 REFUND VOUCHER

In Tally.ERP 9, we have learnt how the advance payment voucher is recorded and also we have learnt to raise the liability in Tally.ERP 9.

In this section we will learn to record the refund voucher and reverse the tax liability. If the advance payment transaction is cancelled fully or partially. Then the details needs to be accounted 9in the receipt voucher by marking it as a refund voucher.

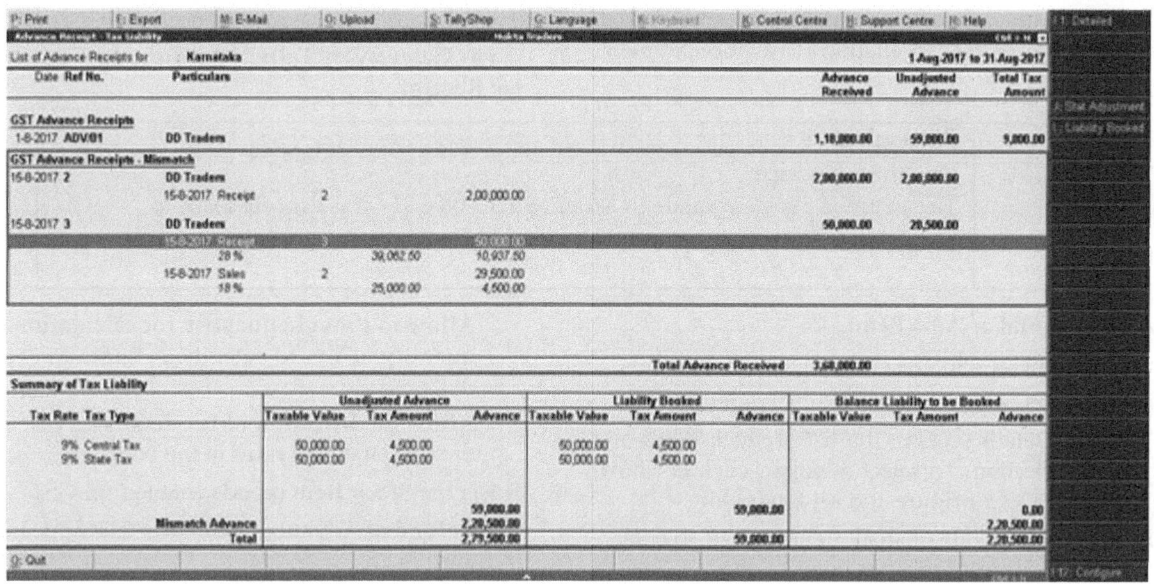

Figure 14.25: Advance Receipt – Tax Liability

*Activity: Record the following advance entry*

| Date | Particulars |
|---|---|
| *30-08-2017* | ***Voucher: Payment***<br>*Made a payment of ₹ 40,000 to Sarathi Traders, location Singapore towards purchase of cartage.*<br>***Hint:** While recording the payment entry use the key Alt+V: Reverse Charge advance and raise a liability using a journal voucher* |

While recording the Advance payment entry enter the following details in the **Advance Payment Details** screen as shown in figure 14.26:

**Note:** The **Advance Payment Details** screen in TallyACE/PRO/GURU book appears as shown here.

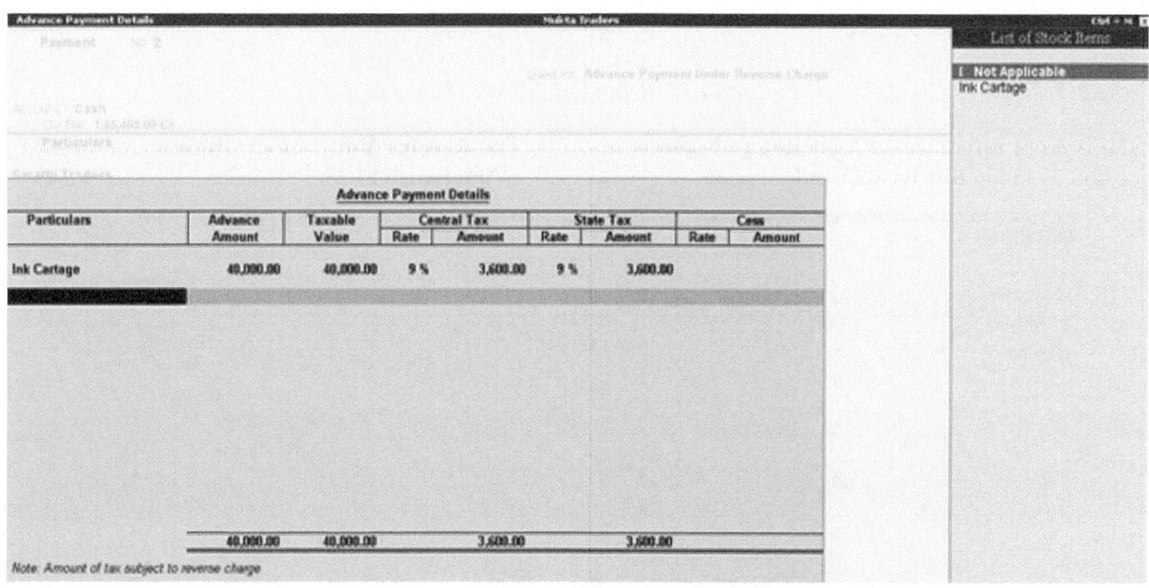

Figure 14.26 :Advance Payment Details Screen

***Activity:***

- *Raise a tax liability by recording a journal voucher in Tally.ERP 9.*
- *Go to GSTR-2 report and check that the advance payment entry will reflect under the head **Tax liability under Reverse Charge on Advance.***

Once after recording the advance payment entry and journal voucher, let us check how the cancellation of advance payment voucher is done.

To record the advance payment cancellation in receipt voucher

1. Go to **Gateway of Tally > Accounting Vouchers >** Press **F6: Receipt.**

| Date | Particulars |
|---|---|
| 31-08-2017 | **Voucher: Receipt**<br>The advance payment made to Sarathi on 30-08-2017 was cancelled due to transportation issue. |

2. Press **Alt+F: Refund of Adv. Pymt.**
3. Under **Account** field, select as cash ledger
4. Under **Particulars** field, select as Sarathi Traders
5. In the **Refund Details** section, the list of stock items are displayed for selection. To select a ledger, click **L: Show Ledgers**. Click **F12: Configure** and set the option:
   - **Allow to provide rate of stock items** to **Yes**, to enter/ alter the slab rate of the stock item.
   - **Allow to provide quantity for calculation of cess on quantity** to **Yes**, to enter the cess rate and cess rate per unit.
   - **Allow modification of tax details** to **Yes**, to override the GST and cess rates in the voucher.
6. Select the **Stock Item** (goods enabled for GST)

   The **Refund of Advance Payment** screen appears as shown in figure 14.27:

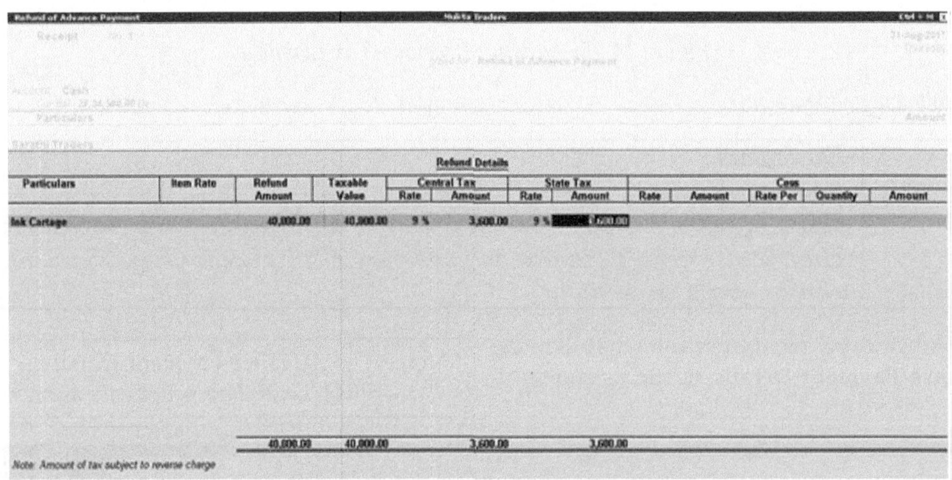


*Figure 14.27: Refund of Advance Payment*

7. Select the type of reference as **Agst Ref** and select the reference details in the **Bill-wise Details** screen.

   The **Receipt Voucher Creation** screen appears as shown in the figure 14.28:

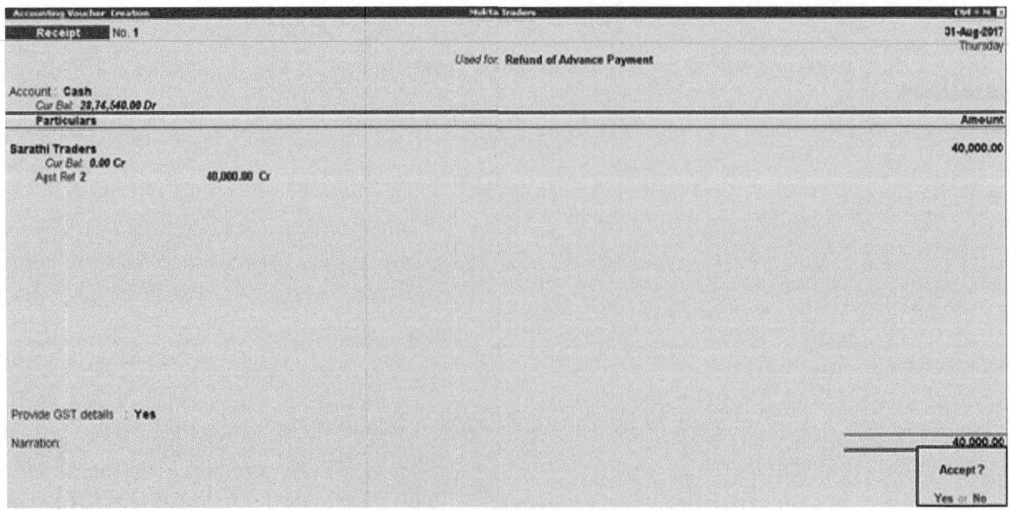


*Figure 14.28: Receipt Voucher Creation*

8. Accept the Voucher.

***Activity**: Go to GSTR-2 report and check that the advance payment amount is removed from the head **Tax liability under Reverse Charge on Advance.***

Once after recording the receipt voucher to cancel the payment voucher, next step is to cancel the tax liability which was raised using journal voucher against the payment voucher.

To reverse the Tax liability to the extent of refund voucher:

1. Go to **Journal Voucher Creation** screen and Press **Alt+J: Stat Adjustment**
2. Select the details as shown in the figure 14.29:

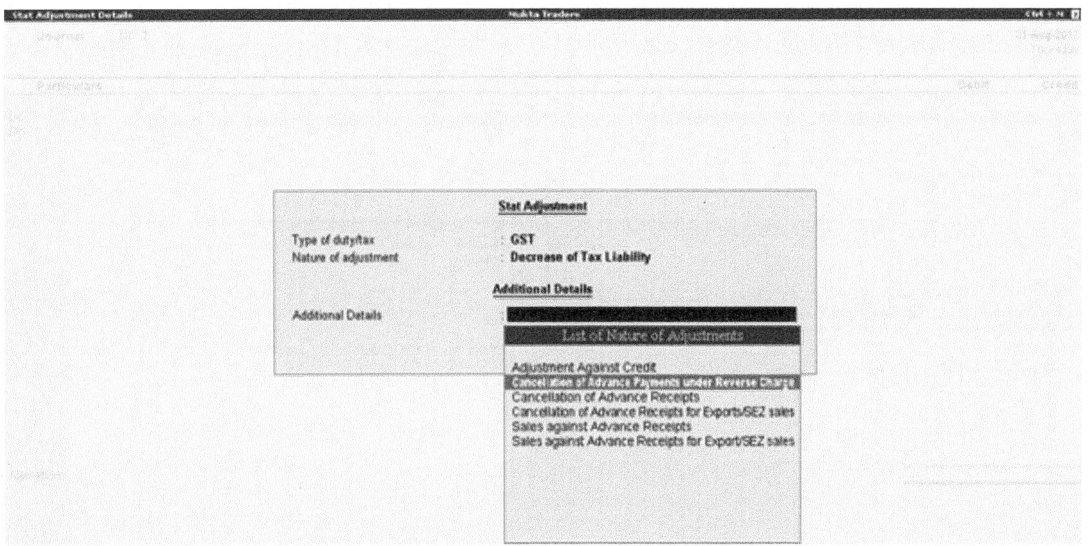


*Figure 14.29: Stat Adjustment Details Screen*

3. **Debit** the **GST tax ledgers** and **Credit** the **Tax on Advance** ledger (Current Asset A/c)

   The **Journal Voucher Creation** screen appears as shown in the figure 14.30:
4. Accept the screen.

This entry will have an impact on books of account.

**Note:**
- Similarly we can record the details of advance receipts for orders cancelled in Tally.ERP 9. In case of advance receipt cancellation, the details need to be accounted in the payment voucher and reverse the tax liability in journal voucher by selecting the flag name as Cancellation of Advance Receipts
- In Tally.ERP 9 Branch Transfer Inward and Branch Transfer Outward is provided in Nature of Transactions to record inward and outward movement of goods to branch offices within the same state.

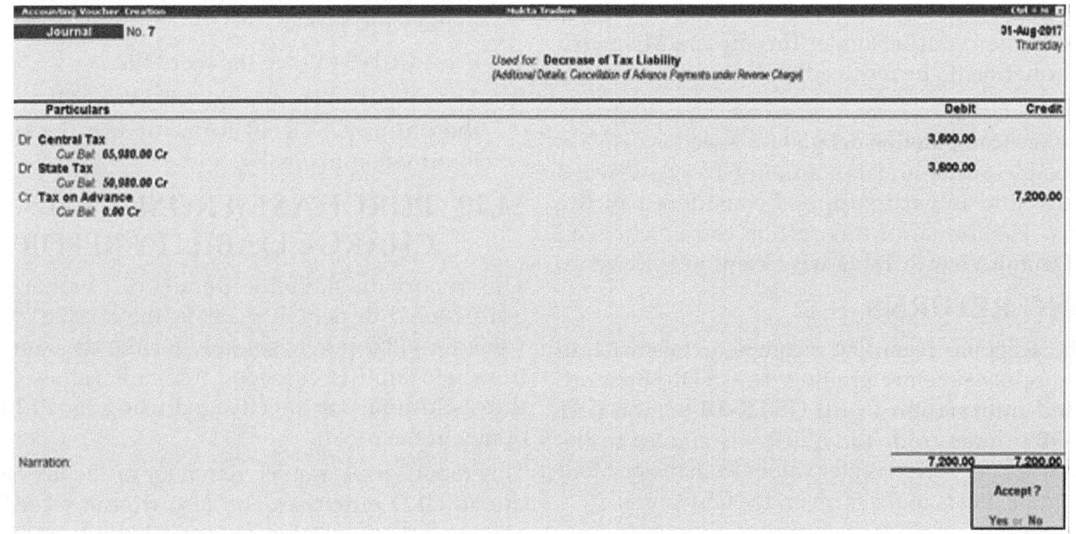


*Figure 14.30: Journal Voucher Creation Screen*

## 14.8 REPORTS

### 14.8.1 Generating Form GSTR-3B

Form GSTR-3B is an interim return form to be used by GST dealers with regular registration for filing returns for the month of July and August. It is an online form where dealers can enter the GST details directly on the GST portal. This report can be printed from Tally.ERP 9 with all transaction details in the required format. The details from the printed report can be used to fill in the online form on the GST portal.

In Tally.ERP 9, GSTR-3B can be viewed in the report format with tax computation details. This report can be changed to the table-wise format (department format) with the click of a button.

**To view GSTR-3B**

1. Go to **Gateway of Tally > Display > Statutory Reports > GST > GSTR–3B**.

   The **GSTR-3B** report appears as shown in the figure 14.31

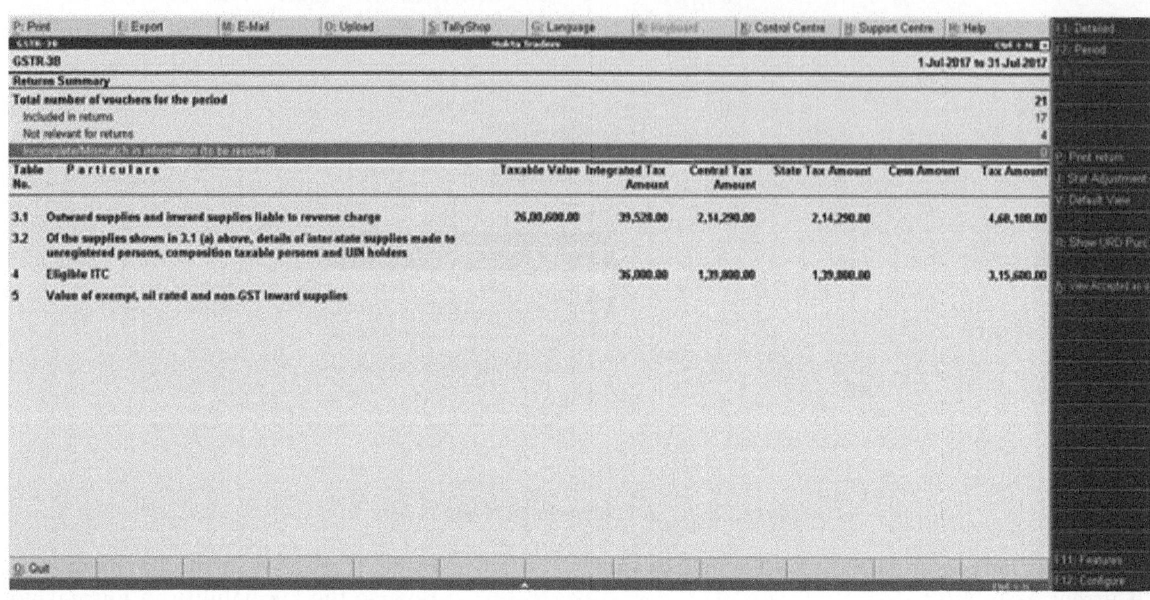


*Figure 14.31*

- **Returns Summary**: This section displays a snapshot of business operations in the given period. Displays the **Total number of vouchers for the period**, vouchers **Included in returns**, vouchers **Not relevant for returns** and vouchers with **Incomplete/Mismatch in information (to be resolved)**for the reporting period.

  Drill down from any row to view the list of vouchers under the respective category. You can resolve the exceptions for voucher under **Incomplete/Mismatch in information (to be resolved)** to include them in the returns.

- **Particulars (computation details)**: This section displays the taxable value and tax amount from outward supplies and inward supplies considered in the returns. The format of this section can be changed from **Default View** to **Table-wise View** and vice versa.

## 14.9 FILING RETURNS

Ensure that all exceptions regarding incomplete/mismatch in information are resolved before printing the **GSTR-3B** report. Use the printed information to fill **GSTR-3B** on the GST portal. **GSTR-3B** printed from Tally.ERP 9 is similar to the online form in structure. You can enter values from the printout in the corresponding fields of the form on the GST portal.

**To print GSTR-3B**

1. Go to **Gateway of Tally** > **Display** > **Statutory Reports** > **GST** > **GSTR-3B**.
2. Press **Ctrl+P** to print the form.

**Note:** Make sure that MS Word application available in the system to view the form.

3. In the **Print Report** screen, press **Enter**. GSTR-3B is created in the word format.
4. Press **Ctrl+S** to save the word file.
5. Then the details from the MS Word file can be copied to the online GSTR-3B form, or use the printout to fill information manually.

## 14.10 PURCHASE FROM URD - REVERSE CHARGE LIABILITY REPORT

This report displays the details of purchases made from unregistered dealers. It displays the taxable amount and tax value for URD purchases only for the days on which the set threshold limit is exceeded. (default value of ₹ 5000). This threshold limit can be changed using the **F12** configuration option in the report.

This report gives a quick reminder of the tax liability created due to URD purchases and also we can record the required adjustment transaction to bring liability into the books of accounts.

To view the Purchase from URD – Reverse Charge Liability report

1. Go to **Gateway of Tally** > **Display** > **Statutory Reports**> **GST** > **GSTR-3B**.

   The **GSTR-3B** with URD purchase option appears as shown in figure 14.32:

2. Press **Alt+R: Show URD Purc.**
3. Press **F1: Detailed** to view in detailed mode.

The **Purchase from URD – Reverse Charge Liability** appears as shown in the figure 14.33:

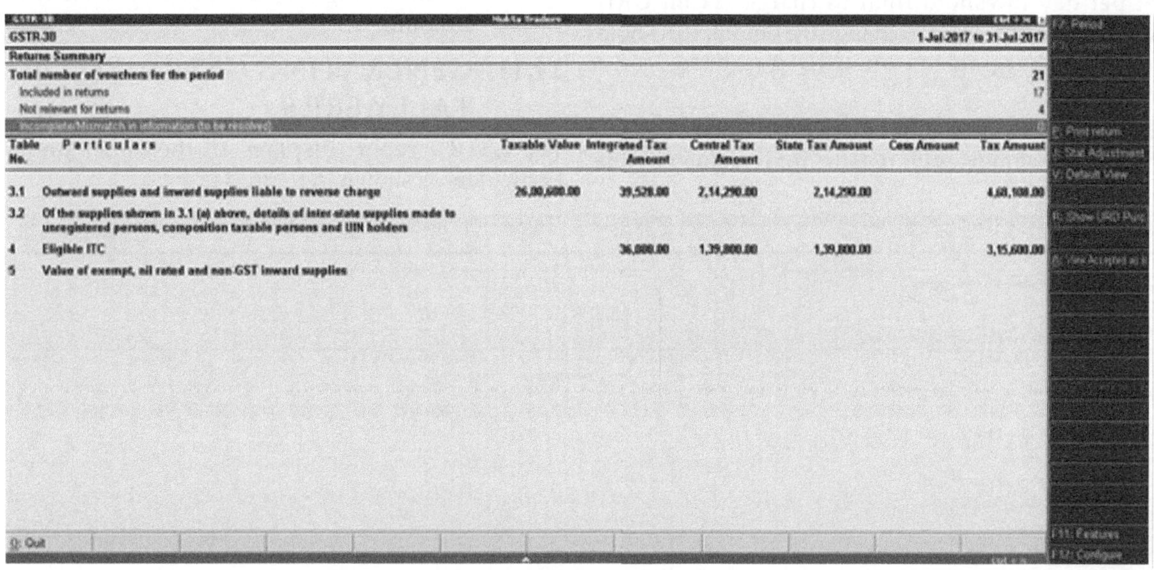


*Figure 14.32: GSTR-3B*

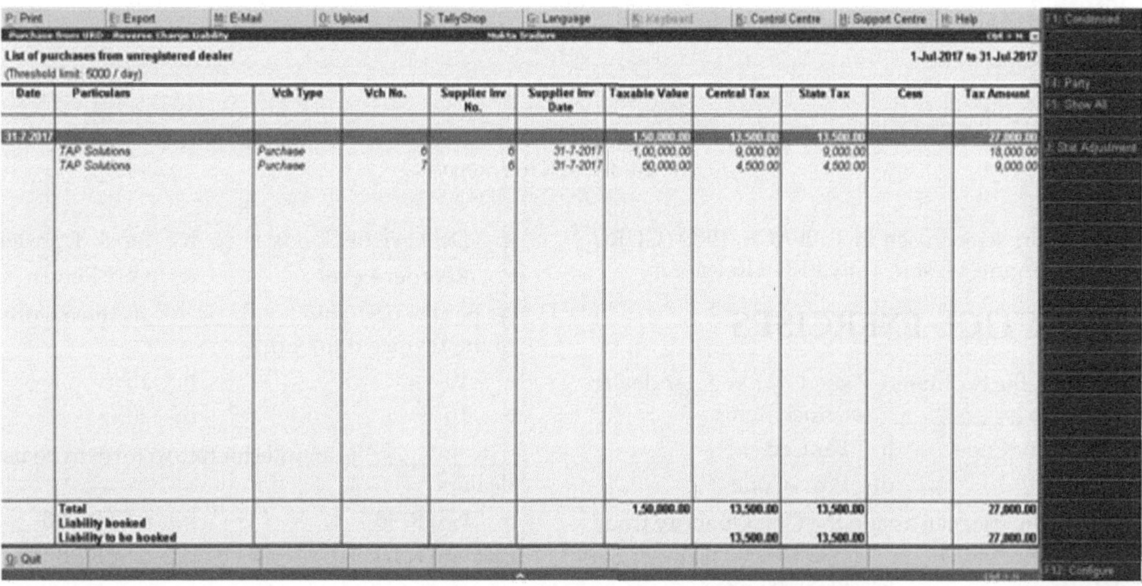


*Figure 14.33: Purchase from URD – Reverse Charge Liability*

## *Observation:*

- *In the Purchase from URD report, we can observe that the Liability booked field is blank and Liability to be booked displaying as 27,000 (Central Tax as 13,500 and State Tax as 13,500).*
- *Once after raising the amount of liability through journal adjustment, the total amount will reflect under the field Liability booked.*

Explanation of different options available in vertical button bar

- **F4: Party -** Click this button to view the vouchers only for a particular supplier.
- **F5: Show All** - Click this button to view URD purchase vouchers for all days without filtering based on the threshold limit. In this view, the **Total**, **Liability booked**, and **Liability to be booked** information is not displayed.

- **J: Stat Adjustment** - Click this button to record journal transactions for booking the pending liability and for updating the liability in books of accounts.
- **F12: Configure** - Click this button to configure the options for the report.
  - o **Set per day threshold limit to charge tax on URD purchases:** Allows you to change the default threshold limit for charging tax on URD purchases for a particular day.
  - o **Show eligible ITC details?** Enable this option to view additional columns with details of tax value eligible for input tax credit out of the liability booked for URD purchases.
  - o **Show tax types in separate columns?** Enable this column to view Integrated Tax, Central Tax, State Tax, and Cess in separate columns. When this option is set to **No**, a single column is displayed with total **Tax Amount**.

## 14.11 GENERATING GSTR-1 REPORT IN TALLY.ERP 9

The GSTR-1 report displays all the tables under the head **Particulars** as shown in figure 14.34:

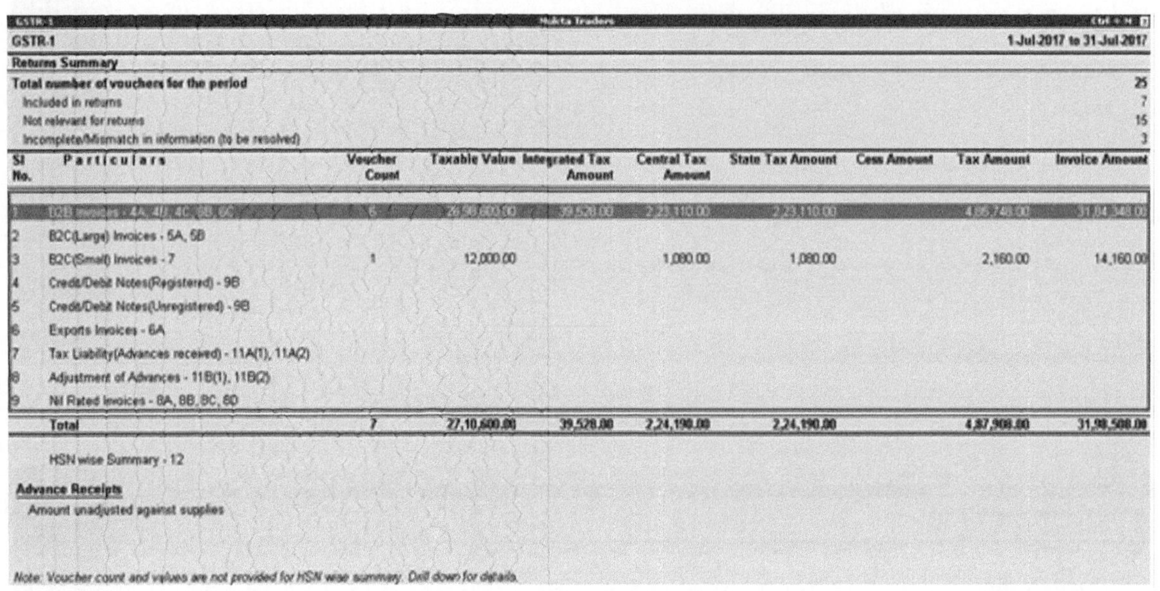

GSTR-1 | Mukta Traders

GSTR-1 — 1-Jul-2017 to 31-Jul-2017

Returns Summary

| | |
|---|---|
| Total number of vouchers for the period | 25 |
| Included in returns | 7 |
| Not relevant for returns | 15 |
| Incomplete/Mismatch in information (to be resolved) | 3 |

| Sl No. | Particulars | Voucher Count | Taxable Value | Integrated Tax Amount | Central Tax Amount | State Tax Amount | Cess Amount | Tax Amount | Invoice Amount |
|---|---|---|---|---|---|---|---|---|---|
| 1 | B2B Invoices - 4A, 4B, 4C, 6B, 6C | 6 | 26,98,600.00 | 39,528.00 | 2,23,110.00 | 2,23,110.00 | | 4,85,748.00 | 31,84,348.00 |
| 2 | B2C(Large) Invoices - 5A, 5B | | | | | | | | |
| 3 | B2C(Small) Invoices - 7 | 1 | 12,000.00 | | 1,080.00 | 1,080.00 | | 2,160.00 | 14,160.00 |
| 4 | Credit/Debit Notes(Registered) - 9B | | | | | | | | |
| 5 | Credit/Debit Notes(Unregistered) - 9B | | | | | | | | |
| 6 | Exports Invoices - 6A | | | | | | | | |
| 7 | Tax Liability(Advances received) - 11A(1), 11A(2) | | | | | | | | |
| 8 | Adjustment of Advances - 11B(1), 11B(2) | | | | | | | | |
| 9 | Nil Rated Invoices - 8A, 8B, 8C, 8D | | | | | | | | |
| | Total | 7 | 27,10,600.00 | 39,528.00 | 2,24,190.00 | 2,24,190.00 | | 4,87,908.00 | 31,98,508.00 |

HSN wise Summary - 12

Advance Receipts

Amount unadjusted against supplies

*Note: Voucher count and values are not provided for HSN wise summary. Drill down for details.*

*Figure 14.34: GSTR-1 Report*

All the GSTR-1 Report screen used in TallyACE/PRO/GURU book appears as the figure 14.34 in Tally.ERP 9 Release 6.1

# PRACTICE EXERCISES

1. As per GST rule, the tax invoice issued by a regular dealer must contain the ___________ for stock items
   a. Unit Quantity Code  b. Bar Code
   c. Serial Code  d. Press Code
2. In Tally.ERP 9, the user can assign the Unit Quantity Code with _____________
   a. Stock Groups  b. Stock Items
   c. Units of Measure  d. Stock Ledger
3. The Unit Quantity Code has to be assigned to units of measure for ________
   a. Delivery of Goods  b. Stock Transfers
   c. Reorder Level  d. GST Return
4. As per the GST rule ____________is the maximum length of the invoice numbering
   a. 10  b. 15
   c. 16  d. 20
5. ____________is an interim return form to be used by GST dealers
   a. GSTR-3B  b. GSTR- AB
   c. GSTR 1B  d. GSTR 2B

### Answers

1. (a) 2. (c) 3. (d) 4. (c) 5. (a)

# Chapter 15

# Tally.ERP 9 Release 6.2 Annexure

## 15.1 GSTR 2 REPORT IN TALLY.ERP 9

GSTR-2 is the monthly GST return which needs to be filed by a taxable person registered under GST. It includes the details of all inward supplies made in the given period.

The inward supply details contains the following details:

- B2B invoices to registered and unregistered dealers
- Import of goods and service
- Adjustments to purchases in debit/credit notes
- Nil rated invoices
- Advances paid and adjusted and
- Tax credit reversed or re-claimed

In GSTR-2, as a buyer we can reconcile the invoices in our books of account with the invoices uploaded by the supplier. And also we can upload the details of invoices that are not available in the portal. To support all types of businesses GST department have made a provision for both manual and automatic reconciliation. Where we can mark the status of the invoices directly on the portal or automate reconciliation by downloading the JSON file.

The JSON file contains the invoices details uploaded by the supplier

### 15.1.1 Filing of GSTR 2 Return in Tally.ERP 9

In Tally.ERP 9, we can file the GSTR 2 return by generating the GSTR-2 file as per the latest e-filing requirements.

In Tally.ERP 9, we can file the GSTR-2 Return in one of the following methods:

- By using the JSON file generated from Tally.ERP 9.
- By using offline tool or,
- Prepare online.

**Note:** JSON stands for JavaScript Object Notation, it is the data interchange format.

#### *Filing of Return by Using the JSON File Generated from Tally.ERP 9*

In this section, we will learn to file the GSTR-2 return by using the JSON file generated from Tally.ERP 9. The following steps are followed to complete the filing of return by using JSON file generated from Tally.ERP 9.

**Step 1:** Download GSTR-2 file from the GST Portal

1. Log in to GST Portal (www.gst.gov.in).
2. Go to **Services** > select **Returns.**
3. In **Returns Dashboard**, select the period for which GSTR-2 needs to be downloaded.

   The **GST File Returns Dashboard** appears as shown in figure 15.1:

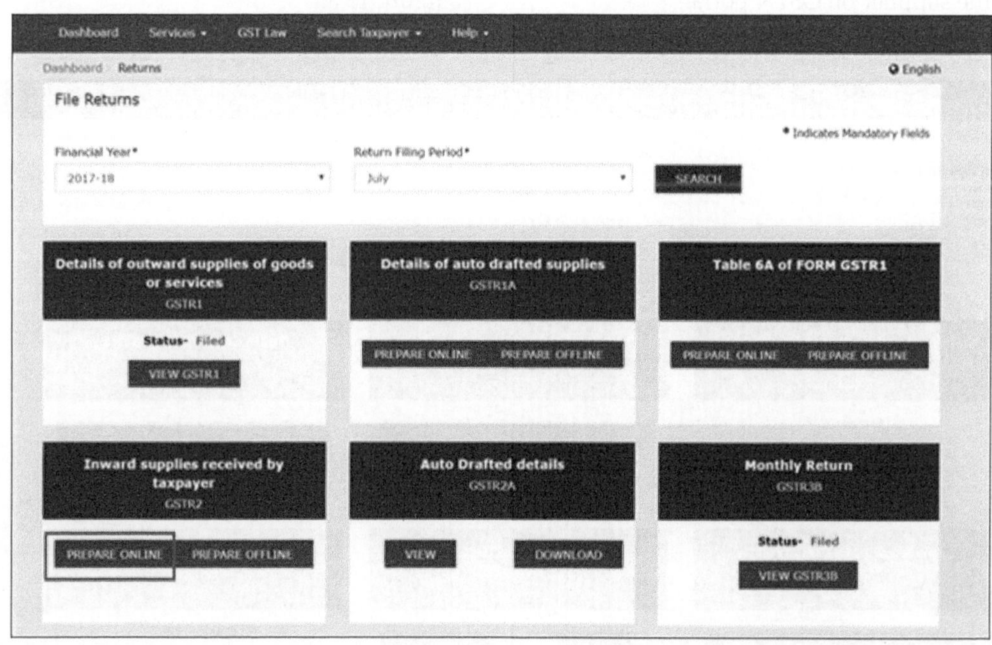


*Figure 15.1: GST File Returns Dashboard*

4. Under **Inward supplies received by taxpayer GSTR2,** click on **PREPARE ONLINE** button.

   The **GSTR-2 Other Details** screen appears as shown in figure 15.2:

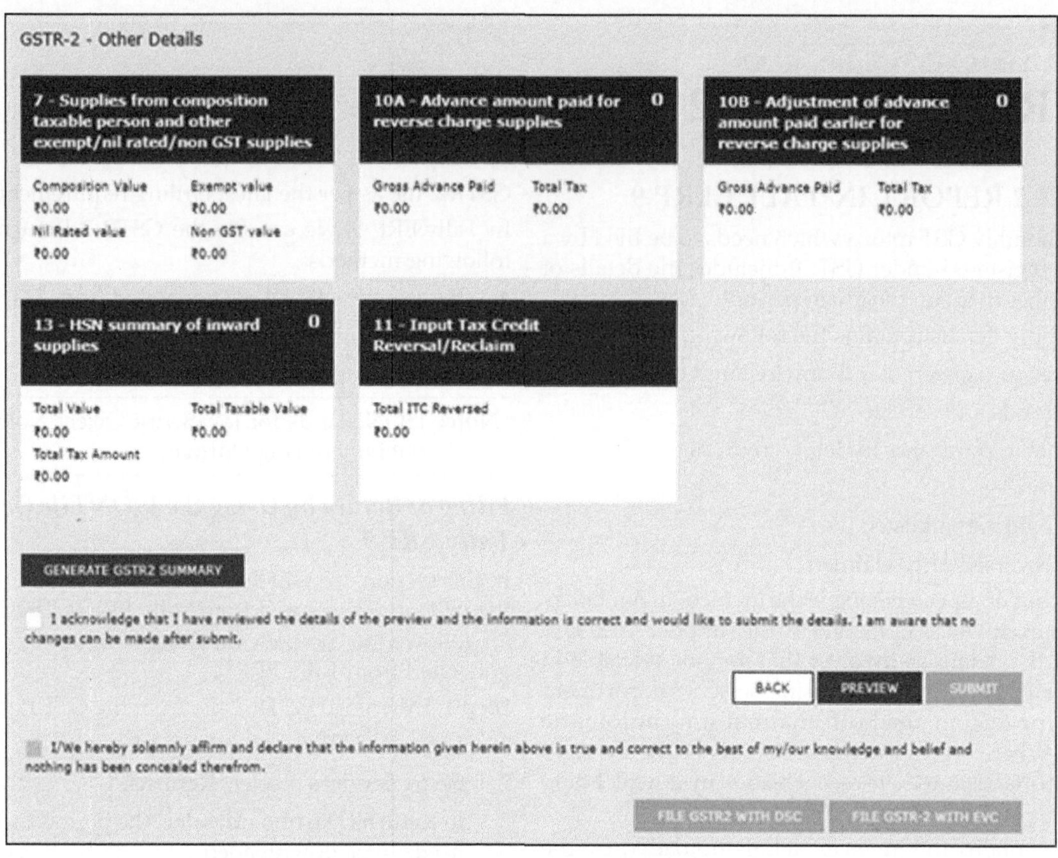


*Figure 15.2: GSTR-2 Other Details*

5. Click **Generate GSTR2 Summary** to view the transactions submitted by the supplier on GSTN portal.
6. Click **BACK** to return to the dashboard.

The **GST File Returns Dashboard** appears as shown in figure 15.3:

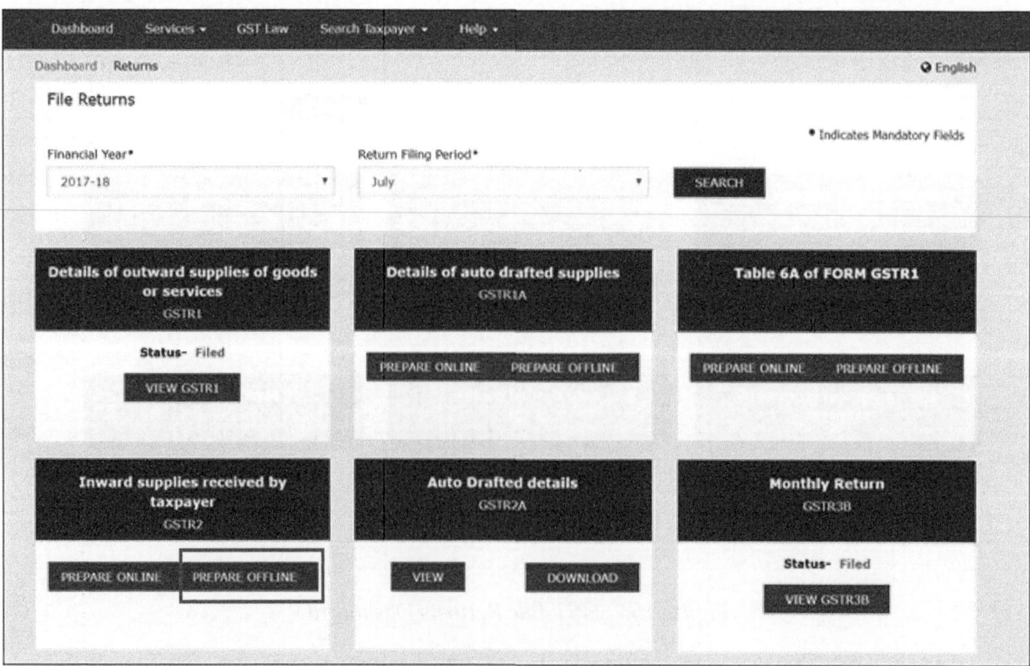


*Figure 15.3: GST File Returns Dashboard*

7. Under **Inward supplies received by taxpayer GSTR2,** click **PREPARE OFFLINE.**

The **Offline Upload and Download for GSTR2** screen appears as shown in figure 15.4:

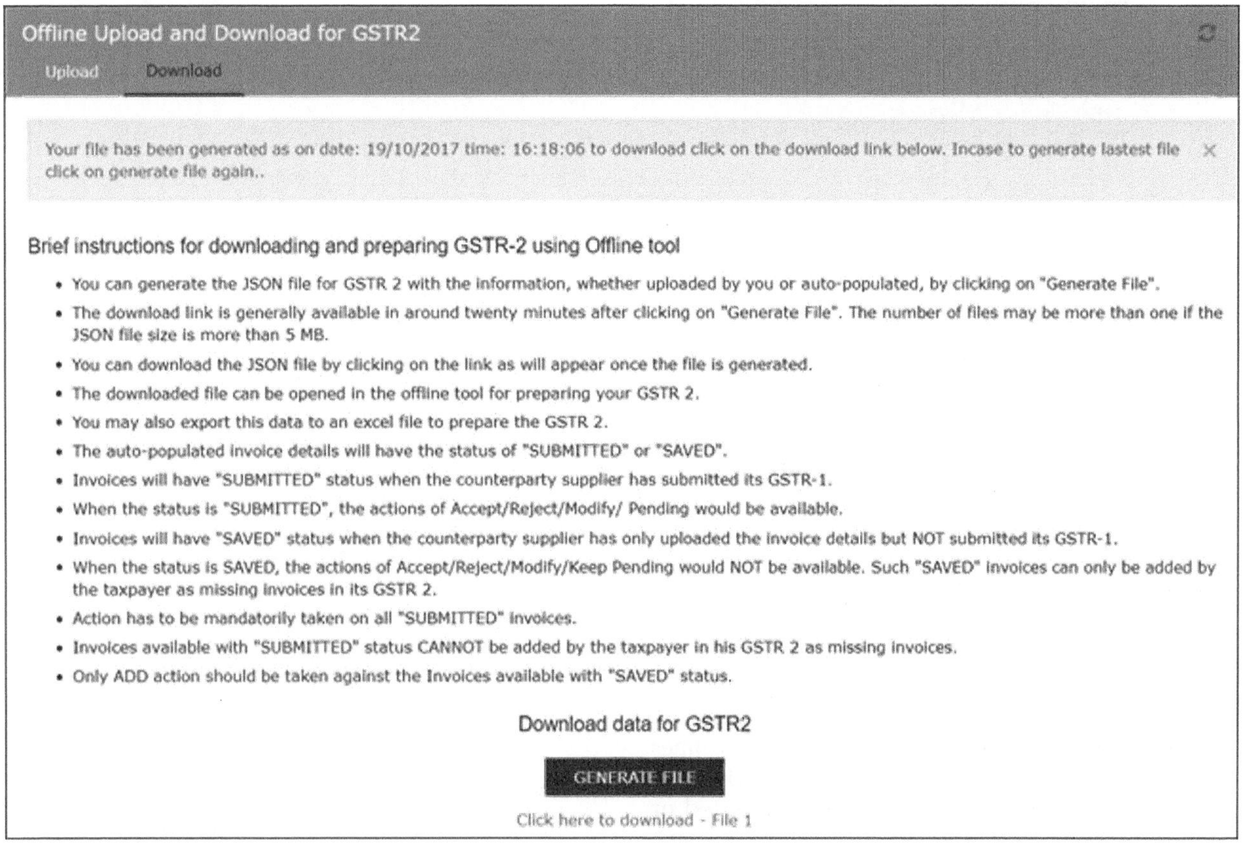

Offline Upload and Download for GSTR2
Upload
Download
Your file has been generated as on date: 19/10/2017 time: 16:18:06 to download click on the download link below. Incase to generate lastest file click on generate file again..
Brief instructions for downloading and preparing GSTR-2 using Offline tool
You can generate the JSON file for GSTR 2 with the information, whether uploaded by you or auto-populated, by clicking on "Generate File".
The download link is generally available in around twenty minutes after clicking on "Generate File". The number of files may be more than one if the JSON file size is more than 5 MB.
You can download the JSON file by clicking on the link as will appear once the file is generated.
The downloaded file can be opened in the offline tool for preparing your GSTR 2.
You may also export this data to an excel file to prepare the GSTR 2.
The auto-populated invoice details will have the status of "SUBMITTED" or "SAVED".
Invoices will have "SUBMITTED" status when the counterparty supplier has submitted its GSTR-1.
When the status is "SUBMITTED", the actions of Accept/Reject/Modify/ Pending would be available.
Invoices will have "SAVED" status when the counterparty supplier has only uploaded the invoice details but NOT submitted its GSTR-1.
When the status is SAVED, the actions of Accept/Reject/Modify/Keep Pending would NOT be available. Such "SAVED" invoices can only be added by the taxpayer as missing invoices in its GSTR 2.
Action has to be mandatorily taken on all "SUBMITTED" invoices.
Invoices available with "SUBMITTED" status CANNOT be added by the taxpayer in his GSTR 2 as missing invoices.
Only ADD action should be taken against the Invoices available with "SAVED" status.
Download data for GSTR2
GENERATE FILE
Click here to download - File 1

*Figure 15.4: Offline Upload and Download for GSTR2*

8. In the **Download** tab, click **GENERATE FILE**. The file will be generated.
9. Click the link **Click here to download** to download the GSTR-2 file.
10. Copy the ZIP/extracted JSON file in the folder to a computer.

Once after saving the extracted JSON file in the computer, then follow the step given below:

**Step 2:** Load the GSTR-2 file and reconcile the transactions.

1. Go to **Gateway of Tally** > **Display** > **Statutory Reports** > **GST** > **GSTR-2.**
2. Click **L: Load File.**
3. In the **Load File** screen, enter the path in which the GSTR-2 file is saved i.e. the downloaded file, and press **Enter.**

---

**Note:** Make sure the period in the GSTR-2 report and the company GSTIN/UIN are same as that of the file, so that the ZIP/JSON file will be listed.

---

4. While selecting the ZIP/JSON file the message will pop up as shown in the figure 15.5:

The **File Loaded Successfully! Message** screen appears as shown in the figure 15.5:

File loaded successfully!
Total no. of invoices loaded is 19
Update reconciliation of invoice status?
Yes or No

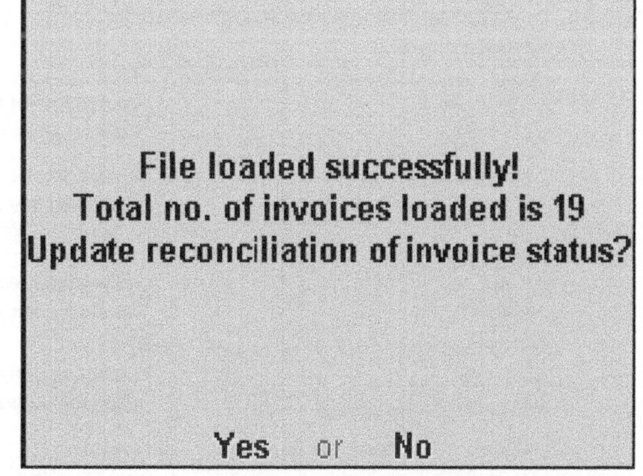

*Figure 15.5: File Loaded Successfully! Message*

5. To update the invoice status in GSTR-2 report select as **Yes** or to load only the file not the status, then select as **No.**

The **GSTR-2** report screen appears as shown in the figure 15.6:

| GSTR-2 | National Enterprises | | | | | Ctrl + M |
|---|---|---|---|---|---|---|
| **GSTIN/UIN : [illegible]** | | | | | | **1-Jul-2017 to 31-Jul-2017** |
| **Path\File Name:** C:\TallyERP9\GSTR-2_[illegible]_July_2017-18_NC.json | | | | | | |
| **Returns Summary** | | | | | | |
| **Number of vouchers for the period** | | | | | | **41** |
| Included in returns | | | | | | 28 |
| *Invoices ready for returns* | 28 | | | | | |
| *Invoices with mismatch in information* | 0 | | | | | |
| Not included in returns due to incomplete information | | | | | | 0 |
| Not relevant for returns | | | | | | 13 |

| **Particulars** | **No. of Invoices** | **Taxable Value** | **Total Tax** | **Total ITC Available** | **Reconciliation Status** |
|---|---|---|---|---|---|
| B2B Invoices - 3, 4A - Portal | 11 | 35,35,000.00 | 6,69,000.00 | 6,69,000.00 | Not Complete(11) |
| *As per books* | 13 | 29,35,000.00 | 4,85,400.00 | 4,85,400.00 | |
| Credit/Debit Notes Regular - 6C - Portal | 2 | 2,14,000.00 | 38,520.00 | 38,520.00 | Not Complete(2) |
| *As per books* | 2 | (-)2,14,000.00 | (-)38,520.00 | (-)38,520.00 | |
| B2BUR Invoices - 4B - Portal | 2 | 3,60,000.00 | 64,800.00 | 64,800.00 | |
| *As per books* | 1 | 90,000.00 | 16,200.00 | 16,200.00 | |
| Import of Services - 4C - Portal | 1 | 2,00,000.00 | 36,000.00 | 36,000.00 | |
| *As per books* | 1 | 2,00,000.00 | 36,000.00 | 36,000.00 | |
| Import of Goods - 5 - Portal | 1 | 44,00,000.00 | 7,92,000.00 | 7,92,000.00 | |
| *As per books* | 1 | 11,00,000.00 | 1,98,000.00 | 1,98,000.00 | |
| Credit/Debit Notes Unregistered - 6C - Portal | 1 | 1,10,000.00 | 19,800.00 | 19,800.00 | |
| *As per books* | 1 | (-)1,10,000.00 | (-)19,800.00 | (-)19,800.00 | |
| Nil Rated Invoices - 7 - Portal (Summary) | 1 | 85,000.00 | | | |
| *As per books* | 1 | 85,000.00 | | | |
| Advance Paid -10A - Portal (Summary) | 1 | 1,23,000.00 | 6,150.00 | | |
| *As per books* | 2 | 1,23,000.00 | 6,150.00 | | |
| Adjustment of Advance - 10B - Portal (Summary) | 1 | 1,23,000.00 | 6,150.00 | | |
| *As per books* | 1 | (-)56,000.00 | (-)2,800.00 | | |
| **Total Inward Supplies** | | **91,50,000.00** | **16,40,520.00** | **16,20,120.00** | |
| ITC Reversal/Reclaim - 11 - Portal (Summary) | 7 | | 8,100.00 | | |
| | | | | | **11 more ...** |

*Figure 15.6: GSTR-2 Report*

**Note:** In the GSTR-2 report of figure 15.6, blue colour lines show the details as per the downloaded GSTR-2 file. This includes the details of invoices submitted or saved by the supplier, and the invoices that we have manually uploaded on the portal. Black colour lines show the details of invoices as per books of account maintained in Tally.ERP 9.

Once after loading the JSON file, let us reconcile the status for invoices/transactions in **GSTR-2** report to do so, select **B2B Invoice -3, 4A** and press **Enter**

1. From **GSTR-2** report, press **Enter** on **B2B Invoice -3, 4A,** to get the **Party Register** details screen.

   The **Party Register** will appear as shown in the figure 15.7:

| Party Register | National Enterprises | | | | | Ctrl + M |
|---|---|---|---|---|---|---|
| Vouchers of : **B2B Invoices - 3, 4A** | | | | | | **1-Jul-2017 to 31-Jul-2017** |
| **Supplier Name** | **Supplier GSTIN/UIN** | **No.of Invoices** | **Taxable Value** | **Tax Paid** | **ITC Availed** | **Reconciliation Status** |
| **Status not Updated** | | | | | | |
| *M TECH* | [illegible] | 5 | 2,64,231.18 | 48,096.40 | 48,096.40 | *Not Complete (5)* |
| *<Not Available>* | [illegible] | 16 | 4,665.68 | 838.04 | 838.04 | *Not Complete (16)* |
| *ARIHANT* | [illegible] | 35 | 3,40,046.00 | 80,968.08 | 80,968.08 | *Not Complete (8)* |
| | | 35 | 3,40,046.00 | 80,963.08 | 80,963.08 | |
| *<Not Available>* | [illegible] | 1 | 30,000.00 | 8,400.00 | 8,400.00 | *Not Complete (1)* |
| *Penton* | [illegible] | 1 | 3,700.00 | 666.00 | 666.00 | *Not Complete (1)* |
| | | 1 | 3,800.00 | 684.00 | 684.00 | |
| **States Updated** | | | | | | |
| *Epso* | [illegible] | 1 | | | | *Completed* |
| *SHRINIDHI* | [illegible] | 1 | 462.00 | 83.16 | 83.16 | *Completed* |
| **Saved Transactions (Create if not available in book)** | | | | | | |
| *VISHWA* | [illegible] | 0(1) | | | | *Completed* |
| *Crown* | [illegible] | 0(2) | | | | *Completed* |
| | | 2 | 35,064.00 | 9,817.92 | 9,817.92 | |
| **Available Only in Books (Can mark as 'New' when exporting)** | | | | | | |
| MAGNIFIED | | 1 | 30,000.00 | 8,400.00 | 8,400.00 | |
| S.V.INFO | [illegible] | 1 | 16,600.00 | 2,988.00 | 2,988.00 | |
| **Grand Total (As per Portal)** | | **63** | **6,33,094.86** | **1,39,051.68** | **1,39,051.68** | |
| **(As per Books)** | | **40** | **4,25,510.00** | **1,02,853.00** | **1,02,853.00** | |

F5: Invoice-wise
C: Contact Details
S: Set Status

*Figure 15.7: Party Register*

Explanation of the options available in Party Register screen as shown in figure 15.7:

- **Status not Updated**: Displays the party-wise details of transactions for which status is not set.
- **Status Updated**: Displays the party-wise details of transactions for which status is set.
- **Saved Transactions (Create if not available in books)**: Displays the transactions which the counter party has submitted but not filed as part of GSTR-1 returns.
- **Available Only in Books (Can mark as 'New' when exporting)**: Displays transactions which are available only in Tally.ERP 9. While exporting the data to JSON format, we can set the status as **New** and export it to JSON file.

2. From the **Party Register** screen press **F5:Invoice-wise**

   The **Party Register – Invoice Wise** report appears as shown in the figure 15.8:

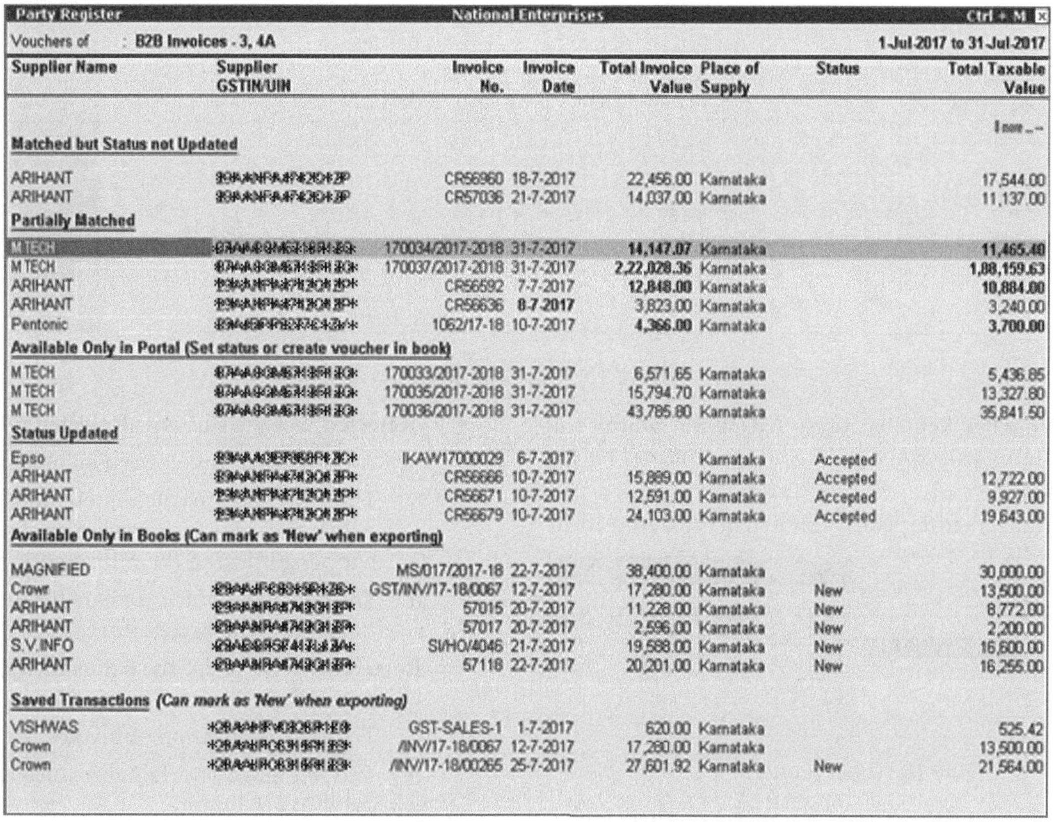

Party Register | National Enterprises | Ctrl + M

Vouchers of : B2B Invoices - 3, 4A | 1-Jul-2017 to 31-Jul-2017

| Supplier Name | Supplier GSTIN/UIN | Invoice No. | Invoice Date | Total Invoice Value | Place of Supply | Status | Total Taxable Value |
|---|---|---|---|---|---|---|---|
| **Matched but Status not Updated** | | | | | | | |
| ARIHANT | [illegible] | CR56960 | 18-7-2017 | 22,456.00 | Karnataka | | 17,544.00 |
| ARIHANT | [illegible] | CR57036 | 21-7-2017 | 14,037.00 | Karnataka | | 11,137.00 |
| **Partially Matched** | | | | | | | |
| M TECH | [illegible] | 170034/2017-2018 | 31-7-2017 | **14,147.07** | Karnataka | | **11,465.40** |
| M TECH | [illegible] | 170037/2017-2018 | 31-7-2017 | **2,22,028.36** | Karnataka | | **1,88,159.63** |
| ARIHANT | [illegible] | CR56592 | 7-7-2017 | **12,848.00** | Karnataka | | **10,884.00** |
| ARIHANT | [illegible] | CR56636 | **8-7-2017** | 3,823.00 | Karnataka | | 3,240.00 |
| Pentonic | [illegible] | 1062/17-18 | 10-7-2017 | **4,366.00** | Karnataka | | **3,700.00** |
| **Available Only in Portal (Set status or create voucher in book)** | | | | | | | |
| M TECH | [illegible] | 170033/2017-2018 | 31-7-2017 | 6,571.65 | Karnataka | | 5,436.85 |
| M TECH | [illegible] | 170035/2017-2018 | 31-7-2017 | 15,794.70 | Karnataka | | 13,327.80 |
| M TECH | [illegible] | 170036/2017-2018 | 31-7-2017 | 43,785.80 | Karnataka | | 35,841.50 |
| **Status Updated** | | | | | | | |
| Epso | [illegible] | IKAW17000029 | 6-7-2017 | | Karnataka | Accepted | |
| ARIHANT | [illegible] | CR56686 | 10-7-2017 | 15,889.00 | Karnataka | Accepted | 12,722.00 |
| ARIHANT | [illegible] | CR56671 | 10-7-2017 | 12,591.00 | Karnataka | Accepted | 9,927.00 |
| ARIHANT | [illegible] | CR56679 | 10-7-2017 | 24,103.00 | Karnataka | Accepted | 19,643.00 |
| **Available Only in Books (Can mark as 'New' when exporting)** | | | | | | | |
| MAGNIFIED | | MS/017/2017-18 | 22-7-2017 | 38,400.00 | Karnataka | | 30,000.00 |
| Crowr | [illegible] | GST/INV/17-18/0067 | 12-7-2017 | 17,280.00 | Karnataka | New | 13,500.00 |
| ARIHANT | [illegible] | 57015 | 20-7-2017 | 11,228.00 | Karnataka | New | 8,772.00 |
| ARIHANT | [illegible] | 57017 | 20-7-2017 | 2,596.00 | Karnataka | New | 2,200.00 |
| S.V.INFO | [illegible] | SI/HO/4046 | 21-7-2017 | 19,588.00 | Karnataka | New | 16,600.00 |
| ARIHANT | [illegible] | 57118 | 22-7-2017 | 20,201.00 | Karnataka | New | 16,255.00 |
| **Saved Transactions** *(Can mark as 'New' when exporting)* | | | | | | | |
| VISHWAS | [illegible] | GST-SALES-1 | 1-7-2017 | 620.00 | Karnataka | | 525.42 |
| Crown | [illegible] | /INV/17-18/0067 | 12-7-2017 | 17,280.00 | Karnataka | | 13,500.00 |
| Crown | [illegible] | /INV/17-18/00265 | 25-7-2017 | 27,601.92 | Karnataka | New | 21,564.00 |

*Figure 15.8: Party Register – Invoice Wise Report*

3. The report of figure 15.8 displays the details of transactions made with all parties.

   The transactions made with all parties in Party Register – Invoice Wise report will be available in the following categories:

   - **Matched but Status not Updated**: We can select the status **Accepted, Accepted with Ineligible ITC, Modified, Pending,** or **Rejected**.
   - **Partially Matched**: We can select the status **Accepted, Accepted with Ineligible ITC, Modified, Pending,** or **Rejected.**
   - **Available Only in Portal (Set status or create voucher in book)**: Click **A: Add Voucher** to create the transaction in Tally.ERP 9.
   - **Status Updated**: We can set the status to be uploaded as **Accepted, Accepted with Ineligible ITC, Modified, Pending,** or **Rejected.**
   - **Available Only in Books (Can Mark as 'New' when exporting)**: While exporting the data to JSON format, we can set the status as New and export it to JSON file.
   - **Saved Transactions (can mark as 'New' when exporting)**: Displays the transactions which the counter party has submitted but not filed as part of GSTR-1 returns.

4. From the **Party Register**, select any party ledger to view the **Voucher Register** report as shown in figure 1.8:

   The **Voucher Register** screen will appears as shown in figure 15.9:

Voucher Register — National Enterprises — Ctrl + M

Vouchers of : ARIHANT — 1-Jul-2017 to 31-Jul-2017

GSTIN/UIN : [illegible]

| Invoice No. | Invoice Date | Total Invoice Value | Place of Supply | Status | Total Taxable Value | Integrated Tax Amount | ITC Available Integrated Tax |
|---|---|---|---|---|---|---|---|
| | | | | | | | 6 more ... — |
| **Matched but Status not Updated** | | | | | | | |
| CR56960 | 18-7-2017 | 22,456.00 | Karnataka | | 17,544.00 | | |
| CR57036 | 21-7-2017 | 14,037.00 | Karnataka | | 11,137.00 | | |
| **Partially Matched** | | | | | | | |
| [illegible] | 7-7-2017 | 12,848.00 | Karnataka | | 10,884.00 | | |
| CR56636 | 8-7-2017 | 3,823.00 | Karnataka | | 3,240.00 | | |
| CR56983 | 19-7-2017 | 18,099.00 | Karnataka | | 14,140.00 | | |
| CR56988 | 19-7-2017 | 11,228.00 | Karnataka | | 8,772.00 | | |
| CR57263 | 27-7-2017 | 11,228.00 | Karnataka | | 8,772.00 | | |
| **Available Only in Portal (Set status or create voucher in book)** | | | | | | | |
| CR57015 | 20-7-2017 | 11,228.00 | Karnataka | | 8,772.00 | | |
| CR57017 | 20-7-2017 | 2,596.00 | Karnataka | | 2,200.00 | | |
| CR57118 | 22-7-2017 | 20,201.00 | Karnataka | | 16,255.00 | | |
| **Status Updated** | | | | | | | |
| CR56666 | 10-7-2017 | 15,889.00 | Karnataka | Accepted | 12,722.00 | | |
| CR56671 | 10-7-2017 | 12,591.00 | Karnataka | Accepted | 9,927.00 | | |
| CR56679 | 10-7-2017 | 24,103.00 | Karnataka | Accepted | 19,643.00 | | |
| CR56717 | 11-7-2017 | 4,280.00 | Karnataka | Accepted | 3,627.00 | | |
| CR56773 | 12-7-2017 | 22,456.00 | Karnataka | Accepted | 17,544.00 | | |
| CR56801 | 13-7-2017 | 9,756.00 | Karnataka | Accepted | 8,268.00 | | |
| **Available Only in Books (Can mark as 'New' when exporting)** | | | | | | | |
| 57017 | 20-7-2017 | 2,596.00 | Karnataka | New | 2,200.00 | | |
| 57015 | 20-7-2017 | 11,228.00 | Karnataka | New | 8,772.00 | | |
| 57118 | 22-7-2017 | 20,201.00 | Karnataka | New | 16,255.00 | | |

*Figure 15.9: Voucher Register*

5. From the **Voucher Register**, press **Alt+S: Set Status** and select the status as per the books of account and as per GSTR-2 file.

   The **Set Status** screen appears as shown in the figure 15.10:

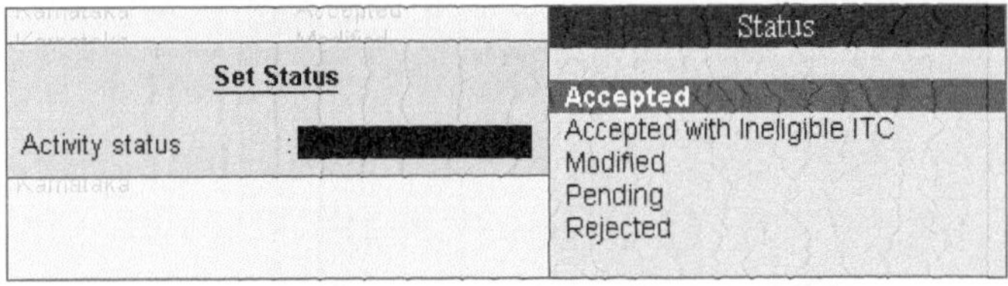


*Figure 15.10: Set Status*

6. Select the relevant status for each transaction displayed.

   When **Status** is selected as:

   - **New**: Set the status of invoices **Available only in Books** as **New** and upload them to portal as new claims. This will reflect in GSTR-1A for the counter party to act on.
   - **Accepted**: Set the status as **Accepted** when the invoices in Tally.ERP 9 are fully matching with the invoices in the GSTR-2 file (downloaded from portal).
   - **Modified**: Set the status as **Modified** when the invoices in Tally.ERP 9 are partially matching with the invoice details in the portal. This will reflect in GSTR-1A for the counter party to act on.
   - **Pending**: Set the status as **Pending** to put the invoice on hold. For example, the invoice is available in books or in portal but the goods have not been delivered during the return period. We can accept, reject or modify the invoice in the next return period based on the transaction status.
   - **Rejected**: Set the status as **Rejected** when:
     - o An unknown invoice is available on the portal.
     - o The purchase invoice is created but the actual delivery of goods or rendering of services has not happened during the return period.
     - o The rejected invoice appears for the counter party in GSTR-1A to accept or reject.
   - **Rejected by GST**: Set the status as **Rejected by GST** when:
     - o There is duplication of invoice.
     - o The reference of original invoice is not found for debit or credit note.
     - o GSTIN of the party has been suspended.

7. Similarly, In GSTR-2, select **Credit/Debit Notes Regular - 6C** and press **Enter**. Reconcile the transactions as per the procedure used for **B2B Invoices - 3, 4A.**

8. Once the reconciliation of B2B Invoices and Debit and Credit, we can save the **GSTR-2 Return** by using the key **Alt+S: Save Returns.**

The information related to invoices reconciled and marked as New is saved to the JSON file loaded in Tally.ERP 9.

**Note:** If the reconciliation of all the invoice statuses is not completed, then we can do it at regular intervals by loading the saved JSON file to continue the reconciliation for the next set of transactions

Once the reconciliation is complete, then follow the step given below:

**Step 3:** Generate the return in JSON format and file the return

1. From **GSTR-2** report, press **F12: Configure**

The **Configuration** screen appears as shown in the figure 15.11:

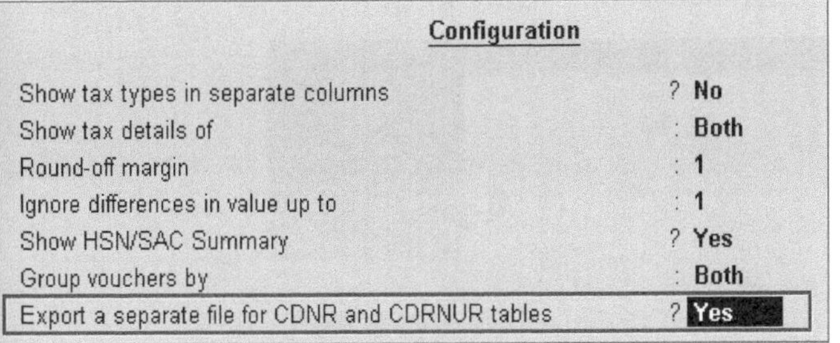


*Figure 15.11: Configuration Screen*

2. Set the option **Export a separate file for CNDR & CDRNUR tables** to **Yes**
3. Accept the configuration screen.
4. Press **Ctrl+E** to export and set the option **Export transactions available only in the book with the status New?** to **Yes**

   The files will be exported in JSON format in the **FiletoUpload** folder (in the path from where the GSTR-2 file downloaded from portal, was loaded in GSTR-2 report of Tally.ERP 9. The status of transactions which are available only in the books will be marked as **New** and exported to JSON file.
5. After exporting the return, Login to the GST Portal (www.gst.gov.in)
6. Click **Services** > **Returns** > **Returns Dashboard.**
7. Select the **Return Filing Period**, and click **SEARCH**.

   The **Returns Dashboard** screen appears as shown in the figure 15.12:

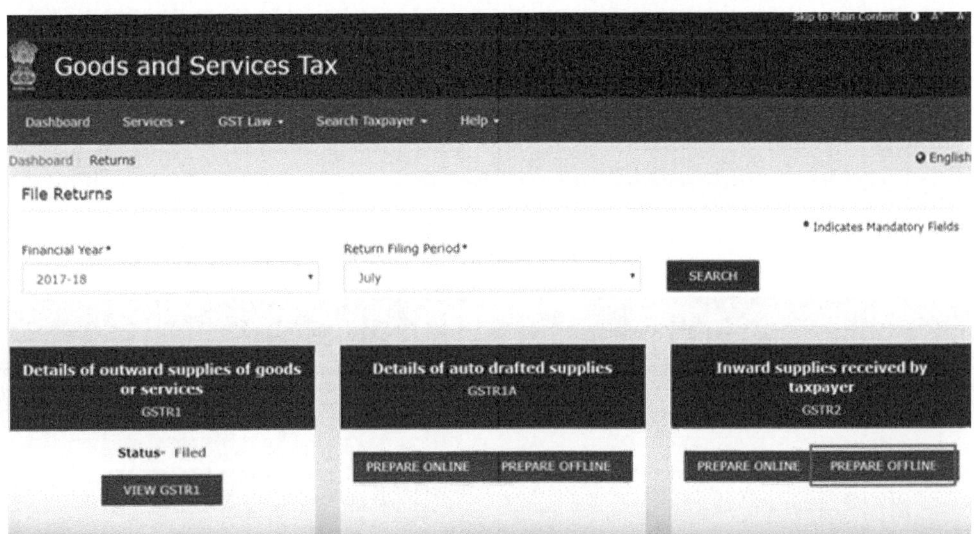


*Figure 15.12: Return Dashboard screen*

8. Click **PREPARE OFFLINE**

   The **Offline Upload and Download for GSTR2** appears as shown in the figure 15.13:
9. Click on **Upload** tab.

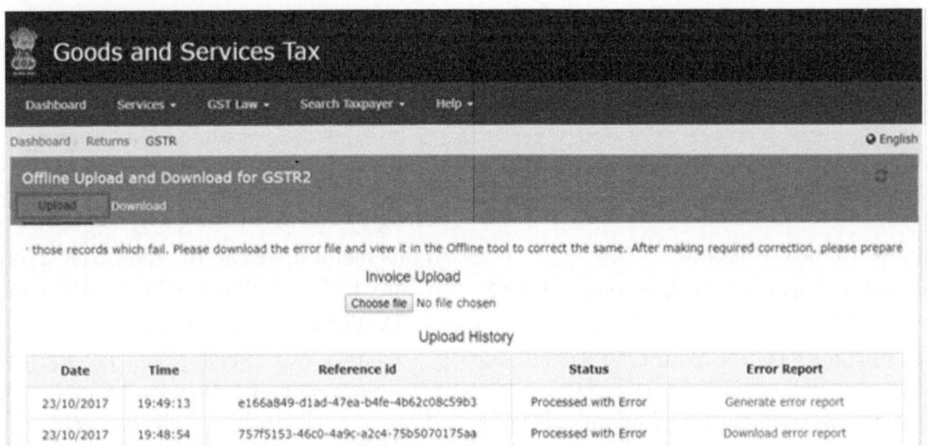


*Figure 15.13: Offline Upload & Download for GSTR2*

10. Browse and select the JSON file generated in Tally.ERP 9 The **JSON File Selection** appears as shown in figure 15.14:

11. Once after selecting the JSON file will be processed an the details will be updated in the respective tables in GSTR as shown in the figure 15.15:

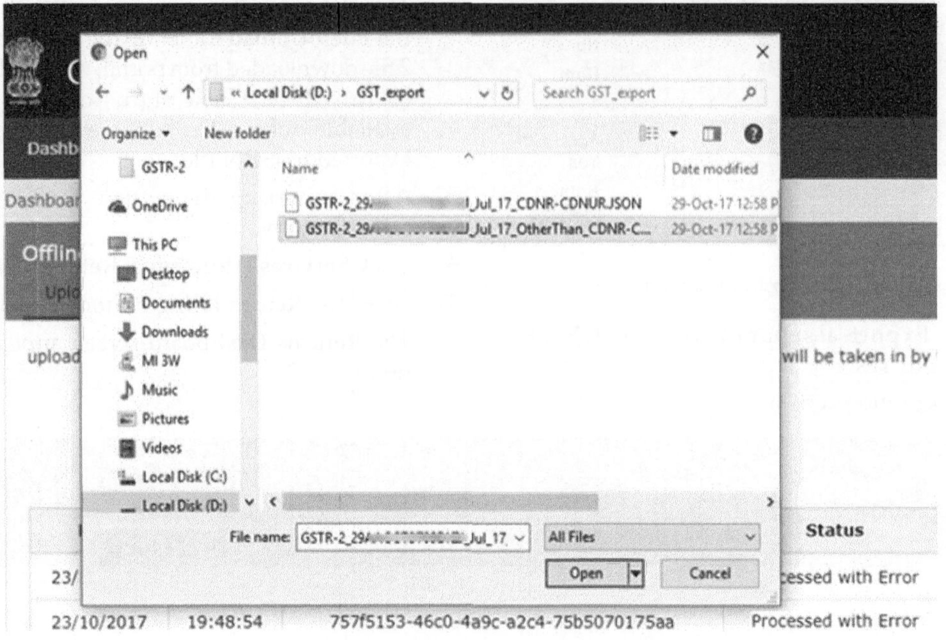


*Figure 15.14: JSON File Selection*

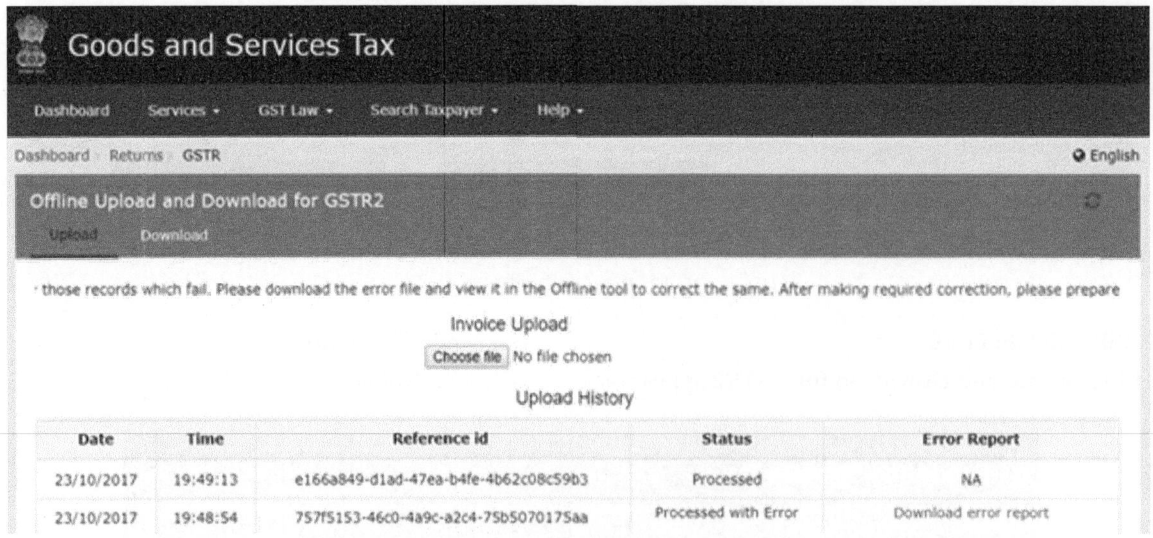


*Figure 15.15: Updated Details in GSTR-2*

12. Preview the uploaded details in **Status** column.
13. Click **BACK** to return to the dashboard.
14. Under **Inward supplies received by taxpayer GSTR2**, click **PREPARE ONLINE**.
15. Click **SUBMIT**, and **FILE RETURN**. Your **GSTR-2** will be filed electronically.

The above procedure is one of the method to file the GSTR-2 return from Tally.ERP 9. Next we will learn about the other two methods used in filing GSTR-2 return, they are:

### *Filing of Return Using Offline Tool*

In this method we can file the GSTR-2 return using offline to in Tally.ERP 9. Follow the below given steps to file the return

1. Download the GSTR-2 file from GST portal
2. Import the GSTR-2 file in the offline tool, reconcil transaction and generate JSON
3. Upload the generated JSON file on the GST portal and fil the GSTR-2 returns.

**Note:** To download GST Offline Tool follow the below given procedure:

- Go to the GST portal > **Downloads**.
- Click **Returns Offline Tool**. A **ZIP** file containing the **GST Offline Tool** will be downloaded. This zip file also contains a detailed document on using the offline tool. Some important information about the tool, and the system requirements for using the tool are also available on the download page.
- Extract the offline tool from the ZIP file and install it.

### *Prepare Online*

In this method, we can refer the data captured in GSTR-2 report of Tally.ERP 9 and enter the transaction details in the portal for filing returns.

## 15.2 GSTR 1 REPORT IN TALLY.ERP 9

GSTR-1 is the monthly GST return to be filed by a taxable person registered under GST. GSTR-1 includes the details of all outward supplies made in the given period. The outward supply details include B2B invoices, B2C invoices, adjustments to sales made in debit/credit notes, exports, nil rated invoices, advances received with tax adjustments.

### 15.2.1 Filing of GSTR-1 Return in Tally.ERP 9

In Tally.ERP 9, we can file the GSTR 1 return by generating the GSTR-1 file as per the latest e-filing requirements.

In Tally.ERP 9, we can file the GSTR-1 return in one of the following methods:

- By using the JSON file generated from Tally.ERP 9.
- By using offline tool or,
- By filing directly on the GST portal.

**Note:** JSON stands for JavaScript Object Notation, it is the data interchange format.

Filing of Return by Using the JSON File Generated from Tally.ERP 9

In this section, we will learn to file the GSTR-1 return by using the JSON file generated from Tally.ERP 9.

**Step 1:** Generating of GSTR-1 Return in JSON from Tally.ERP 9

1. Go to **Gateway of Tally** > **Display** > **Statutory Reports** > **GST** > **GSTR-1**.
2. Press **F2: Period** enter the period for which returns need to be filed.
3. Press **F12: Configure:** To view the export options for HSN/SAC details, enable **Show HSN/SAC Summary?** And accept the configuration screen.
4. Press **Ctrl+E: Export GSTR-1**

   The **Export Report** appears as shown in the figure 15.16:

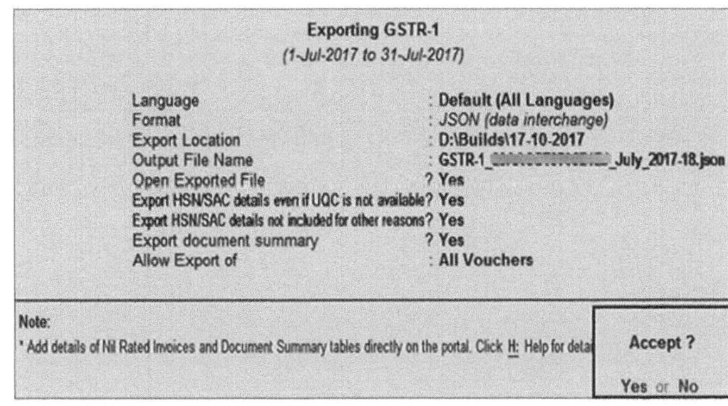


*Figure 15.16: Export Report*

5. Enter the details as shown in figure 15.16, make sure the **Format** is selected as **JSON (data interchange).**
6. Press **Enter** to accept.
7. Compress the **JSON file** generated from Tally.ERP 9 in the **.zip** format and upload it to the portal for filing returns.

**Step 2:** File GSTR-1 Return

1. Login to GST portal.
2. Click **Services** > **Returns** > **Returns Dashboard**.
3. Select the **Return Filing Period**, and click **Search**.

   The **File Returns** screen appears as shown in the figure 15.17:

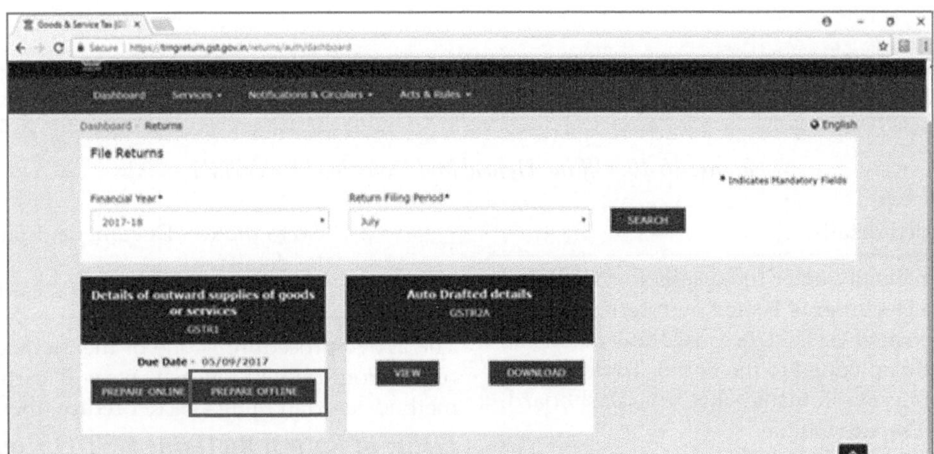


*Figure 15.17: File Returns*

4. Under **Details of outward supplies of goods or services GSTR1,** select **PREPARE OFFLINE.** We will get the screen as shown in figure 15.18:

The **Offline Upload and Download for GSTR-1** appears as shown in the figure 15.18:

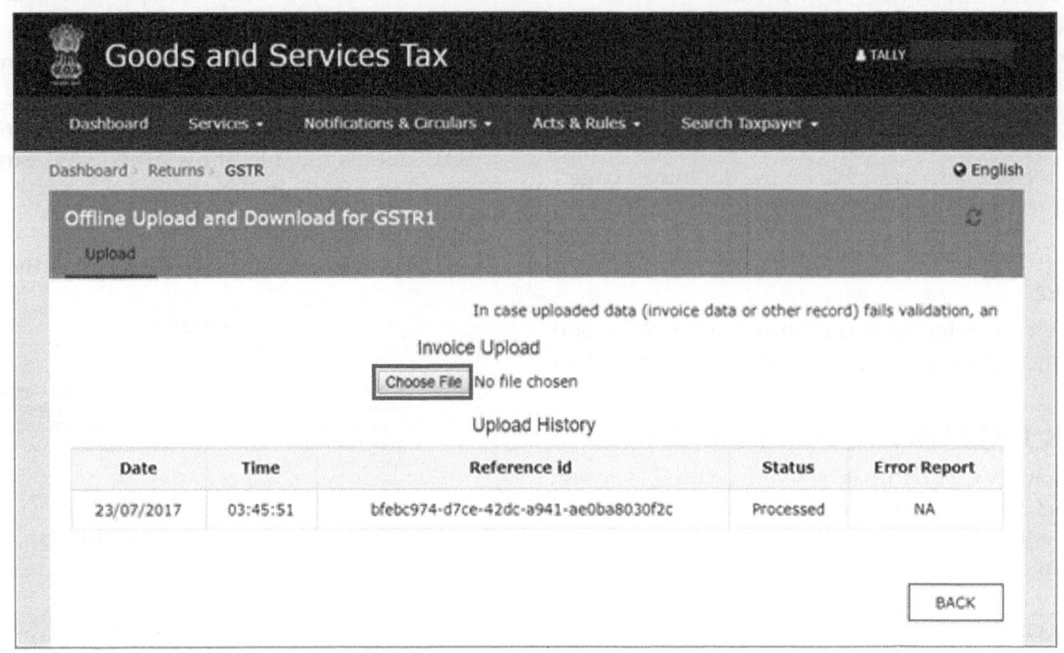


*Figure 15.18: Offline Upload and Download for GSTR-1*

5. Click on **Choose File** tab to import the JSON file generated from Tally.ERP 9 or the offline tool. Once the JSON file is uploaded successfully, we will get the notification as shown in figure 15.19:

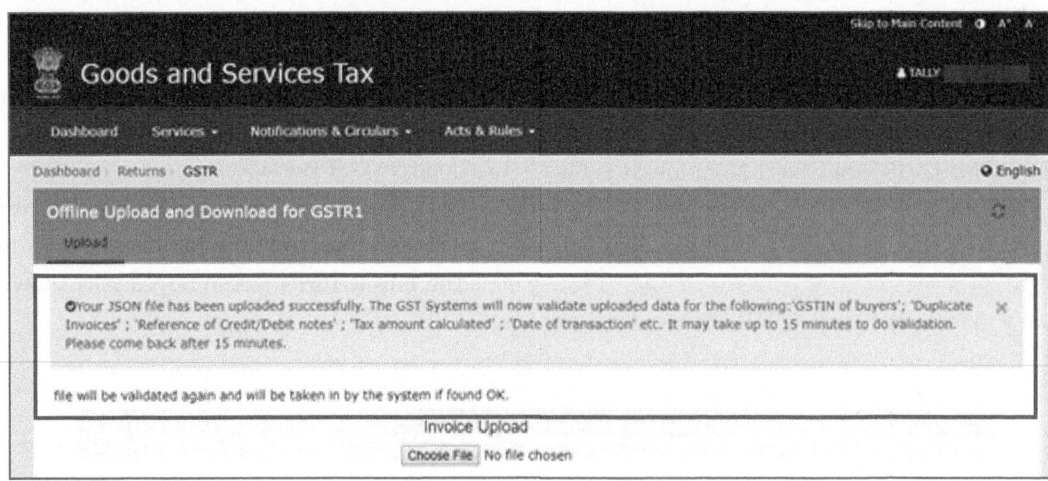


*Figure 15.19: Offline Upload and Download for GSTR1*

6. Verify the uploaded details.

**Note:** We have to manually enter the details for **Nil Rated Supplies** and **Documents Issued** by referring to the table-wise format of GSTR-1, because these details do not get directly uploaded to the portal. To do so:

- Go to Services > Returns > Returns Dashboard, and click Prepare Online.
- Go to the 8A, 8B, 8C, 8D - Nil Rated Supplies page, and enter the details.
- Go to the 13 - Documents Issued page, and enter the details.
- Submit the returns and e-sign.

The above procedure is one of the method to file the GSTR-1 return from Tally.ERP 9. Next we will learn about the other two methods used in filing GSTR-1 return, they are:

### *Filing of Return By Using GST Offline Tool*

In this method we can file the GSTR-2 return using offline tool in Tally.ERP 9. Follow the below given steps to file the return:

1. Exporting of GSTR-1 returns in MS Excel or CSV
2. Import the GSTR-2 file in the offline tool and generate JSON
3. Upload the generated JSON file on the GST portal and file the GSTR-1 returns.

### *Filing of Returns Directly on the GST Portal*

To file the returns directly to GST portal, follow the steps given below:

1. Login to GST Portal
2. Go to **Services** > **Returns** > **Returns Dashboard**, and click **Prepare Online**.
3. Select the **Return Filing Period**, and click **Search**
4. Open each GSTR-1 table, read or copy data from Tally.ERP 9, and fill the tables.
5. Submit the returns and e-sign.

## 15.3 PURCHASES FROM UNREGISTERED DEALERS TRANSACTIONS AFTER DEFERMENT OF REVERSE CHARGE

Reverse charge in case of purchases made from unregistered dealers (URD) is disabled by default due to deferment of reverse charge. It is deferred till 31st March 2018. The deferment is effective from 13th October 2017 onwards.

The purchase from URD transactions will be treated as exempt transactions in **GSTR-2** and **GSTR-3B**. All adjustment transactions recorded for tax liability using the following journal flags will be moved under **Not relevant for returns** in **GSTR-2** and **GSTR-3B** reports.

### Interstate Purchase of Service from Unregistered Dealers

**Illustration:** As on 20-10-2017, National Enterprises, Karnataka procured transportation services from TJ Associates for 1,00,000, Andhra Pradesh and the service is exempted.

**Activity:** Create the following ledgers in Tally.ERP 9

- **Party Ledger:** TJ Associates under sundry creditors, enable the option **Set/alter GST details** to **Yes** and select the **Registration type** as **Unregistered.**
- **Purchase Ledger:** Transportation Services under Purchase Accounts, select **Applicable** in **Is GST Applicable** option and enable the option **Set/alter GST Details** to **Yes** and fill in the GST details as shown in figure 15.20:

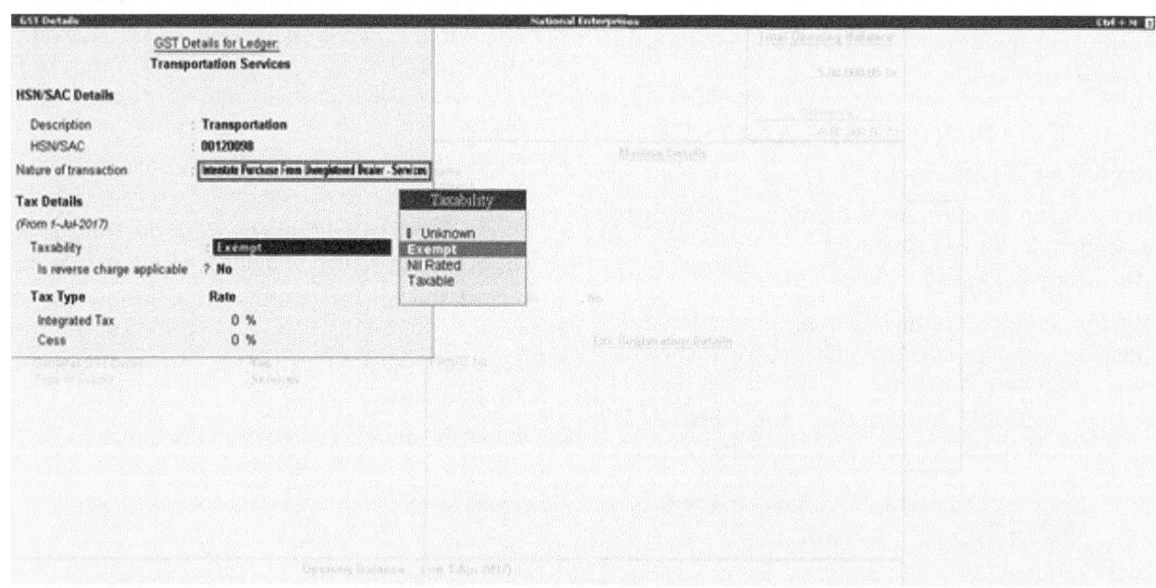


*Figure 15.20: GST Details Screen*

- Make sure to select the **Nature of Transaction** as **Interstate Purchase From Unregistered Dealer – Services** and **Type of Supply** is selected as **Services**
- Save the ledger

To record interstate purchase of service from unregistered dealers, follow the steps given below:

1. Go to **Gateway of Tally > Accounting Vouchers >** press **F9:Purchase**
2. Press **Alt+I** from item invoice mode
3. Enter the details as shown in figure 15.21:

   The **Purchase Invoice** screen appears as shown in the figure 15.21:

*Figure 15.21: Purchase Invoice Screen*

4. Press **Alt+A: Tax Analysis**, to view the calculation details. Press **Esc** to go back to the voucher creation screen.
5. Press **Ctrl+A** to accept the screen.

**Note:** The entry will appear in GSTR-2 report under the head **Nil Rated Invoices.**

## 15.4 NIL RATED PURCHASES AND SEZ TRANSACTIONS

In this section we will learn to record the nil rated purchases and SEZ transaction details in Tally.ERP 9.

### 15.4.1 Nil Rated Purchases

In Tally.ERP 9, we can record the nil rated goods purchases from a local or interstate supplier does not attract GST, and can be recorded using a purchase voucher.

***Illustration:*** *As on 20-10-2017, National Enterprises purchased 100 Kgs. Of Green Apples @ 300per/Kg. from Mani Traders. The item is nil rated.*

***Activity:*** *Create the required masters in Tally.ERP 9.*

- ***Mani Traders*** *under Sundry Creditors, enter Registration type as Regular and enter the valid GSTIN Number.*
- ***Nil Rated – Purchase*** *under Purchase Accounts, In* ***Is GST Applicable*** *field, select as Applicable, In* ***Nature of Transaction*** *field, select as Purchase Nil Rated, In* ***taxability*** *field ,select as Nil Rated.*
- *Create Unit of Measure by name Kgs. and make sure to select the UQC code.*
- *Green Apple under Primary, select the Units as Kgs., GST is applicable but do not configure GST rate details*

To record the nil rated transaction follow the steps given below:

1. Go to **Gateway of Tally > Accounting Vouchers > Press F9: Purchase.**
2. Enter the details as shown in the figure 15.22:

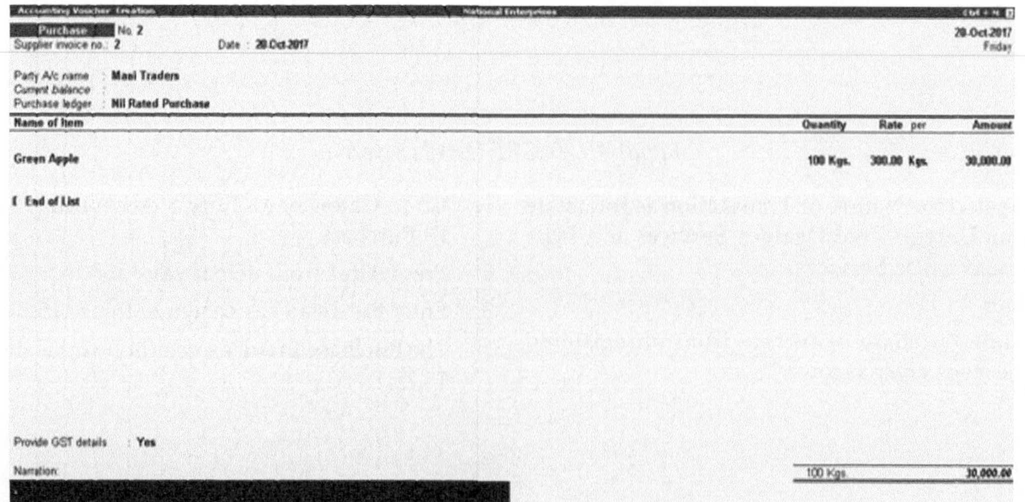

*Figure 15.22: Purchase Voucher Screen*

3. Press **Ctrl +A** to accept the screen.

Once after recording the transaction the details will get captured in GSTR-2 under Nil Rated Invoices and also the value will get captured in GSTR-3B, under the head Value of exempt, nil rated and non-GST inward supplies. Can drill down further to check more details about the transaction.

**Note:** Similarly in Tally.ERP 9, we can record the exempted purchase by configuring the ledger master of the exempted goods or services, **Taxability** to **Exempt** in the **GST Details** screen.

### 15.4.2 SEZ Purchases

SEZ stands for Special Economic Zone and the purchases made from a party in SEZ can be recorded using purchase voucher.

The following are the Nature of SEZ Transactions available in Tally.ERP 9:

- Purchase from SEZ – Taxable
- Purchase from SEZ - Exempt or Nil Rated
- Purchase from SEZ without bill of entry
- Purchase from SEZ - LUT/Bond

***Illustration:*** *As on 20-10-2017, National Traders purchased 100 bottles of Chocolate Butter @300 per bottle from Food Court Ltd. – TFI Agro Tech Park.*

***Activity:*** *Create the required masters in Tally.ERP 9.*

- ***Food Court Ltd. – TFI Agro Tech Park*** *under Sundry Creditors, enter Registration type as Regular, Party Type as SEZ and enter the valid GSTIN Number.*
- ***SEZ Taxable Purchase*** *under Purchase Accounts, In* ***Is GST Applicable*** *field, select as Applicable, In* ***Nature of Transaction*** *field, select as* ***Purchase from SEZ Taxable,*** *In* ***taxability*** *field, by default it will as taxable and enter the GST tax rate as 12%.*
- *Create Unit of Measure by name Btl. and make sure to select the UQC code.*
- ***Chocolate Butter*** *under Primary, select the Units as Btl.., GST is applicable but do not configure GST rate details.*

**Note:** Purchase from SEZ - Taxable: In SEZ purchases, integrated tax is applicable for both local and interstate parties. In the **Party Details** screen of the invoice, set the option **Is BOE not Available?** to **No.**

To record the SEZ Taxable Purchase Transactions, follow the steps given below:

1. Go to **Gateway of Tally** > **Accounting Vouchers** > **F9: Purchases**
2. Enter the details as shown in the figure 15.23:
3. Press **Ctrl+A** to accept.

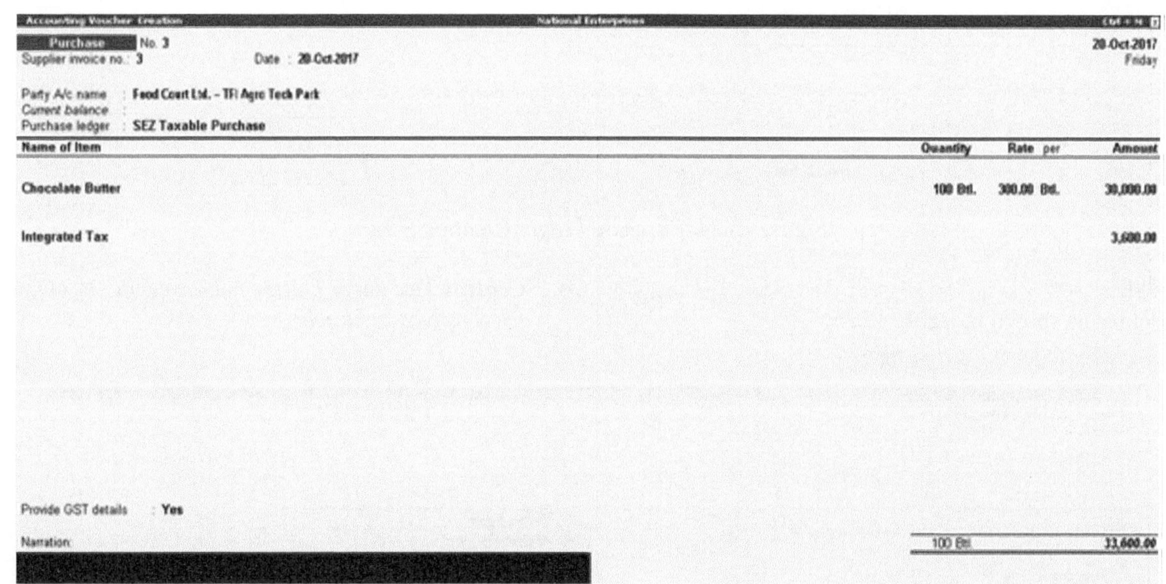


*Figure 15.23: SEZ Taxable Purchase*

In Tally.ERP 9, the SEZ Transactions will get captured in GSTR-2 report.

**Note:** Similarly we can record the SEZ Transactions based on its nature of transactions as shown below:

- Purchase from SEZ - Exempt or Nil Rated: No tax is applicable. In the Party Details screen of the invoice, set the option Is BOE not Available? to No
- Purchase from SEZ without bill of entry: Can be taxable, exempt or nil rated. In the Party Details screen of the invoice, set the option Is BOE not Available? to Yes.
- Purchase from SEZ - LUT/Bond: No tax is applicable. Such purchases can be made when your supplier has signed up a letter of undertaking with the department for the sale of goods without the payment of duty. While passing the purchase transaction, you can select either the ledger created for exempt SEZ purchases or the common purchase ledger.

- o Provide the LUT/Bond details in the Company GST Details screen.
- o Set the option in Is BOE not Available? to Yes in the Party Details screen of the invoice.

In Tally.ERP 9, we have also provided the option to record the details of Deemed Exports and Purchase of Work Contract service as per the filing requirements.

## 15.5 PURCHASE OF SERVICES THAT ATTRACTS GST AND TDS

In Tally.ERP 9, we can record the purchase of services which attracts the GST and TDS. To account the transactions we ca use the purchase voucher.

***Illustration:*** *As on 21-10-2017, National Enterprises, purchase software license from Sky High Solutions Pvt. Ltd. @ 2, 00,000.*

To record the purchase transaction, follow the steps given below

***Activity:*** *Enable TDS option F11: Company Features > F3: Statutor and Taxation.*

**Step 1:** Creation of Required Masters.

### *Purchase of Software License.*

Go to **Gateway of Tally > Accounts Info. > Ledgers > Create** Enter the details as shown in the figure 15.24:

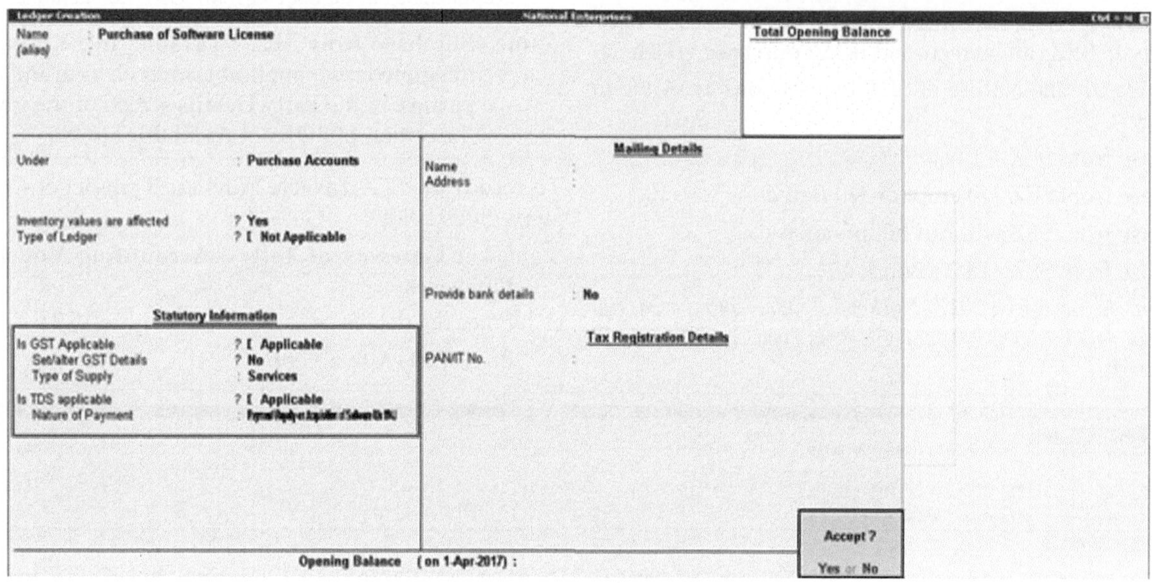


Figure 15.24: Purchase Ledger Creation Screen

### *Party Ledger*

Enter the details as shown in figure 15.25:

***Activity:*** *Create the following duty ledgers:*

- o ***Central Tax*** *under Duties and Taxes, In "Is TDS Applicable select as Not applicable*

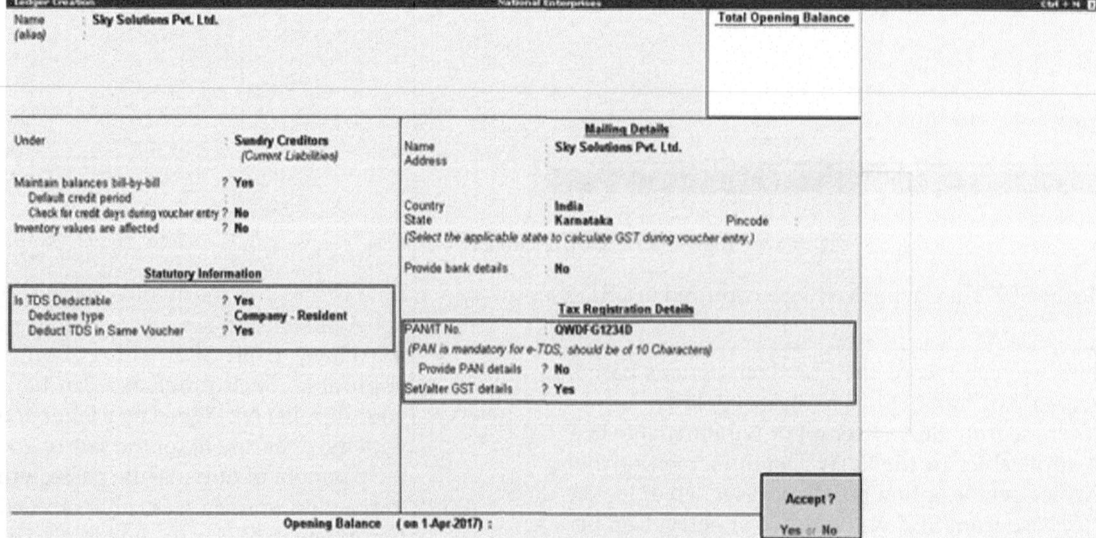


Figure 15.25: Party Ledger Creation Screen

- ***State Tax** under Duties and Taxes, In "Is TDS Applicable" select as Not applicable*
- ***TDS Duty** under Duties and Taxes, In "Nature of Payment" select as Payment/Royalty on Acquisition of software U/s 194J*
- ***Make sure to select the correct tax configuration***

**Step:** Recording of Transaction

1. Go to **Gateway of Tally > Accounting Vouchers >** press **F9: Purchase.**
2. Press **F2: Date** and change the date to 21-10-2017.
3. Press **Alt+I** to move from item invoice mode to accounting invoice mode.
4. Enter the details as shown in figure 15.26:

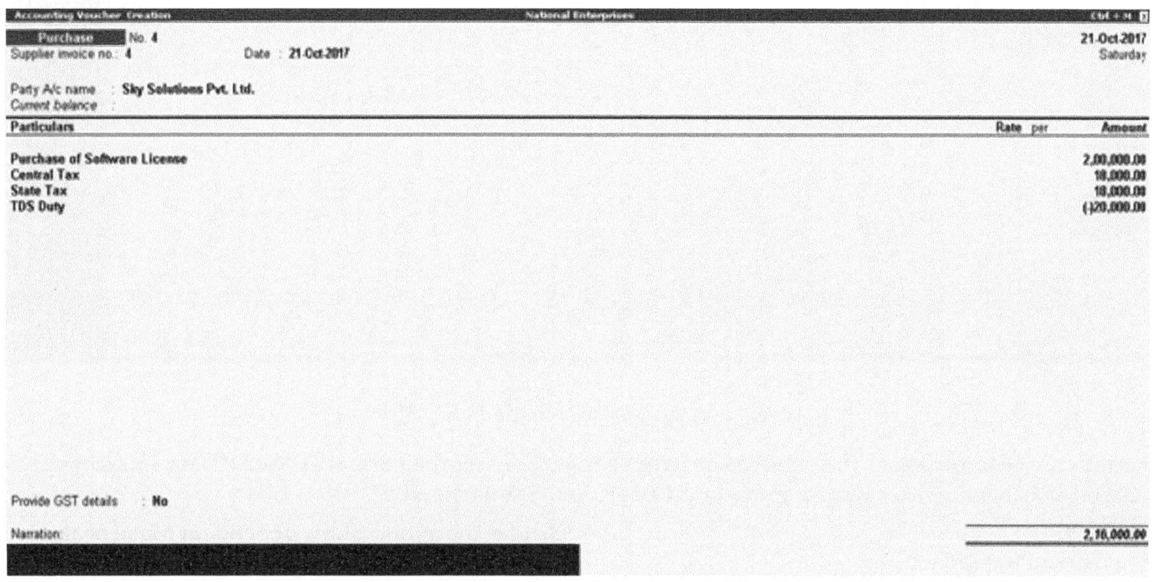


*Figure 15.26: Purchase Invoice*

5. Press Ctrl+A to accept the screen.

The transaction of figure 1.24 will appear in GSTR-2 and in Form 26Q of TDS report under Deduction at Normal Rate field.

## 15.6 MARKING OF MODIFIED VOUCHERS BY CONSULTANTS AND SHARING IT WITH CLIENTS.

At the end of financial period or on frequent basis the books of accounts maintained by many businesses are audited or the returns are filed by taking the help from consultants like Tax consultants, CA, Accountants etc.

As a consultant, if we modify the clients' books, then we have to ensure that their books reflect the final values. To address this need, we can use the **Mark Changed Vouchers** feature. This feature helps to identify the list of changed vouchers, but not the individual changes.

**Note:**
- Client place and consultant place should have Tally.ERP 9 Release 6.2 Installed.
- Once the data is shared with the consultant, the client should not make any changes in the data shared. If the changes are made, then while importing the data received from consultants, the changes will be overwritten.

***Illustration:** As on 31-10-2017, National Traders has send the data for auditing to the tax consultant.*

Let us check the activity done as a consultant and client.

### *As a Consultant*

As a consultant, once the data is received from the client (National Enterprises), need to mark the vouchers in the client's data.

To mark the vouchers in the client's data

1. Open the client's data in Tally.ERP 9 Release 6.2
2. Go to **Gateway of Tally** > **F11: Features** > **Accounting Features**
3. Set the option **Mark changed vouchers** to **Yes**
4. Accept the **Accounting Features** screen
5. Modify the transactions as per the statutory needs. (**For example:** While auditing the data tax consultant have found out that the GSTIN Numbers were not given in the party details screen and in the party ledgers. The same changes were done in the National Enterprises data)

To view the modified vouchers in the clients data

Once after making the necessary changes, we can view the modified transactions details in the following register.

1. Go to **Gateway of Tally** > **Display** > **Exceptions Reports** > **Marked Vouchers**

The **Marked Vouchers Registers** screen appears as shown in the figure 15.27:

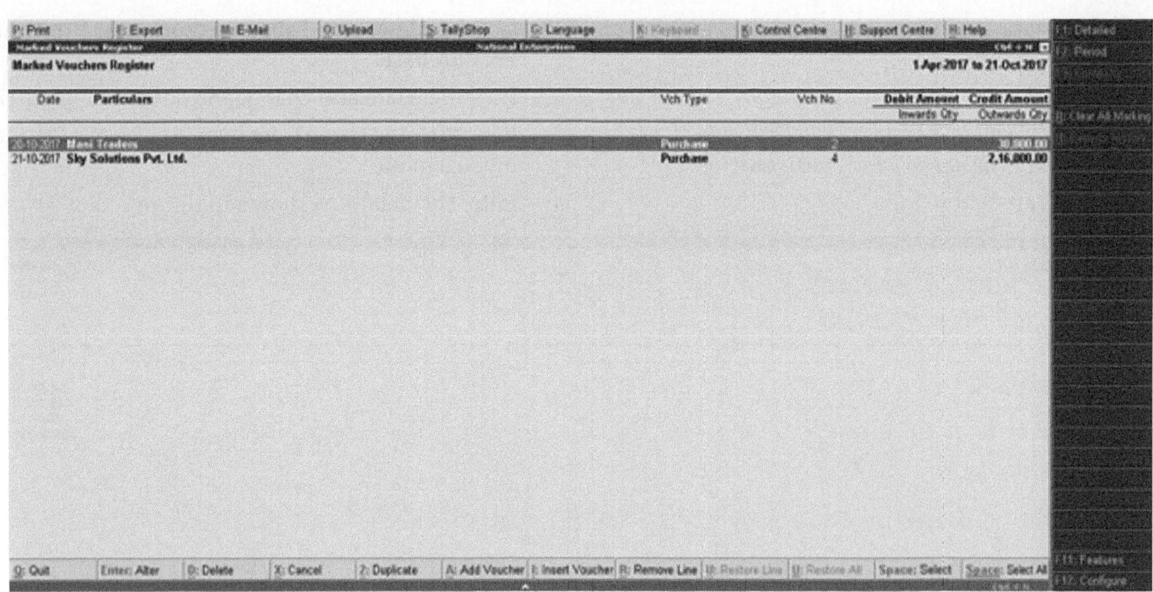

*Figure 15.27: Marked Vouchers Registers*

If by mistake any changes are marked, the same can be removed from the marked vouchers register by using the key **Ctrl+R: Clear All Marking**

To export the marked transaction

1. Press **E: Export** in the **Marked Vouchers Register**
2. Select the **Format** as **XML (Data Interchange for Marked Vouchers)**
3. Set the option **Show dependent Masters also?** to **Yes**, if the masters in the altered transactions are also modified

   The **Export Report** appears as shown in the figure 15.28:

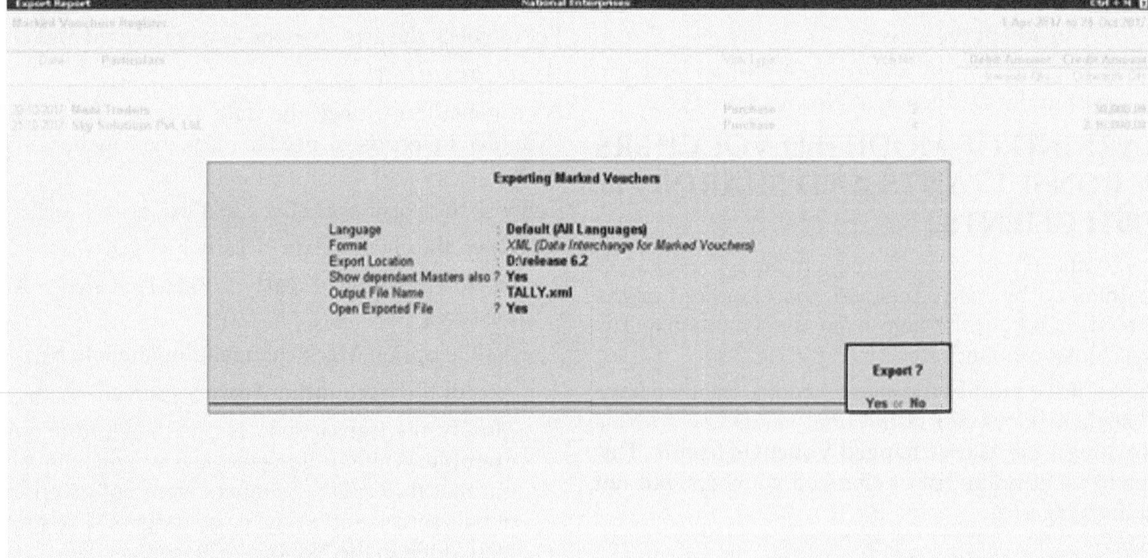


*Figure 15.28: Export report*

4. Press **Enter** to export

**Note:** If the data is shared periodically with the client change the **Output File Name** and export the data.

5. After exporting check the export history or summary of exported voucher use the key **Ctrl+H: Export History** from the **Marked Vouchers Register**

The **Summary of Exported Vouchers** appears as shown in the figure 15.29:

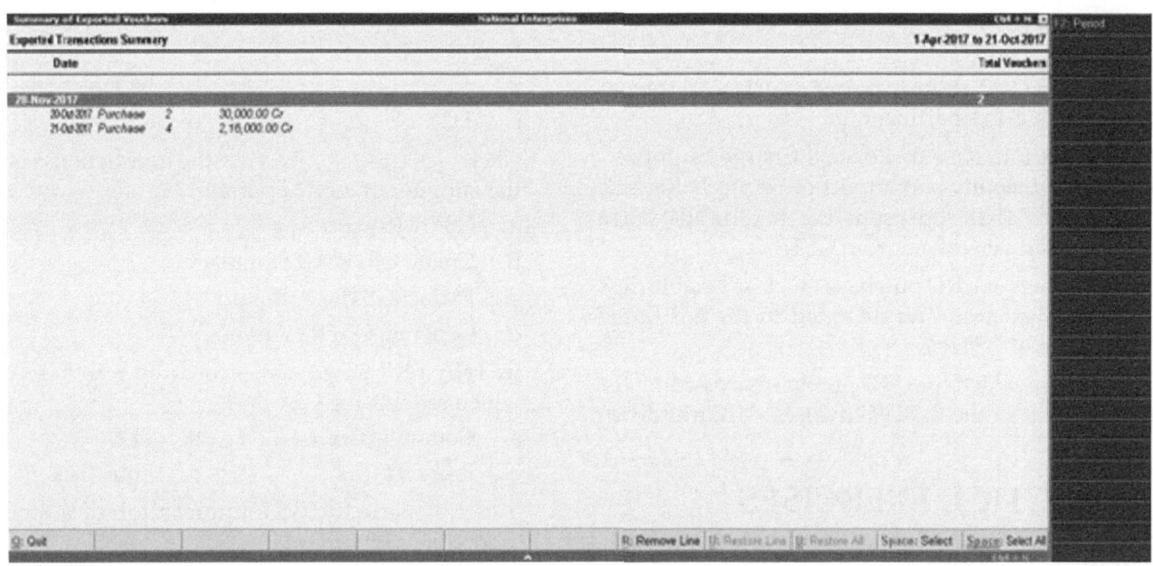

*Figure 15.29 Summary of Exported Vouchers*

### *As a Client*

As a client, once after receiving the data from tax consultant, the modified vouchers can be imported in the present data. The same will be updated.

1. Open your company data. Ensure that the option **Mark changed vouchers?** is set to **No**.
2. Save the XML file received from the consultant in your computer.
3. Go to **Gateway of Tally** > **Import Data** > **Vouchers**. Enter the data path in which the XML file is saved.
4. Press **Enter** to Import the file.

**Note:** Once the data is shared with the consultant, the client should not make any changes in the data shared. If the changes are made, then while importing the data received from consultants, the changes will be overwritten.

## 15.7 OTHER ADDITIONS OF TALLY.ERP 9

The following are the other enhancements or enhancements done in Tally.ERP 9 Release 6.2

- No need to pay GST at the time of receipt of advances on sale of goods for taxpayers with turnover up to Rs. 1.5 Cr.

  By default, Release 6.1.1 does not consider taxes on advances received. For businesses with more than Rs. 1.5 Cr aggregate turnover, use Enable tax liability on advance receipts under F11: Statutory & Taxation to consider tax on advances received.
- **Better GST billing experience:** Specify the discount value for each item in the invoice, and the discount value is considered as part of the assessable value of an item. Cash sales are considered as local sales by default now. Your cash transactions will be much faster and error-free.
- **Improved GSTIN validation:** Tally.ERP 9 validates the party GSTIN (as required by the GSTN portal) when you create a party or export GSTR-1. This helps avoid invoice rejection on the GSTN portal due to incorrect party GSTIN.
- **Better control of round-off mismatches:** We have introduced an option in F12: Configure to define the band for round-off limit for mismatches. With this, you can choose to ignore mismatches in tax calculation that occur due to minor round-off differences, up to a specific amount. Fewer mismatches to resolve means lesser work.
- If you are creating a party ledger for an Embassy or a UN Body, you can select the party type as Embassy/UN Body
- If you are creating a company or a party ledger for a Society, Club, Trust, or AOP, you can enter numbers or alphabets as the last 3 characters while entering the GSTIN/UIN.
- You can enter the discount percentage or amount for each stock item in the invoice by enabling the option Activate cash/trade discount? in the invoice configuration screen. The total discount amount will be displayed against the discount ledger.
- You can print invoices with your company state name and code.
- View export details from GSTR-1 > Export Invoices - 6A and import details from GSTR-2 > Import of Goods - 5 drill-down reports. You can also view these details in the columnar registers by enabling the options Show shipping details?/Show bill of entry details? and Show port code?.
- You can view the contact details and e-mail ID of the party in the Party Ledger level correction report
- Use the new report Advance Payments – Tax Liability to know the amount of advance payments made or reversed in a period. You can create or reverse the liability accordingly.

- You can view the GST Information of a stock item in the Stock Query report.
- We support GSTR-2 report as per the latest format provided by the GST department.
- New reports for Purchase of Reverse Charge Supplies - Reverse Charge Liability and Import of Service - Reverse Charge Liability that represent the tax liability are provided. You can view them from GSTR-2.
- View the net values of URD purchases such as taxable (less than Rs. 5,000), exempt, and nil rated in the Nil Rated Invoices - 7 table of GSTR-2.
- The tax liability recorded for URD purchases exceeding Rs. 5000 now appears in the B2BUR Invoices - 4B drill-down report of GSTR-2.

## PRACTICE EXERCISES

1. In Tally.ERP 9, the user can load __________file and reconcile for filing return
   a. GSTR 2 b. GSTR 10A
   c. GSTR 20B d. GSTR 20
2. In Tally.ERP , the user can export GSTR 2 in __________ format also
   a. APK b. JSON
   c. Txt d. btm
3. Click __________ to view the transactions submitted by the supplier on GSTN portal.
   a. GSTN Reports
   b. Create GSTR AB Summary
   c. Extract GSTR 1A Report
   d. Generate GSTR2 Summary
4. In Tally.ERP 9, we can record the purchase of services which attracts the GST and _______
   a. Common Tax b. TDS
   c. Property Tax d. Entry Tax
5. You can view the GST Information of a stock item in _________ report
   a. Stock Journal b. Inventory Info
   c. Statutory Info d. Stock Query

**Answers**

1. (a) 2. (b) 3. (d) 4. (b) 5. (d)

## Chapter 16

# Tally.ERP 9 Release 6.3 Annexure

## 16.1 EXPORTING OF GSTR-3B IN JASON FORMAT

In Tally.ERP 9, we can now directly export GSTR-3B form in JSON format and upload it to the GST portal. Even we can export the GSTR-3B in in MS Excel MS Excel offline utility tool provided by the department.

In Tally.ERP 9, we can file the GSTR-3B in any one of the following methods.

**Method 1:** By generating the JSON file from Tally.ERP 9 and uploading the same in GST portal.

**Method 2:** By using the GSTR-3B excel offline utility tool.

**Method 3:** By filing the return directly on the portal.

In this section we will learn to export GSTR-3B in JSON format and upload the same in GST portal.

---

**Note:** Ensure that all exceptions regarding incomplete/ mismatch in information are resolved before printing or exporting the **GSTR-3B** report.

---

**Method 1: By generating the JSON file from Tally.ERP 9 and uploading the same in GST portal**

1. To generate GSTR-3B, go to **Gateway of Tally> Display** > **Statutory Reports** > **GST** > **GSTR-3B**.

   The **GSTR-3B** report appears as shown in the figure 16.1:

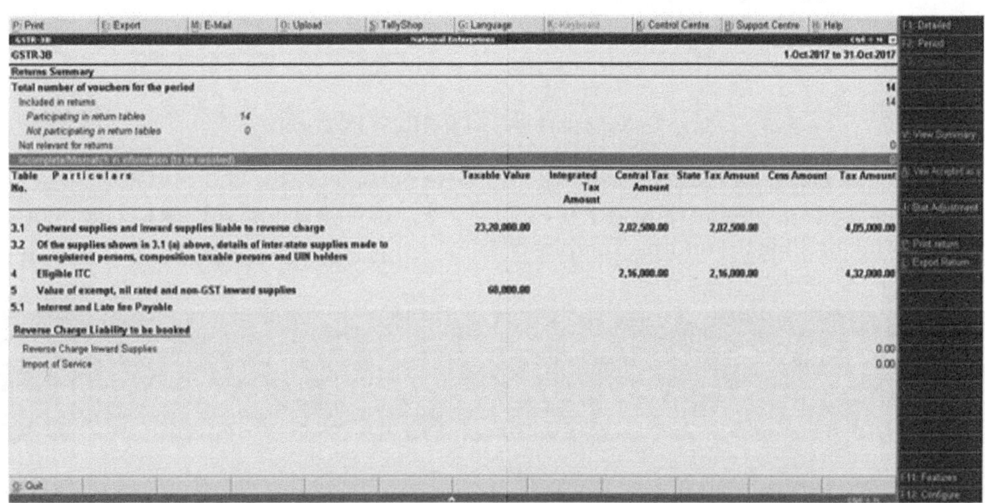

*Figure 16.1: GSTR-3B Report screen*

2. Press **Ctrl+E: Export Return.**
3. Select **JSON (Data Interchange)** as the **Format**.

   The completed **Export Report** screen appears as shown in the figure 16.2:

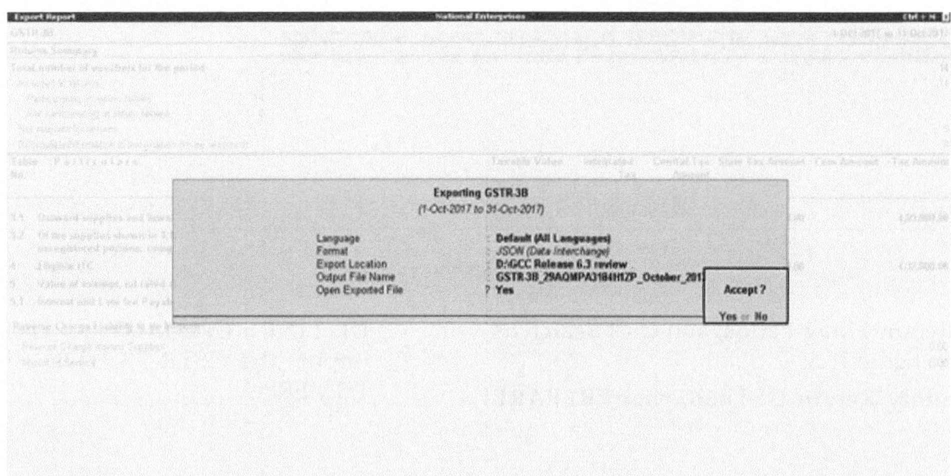


*Figure 16.2: Export Report screen*

4. Press **Enter** to export.

   After exporting the GSTR-3B the file will be available in the location given in export location.

   The **Exported GSTR-3B in JSON Format** appears as shown in figure 16.3:

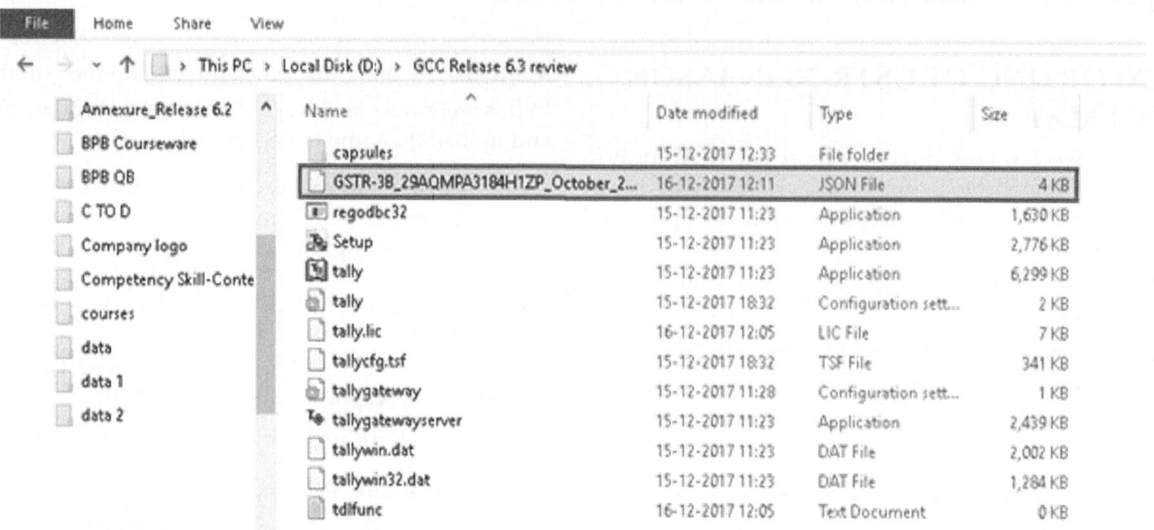


*Figure 16.3: Exported GSTR-3B JSON Format*

5. Upload the JSON file to the portal for filing returns.

   After GSTR-3B JSON file generated from Tally.ERP 9, can be uploaded in GST portal for filing the returns. To upload the same follow the steps given below:

   - Log in to the GST portal.
   - Go to **Dashboard** > **RETURN DASHBOARD**.

     The **Dashboard** appears as shown in the figure 16.4:

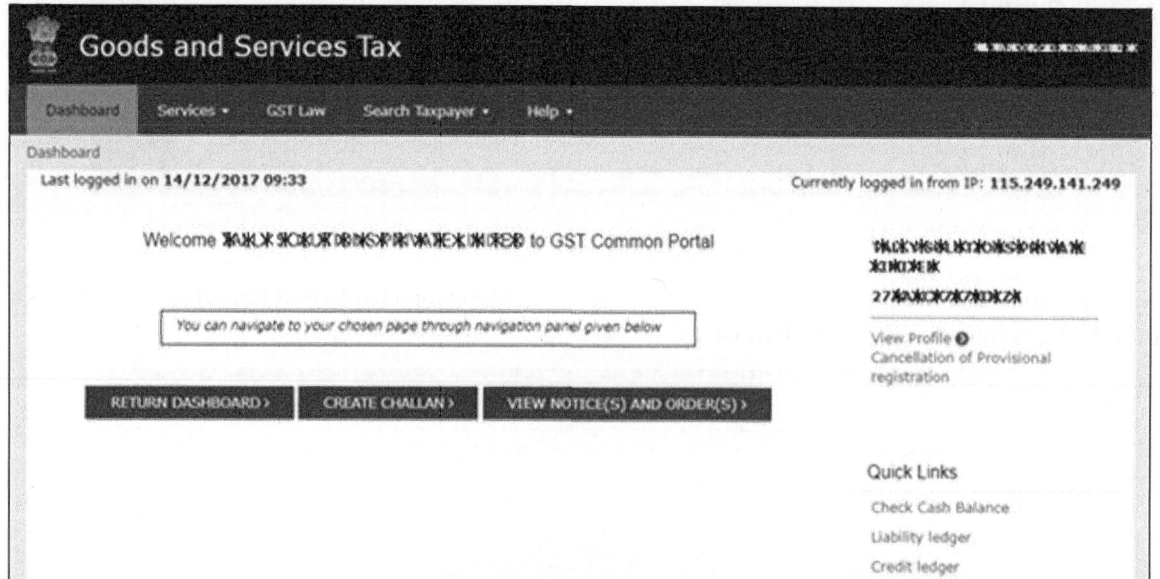


*Figure 16.4:Dashboard screen*

   - Select the **Return Filing Period**, and click **Search** as shown in the figure 16.5:
   - Under **Monthly Return GSTR3B**, click **PREPARE OFFLINE** > **UPLOAD** tab > click **CHOOSE FILE** to import the GSTR-3B JSON file generated from Tally.ERP 9.

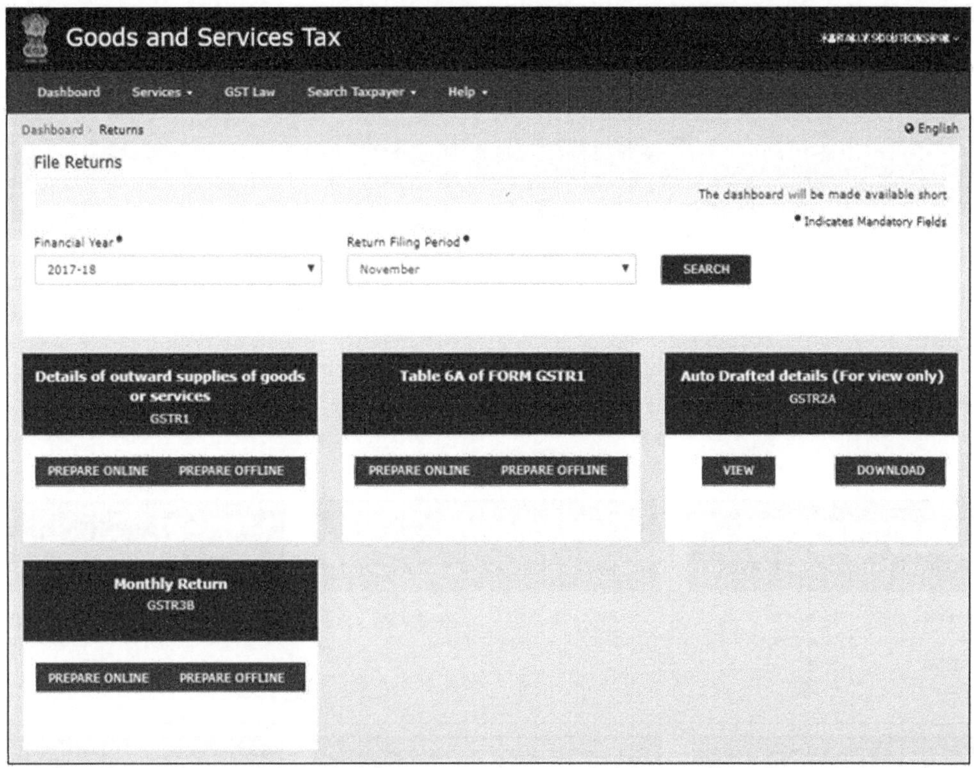


*Figure 16.5: Dashboard – selection of Return filing period*

- Once the JSON files are uploaded successfully, we will be notified with a message. Once the file is successfully uploaded the **Error Report** displays **NA**, as shown in figure 16.6

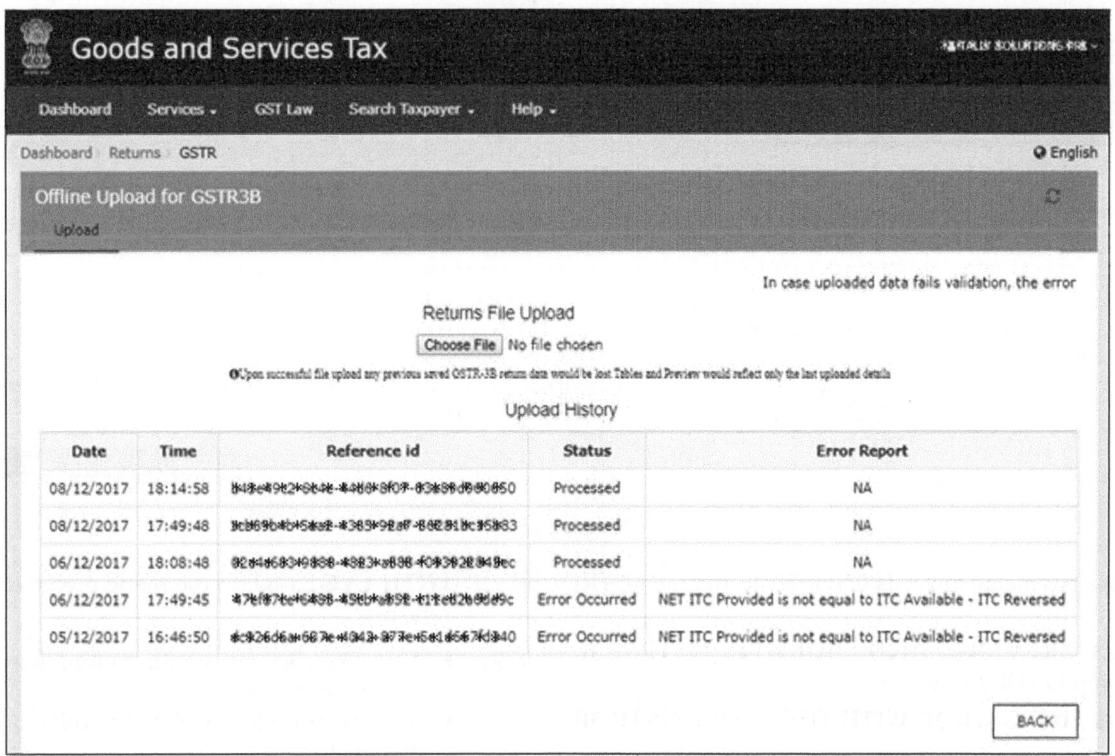


| Date | Time | Reference id | Status | Error Report |
|---|---|---|---|---|
| 08/12/2017 | 18:14:58 | [illegible] | Processed | NA |
| 08/12/2017 | 17:49:48 | [illegible] | Processed | NA |
| 06/12/2017 | 18:08:48 | [illegible] | Processed | NA |
| 06/12/2017 | 17:49:45 | [illegible] | Error Occurred | NET ITC Provided is not equal to ITC Available - ITC Reversed |
| 05/12/2017 | 16:46:50 | [illegible] | Error Occurred | NET ITC Provided is not equal to ITC Available - ITC Reversed |

*Figure 16.6: Offline Upload for GSTR-3B*

- Click **BACK > Monthly Return GSTR3B**, click **PREPARE ONLINE**. The values get posted in the relevant tables of GSTR-3B.
- Click the declaration check box and click **SAVE GSTR3B**.

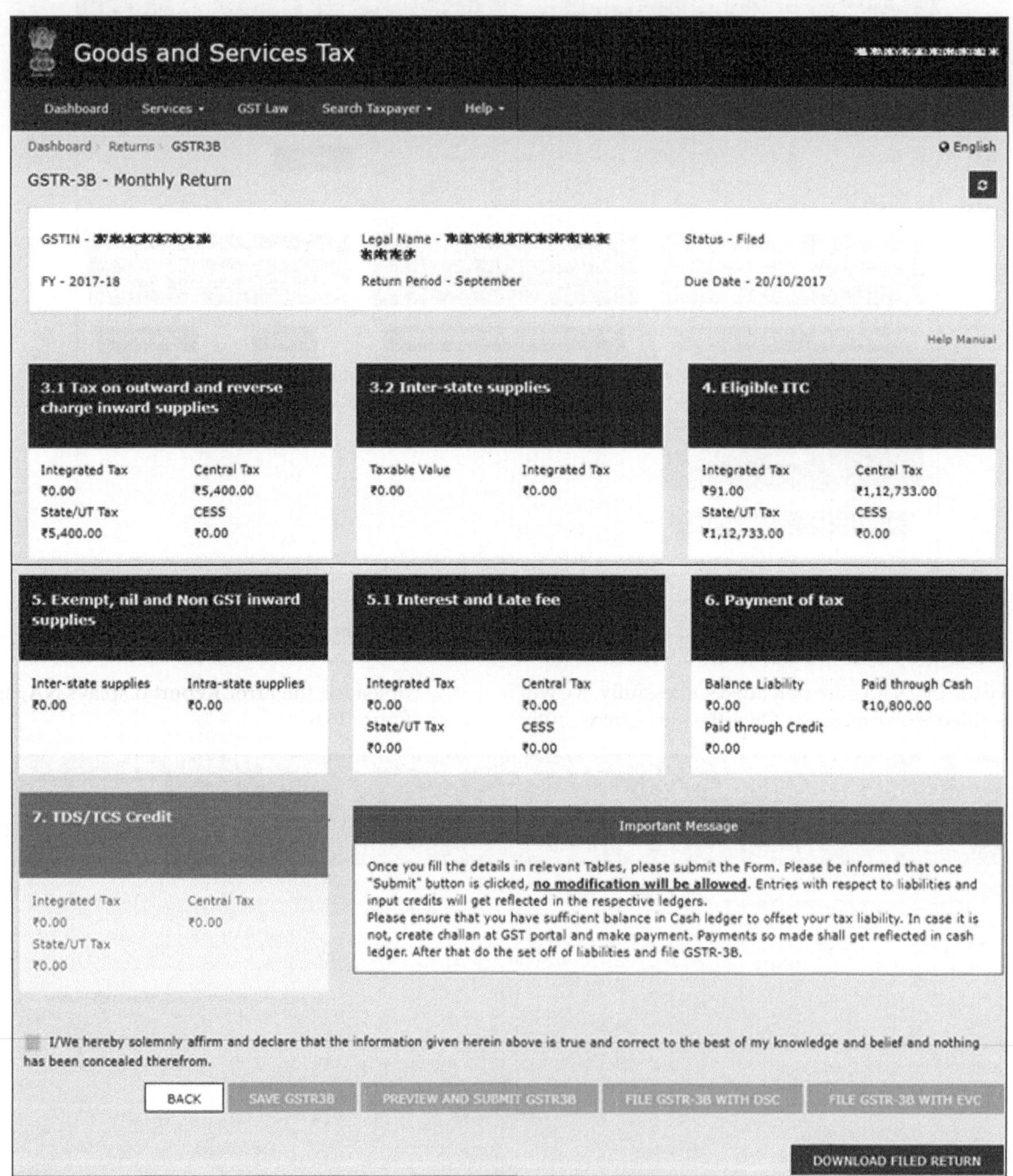


*Figure 16.7*

- Make payments towards GSTR-3B, to file the GSTR-3B returns.
- Click **PREVIEW AND SUBMIT GSTR3B** to submit **GSTR-3B** returns.
- Click **FILE GSTR-3B WITH DSC** or **FILE GSTR-3B WITH EVC** based on the mode preferred to sign the returns.

**Note:**
- Once we click on submit button, then the GSTR-3B cannot be revised.
- We can also file GSTR-3B by following the other two methods also.

## 16.2 GENERATE QUARTERLY GSTR-1 REPORT

As per the announcements made in the 23rd GST Council Meeting, regular dealers with turnover less than 1.5 Cr have to file GSTR-1 on a quarterly basis.

In this section we will learn to generate quarterly GSTR-1 report in Tally.ERP 9.

To generate,

- Go **Gateway of Tally**, **F11** > **F3** > **Statutory** details.
- Enable the option **Set/alter GST details** to **Yes.**
- Select the **Periodicity of GSTR-1** as **Quarterly** as shown in figure 16.8:

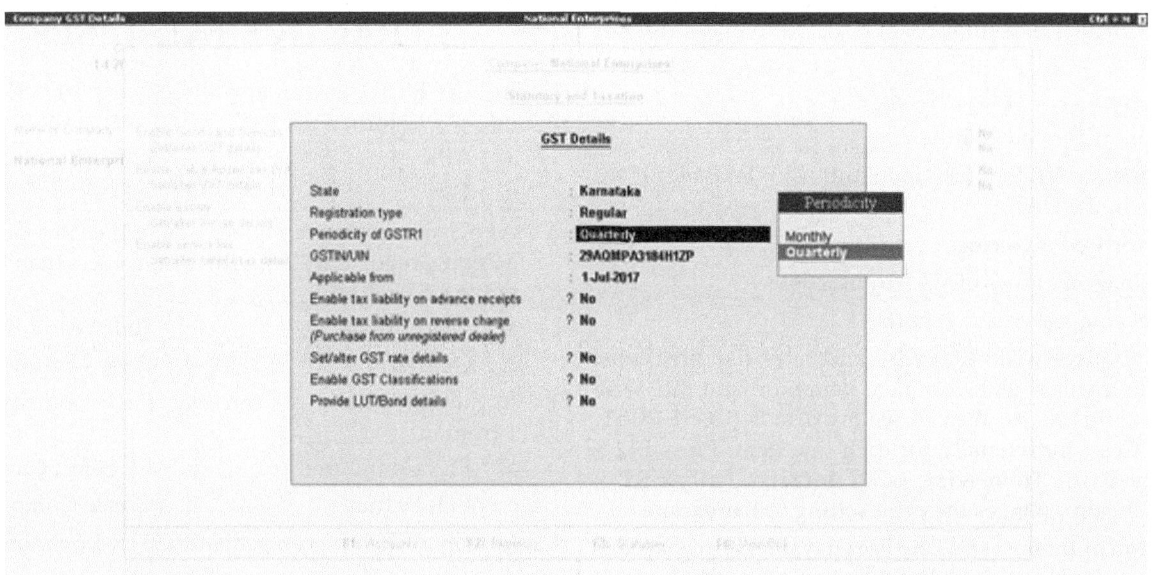


*Figure 16.8: Company GST Details screen*

- After selecting the period accept the screen.

Then the **GSTR-1** report will display the details based on period selected in figure 16.8 i.e., quarterly basis as shown in figure 16.9:

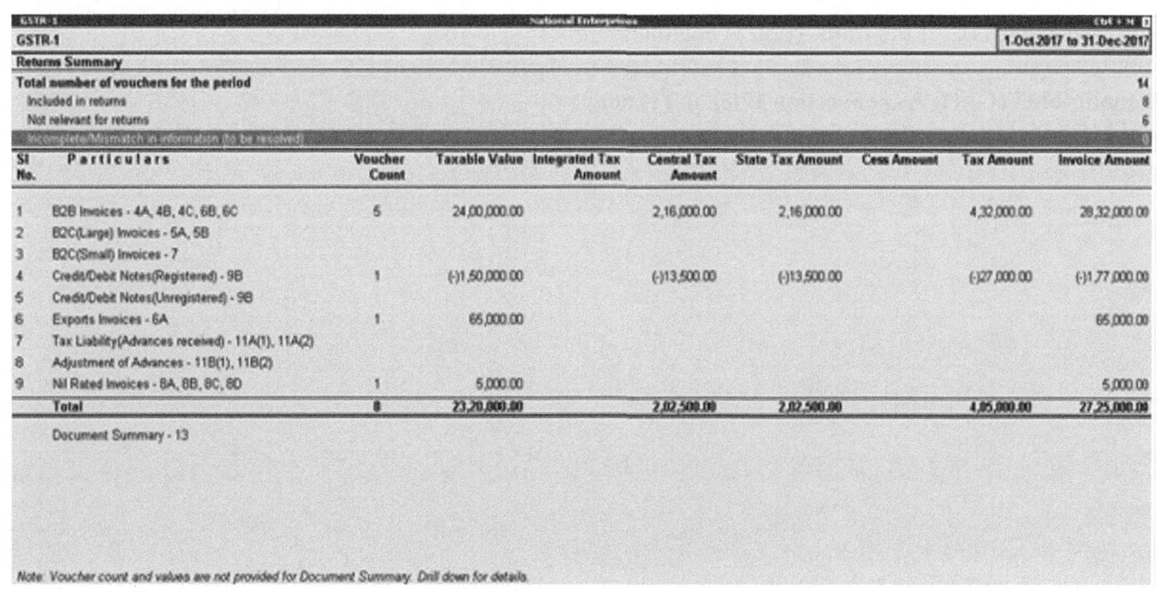

GSTR-1 — 1-Oct-2017 to 31-Dec-2017

Returns Summary

| | |
|---|---|
| Total number of vouchers for the period | 14 |
| Included in returns | 8 |
| Not relevant for returns | 6 |
| Incomplete/Mismatch in information (to be resolved) | 0 |

| Sl No. | Particulars | Voucher Count | Taxable Value | Integrated Tax Amount | Central Tax Amount | State Tax Amount | Cess Amount | Tax Amount | Invoice Amount |
|---|---|---|---|---|---|---|---|---|---|
| 1 | B2B Invoices - 4A, 4B, 4C, 6B, 6C | 5 | 24,00,000.00 | | 2,16,000.00 | 2,16,000.00 | | 4,32,000.00 | 28,32,000.00 |
| 2 | B2C(Large) Invoices - 5A, 5B | | | | | | | | |
| 3 | B2C(Small) Invoices - 7 | | | | | | | | |
| 4 | Credit/Debit Notes(Registered) - 9B | 1 | (-)1,50,000.00 | | (-)13,500.00 | (-)13,500.00 | | (-)27,000.00 | (-)1,77,000.00 |
| 5 | Credit/Debit Notes(Unregistered) - 9B | | | | | | | | |
| 6 | Exports Invoices - 6A | 1 | 65,000.00 | | | | | | 65,000.00 |
| 7 | Tax Liability(Advances received) - 11A(1), 11A(2) | | | | | | | | |
| 8 | Adjustment of Advances - 11B(1), 11B(2) | | | | | | | | |
| 9 | Nil Rated Invoices - 8A, 8B, 8C, 8D | 1 | 5,000.00 | | | | | | 5,000.00 |
| | Total | 8 | 23,20,000.00 | | 2,02,500.00 | 2,02,500.00 | | 4,05,000.00 | 27,25,000.00 |

Document Summary - 13

Note: Voucher count and values are not provided for Document Summary. Drill down for details.

*Figure 16.9 GSTR-1 Report*

In the above screen of figure 16.9, we can observe that it is displaying quarterly details instead of monthly.

## 16.3 OTHER ADDITIONS OF TALLY.ERP 9 RELEASE 6.3

The following are the other enhancements or enhancements done in Tally.ERP 9 Release 6.3

- **GCC VAT:** Tally.ERP 9 is accredited by GAZT (General Authority of Zakat & Tax) in Saudi Arabia. It is also compliant with the VAT guidelines as prescribed by the FTA (Federal Tax Authority) of UAE. Now in Release 6.3, we can:
  - Record VAT Transactions.
  - Print tax invoices in Arabic.
  - Generate VAT return and Audit file (FAF file) if we are in the UAE.
  - Error-free invoicing
  - Manage all types of VAT transactions
  - Get comprehensive reports
- **Print invoices with item-wise and rate-wise breakups:** Printing invoices with complete item-wise and rate-wise tax breakup details. We can see tax details (CGST, IGST, SGST, Cess) individually for each line item. Press **F12** > **Enable Print Item-wise GST details**. Tally.ERP 9 automatically changes the print setting to **Landscape**.
- **Inclusion of Interest and Late Fees payable:** We can record details of any interest or late fees that we might have to pay here and keep the books updated.
- The purchases recorded by selecting the nature of transaction **Purchase from SEZ (Without Bill of Entry) - Taxable** now appear under the following tables of **GSTR-3B**:
  - **4A (5) All other ITC**, if the transaction is eligible for input tax credit
  - **4D Ineligible ITC - (1) As per section 17(5)**, if it is not eligible for input tax credit
- The **e-Sugam no.** is renamed as **e-Way Bill No.**, as per the latest requirements of GST invoice of Karnataka.
- We can print the GST invoice in the landscape orientation by enabling the option **Print Item-wise GST details?**. The printed invoice will display the assessable value by including the apportioned additional ledger amount, and the breakup of GST, for each stock item

# PRACTICE EXERCISES

1. In Tally.ERP 9, we can now directly export GSTR-3B form in _______ format also

   a. APK b. btm

   c. Txt d. JSON

2. As per the announcements made in the 23rd GST Council Meeting, regular dealers with turnover less than 1.5 Cr have to file GSTR-1 on a____________.

   a. Yearly Basis b. Half Yearly Basis

   c. Quarterly Basis d. Forte Nightly Basis

3. In Tally.ERP 9, the user can select the Periodicity of GSTR-1 from in _________

   a. F12: Configure b. F1: Select Cmp

   c. F11: Features d. Create Company

4. In Tally.ERP 9, we can generate GSTR 1 on monthly basis.

   a. True b. False

5. The e-Sugam no. is renamed as _________, as per the latest requirements of GST invoice of Karnataka

   a. Purchase Order Number b. Quotation Number

   c. Register Number d. e-Way Bill No

### Answers

1. (d) 2. (c) 3. (c) 4. (a) 5. (d)

Chapter 17

# Annexure _Tally.ERP 9 Release 6.3.2

## 17.1 Exclusive Economic Zone (Other Territory)

**Exclusive Economic Zone** is a sea zone prescribed by the United Nations Convention on the Law of the Sea over which a state has special rights for fishing, drilling, use of marine resources and other economic activities, which includes production from water and wind. It stretches from the baseline out to 200 nautical miles (nmi) from its coast.

### Other Territory

As per the subsection 81 of section 2 of CGST Act 2017, the term " **Other Territory** " is defined as " **Other territory** " includes territories other than those comprising in a State and those referred to in sub-clauses (a) to (e) of clause (114); the terms ' **other territories** " includes:

1. Territories other than those comprising in a state.
2. Territories referred to in subclause (a) to ( e) of section 2(114)

**Example:** The state of Gujarat, the territory other than Gujarat is covered by the definition of "other territory".

A regular assesse of GST wants to supply the goods and/or services to offshore companies which are registered under GST as "Other Territory".

An Offshore Company refers a corporation, LLC or similar class of entity formed in a foreign country to that of the principals of the organization or one that can only operate outside of its country of formation.

In this section, we will learn to configure the company for the businesses located in other territory and update all details that have to be furnished for generation of relevant returns like GSTR-1, GSTR-3B and GSTR-4.

***Activity:*** *Go to Gateway of Tally > Press F11: Company Feature > F3: Statutory Feature and activate the GST feature in Tally.ERP 9.*

## 17.2 Sales to Exclusive Economic Zones (EEZ or Other Territory)

In this section we will learn to record the sales to other territories. The following are the tax applicability:

| Place of Business | Taxes Applicable |
|---|---|
| Other territory to other territory | Central and UT Tax |
| Other territory to a state or union territory | Integrated Tax |
| State or union territory to other territory | Integrated Tax |

### 17.2.1 Recording of Sales Transaction from Other Territory to Other Territory

In this section, we will learn how a business registered as other territory can make a sales to a traders who is also registered as other territory.

***Illustration:*** *As on 01-03-2018, National Enterprises located in Lakshadweep, sold 100 Nos of Computers to ZIC Solutions located in Lakshadweep @ 10,000 each. GST 28% is applicable.*

**Note:** Make sure to enable the option **Assessee of Other Territory** to **Yes in Company GST Details** .This needs to be enabled in case the business is set up in **Union Territory**

***Activity:*** *Create the following masters*

- **Party Ledger:** ZIC Solution > under **Sundry Debtors** >Enable **Set/Alter GST details** to **Yes**, Make sure to enable the option **Assessee of Other Territory** to **Yes.**
- Sales Ledger: Sales > under **Sales Accounts >** Enable the **option Is GST Applicable** to **Yes > Set/alter GST Details** to **Yes** > **Type of Supply** as **Taxable.**
- **Duty Ledgers**
  - o UT Tax > under Duties and Taxes > In Type of duty/tax select GST > Tax Type select as UT Tax.
  - o Central Tax under Duties and Taxes > In Type of duty/tax select GST > Tax Type select as Central Tax.
- Computer > Enable the option **GST Applicable** to **Yes** and **Set/alter GST Details** to **Yes** and provide the GST details like HSN code, Tax rate etc.

**Recording of sales transactions from other territory to other territory**

1. Go to **Gateway of Tally > Accounting Vouchers >** press **F8: Sales**
2. Enter the details as shown in the figure 17.1:

*Figure 17.1: Sales transaction from other territory to other territory*

3. Accept the screen.
4. Alter the sales invoice and take a print of the sales invoice.

   The **Printed Sales Invoice** appears as shown in the figure 17.2:

**Tax Invoice**

| National Enterprises<br>GSTIN/UIN: 97[illegible]<br>State Name : Other Territory, Code : 97 | Invoice No.<br>**1** | Dated<br>**1-Mar-2018** |
|---|---|---|
| | Delivery Note | Mode/Terms of Payment |
| | Supplier's Ref.<br>**1** | Other Reference(s) |
| Buyer<br>**ZIC Solutions** | Buyer's Order No. | Dated |
| | Despatch Document No. | Delivery Note Date |
| GSTIN/UIN : 97[illegible]<br>State Name : Other Territory, Code : 97 | Despatched through | Destination |
| | Terms of Delivery | |

| Sl No | Description of Goods | HSN/SAC | Quantity | Rate | per | Amount |
|---|---|---|---|---|---|---|
| 1 | **Computer** | 12345675 | **100 Nos** | 10,000.00 | Nos | **10,00,000.00** |
| | ***Central Tax*** | | | | | **1,40,000.00** |
| | ***UT Tax*** | | | | | **1,40,000.00** |
| | Total | | **100 Nos** | | | **₹ 12,80,000.00** |

Amount Chargeable (in words) E. & O.E

**INR Twelve Lakh Eighty Thousand Only**

| HSN/SAC | Taxable Value | Central Tax | | UT Tax | | Total Tax Amount |
|---|---|---|---|---|---|---|
| | | Rate | Amount | Rate | Amount | |
| 12345675 | 10,00,000.00 | 14% | 1,40,000.00 | 14% | 1,40,000.00 | 2,80,000.00 |
| Total | **10,00,000.00** | | **1,40,000.00** | | **1,40,000.00** | **2,80,000.00** |

Tax Amount (in words) : **INR Two Lakh Eighty Thousand Only**

Declaration
We declare that this invoice shows the actual price of the goods described and that all particulars are true and correct.

**for National Enterprises**

Authorised Signatory

This is a Computer Generated Invoice

*Figure 17.2 Printed sales invoice*

## 17.2.2 Recording of Sales Transaction from Other Territory to State/Union Territory

Union territory are the territory which are ruled by the union government (central government), hence it is termed as union territory.

In this section, we will learn how a business registered as othe territory can make a sales to a state or union territory.

***Illustration:*** *As on 01-03-2018, National Enterprises located in Lakshadweep, sold 100 Nos of Computers to High Solutions located in Chennai @ 10,000 each. GST 28% is applicable.*

*Activity: Create the following ledger:*

- **Party Ledger:** High Solution > under **Sundry Debtors** >Enable **Set/Alter GST details** to **Yes**, Make sure not to enable the option **Assessee of Other Territory**.
- **Integrated Tax:** under Duties and Taxes > In Type of duty/ tax select GST > Tax Type select as Integrated Tax.

**Note:** Make sure to enable the option **Assessee of Other Territory** to **Yes in Company GST Details** .This needs to be enabled in case the business is set up in **Union Territory**

Recording of sales transactions from other territory to state/ union territory

1. Go to **Gateway of Tally > Accounting Vouchers >** press **F8: Sales**
2. Enter the details as shown in the figure 17.3:
3. Accept the screen.

**Once after recording the transaction, check the details in GSTR 3B report.**

- Go to Gateway of Tally > Display > Statutory Reports > GST > GSTR 3B.
- Enter the period for which GSTR 3B return needs to be generated.

The **GSTR 3B** report appears as shown in the figure 17.4:

*Figure 17.3: Sales transaction from other territory to state/union territory*

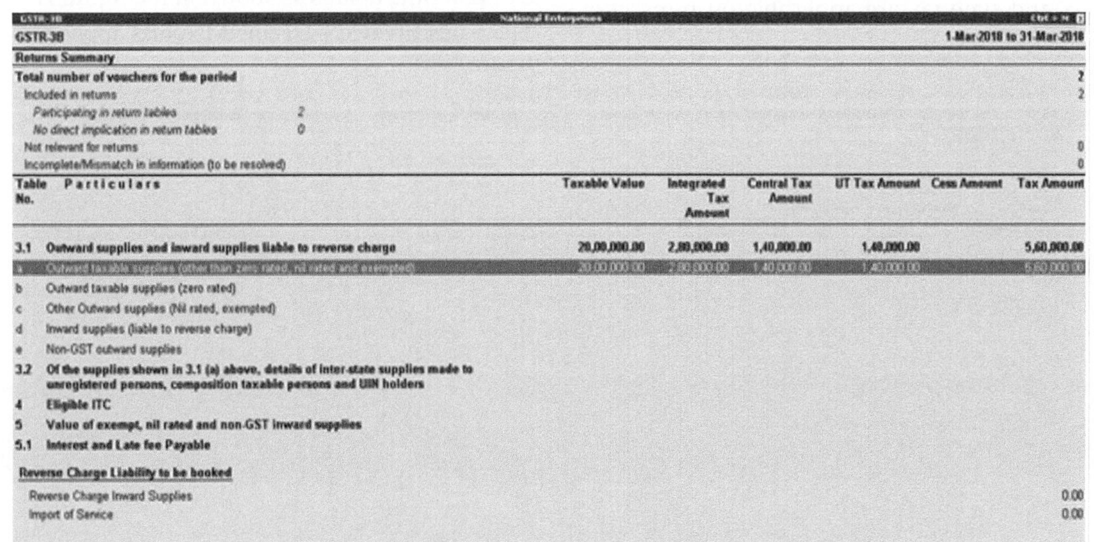

*Figure 17.4: GSTR 3B report*

The details of transactions will get captured under the head Outward supplies and inward supplies liable to reverse charge.

### 17.2.3 Recording of Sales Transaction from State or Union Territory to Other Territory

In this section, we will learn how a business registered as union territory or state can make a sales to a state or other territory.

***Illustration:*** *As on 01-03-2018, National Enterprises located in Karnataka, sold 100 Nos of Computers to ZIC Solutions located in Lakshadweep @ 10,000 each. GST 28% is applicable.*

**Note:** Make sure to enable the option **Assessee of Other Territory** to **No in Company GST Details.**

***Activity:***

1. *Create a new company and select the state as Karnataka and make sure the option* ***Assessee of Other Territory*** *to* ***No in Company GST Details.***
2. *Record the sales transactions from state or union territory to other territory*

## 17.3 Support for Deemed export as per last GST notification

Deemed exports are defined as transactions in which the supply and manufacture of goods takes place within India. Essentially, deemed exports refer to the supply of goods to end-exporters.

For example, if a two-wheeler spare parts manufacturer supplies rear-view mirrors to a motorcycle manufacturer and exporter, then the sale of the rear-view mirrors would be considered as deemed exports.

As per the Latest GST notification from 18th October 2017 onwards:

- Integrated tax is applicable on interstate transactions.
- Central tax and state tax are applicable on transactions made within the state.

**Note:** Prior to this date, integrated tax had to be charged on all taxable deemed exports made within and outside the state.

Following are the tax applicability based on the transaction of deemed exports

| Transaction of Deemed Exports | Tax Applicability |
|---|---|
| Interstate taxable deemed export – Deemed Export Taxable | Integrated Tax |
| Intrastate taxable deemed export | Central Tax and State Tax |
| Intrastate Deemed Exports Exempt<br>Intrastate Deemed Exports Nil Rated<br>Deemed Exports Exempt<br>Deemed Exports Nil Rated | No Tax |

***Illustration:*** *National Enterprises, Karnataka sold the 100 Rear View Mirrors @ 200 each to JAHA Manufacturer, Chennai.*

***Activity:*** *Create the sales ledger*

- ***Interstate deemed exports taxable ledger:*** *While creating the sales ledger make sure to select the* ***Nature of Transaction*** *as* ***Intrastate Deemed Exports Taxable*** *in GST Details screen.*
- ***JAHA Manufacturer:*** *Make sure to select the correct state and configure GST details.*
- ***Rare View Mirror:*** *Make sure to provide the details in GST Details screen.*

Recording of transaction of deemed exports which takes place within the state

1. Go to **Gateway of Tally > Accounting Vouchers >** press **F8: Sales.**
2. Enter the details as shown in the figure 17.5:

The **Sales Invoice – Deemed Exports** appears as shown in the figure 17.5:

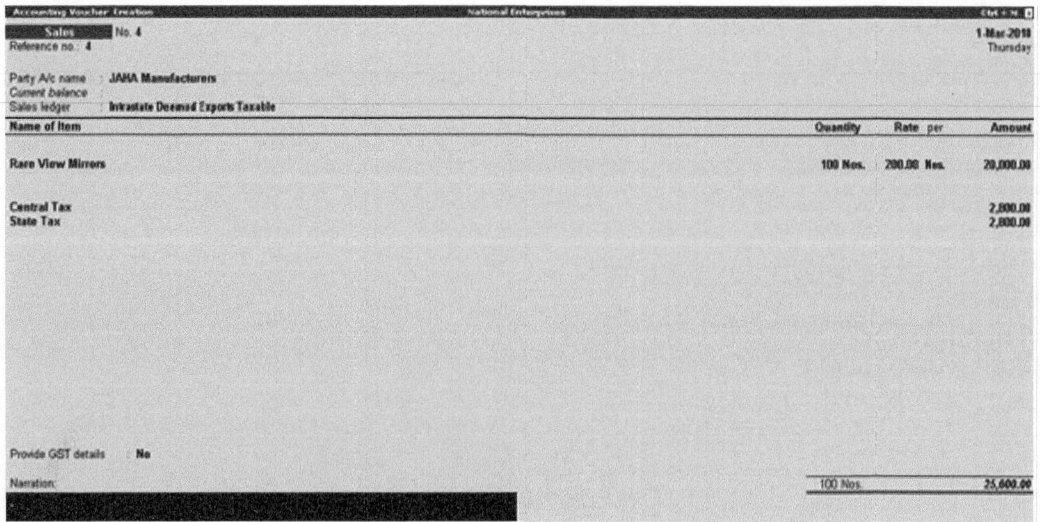


*Figure 17.5: Sales Invoice – Deemed Exports*

In this case we have selected as Central Tax and State Tax ledgers, because as per the latest GST notification the deemed exports which takes place within the state will attract central and state tax instead of integrated tax.

**Note:** Similarly by selecting the required Nature of Transactions in the sales ledger, we can record the other types of deemed exports like Intrastate Deemed Exports – Nil Rates, Intrastate Deemed Exports – Exempt, Deemed Exports Taxable, Deemed Exports Nil Rated and Deemed Exports Exempt. The values of these transactions will be captured in the relevant tables of **GSTR-1**, **GSTR-3B**, and **Advance Receipts Summary** reports.

## 17.4 Other Enhancements in Tally.ERP 9 Release 6.3.2

- In Tally.ERP 9, we can file the Quarterly e-TDS/TCS as per latest tool - latest File Validation Utility 5.7. It supports the applicable remittance code for natures of payment of sections 195/196D.
- We can print, export or email the transactions of the **Voucher with incomplete/mismatch in information** report, and the **Exception Resolution** screen of each exception of the **GSTR-1** and **GSTR-3B** reports.
- The details of GTA services purchased from interstate unregistered dealers are captured in GSTR 3B report.
- GCC VAT designated purchase is supported for UAE and KSA markets.

## Chapter 18

# TallyACE Release 6.4 Annexure

### LEARNING OBJECTIVES

- e-Way Bill
- Enabling e-Way Bill in Tally.ERP 9
- Recording invoice with details required for e-Way Bill generation
- Creating JSON by exporting e-Way Bill details from invoice
- Uploading JSON to portal
- Generating e-Way Bill number from portal
- Printing the invoice with e-Way Bill number
- Resolving exceptions from Export for e-Way Bill report
- Updating e-Way Bill details from Update e-Way Bill report
- Composition Scheme
- Enabling GST as a composition dealer in Tally.ERP 9
- Creating masters for composition dealer
- Accounting of purchase transaction as a composition dealer
- Accounting of sales transaction as a composition dealer
- Accounting sales returns and purchase returns
- Generating GST-4 in Tally.ERP 9
- Other enhancements in release 6.4

## 18.1 E-WAY BILL

Electronic Way Bill (e-way bill) is an electronic document generated on the GST portal for evidencing movement of goods. It is a unique bill number generated for the specific consignment which involves movement of goods. If the invoice value is [1] . 50,000 or above, all registered dealers need to generate e-Way Bill for the interstate movement of goods. In few states, dealers need e-Way Bills even for the intrastate movement of goods.

E-Way Bill has two Components such as Part-A and Part-B, **Part-A** comprises the details of GSTIN of recipient, place of delivery (PIN Code), invoice or challan number and date, value of goods, HSN code, transport document number (Goods Receipt Number or Railway Receipt Number or Airway Bill Number or Bill of Lading Number) and reasons for transportation, and **Part-B** comprises the transporter details (Vehicle number).

**E- Way Bill will be issued by**

- Registered Supplier
- Registered Receiver
- Transporter, in case if both the supplier and the receiver are unregistered

**Conditions for generating E-Way Bills**

- E-Way Bill needs to be generated before the commencement of movement of goods.
- If multiple consignments are transported in one vehicle, then the transporter should generate a consolidated E-Way bill in the Form GST EWB 02 and separately indicate the serial number of E-Way Bill for each of the consignment.
- On generation of E-Way Bill, on the portal a unique E-Way Bill number called 'EBN' will be made available to the supplier, the recipient and the transporter.
- E-Way Bill will be made available for acceptance from the recipient of goods if he is registered under GST, the recipient of goods shall communicate acceptance or rejection of the consignment covered by the E-Way Bill within 72 hours, if the recipient of goods does not communicate the acceptance or rejection within 72 hours, then it will be deemed as accepted by the recipient.
- The validity of E-Way bill for distance less than 100KM is 1 day and for every 100KM or part thereafter is 1 additional day

---

**Note:** The validity period will be counted from the time of generation of the E-Way Bill. The validity period of the E-Way Bill may be extended by the commissioner for certain categories of goods, as specified in the notification issued in this regard.

---

**Modes of generation of e-way bill**

- Via Web (laptop/desktop or phone)
- Via SMS (mobile number should be registered)
- Via API (Application Program Interface).
- Via Android based mobile application.
- Via Suvidha Providers

### 18.1.1 Exporting the Details of E-Way Bill from Tally.ERP 9 to JSON File

In Tally.ERP 9, we can setup e-way bill for the company, record transactions with e-way bill details, export e-way bill details to JSON file, and print invoices with e-way bill details etc.

#### *18.1.1.1 E-Way Bill Setup in Tally.ERP 9*

We will now see how to enable e-way bill for the company in Tally.ERP 9,

To enable e-way bill,

***Activity:*** *Create a company in Tally.ERP 9 with the following details:*

- ***Company:*** *Name: Mukta Traders*
- ***Address:*** *No.209, 19$^{th}$ Cross, Twin Tower, Karnataka-560029*
- ***Financial Year:*** *01-04-2017*

1. Go to **Gateway of Tally**>Click **F11: Features**>Click **F3: Statutory**.
2. Set the options **Enable Goods and Services Tax (GST)** to **Yes** and **Set/alter GST details** to **Yes**

3. From Tally.ERP 9 Release 6.4 onwards, by default the below mentioned options such as,
   - e-Way Bill applicable
   - e-Way Bill applicable from
   - e-Way Bill threshold and
   - e-Way Bill applicable for intrastate, will be enabled and selected with appropriate applicable date and threshold limit.

The **Company GST Details** screen appears as shown in figure 18.1:

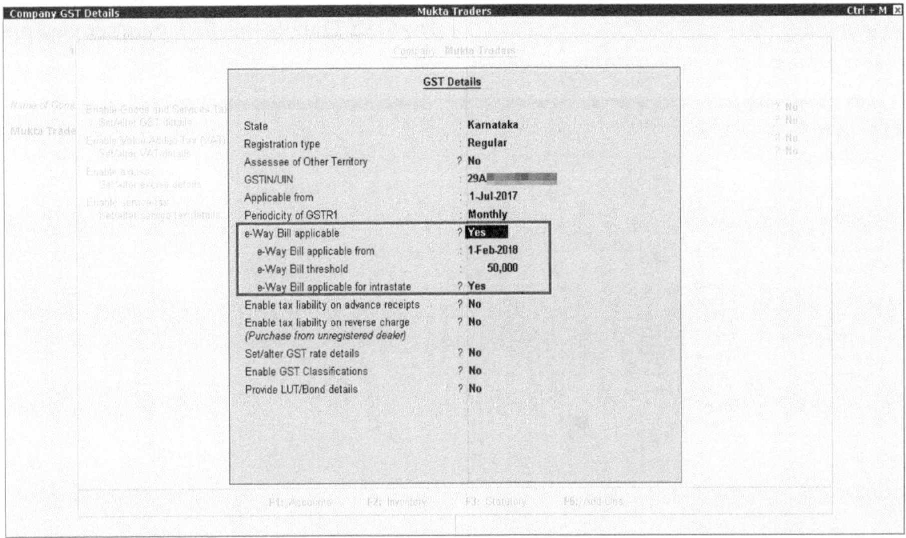


Figure 18.1: Company GST Details

**Note:** In Tally.ERP 9, we can enter e-Way Bill details only when such transactions are recorded with stock items. The provision to enter e-Way Bill details is not available in accounting invoice mode, and in the companies enabled to maintain accounts only.

### 18.1.1.2 *Recording of Invoice with E-Way Bill Details*

Let us now learn to record GST invoice with e-way bill details in Tally.ERP 9.

***Illustration:*** *As on 28-02-2018, Mukta Traders, Karnataka supplied 25 Laptops at ₹ .38,500 each to Kishore Enterprises, Tamil Nadu. Additionally, GST@18% is charged on the invoice and also company wants to generate e-way bill in Tally.ERP 9.*

***Activity:*** *Create the following masters in Tally.ERP 9*

- ***Party Ledger:*** *Create Kishore Enterprises under sundry debtors, select the state as Tamil Nadu, enable the option **Set/alter GST details** to **Yes** and select the **Registration type** as Regular.*

**Note:** In the party ledger if the Registration type is selected as Regular or Composition, the GSTIN/UIN entered is considered as the transporter ID, if the Registration type is selected as Unknown or Unregistered, then 15 digit Transporter ID has to be entered.

The Party **GST Details** screen appears as shown in figure 18.2:

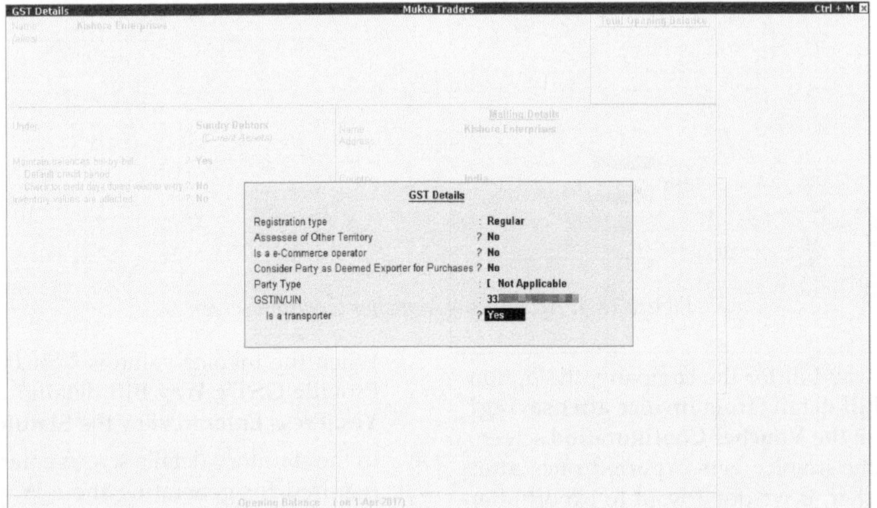


Figure 18.2: Party GST Details

- ***Sales** under Sales Accounts, In **Is GST Applicable** field, select as **Applicable**, do not enable **Set/alter GST Details** as we will configure the GST tax rate in the stock item master, select the **Type of Supply** as **Goods** and save the ledger*
- ***Integrated Tax** under Duties and Taxes, select **Type of duty/ tax** as **GST**, select the **Tax type** as **Integrated Tax** and save the ledger*
- *Create **Units of Measure** as Nos with **Formal name** Numbers and select the **Unit Quantity Code(UQC)***
- *Create the stock item as **Laptop,** In **GST Applicable** field, selec as **Applicable,** enable **Set/alter GST Details** and provide **HSN SAC Details**, select **Calculation type** as **On Value**, selec **Taxability** as **Taxable** and provide the **Tax Rate** . Make sur to provide the Opening quantity as 50 Nos. and Rate as ₹.30,00*

The **GST Details** for stock item screen appears as shown in figur 18.3:

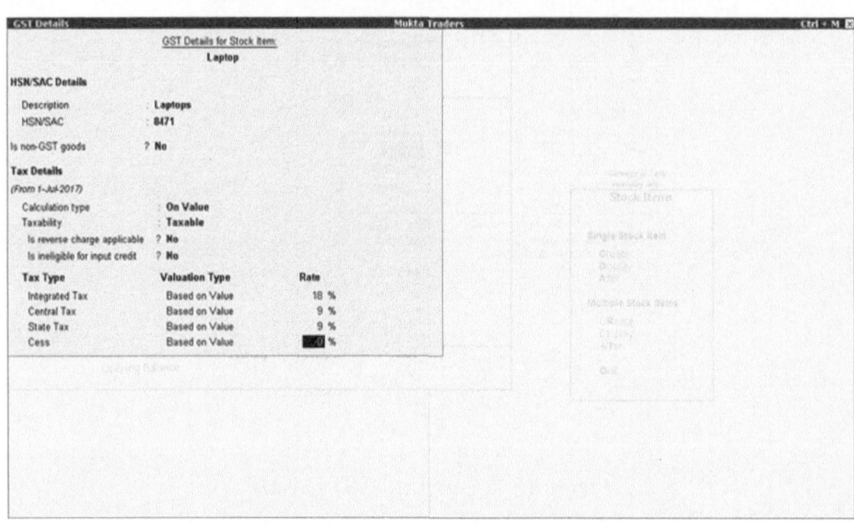


*Figure 18.3: GST Details for Stock Item*

To record the invoice with details required for e-way bill, follow the steps given below:

1. Go to **Gateway of Tally > Accounting Vouchers > Pres F8: Sales.**
2. Enter the details as shown in the figure 18.4:

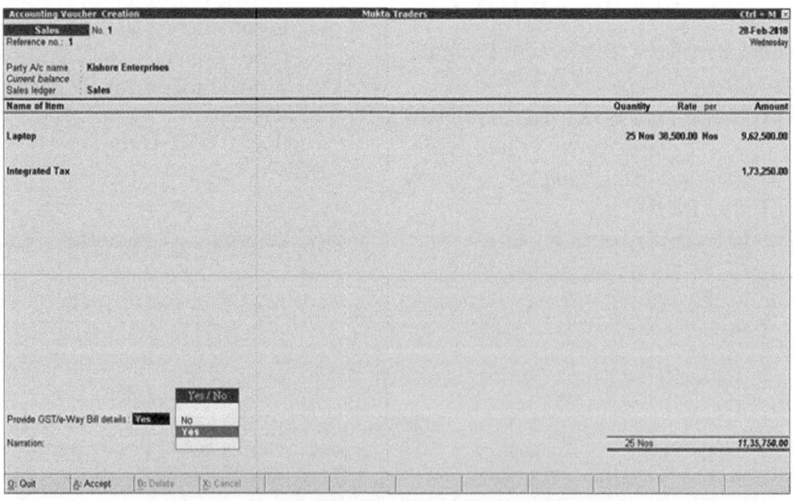


*Figure 18.4: Accounting Voucher Creation screen*

**Note:** On enabling e-way bill for the company, the option **Export e-Way Bill details from invoice after saving?** is also enabled in the **Voucher Configuration** screen, due to which the invoice gets exported once after saving the voucher, if we don't want to export after saving voucher then the same can be disabled.

3. When the invoice value is ₹ .50,000 or more, the optio **Provide GST/e-Way Bill details?** appears which is set t **Yes.** Press **Enter** to view the **Statutory Details** screen.
4. In the statutory details screen enter the mandatory detail required for generating the e-Way Bill as shown in th figure 18.5:

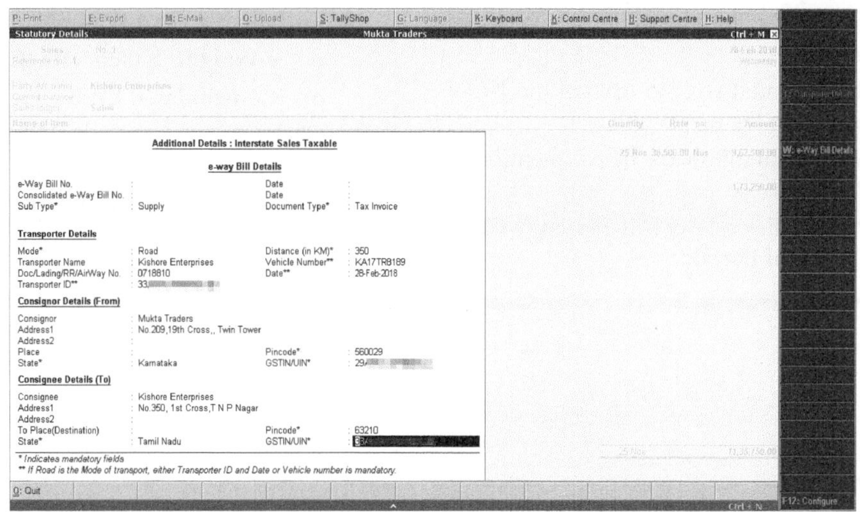


*Figure 18.5: Statutory Details screen*

**Note:**
- If the goods are transported in different modes or vehicles, we can press **Ctrl+T** and enter the bifurcated transporter's details with the distance and vehicle numbers etc.
- We can click **W: e-Way Bill Details** to enter the details of multiple e-Way Bills generated for a single transaction.
- Press **F12: Configure** from Statutory Details screen and enable the option **Enable consolidated e-Way Bill details** to **Yes** and **Show consignor details** to **Yes,** if consignor and consolidated details are not appearing. And also if these options are not enabled then we will not be able to export the e-way bill details.

5. Press **Enter** to accept the statutory details screen

**Note:** If the e-way bill details in invoice or HSN code is not provided for the stock item, then the invoice will not be exported once after saving the voucher, the error message will appear as shown in the figure 18.6

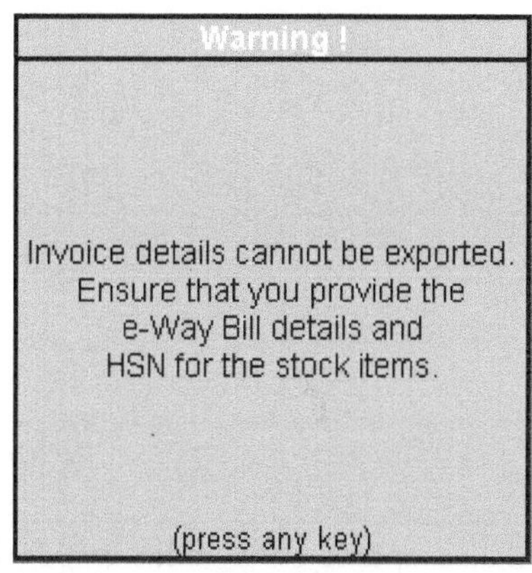


*Figure 18.6: Warning Message*

6. If all the details are correct then on accepting the sales voucher, Tally will automatically ask for exporting the details for e-Way bill

   The **Export Details for e-Way Bill** screen appears as shown in figure 18.7:

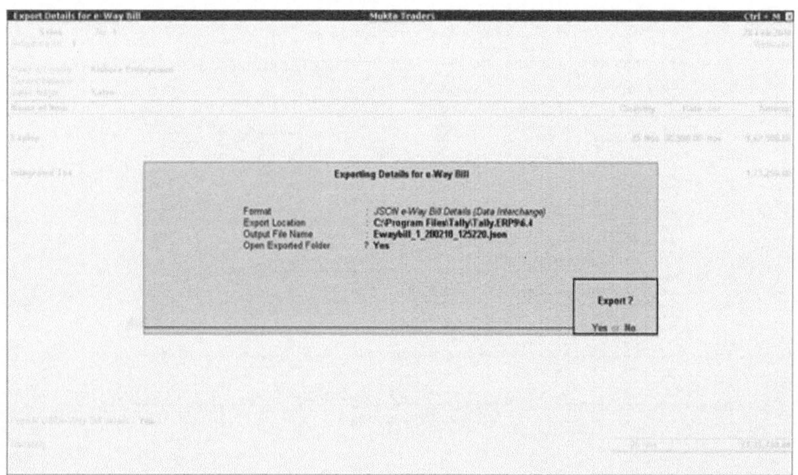


*Figure 18.7: Export Details for e-Way Bill screen*

7. Press **Enter** to create a JSON file. The folder in which the JSON is created now appears.
8. Once after JSON file is created we can upload the JSON file to the portal to generate the e-Way Bill.

   To upload the JSON to portal follow the below mentioned steps:

   - Login to **GST Portal**>click **e-Way Bill System > Click here to go to e-Way Bill Portal.**
   - To generate the e-Way Bill, choose the required links:
     - o **e-Waybill > Generate Bulk**
     - o **Consolidated EWB > Generate Bulk**
   - Click **Choose File** > select the JSON > click **Upload & Generate**. The e-way bill gets generated.
9. After generating the e-way bill no., open Tally.ERP 9 we will get **e-Way Bill Information** screen, enter the **e-Way Bill No.** and **e-Way Bill Date** as shown in the figure 18.8

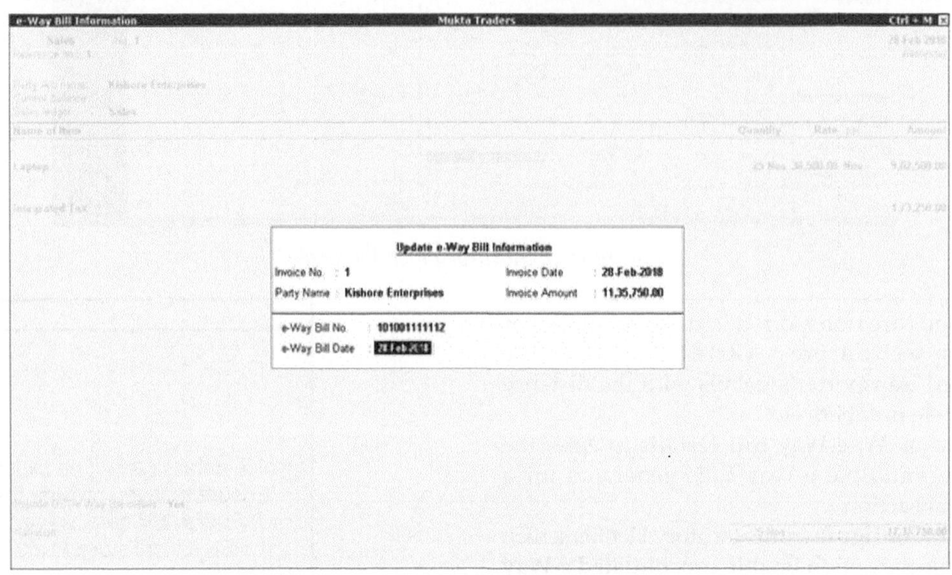


*Figure 18.8: e-Way Bill Information screen*

---

**Note:** We can also update e-way bill number details from Gateway of Tally>Display>Statutory Reports>GST Reports>e-Way Bill>Update e-Way Bill Information.

---

## 18.1.2 Printing of Invoice with E-Way Bill Details

To print the invoice with e-way bill number, open the sales voucher in alteration mode and click **P: Print,** In the voucher printing screen, click **F12: Configure** and ensure the option **Print e-Way Bill No.?** is set to **Yes** as shown in figure 18.9

The **Invoice Print Configuration** screen appears as shown in the figure 18.9:

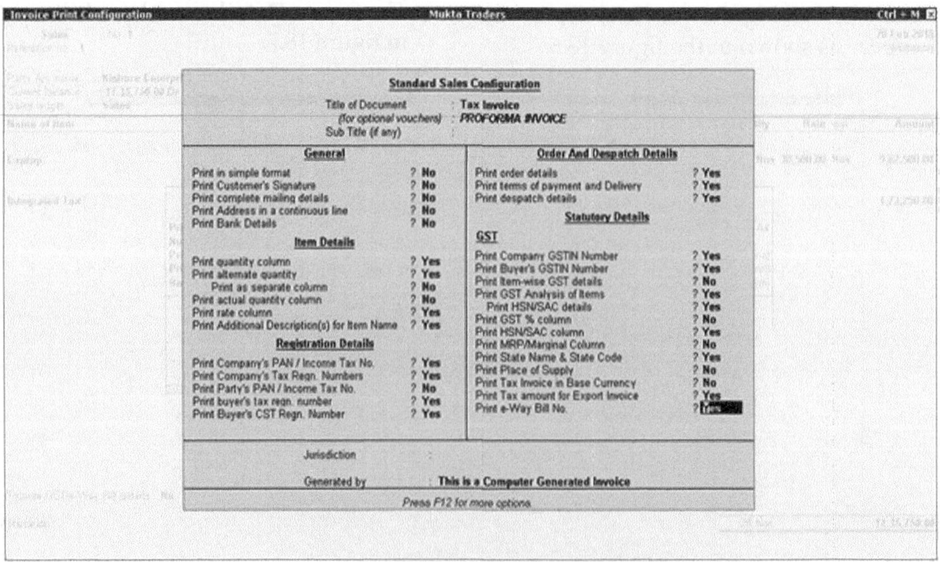


*Figure 18.9: Invoice Print Configuration screen*

The **Sales Invoice Print with e-Way Bill details** appears as shown in the figure 18.10:

**Tax Invoice**

| **Mukta Traders**<br>No.209,19th Cross,<br>Twin Tower<br>GSTIN/UIN:<br>State Name : Karnataka, Code : 29<br>E-Mail : muktatraders@gmail.com | Invoice No.<br>**1** | e-Way Bill No.<br>101001111112 | Dated<br>**28-Feb-2018** |
|---|---|---|---|
| | Delivery Note | | Mode/Terms of Payment |
| | Supplier's Ref.<br>**1** | | Other Reference(s) |
| Buyer<br>**Kishore Enterprises**<br>GSTIN/UIN :<br>State Name : Tamil Nadu, Code : 33 | Buyer's Order No. | | Dated |
| | Despatch Document No. | | Delivery Note Date |
| | Despatched through | | Destination |
| | Terms of Delivery | | |

| Sl No. | Description of Goods | HSN/SAC | Quantity | Rate | per | Amount |
|---|---|---|---|---|---|---|
| 1 | **Laptop** | 8471 | **25 Nos** | 38,500.00 | Nos | **9,62,500.00** |
| | ***Integrated Tax*** | | | | | **1,73,250.00** |
| | Total | | **25 Nos** | | | **₹ 11,35,750.00** |

Amount Chargeable (in words) E. & O.E

**INR Eleven Lakh Thirty Five Thousand Seven Hundred Fifty Only**

| HSN/SAC | Taxable Value | Integrated Tax | | Total Tax Amount |
|---|---|---|---|---|
| | | Rate | Amount | |
| 8471 | 9,62,500.00 | 18% | 1,73,250.00 | 1,73,250.00 |
| **Total** | **9,62,500.00** | | **1,73,250.00** | **1,73,250.00** |

Tax Amount (in words) : **INR One Lakh Seventy Three Thousand Two Hundred Fifty Only**

Declaration
We declare that this invoice shows the actual price of the goods described and that all particulars are true and correct.

**for Mukta Traders**

Authorised Signatory

This is a Computer Generated Invoice

*Figure 18.10: Invoice Print with e-Way Bill No*

### 18.1.3 Export for e-Way Bill Report

In this report, we can:

- Resolve the exceptions by entering the mandatory details that were not provided during voucher entry such as HSN Code and mandatory information's required for e-way bill generation
- Check the invoice status to export or update e-way bill number and date

- View the invoices ready for export and exported invoices
- Create JSON or export data to JSON preparation tool

***Activity :***

***Illustration:*** *As on 28-02-2018, Mukta Traders, Karnataka supplied 12 Printers at ₹ 5000 each to prathima, Tamil Nadu. Additionally, GST@18% is charged on the invoice.*

- *Create* ***Prathima*** *ledger under* ***sundry debtors***
- *Create the stock item as* ***Printers ,*** *In* ***GST Applicable*** *field, select as* ***Applicable,*** *enable* ***Set/alter GST Details,*** *do not provide* ***HSN/SAC Details,*** *Make sure to provide the Opening quantity as 20 Nos. and Rate as ₹. 4500*
- *Record the transaction*

The Navigation to view **Export for e-Way Bill** report from Tally.ERP 9 is, from **Gateway of Tally>Display>Statutory Reports>GST >e-Way Bill>Export for e-Way Bill**

The **Export for e-Way Bill** report appears as shown in figure 18.11:

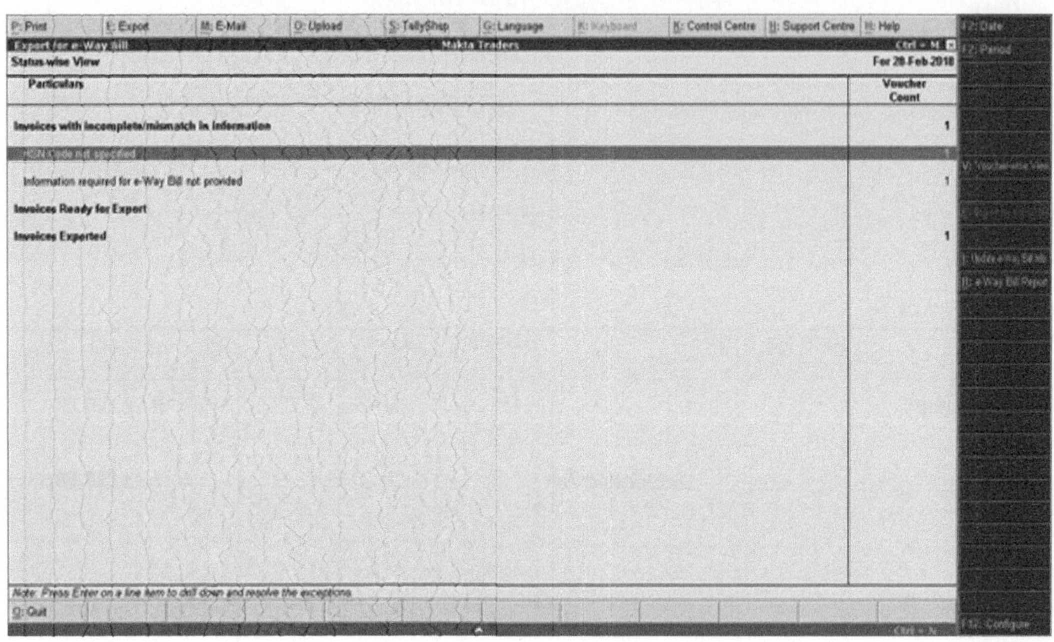


*Figure 18.11: Export for e-Way Bill report*

From **Export for e-Way Bill** report we can click **F12: Configure** and enable the required options, also we can change the **e-Way Bill Threshold for Report**.

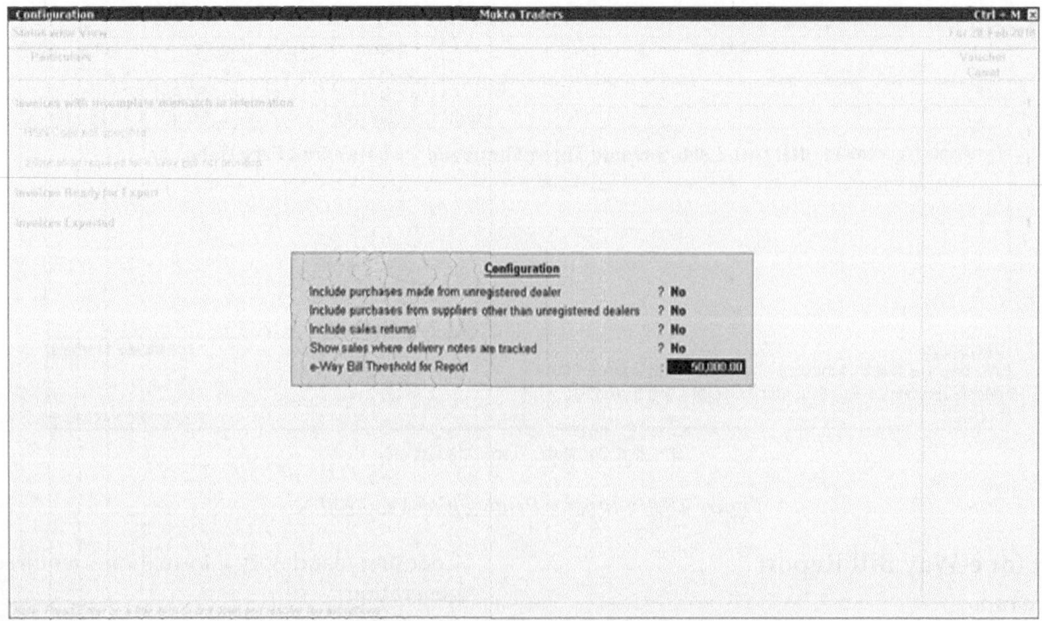


*Figure 18.12: Export for e-Way Bill report configuration screen*

### 18.1.3.1 *Update e-Way Bill Information*

Update e-way bill information report displays the invoices for which e-way bill number and date are not provided.

To view **Update e-Way Bill Information**, Go to **Gateway of Tally> Display> Statutory Reports > GST > e-Way Bill > Update e-Way Bill Information**. Alternatively, we can press **Ctrl+I** from the **Export for e-Way Bill** report to view this report.

### 18.1.3.2 *e-Way Bill Report*

e-Way Bill Report displays the invoices that have e-Way Bill number and date.

The **e-Way Bill Report** appears as shown in the figure 18.13

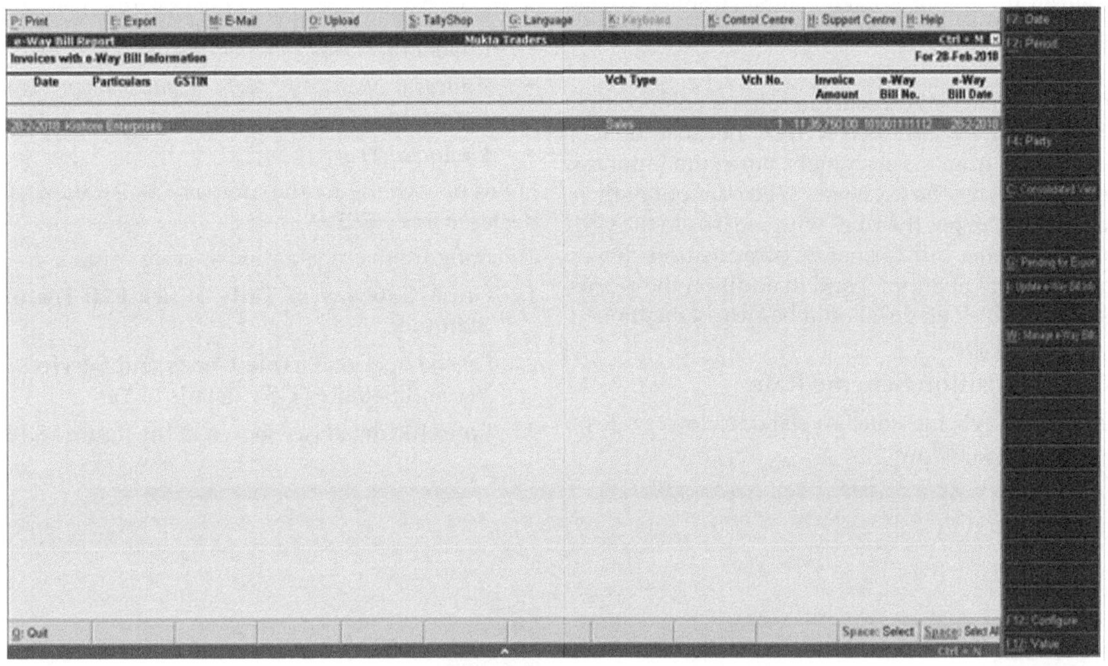


*Figure 18.13: e-Way Bill report*

In e-Way Bill report we can perform below listed activities:

- Click **F4: party** and select the required party ledger
- Press **Ctrl+G** for status-wise view of **Export for e-Way Bill** report
- Press **Ctrl+I** to enter the e-Way Bill number and date in the **Update e-Way Bill Information** report
- Press **Ctrl+W** to enter the e-Way Bill details for the invoice in **Manage e-Way Bill screen** (same as **Statutory Details** screen of the invoice
- Click **C : Consolidated** to group the invoices based on mode, vehicle number, place and state, we can view invoice wise details of individual invoices and also export JSON for consolidated invoices

## 18.2 COMPOSITION SCHEME

Composition Scheme under GST is a simple and easy mechanism for small tax payers, wherein the tax payers have less tedious GST formalities and pay GST at a lower or fixed composition tax rate on their turnover.

### 18.2.1 Turnover Limit for GST Composition Scheme

Any tax payer, whose turnover is less than INR 1.5 Crore, in Rest of India, and less then INR 75 Lakhs in Special Category States (North Eastern States and Himachal Pradesh), can opt for the composition scheme under GST. The point to be noted is that the GST composition scheme limit is based on the turnover of all businesses which are registered with the same PAN, and thus all businesses under the same PAN can either be registered as regular dealers or can be registered as composition dealers but cannot be a combination of both.

### 18.2.2 Persons Ineligible for the GST Composition Scheme

The following taxable persons cannot opt for the composition scheme under GST:

- Taxpayer supplying Exempt supplies
- Supplier of services other than restaurant related services
- Manufacturer of ice cream, pan masala, or tobacco
- Casual Taxable Person or a Non-resident Taxable Person
- Businesses which supply goods through an e-commerce operator

### 18.2.3 Important features of GST Composition scheme

The businesses registered for composition scheme under GST has to comply with the following rules:

- Composition dealers cannot claim Input Tax Credit
- Composition dealers cannot make any inter-state supply of goods

- Composition dealers cannot supply GST Exempted goods
- Composition dealers has to pay tax at normal rates for transactions under Reverse Charge Mechanism
- Composition tax payers has to mention as **Composition Taxable Person** on every notice or signboard displayed prominently at their place of business
- Services worth up to INR 5 Lakh can be supplied under the scheme, by a taxable person who is also supplying goods
- As per the GST composition scheme rules, a composition dealer cannot issue a GST tax invoice, because he can neither charge tax from his customers, nor claim input tax credit. In other words, the tax needs to be paid out of their own pocket. Thus, as per the rules with regards to the GST composition scheme bill format, a composition dealer needs to issue a Bill of Supply, and in addition the words 'composition taxable person' should be clearly mentioned on it, as discussed above.

### 18.2.4 GST Composition Scheme Rate

The GST Composition Scheme Rate is a standard lower rate of tax, which is specified as follows:

1. For Manufacturers and Traders of Goods, the compositio tax rate is 1%
2. For Restaurants not serving alcohol for huma consumption, the composition tax rate is 5%

### 18.2.5 Activation of GST as a Composition Registration Type

***Activity:*** *Create a company in Tally.ERP 9 with the following detail*

- ***Company:*** *Name: National Traders*
- ***Address:*** *No.34, 5th Main Road, Sriman Nagar, Bangalor Karnataka-560078*
- ***Financial Year:*** *01-04-2017*

Let us now configure the company registration as Compositio dealer in Tally.ERP 9,

To configure the registration as composition,

1. Go to **Gateway of Tally** >Click **F11: Features**>Click **F3 Statutory.**
2. Set the options **Enable Goods and Services Tax (GST)** t **Yes** and **Set/alter GST details** to **Yes**
3. Enter the details as shown in the figure 18.14

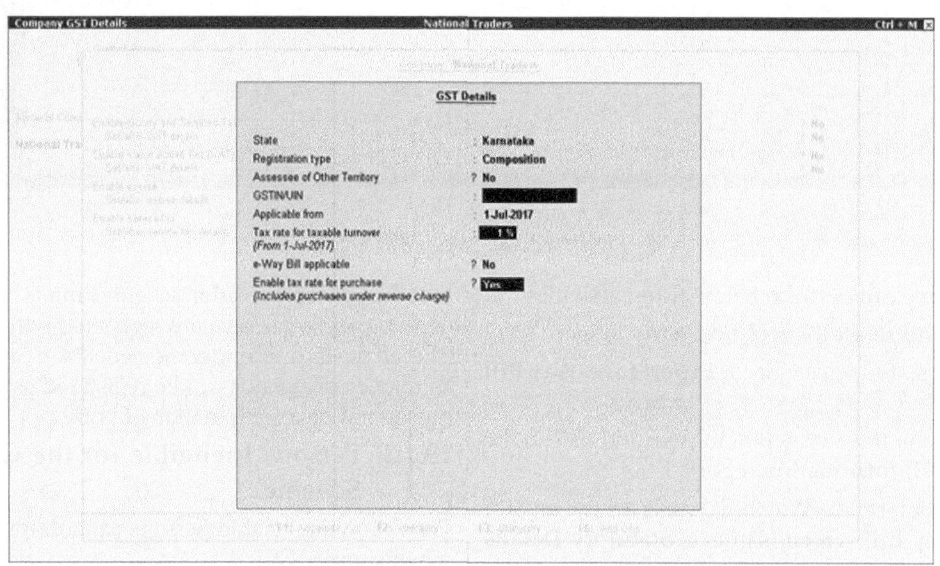


*Figure 18.14: Company GST Details screen*

**Note:**
- The option **Enable tax rate for purchase** allows to enter the tax rate in the purchase ledger, for calculating tax on purchases from regular dealers and reverse charge transactions.
- If GST is already enabled in the company as regular dealer to maintain the books under composition scheme the registration type has to be changed from regular to composition.

### 18.2.6 Recording of Transactions under Composition Scheme

In this section we will learn to record the purchases and sales transaction under composition scheme.

#### *18.2.6.1 Accounting of Purchase Transaction*

We can record purchase of goods or services with or withou reverse charge, under composition scheme of GST.

***Illustration:*** *As on 01-03-2018, National Traders a composition dealer Karnataka purchased 25 Aluminium Ladders worth ₹. 3,980 each fron RKM Hardware Distributors, on which GST@18% is charged*

Let us now record an intrastate purchase transaction, to recor follow the below given steps:

**Step 1: Creation of Stock item**

To create a stock item,

1. Go to **Gateway of Tally>Inventory Info>Create**, create th stock item as shown in the figure 18.15

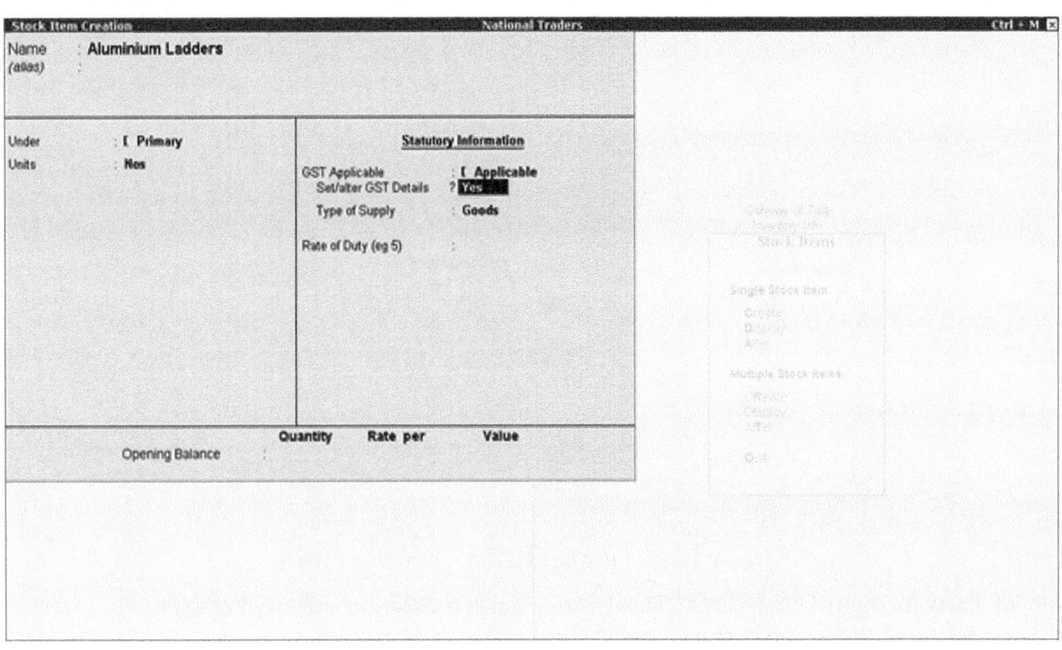


*Figure 18.15: Stock Item Creation Screen*

2. In **GST Applicable** field, select as **Applicable,** enable **Set/ alter GST Details**

3. Configure the GST Details as shown in the figure 18.16

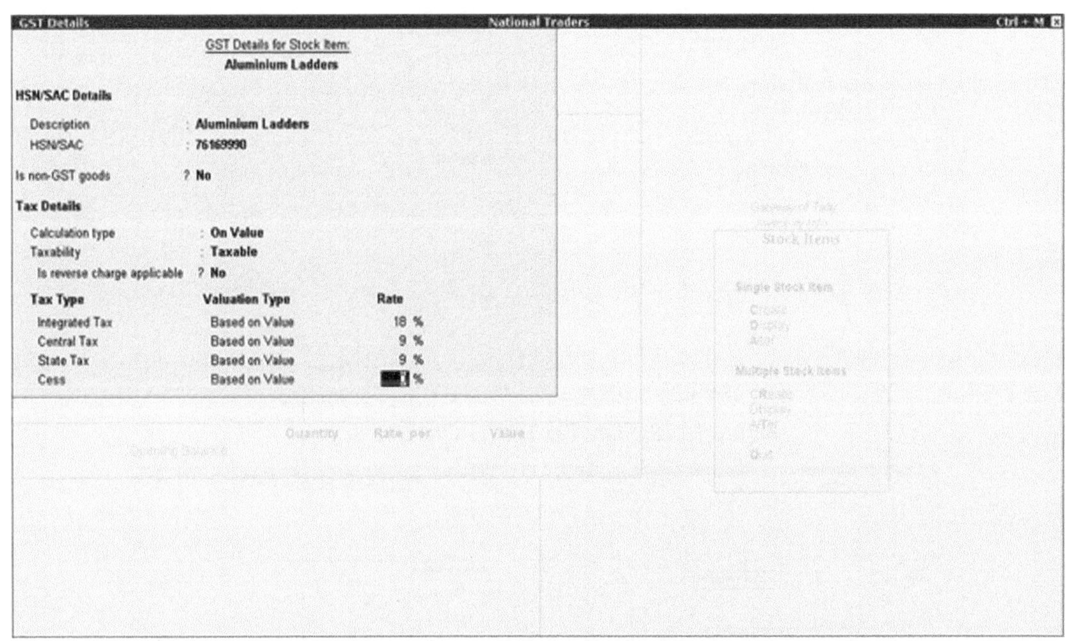


*Figure 18.16: Stock Item GST Details Screen*

4. Select the **Type of Supply** as **Goods** or **Services**, and save the stock item.

**Step 2: Creation of Purchase Ledger**

To create purchase ledger,

1. Go to **Gateway of Tally>Accounts Info>Ledgers>Create**, create the purchase ledger as shown in the figure 18.17

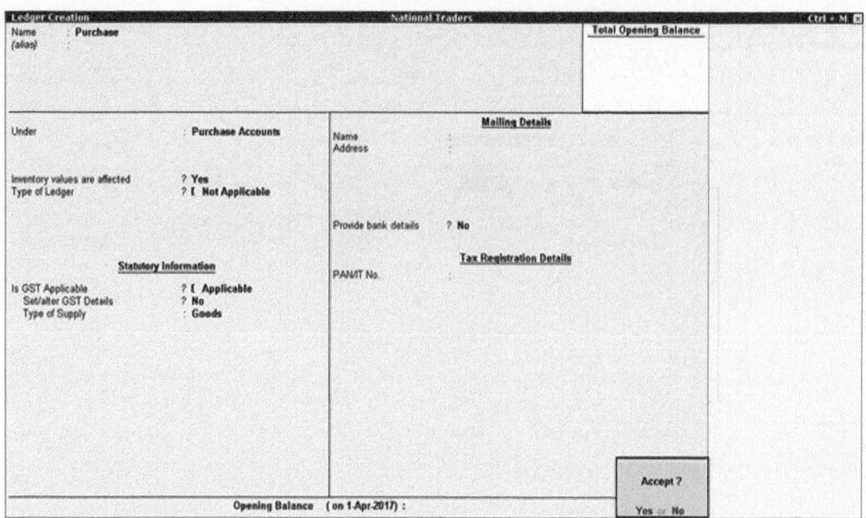


*Figure 18.17: Purchase Ledger Creation Screen*

**Step 3: Creation of Party Ledger:** Create RKM Hardware Distributors under sundry creditors, select state, enable the option **Set/alter GST details** to **Yes** and select the **Registration type** as Regular.

**Step 4: Creation of Duty Ledgers**

1. Create **State Tax ledger** as shown in the figure 18.18
2. Create **Central Tax ledger** as shown in the figure 18.19

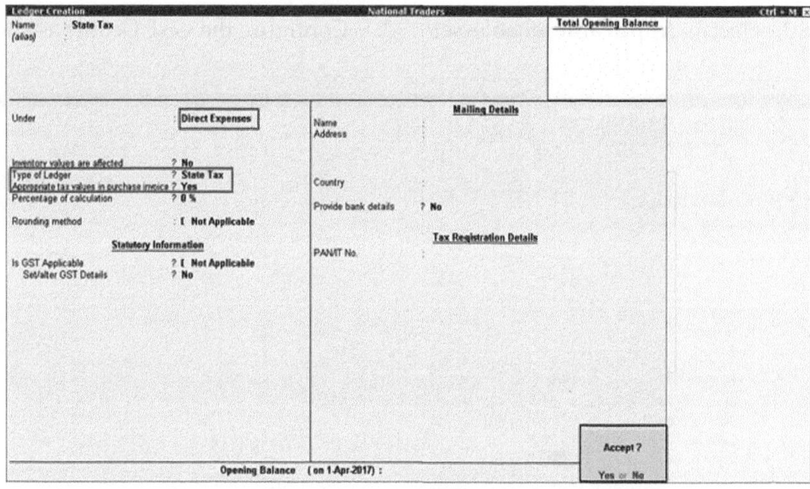


*Figure 18.18: State Tax Ledger Creation Screen*

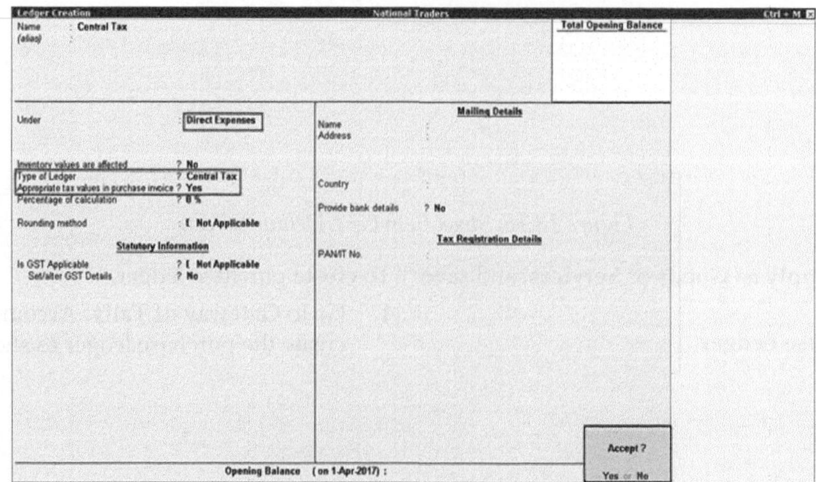


*Figure 18.19: Central Tax Ledger Creation Screen*

**Step 5: Recording intrastate purchase of taxable goods**

To record the intrastate purchase transaction as a composition, follow the steps given below:

1. Go to **Gateway of Tally > Accounting Vouchers > Press F9: Purchases.**
2. Enter the details as shown in the figure 18.20:

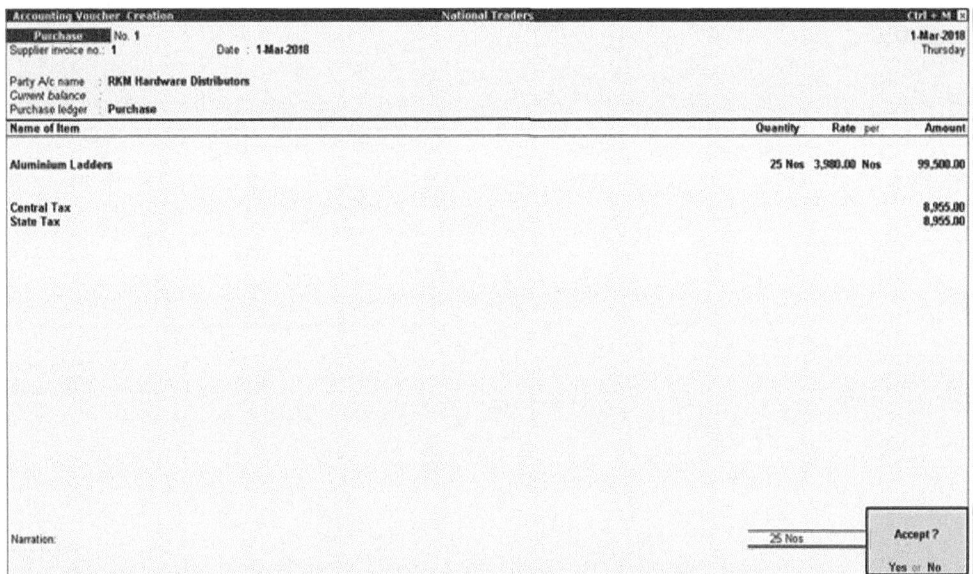


*Figure 18.20: Purchase Voucher Creation Screen*

**Note:**
- The invoice received from composition or unregistered dealers will not have tax in it. Hence, it is not required to select tax ledgers on such purchases.
- Interstate purchase of taxable services can be accounted in **Accounting Invoice** mode.

### 18.2.6.2 *Accounting of Sales Transaction and Printing of Invoice*

Let us now record a sales transaction as a composition dealer.

***Illustration:*** *As on 01-03-2018, Nation Traders a composition dealer, Karnataka sold 20 Aluminium Ladders worth ₹. 4,500 each from SM Hardware Distributors.*

***Activity:*** *Create the following ledgers in Tally.ERP 9*

- ***Party Ledger:*** *Create SM Hardware Distributors under sundry debtors, enable the option **Set/alter GST details** to **Yes** and select the **Registration type** as Regular.*
- *Create **Sales ledger** as shown in the figure 18.21*

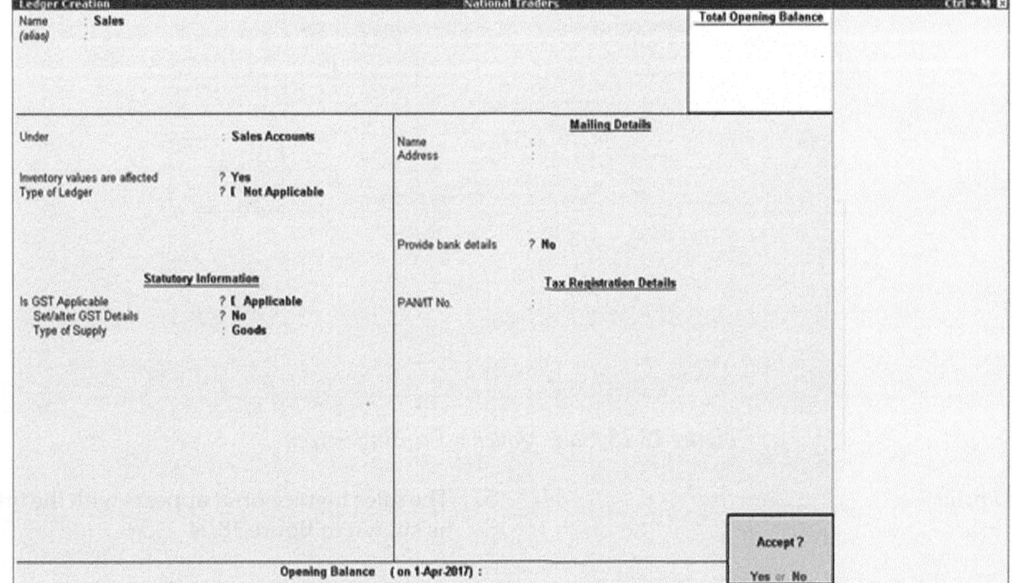


*Figure 18.21: Sales Ledger Creation Screen*

To record the sales transaction as a composition dealer, follow the steps given below:

1. Go to **Gateway of Tally > Accounting Vouchers > Press F8: Sales.**
2. Enter the details as shown in the figure 18.22:

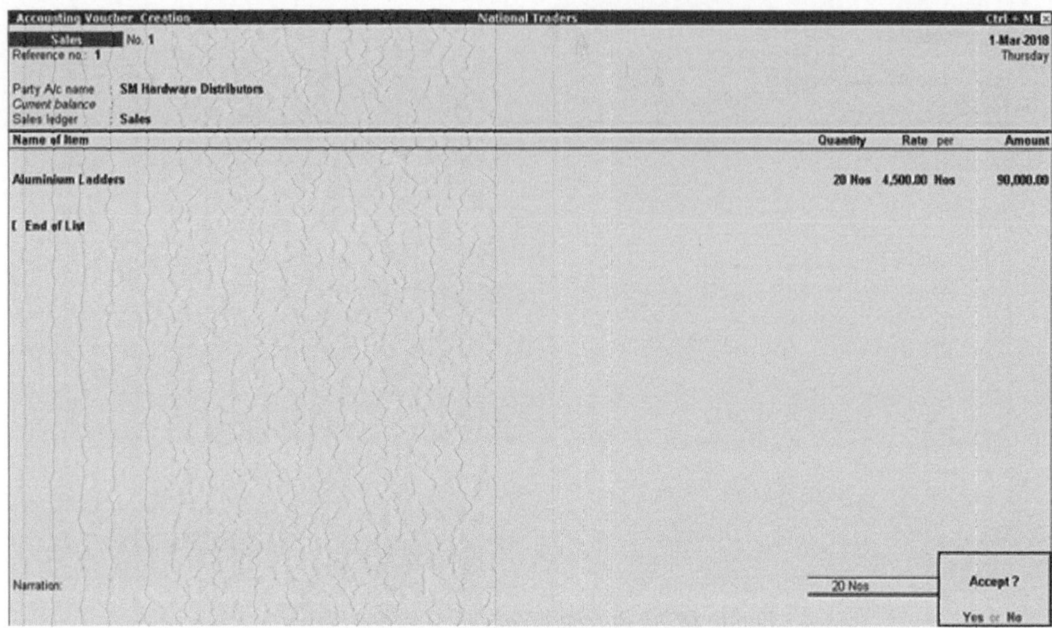

*Figure 18.22: Sales Voucher Creation Screen*

3. To print the Invoice Click **P : Print** from the sales voucher alteration screen . The report titles appear as per GST rules in the **Voucher Printing** screen as shown in figure 18.23

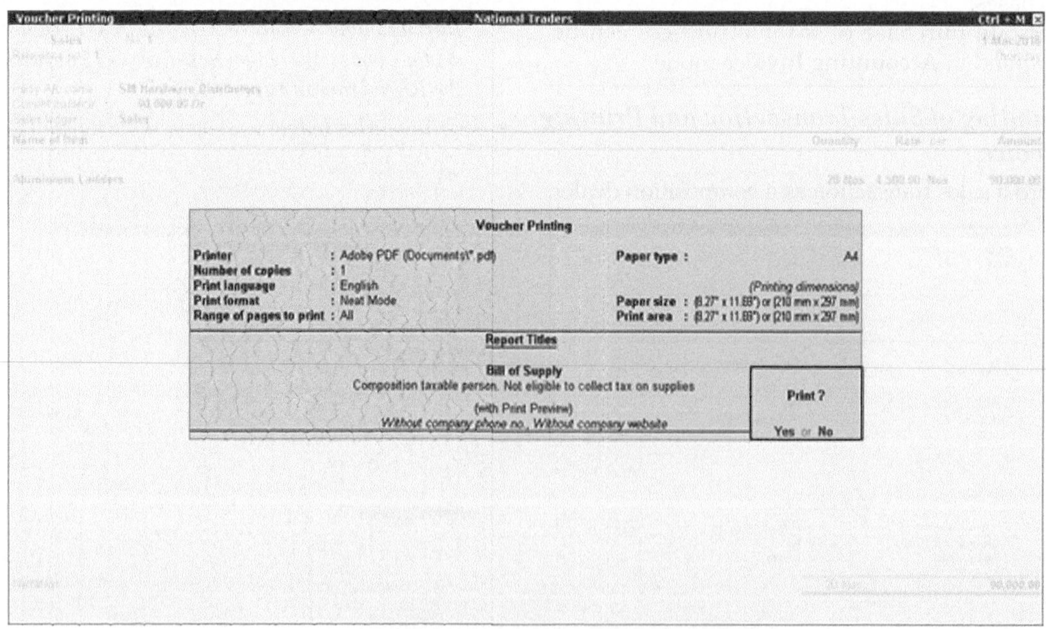

*Figure 18.23: Sales Voucher Printing Screen*

4. Press **Enter** to print
5. The sales invoice print appears with the title **Bill of Supply** as shown in figure 18.24

**Bill of Supply**

Composition taxable person. Not eligible to collect tax on supplies

| **National Traders**<br>#34, 5th Main Road Sriman Nagar<br>Bangalore<br>GSTIN/UIN: 29AACCT3705E1ZJ<br>State Name : Karnataka, Code : 29<br>E-Mail : Nationaltraders@gmail.com | Invoice No.<br>1 | Dated<br>**1-Mar-2018** |
|---|---|---|
| | Delivery Note | Mode/Terms of Payment |
| | Supplier's Ref.<br>1 | Other Reference(s) |
| Buyer<br>**SM Hardware Distributors**<br><br>GSTIN/UIN :<br>State Name : Karnataka, Code : 29 | Buyer's Order No. | Dated |
| | Despatch Document No. | Delivery Note Date |
| | Despatched through | Destination |
| | Terms of Delivery | |

| Sl No. | Description of Goods | HSN/SAC | Quantity | Rate | per | Amount |
|---|---|---|---|---|---|---|
| 1 | **Aluminium Ladders** | 76169990 | **20 Nos** | 4,500.00 | Nos | **90,000.00** |
| | Total | | **20 Nos** | | | **₹ 90,000.00** |

Amount Chargeable (in words) E. & O.E

**INR Ninety Thousand Only**

| HSN/SAC | Value of Supply |
|---|---|
| 76169990 | 90,000.00 |
| **Total** | **90,000.00** |

Tax Amount (in words) : **NIL**

Declaration
We declare that this invoice shows the actual price of the goods described and that all particulars are true and correct.

**for National Traders**

Authorised Signatory

This is a Computer Generated Invoice

*Figure 18.24: Bill of Supply*

## *18.2.6.3 Accounting of Purchase Return*

We can record purchase returns against an earlier purchase transaction using a debit note.

***Illustration:*** *As on 02-03-2018, Nation Traders returned 5 Aluminium Ladders worth ₹. 3,980 each to RKM Hardware Distributors with GST@18%,as the goods were damaged.*

**Recording Purchase Returns**

To record the debit note,

1. Go to **Gateway of Tally**>**Accounting Vouchers**>Click **Ctrl+F9: Debit Note.**
2. Enter the details as shown in the figure 18.25:

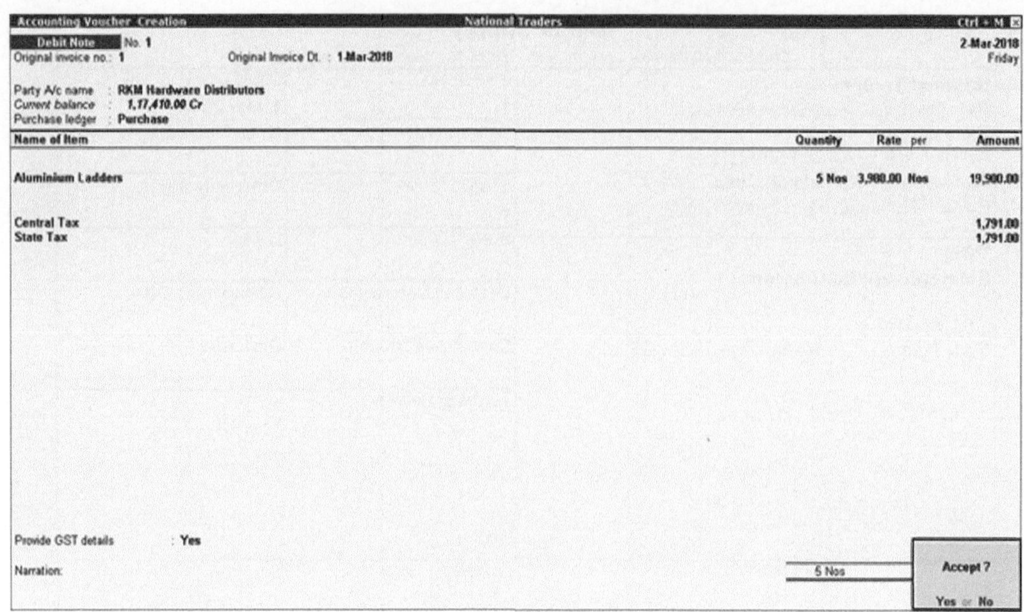


*Figure 18.25: Debit Note voucher*

**Note:** In Debit Note, enable Provide GST details to select Reason for issuing note.

### *18.2.6.4 Accounting of Sales Return*

We can record sales returns against an earlier sales transaction using a credit note.

***Illustration:*** *As on 02-03-2018, SM Hardware Distributors returne 3 Aluminium Ladders worth ₹. 4500 each as the goods were damagec*

**Recording Sales Returns**

To record the credit note,

1. Go to **Gateway of Tally**>**Accounting Vouchers**>Clic **Ctrl+F8: Credit Note.**
2. Enter the details as shown in the figure 18.26:

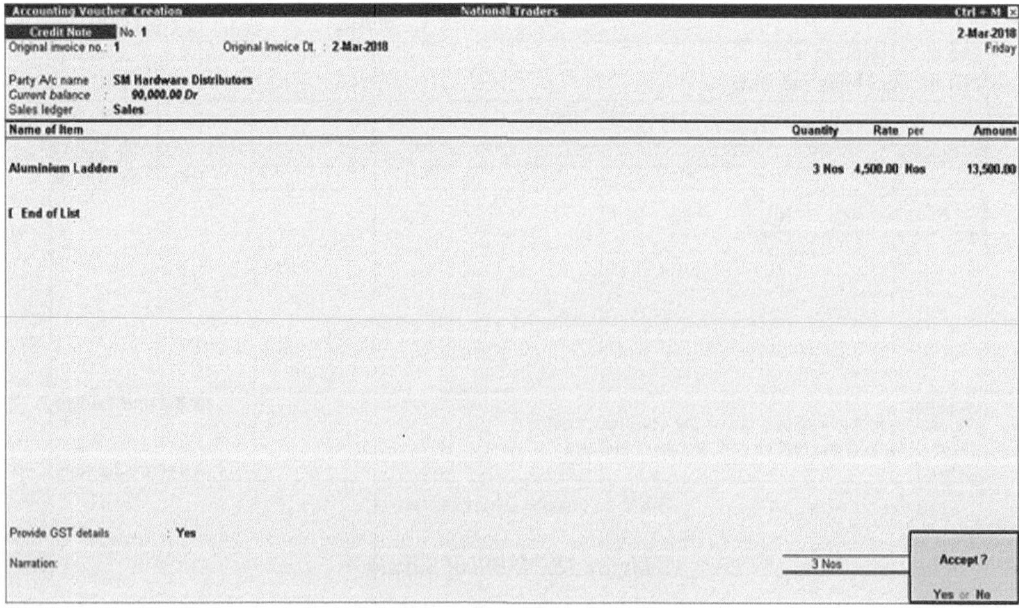


*Figure 18.26: Credit Note voucher*

**Note:** In Credit Note, enable **Provide GST details** to select **Reason for issuing note.**

### 18.2.7 Generating of GSTR-4 Report

The GSTR-4 report includes the details of taxable outward anc inward supplies, including supplies under reverse charge, mad by GST composition dealer in a given period.

We can generate the GSTR-4 with the details required for filing returns.

To view GSTR-4,

Go to **Gateway of Tally** > **Display** > **Statutory Reports** > **GST** > **GSTR–4**, Press **F2** and mention **From** and **To** period as 1-3-2018 and 31-3-2018.

GSTR-4 report appears as shown in figure 18.27

GSTR-4 — National Traders — Ctrl + M

GSTR4 — 1-Mar-2018 to 31-Mar-2018

Returns Summary

| Total number of vouchers for the period | 3 |
|---|---|
| Included in returns | 2 |
| Not relevant for returns | 1 |
| Incomplete/Mismatch in information (to be resolved) | 0 |

| Particulars | Voucher Count | Taxable Value | Integrated Tax Amount | Central Tax Amount | State Tax Amount | Cess Amount | Total Tax Amount |
|---|---|---|---|---|---|---|---|
| **Outward Supplies** | | | | | | | |
| Turnover of Taxable Sales @ 1% | 2 | 76,500.00 | | 382.50 | 382.50 | | 765.00 |
| Total | 2 | 76,500.00 | | 382.50 | 382.50 | | 765.00 |

*Figure 18.27: GSTR-4*

- Click F12: Configure and enable the options shown in figure 18.28

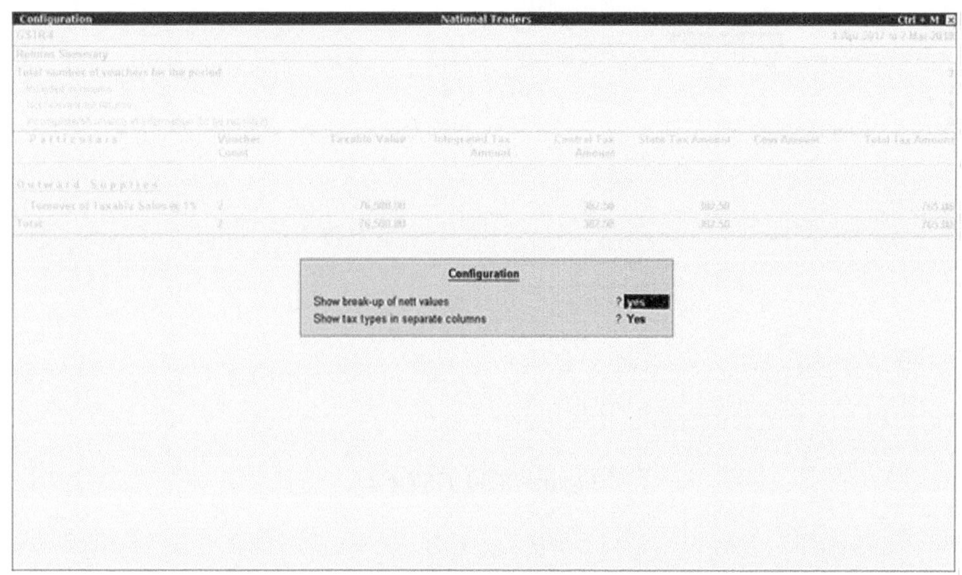


*Figure 18.28: GSTR-4*

- Click **F1 : Detailed** to view the breakup of sales and sales returns as shown in figure 18.29

GSTR-4 — National Traders — Ctrl + M

GSTR4 — 1-Apr-2017 to 2-Mar-2018

Returns Summary

| Total number of vouchers for the period | 3 |
|---|---|
| Included in returns | 2 |
| Not relevant for returns | 1 |
| Incomplete/Mismatch in information (to be resolved) | 0 |

| Particulars | Voucher Count | Taxable Value | Integrated Tax Amount | Central Tax Amount | State Tax Amount | Cess Amount | Total Tax Amount |
|---|---|---|---|---|---|---|---|
| **Outward Supplies** | | | | | | | |
| Turnover of Taxable Sales @ 1% | 2 | 76,500.00 | | 382.50 | 382.50 | | 765.00 |
| *Gross Value* | 90,000.00 | 900.00 | | | | | |
| *Returns* | (-)13,500.00 | (-)135.00 | | | | | |
| Total | 2 | 76,500.00 | | 382.50 | 382.50 | | 765.00 |

*Figure 18.29: GSTR-4*

There are two sections in this report,

- Returns summary, which is a snapshot of the business operations in the given period.
- Particulars, which displays transactions participating in the returns.

## 18.3 OTHER ENHANCEMENTS IN RELEASE 6.4

The following are the other enhancements or enhancements done in Tally.ERP 9 Release 6.4

- On February 20, the GSTN made changes in the GSTR-1 Excel Offline Utility Tool, CSV file format and JSON format, the same has been incorporated in Tally.ERP 9 Release 6.4.
- Enhancements in cess ledger

We can create cess ledger to calculate cess on quantity and value for regular dealers of GST. The cess on quantity ledger will be created as shown in the figure 18.30

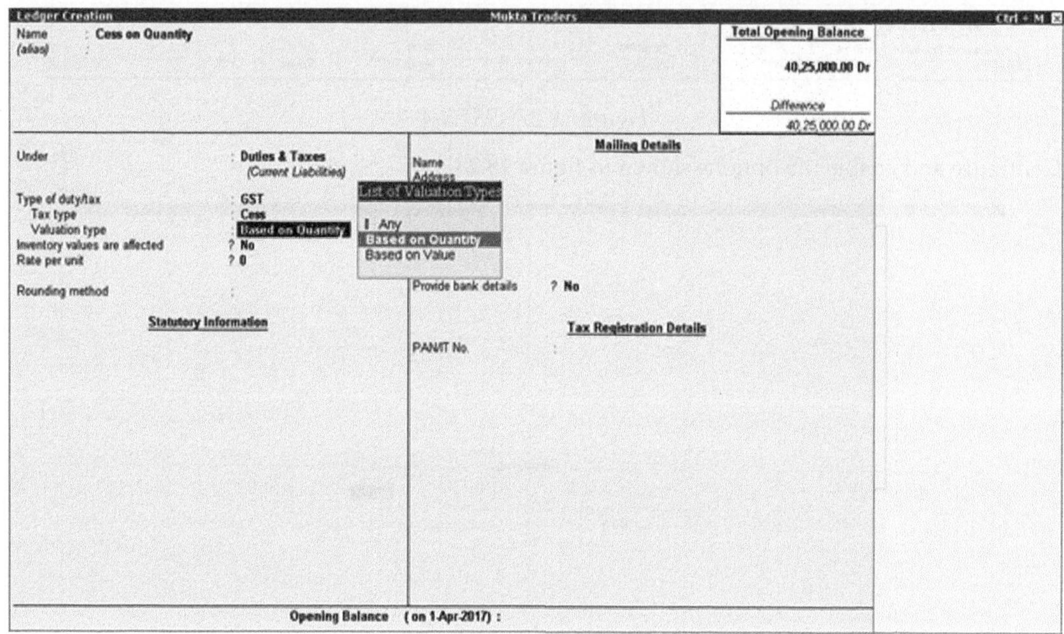


*Figure 18.30: GSTR-4*

Chapter 19

# Tally.ERP 9 Release 6.4.3 Annexure

## 19.1 E-WAY BILL THRESHOLD LIMIT

As per the latest instructions from GST council, e-way bills are now required for movement of taxable goods worth more than ₹. 50, 000 instead of overall invoice value. Earlier, even if the invoice containing taxable and exempted goods valuing above ₹. 50, 000, then all registered dealers had to generate e-way bills for interstate or intrastate movement of goods.

In this section we will learn to configure the e-way bill threshold limit for taxable goods value.

***Activity:***

- *Create a Company in Tally.ERP 9 with the following details:*

  *Company Name: Nisha Traders*

  *Address: No.54, 5th Cross, RC Building- Bangalore, Karnataka-560034*

  *Financial Year: 01-04-2018*

To configure the e-way bill threshold limit for taxable goods value,

1. Go to **Gateway of Tally**> Click **F11: Features** >Click **F3: Statutory.**
2. Set the options **Enable Goods and Services Tax (GST)?** to **Yes** and **Set/alter GST details ?** to **Yes.**
3. Select the option **Threshold limit includes** as **Taxable goods value** as shown in the figure 19.1

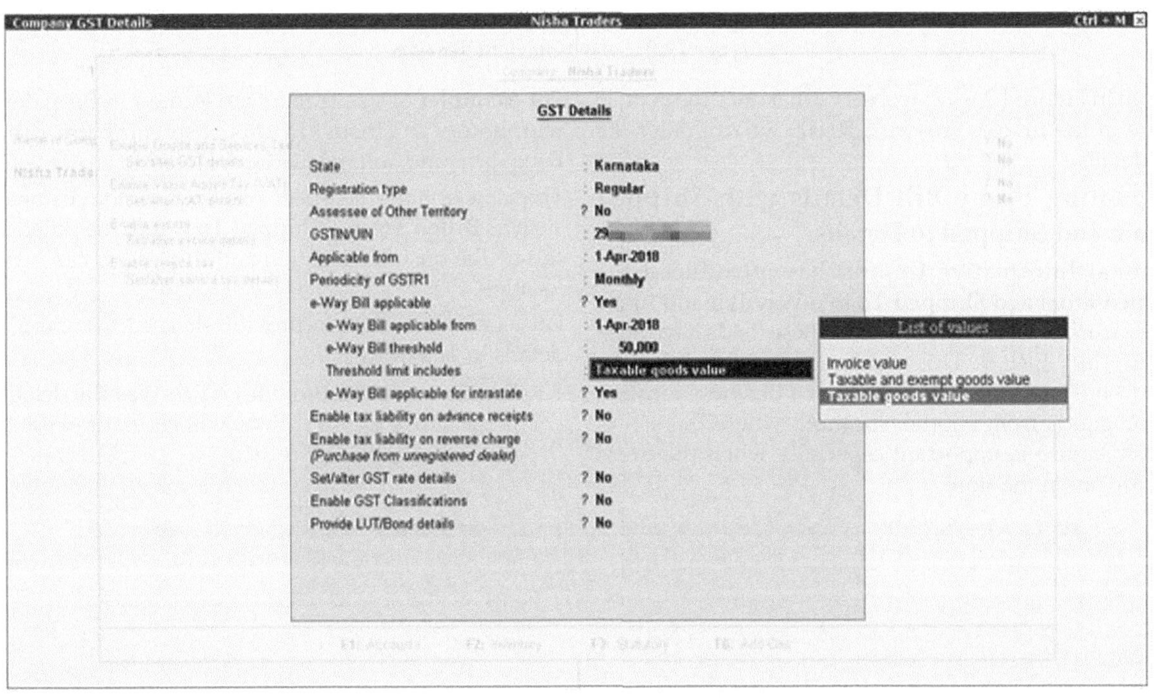


*Figure 19.1: Company GST Details*

However, Tally.ERP 9 has also given the provision to select the 'Threshold limit to include' as **Invoice value** and **Taxable and exempt goods value,** which can be selected if required.

### 19.1.1 Recording e-way Bill for Taxable Goods Value

***Illustration: 1***

*Nisha Traders, Karnataka supplied 2 Nos. of Laptop at ₹ 38,500 each to Gupta Traders, Tamil Nadu, with the reference no NT/1, and additionally GST @ 18% is charged on Laptop.*

***Activity:*** *Create the following Accounting and Inventory masters.*

- *Sales ledger under Sales Accounts, do not configure GST details(GST details will be configured in Stock item).*
- *Gupta Traders under Sundry Debtors, State Tamil Nadu and provide the Valid GSTIN number.*
- *Integrated Tax ledger under Duties and taxes, select type of duty as GST and tax type as Integrated Tax*
- *Stock item as Laptop, select Units, configure GST details and provide the opening balance as 50 Nos.*

Recording of sales transaction and defining of e-way bill details.

1. Go to **Gateway of Tally > Accounting Vouchers > press F8: Sales.**
2. Enter the details as shown in the figure 19.2.

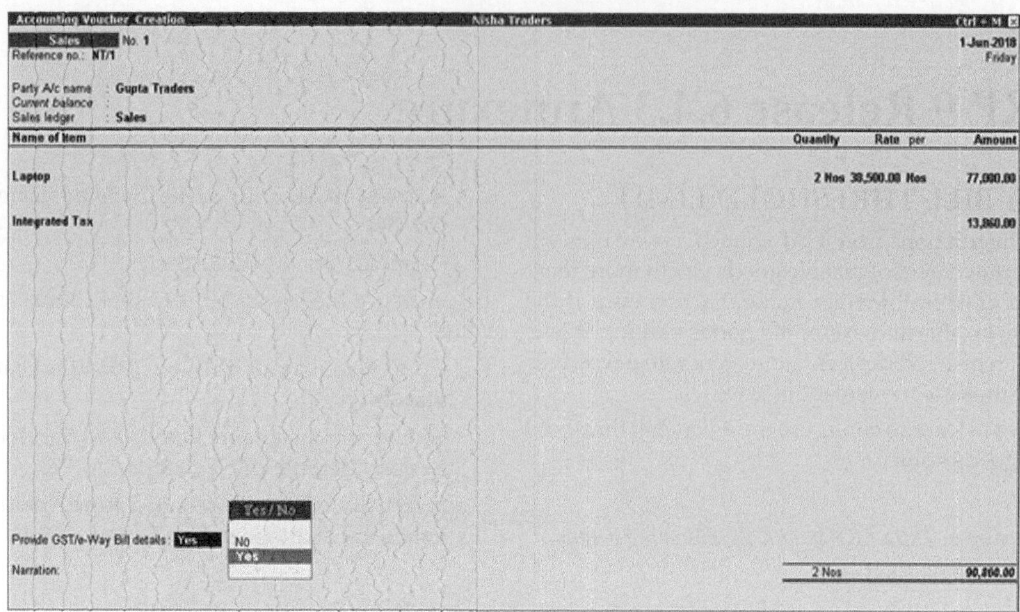


*Figure 19.2: Sales Voucher Creation*

**Observation:** In Figure 1.2 we can observe that once the taxable goods value in the invoice crosses ₹ 50,000 we can enter the e-way bill details.

### 19.1.2 Updating E-way Bill Details with Shipped from and Shipped to Details

NIC (National Informative Centre) has introduced the fields **Shipped From** and **Shipped To** in e-Way Bill and made it mandatory from 23rd May, 2018, hence these fields have been provided in Tally.ERP 9. This fields are provided for the businesses to bill to the customer from the business location and ship the goods from another location (where the stocks stored). This feature is important especially when the items purchased are not in the store.

**For example:** Nisha Traders are located in Bengaluru and has warehouse in Hosur, In this case company can bill from Bengaluru and ship goods from Hosur to customer's location.

The same options have been provided for the customer's as well such as **Billed To** and **Shipped To** where the Billed To address can be the business location and shipped to can be warehouse location.

Let us now see, how to provide shipped from and shipped to details in Tally.ERP 9.

1. Enable the option Provide GST/e-Way Bill details as shown in the above figure 1.2, you will get statutory details screen as shown in the figure 19.3.

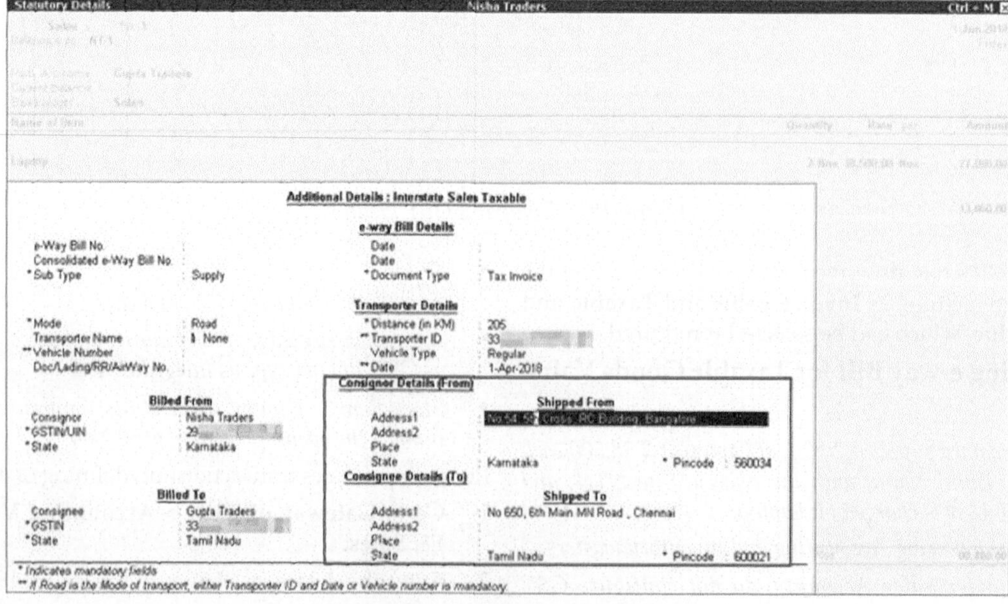


*Figure 19.3: Statutory Details*

In Tally.ERP 9 we can provide the state names for shipped from and shipped to addresses.

To provide state names for shipped from and shipped to addresses from **Statutory Details** screen, click **F12: Configure**, and enable the option **Show state name for Shipped from and Shipped To ?**

### 19.1.3 Clear warning Message is Provided on Missing the Mandatory Fields in E-way Bill Details Screen

Tally.ERP 9 provides a clear warning message of missing information which is mandatory for generation of e-way bill if it is missed out while recording the transaction.

## 19.2 MANAGE DIFFERENCES IN GSTR-1 TRANSACTIONS

As per the latest changes made by GST department, the tax amount can be of any value, earlier there was a condition that tax amount should be equal to taxable value (**x**) tax rate, which is now removed and the same can be handled in Tally.ERP 9.

***Activity: Illustration: 2***

*As on 01-06-2018, Nisha Traders, Karnataka supplied 1 Laptop at ₹ 38,500 each to Gupta Traders, Tamil Nadu. Additionally, charged ₹ 6,935 as integrated tax.*

**Note:** In the above illustration integrated tax will be provided manually and it will not matching with the tax rate configured, hence we will get the warning message as **Tax amount does not match** press enter and accept the transaction.

After recording the transaction, go to **Gateway of Tally >Display >Statutory Reports >GST >GSTR-1,** provide the period for which the transactions are recorded.

If tax amounts are not equal to the computed tax amounts (taxable value (**x**) rate), such transactions are treated as Mismatches by default. We can resolve these differences by adjusting amounts before filing GSTR-1.

Let us now see how to adjust the tax amount individually for each transactions,

To adjust the tax amount individually for each transactions,

1. From GSTR-1 report, enter on **Incomplete/Mismatch in information (to be resolved).**
2. Select **Mismatch due to tax amount modified in voucher.**
3. From the Exception Resolution screen, click **A: Accept as is** to accept the voucher with difference

If we do not want to adjust the differences individually, we can allow tax differences up to required limit in the GSTR-1 report.

To allow the differences in GSTR-1,

1. From **GSTR-1**, click **F12: Configure,**
2. Against the option **Allow tax differences up to** set limit as required.
3. Once after providing the limit, an additional option **Actual tax versus computed tax** appears, with the below mentioned options.
   - Greater
   - Greater or Lesser
   - Lesser
4. Select required parameter for Actual tax versus computed tax to consider the differences in GSTR-1.

## 19.3 ROUNDING OFF INVOICE AMOUNTS AUTOMATICALLY

In Tally.ERP 9, we can now round off the invoice amounts automatically, by creating the round off ledger as shown in the figure 19.4

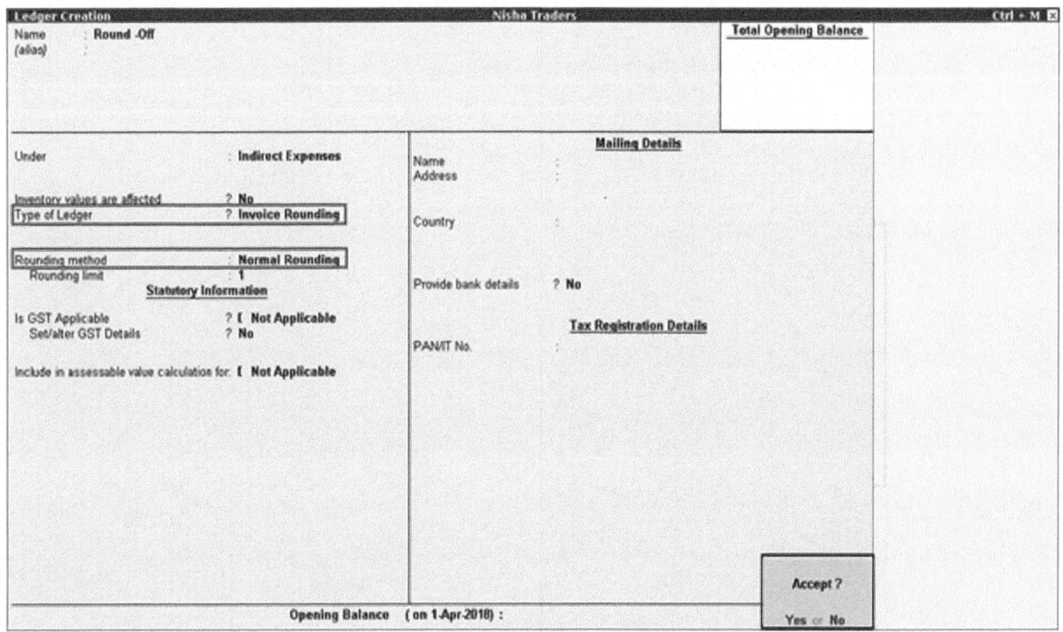


*Figure 19.4: Round off ledger creation screen*

**Note:** Select the required rounding method, based on the rounding method selected, round off happens in the transaction.

## 19.4 PAYROLL UPDATION AS PER FINANCE BILL 2018

We can now compute the salaries for employees as per the latest budgetary changes made in finance bill 2018

Tally.ERP 9 now supports the reintroduction of below mentioned income tax classifications,

1. **Standard Deduction:** As per the latest changes standard deduction of ₹ 40,000 is supported.

**Note:** Load the payroll enabled company to view these changes.

- To view the standard deduction slab, from **Gateway of Tally** > select **Display**> **Payroll Statutory Info**> **Income tax Classifications** > **Standard Deduction.**

2. **Health and Education Cess:** Tally.ERP 9 supports the latest changes of health and education cess slab of 4% tax rate.
   - To view the health and education cess slab rate ,Go t **Gateway of Tally>Display>Payroll Statutor Info>Income Tax Slabs> Health and Education Ces Slab.**
3. Exemption on **Medical Reimbursement** and **Transpor Allowance** is Removed and the same is supported i Tally.ERP 9, to view the income tax classification of medica reimbursement, Go to **Gateway of Tally>Display>Payrol Statutory Info> Income Tax Classifications**>select **Medica Reimbursement/Transport Allowance**
4. Benefits for Senior Citizens, Tally.ERP 9 supports th increase of exemption limit for senior citizens in mediclain insurance and expenditure for specified diseases
   - To view the medical reimbursement and transpor allowance classifications, Go to **Gateway of Tally Display>Payroll Statutory Info>Income Ta Classifications>Mediclaim Insurance/ Mediclain Insurance (Dependent)/ Expenditure for Specifie Disease.**

# Practice Exercises

## Chapter 7: Computerised Accounting Systems using Tally.ERP 9

1. Tally.ERP 9 is one of the most widely used ____________ software
   a. Financial  b. Drawing
   c. Gaming  d. Audio Video
2. The first step towards working with Tally.ERP 9 is to create a ________
   a. Report  b. Ledgers
   c. Folder  d. Company
3. There are ________ pre-defined groups in Tally.ERP 9, which feature in the Chart of Accounts of many organisations
   a. 82  b. 28
   c. 32  d. 48
4. In Tally.ERP 9, the predefined Godown is ___________
   a. Prime Location  b. Warehouse
   c. Main Location  d. Storage
5. In Tally.ERP 9, the accounting transactions are entered from ____________
   a. Accounting Vouchers  b. Payroll Vouchers
   c. Inventory Vouchers  d. Order Vouchers

**Answers**

1. (a) 2. (d) 3. (b) 4. (c) 5. (a)

### (a) Banking

1. ______________ is a written order to the bank to pay the stated sum of money.
   a. Cheque  b. Notice
   c. Authorisation Letter  d. Debentures
2. Cheques can be printed while printing a ___________ voucher.
   a. Material In  b. Payment
   c. Receipt  d. Stock Journal
3. Tally.ERP 9 allows you to print ____________ cheques at the same time
   a. Dual  b. Multiple
   c. Single  d. Parallel
4. Tally.ERP 9 allows you to generate Cheque and _________ Deposit Slip
   a. Credit  b. Stock
   c. Fixed Asset  d. Cash

**Answers**

1. (a) 2. (b) 3. (b) 4. (d)

### (b) Cost Centre and Cost Categories

1. Cost Center is a unit of an organisation where transactions can be allocated to recognise cost or profit.
   a. True  b. False
2. ___________ can be allocated to different cost centres
   a. Stock Group  b. Stock Item
   c. Accounts Group  d. Ledger
3. ___________ report displays the summarised information of all Cost Centres for the selected Group
   a. Group Break-Up  b. Ledger Break-Up
   c. Category Summary  d. Stock Break-Up
4. ___________ are used to automate cost centre allocations in transactions.
   a. Income Classes  b. Centre Classes
   c. Cost Centre Break-up  d. Cost Centre Classes
5. ______________ facilitate third dimensional reporting of Expenditure and Revenue
   a. Accounts Group  b. Ledgers
   c. Balance Sheet  d. Cost Categories

**Answers**

1. (a) 2. (d) 3. (a) 4. (d) 5. (d)

### (c) Order Processing

1. ___________ refers to placing purchase orders with suppliers/receiving order from customers for sale
   a. Order Processing  b. Tender
   c. Acquisition  d. Procurement
2. Purchase Invoice or ____________ can be raised against previously recorded purchase orders
   a. Debit Note  b. Credit Note
   c. Delivery Note  d. Receipt Note
3. In Tally.ERP 9, the user can view all the sales order outstanding from ___________
   a. Inventory Books  b. Statements of Inventory
   c. Statements of Accounts  d. Stock Register
4. Sales Order Outstanding screen, by default will show the report as ___________ of the voucher entry
   a. Last Date  b. Previous Date
   c. Due Date  d. Issue Date

**Answers**

1. (a) 2. (c) 3. (b) 4. (a)

### (d) Data Backup and Restore

1. Tally.ERP 9 helps users to take back up of one or more companies in ______

a. Web directory b. Single directory
c. Tally Server d. Telephone directory

2. In Tally.ERP 9, the ________ functionality allows you to restore the data backup taken earlier
   a. Backup b. Restore
   c. Split Data d. Security Control
3. The user can take backup on external device by providing directory path at ________ field
   a. Source b. Network
   c. Destination d. Tally Server

**Answers**

1. (b) 2. (b) 3. (c)

# Chapter 7 - Part B: Goods and Services Tax

1. A seller supplies goods to a buyer both are located in the same state, then which tax is levied under GST.
   a. Central Tax & State Tax b. Union Territory Tax
   c. Integrated Tax d. No Tax
2. A seller supplies goods to a buyer both are located in the different state, then which Tax Act is effective
   a. Central Tax b. State Tax
   c. Union Territory Tax d. Integrated Tax
3. When a registered dealer sell the goods outside the state to an unregistered dealer then which tax is charged on supplies of goods
   a. Central Tax & State Tax b. Nil Tax
   c. Union Territory Tax d. Integrated Tax
4. The dealer registered under composition scheme will charge ____________ tax to the customer for the supplies of goods
   a. Central Tax & State Tax
   b. Not Allowed to Charge Tax
   c. Union Territory Tax
   d. Integrated Tax
5. A seller supplies 50Pcs of Cooker @ ₹ 2,000/Pcs to a registered dealer located outside the state and the GST is charged on supplies @ 12% what is the amount of tax charged
   a. Central Tax 12,000
   b. State Tax 6,000
   c. Central Tax 60,00 and State Tax 60,000
   d. Integrated Tax 12,000
6. A seller supplies 40Pcs of Cooker @ ₹ 3,000/Pcs to a registered dealer located within the state and the GST is were charged on supplies @ 18% which tax is charged on supplies
   a. Central Tax 21,600
   b. Union Territory Tax 10,800
   c. Central Tax 10,800 and State Tax 10,800
   d. Integrated Tax 10,800
7. On 01 December 2017, an registered service provider rendered professional services @ ₹ 30,000 to a registered client located outside the state, which tax is applicable on the services supplied
   a. Integrated Tax b. Service Tax
   c. Supply Tax d. Central Tax & State Tax
8. A seller supplies 20Nos of Piano @ ₹ 900/Nos to a registered dealer located outside the state and the GST is were charged on supplies @ 12% of which 5 Nos of Piano were returned hence what is the amount of tax on goods returned
   a. ₹ 3,240 b. ₹ 540
   c. ₹ 2,430 d. ₹ 4,050
9. On 01 September 2017, an unregistered service provider rendered advertising services @ ₹ 10,000 to a registered client located outside the state, which tax is applicable on the services supplied
   a. Central Tax & State Tax
   b. Service Tax
   c. Integrated Tax
   d. Not Allowed to Charge Tax

**Answers**

1. (a) 2. (d) 3. (d) 4. (b) 5. (d)
6. (c) 7. (a) 8. (b) 9. (d)

# Chapter 13: Other Features

## (a) Interest

1. If the user want to set the interest calculation only for credit balances then this can be done only if ____________ is enabled
   a. Use advanced parameters
   b. For amounts added
   c. For amounts deducted
   d. Calculate Interest Transaction-by-Transaction
2. If the user want to charge interest on every transaction then __________ need to be done
   a. Override Parameters for each Transaction
   b. Eff. Date of Transaction
   c. Calculate Interest Transaction-by-Transaction
   d. Past Due Date
3. If the interest to be calculated after the due credit period for the customer then __________ have to set
   a. Calculate From: Due Date of Invoice/Ref
   b. Calculate From: Date of Applicability
   c. Calculate From: Eff. Date of Transaction
   d. Applicability: Past Due Date
4. To record the interest accrued for the customers __________ voucher is used in Tally.ERP 9
   a. Journal b. Contra

c. Debit Note d. Credit Note

5. To calculate compounding interest in Tally.ERP 9 ___________ to be set
   a. Journal > Class > Amount to be treated as Compound Interest
   b. Interest Voucher > Class > Amount to be treated as Compound Interest
   c. Receipt/ Payment Voucher > Class > Amount to be treated as Compound Interest
   d. Debit/ Credit Note Voucher > Class > Amount to be treated as Compound Interest

**Answers**

1. (a) 2. (c) 3. (a) 4. (c) 5. (d)

## (b) Point of Sales (POS)

1. In Tally.ERP 9 the POS Voucher is grouped under with Voucher Type
   a. Sales b. Purchase
   c. Journal d. Contra
2. To use the POS function in Tally.ERP 9 ___________ option is set
   a. Use for POS Invoicing
   b. Use for Desk Invoicing
   c. Use for Counter Invoicing
   d. Use for Instant Invoicing
3. To accept the coupons voucher for POS Invoicing ___________ is set in Tally.ERP 9
   a. Coupon Voucher b. Gift Vouchers
   c. Gift Coupon d. Reward Voucher
4. To use only one payment method during POS Voucher entry _______ mode to be switched
   a. Cash Register b. Journal Voucher
   c. POS Receipt d. Single Mode Pymt
5. In Tally.ERP 9, the Single Mode Payment for POS voucher entry _________ is the mode of payment
   a. Cheque b. Online Payment
   c. Cash d. Refund

**Answers**

1. (a) 2. (a) 3. (b) 4. (d) 5. (c)

## (c) Budget

1. When actuals spending are more than the budget then ___________
   a. Under Budget b. Over Budget
   c. Substantial Budget d. Nil Budget
2. In Tally.ERP 9, the difference of actuals and budgeted are available in ___________ report
   a. Common Budget b. Columnar
   c. Daybook d. Budget Variance
3. In Tally.ERP 9, the budgets can be created for ___________ also
   a. Cost Centre b. Bill of Materials
   c. Assets d. Liabilities
4. The type of budget in Tally.ERP 9 can also be set ___________
   a. On Refunds b. On Nett Transactions
   c. On Cost d. On Opening Balance
5. In Tally.ERP 9, budget variance report can be displayed in ___________
   a. Balance Sheet b. Profit & Loss A/c
   c. Income Statement d. Trial Balance

**Answers**

1. (a) 2. (d) 3. (a) 4. (b) 5. (d)

## (d) Bill of Material (BOM)

1. In Tally.ERP 9, Bills of Materials are used in ___________
   a. Production b. Cost Centres
   c. Interest Calculation d. Budgets
2. From ___________ the user can define the BOM in Tally.ERP
   a. Stock Item Creation b. Stock Group Creation
   c. Ledger Creation d. Voucher Types Creation
3. _________ is the minimum number of Unit of manufacture set in BOM
   a. 10 b. 5
   c. 2 d. 1
4. To get the prefilled BOM List for production ___________ voucher is used
   a. Contra b. Stock Journal
   c. Journal d. Reversing Journal
5. Is it possible to create multiple BOM's for a single final stock item
   a. True b. False

**Answers**

1. (a) 2. (a) 3. (d) 4. (b) 5. (a)

## (e) Tax Collected at Source (TCS)

1. The location from where TAN registration number can be provided in Tally.ERP 9
   a. Accounting Features b. Inventory Features
   c. Statutory & Taxation d. Add-On Features
2. The TCS Nature of Goods can be created from ___________
   a. Accounts Info > Statutory Info
   b. Accounts Info > TCS Nature of Goods
   c. Accounts Info > Ledgers > TCS Nature of Goods
   d. F12: Configure > TCS Nature of Goods
3. For ___________ the TCS Nature of Goods needs to be defined
   a. Cost Center b. Unit of measure
   c. Stock Item d. Stock Categories
4. The TCS challan can be printed from_________ voucher

a. Contra b. Payment
c. Receipt d. Journal

5. __________ can be used to reconcile the TCS Payments
a. Cash b. Cheque
c. Challan d. Collections

**Answers**

1. (c) 2. (a) 3. (c) 4. (b) 5. (c)

### (f) Security Control

1. To create the administrator users and password __________ has to be enabled.
a. Security Control b. Admin Control
c. Remote User Control d. Auditor Control

2. To use the Tally Audit Features __________ must be enabled first.
a. Security Control b. Admin Control
c. Remote User Control d. Auditor

3. While opening an password protected company in Tally.ERP 9______ credential has to be entered
a. Name of User and OTP
b. Only Password (if any) (User Auto Selected)
c. Name of User and Password (if any)
d. Only Name of User

4. In Tally.ERP 9, which of the following voucher is the non-accounting voucher?
a. Journal Voucher b. Payment Voucher
c. Sales Voucher d. Memorandum Voucher

5. __________ is a listing of components which will be used to produce a finished goods.
a. Bill of Lading b. Bill of Materials (BoM)
c. Bill of Exchange d. Bill of Trading

**Answers**

1. (a) 2. (a) 3. (c) 4. (d) 5. (b)

## Chapter 18: TallyACE Release 6.4 Annexure

1. E-Way Bill contains the details of __________ from one place to another
a. Supplier of Goods b. Movement of Goods
c. Receiver of Goods d. Receipts of Goods

2. It is mandatory to have __________ number if the value of goods which is transported is more than ₹ 50,000.
a. Invoice Number b. Docket Number
c. Credit Note Number d. E-way bill

3. __________ number can be generated from e-way portal.
a. E-Way bill b. Purchase Order Number
c. Sales Order Number d. Docket Number

4. E-Way bill can also be generated from __________ method.
a. Short Message Service (SMS) b. E-mail
c. Fax d. Pager

**Answers**

1. (b) 2. (d) 3. (a) 4. (a)